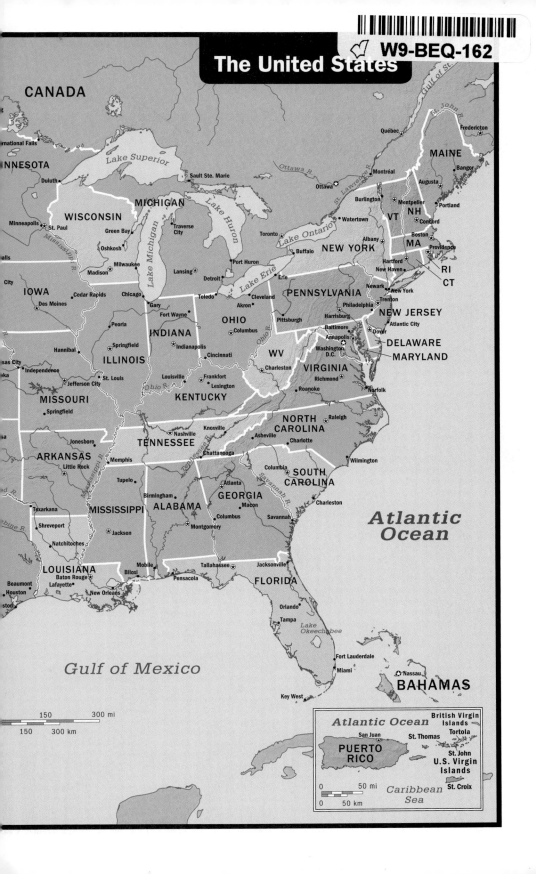

# The United States

W9-BEQ-162

**CANADA**

Atlantic Ocean

Gulf of Mexico

**BAHAMAS**

Lake Superior
Lake Huron
Lake Michigan
Lake Ontario
Lake Erie

MINNESOTA
WISCONSIN
MICHIGAN
IOWA
ILLINOIS
INDIANA
OHIO
MISSOURI
KENTUCKY
TENNESSEE
ARKANSAS
MISSISSIPPI
ALABAMA
GEORGIA
LOUISIANA
FLORIDA
NORTH CAROLINA
SOUTH CAROLINA
VIRGINIA
WV
PENNSYLVANIA
NEW YORK
NEW JERSEY
DELAWARE
MARYLAND
MAINE
VT
NH
MA
RI
CT

International Falls
Duluth
Minneapolis
St. Paul
Green Bay
Oshkosh
Milwaukee
Madison
Traverse City
Sault Ste. Marie
Lansing
Port Huron
Detroit
Toledo
Cleveland
Akron
Columbus
Cincinnati
Indianapolis
Springfield
Fort Wayne
Gary
Chicago
Peoria
Cedar Rapids
Des Moines
Hannibal
St. Louis
Jefferson City
Independence
Springfield
Jonesboro
Memphis
Little Rock
Tupelo
Jackson
Natchitoches
Shreveport
Texarkana
Beaumont
Houston
Lafayette
Baton Rouge
New Orleans
Biloxi
Mobile
Pensacola
Birmingham
Montgomery
Columbus
Macon
Atlanta
Columbia
Savannah
Charleston
Wilmington
Charlotte
Raleigh
Knoxville
Asheville
Nashville
Chattanooga
Louisville
Frankfort
Lexington
Charleston
Richmond
Roanoke
Norfolk
Pittsburgh
Harrisburg
Philadelphia
Baltimore
Annapolis
Washington, D.C.
Dover
Atlantic City
Trenton
Newark
New York
Hartford
New Haven
Providence
Boston
Concord
Montpelier
Portland
Augusta
Bangor
Albany
Buffalo
Watertown
Toronto
Burlington
Ottawa
Montréal
Québec
Fredericton

Québec
St. Lawrence R.
Ottawa R.
Gulf of St.
St. John R.
Ohio R.
Mississippi R.
Tennessee R.
Savannah R.
Red R.
Sabine R.

Orlando
Tampa
Lake Okeechobee
Fort Lauderdale
Miami
Key West
Tallahassee
Jacksonville

Nassau

150   300 mi
150   300 km

### Inset: Puerto Rico / U.S. Virgin Islands

Atlantic Ocean

British Virgin Islands
Tortola
San Juan
St. Thomas
**PUERTO RICO**
St. John
U.S. Virgin Islands
St. Croix

Caribbean Sea

0   50 mi
0   50 km

EIGHTH ESSENTIALS EDITION

# We the People

## AN INTRODUCTION TO AMERICAN POLITICS

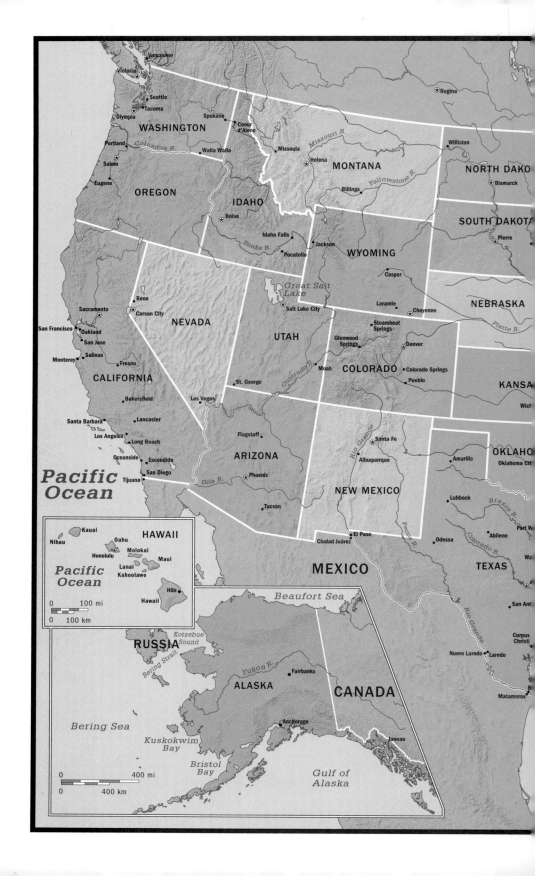

EIGHTH ESSENTIALS EDITION

# We the People

## AN INTRODUCTION TO AMERICAN POLITICS

### Benjamin Ginsberg
JOHNS HOPKINS UNIVERSITY

### Theodore J. Lowi
CORNELL UNIVERSITY

### Margaret Weir
UNIVERSITY OF CALIFORNIA, BERKELEY

### Robert J. Spitzer
SUNY CORTLAND

 W. W. NORTON & COMPANY
NEW YORK   LONDON

*To Teresa Spitzer*
*Sandy, Cindy, and Alex Ginsberg*
*Angele, Anna, and Jason Lowi*
*Nicholas Ziegler*

W. W. Norton & Company has been independent since its founding in 1923, when William Warder Norton and Mary D. Herter Norton first published lectures delivered at the People's Institute, the adult education division of New York City's Cooper Union. The Nortons soon expanded their program beyond the Institute, publishing books by celebrated academics from America and abroad. By mid-century, the two major pillars of Norton's publishing program—trade books and college texts—were firmly established. In the 1950s, the Norton family transferred control of the company to its employees, and today—with a staff of four hundred and a comparable number of trade, college, and professional titles published each year—W. W. Norton & Company stands as the largest and oldest publishing house owned wholly by its employees.

Editor: Ann Shin
Assistant editor: Jake Schindel
Project editor: Melissa Atkin
Senior production manager: Benjamin Reynolds
Book design: Lissi Sigillo
Information graphics design: Kiss Me I'm Polish LLC, New York
Design director: Rubina Yeh
Managing editor, College: Marian Johnson
Composition: Jouve
Manufacturing: R. R. Donnelley & Sons—Jefferson City, MO
Photo editor: Junenoire Mitchell
Photo researcher: Susan Buschhorn
E-media editor: Peter Lesser
Marketing manager: Nicole Netherton

Library of Congress Cataloging-in-Publication Data

We the people : an introduction to American politics / Benjamin Ginsberg ... [et al.].—8th essentials ed.
    p. cm.
Includes bibliographical references and index.

ISBN 978-0-393-93565-3 (pbk.)

1. Ginsberg, Benjamin.

JK276.W45 2011
320. 473—dc22

2010041073

W. W. Norton & Company, Inc., 500 Fifth Avenue, New York, N. Y. 10110
www.wwnorton.com

W. W. Norton & Company Ltd., Castle House, 75/76 Wells Street, London W1T 3QT

3 4 5 6 7 8 9 0

# contents

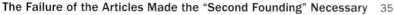

## 4 ● Civil Liberties and Civil Rights 90

# PART II  Politics

## 5 ● Public Opinion   138

## 6 ● The Media   166

# 7 ● Political Parties and Elections   196

## 8 ● Interest Groups   236

# PART III   Institutions

## 9 ● Congress   264

# 10 ● The Presidency   302

## 11 ● Bureaucracy   332

## 12 ● The Federal Courts   362

# PART IV   Policy

## 13 ● Domestic Policy   394

## 14 ● Foreign Policy   428

# preface

This book has been and continues to be dedicated to developing a satisfactory response to the question more and more Americans are asking: Why should we be engaged with government and politics? Through the earlier editions, we sought to answer this question by making the text directly relevant to the lives of the students who would be reading it. As a result, we tried to make politics interesting by demonstrating that students' interests are at stake and that they therefore need to take a personal, even selfish, interest in the outcomes of government. At the same time, we realized that students needed guidance in how to become politically engaged. Beyond providing students with a core of political knowledge, we needed to show them how they could apply that knowledge as participants in the political process. The "Get Involved" sections in each chapter help achieve that goal.

As events from the last several years have reminded us, "what government does" can be a matter of life and death. Recent events have reinforced the centrality of government in citizens' lives. The U.S. government has fought two wars abroad, while claiming sweeping new powers at home that could compromise the liberties of its citizens. America's role in the world is discussed daily both inside and outside the classroom. Moreover, students and younger Americans have become more aware of and involved in politics, as the 2008 elections illustrated. Reflecting all of these trends, this new Eighth Essentials Edition shows more than any other book on the market (1) how students are connected to government; (2) how American government is connected to the world; and (3) why students should think critically about government and politics. These themes are incorporated in the following ways:

- **Chapter introductions focus on "What Government Does and Why It Matters."** In recent decades, cynicism about "big government" has dominated the political zeitgeist. But critics of government often forget that governments do a great deal for citizens. Every year, Americans are the beneficiaries of billions of dollars of goods and services from government programs. Government "does" a lot, and what it does matters to everyone, including college students. At the start of each chapter, this theme is introduced and applied to the chapter's topic. The goal is to show students that government and politics mean something to their daily lives.

- **"Get Involved" units show students how they can make a difference in politics.** The 2008 elections produced a surge in political participation among young Americans, as well as changes in the ways that they participated. These boxes use contemporary examples to explain how young people (even those with busy lives!) can get involved in politics. Specific, step-by-step instructions guide students through a range of possible political activities related to each chapter's topic.

- **Built-in study guldes at the end of each chapter offer valuable learning tools.** A practice quiz and glossary definitions help students review the chapter material. Each chapter also includes a list of recommended readings and Web sites to help students get started on research projects.

We continue to hope that our book will itself be accepted as a form of enlightened political action. The Eighth Essentials Edition is another chance. It is an advancement toward our goal. We promise to keep trying.

# acknowledgments

We are especially pleased to acknowledge the many colleagues who had a direct and active role in criticism and preparation of the manuscript. Our thanks go to:

## First Edition Reviewers

Sarah Binder, Brookings Institution
Kathleen Gille, Office of Representative David Bonior
Rodney Hero, University of Colorado at Boulder
Robert Katzmann, Brookings Institution
Kathleen Knight, University of Houston
Robin Kolodny, Temple University
Nancy Kral, Tomball College
Robert C. Lieberman, Columbia University
David A. Marcum, University of Wyoming
Laura R. Winsky Mattei, State University of New York at Buffalo
Marilyn S. Mertens, Midwestern State University
Barbara Suhay, Henry Ford Community College
Carolyn Wong, Stanford University
Julian Zelizer, State University of New York at Albany

## Second Edition Reviewers

Lydia Andrade, University of North Texas
John Coleman, University of Wisconsin at Madison
Daphne Eastman, Odessa College
Otto Feinstein, Wayne State University
Elizabeth Flores, Delmar College
James Gimpel, University of Maryland at College Park

Jill Glaathar, Southwest Missouri State University
Shaun Herness, University of Florida
William Lyons, University of Tennessee at Knoxville
Andrew Polsky, Hunter College, City University of New York
Grant Reeher, Syracuse University
Richard Rich, Virginia Polytechnic
Bartholomew Sparrow, University of Texas at Austin

## Third Edition Reviewers

Bruce R. Drury, Lamar University
Andrew I. E. Ewoh, Prairie View A&M University
Amy Jasperson, University of Texas at San Antonio
Loch Johnson, University of Georgia
Mark Kann, University of Southern California
Robert L. Perry, University of Texas of the Permian Basin
Wayne Pryor, Brazosport College
Elizabeth A. Rexford, Wharton County Junior College
Andrea Simpson, University of Washington
Brian Smentkowski, Southeast Missouri State University
Nelson Wikstrom, Virginia Commonwealth University

## Fourth Edition Reviewers

M. E. Banks, Virginia Commonwealth University
Lynn Brink, North Lake College
Mark Cichock, University of Texas at Arlington
Del Fields, St. Petersburg College
Nancy Kinney, Washtenaw Community College
William Klein, St. Petersburg College
Dana Morales, Montgomery College
Christopher Muste, Louisiana State University
Larry Norris, South Plains College
David Rankin, State University of New York at Fredonia
Paul Roesler, St. Charles Community College
J. Philip Rogers, San Antonio College
Greg Shaw, Illinois Wesleyan University
Tracy Skopek, Stephen F. Austin State University
Don Smith, University of North Texas
Terri Wright, Cal State, Fullerton

## Fifth Edition Reviewers

Annie Benifield, Tomball College
Denise Dutton, Southwest Missouri State University
Rick Kurtz, Central Michigan University
Kelly McDaniel, Three Rivers Community College
Eric Plutzer, Pennsylvania State University
Daniel Smith, Northwest Missouri State University
Dara Strolovitch, University of Minnesota
Dennis Toombs, San Jacinto College– North
Stacy Ulbig, Southwest Missouri State University

## Sixth Edition Reviewers

Janet Adamski, University of Mary Hardin–Baylor
Greg Andrews, St. Petersburg College
Louis Bolce, Baruch College
Darin Combs, Tulsa Community College
Sean Conroy, University of New Orleans

Paul Cooke, Cy Fair College
Vida Davoudi, Kingwood College
Robert DiClerico, West Virginia University
Corey Ditslear, University of North Texas
Kathy Dolan, University of Wisconsin, Milwaukee
Randy Glean, Midwestern State University
Nancy Kral, Tomball College
Mark Logas, Valencia Community College
Scott MacDougall, Diablo Valley College
David Mann, College of Charleston
Christopher Muste, University of Montana
Richard Pacelle, Georgia Southern University
Sarah Poggione, Florida International University
Richard Rich, Virginia Tech
Thomas Schmeling, Rhode Island College
Scott Spitzer, California State University–Fullerton
Dennis Toombs, San Jacinto College– North
John Vento, Antelope Valley College
Robert Wood, University of North Dakota

## Seventh Edition Reviewers

Molly Andolina, DePaul University
Nancy Bednar, Antelope Valley College
Paul Blakelock, Kingwood College
Amy Brandon, San Jacinto College
Jim Cauthen, John Jay College
Kevin Davis, North Central Texas College
Louis DeSipio, University of California– Irvine
Brandon Franke, Blinn College
Steve Garrison, Midwestern State University
Joseph Howard, University of Central Arkansas
Aaron Knight, Houston Community College
Paul Labedz, Valencia Community College
Elise Langan, John Jay College
Mark Logas, Valencia Community College
Eric Miller, Blinn College
Anthony O'Regan, Los Angeles Valley College
David Putz, Kingwood College
Chis Soper, Pepperdine University
Kevin Wagner, Florida Atlantic University
Laura Wood, Tarrant County College

## Eighth Edition Reviewers

Andrea Aleman, University of Texas at San Antonio

Stephen Amberg, University of Texas at San Antonio

Steve Anthony, Georgia State University

Brian Arbour, John Jay College, CUNY

Greg Arey, Cape Fear Community College

Ellen Baik, University of Texas–Pan American

David Birch, Lone Star College–Tomball

Bill Carroll, Sam Houston State University

Ed Chervenak, University of New Orleans

Gary Church, Mountain View College

Adrian Stefan Clark, Del Mar College

Casey Klofstad, University of Miami

Annie Cole, Los Angeles City College

Greg Combs, University of Texas at Dallas

Cassandra Cookson, Lee College

Brian Cravens, Blinn College

John Crosby, California State University–Chico

Scott Crosby, Valencia Community College

Courtenay Daum, Colorado State University, Fort Collins

Paul Davis, Truckee Meadows Community College

Peter Doas, University of Texas–Pan American

Vida Davoudi, Lone Star College–Kingwood

John Domino, Sam Houston State University

Doug Dow, University of Texas–Dallas

Jeremy Duff, Midwestern State University

Heather Evans, Sam Houston State University

Hyacinth Ezeamii, Albany State University

Bob Fitrakis, Columbus State Community College

Brian Fletcher, Truckee Meadows Community College

Paul Foote, Eastern Kentucky University

Frank Garrahan, Austin Community College

Jimmy Gleason, Purdue University

Steven Greene, North Carolina State University

Jeannie Grussendorf, Georgia State University

M. Ahad Hayaud-Din, Brookhaven College

Virginia Haysley, Lone Star College–Tomball

Alexander Hogan, Lone Star College–CyFair

Glen Hunt, Austin Community College

Mark Jendrysik, University of North Dakota

Krista Jenkins, Fairleigh Dickinson University

Carlos Juárez, Hawaii Pacific University

Melinda Kovács, Sam Houston State University

Paul Labedz, Valencia Community College

Boyd Lanier, Lamar University

Jeff Lazarus, Georgia State University

Jeffrey Lee, Blinn College

Alan Lehmann, Blinn College

Julie Lester, Macon State College

Steven Lichtman, Shippensburg University

Mark Logas, Valencia Community College

Fred Lokken, Truckee Meadows Community College

Shari MacLachlan, Palm Beach Community College

Guy Martin, Winston-Salem State University

Fred Monardi, College of Southern Nevada

Vincent Moscardelli, University of Connecticut

Jason Mycoff, University of Delaware

Sugumaran Narayanan, Midwestern State University

Adam Newmark, Appalachian State University

Larry Norris, South Plains College

Anthony Nownes, University of Tennessee, Knoxville

Elizabeth Oldmixon, University of North Texas

Anthony O'Regan, Los Angeles Valley College

John Osterman, San Jacinto College–Central

Mark Peplowski, College of Southern Nevada

Maria Victoria Perez-Rios, John Jay College, CUNY

Sara Rinfret, University of Wisconsin, Green Bay

Andre Robinson, Pulaski Technical College

Paul Roesler, St. Charles Community College

Susan Roomberg, University of Texas at San Antonio

Ryan Rynbrandt, Collin County Community College

Mario Salas, Northwest Vista College

Michael Sanchez, San Antonio College

Mary Schander, Pasadena City College

Laura Schneider, Grand Valley State University

Ronnee Schreiber, San Diego State University

Subash Shah, Winston-Salem State University

Mark Shomaker, Blinn College

Roy Slater, St. Petersburg College

Scott Spitzer, California State University–Fullerton

Debra St. John, Collin College

John Vento, Antelope Valley College

Eric Whitaker, Western Washington University

Clay Wiegand, Cisco College

Walter Wilson, University of Texas at San Antonio

Kevan Yenerall, Clarion University

Rogerio Zapata, South Texas College

We also must pay thanks to the many collaborators we have had on this project: Dannagal Young of the University of Delaware, who contributed the "Politics and Popular Culture" boxes; Molly Andolina of DePaul University and Krista Jenkins of Fairleigh Dickinson University, who together contributed the new "Get Involved" boxes; and Erin Ackerman and Brian Arbour, both of John Jay College, who contributed "Who Are Americans?" boxes.

We are also grateful for the talents and hard work of several research assistants, whose contributions can never be adequately compensated. In particular, for his work on this Eighth Edition, we thank Peter Ryan.

Perhaps above all, we wish to thank those at W. W. Norton. For its first five editions, editor Steve Dunn helped us shape the book in countless ways. Our current editor, Ann Shin, has carried on the Norton tradition of splendid editorial work. We thank Kelly Mitchell, Patty Cateura, Elyse Rieder, and Rae Grant for devoting an enormous amount of time to finding new photos. For our student Web site and other media resources for the book, Peter Lesser has been an energetic and visionary editor, and Lorraine Klimowich has efficiently managed the test bank and instructor's manual. Patterson Lamb copyedited the manuscript with Marian Johnson's superb direction, and project editor Melissa Atkin devoted countless hours keeping on top of myriad details. Ben Reynolds has been dedicated in managing production. Finally, we wish to thank Roby Harrington, the head of Norton's college department.

Benjamin Ginsberg
Theodore J. Lowi
Margaret Weir
Robert J. Spitzer

*November 2010*

EIGHTH ESSENTIALS EDITION

# We the People

## AN INTRODUCTION TO AMERICAN POLITICS

Most Americans share the core political values of liberty, equality, and democracy and want their government and its policies to reflect these values. However, people often disagree on the meanings of these values and what government should do to protect them.

# Introduction: The Citizen and Government

**WHAT GOVERNMENT DOES AND WHY IT MATTERS** Americans sometimes appear to believe that the government is an institution that does things to them and from which they need protection. Business owners complain that federal health and safety regulations threaten their ability to make a profit. Farmers and ranchers complain that federal and state environmental rules intrude on their property rights. Motorists allege that municipal "red light" cameras, designed to photograph traffic violators, represent the intrusion of "Big Brother" into their lives. Civil libertarians—including groups such as the American Civil Liberties Union (ACLU), organized to defend First Amendment freedoms—express concern over what they view as sometimes overly aggressive police and prosecutorial practices. Everyone complains about federal, state, and local taxes.

Yet many of the same individuals who complain about what the government does *to* them also want the government to do a great deal *for* them. When the mortgage and banking crisis in 2008 threatened to throw the world economy into depression, all eyes turned to the federal government for help. The Treasury Department and the Federal Reserve responded with an unprecedented $787 billion rescue plan that they hoped would restore confidence in financial institutions and prevent a major economic downturn. Americans also look to government for assistance with more routine matters. Farmers are the beneficiaries of billions in federal subsidies and research programs. Motorists would have no roads upon which to be photographed by those hated cameras if not for the tens of billions of dollars spent each year on road construction and maintenance by federal, state, and municipal authorities. Individuals accused of crimes benefit from procedural safeguards and state-funded defense attorneys. Most Americans would not be here at all if it were not for federal immigration policies, which set the terms for entry into the United States and for obtaining citizenship. And, as for those detested taxes, without them there would be no government benefits.

Americans' dependence on the government is brought into particularly sharp focus during times of danger. After the September 11, 2001, terrorist attacks on the World Trade Center and the Pentagon, Americans demanded government action. President George W. Bush responded by mobilizing powerful military forces and organizing an international coalition for what he defined as a lengthy and worldwide campaign against terrorism. Bush also created an Office of Homeland Security (later reorganized as a cabinet department) and instituted massive new law-enforcement measures to combat terrorism. Subsequently, the president ordered that suspected foreign terrorists be tried before special military tribunals, bypassing the civilian courts and their numerous procedural safeguards. The Centers for Disease Control moved to develop methods for preventing bioterrorism. The Treasury Department began tracking funds used to support terrorist activities worldwide. The State Department sought to enhance international support for American antiterrorism efforts. Congress authorized tens of billions of dollars in new federal expenditures to combat terrorism and to repair the damage already caused by terrorists. The states mobilized their own police and national guard forces for duties such as airport security.

As the government seeks to protect its citizens, it faces the challenge of doing so in ways that are true to American values. Liberty, equality, and democracy are key American political values. Liberty means personal freedom and a government whose powers are limited by law. Equality is the idea that all individuals should have the right to participate in political life and society on equivalent terms. Democracy implies placing considerable political power in the hands of ordinary people. Most Americans find it easy to affirm all three values in principle. In practice, however, matters are not always so clear. Policies and practices that seem to affirm one of these values may contradict another. Americans, moreover, are sometimes willing to subordinate liberty to security and have frequently tolerated significant departures from the principles of equality and democracy.

# key concepts

- Even though the relationship between the citizen and the government is central to American government, the government does not necessarily do what the majority of the people want.
- Government affects our lives every day.
- Different types of government are defined by how powerful the government is and how free the people are.
- Politics in America changed when more people won the right to participate.
- The identity and characteristics of Americans have changed over time.
- Liberty, equality, and democracy are core American values, though they often come into conflict with each other.

## Government Affects Our Lives Every Day

Since the United States was established as a nation, Americans have been reluctant to grant government too much power, and they have often been suspicious of politicians. But over the course of the nation's history, Americans have also turned to government for assistance in times of need and have strongly supported the government in periods of war. In 1933, the power of the government began to expand to meet the crises created by the stock market crash of 1929, the Great Depression, and the run on banks of 1933. Congress passed legislation that brought the government into the businesses of home mortgages, farm mortgages, credit, and relief of personal distress. More recently, when the economy fell into a recession in 2008 and 2009, the federal government stepped in to shore up the financial system, oversee the restructuring of the ailing auto companies, and inject hundreds of billions of dollars into the faltering economy.

Yet even in times when politics seems far removed from students' daily lives, it turns out that much of what students think about is political. Figure 1.1 shows an array of first-year college student attitudes. Although being "very well-off financially" is by far the most important goal, all the others are, in some way, political.

The government affects people's lives in good times as well as bad. One important reason for citizens to pay attention to their government in good times is to make sure that the government does not make decisions that might result in unjustified wars, riots, or an economic downturn. The numerous ways in which government affects people daily are nicely summarized in Box 1.1, which shows how many of the routine events in the life of an average college student are affected by the hand of government.

In this chapter, and in this book, we will argue that the key to understanding American government is to understand the relationship between the citizen and the government. This does *not* mean that every government decision is based on

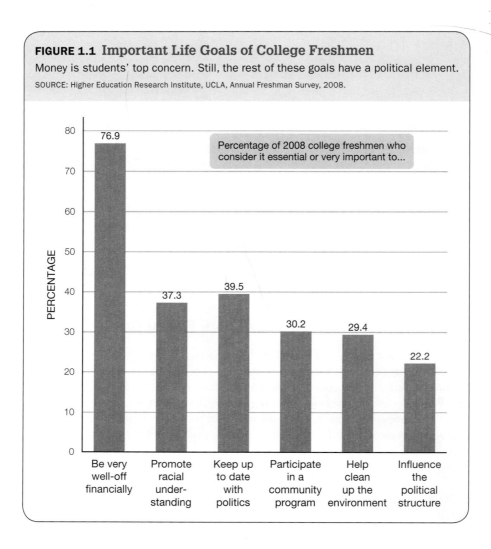

**FIGURE 1.1 Important Life Goals of College Freshmen**

Money is students' top concern. Still, the rest of these goals have a political element.

SOURCE: Higher Education Research Institute, UCLA, Annual Freshman Survey, 2008.

Percentage of 2008 college freshmen who consider it essential or very important to...

| Be very well-off financially | Promote racial under-standing | Keep up to date with politics | Participate in a community program | Help clean up the environment | Influence the political structure |
|---|---|---|---|---|---|
| 76.9 | 37.3 | 39.5 | 30.2 | 29.4 | 22.2 |

what the majority of people want. In fact, there are many instances when the government makes decisions contrary to what most people want.

Sometimes the government contradicts public opinion because well-placed, influential elites exert a great deal of influence over those who make decisions—a circumstance that riles most Americans. At other times, the government may oppose majority wishes because it is acting to protect the fundamental civil or political rights of a few—a circumstance that most citizens would support, at least in principle. The point is that politics takes on a different character according to the extent to which people are informed and involved. In order to understand this complex relationship, we must begin with an understanding of "citizen," "government," and how the two relate to each other. We will then consider three key values that organize American politics: liberty, equality, and democracy.

## The Presence of Government in the Daily Life of a Student at "State University"

| TIME OF DAY | SCHEDULE |
|---|---|
| 7:00 A.M. | Wake up. Standard time set by the national government. |
| 7:10 A.M. | Shower. Water courtesy of local government, either a public entity or a regulated private company. Brush your teeth with toothpaste whose cavity-fighting claims have been verified by a federal agency. Dry your hair with electric dryer, manufactured according to federal government agency guidelines. |
| 7:30 A.M. | Have a bowl of cereal with milk for breakfast. "Nutrition Facts" on food labels are a federal requirement, pasteurization of milk required by state law, freshness dating on milk based on state and federal standards, recycling the empty cereal box and milk carton enabled by state or local laws. |
| 8:30 A.M. | Drive or take public transportation to campus. Air bags and seat belts required by federal and state laws. Roads and bridges paid for by state and local governments, speed and traffic laws set by state and local governments, public transportation subsidized by all levels of government. |
| 8:45 A.M. | Arrive on campus of large public university. Buildings are 70 percent financed by state taxpayers. |
| 9:00 A.M. | First class: Chemistry 101. Tuition partially paid by a federal loan (more than half the cost of university instruction is paid for by taxpayers), chemistry lab paid for with grants from the National Science Foundation (a federal agency) and smaller grants from business corporations made possible by federal income tax deductions for charitable contributions. |
| Noon | Eat lunch. College cafeteria financed by state dormitory authority on land grant from federal Department of Agriculture. |
| 2:00 P.M. | Second class: American Government 101 (your favorite class!). You may be taking this class because it's required by the state legislature or because it fulfills a university requirement. |
| 4:00 P.M. | Third class: Computer lab. Free computers, software, and Internet access courtesy of state subsidies plus grants and discounts from IBM and Microsoft, the costs of which are deducted from their corporate income taxes; Internet built in part by federal government. Duplication of software protected by federal copyright laws. |
| 6:00 P.M. | Eat dinner: hamburger and french fries. Meat inspected for bacteria by federal agencies. |

*(continued)*

(continued)

| | |
|---|---|
| 7:00 P.M. | Work at part-time job at the campus library. Minimum wage set by federal government, books and journals in library paid for by state taxpayers. |
| 10:00 P.M. | Go home. Street lighting paid for by county and city governments, police patrols by city government. |
| 10:15 P.M. | Watch TV. Networks regulated by federal government, cable public-access channels required by city law. Weather forecast provided to broadcasters by a federal agency. |
| Midnight | Put out the garbage before going to bed. Garbage collected by city sanitation department, financed by "user charges." |

## ● Citizenship Is Based on Political Knowledge and Participation

Beginning with the ancient Greeks, citizenship has meant membership in one's community. In fact, the Greeks did not even conceive of the individual as a complete person. The complete person was the public person, the *citizen*; a noncitizen or a private person was referred to as an *idiōtēs*. Participation in public affairs was virtually the definition of citizenship.

Today, voting is considered the building block of **citizenship**—informed and active membership in a political community—as it is the method by which Americans choose their elected leaders. Citizens can influence their government in many ways, including serving on a jury, lobbying, writing a letter to the editor of a local newspaper, and engaging in a public rally or protest. The point of these activities is to influence the government.

Citizens need political knowledge to figure out how best to act in their own interests. To take a simple example, if the garbage is not collected from in front of people's homes, in order to respond effectively people need to know that this job is the responsibility of their local government, not the national government. Americans often complain that government does not respond to their needs, but sometimes the failure of government to act may simply result from citizens' lacking the information necessary to present their problems to the correct government office or agency. To put the matter more simply, effective participation requires knowledge. (It should come as no surprise, then, that people who do not vote have less knowledge of politics than people who do vote.)

Numerous studies and surveys show that many Americans have significant gaps in their political knowledge. For example, in 2010 only 39 percent of those surveyed could identity Harry Reid as the Senate majority leader, and in 2009, only 45 percent could name Federal Reserve Chairman Ben Bernanke. On the other hand, the public is more knowledgeable about politicians who have been prominent in national politics. For example, in the same 2009 survey, 85 percent or more could identify Secretary of State Hillary Clinton.[1]

Greater political knowledge increases the ability of people to influence their government. It is to the nature of government that we now turn.

# ● Government Is Made Up of the Institutions and Procedures by which People Are Ruled

**Government** is the term that describes the formal institutions and procedures through which a territory and its people are ruled. To govern is to rule. A government may be as simple as a tribal council that meets occasionally to advise the chief, or as complex as the vast establishments, with their forms, rules, and bureaucracies, found in the United States and the countries of Europe. A more complex government is sometimes referred to as "the state." In the history of civilization, governments have not been difficult to establish. There have been thousands of them. The hard part is establishing a government that lasts. Even more difficult is developing a stable government that promotes liberty, equality, and democracy.

## Different Forms of Government Are Defined by Power and Freedom

Governments vary in their structure, in their size, and in the way they operate. Two questions are of special importance in determining how governments differ: Who governs? And how much government control is permitted?

In some nations, government power is held by a single individual, such as a king or dictator, or by a small group of powerful individuals, such as military leaders or wealthy landowners. Such a system of government normally pays little attention to popular preferences; it tends to hold power by violence or the threat of violence and is referred to as an **authoritarian** system, meaning that the government recognizes no formal limit but may nevertheless be restrained by the power of other social institutions. A system of government in which the degree of control is even greater is a **totalitarian** system, where the government not only exercises great power, but seeks to impose its will by suppressing any and all other groups and individuals in society that might pose a challenge to its power. Nazi Germany under Adolf Hitler and the Soviet Union under Joseph Stalin are classic examples of totalitarian rule.

In contrast, a **democracy** is a political system where popular wishes and preferences regularly and systematically shape who controls the government and what the government does. Under such a system, **constitutional government** is the norm, in that governmental power is both described in, and limited by, a governing constitution. At times, an authoritarian government might bend to popular wishes, and as we have already pointed out, democratic governments do not automatically follow the wishes of the majority. The point, however, is that these contrasting systems of government are based on very different assumptions and practices (see Box 1.2).

Americans have the good fortune to live in a nation in which limits are placed on what governments can do and how they can do it. But such constitutional democracies are relatively rare in today's world; it is estimated that only twenty or so of the world's nearly two hundred governments could be included in this category. And constitutional democracies were unheard of before the modern era. Prior to the eighteenth and nineteenth centuries, governments seldom sought—and rarely received—the support of their ordinary subjects. The available evidence strongly

## Constitutional, Authoritarian, and Totalitarian Governments

Most Western *democracies* have constitutions that actually define the limits and scope of governmental power. But the mere existence of a constitution does not, by itself, define a regime as constitutional. Some governments have constitutions that they ignore. At least until recently, this was the case in such Eastern European nations as Romania and Bulgaria. In the true constitutional setting, the actual processes of government follow the forms prescribed by the constitution, and groups in society have sufficient freedom and power to oppose efforts by the government to overstep these limits. The governments in the United States and Western Europe provide the best examples.

*Authoritarian* governments must sometimes be responsive to a small number of powerful social groups and institutions such as the army, but such governments recognize no formal obligations to consult their citizens or to respect limits on their actions. Examples of authoritarian governments in the recent past include Spain under the leadership of General Francisco Franco and Portugal under Prime Minister Antonio Salazar.

*Totalitarian* governments can be distinguished from both democratic and authoritarian governments by the lack of any distinction between the government and other important social institutions. Indeed, totalitarian governments generally seek to destroy all other social institutions—for example, churches, labor unions, and political parties—that may function as rival sources of power. Examples of totalitarian governments include the Third Reich in Germany under Hitler in the 1930s and 1940s and the government of the Soviet Union under Stalin between the 1930s and 1950s.

In recent decades, a number of authoritarian regimes in Eastern Europe, including the Soviet Union and its satellite states, faced severe economic hardship and popular discontent. After 1989, most of these regimes, including those in Czechoslovakia, Poland, Hungary, East Germany, and the Soviet Union itself, collapsed and were replaced by new, democratically elected governments.

suggests that the ordinary people had little love for the government or for the social order. After all, they had no stake in it. They equated government with the police officer, the bailiff, and the tax collector.[2]

Beginning in the seventeenth century, in a handful of Western nations, two important changes began to take place in the character and conduct of government. First, governments began to acknowledge formal limits on their power. Second, a small number of governments began to provide the ordinary citizen with a formal voice in public affairs—through the vote. Obviously, the desirability of limits on government and the expansion of popular influence were at the heart of the American Revolution in 1776. "No taxation without representation" was hotly debated from the beginning of the Revolution through the adoption of the modern Constitution in 1789. But even before the Revolution, a tradition of limiting government and expanding citizen participation in the political process had developed throughout western Europe. Thus, to understand how the relationship between rulers and the ruled was transformed, we must broaden our focus to take into account events in Europe as well as in America. We will divide the transformation into its two separate parts. The first is the effort to put limits on government. The second is the effort to expand the influence of the people through access to government and politics.

## Limits on Governments Encouraged Freedom

The key force behind the imposition of limits on government power was a new social class, the bourgeoisie. *Bourgeoisie* is a French word for freeman of the city, or *bourg*. Being part of the bourgeoisie later became associated with being "middle class" and with being in commerce or industry. In order to gain a share of control of government, joining or even displacing the kings, aristocrats, and gentry who had dominated government for centuries, the bourgeoisie sought to change existing institutions—especially parliaments—into instruments of real political participation. Parliaments had existed for centuries but were generally controlled by the aristocrats. The bourgeoisie embraced parliaments as means by which they could exert the weight of their superior numbers and growing economic advantage against their aristocratic rivals. At the same time, the bourgeoisie sought to place restraints on the capacity of governments to threaten these economic and political interests by placing formal or constitutional limits on governmental power.

Although motivated primarily by the need to protect and defend their own interests, the bourgeoisie advanced many of the principles that became the central underpinnings of individual liberty for all citizens—freedom of speech, freedom of assembly, freedom of conscience, and freedom from arbitrary search and seizure. It is important to note here that the bourgeoisie generally did not favor democracy as we know it. They were advocates of electoral and representative institutions, but they favored property requirements and other restrictions so as to limit participation to the middle classes. Yet once these institutions of politics and the protection of the right to engage in politics were established, it was difficult to limit them to the bourgeoisie.

## Expansion of Participation in America Changed the Political Balance

In America, the expansion of participation to ever-larger segments of society, seen mostly in the expansion of voting rights, occurred because of pressure from those who were not a part of the political process, as well as from those already in power who tried to gain political advantage by "lining up the unwashed," as one American historian put it.[3] In the first thirty years of America's history, for example, property qualifications for voting kept most white males out of the voting booths (obviously, African Americans and women did not win the right to vote until much later). In the 1820s, leaders like Andrew Jackson came to power by helping to put an end to property qualifications. These millions of grateful new voters threw overwhelming support behind Jackson and what came to be known as "Jacksonian democracy."

This pattern of suffrage expansion by groups hoping to derive some political advantage has been typical in American history. After the Civil War, one of the chief reasons that Lincoln's Republican Party moved to enfranchise newly freed slaves was to use the support of the former slaves to maintain Republican control over the defeated southern states. Similarly, in the early twentieth century, upper-middle-class "Progressives" advocated women's suffrage because they believed that women were likely to support the reforms espoused by the Progressive movement.

## The Goal of Politics Is Having a Say in What Happens

Expansion of participation means that more and more people have a legal right to take part in politics. Politics is an important term. In its broadest sense, "politics" refers to conflicts over the character, membership, and policies of any organization to which people belong. As Harold Lasswell, a famous political scientist, once put it, politics is the struggle over "who gets what, when, how."[4] Although politics is a phenomenon that can be found in any organization, our concern in this book is more narrow. Here, **politics** will be used to refer only to conflict over the leadership, structure, and policies of governments. The goal of politics, as we define it, is to have a share or a say in the composition of the government's leadership, how the government is organized, or what its policies are going to be. Having a share is called **power** (influence over a government's leadership, organization, or policies) or influence.

Politics can take many forms, including voting, sending letters to government officials, lobbying legislators on behalf of particular programs, and participating in protest marches and even violent demonstrations. A system of government that gives citizens a regular opportunity to elect government officials is usually called a **representative democracy** or **republic.** A system that permits citizens to vote directly on laws and policies is often called a **direct democracy.** At the national level, America is a representative democracy in which citizens select government officials but do not vote on legislation. Some states, however, have provisions for direct legislation through ballot initiative and popular referendum. In 2010, 184 initiatives appeared on state ballots.

# ● The Identity of Americans Has Changed over Time

While American democracy aims to give the people a voice in government, the meaning of "we the people" has changed over time. Who are Americans? Over the course of American history, politicians, religious leaders, prominent scholars, and ordinary Americans have puzzled over and fought about the answer to this fundamental question. It is not surprising that such a simple question could provoke so much conflict: since the Founding, the American population has been a moving target, growing from 3.9 million in 1790, the year of the first official census, to 307 million in 2009. As the American population grew, it became more diverse in nearly every dimension imaginable.[5]

At the time of the Founding, when the United States consisted of thirteen states arrayed along the Eastern Seaboard, 81 percent of Americans traced their roots to Europe, mostly England and northern Europe; nearly one in five were of African origin, the vast majority of whom had been brought to the United States

*Native American societies, with their own forms of government, had existed for thousands of years before the first European settlers arrived. By the time this photo of Red Cloud and other Sioux warriors was taken around 1870, Native Americans made up about 1 percent of the American population.*

against their wills to work as slaves.[6] There was also an unknown number of Native Americans, not counted by the census since the government did not consider them Americans.[7]

Fast-forward to 1900. The country, now stretched out across the continent, had a sharply altered racial and ethnic composition. Waves of immigrants, mainly from Europe, boosted the population to 76 million. The black population stood at 12 percent. Residents who traced their origins to Latin America or Asia each accounted for less than 1 percent of the entire population.[8] Although principally of European origin, the American population had become much more ethnically diverse as immigrants, first from Germany, then Ireland, and finally from Southern and Eastern Europe, made their way to the United States. The foreign-born population of the United States reached its height at 14.7 percent in 1910.[9]

## Immigration and Increasing Ethnic Diversity Have Always Caused Intense Debate

As the population grew more diverse, anxiety about Americans' ethnic identity mounted, and, much as today, politicians and scholars argued about whether the country could absorb such large numbers of immigrants. The debate encompassed such issues as concerns about whether immigrants' political and social values were compatible with American democracy, whether they would learn English, and alarm about the diseases they might bring into the United States. Even the different cooking styles of immigrants—whose cuisines used more garlic than the typical Anglo-American diet—caused anxiety.

Immigrants' religious affiliations also aroused concern. The first immigrants to the United States were overwhelmingly Protestants, many of them fleeing religious persecution. The arrival of Germans and Irish in the middle of the 1800s meant increasing numbers of Catholics, and the large-scale immigration of the early twentieth century threatened to reduce the percentage of Protestants significantly: Eastern European immigrants pouring into the country were heavily Jewish, while the Southern Europeans were mostly Catholic. A more religiously diverse country challenged the implicit Protestantism embedded in many aspects of American public life.

After World War I, Congress responded to the fears swirling around immigration with new laws that sharply limited the number of immigrants who could enter the country each year. Congress also established a new National Origins Quota System based on the nation's population in 1890 before the wave of immigrants from Eastern and Southern Europe arrived.[10] Supporters of ethnic quotas hoped to turn back the clock and return to an earlier America in which Northern Europeans dominated. The new system set up a hierarchy of admissions: Northern European countries received generous quotas, whereas Eastern and Southern European countries were granted very small quotas for new immigrants. These restrictions ratcheted down the numbers of immigrants, so that by 1970, the foreign-born population in the United States reached an all-time low of 5 percent.

## Changing Government Criteria for Racial Classification Reflect America's Changing Identity

Official efforts to use racial and ethnic criteria to restrict the American population were not new. The very first census, as we have seen, did not count Native Americans; in fact, Native Americans were not granted the right to vote until 1924. Most people of African descent were not officially citizens until 1868, when the Fourteenth Amendment to the Constitution conferred citizenship upon the freed slaves.

In 1790 the federal government had sought to limit the nonwhite population with a law stipulating that only free whites could become naturalized citizens. Not until 1870 did Congress lift the ban on the naturalization of nonwhites. Restrictions applied to Asians as well. The Chinese Exclusion Act of 1882 outlawed the entry of Chinese laborers to the United States, and additional barriers enacted after World War I meant that virtually no Asians entered the country as immigrants until 1943, when China became our ally in World War II and these provisions were lifted. People of Hispanic origin do not fit simply into the American system of racial classification. In 1930, for example, the census counted people of Mexican origin as nonwhite but reversed this decision a decade later. Not until 1970 did the census officially begin counting persons of Hispanic origin, noting that they could be any race.[11]

## Today the Country Still Confronts the Question "Who Are Americans?"

By 2000 immigration had profoundly transformed the nation's racial and ethnic profile once again. The primary cause was Congress's decision in 1965 to lift the tight immigration restrictions of the 1920s, a decision that resulted, among other things, in the growth of the Hispanic, or Latino, population. The 2008 census estimates show that the total Hispanic proportion of the population is now 15 percent, while the black, or African American, population is under 13 percent of the total population. Asians compose 4 percent of the population. European Americans account for only two-thirds of the population—their lowest share ever. Moreover, 1.6 percent of the population now identified itself as of "two or more races," a new category added to the census in 2000.[12] Although it is only a small percentage of the population, the biracial category points toward a future in which the traditional labels of racial identification may be blurring. The increasing ambiguity of racial categories poses challenges to a host of policies—many of them put into place to remedy past discrimination—that rely on racial counts of the population.

In 2005, 12 percent of the population was born outside the United States, a figure comparable to the rates of foreign-born at the turn of the previous century. Over half of the foreign-born came from Latin America: one in ten from the Caribbean, nearly four in ten from Central America (including Mexico), and 6 percent from South America. Those born in Asia constituted the next largest group, making up one-quarter of foreign-born residents. In sharp contrast to the immigration patterns of a century earlier, in 2004 only 14 percent of those born outside the United States came from Europe.[13]

These figures represent only legally authorized immigrants, while estimates put the number of unauthorized immigrants at 11.5 to 12 million, the majority of whom are from Mexico and Central America.[14] State and local governments have passed a variety of conflicting laws affecting unauthorized immigrants. Some states have offered driver's licenses to undocumented immigrants, while others have sought to bar them from public services, such as education and emergency health care, both of which are constitutionally guaranteed to unauthorized immigrants.[15] The presence of such a significant proportion of residents who are barred from participating in American politics also poses troubling questions about the health of our democracy.

The new patterns of immigration combined with a number of other factors meant new patterns of religious affiliation in the United States. In 1900, 80 percent of the population was Protestant; by 2000 a little over half of Americans identified themselves as Protestants.[16] Catholics now made up a quarter of the population and Jews accounted for close to 2 percent. A small Muslim population had also grown, with nearly one half of one percent of the population. One of the most important shifts in religious affiliation during the latter half of the twentieth century was the percentage of people who professed no organized religion. In 2006, 12 percent of the population was not affiliated with an organized church. These changes suggest an important shift in American religious identity: although the United States thinks of itself as a "Judeo-Christian" nation, and indeed was 95 percent Protestant,

Catholic, or Jewish from 1900 to 1968, by 2008 the numbers had fallen to only 80 percent of the population.[17] The presence of such religious diversity and a growing secular population set the stage for deep conflicts over policy. For example, many religious groups welcomed President George W. Bush's faith-based initiative, which sought to channel more funds to religious groups to administer social services, while secularists viewed the policy as abrogating the division between church and state.

As America grew and its population expanded and diversified, the country's age profile shifted with it. In 1900 only 4 percent of the population was over sixty-five. As life expectancy increased, the number of older Americans grew with it: by 2008 13 percent of the population was over sixty-five. The number of children under the age of eighteen also changed; in 1900 this group composed 43 percent of the American population; by 2008, children eighteen and under had fallen to less than a quarter of the population.[18] An aging population poses challenges to the United States. As the elderly population grows and the working-age population shrinks, questions arise about how we will fund programs for the elderly, such as Social Security.

Over the course of American history, Americans have changed in other ways as well, moving from mostly rural settings and small towns to large urban areas. Before 1920 less than half the population lived in urban areas; today three-quarters of Americans do.[19] Critics charge that the American political system, created when America was a largely rural society, underrepresents urban areas. The constitutional provision allocating each state two senators, for example, overrepresents sparsely populated rural states and underrepresents urban states, where the population is far more concentrated. The American population has also shifted regionally. In the past fifty years, especially, many Americans left the Northeast and Midwest and moved to the South and Southwest. As congressional seats have been reapportioned to reflect the population shift, many problems that particularly plague the Midwest and Northeast, such as the decline of manufacturing jobs, receive less attention in national politics.

The shifting contours of the American people have regularly raised challenging questions about our politics and governing arrangements. Population growth has spurred politically charged debates about how the population should be apportioned among congressional districts and has also transformed the close democratic relationship between congressional representatives and their constituents envisioned by the framers. For example, the framers stipulated that the number of representatives in the House "shall not exceed one for every thirty Thousand" constituents; today the average member of Congress represents 646,952 constituents.[20] Immigration and the cultural and religious changes it entails provoked heated debates a hundred years ago and still do today. The different languages and customs that immigrants bring to the United States trigger fears that the country is changing in ways that may undermine American values and alter fundamental identities. The large number of unauthorized immigrants in the country today makes these anxieties even more acute. Yet a changing population has been one of the constants of American history: indeed, each generation has confronted the myriad political challenges associated with answering anew, "Who are Americans?"

## America Is Built on the Ideas of Liberty, Equality, and Democracy

A few fundamental values underlie the American system. These values are reflected in such Founding documents as the Declaration of Independence, the Constitution, and the Bill of Rights. The three values on which the American system of government is based are liberty, equality, and democracy.

### Liberty Means Freedom

No ideal is more central to American values than liberty. The Declaration of Independence defined three inalienable rights: "life, liberty and the pursuit of happiness." The preamble of the Constitution likewise identified the need to secure "the blessings of liberty" as one of the key reasons for drawing up the Constitution. For Americans, **liberty** means freedom from government control, and also economic freedom. Both are closely linked to the idea of **limited government,** meaning that powers are defined and limited by a constitution.

The Constitution's first ten amendments, known collectively as the Bill of Rights, above all preserve individual personal liberties and rights. In fact, liberty has come to mean many of the freedoms guaranteed in the Bill of Rights: freedom of speech and writing, the right to assemble freely, and the right to practice religious beliefs without interference from the government. Over the course of American history, the scope of personal liberties has expanded, as laws have become more tolerant and as individuals have successfully used the courts to challenge restrictions on their individual freedoms. Far fewer restrictions exist today on the press, political speech, and individual moral behavior than in the early years of the nation. Even so, conflicts persist over how personal liberties should be extended and when personal liberties violate community norms. For example, one of the most contentious issues in the last forty years has been that of abortion. Whereas defenders of the right to choose abortion view it as

*The issue of freedom plays out in a personal way in abortion rights. In political terms, the debate hinges on the extent of government control over personal liberty.*

# Honing Your Political Radar

Numerous surveys have shown that the vast majority of college students view the world of government as a remote, far-off land dominated by "old white guys in suits." For many people politics seems like something that doesn't really have an impact on their lives, largely because the political system does so little to help younger Americans recognize how important government can be.

As you'll see throughout this book, the political decisions that government officials make can have a real impact on your life. Whom you can and cannot marry, how clean the environment is where you live—these are just two of many examples. The following are a few steps you can take to better understand where you fit into policy debates today and how core political values play out in the real world.

- Investigate a political or social issue that you have an opinion on yet know little about. This sounds odd at first, but we are often asked to offer opinions on things that we haven't had time to examine carefully. Try doing an Internet search on the issue of your choice and reading up on it. Be sure to read things that both contradict and reinforce your opinion. As you do this, think about how your interpretation of one or more core political values (liberty, equality, or democracy) shapes your understanding of this issue. Did thinking through other people's opinions change yours?

- Talk to friends and family about a political or social issue that tends to promote a variety of opinions, such as abortion laws, the environment, health care, or the "right to die." Ask questions about their positions and listen to the differences of opinion that emerge in your conversations. Do the differences have anything to do with disagreements over liberty and equality?

- Watch a TV show with political content, like *The Daily Show with Jon Stewart* or *The O'Reilly Factor* and examine an issue that's covered in the broadcast. What you hear may be just one side of the issue, but a good place to explore other sides of many controversial issues is the Public Agenda Foundation Web site (www.publicagenda.org). If you click on the "Issue Guides" link at the top of the page, you can see what others say about an issue.

- Read the other "Get Involved" sections in this book for specific ways that you can influence government and politics at the national level, at the state level, on your campus, and in your community.

an essential personal freedom for women, opponents view it as murder—something that no society should allow.

In addition to personal freedom, the American concept of liberty means economic freedom. Since the Founding, economic freedom has been linked to capitalism, free markets, and the protection of private property. Free competition, unfettered movement of goods, and the right to enjoy the fruits of one's labor are all essential aspects of economic freedom and American capitalism.[21] In the first century of the Republic, support for capitalism often meant support for the doctrine of *laissez faire* (translated literally as "to leave alone"), an economic system in which the means of production and distribution are privately owned and operated for profit with minimal or no government interference. **Laissez-faire capitalism** allowed very little room for the national government to regulate trade or restrict the use of private property, even in the public interest. Americans still strongly support capitalism and economic liberty, but they now also endorse some restrictions on economic freedoms to protect the public. Federal and state governments now deploy a wide array of regulations in the name of public protection. These include health and safety laws, environmental rules, and workplace regulations. Not surprisingly, fierce disagreements often erupt over what the proper scope of government regulation should be. What some people regard as protecting the public, others see as an infringement of their own freedom to run their businesses and use their property as they see fit.

## Equality Means Treating People Fairly

The Declaration of Independence declares as its first "self-evident" truth that "all men are created equal." As central as it is to the American political creed, however, equality has been a less defined ideal than liberty because people interpret "equality" in different ways. Most Americans share the ideal of **equality of opportunity** wherein all people should have the freedom to use whatever talents and wealth they have to reach their fullest potential. Yet it is hard for Americans to reach an agreement about what constitutes equality of opportunity. Must past inequalities be remedied in order to ensure equal opportunity in the present? Should inequalities in the legal, political, and economic spheres be given the same weight? In contrast to liberty, which requires limits on the role of government, equality implies an obligation of the government to the people.[22]

Americans do make clear distinctions between political equality and social or economic equality. **Political equality** refers to the right to participate in politics equally, based on the principle of "one person, one vote." Beginning from a very restricted definition of political community, which originally included only propertied white men, the United States has moved much closer to an ideal of political equality. Broad support for the ideal of political equality has helped expand the American political community and extend the right to participate to all. Although considerable conflict remains over whether the political system makes it harder for some people to participate and easier for others and about whether the role of money in politics has drowned out the public voice, Americans agree that all citizens should have equal rights to participate and that government should enforce that right.

In part because Americans believe that individuals are free to work as hard as they choose, they have always been less concerned about social or economic inequality. Many Americans regard economic differences as the consequence of individual choices, virtues, or failures. Because of this, Americans tend to be less supportive than most Europeans of government action to ensure equality. Yet when major economic forces, such as the Great Depression of the 1930s, affect many people or when systematic barriers appear to block equality of opportunity, Americans support government action to promote equality. Even then, however, Americans have endorsed only a limited government role designed to help people get back on their feet or to open up opportunity.

## Democracy Means That What the People Want Matters

The essence of democracy is the participation of the people in choosing their rulers and the people's ability to influence what those rulers do. In a democracy, political power ultimately comes from the people. The principle of democracy in which political authority rests ultimately in the hands of the people is known as **popular sovereignty.** In the United States, popular sovereignty and political equality make politicians accountable to the people. Ideally, democracy envisions an engaged citizenry prepared to exercise its power over rulers. As we saw earlier, the United States is a representative democracy, meaning that the people do not rule directly but instead exercise power through elected representatives. Forms of participation

*Political participation was greatest during the nineteenth century. But as this 1854 painting indicates, white men were virtually the only people who could vote at the time.*

in a democracy vary greatly, but voting is a key element of the representative democracy that the American Founders established.

American democracy rests on the principle of **majority rule** with **minority rights,** the democratic principle that a government follows the preferences of the majority of voters but protects the interests of the minority. Majority rule means that the wishes of the majority determine what government does. The House of Representatives—a large body elected directly by the people—was designed in particular to ensure majority rule. But the Founders feared that popular majorities could turn government into a "tyranny of the majority" that would violate individual liberties. Concern for individual rights has thus been a part of American democracy from the beginning. The rights enumerated in the Bill of Rights and enforced through the courts provide an important check on the power of the majority.

## American Political Values Conflict

The ideals of liberty, equality, and democracy can be interpreted in many different ways. Moreover, these ideals can easily conflict with one another in practice. When we examine American history, we can see that there have been large gaps between these ideals and the practice of American politics. We can also see that some ideals have been prized more than others at different historical moments. But it is also clear that as Americans have engaged in political conflict about who should participate in politics and how political institutions should be organized, they have called upon these ideals to justify their actions. So, for example, affirmative action programs, or laws designed to prevent discrimination against the handicapped, such as the Americans with Disabilities Act, may promote equality but may also infringe upon the liberty of employers to hire whomever they wish.

Conversely, in the name of equality or liberty, courts often hand down verdicts that undo decisions of democratically elected legislatures and even decisions reached in popular votes. Principles that seem universal in the abstract become more complicated in operation. In the process of resolving conflicts among core beliefs, America's political principles change and evolve. Even core values should be understood as works in progress rather than immutable facts.

# studyguide

## Practice Quiz

 Find a diagnostic Web Quiz with 20 additional questions on the StudySpace Web site: www.wwnorton.com/we-the-people

1. Generally speaking, Americans know *(p. 8)*
   a) very little about current political issues but are able to identify high-profile political leaders.
   b) a great deal about current political issues but are not able to identify high-profile political leaders.
   c) very little about current political issues and are not able to identify high-profile political leaders.
   d) a great deal about current political issues and are able to identify high-profile political leaders.

2. According to the authors, good citizenship requires *(p. 8)*
   a) political knowledge.
   b) political engagement.
   c) a good education.
   d) both a and b

3. What is the difference between a totalitarian government and an authoritarian one? *(p. 9)*
   a) Authoritarian governments allow for popular participation.
   b) Totalitarian governments are generally religiously based.
   c) In an authoritarian government, certain institutions may operate independently of the government.
   d) There is no difference between the two.

4. The bourgeoisie championed *(p. 11)*
   a) democracy.
   b) "taxation without representation."
   c) limitations on government power.
   d) societal revolution.

5. The famous political scientist Harold Lasswell defined politics as the struggle over *(p. 12)*
   a) who gets elected.
   b) who gets what, when, how.
   c) who protests.
   d) who gets to vote.

6. Although not present at the national level, a number of states and cities permit citizens to vote directly on laws and policies. This form of rule is called *(p. 12)*
   a) representative democracy.
   b) direct democracy.
   c) pluralism.
   d) laissez-faire capitalism.

7. Since 1900, which of the following groups has increased as a percentage of the overall population in the United States? *(pp. 13–14)*
   a) black
   b) Hispanic
   c) Asian
   d) All of the above have increased as a percentage of the overall population.

8. The percentage of foreign-born individuals living in the United States *(pp. 15–16)*
   a) has increased significantly since reaching its low point in 1970.
   b) has decreased significantly since reaching its high point in 1970.
   c) has remained the same since 1970.
   d) has not been studied since 1970.

9. Which of the following is *not* related to the American conception of "liberty"? *(p. 17)*
   a) freedom of speech
   b) free enterprise
   c) freedom of religion
   d) All of the above are related to liberty.

10. Which of the following is an important principle of American democracy? *(pp. 17–21)*
    a) popular sovereignty
    b) majority rule, minority rights
    c) limited government
    d) All of the above are important principles of American democracy.

11. The principle of political equality can be best summed up as *(p. 19)*
    a) "equality of results."
    b) "equality of opportunity."
    c) "one person, one vote."
    d) "equality between the sexes."

12. Which of the following is *not* part of American political culture? *(pp. 20–21)*
    a) belief in equality of results
    b) belief in equality of opportunity
    c) belief in individual liberty
    d) belief in free competition

## Chapter Outline

 Find a detailed Chapter Outline on the StudySpace Web site: www.wwnorton.com/we-the-people

## Key Terms

 Find Flashcards to help you study these terms on the StudySpace Web site: www.wwnorton.com/we-the-people

**authoritarian government** *(p. 9)* a system of rule in which the government recognizes no formal limit but may nevertheless be restrained by the power of other social institutions

**citizenship** *(p. 8)* informed and active membership in a political community

**constitutional government** *(p. 9)* a system of rule in which governmental power is both described in, and limited by, a governing constitution

**democracy** *(p. 9)* a system of rule where popular wishes and preferences regularly and systematically shape who controls the government and what the government does

**direct democracy** *(p. 12)* a system of rule that permits citizens to vote directly on laws and policies

**equality of opportunity** *(p. 19)* a widely shared American ideal that all people should have the freedom to use whatever talents and wealth they have to reach their fullest potential

**government** *(p. 9)* institutions and procedures through which a territory and its people are ruled

**laissez-faire capitalism** *(p. 19)* an economic system in which the means of production and distribution are privately owned and operated for profit with minimal or no government interference

**liberty** *(p. 17)* freedom from government control

**limited government** *(p. 17)* a government whose powers are defined and limited by a constitution

**majority rule/minority rights** *(p. 21)* the democratic principle that a government follows the preferences of the majority of voters but protects the interests of the minority

**political equality** *(p. 19)* the right to participate in politics equally, based on the principle of "one person, one vote"

**politics** *(p. 12)* conflict over the leadership, structure, and policies of governments

**popular sovereignty** *(p. 20)* a principle of democracy in which political authority rests ultimately in the hands of the people

**power** *(p. 12)* influence over a government's leadership, organization, or policies

**representative democracy/republic** *(p. 12)* a system of government that gives citizens a regular opportunity to elect government officials

**totalitarian government** *(p. 9)* a system of rule in which the government not only

exercises great power, but seeks to impose its will by suppressing any and all other groups and individuals in society that might pose a challenge to its power

# For Further Reading

Craig, Stephen C., and Stephen Earl Bennett, eds. *After the Boom: The Politics of Generation X.* Lanham, MD: Rowman and Littlefield, 1997.

Dahl, Robert. *How Democratic Is the American Constitution?* New Haven, CT: Yale University Press, 2002.

Delli Carpini, Michael X., and Scott Keeter. *What Americans Know about Politics and Why It Matters.* New Haven, CT: Yale University Press, 1996.

Hochschild, Jennifer L. *Facing Up to the American Dream: Race, Class, and the Soul of the Nation.* Princeton, NJ: Princeton University Press, 1995.

Huntington, Samuel P. *American Politics: The Promise of Disharmony.* Cambridge, MA: Harvard University Press, 1981.

Lasswell, Harold. *Politics: Who Gets What, When, How.* New York: Meridian Books, 1958.

McClosky, Herbert, and John Zaller. *The American Ethos: Public Attitudes toward Capitalism and Democracy.* Cambridge, MA: Harvard University Press, 1984.

Nie, Norman H., Jane Junn, and Kenneth Stehlik-Barry. *Education and Democratic Citizenship in America.* Chicago: University of Chicago Press, 1996.

Nye, Joseph S., Jr., Philip D. Zelikow, and David C. King, eds. *Why People Don't Trust Government.* Cambridge, MA: Harvard University Press, 1997.

Putnam, Robert. *Making Democracy Work: Civic Traditions in Modern Italy.* Princeton, NJ: Princeton University Press, 1993.

Tocqueville, Alexis de. *Democracy in America.* Trans. Phillips Bradley. New York: Knopf, Vintage Books, 1945; orig. published 1835.

# Recommended Web Sites

**American Democracy Project**
www.aascu.org/programs/adp/
This is an effort by the Association of State Colleges and Universities to increase political engagement among college students. See what opportunities are available for you to become politically active.

**Americans for Informed Democracy**
www.aidemocracy.org
A nonpartisan organization that promotes democracy and seeks to build a new generation of globally conscious leaders. Find out how you can be politically active and coordinate a town hall meeting on campus, attend a leadership retreat, or publish your opinions on democracy.

**DiversityInc**

http://diversityinc.com

This site is dedicated to the promotion of American diversity and education. Here you can read about the issues that directly affect American minorities.

**For Democracy**

www.fordemocracy.com

Most Americans know little about our government. Log on to this independent site to find a plethora of information on the history of American democracy and related current events.

**Future of Freedom Foundation**

www.fff.org

This organization promotes individual liberty, free markets, private property, and limited government. Find out how some people are trying to protect freedom in the United States.

**Institute for Learning Technologies**

www.ilt.columbia.edu/publications/digitext.html

Columbia University's Institute for Learning Technologies provides general information on early political thinkers such as Aristotle, Hobbes, Locke, and Rousseau. Take a moment to read some of the writings on topics such as popular sovereignty, democracy, and limited government.

**Mobilize.org**

http://mobilize.org

This all-partisan network is dedicated to educating, empowering, and energizing young people. Find out how politics affects America's youth and what they are doing about it by being engaged and active.

**SpeakOut.com**

www.speakout.com

This site encourages citizens to be politically informed and active. Visitors with a sense of political efficacy can participate in online polls, contact public officials, and sign petitions on important political issues.

**U.S. Census Bureau**

www.census.gov

The Web site for the Bureau of the Census offers a statistical look at our country's population and economy. Check out some of the statistics to get a better idea of American diversity.

When the framers of the Constitution met in 1787, they set out to establish a political system that would protect liberty and place limits on government. They also believed a powerful government required a broad popular base. However, they debated how best to protect liberty and how to balance democracy with other concerns.

# The Founding and the Constitution

**WHAT GOVERNMENT DOES AND WHY IT MATTERS** The framers of the U.S. Constitution knew why government mattered. In the Constitution's preamble, the framers tell us that the purposes of government are to promote justice, to maintain peace at home, to defend the nation from foreign foes, to provide for the welfare of the citizenry, and, above all, to secure the "Blessings of Liberty" for Americans. The remainder of the Constitution spells out a plan for achieving these great objectives. The plan includes provisions for the exercise of legislative, executive, and judicial powers and a recipe for the division of powers among the federal government's branches and between the national and state governments.

The story of America's Founding and the Constitution is generally presented as something both inevitable and glorious: it was inevitable that the American colonies would break away from England to establish their own country successfully; and it was glorious in that it established the best of all possible forms of government under a new Constitution, which was easily adopted and quickly embraced, even by its critics. In reality, though, America's successful breakaway from England was by no means assured, and the Constitution that we revere today as one of the most brilliant creations of any nation was in fact highly controversial. Moreover, its ratification and durability were often in doubt.

George Washington, the man revered as the father of the country and the person chosen to preside over the Constitutional Convention of 1787, thought the document produced that hot summer in Philadelphia would probably last no more than twenty years, at which time leaders would have to convene again to come up with something new.

That Washington's prediction proved wrong is, indeed, a testament to the enduring strength of the Constitution. But none of the Founders was Moses, and the Constitution was no Ten Commandments, carved by lightning in stone. The Constitution was a product of political bargaining and compromise, formed in very much the same way political decisions are made today. This fact is often overlooked because of what historian Michael Kammen has called the "cult of the Constitution"—a tendency of Americans, going back more than a century, to venerate blindly, sometimes to the point of near worship, the Founders and the document they created.[1]

As we noted in Chapter 1, many governments in the world do not function democratically. In the eighteenth century, authoritarian governments were the norm around the world, so there was much apprehension in America that its new democracy was fragile—that the hard-won freedoms might easily be lost to military or monarchical rule in America. In fact, many who opposed the new constitution did so precisely because they thought it moved the country too close to what would today be labeled an authoritarian form of government.

The proposed new system of government faced considerable opposition. The objections raised by opponents of the proposed constitution—who called themselves Antifederalists—were profound and important. The Antifederalists thought that the state governments would be able to represent the people much better than the national government could. They also were concerned that the officials of a large and powerful government would inevitably abuse their authority.

The founding era was also the period during which Americans first confronted the great question of who was to be included and who was to be excluded from full citizenship. The answer given by the Founders—all white men were entitled to full citizenship rights—was an extremely democratic position for its time. America was one of the few nations that extended citizenship so broadly. Yet the founding generation did not resolve the question once and for all. Over the more than two hundred years since the founding era, as we shall see, the question of who is and who is not a full citizen of the United States has been debated many times and has never been completely resolved.

## ● Political Philosophers Contributed to the Founders' Ideas

The government created by the country's founders was the product of British legal and political traditions, colonial experience, and new ideas about governance that gained currency in the century before America broke with Britain. While America's leaders were first and foremost practical politicians, they also read political philosophy and were influenced by the important thinkers of their day, including Hobbes, Locke, and Montesquieu.

The seventeenth-century British political thinker Thomas Hobbes (1588–1679) was no advocate of democratic government, but he wrote persuasively in *Leviathan* about the necessity of a government authority as an antidote to human existence in a government-less state of nature, where life was "solitary, poor, nasty, brutish, and short." He also believed that governments should have limits on the powers they exercised, and that political systems are based on the idea of "contract theory," meaning that political systems are based on the idea that the people of a country voluntarily gave up some freedom in exchange for an ordered society. The monarchs who ruled that society therefore derived their legitimacy from this contract, not from a God-given right to rule.

Another British political thinker, John Locke (1632–1704), advanced the principles of republican government by arguing not only that monarchical power was not absolute, but that such power was dangerous and should therefore be limited. In a break with Hobbes, Locke argued that the people retained rights despite the social contract they had made with the monarch. Preserving safety in society was not enough; people's property also required protection, as did their lives and liberty. Further, Locke wrote in his *Second Treatise of Civil Government* that the people of a country have a right to overthrow a government they believe to be unjust or tyrannical. This key idea shaped the thinking of the Founders, including Thomas Jefferson, the primary author of the Declaration of Independence, who said that the document was "pure Locke." Locke advanced the important ideas of limited government and consent of the governed.

Baron de la Brède et de Montesquieu (1689–1755) was a French political thinker who advocated the key idea that power needed to be balanced by power as a bulwark against tyranny. The way in which this could be achieved was through the separation of governing powers. This idea was already in practice in Britain, where legislative and executive powers were divided between Parliament and the monarch. In *The Spirit of the Laws*, Montesquieu argued for the separation and elevation of judicial power, which in Britain was still held by the monarch. Montesquieu did not argue for a pure separation of powers; rather, basic functions would be separated, but there would also be some overlap of functions. These ideas were central in shaping the three-branch system of government produced by America's founders in the Constitution of 1787.

## ● Narrow Interests and Political Conflicts Shaped the First Founding

The American Revolution and the U.S. Constitution were outgrowths of a struggle among competing economic and political forces within the colonies. Five sectors of society had interests that were important in colonial politics: (1) the New England merchants; (2) the southern planters; (3) the "royalists"—holders of royal lands, offices, and patents (licenses to engage in a profession or business activity); (4) shopkeepers, artisans, and laborers; and (5) small farmers. Throughout the eighteenth century, these groups were in conflict over issues of taxation, trade, and commerce. For the most part, however, the southern planters, the New England merchants, and the royal office and patent holders—groups that together made up the colonial elite—were able to maintain a political alliance that held in check the more radical forces representing shopkeepers, laborers, and small farmers. After 1760, however, by seriously threatening the interests of New England merchants and southern planters, British tax and trade policies split the colonial elite, permitting radical forces to expand their political influence, and set into motion a chain of events that culminated in the American Revolution.[2]

### British Taxes Hurt Colonial Economic Interests

Beginning in the 1760s, the debts and other financial problems faced by the British government forced it to search for new revenue sources. This search rather quickly led to the Crown's North American colonies, which, on the whole, paid remarkably little in taxes to their parent country. The British government reasoned that a sizable fraction of its debt arose from the expenses it had incurred in defense of the colonies during the recent French and Indian wars (1756–63), as well as from the continuing protection that British forces were giving the colonists from Indian attacks and that the British navy was providing for colonial shipping. Thus, during the 1760s, England sought to impose new, though relatively modest, taxes on the colonists.

Like most governments of the period, the British regime had limited ways in which to collect revenues. The income tax, which in the twentieth century became the single most important source of governmental revenues, had not yet been developed. For the most part, in the mid-eighteenth century, governments relied on tariffs, duties, and other taxes on commerce, and it was to such taxes, including the Stamp Act, that the British turned during the 1760s.

The Stamp Act and other taxes on commerce, such as the Sugar Act of 1764, which taxed sugar, molasses, and other commodities, most heavily affected the two groups in colonial society whose commercial interests and activities were most extensive—the New England merchants and the southern planters. Under the famous slogan "no taxation without representation," the merchants and planters together sought to organize opposition to these new taxes. In the course of the struggle against British tax measures, the planters and merchants broke with their royalist allies and turned to their former adversaries—the shopkeepers, small farmers, laborers, and artisans—for help. With the assistance of these groups, the merchants and planters organized demonstrations and a boycott of British goods that ultimately forced the Crown to rescind most of its new taxes.

From the perspective of the merchants and planters, the British government's decision to eliminate most of the hated taxes represented a victorious end to their struggle with the parent country. They were anxious to end the unrest they had helped to arouse, and they supported the British government's efforts to restore order. Indeed, most respectable Bostonians supported the actions of the British soldiers involved in the Boston Massacre (1770). In their subsequent trial, the soldiers were defended by John Adams, a pillar of Boston society and a future president of the United States. Adams asserted that the soldiers' actions were entirely justified, provoked by "a motley rabble of saucy boys, Negroes and mulattos, Irish teagues and outlandish Jack tars." All but two of the soldiers were acquitted.[3]

Despite the efforts of the British government and the better-off strata of colonial society, political strife persisted. The more radical forces representing shopkeepers, artisans, laborers, and small farmers, who had been mobilized and energized by the struggle over taxes, continued to agitate for political and social change within the colonies. These radicals, led by individuals such as Samuel Adams, a cousin of John Adams, asserted that British power supported an unjust political and social structure within the colonies and began to advocate an end to British rule.[4]

## Political Strife Radicalized the Colonists

The political strife within the colonies was the background for the events of 1773–74. In 1773, the British government granted the politically powerful but ailing East India Company a monopoly on the export of tea from Britain, eliminating

*The British helped radicalize colonists through bad policy decisions in the years before the Revolution. For example, Britain gave the ailing East India Company a monopoly on the tea trade in the American colonies. Colonists feared the monopoly would hurt colonial merchants' business and protested by throwing East India Company tea into Boston Harbor in 1773.*

a lucrative form of trade for colonial merchants. To add to the injury, the East India Company sought to sell the tea directly in the colonies instead of working through the colonial merchants. Tea was an extremely important commodity in the 1770s, and these British actions posed a mortal threat to the New England merchants. Together with their southern allies, the merchants once again called upon the radicals for support. The most dramatic result was the Boston Tea Party of 1773, led by Samuel Adams.

This event was of decisive importance in American history. The merchants had hoped to force the British government to rescind the Tea Act, but they did not support any demands beyond this one. They certainly did not seek independence from Britain. Samuel Adams and the other radicals, however, hoped to provoke the British government to take actions that would alienate its colonial supporters and pave the way for a rebellion. This was precisely the purpose of the Boston Tea Party, and it succeeded. By dumping the East India Company's tea into Boston Harbor, Adams and his followers goaded the British into enacting a number of harsh reprisals. Within five months of the incident in Boston, the House of Commons passed a series of acts that closed the port of Boston to commerce, changed the provincial government of Massachusetts, provided for the removal of accused persons to England for trial, and most important, restricted movement to the West—further alienating the southern planters, who depended upon access to new western lands. These acts of retaliation confirmed the worst criticisms of England and helped radicalize Americans. Radicals such as Samuel Adams and Christopher Gadsden of South Carolina had been agitating for more violent measures to deal with England. But it was Britain's political repression that fanned support for independence.

Thus, the Boston Tea Party set in motion a cycle of provocation and retaliation that in 1774 resulted in the convening of the First Continental Congress—an assembly of delegates from all parts of the colonies which called for a total boycott of British goods and, under the prodding of the radicals, began to consider the possibility of independence from British rule. The eventual result was the Declaration of Independence.

## The Declaration of Independence Explained
## Why We Wanted to Break with England

In 1776, the Second Continental Congress appointed a committee consisting of Thomas Jefferson of Virginia, Benjamin Franklin of Pennsylvania, Roger Sherman of Connecticut, John Adams of Massachusetts, and Robert Livingston of New York to draft a statement of American independence from British rule. The Declaration of Independence, written by Jefferson and adopted by the Second Continental Congress, was an extraordinary philosophical and political document. Philosophically, the Declaration was remarkable for its assertion that certain rights, called "unalienable rights"—including life, liberty, and the pursuit of happiness—could not be abridged by governments. In the world of 1776, a world in which some

THE DECLARATION OF INDEPENDENCE.
JULY 4TH 1776.

*The year after fighting began between American colonists and the British army, the Continental Congress voted for independence on July 2, 1776, and approved the Declaration of Independence two days later, on July 4.*

kings still claimed to rule by divine right, this was a dramatic statement. Politically, the Declaration was remarkable because, despite the differences of interest that divided the colonists along economic, regional, and philosophical lines, the Declaration identified and focused on problems, grievances, aspirations, and principles that might unify the various colonial groups. The Declaration was an attempt to identify and articulate a history and set of principles that might help to forge national unity.[5] It also explained to the rest of the world why American colonists were attempting to break away from England.

## The Articles of Confederation Created Our First National Government

Having declared their independence, the colonies needed to establish a governmental structure. In November 1777, the Continental Congress adopted the **Articles of Confederation**—the United States' first written constitution. Although it was not ratified by all the states until 1781, it was the country's operative constitution for almost twelve years, until March 1789.

The Articles of Confederation was a constitution concerned primarily with limiting the powers of the central government. The central government, first of all, was based entirely in a Congress. Since it was not intended to be a powerful government, it was given no executive branch. Execution of its laws was to be left to the individual states. Second, the Congress had little power. Its members were not much more than delegates or messengers from the state legislatures. They were chosen by the state legislatures, their salaries were paid out of the state treasuries, and they were subject to immediate recall by state authorities. In addition, each state, regardless of its size, had only a single vote.

The Congress was given the power to declare war and make peace, to make treaties and alliances, to coin or borrow money, and to regulate trade with the Native Americans. It could also appoint the senior officers of the United States Army. But it could not levy taxes or regulate commerce among the states. Moreover, the army officers it appointed had no army to serve in because the nation's armed forces were composed of the state militias. And in order to amend the Articles, all thirteen states had to agree—a virtual impossibility. Probably the most unfortunate part of the Articles of Confederation was that the central government could not prevent one state from discriminating against other states in the quest for foreign commerce.

In brief, the relationship between the Congress and the states under the Articles of Confederation was much like the contemporary relationship between the United Nations and its member states, a relationship in which the states retained virtually all governmental powers. It was properly called a **confederation** (a system of government in which states retain sovereign authority except for the powers expressly delegated to the national government) because, as provided under Article II, "each state retains its sovereignty, freedom and independence, and every Power, Jurisdiction and right, which is not by this confederation expressly delegated to the United States, in Congress assembled." Not only was there no executive, there also was no judicial authority and no other means of enforcing the Congress's will. If there was to be any enforcement at all, the states would do it for the Congress.[6]

# The Failure of the Articles Made the "Second Founding" Necessary

The Declaration of Independence and the Articles of Confederation were not sufficient to hold the new nation together as an independent and effective nation-state. From almost the moment of armistice with the British in 1783, moves were afoot to reform and strengthen the Articles of Confederation.

## America's Weakness at Home Made It Weak Abroad

There was a special concern for the country's international position. Competition among the states for foreign commerce allowed the European powers to play the states against one another, which not only made America seem weak and vulnerable abroad but created confusion on both sides of the Atlantic. At one point during the winter of 1786–87, John Adams of Massachusetts, a leader in the independence struggle, was sent to negotiate a new treaty with the British, one that would cover disputes left over from the war. The British government responded that, since the United States under the Articles of Confederation was unable to enforce existing treaties, it would negotiate with each of the thirteen states separately.

At the same time, well-to-do Americans—in particular the New England merchants and southern planters—were troubled by the influence that "radical" forces exercised in the Continental Congress and in the governments of several of the states. The colonists' victory in the Revolutionary War had not only meant the end of British rule, but also significantly changed the balance of political power within the new states. As a result of the Revolution, one key segment of the colonial elite—the royal land, office, and patent holders—was stripped of its economic and political privileges. In fact, many of these individuals, along with tens of thousands of other colonists who considered themselves loyal British subjects, left for Canada after the British surrender. And while the pre-Revolutionary elite was weakened, the pre-Revolutionary radicals were now better organized and were the controlling forces in such states as Pennsylvania and Rhode Island, where they pursued economic and political policies that struck terror into the hearts of the pre-Revolutionary political establishment. In Rhode Island, for example, between 1783 and 1785, a legislature dominated by representatives of small farmers, artisans, and shopkeepers had instituted economic policies, including drastic currency inflation, that frightened business and property owners throughout the country. Of course, the central government under the Articles of Confederation was powerless to intervene.

## The Annapolis Convention Was Key to Calling a National Convention

The continuation of international weakness and domestic economic turmoil led many Americans to consider whether their newly adopted form of government might not already require revision. In the fall of 1786, many state leaders accepted an invitation from the Virginia legislature for a conference of representatives of all the states. Delegates from five states actually attended. This conference, held in Annapolis, Maryland, was the first step toward the second founding. The one positive thing that came out of the Annapolis Convention was a carefully worded resolution calling on the Congress to send commissioners to Philadelphia at a later time "to devise such further provisions as shall appear to them necessary to render the Constitution of the Federal Government adequate to the exigencies of the Union."[7] This resolution was drafted by Alexander Hamilton, a thirty-four-year-old New York lawyer who had played a significant role in the Revolution as George Washington's secretary and who played a still more significant role in framing the Constitution and forming the new government in the 1790s. But the resolution did not necessarily imply any desire to do more than improve and reform the Articles of Confederation.

## Shays's Rebellion Showed How Weak the Government Was

It is quite possible that the Constitutional Convention of 1787 in Philadelphia would never have taken place at all except for a single event that occurred during the winter following the Annapolis Convention: Shays's Rebellion.

Daniel Shays, a former army captain, led a mob of farmers in a rebellion against the government of Massachusetts. The purpose of the rebellion was to prevent foreclosures on their debt-ridden land by keeping the county courts of western Massachusetts from sitting until after the next election. The state militia dispersed the mob, but for several days Shays and his followers terrified the state government by attempting to capture the federal arsenal at Springfield, provoking an appeal to the Congress to help restore order. Within a few days, the state government regained control and captured fourteen of the rebels (all were eventually pardoned). In 1787, a newly elected Massachusetts legislature granted some of the farmers' demands.

Although the incident ended peacefully, its effects lingered and spread. George Washington summed it up: "I am mortified beyond expression that in the moment of our acknowledged independence we should by our conduct verify the predictions of our transatlantic foe, and render ourselves ridiculous and contemptible in the eyes of all Europe."[8]

The Congress under the Confederation had been unable to act decisively in a time of crisis. This provided critics of the Articles of Confederation with precisely the evidence they needed to push Hamilton's Annapolis resolution through the Congress. Thus, the states were asked to send representatives to Philadelphia to discuss constitutional revision. Delegates were eventually sent by every state except Rhode Island.

*In the winter of 1787, Daniel Shays led a makeshift army against the federal arsenal at Springfield to protest heavy taxes levied by the Massachusetts legislature.*

## The Constitutional Convention Didn't Start Out to Write a New Constitution

Delegates selected by the state governments convened in Philadelphia in May 1787. Seventy-four delegates were chosen; fifty-five attended; and thirty-nine eventually signed the Constitution. On the minds of all the delegates were political strife, international embarrassment, national weakness, and local rebellion. Recognizing that these issues were symptoms of fundamental flaws in the Articles of Confederation, the delegates soon abandoned the plan to revise the Articles and committed themselves to a second founding—a second, and ultimately successful, attempt to create a legitimate and effective national system of government. This effort occupied the convention for the next five months.

**A Marriage of Interest and Principle** Scholars have for years disagreed about the motives of the Founders in Philadelphia. Among the most controversial views of the framers' motives is the "economic interpretation" put forward by historian Charles Beard and his disciples.[9] According to Beard's account, America's Founders were a collection of securities speculators and property owners whose only aim was personal enrichment. From this perspective, the Constitution's lofty principles were little more than sophisticated masks behind which the most venal interests sought to enrich themselves.

Contrary to Beard's approach is the view that the framers of the Constitution *were* concerned with philosophical and ethical principles. Indeed, the framers did try to devise a system of government consistent with the dominant philosophical and moral principles of the day. But, in fact, these two views belong together: the Founders' interests were reinforced by their principles. The convention that drafted

*Opponents of the Articles called for a new Constitutional Convention to explore a stronger form of national government. George Washington, a hero of the Revolution, presided over the convention.*

the American Constitution was chiefly organized by the New England merchants and southern planters. Although the delegates representing these groups did not all hope to profit personally from an increase in the value of their securities, as Beard would have it, they did hope to benefit in the broadest political and economic sense by breaking the power of their radical foes and establishing a system of government more compatible with their long-term economic and political interests. Thus, the framers sought to create a new government capable of promoting commerce and protecting property from radical state legislatures. At the same time, they hoped to fashion a government less susceptible than the existing state and national regimes to populist forces hostile to the interests of the commercial and propertied classes.

**The Great Compromise** The proponents of a new government fired their opening shot on May 29, 1787, when Edmund Randolph of Virginia offered a resolution that proposed corrections and enlargements in the Articles of Confederation. The proposal, which showed the strong influence of his fellow Virginian James Madison, was not a simple motion, but a package of his fifteen resolutions that, in effect, created a new government. Randolph later admitted it was intended to be an alternative draft constitution, and it did in fact serve as the framework for what ultimately became, after much debate and amendment, the Constitution. (There is no verbatim record of the debates, but Madison was present during virtually all of the deliberations and kept full notes on them.[10])

The portion of Randolph's motion that became most controversial was called the **Virginia Plan.** This plan provided for a system of representation in the national legislature based upon the population of each state or the proportion of each state's revenue contribution to the national government, or both. (Randolph also proposed a second branch of the legislature, but it was to be elected by the members of the first branch.) Since the states varied enormously in size and wealth, the Virginia Plan was heavily biased in favor of the large states.

While the convention was debating the Virginia Plan, more delegates were arriving in Philadelphia and were beginning to mount opposition to it. Their resolution was introduced by William Paterson of New Jersey and known as the **New Jersey Plan** (which called for equal state representation in the national legislature regardless of population). The main supporters of the New Jersey Plan were delegates from the less-populous states, which included Delaware, New Jersey, Connecticut, and New York, who asserted that the more populous states, such as Virginia, Pennsylvania, North Carolina, Massachusetts, and Georgia, would dominate the new government if representation were determined by population. The smaller states argued that each state should be equally represented in the new regime regardless of that state's population.

The issue of representation was one that threatened to wreck the entire constitutional enterprise. Delegates conferred, factions maneuvered, and tempers flared. James Wilson of Pennsylvania told the small-state delegates that if they wanted to disrupt the union they should go ahead. The separation could, he said, "never happen on better grounds." Small-state delegates were equally blunt. Gunning Bedford of Delaware declared that the small states might look elsewhere for friends if they were forced. "The large states," he said, "dare not dissolve the confederation. If they do the small ones will find some foreign ally of more honor and good faith, who will take them by the hand and do them justice." These sentiments were widely shared. The union, as Oliver Ellsworth of Connecticut put it, was "on the verge of dissolution, scarcely held together by the strength of a hair."

The outcome of this debate was the Connecticut Compromise, also known as the **Great Compromise.** Under the terms of this compromise, in the first branch of Congress—the House of Representatives—the representatives would be apportioned according to the number of inhabitants in each state. This, of course, was what delegates from the large states had sought. But in the second branch—the Senate—each state would have an equal vote regardless of its population; this provision addressed the concerns of the small states. This compromise was not immediately satisfactory to all the delegates. Indeed, two of the most vocal members of the small-state faction, John Lansing and Robert Yates of New York, were so incensed by the concession that their colleagues had made to the large-state forces that they stormed out of the convention. In the end, however, both sets of forces preferred compromise to the breakup of the Union, and the plan was accepted.

### The Question of Slavery: The Three-Fifths Compromise

As important as the Great Compromise was, the notion of a **bicameral** (two-chambered) legislature was no novelty in 1787. Some of the states had had bicameral legislatures for years. A far more fundamental issue had to be confronted before the Great Compromise could take place: the issue of slavery.

Many of the conflicts that emerged during the Constitutional Convention were reflections of the fundamental differences between the slave and the nonslave states—differences that pitted the southern planters and New England merchants against one another. This was the first premonition of a conflict that would later almost destroy the Republic.

More than 90 percent of the country's slaves resided in five states—Georgia, Maryland, North Carolina, South Carolina, and Virginia—where they accounted for 30 percent of the total population. In some places, slaves outnumbered nonslaves by as much as ten to one. For the Constitution to embody any principle of national supremacy, some basic decisions would have to be made about the place of slavery in the general scheme. Madison hit on this point on several occasions as different aspects of the Constitution were being discussed. For example, he observed,

> It seemed now to be pretty well understood that the real difference of interests lay, not between the large and small but between the northern and southern states. The institution of slavery and its consequences formed the line of discrimination.[11]

Northerners and southerners eventually reached agreement through the **Three-fifths Compromise.** The seats in the House of Representatives would be apportioned according to a "population" in which five slaves would count as three free persons. The slaves would not be allowed to vote, of course, but the number of representatives would be apportioned accordingly.

The issue of slavery was the most difficult one faced by the framers and nearly destroyed the Union. Although some delegates believed slavery to be morally wrong, an evil and oppressive institution that made a mockery of the ideals and values

*The new country did not provide freedom for everyone. Samuel Jennings painted this work,* Liberty Displaying the Arts and Sciences, *in 1792. The books, instruments, and classical columns at the left of the painting contrast with the kneeling slaves at the right—illustrating the divide between America's rhetoric of liberty and equality and the political and ecnomic reality of slavery.*

espoused in the Constitution, morality was not the issue that caused the framers to support or oppose the Three-fifths Compromise. Whatever they thought of the institution of slavery, most delegates from the northern states opposed counting slaves in the distribution of congressional seats. Wilson of Pennsylvania, for example, argued that if slaves were citizens they should be treated and counted like other citizens. If, on the other hand, they were property, then why should not other forms of property be counted toward the apportionment of representatives? But southern delegates made it clear that if the northerners refused to give in, they would never agree to the new government. William R. Davie of North Carolina heatedly said that it was time "to speak out." He asserted that the people of North Carolina would never enter the Union if slaves were not counted as part of the basis for representation. Without such agreement, he asserted ominously, "the business was at an end." Even southerners such as Edmund Randolph of Virginia, who conceded that slavery was immoral, insisted upon including slaves in the allocation of congressional seats. This conflict between the southern and northern delegates was so divisive that many came to question the possibility of creating and maintaining a union of the two. Pierce Butler of South Carolina declared that the North and South were as different as Russia and Turkey. Eventually, the North and South compromised on the issue of slavery and representation. Indeed, northerners even agreed to permit a continuation of the odious slave trade until 1808 to keep the South in the Union. The price paid to placate southern slaveholders was to provide a political reward—greater representation in the House of Representatives to slaveholders. As such, the Three-fifths Compromise was an early example of what is now called institutional racism—rules or laws that protect or perpetuate the oppression of racial groups. In due course, Butler proved to be correct, and a bloody war was fought when the disparate interests of the North and the South could no longer be reconciled.

## ● The Constitution Created Both Bold Powers and Sharp Limits on Power

The political significance of the Great Compromise and the Three-fifths Compromise was to reinforce the unity of the mercantile and planter forces that sought to create a new government. The Great Compromise reassured those who feared this new governmental framework would reduce the importance of their own local or regional influence. The Three-fifths Compromise temporarily defused the rivalry between the merchants and planters. Their unity secured, members of the alliance supporting the establishment of a new government moved to fashion a constitutional framework consistent with their economic and political interests.

In particular, the framers sought a new government that, first, would be strong enough to promote commerce and protect property from radical state legislatures such as Rhode Island's. This became the constitutional basis for national control over commerce and finance, as well as for the establishment of national judicial supremacy and the effort to construct a strong presidency. Second, the framers sought to prevent what they saw as the threat posed by the "excessive democracy" of the state and national governments under the Articles of Confederation. This led to such constitutional principles as bicameralism (division of the Congress into two chambers), **checks and balances** (mechanisms through which each branch of government is able to participate in and influence the activities of the other branches), staggered terms in office with longer terms for senators, and indirect election (selection of the president not by voters directly but by an **electoral college,** whereby presidential electors from each state who meet after the popular election cast ballots for president and vice president; and senators chosen by state legislatures). Third, the framers, lacking the power to force the states or the public at large to accept the new form of government, sought to identify principles that would help to secure support. This became the basis of the constitutional provision for direct popular election of representatives and, subsequently, for the addition of the **Bill of Rights** (the first ten amendments to the Constitution, which guarantee certain rights and liberties to the people). Finally, the framers wanted to be certain that the government they created did not pose even more of a threat to its citizens' liberties and property rights than did the radical state legislatures they feared and despised. To prevent the new government from abusing its power, the

BOX 2.1

## The Seven Articles of the Constitution

**I. The Legislative Branch**
House: two-year terms, elected directly by the people.
Senate: six-year terms (staggered so that only one-third of the Senate changes in any given election), appointed by state legislature (changed in 1913 to direct election).
Expressed powers of the national government: collecting taxes, borrowing money, regulating commerce, declaring war, and maintaining an army and a navy; all other power belongs to the states, unless deemed otherwise by the elastic (necessary and proper) clause.
Exclusive powers of the national government: states are expressly forbidden to issue their own paper money, tax imports and exports, regulate trade outside their own borders, and impair the obligation of contracts; these powers are the exclusive domain of the national government.

**II. The Executive Branch**
Presidency: four-year terms (limited in 1951 to a maximum of two terms), elected indirectly by the electoral college.
Powers: can recognize other countries, negotiate treaties, grant reprieves and pardons, convene Congress in special sessions, and veto congressional enactment.

**III. The Judicial Branch**
Supreme Court: lifetime terms, appointed by the president with the approval of the Senate.
Powers: include resolving conflicts between federal and state laws, determining whether power belongs to the national government or the states, and settling controversies between citizens of different states.

**IV. National Unity and Power**
Reciprocity among states: establishes that each state must give "full faith and credit" to official acts of other states, and guarantees citizens of any state the "privileges and immunities" of every other state.

**V. Amending the Constitution**
Procedure: requires approval by two-thirds of Congress and adoption by three-fourths of the states.

**VI. National Supremacy**
The Constitution and national law are the supreme law of the land and cannot be overruled by state law.

**VII. Ratification**
The Constitution became effective when approved by nine states.

framers incorporated principles such as the **separation of powers** (the division of governmental power among several institutions that must cooperate in decision making) and **federalism** (a system of government in which power is divided, by a constitution, between a central government and regional governments) into the Constitution. Let us assess the major provisions of the Constitution's seven articles (listed in Box 2.1) to see how each relates to these objectives.

## The Legislative Branch Was Designed to Be the Most Powerful

In Article I, Sections 1–7, the Constitution provided for a Congress consisting of two chambers—a House of Representatives and a Senate. Members of the House of Representatives were given two-year terms in office and were to be elected directly by the people. Members of the Senate were to be appointed by the state legislatures (this was changed in 1913 by the Seventeenth Amendment, which instituted direct election of senators) for six-year terms. These terms were staggered so that the appointments of one-third of the senators would expire every two years. The Constitution assigned somewhat different tasks to the House and Senate. Although the approval of each body was required for the enactment of a law, the Senate alone was given the power to ratify treaties and approve presidential appointments. The House, on the other hand, was given the sole power to originate revenue bills.

The character of the legislative branch was directly related to the framers' major goals. The House of Representatives was designed to be directly responsible to the people in order to encourage popular consent for the new Constitution and to help enhance the power of the new government. At the same time, to guard against "excessive democracy," the Constitution checked the power of the House of Representatives with that of the Senate, whose members were to be appointed by the states for long terms rather than be elected directly by the people. The purpose of this provision, according to Alexander Hamilton, was to avoid "an unqualified complaisance to every sudden breeze of passion, or to every transient impulse which the people may receive."[12] Staggered terms of service in the Senate, moreover, were intended to make that body even more resistant to popular pressure. Since only one-third of the senators would be selected at any given time, the composition of the institution would be protected from changes in popular preferences transmitted by the state legislatures. This would prevent what James Madison called "mutability in the public councils arising from a rapid succession of new members."[13] Thus, the structure of the legislative branch was designed to contribute to governmental power, to promote popular consent for the new government, and at the same time to place limits on the popular political currents that many of the framers saw as a radical threat to the economic and social order.

The issues of power and consent were important throughout the Constitution. Section 8 of Article I specifically listed the powers of Congress, which include the authority to collect taxes, to borrow money, to regulate commerce, to declare war, and to maintain an army and navy. By granting Congress these powers, the framers indicated very clearly that they intended the new government to be far more powerful than its predecessor. At the same time, by defining the new government's most important powers as belonging to Congress, the framers sought to promote popular acceptance of this critical change by reassuring citizens that their views would be fully represented whenever the government exercised its new powers.

As a further guarantee to the people that the new government would pose no threat to them, the Constitution seemed to say that any powers not listed were not granted at all. Specific powers granted to Congress in the Constitution are **expressed powers.** But the framers intended to create an active and powerful government, and so they included the **elastic clause,** sometimes known as the necessary and proper clause, a phrase found in Article I, Section 8, of the Constitution that provides Congress with the authority to make all laws necessary and proper to carry out the other powers given to Congress. The elastic clause signified that the enumerated powers were meant to be a source of strength to the national government, not a limitation on it. The national government could use each power with the utmost vigor, but could seize upon no new powers without a constitutional amendment. In the absence of such an amendment, any power not enumerated was conceived to be "reserved" to the states (or the people).

## The Executive Branch Created a Brand-New Office

The Constitution provided for the establishment of the presidency in Article II. As Hamilton commented, the presidential article aimed toward "energy in the Executive." It did so in an effort to overcome the natural tendency toward stalemate that was built into the bicameral legislature as well as into the separation of powers among the three branches. The Constitution afforded the president a measure of independence from the people and from the other branches of government—particularly the Congress.

In line with the framers' goal of increasing power to the national government, the president was granted the power to receive ambassadors from other countries, which has amounted to the power to "recognize" other countries. The president was also given the power to negotiate treaties, although their acceptance required the approval of two-thirds of the Senate. The president was given the unconditional right to grant reprieves and pardons, except in cases of impeachment. And the president was provided with the power to appoint major departmental personnel, to convene Congress in special session, and to veto congressional enactments. (The veto power is formidable, but it is not absolute, since Congress can override it by a two-thirds vote.)

The framers hoped to create a presidency that would help the federal government operate more efficiently. At the same time, however, the framers sought to help the president withstand excessively democratic pressures by creating a system of indirect rather than direct election through a separate electoral college.

## The Judicial Branch Was a Check on Too Much Democracy

In establishing the judicial branch in Article III, the Constitution reflected the framers' preoccupations with nationalizing governmental power and checking radical democratic impulses while guarding against potential interference with liberty and property from the new national government itself.

Under the provisions of Article III, the framers created a court that was to be literally a supreme court of the United States, and not merely the highest court of the national government. The most important expression of this intention was granting the Supreme Court the power to resolve any conflicts that might emerge between federal and state laws. In particular, the Supreme Court was given the right to determine whether a power was exclusive to the national government, concurrent with the states, or exclusive to the states. In addition, the Supreme Court was assigned jurisdiction over controversies between citizens of different states. The long-term significance of this provision was that as the country developed a national economy, it came to rely increasingly on the federal judiciary, rather than on the state courts, for the resolution of disputes.

Judges were given lifetime appointments in order to protect them from popular politics and from interference by the other branches. This did not mean that the judiciary would remain totally impartial to political considerations or to the other branches, for the president was to appoint the judges, and the Senate to approve the appointments. Congress would also have the power to create inferior (lower) courts, to change the jurisdiction of the federal courts, to add or subtract federal judges, and even to change the size of the Supreme Court.

No direct mention is made in the Constitution of **judicial review**—the power of the courts to review and, if necessary, declare actions of the legislative and executive branches, invalid or unconstitutional. The Supreme Court asserted this power in *Marbury v. Madison* (1803). The Supreme Court eventually assumed the power of judicial review. Its assumption of this power was based not on the Constitution itself but on the politics of later decades and the membership of the Court.

## National Unity and Power Set the New Constitution Apart from the Old Articles

Various provisions in the Constitution addressed the framers' concern with national unity and power, including Article IV's provisions for comity (reciprocity) among states and among citizens of all states. Each state was prohibited from discriminating against the citizens of other states in favor of its own citizens, with the Supreme Court charged with deciding in each case whether a state had discriminated against goods or people from another state. The Constitution restricted the power of the states in favor of ensuring enough power to the national government to give the country a free-flowing national economy.

The framers' concern with national supremacy was also expressed in Article VI, in the **supremacy clause,** which states that laws passed by the national government and all treaties "shall be the supreme law of the land" and superior to all laws adopted by any state or any subdivision. This meant that states would be expected to respect all laws made under the "authority of the United States." The supremacy clause also bound the officials of all state and local governments as well as the federal government to take an oath of office to support the national Constitution. This meant that every action taken by the United States Congress would have to be applied within each state as though the action were in fact state law.

## The Constitution Established the Process for Amendment

The Constitution established procedures for its own revision in Article V. Its provisions are so difficult that the document has been successfully amended only seventeen times since 1791, when the first ten amendments were adopted. Thousands of other amendments have been proposed in Congress, but fewer than forty of them have even come close to fulfilling the Constitution's requirement of a two-thirds vote in Congress, and only a fraction have gotten anywhere near adoption by three-fourths of the states. Article V also provides that the Constitution can be amended by a constitutional convention. Occasionally, proponents of particular measures, such as a balanced-budget amendment, have called for a constitutional convention to consider their proposals. Whatever the purpose for which it would be called, however, such a convention would presumably have the authority to revise America's entire system of government.

## The Constitution Set Forth Rules for Its Own Ratification

The rules for the ratification of the Constitution were set forth in Article VII. Nine of the thirteen states would have to ratify, or agree upon, the terms in order for the Constitution to pass. This ratification was to occur by approval of special state conventions instead of by the state legislatures, a move to avoid some state legislatures known to be hostile to the new Constitution.

## The Constitution Limits the National Government's Power

As we have indicated, although the framers sought to create a powerful national government, they also wanted to guard against possible misuse of that power. To that end, the framers incorporated two key principles into the Constitution: the separation of powers and federalism. A third set of limitations, in the form of the Bill of Rights, was added to the Constitution to help secure its ratification when opponents of the document charged that it paid insufficient attention to citizens' rights.

**The Separation of Powers** No principle of politics was more widely shared at the time of the 1787 founding than the principle that power must be used to balance power. The French political theorist Baron de la Brède et de Montesquieu (1689–1755) believed that this balance was an indispensable defense against tyranny. His writings, especially his major work, *The Spirit of the Laws*, "were taken as political gospel" at the Philadelphia Convention.[14] Although the principle of the separation of powers was not explicitly stated in the Constitution, the entire structure of the national government was built precisely on Article I, the legislature; Article II, the executive; and Article III, the judiciary (see Figure 2.1).

However, separation of powers is nothing but mere words on parchment without a method to maintain the separation. The method became known by the popular label "checks and balances" (see Figure 2.2). Each branch is given not only its own powers but also some power over the other two branches. Among the most familiar checks and balances are the president's veto as a power over Congress and Congress's power over the president through its control of appointments to high executive posts and to the judiciary. Congress also has power over the president with its control of appropriations and (by the Senate) the right of approval of treaties. The judiciary was assumed to have the power of judicial review over the other two branches.

Another important feature of the separation of powers is the principle of giving each of the branches a distinctly different constituency. Theorists such as Montesquieu called this a "mixed regime," with the president chosen indirectly by electors, the House by popular vote, the Senate (originally) by state legislature, and the judiciary by presidential appointment. By these means, the occupants of each branch would tend to develop very different outlooks on how to govern, different definitions of the public interest, and different alliances with private interests.

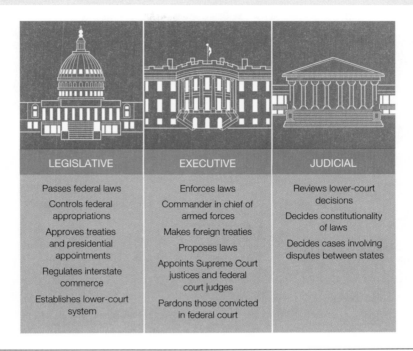

**FIGURE 2.1 Separation of Powers**

The Constitution provides for the separation of powers to ensure that no one branch of American government holds too much power.

| LEGISLATIVE | EXECUTIVE | JUDICIAL |
|---|---|---|
| Passes federal laws | Enforces laws | Reviews lower-court decisions |
| Controls federal appropriations | Commander in chief of armed forces | Decides constitutionality of laws |
| Approves treaties and presidential appointments | Makes foreign treaties | Decides cases involving disputes between states |
| Regulates interstate commerce | Proposes laws | |
| Establishes lower-court system | Appoints Supreme Court justices and federal court judges | |
| | Pardons those convicted in federal court | |

One clever formulation of the separation of powers is that of a system not of separated powers but of "separated institutions sharing power,"[15] thus diminishing the chance that power will be misused.

**Federalism** Compared to the confederation principle of the Articles of Confederation, federalism was a step toward greater centralization of power. The delegates agreed that they needed to place more power at the national level, without completely undermining the power of the state governments. Thus, they devised a system of two sovereigns—the states and the nation—with the hope that competition between the two would be an effective limitation on the power of both.

**The Bill of Rights** Late in the Philadelphia Convention, a motion was made to include a list of citizens' rights in the Constitution. After a brief debate in which hardly a word was said in its favor and only one speech was made against it, the motion was almost unanimously turned down. Most delegates sincerely believed that since the federal government was already limited to its expressed powers, further protection of citizens was not needed. The delegates argued that the states

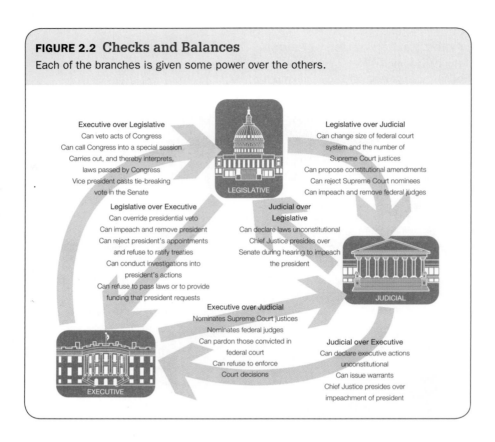

**FIGURE 2.2  Checks and Balances**

Each of the branches is given some power over the others.

**Executive over Legislative**
Can veto acts of Congress
Can call Congress into a special session
Carries out, and thereby interprets,
laws passed by Congress
Vice president casts tie-breaking
vote in the Senate

LEGISLATIVE

**Legislative over Judicial**
Can change size of federal court
system and the number of
Supreme Court justices
Can propose constitutional amendments
Can reject Supreme Court nominees
Can impeach and remove federal judges

**Legislative over Executive**
Can override presidential veto
Can impeach and remove president
Can reject president's appointments
and refuse to ratify treaties
Can conduct investigations into
president's actions
Can refuse to pass laws or to provide
funding that president requests

**Judicial over
Legislative**
Can declare laws unconstitutional
Chief Justice presides over
Senate during hearing to impeach
the president

JUDICIAL

**Executive over Judicial**
Nominates Supreme Court justices
Nominates federal judges
Can pardon those convicted in
federal court
Can refuse to enforce
Court decisions

EXECUTIVE

**Judicial over Executive**
Can declare executive actions
unconstitutional
Can issue warrants
Chief Justice presides over
impeachment of president

should adopt bills of rights because their greater powers needed greater limitations. But almost immediately after the Constitution was ratified, there was a movement to adopt a national bill of rights. This is why the Bill of Rights, adopted in 1791, comprises the first ten amendments to the Constitution rather than being part of the body of it. We will have a good deal more to say about the Bill of Rights in Chapter 4.

# ● Ratification of the Constitution Was Difficult

The first hurdle faced by the new Constitution was ratification by state conventions of delegates elected by the people of each state. This struggle for ratification was carried out in thirteen separate campaigns. Each involved different people, moved at a different pace, and was influenced by local as well as national considerations. Two sides faced off throughout the states, however; the two sides called themselves Federalists and Antifederalists (see Table 2.1). The **Federalists** (those who favored a strong national government and supported the constitution proposed at the American Constitutional Convention of 1787, and who more accurately should have called themselves "Nationalists" but who took their name to appear to follow in the revolutionary tradition) supported the Constitution and preferred a strong

**TABLE 2.1**

## Federalists versus Antifederalists

| | FEDERALISTS | ANTIFEDERALISTS |
|---|---|---|
| Who were they? | Property owners, creditors, merchants | Small farmers, frontiersmen, debtors, shopkeepers |
| What did they believe? | Believed that elites were best fit to govern; feared "excessive democracy" | Believed that government should be closer to the people; feared concentration of power in hands of the elites |
| What system of government did they favor? | Favored strong national government; believed in "filtration" so that only elites would obtain governmental power | Favored retention of power by state governments and protection of individual rights |
| Who were their leaders? | Alexander Hamilton, James Madison, George Washington | Patrick Henry, George Mason, Elbridge Gerry, George Clinton |

national government. The **Antifederalists** favored strong state governments and a weak national government, and were opponents of the constitution proposed at the American Constitutional Convention of 1787. They preferred a federal system of government that was decentralized; they took their name by default, in reaction to their better-organized opponents. The Federalists were united in their support of the Constitution, while the Antifederalists were divided as to what they believed the alternative to the Constitution should be.

During the struggle over ratification of the Constitution, Americans argued about great political issues and principles. How much power should the national government be given? What safeguards were most likely to prevent the abuse of power? What institutional arrangements could best ensure adequate representation for all Americans? Was tyranny to be feared more from the many or from the few?

## Federalists and Antifederalists Fought Bitterly over the Wisdom of the New Document

During the ratification struggle, thousands of essays, speeches, pamphlets, and letters were written in support of and in opposition to the proposed Constitution. The best-known pieces supporting ratification of the Constitution were the eighty-five essays written, under the name of "Publius," by Alexander Hamilton, James Madison, and John Jay between the fall of 1787 and the spring of 1788—known today as the **Federalist Papers.** They not only defended the principles of the Constitution, but also sought to dispel fears of a strong national authority. Originally published in New York newspapers as a kind of eighteenth-century political advocacy campaign designed to persuade dubious New Yorkers (where the new Constitution met an especially chilly reception), the Federalist Papers were cranked our by Hamilton, Madison, and Jay at a rapid pace—three or four a week. The sheer volume of their writing did much to overcome the Constitution's many critics. Even though these essays were designed to present the new Constitution in a favorable light, their depth and brilliance were recognized even in their own time, and they continue to be read and cited as a key source of information on the meaning of our founding document. The Antifederalists published essays of their own, arguing that the new Constitution betrayed the Revolution and was a step toward monarchy. Among the best of the Antifederalist works were the essays, usually attributed to New York Supreme Court Justice Robert Yates, that were written under the name of "Brutus" and published in the *New York Journal* at the same time the Federalist Papers appeared. The Antifederalist view was also ably presented in the pamphlets and letters written by a former delegate to the Continental Congress and future U.S. senator, Richard Henry Lee of Virginia, using the pen name "The Federal Farmer." These essays highlight the major differences of opinion between Federalists and Antifederalists. Federalists appealed to basic principles of government in support of their nationalist vision. Antifederalists cited equally fundamental precepts to support their vision of a looser confederacy of small republics. Three areas of disagreement were representation, majority tyranny, and governmental power.

**Representation** The Antifederalists believed that the best and most representative government was that closest to the people, what we would think of as local and state governments. These smaller, more homogeneous governing units would provide "a true picture of the people . . . [possessing] the knowledge of their circumstances and their wants."[16] A strong national government could not represent the interests of the nation as effectively, the Antifederalists argued, because the nation as a whole was simply too large and diverse.

The Federalists, on the other hand, thought that some distance between the people and their representatives might be a good thing, because it would encourage the selection of a few talented and experienced representatives to serve in a national legislature who could balance the wishes of the people with their own considered judgment. In James Madison's view, representatives would not simply mirror society; rather, they must be "[those] who possess [the] most wisdom to discern, and [the] most virtue to pursue, the common good of the society."[17]

**Tyranny of the Majority** Both Federalists and Antifederalists feared **tyranny**— oppressive and unjust government that employs cruel and arbitrary use of power and authority. But each painted a different picture of what kind of tyranny to fear.

The Antifederalists feared that tyranny would arise from the tendency of governments to become more "aristocratic," wherein a few individuals in positions of authority would use their positions to gain more and more power over the people. For this reason, Antifederalists were sharply critical of those features of the Constitution that limited direct popular influence over the government, including the election of senators by state legislatures, election of the president by the electoral college, and selection of federal judges by the president and the Senate. Judges, who are appointed for life, were seen as an especially dire threat:

"I wonder if the world ever saw . . . a court of justice invested with such immense powers, and yet placed in a situation so little responsible," protested the Antifederalist Brutus.[18]

For the Federalists, tyranny in a republic was less likely to come from aristocrats, and more likely to come from the majority. They feared that a popular majority, "united and actuated by some common impulse of passion, or of interest, adverse to the rights of other citizens," would attempt to "trample on the rules of justice."[19] Those features of the Constitution opposed by the Antifederalists were the very ones that the Federalists defended as the best hope of avoiding tyranny. The sheer size and diversity of the American nation, as represented in the two houses of Congress, would provide a built-in set of balances that would force competing interests to moderate and compromise.

**Governmental Power** A third difference between Federalists and Antifederalists was over the matter of governmental power. Both sides agreed on the principle of **limited government,** meaning a government whose powers are defined and limited by a constitution, but they differed on how best to limit the government.

Antifederalists wanted the powers of the national government to be carefully specified and limited. Otherwise, it would "swallow up all the power of the state governments." Antifederalists bitterly attacked the supremacy clause and the elastic clause of the Constitution, saying that these provisions gave the national government dangerously unlimited grants of power. They also insisted that a bill of rights be added to the Constitution to place limits on the government's power over citizens.

Federalists favored a national government with broad powers. They insisted that the new government must have the power to defend the nation from foreign threats, guard against domestic strife and insurrection, promote commerce, and expand the nation's economy. Federalists agreed that such power could be abused, but believed that the best safeguard against such abuse was through the Constitution's internal checks and controls, not by keeping the national government weak. As Madison said, "[T]he power surrendered by the people is first divided between two distinct governments [federal and state], and then the portion allotted to each subdivided among distinct and separate departments. Hence, a double security arises to the rights of the people. The different governments will control each other, at the same time that each will be controlled by itself."[20] The Federalists considered a bill of rights to be unnecessary, although this Antifederalist demand was eventually embraced by Federalists, including Madison.

## Both Federalists and Antifederalists Contributed to the Success of the New System

In general, the Federalist vision of America triumphed. The Constitution adopted in 1789 created the framework for a powerful national government that for more than two hundred years has defended the nation's interests, promoted its commerce, and maintained national unity. In one notable instance, the national government fought and won a bloody war to prevent the nation from breaking apart. And despite this powerful government, the system of internal checks and balances has functioned reasonably well, as the Federalists predicted, to prevent the national government from tyrannizing its citizens.

Although they were defeated in 1789, the Antifederalists present us with an important picture of a road not taken and of an America that might have been. Would the country have been worse off if it had been governed by a confederacy of small republics linked by a national administration with severely limited powers? Were the Antifederalists correct in predicting that a government given great power in the hope that it might do good would, through "insensible progress," inevitably turn to evil purposes? The verdict of history supports both the Federalist blueprint for American government and the Antifederalist concern for individual rights. In modern politics, many Americans continue to identify with the Antifederalist suspicion of government and its powers. Yet the success of the Federalist plan that has prevailed for over two hundred years surely supports the idea that government is less a "necessary evil" than it is, in historian Garry Wills's phrase, "a necessary good."[21]

## ● Constitutional Amendments Dramatically Changed the Relationship between Citizens and the Government

The Constitution has endured for more than two centuries as the framework of government because it has changed. Without change, the Constitution might have become merely a sacred but obsolete relic of a bygone era.

### Amendments: Many Are Called, Few Are Chosen

The need for change was recognized by the framers of the Constitution, and the provisions for **amendment** (a change added to a bill, law, or constitution) were incorporated into Article V. The Constitution has proven to be extremely difficult to amend. In the history of efforts to amend the Constitution, the most appropriate characterization is "many are called, few are chosen." Since 1789, more than eleven thousand amendments have been formally offered in Congress. Of these, Congress officially proposed only twenty-nine, and twenty-seven of these were eventually ratified by the states.

Four methods of amendment are provided for in Article V:

1. Passage in House and Senate by two-thirds vote, then ratification by majority vote of the legislatures of three-fourths (thirty-eight) of the states.

2. Passage in House and Senate by two-thirds vote, then ratification by conventions called for the purpose in three-fourths of the states.

3. Passage in a national convention called by Congress in response to petitions by two-thirds of the states, then ratification by majority vote of the legislatures of three-fourths of the states.

4. Passage in a national convention, as in (3), then ratification by conventions called for the purpose in three-fourths of the states.

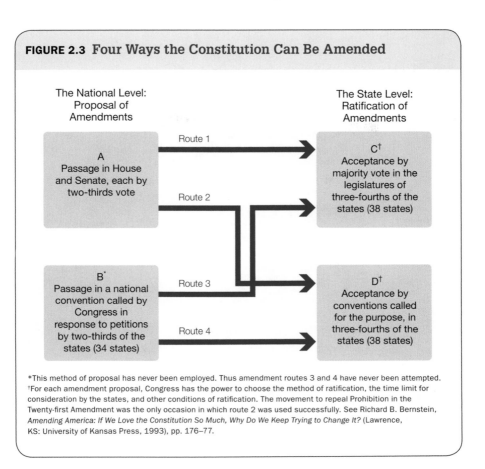

**FIGURE 2.3 Four Ways the Constitution Can Be Amended**

The National Level:
Proposal of
Amendments

The State Level:
Ratification of
Amendments

**A**
Passage in House
and Senate, each by
two-thirds vote

Route 1

Route 2

**C†**
Acceptance by
majority vote in the
legislatures of
three-fourths of the
states (38 states)

**B\***
Passage in a national
convention called by
Congress in
response to petitions
by two-thirds of the
states (34 states)

Route 3

Route 4

**D†**
Acceptance by
conventions called
for the purpose, in
three-fourths of the
states (38 states)

\*This method of proposal has never been employed. Thus amendment routes 3 and 4 have never been attempted.
†For each amendment proposal, Congress has the power to choose the method of ratification, the time limit for consideration by the states, and other conditions of ratification. The movement to repeal Prohibition in the Twenty-first Amendment was the only occasion in which route 2 was used successfully. See Richard B. Bernstein, *Amending America: If We Love the Constitution So Much, Why Do We Keep Trying to Change It?* (Lawrence, KS: University of Kansas Press, 1993), pp. 176–77.

Figure 2.3 illustrates each of these possible methods. Since no amendment has ever been proposed by national convention, methods (3) and (4) have never been employed. And method (2) has only been employed once (the Twenty-first Amendment, which repealed the Eighteenth, or Prohibition, Amendment). Thus, method (1) has been used for all the others.

Now it should be clear why it has been so difficult to amend the Constitution. The requirement of a two-thirds vote in the House and the Senate means that any proposal for an amendment in Congress can be killed by only 34 senators or 136 members of the House. What is more, if the necessary two-thirds vote is obtained, the amendment can still be killed by the refusal or inability of only thirteen out of fifty state legislatures to ratify it. Since each state has an equal vote regardless of its population, the thirteen holdout states may represent a very small fraction of the total American population.

## The Amendment Process Reflects "Higher Law"

The very high failure rate of nearly all amendment attempts suggests that only a limited number of changes can actually be made through the Constitution. Most efforts to amend the Constitution have failed because they were simply attempts

**TABLE 2.2**

## Amendments to the Constitution

| AMENDMENT | PURPOSE | YEAR PROPOSED | YEAR ADOPTED |
| --- | --- | --- | --- |
| XI | Limited jurisdiction of federal courts over suits involving the states. | 1794 | 1798 |
| XII | Provided separate ballot for vice president in the electoral college. | 1803 | 1804 |
| XIII | Eliminated slavery and eliminated the right of states to allow property in persons. | 1865* | 1865 |
| XIV | (Part 1) Provided a national definition of citizenship.† | 1866 | 1868 |
| XIV | (Part 2) Applied due process of Bill of Rights to the states. | 1866 | 1868 |
| XV | Extended voting rights to all races. | 1869 | 1870 |
| XVI | Established national power to tax incomes. | 1909 | 1913 |
| XVII† | Provided direct election of senators. | 1911 | 1913 |
| XIX | Extended voting rights to women. | 1919 | 1920 |
| XX | Eliminated "lame duck" session of Congress. | 1932 | 1933 |
| XXII | Limited presidential term. | 1947 | 1951 |
| XXIII | Extended voting rights to residents of the District of Columbia. | 1960 | 1961 |
| XXIV | Extended voting rights to all classes by abolition of poll taxes. | 1962 | 1964 |
| XXV | Provided presidential succession in case of disability. | 1965 | 1967 |
| XXVI | Extended voting rights to citizens aged 18 and over. | 1971 | 1971§ |
| XXVII | Limited Congress's power to raise its own salary. | 1789 | 1992 |

*The Thirteenth Amendment was proposed January 31, 1865, and adopted less than a year later, on December 18, 1865.
†In defining *citizenship*, the Fourteenth Amendment actually provided the constitutional basis for expanding the electorate to include all races, women, and residents of the District of Columbia. Only the "eighteen-year-olds' amendment" should have been necessary, since it changed the definition of citizenship. The fact that additional amendments were required following the Fourteenth suggests that voting is not considered an inherent right of U.S. citizenship. Instead, it is viewed as a privilege.
†The Eighteenth Amendment, satified in 1919, outlawed the sale and transportation of liquor. It was repealed by the Twenty-first Amendment ratified in 1933.
§The Twenty-sixth Amendment holds the record for speed of adoption. It was proposed on March 23, 1971, and adopted on July 5, 1971.

to use the Constitution as an alternative to legislation for dealing directly with a public problem.

Successful amendments, on the other hand, are concerned with the structure or composition of government (see Table 2.2; the first ten amendments will be discussed in Chapter 4). This is consistent with the dictionary, which defines *constitution* as the makeup or composition of something. And it is consistent with the concept of a constitution as "higher law," because the whole point and purpose of a higher law is to establish a framework within which government and the process of making ordinary law can take place. Even those who would have preferred more changes in the Constitution have to agree that there is great wisdom in this principle. A constitution ought to enable legislation and public policies to take place, but it should not determine what that legislation or those public policies ought to be.

For those whose hopes for change center on the Constitution, it must be emphasized that the amendment route to social change is, and always will be, extremely limited. Through a constitution it is possible to establish a working structure of government and basic rights of citizens by placing limitations on the powers of that government. Once these things have been accomplished, the real problem is how to extend rights to those people who do not already enjoy them. Of course, the Constitution cannot enforce itself. But it can and does have a real influence on everyday life because a right or an obligation set forth in the Constitution can become a cause of action in the hands of an otherwise powerless person.

Private property is an excellent example. Property is one of the most fundamental and well-established rights in the United States; but it is well established not because it is recognized in so many words in the Constitution but because legislatures and courts have made it a crime for anyone, including the government, to trespass or to take away property without compensation.

A constitution is good if it produces the cause of action that leads to good legislation, good case law, and appropriate police behavior. A constitution cannot eliminate power. But its principles can be a citizen's dependable defense against the abuse of power.

# Amending the Constitution

Although only one other amendment has been ratified since the Twenty-sixth, countless others have been introduced by members of Congress or promoted by interested members of the public. All of them have the potential to affect the lives of Americans of all ages. Some of the better-known proposals include:

- The Federal Marriage Amendment, which would define marriage as a union between a man and a woman and expressly prohibit gay marriage.

- The Every Vote Counts Amendment, which would replace the Electoral College with the direct election of the president and vice president.

- The English Language Amendment, which would make English the official language of the United States.

- The Flag Desecration Amendment, which would prohibit the desecration (including burning) of the American flag.

If you get involved in these debates, either by pushing for passage of an amendment or by working to defeat a proposal, you can have an impact on the actual content of our Constitution. There are several ways to get involved:

- To see exactly what amendments have been proposed in Congress, you can search the Library of Congress archives (at www.thomas.gov) using the phrase "proposing an amendment to the Constitution" (since most resolutions begin this way).

- When you see the sponsor of the bill, you can contact him or her directly to voice your support or opposition via telephone, letter, or e-mail. An alphabetical list of all members of the House is available at www.house.gov. You can contact senators at www.senate.gov.

- Find an organization that is working on your side of this issue with a quick Internet search of the amendment. Once you identify an organization, you can decide if you want to contribute money to the group, or perhaps sign an online petition, or participate in one of their rallies or meetings.

- Each of the fifty states is governed by a constitution, most of which are much easier to amend than the U.S. Constitution. For example, while the Federal Marriage Amendment has not passed in Congress, many states have amended their constitutions to ban same-sex marriage. Getting involved at the state level can have a true impact. A good resource on state-level policy is the Pew Research Center's www.stateline.org.

# studyguide

## Practice Quiz

 Find a diagnostic Web Quiz with 33 additional questions on the StudySpace Web site: www.wwnorton.com/we-the-people

1. In their fight against British taxes such as the Stamp Act and the Sugar Act of 1764, New England merchants allied with which of the following groups? *(p. 31)*
   a) artisans
   b) southern planters
   c) laborers
   d) all of the above

2. The first governing document in the United States was *(p. 34)*
   a) the Declaration of Independence.
   b) the Articles of Confederation and Perpetual Union.
   c) the Constitution.
   d) none of the above.

3. Where was the execution of laws conducted under the Articles of Confederation? *(p. 34)*
   a) the presidency
   b) the Congress
   c) the states
   d) the expanding federal bureaucracy

4. Which of the following was *not* a reason that the Articles of Confederation seemed too weak? *(pp. 35–36)*
   a) the lack of a single voice in international affairs
   b) the power of radical forces in the Congress
   c) the impending "tyranny of the states"
   d) the power of radical forces in several states

5. Which event led directly to the Constitutional Convention by providing evidence that the government created under the Articles of Confederation was unable to act decisively in times of national crisis? *(p. 36)*
   a) the Boston Tea Party
   b) the Boston Massacre
   c) Shays's Rebellion
   d) the Annapolis Convention

6. Which state's proposal embodied a principle of representing states in the Congress according to their size and wealth? *(p. 38)*
   a) Connecticut
   b) Maryland
   c) New Jersey
   d) Virginia

7. The agreement reached at the Constitutional Convention that determined that every slave would be counted as a fraction of a person for the purposes of taxation and representation in the House of Representatives was called the *(p. 39)*
   a) Connecticut Compromise.
   b) Three-fifths Compromise.
   c) Great Compromise.
   d) Virginia Plan.

8. What mechanism was instituted in the Congress to guard against "excessive democracy"? *(pp. 39–41)*
   a) bicameralism
   b) staggered Senate terms
   c) appointment of senators for long terms
   d) all of the above

9. Which of the following best describes the Supreme Court as understood by the Founders? *(pp. 44–45)*
   a) the highest court of the national government
   b) arbiter of disputes within the Congress
   c) a figurehead commission of elders
   d) a supreme court of the nation and its states

10. Theorists such as Montesquieu referred to the principle of giving each branch of government a distinctly different constituency as *(p. 46)*
    a) mixed regime.
    b) confederation.

c) limited government.

d) federalism.

11. Which of the following was a concern of the Antifederalists? *(p. 49)*
   a) a national government would "swallow up all the power of the state governments"
   b) the potential for tyranny in the central government
   c) a strong national government would not truly reflect the needs of a large and diverse nation
   d) all of the above

12. Which of the following best describes the process of amending the Constitution? *(p. 52)*
   a) It is difficult and has rarely been used successfully to address specific public problems.
   b) It is difficult and has frequently been used successfully to address specific public problems.
   c) It is easy and has rarely been used successfully to address specific public problems.
   d) It is easy and has frequently been used successfully to address specific public problems.

## Chapter Outline

 Find a detailed Chapter Outline on the StudySpace Web site: www.wwnorton.com/we-the-people

## Key Terms

 Find Flashcards to help you study these terms on the StudySpace Web site: www.wwnorton.com/we-the-people

**amendment** *(p. 52)* a change added to a bill, law, or constitution

**Antifederalists** *(p. 49)* those who favored strong state governments and a weak national government and were opponents of the constitution proposed at the American Constitutional Convention of 1787

**Articles of Confederation** *(p. 34)* America's first written constitution; served as the basis for America's national government until 1789

**bicameral** *(p. 39)* a two-chambered legislature; opposite of unicameral

**Bill of Rights** *(p. 41)* the first ten amendments to the Constitution, which guarantee certain rights and liberties to the people

**checks and balances** *(p. 41)* mechanisms through which each branch of government is able to participate in and influence the activities of the other branches. Major examples include the presidential veto power over congressional legislation, the

power of the Senate to approve presidential appointments, and judicial review of congressional enactments

**confederation** *(p. 34)* a system of government with a weak national government but strong states or provinces

**elastic clause** *(p. 44)* a phrase in Article I, Section 8, of the Constitution (also known as the necessary and proper clause), which provides Congress with the authority to make all laws necessary and proper to carry out the other powers given to Congress

**electoral college** *(p. 41)* the presidential electors from each state who meet after the popular election to cast ballots for president and vice president

**expressed powers** *(p. 43)* specific powers granted to Congress in the Constitution

**federalism** *(p. 42)* a system of government in which power is divided, by a constitution, between the central (national) government and regional (state) governments

**Federalist Papers** *(p. 49)* a series of essays written by James Madison, Alexander Hamilton, and John Jay supporting the ratification of the Constitution

**Federalists** *(p. 48)* those who favored a strong national government and supported the constitution proposed at the American Constitutional Convention of 1787

**Great Compromise** *(p. 39)* the agreement reached at the Constitutional Convention of 1787 where representation in the House of Representatives would be apportioned according to the number of inhabitants in each state, but in the Senate each state would have an equal vote regardless of its population

**judicial review** *(p. 45)* the power of the courts to review and, if necessary, declare actions of the legislative and executive branches invalid or unconstitutional. The Supreme Court asserted this power in *Marbury v. Madison* (1803)

**limited government** *(p. 51)* a government whose powers are defined and limited by a constitution

**New Jersey Plan** *(p. 38)* a framework for the Constitution, introduced by William Paterson, which called for equal state representation in the national legislature regardless of population

**separation of powers** *(p. 42)* the division of governmental power among several institutions that must cooperate in decision making

**supremacy clause** *(p. 45)* Article VI of the Constitution, which states that laws passed by the national government and all treaties "shall be the supreme law of the land" and superior to all laws adopted by any state or any subdivision

**Three-fifths Compromise** *(p. 39)* the agreement reached at the Constitutional Convention of 1787 that stipulated that for purposes of the apportionment of congressional seats, five slaves would count as three free persons

**tyranny** *(p. 50)* oppressive and unjust government that employs cruel and unjust use of power and authority

**Virginia Plan** *(p. 38)* a framework for the Constitution, introduced by Edmund Randolph, which provided for a system of representation in the national legislature based upon the population of each state

# For Further Reading

Beard, Charles. *An Economic Interpretation of the Constitution of the United States.* New York: Macmillan, 1913.

Breyer, Stephen. *Active Liberty: Interpreting Our Democratic Constitution.* New York: Knopf, 2005.

Cohler, Anne M. *Montesquieu's Politics and the Spirit of American Constitutionalism.* Lawrence: University Press of Kansas, 1988.

Ellis, Joseph. *American Creation: Triumphs and Tragedies at the Founding of the Republic.* New York: Knopf, 2007.

Farrand, Max, ed. *The Records of the Federal Convention of 1787.* 4 vols. New Haven, CT: Yale University Press, 1966.

Hamilton, Alexander, James Madison, and John Jay. *The Federalist Papers.* Edited by Isaac Kramnick. New York: Viking, 1987.

Jensen, Merrill. *The Articles of Confederation.* Madison: University of Wisconsin Press, 1963.

Lewis, Anthony. *Freedom for the Thought That We Hate: A Biography of the First Amendment.* New York: Basic Books, 2008.

Main, Jackson Turner. *The Social Structure of Revolutionary America*. Princeton, NJ: Princeton University Press, 1965.

Rossiter, Clinton. *1787: Grand Convention*. New York: Macmillan, 1966.

Storing, Herbert, ed. *The Complete Anti-Federalist*. 7 vols. Chicago: University of Chicago Press, 1981.

Wills, Garry. *A Necessary Evil*. New York: Simon & Schuster, 1999.

Wood, Gordon S. *The Creation of the American Republic*. New York: Norton, 1982.

# Recommended Web Sites

**The American Civil Liberties Union**
**www.aclu.org**
> The ACLU is committed to protecting, for all individuals, the freedoms found in the Bill of Rights. This sometimes controversial organization continuously monitors the government for violations of liberty and encourages its members to take political action.

**Archiving Early America**
**www.earlyamerica.com**
> Revolutionary Americans were motivated by a variety of competing ideals, principles, and interests. Visit this Web site to learn more about the early colonists and the founding of our government.

**Constitution Finder**
**http://confinder.richmond.edu**
> Is the American Constitution a model for the world? Explore the constitutions of many different nations and see what elements of the U.S. Constitution can be found in the governing documents of other countries.

**FindLaw**
**http://findlaw.com/11stategov**
> The Find Law Web site provides all fifty states' constitutions. Click on your state and try to identify such constitutional principles as bicameralism, staggered terms of office, checks and balances, and separation of powers.

**The National Archives**
**www.archives.gov**
> This government site provides information about and actual digital images of such founding documents as the Declaration of Independence, the U.S. Constitution, and the Bill of Rights.

**National Constitution Center**
**www.constitutioncenter.org**
> The National Constitution Center in Philadelphia maintains a Web site that provides in-depth instructional analysis of the U.S. Constitution. Check out the Interactive Constitution function and follow the document from its Preamble through the Twenty-seventh Amendment.

**Oyez**
**www.oyez.org**
> This Web site for U.S. Supreme Court Media has a great search engine for finding information on Supreme Court cases. See how the Court has interpreted the Constitution over time.

**The PBS *Liberty!* Series**
**www.pbs.org/ktca/liberty**
   The PBS *Liberty!* series on the American Revolution offers an in-depth look at the Revolutionary War and includes information on historical events such as the Constitutional Convention.

**The Supreme Court of the United States**
**www.supremecourtus.gov**
   The Web site for the U.S. Supreme Court provides information on recent decisions. Take a moment to read some oral arguments, briefs, and opinions.

In a federal system, state and local governments establish many of the rules that affect people's everyday lives. For example, in 2008, California passed a law that made it illegal to send text messages while driving. Other states have passed their own laws related to using cell phones and e-mail while behind the wheel.

# 3

# Federalism

**WHAT GOVERNMENT DOES AND WHY IT MATTERS** In 2009, the federal Department of Transportation held a summit on the dangers of using cell phones while behind the wheel. Scientists presented evidence that talking, texting, or sending e-mail on cell phones while driving is as dangerous as driving under the influence of alcohol. Yet it is the states, not the federal government, that are responsible for the laws that govern driving. At the time of the national summit, several states had already adopted a variety of laws related to driving and cell-phone use, but with varying penalties. To influence state law, members of Congress introduced legislation that would require states to enact tough laws prohibiting drivers' cell-phone use while driving or risk losing federal highway funds. A competing bill offered states extra transportation funds as an incentive to enact texting bans.[1] These concerns about distracted driving engaged one of the oldest questions in U.S. government: What is the responsibility of the federal government and what is the responsibility of the states? The United States is a federal system, in which the national government shares power with lower levels of government. Throughout American history, lawmakers, politicians, and citizens have wrestled with questions about how responsibilities should be allocated across the different levels of government. Some responsibilities, such as international relations, clearly lie with the federal government. Others, such as divorce laws, are controlled by state governments. In fact, most of the rules and regulations that Americans face in their daily lives are set by state and local governments. However, many government responsibilities are shared in American federalism and require cooperation among local, state, and federal governments. These include such activities as responding to natural disasters, including hurricanes; building transportation systems that include roads, bridges, airports, and mass transit; providing education; protecting the health and safety of citizens; providing social benefits; protecting civil liberties; and administering criminal justice.

The debate about "who should do what" remains one of the most important discussions in American politics. Much is at stake in how authority is divided up among national, state, and local governments. Reflecting the Founders' mistrust of centralized power and Americans' long-standing preference for local self-government, American federalism promotes the value of democracy by allowing states to set their own standards for many of the issues that most affect people's lives. Variations in state laws reflect the distinctive priorities of each state. Yet since the 1930s, the federal government has played an expanded role in ensuring democracy, equality, and liberty. During the 1960s, it outlawed many obstacles to political participation in the American South. By funding social welfare programs and setting national standards, the federal government helps to limit inequality across the states. Federal laws also ensure that basic liberties are enforced in every state. In recent years, a trend to return more power to the states has allowed greater differences in the laws and social protections in the states. Though this trend has slowed the move toward greater equality, its proponents believe that it has in fact enhanced democracy.

## key concepts

- Federalism has shaped American politics from the country's beginnings to the present.
- The definition of federalism has changed radically in the last two centuries. The federal government has done far more since the 1930s than it did during the "traditional system," from 1789 to the 1930s.
- The states continue to exert great power over citizens' everyday lives.
- The "New Federalism" of recent years has turned more power back to the states.
- Sometimes the federal government requires the states to do things but does not give the states the money to do them.

# Federalism Shapes American Politics

Even though the word "federalism" never appears in the Constitution, the concept arises directly from the document. **Federalism** can be defined with misleading ease as the division of powers and functions between the central (national) government and regional (state) governments. This simple definition causes confusion, however, as many assume that federalism means giving most power to the "federal" government, when in fact it does not. Aside from America, other nations with diverse ethnic or language groupings, such as Switzerland and Canada, also have federalist systems (although the specific ways in which power is shared in these nations varies, so that no two federal systems are exactly alike).

A governing system that does give most power to the federal or national government is called a **unitary system.** In this system, lower levels of government have little independent power. In France, for example, the central government was once so involved in the smallest details of local activity that the minister of education boasted that by looking at his watch he could tell what all French schoolchildren were learning at that time because the central government set the school curriculum. At the other end of the spectrum, a confederation is a system with a weak national government but strong states or provinces. America's first constitution, the Articles of Confederation, is such an example.

## Federalism Comes from the Constitution

The United States was the first nation to adopt federalism as its governing framework. With federalism, the framers sought to limit the national government by creating a second layer of state governments. American federalism recognized two sovereigns in the original Constitution and reinforced the principle in the Bill of Rights by granting a few **expressed powers** (powers specifically granted to Congress in the Constitution) to the national government and reserving all the rest to the states.

**The Powers of the National Government** As we saw in Chapter 2, the "expressed powers" granted to the national government are found in Article I, Section 8, of the Constitution. These seventeen powers include the power to collect taxes, to coin money, to declare war, and to regulate commerce (which, as we will see, became a very important power for the national government). Article I, Section 8, also contains another important source of power for the national government: the **implied powers** that enable Congress "to make all Laws which shall be necessary and proper for carrying into Execution the foregoing Powers." Such powers are not specifically expressed but are implied through the expansive interpretation of delegated powers. Not until several decades after the Founding did the Supreme Court allow Congress to exercise the power granted in this **necessary and proper clause,** but, as we shall see later in this chapter, this doctrine allowed the national government to expand considerably the scope of its authority, although the process was a slow one.

Aside from these powers, the federal government operates with one other advantage over the states: as mentioned in the last chapter, Article VI of the Constitution says that whenever there is a conflict between a national law and a state law, the national law shall prevail. This doctrine of *national supremacy* says that

*Should same-sex marriages performed in one state be legally recognized in another state? State laws vary, and despite the Constitution's "full faith and credit" clause, these differences can lead to debate over controversial issues.*

"[t]his Constitution, and the Laws of the United States . . . and all Treaties made . . . shall be the supreme Law of the Land," even extending to state courts and constitutions.

## The Powers of State Government

One way in which the framers sought to preserve a strong role for the states was through the Tenth Amendment to the Constitution. The Tenth Amendment states that the powers that the Constitution does not delegate to the national government or prohibit to the states are "reserved to the States respectively, or to the people." The Antifederalists, who feared that a strong central government would encroach on individual liberty, repeatedly pressed for such an amendment as a way of limiting national power. Federalists agreed to the amendment because they did not think it would do much harm, given the powers of the Constitution already granted to the national government. The Tenth Amendment is also called the **reserved powers** amendment because it aims to reserve powers to the states.

The most fundamental power that is retained by the states is that of coercion—the power to develop and enforce criminal codes, to administer health and safety rules, and to regulate the family via marriage and divorce laws. The states have the power to regulate individuals' livelihoods; if you're a doctor or a lawyer or a plumber or a hair stylist, you must be licensed by the state. Even more fundamentally, the states have the power to define private property— private property exists because state laws against trespass define who is and is not entitled to use a piece of property. If you own a car, your ownership isn't worth much unless the state is willing to enforce your right to possession by making it a crime for anyone else to drive your car without your permission. These laws are essential to citizens' everyday lives, and the powers of the states regarding such domestic issues are much greater than the powers of the national government, even today.

A state's authority to regulate the health, safety, and morals of its citizens is commonly referred to as the **police power** of the state. Policing is what states do—they coerce you in the name of the community in order to maintain public order. And this was exactly the type of power that the Founders intended the states to exercise.

In some areas, the states share **concurrent powers** (powers exercised by both the federal and the state governments) with the national government, wherein they retain and share some power to regulate commerce and to affect the currency—for example, by being able to charter banks, grant or deny corporate charters, grant or deny licenses to engage in a business or practice a trade, and regulate the quality of products or the conditions of labor. This issue of concurrent versus exclusive power has come up from time to time in our history, but wherever there is a direct conflict of laws between the federal and the state levels, the issue will most likely be resolved in favor of national supremacy.

**States' Obligations to One Another** The Constitution also creates obligations among the states. These obligations, spelled out in Article IV, were intended to promote national unity. By requiring the states to recognize actions and decisions taken in other states as legal and proper, the framers aimed to make the states less like independent countries and more like parts of a single nation.

Article IV, Section I, establishes the **full faith and credit clause** applying to states, meaning that each state is normally expected to honor the "public Acts, Records, and judicial Proceedings" that take place in any other state. So, for example, if a couple is married in Texas—marriage being regulated by state law—Missouri must also recognize that marriage, even though they were not married under Missouri state law.

The "full faith and credit" clause has become embroiled in the controversy over gay and lesbian marriage. The matter first received nationwide attention when the Vermont Supreme Court ruled in 1999 that gay and lesbian couples should have the same rights as heterosexuals. The following year, Vermont's legislature enacted legislation to allow "civil unions," granting many legal rights to gay and lesbian couples, such as eligibility for the partner's health insurance, inheritance rights, and the right to transfer property. In 2009, the legislature legalized gay marriage. In 2010, five states allow gay marriage: Connecticut, Iowa, Massachusetts, New Hampshire, and Vermont. The District of Columbia recognized gay marriage in 2010. Of these, Massachusetts was the first state to adopt such a law, in 2004. In the first year of the law, 6,200 same-sex marriages were performed. The second year, the number dropped to 1,900.[2]

Three other states, Maryland, New York, and Rhode Island, recognize gay marriages performed elsewhere. Maine's state legislature enacted a similar law, but it was defeated in a statewide voter referendum in 2009. Gay marriage was legal in California for six months until the state's same-sex marriage law was defeated by voter referendum in 2008. Most states have reacted against gay marriage by enacting their own laws. As of 2009, forty-one states have adopted laws defining marriage solely as a union of a man and woman, and thirty states have amended their state constitutions to say the same thing.[3]

The principle of "full faith and credit" would seem to suggest that states without gay marriage would be obliged to recognize such unions in their states, just as they would recognize heterosexual marriages performed in other states. But to forestall this possibility, in 1996 Congress passed the Defense of Marriage Act (DOMA), which declared that states did *not* have to recognize same-sex marriage even if it is legal in other states. The law also said that the federal government will not recognize gay marriage,

## TABLE 3.1

### 89,527 Governments in the United States

| TYPE | NUMBER |
| --- | --- |
| National | 1 |
| State | 50 |
| County | 3,033 |
| Municipal | 19,492 |
| Townships | 16,519 |
| School districts | 13,051 |
| Other special districts | 37,381 |

SOURCE: U.S. Census Bureau, www.census.gov/govs/cog/GovOrg Tab03ss.html (accessed 2/2/10).

even if legal in some states, and that same-sex partners are not eligible for federal benefits such as Medicare and Social Security. Legal efforts are under way to challenge the constitutionality of both the federal and the state DOMA laws.

Article IV, Section 2, known as the "comity clause," also seeks to promote national unity. This clause provides that citizens enjoying the **"privileges and immunities"** of one state should be entitled to similar treatment in other states. What this has come to mean is that a state cannot discriminate against someone from another state or give special privileges to its own residents. For example, in the 1970s, when Alaska passed a law that gave residents preference over nonresidents in obtaining work on the state's oil and gas pipelines, the Supreme Court ruled the law illegal because it discriminated against citizens of other states.[4] This clause also regulates criminal justice among the states by requiring states to return fugitives to the states from which they have fled. Thus, in 1952, when an inmate escaped from an Alabama prison and sought to avoid being returned to Alabama on the grounds that he was being subjected to "cruel and unusual punishment" there, the Supreme Court ruled that he must be returned according to Article IV, Section 2.[5] This example highlights the difference between the obligations among states and those among different countries. In 1997, France refused to return an American fugitive because he might be subject to the death penalty, which does not exist in France.[6] The Constitution clearly forbids states from doing something similar.

**Local Government and the Constitution** Local government occupies a peculiar but very important place in the American system. In fact, the status of American local government is probably unique in world experience. First, it must be pointed out that local governments have no status in the U.S. Constitution. *State* legislatures created local governments, and *state* constitutions and laws permit local governments to take on some of the responsibilities of the state governments. Most states amended their own constitutions to give their larger cities **home rule**—powers delegated by the state to a local unit of government to manage its own affairs. But local governments enjoy no such recognition in the Constitution. Local governments have always been mere conveniences of the states.[7]

Local governments became administratively important in the early years of the Republic because the states possessed little administrative capability. They relied on local governments—cities and counties—to implement the laws of the state. Local government was an alternative to a statewide bureaucracy (see Table 3.1).

# The Definition of Federalism Has Changed Radically over Time

Many of the fiercest political controversies in American history have revolved around competing views of federalism. The best way to understand these disputes, and how federalism has been redefined throughout American history, is to examine how its conception has changed over time. During the "traditional system" in America, from 1789 to 1933, the political balance scales clearly favored the states over the federal government. From the New Deal period of the 1930s to the present, some important limits were placed on state governments, and the federal government exerted far more power than it had under the traditional system, despite efforts to roll back national government powers in recent decades.

## Federalism under the "Traditional System" Gave Most Powers to the States

The prevailing view of national government–state government relations under the traditional system was one of **dual federalism,** meaning the system of government that prevailed in the United States from 1789 to 1937, in which most fundamental governmental powers were shared between the federal and state governments; during this time, the states possessed a vast amount of governing power. Virtually all of the important policies affecting the lives of Americans were made by the state governments during this period. Remember that at the time of the country's founding, the states had existed as former colonies and then as virtually autonomous units for about thirteen years under the Articles of Confederation. The Constitution imposed a stronger national government upon the states, but the tradition of strong states continued. The novelty of this arrangement can be appreciated by noting that each of the major European countries at that time had a unitary government, composed of a strong single national government with national ministries, a national police force, and a national code of laws covering crime, commerce, public works, education, and all other areas.

As we mentioned earlier, during the period of dual federalism, the states did most of the actual governing. For evidence, look at Table 3.2. It lists the major types of public policies by which Americans were governed for the first century and a half under the Constitution. We call this period of dual federalism the "traditional system" because it covers three-quarters of American history and because the style of national and state governing during this time closely approximates the intentions of the framers of the Constitution.

Under the traditional system, the national government was quite small by comparison both to the state governments and to the governments of other Western nations. Not only was it smaller than most governments of that time, it was actually very narrowly specialized in the functions it performed. The national government built or sponsored the construction of roads, canals, and bridges (internal improvements). It provided cash subsidies to shippers and shipbuilders and distributed free or low-priced public land to encourage western settlement and business ventures. It placed relatively heavy taxes on imported goods (tariffs), not only to raise revenues

**TABLE 3.2**

## The Federal System: Specialization of Governmental Functions in the Traditional System (1789–1933)

| NATIONAL GOVERNMENT POLICIES (DOMESTIC) | STATE GOVERNMENT POLICIES | LOCAL GOVERNMENT POLICIES |
|---|---|---|
| Internal improvements | Property laws (including | Adaptation of state laws |
| Subsidies | slavery) | to local conditions |
| Tariffs | Estate and inheritance | ("variances") |
| Public lands disposal | laws | Public works |
| Patents | Commerce laws | Contracts for public |
| Currency | Banking and credit laws | works |
| | Corporate laws | Licensing of public |
| | Insurance laws | accommodations |
| | Family laws | Assessible improvements |
| | Morality laws | Basic public services |
| | Public health laws | |
| | Education laws | |
| | General penal laws | |
| | Eminent domain laws | |
| | Construction codes | |
| | Land-use laws | |
| | Water and mineral laws | |
| | Criminal procedure | |
| | laws | |
| | Electoral and political | |
| | parties laws | |
| | Local government laws | |
| | Civil service laws | |
| | Occupations and | |
| | professions laws | |

but to protect "infant industries" from competition from the more advanced European enterprises. It protected patents and provided for a common currency, also to encourage and facilitate enterprises and to expand markets.

What do these functions of the national government reveal? First, virtually all the national government's functions were aimed at assisting commerce. It is quite appropriate to refer to the traditional American system as a "commercial republic." Second, virtually none of the national government's policies directly coerced citizens. The emphasis of governmental programs was on assistance, promotion, and encouragement—the allocation of land or capital where they were insufficiently available for economic development.

Meanwhile, state legislatures were actively involved in economic regulation during the nineteenth century. In the United States, then and now, private property exists only in state laws and state court decisions regarding property, trespass, and real estate. American capitalism took its form from state property and trespass laws, as well as from state laws and court decisions regarding contracts, markets, credit, banking, incorporation, and insurance. Laws concerning slavery were a subdivision of property law in states where slavery existed. The practice of important professions, such as law and medicine, was and is illegal except as provided for by state law. Marriage, divorce, and the birth or adoption of a child have always been regulated by state law. To educate or not to educate a child has been a decision governed more by state laws than by parents, and not at all by national law. It is important to note also that virtually all criminal laws—regarding everything from trespass to murder—have been state laws. Most of the criminal laws adopted by Congress are concerned with the District of Columbia and other federal territories. Thus, most of the fundamental governing in the United States was done by the states.

Here lies the most important point of all: The fundamental impact of federalism on the way the United States is governed comes not from any particular provision of the Constitution but from the framework itself, which has determined the flow of government functions and, through that, the political development of the country. By allowing state governments to do most of the fundamental governing, the Constitution saved the national government from many policy decisions that might have proved too divisive for a large and very young country. There is no doubt that if the Constitution had provided for a unitary rather than a federal system, the war over slavery would have come in 1789 or 1809 rather than in 1861; and if it had come that early, the South might very well have seceded and established a separate and permanent slaveholding nation.

*In 1815, President James Madison called for a federally funded program of "internal improvements," which was one of the few policy roles for the national government during the first half of the nineteenth century. By improving transportation through the construction of roads and canals, the government fostered the growth of the market economy and boosted federal power.*

In helping the national government remain small and apart from the most divisive issues of the day, federalism contributed significantly to the political stability of the young nation, even as the social, economic, and political systems of many of the states and regions of the country were undergoing tremendous, profound, and sometimes violent change.[8] As we shall see, some important aspects of federalism have changed, but the federal framework has survived over two centuries and through a devastating civil war.

## The Supreme Court Paved the Way for the End of the "Traditional System"

Having created the national government, and recognizing the potential for abuse of power, the states sought through federalism to constrain the national government. The "traditional system" of a weak national government prevailed for over a century despite economic forces favoring the national government's expansion and despite Supreme Court cases giving a pro-national interpretation to Article I, Section 8, of the Constitution.

That article delegates to Congress the power "to regulate Commerce with foreign Nations, and among the several States and with the Indian Tribes." For most of the nineteenth century, the Supreme Court consistently interpreted this **commerce clause** *in favor* of national power. The first and most important case favoring national power over the economy was *McCulloch v. Maryland* (1819).[9] This case involved the question of whether Congress had the power to charter a national bank, since such an explicit grant of power was nowhere to be found in Article I, Section 8. Chief Justice John Marshall answered that the power could be "implied" from other powers that were expressly delegated to Congress, such as the "powers to lay and collect taxes; to borrow money; to regulate commerce; and to declare and conduct a war."

By allowing Congress to use the necessary and proper clause to interpret its delegated powers expansively, the Supreme Court created the potential for an unprecedented increase in national government power. Marshall also concluded that whenever a state law conflicted with a federal law (as in the case of *McCulloch v. Maryland*), the state law would be deemed invalid since the Constitution states that "the Laws of the United States . . . shall be the supreme Law of the Land." Both parts of this great case are pro-national, including the verification of the principle of "national supremacy," yet Congress did not immediately seek to expand the policies of the national government.

Another major case, *Gibbons v. Ogden* in 1824, reinforced this nationalistic interpretation of the Constitution. The important but relatively narrow issue was whether the state of New York could grant a monopoly to Robert Fulton's steamboat company to operate an exclusive service between New York and New Jersey. Chief Justice Marshall argued that New York State did not have the power to grant this particular monopoly. In order to reach this decision, it was necessary for Marshall to define what Article I, Section 8, meant by "commerce among the several states." He insisted that the definition was "comprehensive," extending to "every species of commercial intercourse." He did say that this comprehensiveness was limited "to that commerce which concerns more states than one," giving rise to what later came to be called "interstate commerce." *Gibbons* is important because it established the supremacy of the national government in all matters affecting interstate commerce.[10] But what would remain uncertain during several decades of constitutional discourse was the precise meaning of "interstate commerce."

Article I, Section 8, backed by the implied powers and national supremacy decision in *McCulloch* and by the broad definition of "interstate commerce" in *Gibbons*, was a source of power for the national government as long as Congress sought to facilitate commerce through subsidies, services, and land grants. But later in the nineteenth century, when the national government sought to use those powers to *regulate* the economy rather than merely to promote economic development, federalism and the concept of interstate commerce began to operate as restraints on, rather than sources of, national power. This is why the Court rulings of *McCulloch* and *Gibbons* did not bring the "traditional system" to an end. The Supreme Court declared any effort of the national government to regulate commerce in such areas as fraud, the production of impure goods, the use of child labor, or the existence of dangerous working conditions or long hours to be unconstitutional as a violation of the concept of interstate commerce. Such legislation meant that the federal government was entering the factory and the workplace—local areas—and was attempting to regulate goods that had not passed into commerce. To enter these local workplaces was to exercise police power—the power reserved to the states for the protection of the health, safety, and morals of their citizens. No one questioned the power of the national government to regulate businesses that intrinsically involved interstate commerce, such as railroads, gas pipelines, and waterway transportation. But well into the twentieth century, the Supreme Court used the concept of

*States' rights have been embraced by many causes in the past fifty years. Governor George Wallace of Alabama, a vocal supporter of states' rights, defiantly turned back U.S. Deputy Attorney General Nicholas Katzenbach, who tried to enroll two black students at the University of Alabama at Tuscaloosa in 1963.*

interstate commerce as a barrier against most efforts by Congress to regulate local conditions.

This interpretation of federalism gave the American economy a freedom from federal government control that closely approximated the ideal of free enterprise. The economy was never entirely free, of course; in fact, entrepreneurs themselves did not want complete freedom from government. They needed law and order. They needed a stable currency. They needed courts and police to enforce contracts and prevent trespass. They needed roads, canals, and railroads. But federalism, as interpreted by the Supreme Court for seventy years after the Civil War, made it possible for business to eat its cake and have it, too. Entrepreneurs enjoyed the benefits of national policies facilitating commerce but were protected by the courts from policies regulating commerce.[11]

In addition, the Tenth Amendment was used to bolster arguments about **states' rights**, the principle that the states should oppose the increasing authority of the national government. This principle was most popular in the period before the Civil War. In the early twentieth century, however, the Tenth Amendment appeared to lose its force as reformers began to press for national regulations to limit the power of large corporations and to protect the health and welfare of citizens.

## FDR's New Deal Remade the Government

The New Deal of the 1930s marked two key changes: the rise of a more active national government and a major change in how the courts interpreted national power. The door to increase federal action opened when states proved unable to cope with the demands brought on by the Great Depression. Before the Depression, states and localities took responsibility for addressing the needs of the poor, usually through private charity. But the extent of the need created by the Depression quickly exhausted local and state capacities. By 1932, 25 percent of the workforce was unemployed. The jobless lost their homes and settled into camps all over the country, called "Hoovervilles" after President Herbert Hoover. Elected in 1928, the year before the Depression hit, Hoover steadfastly maintained that there was little the federal government could do to alleviate the misery caused by the Depression. It was a matter for state and local governments, he said.

Yet demands mounted for the federal government to take action. In Congress, some Democrats proposed that the federal government finance public works to aid the economy and put people back to work. Other members of Congress introduced legislation to provide federal grants to the states to assist them in their relief efforts. None of these measures passed while Hoover remained in the White House.

When Franklin D. Roosevelt took office in 1933, he energetically threw the federal government into the business of fighting the Depression. He proposed a variety of temporary measures to provide federal relief and work programs. Most of the programs he proposed were to be financed by the federal government but administered by the states. In addition to these temporary measures, Roosevelt presided over the creation of several important federal programs designed to provide future economic security for Americans.

For the most part, the new national programs that the Roosevelt administration developed did not directly take power away from the states. Instead, Washington

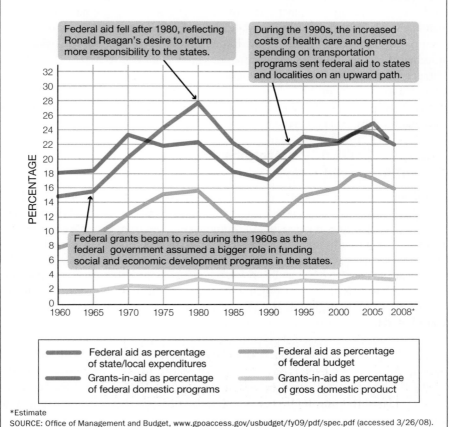

**FIGURE 3.1 The Rise, Decline, and Recovery of Federal Aid**

The level of federal aid has varied over the past several decades as program costs and politics have affected the role the national government plays in funding state and local services. The data in this figure show a rise, decline, and recovery of federal aid. What factors contributed to each of these trends?

Federal aid fell after 1980, reflecting Ronald Reagan's desire to return more responsibility to the states.

During the 1990s, the increased costs of health care and generous spending on transportation programs sent federal aid to states and localities on an upward path.

Federal grants began to rise during the 1960s as the federal government assumed a bigger role in funding social and economic development programs in the states.

Federal aid as percentage of state/local expenditures

Grants-in-aid as percentage of federal domestic programs

Federal aid as percentage of federal budget

Grants-in-aid as percentage of gross domestic product

*Estimate

SOURCE: Office of Management and Budget, www.gpoaccess.gov/usbudget/fy09/pdf/spec.pdf (accessed 3/26/08).

typically redirected states by offering them **grants-in-aid,** programs through which Congress provided money to state and local governments on the condition that the funds be employed for purposes defined by the federal government.

Franklin Roosevelt did not invent the idea of grants-in-aid, but his New Deal vastly expanded the range of grants-in-aid to include social programs, providing grants to the states for financial assistance to poor children. Congress added new grants after World War II, creating programs to help states fund activities such as providing school lunches and building highways. Sometimes the national government required state or local governments to match the national contribution dollar for dollar, but in some programs, such as the development of the interstate highway system, the congressional grants provided 90 percent of the cost of the program.

These newer types of federal grants-in-aid are called **categorical grants,** because the grants are given to states and localities by the national government on the condition that expenditures be limited to a problem or group specified by law. For the most part, the categorical grants created before the 1960s simply helped the states perform their traditional functions.[12] In the 1960s, however, the national role expanded and federal aid in the form of categorical grants increased dramatically (see Figure 3.1). For example, during the Eighty-ninth Congress (1965–66) alone, the number of categorical grant-in-aid programs grew from 221 to 379.[13] The value of categorical grants also has risen dramatically, from $2.3 billion in 1950 to an estimated $467 billion in 2008. The grants authorized during the 1960s addressed national purposes much more strongly than did earlier grants. Central to these national purposes was the need to provide opportunities to the poor.

## Changing Court Interpretations of Federalism Helped Roosevelt's New Deal

In a dramatic change beginning in 1937, the Supreme Court threw out the old distinction between interstate and intrastate commerce on which it had relied in the late 1800s and early 1900s. It converted the commerce clause from a source of limitations to a source of power for the national government. The Court began to refuse to review appeals that challenged acts of Congress protecting the rights of employees to organize and engage in collective bargaining, regulating the amount of farmland in cultivation, extending low-interest credit to small businesses and farmers, and restricting the activities of corporations dealing in the stock market; it upheld many other laws that contributed to the construction of the modern "welfare state."[14]

The Court also reversed its position on the Tenth Amendment, which it had used to strike down national laws as violations of state power. Instead, the Court approved numerous expansions of national power, to such an extent that the Tenth Amendment appeared irrelevant. In fact, in 1941, Justice Harlan Fiske Stone declared that the Tenth Amendment was simply a "truism" that had no real meaning.[15]

Yet the idea that some powers should be reserved to the states did not go away. Indeed, in the 1950s, southern opponents of the civil rights movement revived the idea of states' rights. In 1956, ninety-six southern members of Congress issued a "Southern Manifesto" in which they declared that southern states were not constitutionally bound by Supreme Court decisions outlawing racial segregation. They believed that states' rights should override individual rights to liberty and formal equality. With the triumph of the civil rights movement, the slogan of "states' rights" became tarnished by its association with racial inequality.

The 1990s saw a revival of interest in the Tenth Amendment and important Supreme Court decisions limiting federal power. Much of the recent interest in the Tenth Amendment stems from conservatives who believe that a strong federal government encroaches on individual liberties. They believe such freedoms are better protected by returning more power to the states through the process of **devolution,** whereby programs are removed from one level of government by delegating it or passing it down to a lower level of government, such as from the national government to the state and local governments. In 1996, Republican presidential candidate Robert Dole carried a copy of the Tenth Amendment in his pocket as he campaigned, pulling it out to read at rallies.[16] The Supreme Court's ruling in *United States v. Lopez* in 1995 fueled further interest in the Tenth Amendment. In that case, the Court, stating that Congress had exceeded its authority under the commerce clause, struck down a federal law that barred handguns near schools. This was the first time since the New Deal that the Court had limited congressional powers in this way. In 1997, the Court again relied on the Tenth Amendment to limit federal power in *Printz v. United States.*[17] The decision declared unconstitutional a provision of the Brady Handgun Violence Prevention Act that required state and local law enforcement officials to conduct background checks on handgun purchasers. The Court declared that this provision violated state sovereignty guaranteed in the Tenth Amendment because it required state and local officials to administer a federal regulatory program. The Supreme Court's rulings appeared to signal a much broader limitation on national power by raising new questions about whether individuals can sue a state if it fails to uphold federal law.[18]

In 2002, the Court used the Eleventh Amendment, which grants states immunity from private lawsuits, to limit federal government power. In the case of *Federal Maritime Commission v. South Carolina Ports Authority*, the Court expanded state sovereignty to protect states from having to respond to private complaints brought before federal government agencies.[19] In 2003, however, the Court ruled in favor of federal power in *Nevada Department of Human Resources v. Hibbs*, saying that state employees may sue states for violating a federal law that provides workers the right to take time off for family medical emergencies under the federal Family and Medical Leave Act.[20]

## Cooperative Federalism Pushes States to Achieve National Goals

The growth of categorical grants, along with favorable court rulings, created a new kind of federalism. If the traditional system of two sovereigns performing highly different functions could be called dual federalism, historians of federalism suggest that the system since the New Deal could be called **cooperative federalism,** in which grants-in-aid have been used strategically to encourage states and localities to pursue nationally defined goals, with national and state governments sharing powers and resources via intergovernmental cooperation. One expert on the history of American federalism, Morton Grodzins, characterized this as a move from "layer-cake federalism" to "marble-cake federalism,"[21] in which intergovernmental cooperation and sharing have blurred a once-clear distinguishing line, making it difficult to say where the national government ends and the state and local governments begin (see Figure 3.2).

For a while in the 1960s, it appeared as if the state governments would become increasingly irrelevant to American federalism. Many of the new federal grants bypassed the states and instead sent money directly to local governments and even to local nonprofit organizations. The theme heard repeatedly in Washington was that the states simply could not be trusted to carry out national purposes.[22]

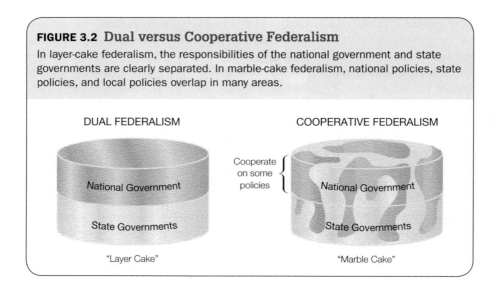

**FIGURE 3.2 Dual versus Cooperative Federalism**

In layer-cake federalism, the responsibilities of the national government and state governments are clearly separated. In marble-cake federalism, national policies, state policies, and local policies overlap in many areas.

DUAL FEDERALISM

COOPERATIVE FEDERALISM

Cooperate on some policies

National Government

State Governments

"Layer Cake"

National Government

State Governments

"Marble Cake"

One of the reasons that Washington distrusted the states was because of the way African American citizens were treated in the South. The southern states' forthright defense of segregation, justified on the grounds of states' rights, helped to tarnish the image of the states as the civil rights movement took hold. The national officials who planned the War on Poverty in the 1960s pointed to the racial exclusion practiced in the southern states as a reason for bypassing state governments. Political scientist James Sundquist described how the "Alabama syndrome" affected the War on Poverty: "In the drafting of the Economic Opportunity Act, an 'Alabama syndrome' developed. Any suggestion within the poverty task force that the states be given a role in the administration of the act was met with the question, 'Do you want to give that kind of power to [Alabama governor] George Wallace?'"[23]

Yet, even though many national policies of the 1960s bypassed the states, other new programs, such as Medicaid—the health program for the poor and disabled—relied on state governments for their implementation. In addition, as the national government expanded existing programs run by the states, states had to take on more responsibility. These new responsibilities meant that the states were now playing a very important role in the federal system.

## National Standards Have Been Advanced through Federal Programs

Over time, the Supreme Court has pushed for greater uniformity in rules and procedures across the states. In addition to legal decisions, the national government uses two other tools to create similarities across the states: grants-in-aid and regulations.

Grants-in-aid, as we have seen, are a little like bribes: Congress gives money to state and local governments if they agree to spend it for the purposes Congress specifies. But as Congress began to enact legislation in new areas, such as environmental policy, it also imposed additional regulations on states and localities. Some political scientists call this a move toward regulated federalism.[24] The effect of these national standards is that state and local policies in the areas of environmental protection, social services, and education are more uniform from coast to coast than are other nationally funded policies.

Some national standards require the federal government to take over areas of regulation formerly overseen by state or local governments. Such **preemption** (the principle that allows the national government to override state or local actions in certain policy areas) occurs when state and local actions are found to be inconsistent with federal requirements. If this occurs, all regulations in the preempted area must henceforth come from the national government. In many cases, the courts determine the scope of the federal authority to preempt. For example, in 1973 the Supreme Court struck down a local ordinance prohibiting jets from taking off from the airport in Burbank, California, between 11 P.M. and 7 A.M. It ruled that the Federal Aeronautics Act granted the Federal Aviation Administration all authority over flight patterns, takeoffs, and landings and that local governments could not impose regulations in this area. As federal regulations increased after the 1970s, Washington increasingly preempted state and local action in many different policy areas. This preemption has escalated since 1994, when Republicans gained control of Congress. Although the Republicans came to power promising to grant more responsibility to the states, they reduced state control in many areas by preemption. For example, in 1998 Congress passed a law that prohibited states and localities from taxing Internet access services. The 1996 Telecommunications Act reduced local control by giving broadcasters and digital companies broad discretion over where they could erect digital television and cellular phone towers even if local citizens objected.[25]

The growth of national standards has created some new problems and has raised questions about how far federal standardization should go. One problem that emerged in the 1980s was the increase in **unfunded mandates**—regulations or new conditions for receiving grants that impose costs on state and local governments for which they are not reimbursed by the national government. The growth of unfunded mandates was the product of a Democratic Congress, which wanted to achieve liberal social objectives, and a Republican president, who opposed increased social spending. Between 1983 and 1991, Congress mandated standards in many policy areas, including social services and environmental regulations, without providing additional funds to meet those standards. Altogether, Congress enacted twenty-seven laws that imposed new regulations or required states to expand existing programs.[26] For example, in the late 1980s, Congress ordered the states to extend the coverage provided by Medicaid, the medical insurance program for the poor and disabled. The aim was to make the program serve more people, particularly poor children, and to expand services. But Congress did not supply additional funding to help states meet these new requirements; the states had to shoulder the increased financial burden themselves. States complained that mandates took up so much of their budgets that they were not able to set their own priorities.[27]

These burdens became part of a rallying cry to reduce the power of the federal government—a cry that took center stage when a Republican Congress was elected in 1994. One of the first measures the new Congress passed was an act to limit the cost of unfunded mandates, the Unfunded Mandate Reform Act

(UMRA). Under this law, Congress must estimate the cost of any proposal it believes will cost more than $50 million. It must then vote to approve the regulation, acknowledging the expenditure. At most, UMRA represented an effort to move the national-state relationship a bit more to the state side. But it has had no significant impact on mandates. The act does not prevent congressional members from passing unfunded mandates, it only makes them think twice before they do. Moreover, the act exempts several areas of regulation. States must still enforce antidiscrimination laws and meet other requirements to receive federal assistance. New national problems inevitably raise the question of who pays. Since the terrorist attacks of 2001, state governments have grown deeply concerned about the costs of security. Although ensuring the common defense is traditionally a federal responsibility, where responsibility for homeland security lies is far less clear. Since 2001, the costs of homeland security have fallen heavily on the states. In 2003, states, faced with their worst fiscal crises in sixty years, complained that the federal assistance provided for homeland security was far too little. At its annual meeting that year, the National Governors' Association declared homeland security an unfunded mandate for which the federal government should provide more assistance. The relationship between national security needs and state and local capabilities remains unsettled.

## New Federalism Means More State Control

Since the 1970s, as states have become more capable of administering large-scale programs, the idea of devolution—transferring responsibility for policy from the federal government to the states and localities—has become popular.

Proponents of more state authority have looked to **block grants** as a way of reducing federal control. Block grants are federal grants that allow the states considerable leeway in how the funds should be spent. President Richard Nixon led the first push for block grants in the early 1970s. Nixon's block grants consolidated programs in the areas of job training, community development, and social services into three large block grants. These grants imposed some conditions on states and localities for how the money should be spent but not the narrow regulations contained in the categorical grants discussed earlier. In addition, Congress approved a fourth block grant called **general revenue sharing,** whereby the federal government provided money to local governments and counties with no strings attached; localities could spend the money as they wished. Ronald Reagan's version of **New Federalism** (returning power to the states through block grants) also looked to block grants. Like Nixon, Reagan wanted to reduce the national government's control and return power to the states. In all, Congress created twelve new block grants between 1981 and 1990.[28]

But these new approaches (summarized in Figure 3.3) have not provided magic solutions to the problems of federalism. For one thing, there is always a trade-off between accountability, that is, whether the states are using funds for the purposes intended, and flexibility. Even after block grants were created, Congress reimposed regulations in order to increase the states' accountability. For example, the first major bipartisan legislation of the George W. Bush administration was an education bill, passed in 2002, that gave schools more discretion over how they used federal

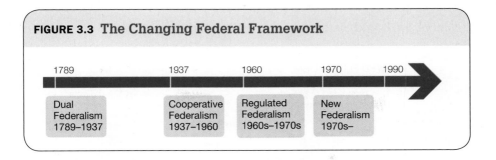

**FIGURE 3.3** The Changing Federal Framework

1789    1937    1960    1970    1990

Dual
Federalism
1789–1937

Cooperative
Federalism
1937–1960

Regulated
Federalism
1960s–1970s

New
Federalism
1970s–

dollars but at the same time imposed educational standards by requiring annual reading and math tests, called "No Child Left Behind." If the objective is to have accountable and efficient government, state bureaucracies are not necessarily any more efficient or more capable than national agencies. In Mississippi, for example, the state Department of Human Services spent money from the child care block grant for office furniture and designer salt and pepper shakers that cost $37.50 a pair. As one Mississippi state legislator said, "I've seen too many years of good ol' boy politics to know they shouldn't [transfer money to the states] without stricter controls and requirements."[29] Both liberals and conservatives have charged that block grants are a way for politicians to avoid the big, controversial policy questions. Instead of facing problems head-on, these critics say, the federal government uses block grants to kick the problems down to the states.[30]

## There Is No Simple Answer to Finding the Right National-State Balance

As Figure 3.4 indicates, federalism has changed dramatically over the course of American history. Finding the right balance among states and the federal government is an evolving challenge for American democracy. In 2005, for example, Congress passed the Real ID Act, which called for minimum national standards for state-issued driver's licenses to be implemented by 2013. The goals of the law—to make uniform and improve the quality of Americans' identification—were widely praised, but also rapidly criticized in the states as an unfunded mandate and a measure that would invade privacy while doing little to improve security. As of 2007, no state in the union had yet complied with these new standards, which require the use of special paper with secret markers, in-person license renewal (eliminating mail renewals), proof of residence, laser engraving, and in virtually every instance a Social Security card, among other restrictions. Several states enacted measures stating that they refused to comply with the law. To complicate matters, as of 2007 eight states have moved in the opposite direction, making it easier for state residents to obtain driver's licenses. The purpose is to allow undocumented immigrants to obtain licenses by eliminating the requirement that applicants must have a Social Security number, so that these individuals will have proper driving instruction and insurance. These efforts have also been controversial because of the fear that criminals or terrorists might exploit the system. Yet driver's license regulations have always been a state matter, and the national government's attempt to

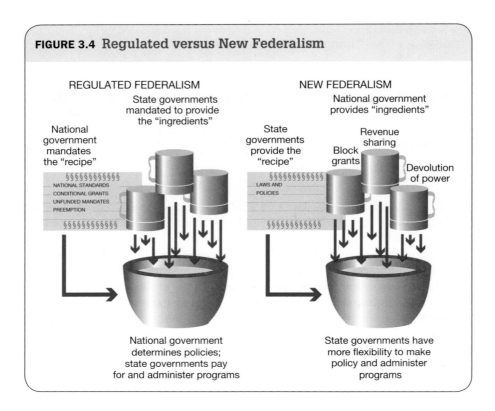

**FIGURE 3.4** Regulated versus New Federalism

REGULATED FEDERALISM

National government mandates the "recipe"

State governments mandated to provide the "ingredients"

NATIONAL STANDARDS
CONDITIONAL GRANTS
UNFUNDED MANDATES
PREEMPTION

National government determines policies; state governments pay for and administer programs

NEW FEDERALISM

National government provides "ingredients"

State governments provide the "recipe"

LAWS AND POLICIES

Revenue sharing

Block grants

Devolution of power

State governments have more flexibility to make policy and administer programs

federalize such licenses by 2013 will continue to encounter stiff legal and political resistance.[31]

Also in 2007, President Bush adopted stricter eligibility requirements for a federal insurance program for poor children whose families did not quality for Medicaid, called the State Children's Health Insurance Program (SCHIP), enacted in 1997. Under the new federal guidelines, eligibility was limited to children living at or below 250 percent of the poverty level. The effect of the change was to force tens of thousands of children out of the program. Eight states banded together to sue the federal government, arguing that the eligibility changes violated the intent of the law. In addition, states where the cost of living is higher argued that the eligibility cutoff needed to be raised so that deserving children were not omitted from the program's coverage. In part because of this federal-state dispute and the popularity of the SCHIP program, Congress passed an expansion of the program in fall 2007, only to have the expansion vetoed by President Bush.[32]

Under contemporary federalism, hot-button issues, including immigration, terrorism, the environment, health care, and abortion, invite a variety of state policies. It is rare that the national government has the ability, or willingness, to impose a single, national rule or standard to resolve even the most pressing national problems. In some instances, enterprising states may wind up providing leadership that eventually pushes the country in new policy directions. For example, the Environmental Protection Agency (EPA) under the George W. Bush administration refused to regulate the emission of "greenhouse gases" such as carbon dioxide that contribute to global warming.

# Take Action at the State Level

College campuses across the country are largely alcohol-free zones, as the majority of their student populations are under twenty-one and thus ineligible to purchase alcoholic drinks. This national standard is a relatively new phenomenon. The legal drinking age had traditionally been a state-level issue, with Congress unable to legislate directly on age requirements. However, in 1984, Congress threatened to withhold national transportation funds from any state that refused to pass a law prohibiting the sale of alcohol to those under twenty-one. Because most states relied heavily on these federal funds, every state except Louisiana quickly raised its legal drinking age. (Louisiana signed on in 1995.)

The debate over the legal drinking age illustrates the essence of federalism—determining which policy areas should be the domain of the federal government and which issues should be reserved to the states. Many of the key issues currently facing us as a nation have been caught in this struggle between federal and state power. Untangling this web can be tricky, but resources are available that can help you learn more about an issue, contact groups involved in the debate, and lend your own voice to the discussion.

- To begin, you can educate yourself about how your state addresses a host of issues ranging from health to the environment to civil rights by visiting the Pew Research Center's Web site: www.stateline.org/live/. This site provides an in-depth look at key issues facing the states, presents comparisons among various state policies, and sometimes offers links to advocacy groups on different sides of the debate.

- If one issue captures your interest or passion or anger, you might have a better chance of affecting policy at the state level (where there is generally greater access to legislators and fewer competing activists) than on the national level.

- In the abortion debate, for example, you might choose to write a letter or e-mail to your state representative or senator advocating either an expansion or restriction of abortion rights in your state.

- You might even want to circulate a petition to get an initiative on the ballot that will set state law on the issue. The Initiative and Referendum Institute at the University of Southern California (www.iandrinstitute.org) has information on this process.

Whatever your choice—to educate yourself, to express your opinion, or to join with others in action—the states provide fifty different arenas for affecting political change.

When the EPA said that it did not have the power to do so under the Clean Air Act, several states, including Massachusetts, sued in 2006, arguing that greenhouse gases were subject to such regulation. In 2007, the Supreme Court ruled in favor of the states in the case of *Massachusetts v. Environmental Protection Agency,* saying that the EPA did have such authority, and in fact was obliged to regulate greenhouse gases unless it could produce scientific evidence to the contrary.[33]

In its first year, the Obama administration signaled a much stronger role for the federal government in some areas but more flexibility for state action in other matters. The stronger federal role was most evident in the measures to reinvigorate the failing economy. In February 2009, Congress enacted the American Recovery and Reinvestment Act (ARRA), a $787 billion measure that, in addition to tax cuts, offered states substantial one-time funds for a variety of purposes, including education, road building, unemployment insurance, and health care. Many governors, strapped for cash, welcomed the new funds. Others worried that the federal government was using ARRA to dictate state spending priorities. Some of these governors sought to use the funds for purposes not allowed in the legislation or refused parts of the funds that they believed would tie their hands in the future. For example, Governor Mark Sanford of South Carolina, a Republican, asked the federal government for a waiver that would permit his state to use approximately $700 million of its estimated $2.8 billion ARRA allocation to pay down the state's debt. When the waiver was denied, Sanford vowed to reject the federal funds; the state legislature overrode his decision.[34] Several states objected to the unemployment funds, which required states to expand eligibility for unemployment insurance to many part-time and temporary workers. A handful of Republican governors, including Haley Barbour of Mississippi, Bobby Jindal of Louisiana, Sarah Palin of Alaska, and Rick Perry of Texas, refused to accept the funds on the grounds that expanded eligibility would place a burden on employers in the future. A majority of states, however, changed their laws in response to the federal requirements.[35]

In other ways, the Obama White House signaled that it would allow the states more leeway for action than they had under the Bush administration. This was particularly true in the domains of social policy and the environment when states sought to enact laws more stringent than those of the federal government. In the memo reversing the Bush policy of preemption, the White House noted, "Throughout our history, State and local governments have frequently protected health, safety, and the environment

*The debate over health care legislation raised concern about unfunded mandates, as state governments worried that Congress would require them to pay some of the costs of universal health care. Although the final legislation did not place the burden on states, several states threatened not to comply with a national health plan.*

more aggressively than has the national Government."[36] This new policy aimed to keep the federal government from infringing on these more aggressive state actions. In one notable example, the Obama administration announced in 2009 that it would not pursue drug prosecutions against those using marijuana for medical purposes—a practice legal in fourteen states.[37]

# studyguide

## Practice Quiz

 Find a diagnostic Web Quiz with 33 additional questions on the StudySpace Web site: www.wwnorton.com/we-the-people

1. Which term describes the sharing of powers between the national government and the state governments? *(p. 65)*
   a) separation of powers
   b) federalism
   c) checks and balances
   d) shared powers

2. Which amendment to the Constitution stated that the powers not delegated to the national government or prohibited to the states were "reserved to the states"? *(p. 66)*
   a) First Amendment
   b) Fifth Amendment
   c) Tenth Amendment
   d) Twenty-sixth Amendment

3. A state government's authority to regulate the health, safety, and morals of its citizens is frequently referred to as *(p. 66)*
   a) the reserved power.
   b) the police power.
   c) the concurrent power.
   d) the implied power.

4. Which constitutional clause has been central in debates over gay and lesbian marriage because it requires that states normally honor the public acts and judicial decisions of other states? *(p. 67)*
   a) full faith and credit clause
   b) privileges and immunities clause

   c) necessary and proper clause
   d) interstate commerce clause

5. Many states have amended their constitutions to guarantee that large cities will have the authority to manage local affairs without interference from state government. This power is called *(p. 68)*
   a) home rule.
   b) preemption.
   c) states' rights.
   d) New Federalism.

6. The system of federalism that allowed states to do most of the fundamental governing from 1789 through the 1930s was *(p. 69)*
   a) home rule.
   b) regulated federalism.
   c) dual federalism.
   d) cooperative federalism.

7. The process of returning more of the responsibilities of governing from the national level to the state level is known as *(p. 76)*
   a) dual federalism.
   b) devolution.
   c) preemption.
   d) home rule.

8. In which case did the Supreme Court create the potential for increased national power by ruling that Congress could use the necessary and proper

clause to interpret its delegated powers broadly? *(p. 72)*
a) *United States v. Lopez*
b) *Printz v. United States*
c) *McCulloch v. Maryland*
d) *Gibbons v. Ogden*

9. One of the most powerful tools by
which the federal government has
attempted to get the states to act in
ways that are desired by the federal
government is by *(p. 75)*
a) providing grants-in-aid.
b) requiring licensing.
c) granting home rule.
d) defending states' rights.

10. The form of regulated federalism that
allows the federal government to take
over areas of regulation formerly overseen by states or local governments is
called *(p. 79)*
a) categorical grants.
b) formula grants.
c) project grants.
d) preemption.

11. When state and local governments
must conform to costly regulations or
conditions in order to receive grants
but do not receive reimbursements
for their expenditures from the federal
government, it is called *(p. 79)*
a) a reciprocal grant.
b) an unfunded mandate.
c) general revenue sharing.
d) a counterfunded mandate.

12. To what does the term "New Federalism" refer? *(p. 80)*
a) the national government's regulation of state action through grants-
in-aid
b) the type of federalism relying on
categorical grants
c) efforts to return more policy-making
discretion to the states through the
use of block grants
d) the recent emergence of local
governments as important political
actors

## Chapter Outline

Find a detailed Chapter Outline on the StudySpace Web site:
www.wwnorton.com/we-the-people

## Key Terms

Find Flashcards to help you study these terms on the
StudySpace Web site: www.wwnorton.com/we-the-people

**block grants** *(p. 80)* federal grants that allow
states considerable leeway or discretion in
how the funds should be spent

**categorical grants** *(p. 76)* congressional
grants given to states and localities on the
condition that expenditures be limited to a
problem or group specified by law

**commerce clause** *(p. 72)* Article I, Section 8,
of the Constitution, which delegates to
Congress the power "to regulate Commerce
with foreign Nations, and among the several
States and with the Indian Tribes." The
Supreme Court interpreted this clause in
favor of national power over the economy

**concurrent powers** *(p. 67)* powers exercised by
both the federal and the state governments

**cooperative federalism** *(p. 77)* federalism
existing since the New Deal era in which
grants-in-aid have been used strategically to
encourage states and localities to pursue nationally defined goals, with national and state
governments sharing powers and resources
via intergovernmental cooperation

**devolution** *(p. 76)* a policy to remove a
program from one level of government by delegating it or passing it down to a lower level
of government, such as from the national government to the state and local governments

**dual federalism** *(p. 69)* the system of government that prevailed in the United States from 1789 to 1937, in which most fundamental governmental powers were shared between the federal and state government

**expressed powers** *(p. 65)* specific powers granted to Congress in the Constitution

**federalism** *(p. 65)* a system of government in which power is divided, by a constitution, between the central (national) government and regional (state) governments

**full faith and credit clause** *(p. 67)* provision from Article IV, Section 1, of the Constitution requiring that the states normally honor the public acts and judicial decisions that take place in another state

**general revenue sharing** *(p. 80)* the process by which one unit of government yields a portion of its tax income to another unit of government, according to an established formula. Revenue sharing typically involves the national government providing money to state governments

**grants-in-aid** *(p. 75)* programs through which Congress provides money to state and local governments on the condition that the funds be employed for purposes defined by the federal government

**home rule** *(p. 68)* power delegated by the state to a local unit of government to manage its own affairs

**implied powers** *(p. 65)* powers derived from the necessary and proper clause of Article I, Section 8, of the Constitution. Such powers are not specifically expressed, but are implied through the expansive interpretation of delegated powers

**necessary and proper clause** *(p. 65)* provision from Article I, Section 8, of the Constitution providing Congress with the authority to make all laws necessary and proper to carry out its expressed powers

**New Federalism** *(p. 80)* policy of Presidents Nixon and Reagan to return power to the states through block grants

**police power** *(p. 66)* power reserved to the government to regulate the health, safety, and morals of its citizens

**preemption** *(p. 79)* the principle that allows the national government to override state or local actions in certain policy areas

**privileges and immunities clause** *(p. 68)* provision from Article IV, Section 2, of the Constitution that citizens of one state should be entitled to similar treatment in other states

**reserved powers** *(p. 66)* the Tenth Amendment to the Constitution, which aims to reserve powers to the states

**states' rights** *(p. 74)* the principle that the states should oppose the increasing authority of the national government. This principle was most popular in the period before the Civil War

**unfunded mandates** *(p. 79)* regulations or conditions for receiving grants that impose costs on state and local governments for which they are not reimbursed by the federal government

**unitary system** *(p. 65)* a governing system that gives most power to the federal or national government

# For Further Reading

Anton, Thomas. *American Federalism and Public Policy.* Philadelphia: Temple University Press, 1989.

Bensel, Richard. *Sectionalism and American Political Development: 1880–1980.* Madison: University of Wisconsin Press, 1984.

Bowman, Ann O'M., and Richard Kearny. *The Resurgence of the States.* Englewood Cliffs, NJ: Prentice Hall, 1986.

Dye, Thomas R. *American Federalism: Competition among Governments.* Lexington, MA: Lexington Books, 1990.

Elazar, Daniel. *American Federalism: A View from the States.* 3rd ed. New York: Harper & Row, 1984.

Feiock, Richard C., and John T. Scholz. *Self-Organizing Federalism: Collaborative Mechanisms to Mitigate Institutional Collective Action Dilemmas.* New York: Cambridge University Press, 2009.

Gerston, Larry N. *American Federalism: A Concise Introduction.* Armonk, NY: M. C. Sharpe, 2007.

Grodzins, Morton. *The American System.* Chicago: Rand McNally, 1974.

Johnson, Kimberly S. *Governing the American State: Congress and the New Federalism, 1877–1929.* Princeton, NJ: Princeton University Press, 2007.

Kelley, E. Wood. *Policy and Politics in the United States: The Limits of Localism.* Philadelphia: Temple University Press, 1987.

Kettl, Donald. *The Regulation of American Federalism.* Baltimore: Johns Hopkins University Press, 1987.

Peterson, Paul E. *The Price of Federalism.* Washington, DC: Brookings, 1995.

# Recommended Web Sites

**Constitution Finder**
**http://confinder.richmond.edu**
Governments can organize power in either unitary or federal systems. Examine the constitutions of different countries throughout the world and try to identify how those governments organize power.

**Council of State Governments**
**www.csg.org**
This organization provides information on a variety of state-federal policy areas. See what current issues concerning federalism are of prime importance to the state governments on this site.

**Federalism Project**
**www.federalismproject.org**
The Federalism Project of the American Enterprise Institute advocates competitive federalism and the empowering of states through devolution.

**Governing.com**
**www.governing.com**
See which state-federal issues are important to your local government officials on the Web site for *Governing* magazine.

**National Conference of State Legislatures**
**www.ncsl.org**
**National Governors Association**
**www.nga.org**
These are two of the largest organizations dedicated to representing state and local government interests at the federal level.

**Oyez: U.S. Supreme Court Media**
**www.oyez.org/cases/1792-1850/1819/1819_0/**
Read here about one of the most important U.S. Supreme Court decisions regarding the division of federal and state powers, in the case of *McCulloch v. Maryland*.

**Urban Institute**
**www.newfederalism.urban.org**
New Federalism gives state governments more flexibility to make public policy and administer programs. The Urban Institute's "Assessing the New Federalism" policy center takes a statistical look at the success and failure of recent government programs.

**U.S. Census Bureau**
**www.census.gov**
The Census Bureau maintains one of the largest collections of data about social and economic conditions in the nation's fifty states.

**World Federalist Movement**
**www.wfm-19P.org/site/**
This international organization is dedicated to the division of power and authority among all local, state, and international governmental agencies. Generally, it promotes federalism and constitutional democracy throughout the world.

Freedom of speech is one of the liberties protected by the First Amendment. Even speech that is hostile or offensive—such as the views expressed by these Ku Klux Klan members—cannot be prohibited as long as it does not incite illegal action.

# 4

# Civil Liberties and Civil Rights

**WHAT GOVERNMENT DOES AND WHY IT MATTERS** Today in the United States, we often take for granted the liberties contained in the first ten amendments to the Constitution, known as the **Bill of Rights**. Citizens of only very few other countries can claim to take liberties for granted. In fact, few people in recorded history have enjoyed such protections, including American citizens before the 1960s. For more than 170 years after its ratification by the states in 1791 the Bill of Rights meant little to most Americans. As we shall see in this chapter, guaranteeing the liberties articulated in the Bill of Rights to all Americans required a long struggle. As recently as the early 1960s, many of the freedoms we have today were not guaranteed. At that time, abortion was illegal everywhere in the United States, criminal suspects in state cases did not have to be informed of their rights, some states required daily Bible readings and prayers in their public schools, and some communities regularly censored reading material that they deemed to be obscene.

Since the early 1960s, the Supreme Court has expanded considerably the scope of **civil liberties**, defined as individual rights and personal freedoms with which governments are prevented from interfering. But since these liberties are constantly subject to judicial interpretation, their provisions are fragile and need to be safeguarded vigilantly, especially during times of war or a threat to national security, such as in the aftermath of September 11, 2001.

Civil rights—protections of citizen equality provided by the government—have also expanded dramatically since the middle of the twentieth century. In 1960, four black students from North Carolina A&T State University sat down at Woolworth's whites-only lunch counter in Greensboro, North Carolina, challenging the policies of segregation that kept blacks and whites in separate public and private accommodations across the South. Day after day the students sat at the counter, ignoring the taunts of onlookers, determined to break the system of segregation. Their actions and those of many other students, clergy members, and ordinary citizens finally did abolish such practices as separate white and black park benches, water fountains, and waiting rooms; the end of segregation meant opening access to public and private institutions on equal terms to all. But the victories of the civil rights movement did not come cheaply; many marchers, freedom riders, and sit-in participants were beaten; some were murdered.

Civil liberties—protections of citizens *from* the government—and civil rights—protections of citizens *by* the government—are two sides of the same coin, because they both pertain to the ability of citizens to exercise personal freedoms and because they both arise from the Fourteenth Amendment. In both cases, we will see that the Fourteenth Amendment was key to these liberties and rights.

## key concepts

- Civil liberties are protections of citizens *from* the government; civil rights are protections of citizens *by* the government.

- We can thank the opponents of the Constitution (the Antifederalists) for the fact that a Bill of Rights was added to the Constitution.

- The Fourteenth Amendment made it possible for citizens to enjoy key Bill of Rights protections in their daily lives through the process of incorporation.

- African Americans fought long and hard to win basic civil rights.

- Other disadvantaged groups followed the trail blazed by the civil rights movement.

- Affirmative action programs were designed to right past wrongs.

## The Origin of the Bill of Rights Lies in Those Who Opposed the Constitution

When the first Congress under the newly ratified Constitution met in late April of 1789, the most important item of business was the consideration of a proposal to add a bill of rights to the Constitution. Such a proposal had been turned down with little debate in the waning days of the Philadelphia Constitutional Convention in 1787, not because the delegates were against rights, but because, as the Federalists, led by Alexander Hamilton, later argued, such a bill was "not only unnecessary in the proposed Constitution but would even be dangerous."[1] First, according to Hamilton, a bill of rights would be irrelevant to a national government that was given only delegated powers. To put restraints on "powers which are not granted" could provide a pretext for governments to claim more powers than were in fact granted: "For why declare that things shall not be done which there is no power to do?"[2] Second, the Constitution was to Hamilton and the Federalists a bill of rights in itself, or contained provisions that amounted to a bill of rights without requiring additional amendments (see Table 4.1). For example, Article I, Section 9, included the right of **habeas corpus,** a court order demanding that an individual in custody be brought into court and shown the cause for detention. This prohibits the government from depriving a person of liberty without explaining the reason before a judge.

Despite the power of Hamilton's arguments, when the Constitution was submitted to the states for ratification, Antifederalists, most of whom had not been delegates in Philadelphia, picked up on the argument of Thomas Jefferson (who also had not been a delegate) that the omission of a bill of rights was a major imperfection of the new Constitution. The Federalists conceded that in order to gain ratification they would have to make an "unwritten but unequivocal pledge" to add a bill of rights.

**TABLE 4.1**

### Rights in the Original Constitution (Not in the Bill of Rights)

| CLAUSE | RIGHT ESTABLISHED |
| --- | --- |
| Article I, Sec. 9 | guarantee of *habeas corpus* |
| Article I, Sec. 9 | prohibition of **bills of attainder** (laws that decree a person guilty of a crime without a trial) |
| Article I, Sec. 9 | prohibition of **ex post facto laws** (laws that declare an action to be illegal after it has been committed) |
| Article I, Sec. 9 | prohibition against acceptance of titles of nobility, etc., from any foreign state |
| Article III | guarantee of trial by jury in state where crime was committed |
| Article III | treason defined and limited to the life of the person convicted, not to the person's heirs |

The Bill of Rights might well have been titled the "Bill of Liberties," because the provisions that were incorporated in the Bill of Rights were seen as defining a private sphere of personal liberty, free from governmental restrictions.[3] As Jefferson put it, a bill of rights "is what people are entitled to against every government on earth. . . ." Note the emphasis—citizen *against* government. Civil liberties are *protections of citizens from* improper government action. Thus, the Bill of Rights is a series of "thou shalt nots"—restraints imposed upon government (see Table 4.2). Some of these restraints are substantive liberties, which put limits on *what* the government shall and shall not have power to do—such as establishing a religion, quartering troops in private homes without consent, or seizing private property without just compensation. Other restraints are procedural liberties, which are restraints on *how* the government is supposed to act. These procedural liberties are usually grouped under the general category of **due process of law,** which is the right of every citizen to be protected against arbitrary action by national or state governments. It first appears in the Fifth Amendment provision that "no person shall be . . . deprived of life, liberty, or property, without due process of law." For example, even though the government has the substantive power to declare certain acts to be crimes and to arrest and imprison persons who violate criminal laws, it may not do so without meticulously observing procedures designed to protect the accused person. The best-known procedural rule is that an accused person is presumed innocent until proven guilty. This rule does not question the government's power to punish someone for committing a crime; it questions only the way the government determines who committed the crime. Substantive and procedural restraints together identify the realm of civil liberties.

In contrast, civil rights as a category refers to the obligations imposed on government to *take positive action* to protect citizens from any illegal actions of government agencies as well as of other private citizens. Civil rights did not become part of the Constitution until 1868, with the adoption of the Fourteenth Amendment, which sought to provide for each citizen "the equal protection of the laws."

**TABLE 4.2**

## Civil Liberties in the Bill of Rights

| AMENDMENT | EXAMPLE |
| --- | --- |
| I | "Congress shall make *no* law . . ." |
| II | "The right . . . to . . . bear Arms, shall *not* be infringed." |
| III | "*No* soldier shall . . . be quartered . . ." |
| IV | "*No* warrants shall issue, but upon probable cause . . ." |
| V | "*No* person shall be held to answer for a . . . crime, unless on presentment or indictment of a Grand Jury . . ." |
| VIII | "Excessive bail shall *not* be required . . . *nor* cruel and unusual punishments inflicted." |

# The Fourteenth Amendment Created the Doctrine of Incorporation

In the first 70 years of the country's history, the Bill of Rights was understood to apply only to the national government and not to the states. In fact, the Supreme Court said this in a decision in 1833.[4] But the Civil War cast new light on the large question of state versus national governmental power. After the war, the Fourteenth Amendment was added to the Constitution. Part of the amendment reads as though it were meant to tell the states that they must now adhere to the Bill of Rights:

> No *State* shall make or enforce any law which shall abridge the privileges or immunities of citizens of the United States; nor shall any *State* deprive any person of life, liberty, or property, without due process of law; nor deny to any person within its jurisdiction the equal protection of the laws. [emphasis added]

This language sounds like an effort to extend the Bill of Rights to all citizens, wherever they might reside.[5] Yet this was not the Supreme Court's interpretation of the amendment for many decades. Within five years of ratification of the Fourteenth Amendment, the Court was making decisions as though the amendment had never been adopted.[6]

The first change in civil liberties following the adoption of the Fourteenth Amendment came in 1897, when the Supreme Court held that the due process clause of the Fourteenth Amendment did in fact prohibit states from taking property for a public use without just compensation, overruling the *Barron* case.[7] However, the Supreme Court had selectively "incorporated" under the Fourteenth Amendment only the property protection provision of the Fifth Amendment and no other clause of the Fifth or any other amendment of the Bill of Rights. In other words, although according to the Fifth Amendment "due process" applied to the taking of life and liberty as well as property, only property was incorporated into the Fourteenth Amendment as a limitation on state power.

No further expansion of civil liberties via the Fourteenth Amendment occurred until 1925, when the Supreme Court held that freedom of speech is "among the fundamental personal rights and 'liberties' protected by the due process clause of the Fourteenth Amendment from impairment by the states."[8] In 1931, the Court added freedom of the press to that short list protected by the Bill of Rights from state action; by 1937, it had added freedom of assembly and petitioning the government for redress of grievances.[9]

But that was as far as the Court was willing to go. As late as 1937, the Supreme Court was still unwilling to nationalize civil liberties beyond the First Amendment. The Constitution, as interpreted by the Supreme Court in *Palko v. Connecticut* (discussed later in this chapter), left standing the framework in which the states had the power to determine their own law on a number of fundamental issues.

As Table 4.3 shows, **selective incorporation**—the process by which different protections in the Bill of Rights were incorporated in the Fourteenth Amendment, thus guaranteeing citizens' protection from state as well as national

**TABLE 4.3**

## Incorporation of the Bill of Rights into the Fourteenth Amendment

| SELECTED PROVISIONS AND AMENDMENTS | NOT INCORPORATED UNTIL | KEY CASE |
| --- | --- | --- |
| Eminent domain (V) | 1897 | Chicago, Burlington, and Quincy R.R. v. Chicago |
| Freedom of speech (I) | 1925 | Gitlow v. New York |
| Freedom of press (I) | 1931 | Near v. Minnesota |
| Free exercise of religion (I) | 1934 | Hamilton v. Regents of the University of California |
| | 1937 | DeJonge v. Oregon |
| Freedom of assembly (I) | 1939 | Hague v. CIO |
| | 1947 | Everson v. Board of Education |
| Freedom from unnecessary search and seizure (IV) | 1949 | Wolf v. Colorado |
| Freedom from warrantless search and seizure (IV) ("exclusionary rule") | 1961 | Mapp v. Ohio |
| Freedom from cruel and unusual punishment (VIII) | 1962 | Robinson v. California |
| Right to counsel in any criminal trial (VI) | 1963 | Gideon v. Wainwright |
| Right against self-incrimination and forced confessions (V) | 1964 | Mallory v. Hogan Escobedo v. Illinois |
| Right to counsel and remain silent (V) | 1966 | Miranda v. Arizona |
| Right against double jeopardy (V) | 1969 | Benton v. Maryland |
| Right to bear arms (II) | 2010 | McDonald v. Chicago |

governments—continued to occur gradually, up until the last incorporation case in 1969 (incorporation is also sometimes referred to as the "absorption" or the "nationalizing" of the Bill of Rights).

The pattern or sequence by which this process of incorporation occurred reveals that all Bill of Rights protections are not considered equally important. Some are clearly more important than others. These **preferred freedoms** (certain protections in the Bill of Rights, such as free speech and free press, that are considered even more important than other freedoms) are critically important because, according to Supreme Court Justice Benjamin Cardozo, they are "the matrix, the indispens-able condition, of nearly every other form of freedom."[10] By comparison, the Third Amendment prohibition against the quartering of troops in people's homes is a relic of the 1700s, in that it was included in the Bill of Rights as a reaction to British troops that engaged in this practice. Since the American Revolution, the practice has not been a problem or concern, unlike the First Amendment, which has spawned numerous legal disputes. The end result of the incorporation process is that, on the whole, the most important civil liberties in the Bill of Rights have now been applied to the states, so that the states must adhere to these protections of individual liberties.

The best way to examine the Bill of Rights today is the simplest way—to take each of the major provisions one at a time. Some of these provisions are settled areas of law and others are not. The Court can reinterpret any one of them at any time.

## ● The First Amendment Guarantees Freedom of Religion

> Congress shall make no law respecting an establishment of religion, or prohibiting the free exercise thereof; or abridging the freedom of speech, or of the press; or the right of the people peaceably to assemble, and to petition the Government for a redress of grievances.

The Bill of Rights begins by guaranteeing freedom, and the First Amendment provides for that freedom in two distinct clauses: "Congress shall make no law [1] respecting an establishment of religion, or [2] prohibiting the free exercise thereof." The first clause is called the "establishment clause," and the second is called the "free exercise clause."

### Separation between Church and State Comes from the First Amendment

The **establishment clause** and the idea of "no law" regarding the establishment of religion can be interpreted in several ways. One interpretation, which probably reflects the views of many of the First Amendment's authors, is that the government is prohibited from establishing an official church. Official state churches, such as the Church of England, were common in the eighteenth century and were viewed by many Americans as inconsistent with a republican form of government. Indeed, many American colonists had fled Europe to escape persecution for having rejected state-sponsored churches. A second interpretation is the "nonpreferential-ist," or "accommodationist," view, which holds that the government may not take sides among competing religions but is not prohibited from providing assistance to religious institutions or ideas as long as it shows no favoritism. The United States accommodates religious beliefs in a variety of ways, from the reference to God on U.S. currency to the prayer that begins every session of Congress. These forms of establishment have never been struck down by the courts.

The third view regarding establishment, which for many years dominated Supreme Court decisions in this realm, is the idea of a "wall of separation" between church and state that cannot be breached by the government. The concept of a wall of separation was Thomas Jefferson's own formulation and has figured in many Supreme Court cases arising under the establishment clause. For two centuries, Jefferson's words have had a powerful impact on our understanding of the proper relationship between church and state in America.

Despite the absolute sound of the phrase "wall of separation," there is ample room to disagree on how high or strong this wall is. For example, the Court has been consistently strict in cases of school prayer, striking down such practices as Bible reading,[11] nondenominational prayer,[12] reading prayers over a public address system during a football game,[13] and even a moment of silence for meditation.[14] In each of these cases, the Court reasoned that school-sponsored observations, even of an apparently nondenominational character, are highly suggestive of school sponsorship and therefore violate the prohibition against establishment of religion. On the other hand, the Court has been quite permissive (and some would say inconsistent) about the public display of religious symbols, such as city-sponsored Nativity scenes in commercial or municipal areas.[15] And although the Court has consistently disapproved of government financial support for religious schools, even when the purpose has been purely educational and secular, the Court has permitted certain direct aid to students of such schools in the form of busing, for example. It also upheld a voucher system that allows the use of public money for religious school tuition.[16] In 2002, in the case of *Zelman v. Simmons-Harris*, the Supreme Court said that tax-supported vouchers could be used at religious schools as long as parents had a choice between religious and secular institutions.[17]

*The First Amendment affects everyday life in a multitude of ways. Because of its ban on state-sanctioned religion, the Supreme Court ruled in 2000 that student-initiated public prayer at school is illegal. Pregame prayer at public schools violates the establishment clause of the First Amendment.*

In 2005 the Supreme Court ruled in two cases on government-sponsored displays of religious symbols. In *Van Orden v. Perry*, the Court decided by a 5–4 margin that a display of the Ten Commandments at the Texas State Capitol did not violate the Constitution.[18] However, in *McCreary v. ACLU*, decided at the same time and also by a 5–4 margin, the Court determined that a display of the Ten Commandments inside two Kentucky courthouses was unconstitutional.[19] Justice Stephen Breyer, the swing vote in the two cases, said that the displays in *Van*

*Orden* had a secular purpose while the displays in *McCreary* had a purely religious purpose. The key difference between the two cases is that the Texas display had been exhibited in a large park for forty years with other monuments related to the development of American law without any objections raised until this case, whereas the Kentucky display was erected much more recently and initially by itself, suggesting to some justices that its posting had a religious purpose. But most observers saw little difference between the two cases, and even Breyer was hard-pressed to explain his shifting votes except to say that *Van Orden* was a "borderline" case. Obviously, the issue of government-sponsored displays of religious symbols has not been settled.

## Free Exercise of Religion Means You Have a Right to Worship

The **free exercise clause** protects the citizen's right to believe and to practice whatever religion one chooses; it also protects the right to be a nonbeliever. The precedent—setting case involving free exercise is *West Virginia State Board of Education v. Barnette* (1943), which involved the children of a family of Jehovah's Witnesses who refused to salute and pledge allegiance to the American flag on the grounds that their religious faith did not permit it. Three years earlier, the Court had upheld such a requirement and had permitted schools to expel students for refusing to salute the flag. But the entry of the United States into a war to defend democracy coupled with the ugly treatment to which the Jehovah's Witnesses children

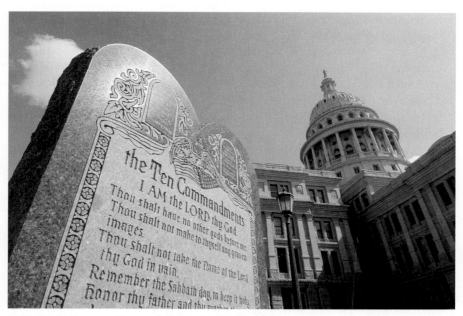

*In 2005, the Supreme Court ruled that this display of the Ten Commandments at the Texas State Capitol in Austin did not violate the separation of church and state. However, the Court found that displays of the Ten Commandments inside two courthouses in Kentucky were unconstitutional.*

had been subjected induced the Court to reverse itself and to endorse the free exercise of religion even when it may be offensive to the beliefs of the majority.[20]

Although the Supreme Court has been fairly consistent and strict in protecting the free exercise of religious belief, it has taken pains to distinguish between religious beliefs and *actions* based on those beliefs. In one case, for example, two Native Americans had been fired from their jobs for smoking peyote, an illegal drug. They claimed that they had been fired from their jobs illegally because smoking peyote was a religious sacrament protected by the free exercise clause. The Court disagreed with their claim in an important 1990 decision.[21]

In a different case, Amish parents refused to send their children to school beyond eighth grade because exposing their children to "modern values" would undermine their religious commitment. In this case, the Court decided in favor of the Amish and endorsed a very strong interpretation of the protection of free exercise.[22]

## ● The First Amendment and Freedom of Speech and the Press Assure Free Exchange of Ideas

Congress shall make no law . . . abridging the freedom of speech, or of the press. . . .

Freedom of speech and of the press have a special place in American political thought. To begin with, democracy depends upon the ability of individuals to talk to one another and to disseminate information and ideas. It would be difficult to conceive how democratic politics could function without free and open debate. Such debate, moreover, is seen as an essential mechanism for determining the quality or validity of competing ideas. As Justice Oliver Wendell Holmes said, "the best test of truth is the power of the thought to get itself accepted in the competition of the market . . . that at any rate is the theory of our Constitution."[23] What is sometimes called the "marketplace of ideas" receives a good deal of protection from the courts. In 1938, the Supreme Court held that any legislation that attempts to restrict these fundamental freedoms "is to be subjected to a more exacting judicial scrutiny . . . than are most other types of legislation."[24] This higher standard of judicial review came to be called **strict scrutiny.**

The doctrine of strict scrutiny places a heavy burden of proof on the government if it seeks to regulate or restrict speech. Americans are assumed to have the right to speak and to broadcast their ideas unless some compelling reason can be identified to stop them. But strict scrutiny does not mean that speech can never be regulated. According to the courts, although virtually all speech is protected by the Constitution, some forms of speech are entitled to a greater degree of protection than others. Let us examine what the federal courts have said about some of the major forms of speech.

### Political Speech Is Consistently Protected

Over the past 200 years, the courts have scrutinized many different forms of speech and constructed different principles and guidelines for each. And of all forms of speech, political speech is the most consistently protected.

**Political Speech** Political speech was the activity of greatest concern to the framers of the Constitution, even though some found it the most difficult provision to protect. Within seven years of the ratification of the Bill of Rights in 1791, Congress adopted the infamous Alien and Sedition Acts, which, among other things, made it a crime to say or publish anything that might tend to defame or bring into disrepute the government of the United States. Quite clearly, the acts' intentions were to criminalize the very conduct given absolute protection by the First Amendment. Fifteen violators—including several newspaper editors—were indicted, and a few were actually convicted before the relevant portions of the acts were allowed to expire.

The first modern free speech case arose immediately after World War I. It involved persons who had been convicted under the federal Espionage Act of 1917 for opposing U.S. involvement in the war. The Supreme Court upheld the Espionage Act and refused to protect the speech rights of the defendants on the grounds that their activities—appeals to draftees to resist the draft—constituted a **"clear and present danger"** to security.[25] This is the first and most famous "test" to determine whether speech is protected or unprotected, based on its capacity to present a "clear and present danger" to society.

It was only after the 1920s that real progress toward a genuinely effective First Amendment was made. Since then, the courts have consistently protected political speech even when it has been deemed "insulting" or "outrageous."

A key source of controversy regarding political speech has been the regulation of campaign spending by wealthy people and corporations. In order to limit the corrupting influence of "big money" in political campaigns, Congress has enacted legislation to regulate or limit such spending (the spending of money in political campaigns has been considered a kind of speech, protected under the First Amendment). In 2002, Congress passed the Bipartisan Campaign Reform Act, which limited "soft money" (money contributed to a political party, not a specific candidate) and regulated "issue advocacy ads" designed to help or hurt candidates but not financed by the candidates. The law survived a constitutional challenge in 2003, but in 2007 the Supreme Court ruled that issue ads could not be restricted. In 2008, it ruled against a part of the law that imposed greater restrictions on giving by wealthy donors.

And in a major decision in 2010, the Supreme Court overturned decades of laws and court cases that had restricted the ability of corporations to spend money from their treasuries on political campaign advertisement (corporations have been allowed to spend money on campaigns only through separate political actions committees; see Chapter 8). In the case of *Citizens United v. Federal Election Commission*, a hotly divided court said that corporations were now entitled under the First Amendment to spend money without limits on political ads, based on the principle that the government had no right to regulate corporate political spending because it is a protected form of political speech. The court left in place restrictions on corporate contributions given directly to candidates running for office and to political parties, and also requirements that corporations must disclose their spending. Although the decision did not say so, most assumed that the lifting of spending restrictions would also apply to labor unions. Writing for the majority, Justice Anthony Kennedy said that the First Amendment barred the government from punishing citizens, "or associations of citizens, for simply engaging in political speech." The ruling prompted fierce criticism. Writing for the four dissenting justices, John Paul Stevens said that it was a serious mistake to equate corporate speech (the spending of money for political ads is considered a kind of speech) with that of individual citizens. Stevens wrote that the decision "threatens to undermine the integrity of elected institutions around the nation."[26] Many critics fear that corporations can now sink unlimited amounts of money into election spending to change the outcome of elections from the national to the local level. By one account, "If you vote wrong, a lobbyist can now tell any elected official, my company, labor union or interest group will spend unlimited sums explicitly advertising against your re-election."[27]

## Symbolic Speech, Speech Plus, and the Rights of Assembly and Petition

The First Amendment treats the freedoms of assembly and petition as equal to the freedoms of religion and political speech. Freedom of assembly and freedom of petition are closely associated with speech but go beyond it to speech associated with action. Since at least 1931, the Supreme Court has sought to protect actions that are designed to send a political message. (Usually the purpose of a symbolic act is not only to send a direct message but to draw a crowd—to do something spectacular in order to draw spectators to the action and thus strengthen the message.) Thus the Court held unconstitutional a California law making it a felony to display a red flag "as a sign, symbol or emblem of opposition to organized government."[28] Although today there are limits on how far one can go with actions that symbolically convey a message, the protection of such actions is very broad.

The Supreme Court has interpreted the freedom of speech as extending to symbolic acts of political protest, such as flag burning. On several occasions—most recently in 2006—a resolution for a constitutional amendment to ban flag burning has passed in the House of Representatives but never found enough support in the Senate.

Another example is the burning of the American flag as a symbol of protest. In 1984, at a political rally held during the Republican National Convention in Dallas, Texas, a political protester burned an American flag in violation of a Texas statute that prohibited desecration of a venerated object. By a 5–4 margin, the Supreme Court declared the Texas law unconstitutional on the grounds that flag burning was expressive conduct protected by the First Amendment.[29] Congress reacted immediately with a proposal for a constitutional amendment reversing the Court's Texas decision, and when the amendment failed to receive the necessary two-thirds majority in the Senate, Congress passed the Flag Protection Act of 1989. Protesters promptly violated this act and their prosecution moved quickly into the federal district court, which declared the new law unconstitutional. The Supreme Court, in another 5–4 decision, affirmed the lower court decision[30] to strike down the law.

In 2003, the Supreme Court struck down a Virginia law that made it a crime to burn a cross. Even though the Court considered cross-burning a protected form of speech, it said in its decision that states could enact laws against cross-burning if such an action was intended as a threat and was not merely a form of symbolic expression. The Court noted that cross-burning is a "particularly virulent form of intimidation," but it nevertheless can be allowed as "a form of symbolic expression."[31]

Closer to the original intent of the assembly and petition clause is the category of **"speech plus"**—speech accompanied by conduct or physical activity such as sit-ins, picketing, and demonstrations; protection of this form of speech under the First Amendment is conditional, and restrictions imposed by state or local authorities are acceptable if properly balanced by considerations of public order. Courts consistently protect such assemblies under the First Amendment; state and local laws regulating such activities are closely scrutinized and frequently overturned. But the same assembly on private property is quite another matter and can in many circumstances be regulated. For example, the directors of a shopping center can lawfully prohibit an assembly protesting a war or supporting a ban on abortion. Assemblies in public areas can also be restricted in some circumstances, especially when the assembly or demonstration jeopardizes the health, safety, or rights of others. This condition was the basis of the Supreme Court's decision to uphold a lower court order that restricted the access abortion protesters had to the entrances of abortion clinics.[32]

## Freedom of the Press Is Broad

For all practical purposes, freedom of speech implies and includes freedom of the press. With the exception of the broadcast media, which are subject to federal regulation, the press is protected under the doctrine against **prior restraint** (efforts by a governmental agency to block the publication of material it deems libelous or harmful in some other way; censorship). Beginning with the landmark 1931 case of *Near v. Minnesota*, the U.S. Supreme Court has held that, except under the most extraordinary circumstances, the First Amendment of the Constitution prohibits government agencies from seeking to prevent newspapers or magazines from publishing whatever they wish.[33] In the case of *New York Times v. U.S.*, the so-called *Pentagon Papers* case, the Supreme Court ruled that the government could not block publication of secret Defense Department documents given to the *New York Times* by an opponent of the Vietnam War who had obtained the documents illegally.[34]

By comparison, greater restrictions are allowed for the electronic media. In a 1990 case, the Supreme Court upheld a lower-court order restraining Cable News Network (CNN) from broadcasting tapes of conversations between former Panamanian dictator Manuel Noriega and his lawyer, supposedly recorded by the U.S. government. The Court held that CNN could be restrained from broadcasting the tapes until the trial court in the Noriega case had decided whether their broadcast would violate Noriega's right to a fair trial.

Another press freedom issue that the courts have often been asked to decide is the question of whether journalists can be compelled to reveal their sources of information. Journalists assert that if they cannot assure sources of confidentiality, the flow of information will be reduced and press freedom effectively curtailed. Government agencies, however, assert that the names of news sources may be relevant to criminal or even national security investigations. Nearly all states have "shield laws" that to varying degrees protect journalistic sources. There is, however, no federal shield law, and the Supreme Court has held that the press has no constitutional right to withhold information in court.[35] In 2005, Judith Miller, a *New York Times* reporter, was jailed for contempt of court for refusing to tell a federal grand jury the name of a confidential source in a case involving the leaked identity of the CIA analyst Valerie Plame, whose husband, Joseph Wilson, had been critical of the Bush administration's Iraq policies.

## Some Speech Has Only Limited Protection

At least four forms of speech fall outside the absolute guarantees of the First Amendment and therefore outside the realm of absolute protection: (1) libel and slander, (2) obscenity and pornography, (3) fighting words, and (4) commercial speech. It should be emphasized once again that these four types of speech still enjoy considerable protection by the courts.

**Libel and Slander** If a written statement is made in "reckless disregard of the truth" and is considered damaging to the victim because it is "malicious, scandalous, and defamatory," it can be punished as **libel.** If an oral statement of such a nature is made, it can be punished as **slander.**

Today, most libel suits involve freedom of the press, and the realm of free press is enormous. Historically, newspapers were subject to the law of libel, which provided that newspapers that printed false and malicious stories could be compelled to pay damages to those they defamed. In recent years, however, American courts have greatly narrowed the meaning of libel and made it extremely difficult, particularly for politicians or other public figures, to win a libel case against a newspaper. In the important 1964 case of *New York Times v. Sullivan*, the Court held that to be deemed libelous, a story about a public official not only had to be untrue but also had to result from "actual malice" or "reckless disregard" for the truth.[36] In other words, the newspaper had to print false and malicious material *deliberately.* In practice, this is a very difficult legal standard to meet.

**Obscenity and Pornography** If libel and slander cases can be difficult because of the problem of determining the truth of statements and whether those statements are malicious and damaging, cases involving pornography and obscenity can be even more sticky. It is easy to say that pornography and obscenity fall outside the realm of protected speech, but it is impossible to draw a clear line defining exactly where protection ends and unprotected speech begins. Not until 1957 did the Supreme Court confront this problem, and it did so with a definition of obscenity that may have caused more confusion than it cleared up. Justice William Brennan, in writing the Court's opinion, defined obscenity as speech or writing that appeals to the "prurient interest"—that is, books, magazines, films, and so on, whose purpose is to excite lust as this appears "to the average person, applying contemporary community standards. . . ." Even so, Brennan added, the work should be judged obscene only when it is "utterly without redeeming social importance."[37] Brennan's definition, instead of clarifying the Court's view, actually caused more confusion. In 1964, Justice Potter Stewart confessed that, although he found pornography impossible to define, "I know it when I see it."[38]

An effort was made to strengthen the restrictions in 1973, when the Supreme Court expressed its willingness to define pornography as a work which (1) as a whole, is deemed prurient by the "average person" according to "community standards"; (2) depicts sexual conduct "in a patently offensive way"; and (3) lacks "serious literary, artistic, political, or scientific value." This definition meant that pornography would be determined by local rather than national standards. Thus, a local bookseller might be prosecuted for selling a volume that was a best-seller nationally but that was deemed pornographic locally.[39] This new definition of standards did not help much either, and not long after 1973 the Court began again to review all such community antipornography laws, reversing most of them.

In recent years, the battle against obscene speech has been against "cyberporn"—pornography on the Internet. Opponents of this form of expression argue that it should be banned because of the easy access children have to the Internet. The first major effort to regulate the content of the Internet occurred in 1996, when Congress passed the Communications Decency Act (CDA), designed to regulate the online transmission of obscene material. The constitutionality of the CDA was immediately challenged in court by a coalition of interests led by the American Civil Liberties Union (ACLU). In the 1997 Supreme Court case of *Reno v. ACLU*, the Court struck down the CDA, ruling that it suppressed speech that "adults have a constitutional right to receive," saying that "the level of discourse reaching the mailbox simply cannot be limited to that which would be suitable for a sandbox." Supreme Court Justice John Paul Stevens described the Internet as the "town crier" of the modern age and said that the Internet was entitled to the greatest degree of First Amendment protection possible. By contrast, radio and television are subject to more control than the Internet.[40] In 2003, however, the Supreme Court upheld a federal law, the Children's Internet Protection Act, that requires public libraries to install antipornography filters on all Internet-accessible computers. Librarians are allowed to unblock some sites at the request of adult patrons.[41] In 2008, the Supreme Court upheld a law that made it a crime to sell child pornography on the Internet.

In 2000, the Supreme Court extended the highest degree of First Amendment protection to cable (not broadcast) television. In *U.S. v. Playboy Entertainment Group*, the Court struck down a portion of the Telecommunications Act of 1996 that required cable TV companies to limit the broadcast of sexually explicit programming to late-night hours. In its decision, the Court noted that the law already provided parents with the means to restrict access to sexually explicit cable channels through various blocking devices. Moreover, such programming could come into the home only if parents decided to purchase such channels in the first place.

**Fighting Words** Speech can also lose its protected position when it moves toward the sphere of action. "Expressive speech," for example, is protected until it moves from the symbolic realm to the realm of actual conduct—to direct incitement of damaging conduct with the use of so-called **fighting words.** In 1942, the Supreme Court upheld the arrest and conviction of a man who had violated a state law forbidding the use of offensive language in public. He had called the arresting officer a "goddamned racketeer" and "a damn Fascist." When his case reached the Supreme Court, the arrest was upheld on the grounds that the First Amendment provides no protection for such offensive language because such words "are no essential part of any exposition of ideas."[42] Since that time, however, the Supreme Court has reversed almost every conviction based on arguments that the speaker had used "fighting words."

**Commercial Speech** Commercial speech, such as newspaper or television advertisements, does not have full First Amendment protection because it cannot be considered political speech. Initially considered to be entirely outside the protection of the First Amendment, commercial speech has made gains during the twentieth century. Some commercial speech is still unprotected and therefore regulated. For example, the regulation of false and misleading advertising by the Federal Trade Commission is an old and well-established power of the federal government. The Supreme Court long ago approved the constitutionality of laws prohibiting the electronic media from carrying cigarette advertising.[43] The Court has also upheld a state university ban on Tupperware parties in college dormitories.[44] It has also upheld city ordinances prohibiting the posting of all signs on public property (as long as the ban is total, so that there is no hint of censorship).[45] And the Court upheld Puerto Rico's statute restricting gambling advertising aimed at residents of Puerto Rico.[46]

**Speech by Public School Students** One group that seems to enjoy only a limited right of free speech is public school students. In 1986, the Supreme Court upheld the punishment of a high school student for making sexually suggestive speech. The Court opinion held that such speech interfered with the school's goal of teaching students the limits of socially acceptable behavior.[47] Two years later, the Supreme Court restricted student speech and press rights even further by defining them as part of the educational process not to be treated with the same standard as adult speech in a regular public forum.[48] In 2007, in the case of *Morse v. Frederick*, the Court held that a principal did not violate a student's free speech rights by suspending him for displaying a banner proclaiming, "BONG HiTS 4 JESUS."[49] The decision affirmed the principle that school officials can censor student speech that advocates or celebrates the use of illegal drugs.

## ● The Second Amendment Protects the Right to Bear Arms in a Militia

A well regulated Militia, being necessary to the security of a free State, the right of the people to keep and bear Arms, shall not be infringed.

The Second Amendment was included in the Bill of Rights to protect the right of citizens to keep and bear arms if called into militia service by the government.

*The Second Amendment arouses at least as much controversy as the First. The right to bear arms is constitutionally guaranteed, although an estimated 80 percent of Americans support some form of gun control.*

When the amendment was written, part-time citizen militias provided an important military force to supplement the small professional standing army at a time when the government possessed limited financial means to supply militiamen with weapons. Thus, the reference to the right of the people "to keep and bear Arms" meant that militia-eligible citizens (white males between the ages of eighteen and forty-five) were expected to keep their own firearms at the ready. As the Supreme Court ruled in 1939, the amendment has as its "obvious purpose" the protection of gun ownership only when related to "the preservation or efficiency of a well regulated militia."[50]

When the nation was governed under the Articles of Confederation, the states maintained exclusive control over militias, but the modern Constitution of 1787 gave control over militias to the national government in Article I, as well as the additional sweeping power to create a national standing army. Fearing both a loss of control over militias and the power of a new national army, Antifederalists insisted on reassurance that the states could continue to organize their own militias to meet their own military needs, resulting in the Second Amendment. The military inadequacies of the old militia system, seen especially in the disastrous performance of these part-time amateur soldiers during the War of 1812, rendered it obsolete, and militia call-ups were replaced with the military draft, which is used to expand the standing army in times of need.

Recent controversy has arisen concerning some citizens who have sought to form their own *private* militias, unconnected with the government. Yet the Supreme

Court made clear that the Second Amendment does not allow citizens to form their own militias free from government control. When these private militias tried to assert such a right, the Supreme Court denied it.[51]

Constitutional interpretation of the Second Amendment underwent a seismic change in 2008 when, for the first time in history, the Supreme Court struck down a gun control law as in violation of the right to bear arms by a 5–4 vote. In the high court's ruling in *D.C. v. Heller*,[52] the majority also ruled for the first time that the Second Amendment protected a personal right to own a gun, for personal self-defense at home. The case arose in the early 2000s, when several residents of the District of Columbia filed suit against D.C.'s strict no-handgun law. In 2007, the court of appeals for the D.C. circuit struck the law down as a violation of the Second Amendment. The following year, the Supreme Court upheld the lower court ruling. While the majority decision, written by Justice Antonin Scalia, admitted that the right was not unlimited, and that most gun regulations would continue to be legal, the decision for the first time separated the right stipulated in the amendment from service in a "well-regulated militia." The decision represented a major victory for gun rights organizations, who had long sought such an interpretation of the amendment.

In 2010, the Supreme Court extended its ruling in *Heller* by applying the Second Amendment to the states in *McDonald v. Chicago*,[53] making this the first new incorporation decision by the high court in forty years (see Table 4.3).

## ● Rights of the Criminally Accused Are Based on Due Process of Law

Except for the First Amendment, most of the battle to apply the Bill of Rights to the states was fought over the various protections granted to individuals who are accused of a crime, who are suspects in the commission of a crime, or who are brought before the court as a witness to a crime. The Fourth, Fifth, Sixth, and Eighth Amendments, taken together, are the essence of the due process of law, even though this fundamental concept does not appear until the very last words of the Fifth Amendment.

### The Fourth Amendment Protects against Unlawful Searches and Seizures

> The right of the people to be secure in their persons, houses, papers, and effects, against unreasonable searches and seizures, shall not be violated, and no Warrants shall issue, but upon probable cause, supported by Oath or affirmation, and particularly describing the place to be searched, and the persons or things to be seized.

The purpose of the Fourth Amendment is to guarantee the security of citizens against unreasonable (that is, improper) searches and seizures. In 1990 the Supreme Court summarized its understanding of the Fourth Amendment brilliantly and succinctly: "A search compromises the individual interest in privacy; a seizure deprives the individual of dominion over his or her person or property."[54] But how are we to define what is reasonable and what is unreasonable?

The 1961 case of *Mapp v. Ohio* illustrates the beauty and the agony of one of the most important procedures that has grown out of the Fourth Amendment—the **exclusionary rule,** which is the ability of courts to exclude evidence obtained in violation of the Fourth Amendment, such as barring evidence obtained during an illegal search from being introduced in a trial. Acting on a tip that Dolly Mapp was harboring a suspect in a bombing incident, several police officers forcibly entered Mapp's house claiming they had a warrant to look for the bombing suspect. The police did not find the bombing suspect but did find some materials connected to the local numbers racket (an illegal gambling operation) and a quantity of "obscene materials," in violation of an Ohio law banning possession of such materials. Although the warrant was never produced, the evidence that had been seized was admitted by a court, and Mapp was charged and convicted for illegal possession of obscene materials.

By the time Mapp's appeal reached the Supreme Court, the question was whether any evidence produced under the circumstances of the search of her home was admissible. The Court's opinion affirmed the exclusionary rule: Under the Fourth Amendment (applied to the states through the Fourteenth Amendment), "all evidence obtained by searches and seizures in violation of the Constitution . . . is inadmissible."[55] This means that even people who are clearly guilty of the crime of which they are accused must not be convicted if the only evidence for their conviction was obtained illegally. This idea was expressed by Supreme Court Justice Benjamin Cardozo nearly a century ago when he wrote that "the criminal is to go free because the constable has blundered."

The exclusionary rule is so dramatic a restriction because it rules out precisely the evidence that produces a conviction; it frees those people who are *known* to have committed the crime of which they have been accused. Because it works so dramatically in favor of persons known to have committed a crime, the Court has since softened the application of the rule. In recent years, the federal courts have relied upon a discretionary use of the exclusionary rule, whereby they make a judgment as to the "nature and quality of the intrusion." It is thus difficult to know ahead of time whether a defendant will or will not be protected from an illegal search under the Fourth Amendment.[56] In 2007, the Court extended protection against unlawful searches to the passengers in cars that have been stopped by the police. Passengers, said the Court, have the same right as drivers to challenge the validity of a search.[57]

In 2009, the Court ruled against an Arizona school district that had conducted a strip search of a 13-year-old student suspected of hiding ibuprofen in her underwear,[58] placing clear limits on the ability of schools to engage in intrusive bodily searches of students.

## The Fifth Amendment Covers Court-Related Rights

No person shall be held to answer for a capital, or otherwise infamous crime, unless on a presentment or indictment of a Grand Jury, except in cases arising in the land or naval forces, or in the Militia, when in actual service in time of War or public danger; nor shall any person be subject for the same offence to be twice put in jeopardy of life or limb; nor shall be compelled in any criminal case to be a witness against himself, nor be deprived of life, liberty, or property, without due process of law; nor shall private property be taken for public use, without just compensation.

**Grand Juries** The first clause of the Fifth Amendment sets forth the right to a **grand jury** (a jury that determines whether sufficient evidence is available to justify a trial; grand juries do not rule on the accused's guilt or innocence) to determine whether a trial is warranted. Grand juries play an important role in federal criminal cases. However, the provision for a grand jury is the one important civil liberties provision of the Bill of Rights that was not incorporated by the Fourteenth Amendment to apply to state criminal prosecutions. Thus, some states operate without grand juries. In such states, the prosecuting attorney simply files a "bill of information" affirming that there is sufficient evidence available to justify a trial. If the accused person is to be held in custody, the prosecutor must take the available information before a judge to determine that the evidence shows probable cause.

**Double Jeopardy** "Nor shall any person be subject for the same offence to be twice put in jeopardy of life or limb" is the constitutional protection from **double jeopardy,** a protection to prevent a person from being tried more than once for the same crime. The protection from double jeopardy was at the heart of the *Palko v. Connecticut* case in 1937. In that case, the state of Connecticut had indicted Frank Palko for first-degree murder, but a lower court had found him guilty of only second-degree murder and sentenced him to life in prison. Unhappy with the verdict, the state of Connecticut appealed the conviction to its highest state court, won the appeal, got a new trial, and then succeeded in getting Palko convicted of first-degree murder. Palko appealed to the Supreme Court on what seemed an open and shut case of double jeopardy. Yet, although the majority of the Court agreed that this could indeed be considered a case of double jeopardy, they decided that double jeopardy was not one of the provisions of the Bill of Rights incorporated in the Fourteenth Amendment as a restriction on the powers of the states. It took more than thirty years for the court to nationalize the constitutional protection against double jeopardy. Palko was eventually executed for the crime, because he lived in the state of Connecticut rather than in some state whose constitution included a guarantee against double jeopardy.

**Self-incrimination** Perhaps the most significant liberty found in the Fifth Amendment, and the one most familiar to many Americans who watch television crime shows, is the guarantee that no citizen "shall be compelled in any criminal case to be a witness against himself. . . ." The most famous case concerning self-incrimination involved twenty-three-year-old Ernesto Miranda, who was sentenced to between twenty and thirty years in prison for the kidnapping and rape of an eighteen-year-old woman. The woman had identified him in a police lineup, and, after two hours of questioning, Miranda confessed, subsequently signing a statement that his confession had been made voluntarily, without threats or promises of immunity. These confessions were admitted into evidence, served as the basis for Miranda's conviction, and also served as the basis of the appeal of his conviction all the way to the Supreme Court. In one of the most intensely and widely criticized decisions ever handed down by the

Supreme Court, Miranda's case produced the rules the police must follow before questioning an arrested criminal suspect. The reading of a person's "*Miranda* rights" became a standard scene in every police station and on virtually every dramatization of police action on television and in the movies. *Miranda* advanced the civil liberties of accused persons not only by expanding the scope of the Fifth Amendment clause covering coerced confessions and self-incrimination, but also by

*The modern interpretation of the Fifth Amendment was shaped by the 1966 case* Miranda v. Arizona. *Ernesto Miranda confessed to kidnapping and rape. Since he was never told that he was not required to answer police questions, his case was appealed on the grounds that his right against self-incrimination had been violated.*

confirming the right to counsel (discussed later). The Supreme Court under Warren Burger and William Rehnquist considerably softened the *Miranda* restrictions, making the job of the police easier, but the **Miranda** rule (the requirement, established by the Supreme Court in *Miranda v. Arizona*, that persons under arrest must be informed prior to police interrogation of their rights to remain silent and to have the benefit of legal counsel) still stands as a protection against egregious police abuses of arrested persons.

**Eminent Domain** The other fundamental clause of the Fifth Amendment is the "takings clause," which extends to each citizen a protection against the "taking" of private property "without just compensation." Although this part of the Fifth Amendment is not specifically concerned with protecting persons accused of crimes, it is nevertheless a fundamentally important instance where the government and the citizen are adversaries. The power of any government to take private property for a public use is called **eminent domain.** The Fifth Amendment puts limits on that inherent power through procedures that require a showing of a public purpose and the provision of fair payment for the taking of someone's property.

## The Sixth Amendment's Right to Counsel Is Crucial for a Fair Trial

In all criminal prosecutions, the accused shall enjoy the right to a speedy and public trial, by an impartial jury of the State and district wherein the crime shall have been committed, which district shall have been ascertained by law, and to be informed of the nature and the cause of the accusation; to be confronted with the witnesses against him; to have compulsory process for obtaining witnesses in his favor, and to have the Assistance of Counsel for his defence.

Like the exclusionary rule of the Fourth Amendment and the self-incrimination clause of the Fifth Amendment, the "right to counsel" provision of the Sixth Amendment is notable for freeing defendants who seem to the public to be guilty as charged. Other provisions of the Sixth Amendment, such as the right to a speedy trial and the right to confront witnesses before an impartial jury, are less controversial.

*Gideon v. Wainwright* (1963) is the perfect example because it involved a disreputable person who seemed patently guilty of the crime for which he was convicted. In and out of jails for most of his fifty-one years, Clarence Earl Gideon received a five-year sentence for breaking and entering a poolroom in Panama City, Florida. While serving time in jail, Gideon became a fairly well-qualified "jailhouse lawyer," made his own appeal on a handwritten petition, and eventually won the landmark ruling on the right to counsel in all felony cases.[59]

The right to counsel has been expanded rather than contracted during the past few decades, even though the courts have become more conservative. The right to counsel extends beyond serious crimes to any trial, with or without jury, that holds the possibility of imprisonment.

## The Eighth Amendment Bars Cruel and Unusual Punishment

The Eighth Amendment prohibits "excessive bail," "excessive fines," and "cruel and unusual punishment." Virtually all the debate over Eighth Amendment issues focuses on the last clause of the amendment: the protection from "cruel and unusual punishment." One of the greatest challenges in interpreting this provision consistently arises over the death penalty. In 1972, the Supreme Court overturned several state death penalty laws, not because they were cruel and unusual but because they were being applied in a capricious manner—that is, blacks were much more likely than whites to be sentenced to death, the poor more likely than the rich, and men more likely than women.[60] Very soon after that decision, a majority of states revised their capital punishment provisions to meet the Court's standards.[61] Since 1976, the Court has consistently upheld state laws providing for capital punishment, although the Court also continues to review numerous death penalty appeals each year.

Between 1976 and 2009, states executed 1,161 people. Most of those executions occurred in southern states, with Texas leading the way at 430. As of 2009, thirty-six states had adopted some form of capital punishment, a move approved of by a majority of Americans, according to polls.

Despite the seeming popularity of the death penalty, the debate has become, if anything, more intense. In 1997, for example, the American Bar Association passed a resolution calling for a halt to the death penalty until concerns about its fairness—that is, whether its application violates the principle of equality—and about ensuring due process are addressed. In 2000, the governor of Illinois imposed a moratorium on the death penalty and created a commission to review the capital punishment system. After a two-year study by the commission, Illinois adopted a number of reforms, including a ban on executions of the mentally retarded. In 2002, the U.S. Supreme Court banned all executions of mentally retarded defendants, a decision that affected more than two hundred people then on death row.

In 2004, the Supreme Court blocked the execution of juveniles charged with capital crimes, but in 2008 it upheld execution by lethal injection despite arguments that the method caused great pain.[62]

## The Right to Privacy Means the Right to Be Left Alone

Although the word, "privacy" never appears in the Bill of Rights, there is general agreement that a **right to privacy** emanates from the first ten amendments—even though judges and legal scholars continue to disagree about where the right comes from. The idea behind the right to privacy is simple: People have a right to be left alone from government or other persons' interference in certain personal areas.

The sphere of privacy was drawn in earnest by the Supreme Court in 1965, when it ruled that a Connecticut statute forbidding the use of contraceptives violated the right of marital privacy. Estelle Griswold, the executive director of the Planned Parenthood League of Connecticut, was arrested by the state of Connecticut for providing information, instruction, and medical advice about contraception to married couples. She and her associates were found guilty as accessories to the crime and fined $100 each. The Supreme Court reversed the lower court decisions and declared the Connecticut law unconstitutional because it violated "a right of privacy older than the Bill of Rights—older than our political parties, older than our school system."[63] Justice William O. Douglas, author of the majority decision in the *Griswold v. Connecticut* case, argued that this right of privacy is also grounded in the Constitution, because it fits into a "zone of privacy" created by a combination of the Third, Fourth, and Fifth Amendments. A concurring opinion, written by Justice Arthur Goldberg, attempted to strengthen Douglas's argument by adding that "the concept of liberty . . . embraces the right of marital privacy though that right is not mentioned explicitly in the Constitution [and] is supported by numerous decisions of this Court . . . and *by the language and history of the Ninth Amendment*" (emphasis added).[64]

The right to privacy was confirmed and extended in 1973 in the most important of all privacy decisions, and one of the most important and controversial Supreme Court decisions in American history: *Roe v. Wade*. This decision established a woman's right to seek an abortion and prohibited states from making abortion a criminal act.[65] It is important to emphasize that the preference for privacy rights and for their extension to include the rights of women to control their own bodies was not something invented by the Supreme Court in a vacuum. Most states did not regulate abortions in any fashion until the 1840s, at which time only six of the twenty-six existing states had any regulations governing abortion at all. In addition, many states had begun to ease their abortion restrictions well before the 1973 *Roe* decision, although in recent years a number of states have reinstated some restrictions on abortion.

Like any important principle, once privacy was established as an aspect of civil liberties protected by the Bill of Rights through the Fourteenth Amendment, it took on a life of its own. In a number of important decisions, the Supreme Court and the lower federal courts sought to protect rights that could not be found in the text of the Constitution but could be discovered through the study of the philosophic sources of fundamental rights. Increasingly in recent years, right-to-privacy claims have been made by those attempting to preserve the right to obtain legal abortions, as well as those seeking to obtain greater rights for homosexuals, and supporters of physician-assisted suicide (also known as the "right to die" movement). In the case of homosexuals, the Supreme Court extended privacy protections to them in 2003 when it ruled that they are "entitled to respect for their private lives" in the case of *Lawrence v. Texas*.[66] For the first time, gays and lesbians could claim right-to-privacy protection. These subjects are inherently controversial, which helps explain why the concept of privacy itself continues to spark controversy.

## ● Civil Rights Are Protections by the Government

With the adoption of the Fourteenth Amendment in 1868, civil rights became part of the Constitution, guaranteed to each citizen through "equal protection of the laws." These words launched a century of political movements and legal efforts to press for racial equality. The African American quest for civil rights in turn inspired many other groups, including members of other racial and ethnic groups, women, the disabled, and gays and lesbians, to seek new laws and constitutional guarantees of their civil rights.

*The 1896 Supreme Court case of* Plessy v. Ferguson *upheld legal segregation and created the "separate but equal" rule, which fostered national segregation. Overt discrimination in public accommodations was common.*

Congress passed the **Fourteenth Amendment**, guaranteeing equal protection and due process, and the states ratified it in the aftermath of the Civil War. Together with the **Thirteenth Amendment**, which abolished slavery, and the **Fifteenth Amendment**, which guaranteed voting rights for black men, it seemed to provide a guarantee of civil rights for the newly freed black slaves. But the general language of the Fourteenth Amendment meant that its support for civil rights could be far-reaching. The very simplicity of the **equal protection clause** of the Fourteenth Amendment left it open to interpretation:

> No State shall make or enforce any law which shall . . . deny to any person within its jurisdiction the equal protection of the laws.

This provision of the Fourteenth Amendment guarantees citizens "the equal protection of the laws." This clause has served as the basis for protecting the civil rights of African Americans, women, and other groups.

## *Plessy v. Ferguson* Established "Separate but Equal"

The Supreme Court was no more ready to enforce the civil rights aspects of the Fourteenth Amendment than it was to enforce the civil liberties provisions. The Court declared the Civil Rights Act of 1875 unconstitutional on the grounds that the act sought to protect blacks against discrimination by *private* businesses, while the Fourteenth Amendment, according to the Court's interpretation, was intended to protect individuals only from discrimination that arose from actions by *public* officials of state and local governments.

In 1896, the Court went still further, in the infamous case of *Plessy v. Ferguson*, by upholding a Louisiana statute that *required* segregation of the races on trolleys and other public carriers (and by implication in all public facilities, including schools). Plessy, a man defined as "one-eighth black," had violated a Louisiana law that provided for "equal but separate accommodations" on trains and a $25 fine for any white passenger who sat in a car reserved for blacks or any black passenger who sat in a car reserved for whites. The Supreme Court held that the Fourteenth Amendment's "equal protection of the laws" was not violated by laws requiring segregation of the races in public accommodations as long as the facilities were equal, thus establishing the **"separate but equal" rule** that prevailed through the mid-twentieth century. People generally pretended that segregated accommodations were equal as long as some accommodation for blacks existed. Thus, racial inequality in the guise of the separate but equal doctrine persisted for decades.

## Racial Discrimination Began to Subside after World War II

The Supreme Court had begun to change its position on racial discrimination before World War II by being stricter about the criterion of equal facilities in the "separate but equal" rule. In 1938, for example, the Court rejected Missouri's policy of paying the tuition of qualified blacks to out-of-state law schools rather than admitting them to the University of Missouri Law School.[67] Similar rulings in the 1940s and 1950s began to nibble away at "separate but equal."

Although none of those pre-1954 cases confronted "separate but equal" and the principle of racial discrimination as such, they were extremely significant to black leaders and gave them encouragement enough to believe that there was at last an opportunity and enough legal precedent to change the constitutional framework itself. Much of this legal work was done by the Legal Defense and Educational Fund of the National Association for the Advancement of Colored People (NAACP). Formed in 1909 to fight discrimination against African Americans, the NAACP was the most important civil rights organization during the first half of the twentieth century.

In the fall of 1952, the Court had on its docket cases from Kansas, South Carolina, Virginia, Delaware, and the District of Columbia challenging the constitutionality of school segregation. Of these, the case filed in Kansas became the chosen one.

Oliver Brown, the father of three girls, lived "across the tracks" in a low- income, racially mixed Topeka neighborhood. Every schoolday morning, Linda Brown took the school bus to the Monroe School for black children about a mile away. In September 1950, Oliver Brown took Linda to the all-white Sumner School, which was closer to home, to enter her into the third grade in defiance of state law and local segregation rules. When they were refused, Brown took his case to the NAACP, and soon thereafter *Brown v. Board of Education* was born.

In deciding the *Brown* case, the Court, to the surprise of many, basically rejected as inconclusive all the learned arguments about the intent and the history of the Fourteenth Amendment and committed itself to considering only the consequences of segregation:

> Does segregation of children in public schools solely on the basis of race, even though the physical facilities and other "tangible" factors may be equal, deprive the children of the minority group of equal educational opportunities? We believe that it does. . . . We conclude that in the field of public education the doctrine of "separate but equal" has no place. Separate educational facilities are inherently unequal.[68]

Thus, the 1954 *Brown* decision struck down the "separate but equal" doctrine as fundamentally unequal. This case eliminated state power to use race as a criterion of discrimination in law and provided the national government with the power to intervene by exercising strict regulatory policies against discriminatory actions. It altered the constitutional framework in two fundamental respects. First, after *Brown*, the states no longer had the power to use race as a criterion of discrimination in law. Second, the national government from then on had the power (and eventually the obligation) to intervene with strict regulatory policies against the discriminatory actions of state or local governments, school boards, employers, and many others in the private sector.

## The Civil Rights Struggle Escalated after *Brown v. Board of Education*

The historic decision in *Brown v. Board of Education* was merely a small opening move. First, most states refused to cooperate until sued, and many ingenious schemes were employed to delay obedience (such as paying the tuition for white students to attend newly created "private" academies). Second, school boards began to cooperate by eliminating legally enforced school segregation (what is referred to as *de jure* segregation, meaning literally "by law" or legally enforced practices as seen in schools racially segregated by law before the 1960s). Despite this change, extensive actual segregation remained (what is referred to as *de facto* segregation, meaning literally "by fact," wherein races are still segregated even though the law does not require it). Thus, school segregation in the North as well as in the South remained as a consequence of racially segregated housing patterns that were untouched by the 1954–55 *Brown* principles. Third, discrimination in employment, public accommodations, juries, voting, and other areas of social and economic activity were not directly touched by *Brown*.

**Social Protest and Congressional Action** Ten years after *Brown*, fewer than 1 percent of black school-age children in the Deep South were attending schools with whites.[69] A decade of frustration made it fairly obvious to all observers that adjudication alone would not succeed. The goal of "equal protection" required positive, or affirmative, action by Congress and by federal agencies. And given massive southern resistance and a generally negative national public opinion toward racial integration, progress would not be made through courts, Congress, or federal agencies without intense, well-organized support. Organized civil rights demonstrations began to mount slowly but surely after *Brown v. Board of Education*. By the 1960s, the many organizations that made up the civil rights movement had accumulated experience and built networks capable of launching massive direct-action campaigns against southern segregationists. The Southern Christian Leadership Conference, the Student Nonviolent Coordinating Committee, and many other organizations had built a movement that stretched across the South. The movement used the media to attract nationwide attention and support. In the massive March on Washington in 1963, the Reverend Martin Luther King Jr., staked out the movement's moral claims in his famous "I Have a Dream" speech. The image of protesters being beaten, attacked by police dogs, and set upon with fire hoses did much to win broad sympathy for the cause of black civil rights and to discredit state and local governments in the South. In this way, the movement created intense pressure for reluctant federal government to take more assertive steps to defend black civil rights.

## The Civil Rights Acts Made Equal Protection a Reality

The right to equal protection of the laws could be established and, to a certain extent, implemented by the courts. But after a decade of very frustrating efforts, the courts and Congress ultimately came to the conclusion that the federal courts alone were not adequate to the task of changing the social rules, and that legislation and administrative action would be needed.

Congress used its legislative powers to help make equal protection of the laws a reality by passing the Civil Rights Act of 1964. The act seemed bold at the time, but it was enacted ten years after the Supreme Court had declared racial discrimination "inherently unequal" under the Fifth and Fourteenth Amendments. And it was enacted long after blacks had demonstrated that discrimination was no longer acceptable. The choice in 1964 was not between congressional action or inaction but between legal action and expanded violence.

**Public Accommodations** After the passage of the 1964 Civil Rights Act, public accommodations quickly removed some of the most visible forms of racial discrimination. Signs defining "colored" and "white" restrooms, water fountains, waiting rooms, and seating arrangements were removed and a host of other practices that relegated black people to separate and inferior arrangements were ended. In addition, the federal government filed more than four hundred antidiscrimination suits in federal courts against hotels, restaurants, taverns, gas stations, and other "public accommodations."

Many aspects of legalized racial segregation—such as separate Bibles in the courtroom—seem like ancient history today. But the issue of racial discrimination in public settings is by no means over. In 1993, six African American Secret Service agents filed charges against the Denny's restaurant chain for failing to serve them; white Secret Service agents at a nearby table had received prompt service. Similar charges citing discriminatory service at Denny's restaurants surfaced across the country. Faced with evidence of a pattern of systematic discrimination and

*The 1964 Civil Rights Act made desegregation a legal requirement. The policy of busing from black neighborhoods to white schools bitterly divided the black and white communities in Boston. In 1976, a protestor waved an American flag threateningly at an innocent black bystander—a lawyer on his way to his office—as another white man sought to help him get out of the way.*

numerous lawsuits, Denny's paid $45 million in damages to plaintiffs in Maryland and California in what is said to be the largest settlement ever in a public accommodation case.[70] The Denny's case shows how effective the Civil Rights Act of 1964 can be in challenging racial discrimination. In addition to the settlement, the chain vowed to expand employment and management opportunities for minorities in Denny's restaurants.

**School Desegregation** The 1964 Civil Rights Act also declared discrimination by private employers and state governments (school boards, etc.) illegal, then went further to provide for administrative agencies to help the courts implement these laws. The act, for example, authorized the executive branch, through the Justice Department, to implement federal court orders to desegregate schools, and to do so without having to wait for individual parents to bring complaints. The act also vastly strengthened the role of the executive branch and the credibility of court orders by providing that federal grants-in-aid to state and local governments for education must be withheld from any school system practicing racial segregation.

In recent years, a series of court rulings have slowed race-based integration efforts. In 2007, the Supreme Court's ruling in *Parents Involved in Community Schools v. Seattle School District No. 1* limited the measures that can be used to promote school integration. The case involved school assignment plans voluntarily initiated by the city of Seattle and, in another, related case, the city of Louisville, Kentucky. By making race one factor in assigning students to schools, the cities hoped to achieve greater racial balance across the public schools. The court ruled that these plans—even though they were voluntarily adopted by cities—were unconstitutional because they discriminated against white students on the basis of race. Many observers described the decision as the end of the Brown era because it eliminated one of the few public strategies left to promote racial integration. Others argued that Justice Anthony Kennedy's concurring opinion, which recognized the harm of racial isolation, may provide the basis for new efforts to promote integration in the future.[71]

**Outlawing Discrimination in Employment** The federal courts and the Justice Department also fought employment discrimination through the Civil Rights Act of 1964, which outlawed job discrimination by all private and public employers, including governmental agencies (such as fire and police departments) that employed more than fifteen workers. We have already seen (in Chapter 3) that the Supreme Court gave "interstate commerce" such a broad definition that Congress had the constitutional authority to cover discrimination by virtually any local employers.[72] The 1964 act makes it unlawful to discriminate in employment on the basis of color, religion, sex, or national origin, as well as race.

In order to enforce fair employment practices, the national government could revoke public contracts for goods and services and refuse to engage in contracts for goods and services with any private company that could not guarantee that its rules for hiring, promotion, and firing were nondiscriminatory.

But one problem was that the complaining party had to show that deliberate discrimination was the cause of the failure to get a job or a training opportunity.

*The mortgage crisis that led to forclosures on many homes hit minority communities especially hard. Civil rights organizations argued that some lenders discriminated against African American and Hispanic home buyers, making it harder for them to get a fair deal on a mortgage.*

Rarely does an employer explicitly admit discrimination on the basis of race, sex, or any other illegal reason. Recognizing the rarity of such an admission, the courts have allowed aggrieved parties (the plaintiffs) to make their case if they can show that an employer's hiring practices had the *effect* of exclusion, even if they cannot show the *intention* to discriminate.

**Voting Rights** Although 1964 was the *most* important year for civil rights legislation, it was not the only important year. In 1965, Congress significantly strengthened legislation protecting voting rights by barring literacy and other tests as a condition for voting in six southern states,[73] by making it a crime to interfere with voting, and by providing for the replacement of local registrars with federally appointed registrars in counties designated by the attorney general as significantly resistant to registering eligible blacks to vote. The right to vote was further strengthened with ratification in 1964 of the Twenty-fourth Amendment, which abolished the poll tax, and later with legislation permanently outlawing literacy tests in all fifty states and mandating bilingual ballots or oral assistance for Spanish-speakers, Chinese, Japanese, Koreans, Native Americans, and Eskimo. This 1965 law finally broke the back of voting segregation, meaning that it took almost one hundred years to carry out the Fifteenth Amendment.

In the long run, the laws extending and protecting voting rights could prove to be the most effective of all the great civil rights legislation, because the progress in black political participation produced by these acts has altered the shape of American politics. In 1965, in the seven states of the Old Confederacy covered by the Voting Rights Act, 29.3 percent of the eligible black residents were registered to vote, compared to 73.4 percent of the white residents (see Table 4.4). Mississippi was the extreme case, with 6.7 percent black and 69.9 percent white registration. In 1967, a mere two years after implementation of the voting rights laws, 52.1 percent of the eligible blacks in the seven states were registered, comparing favorably to 79.5 percent of the eligible whites, a gap of 27.4 points. By 1972, the gap between black and white registration in the seven states was only 11.2 points.

**Housing** The Civil Rights Act of 1964 did not address housing, but in 1968, Congress passed another civil rights act specifically to outlaw housing discrimination. Called the Fair Housing Act, the law prohibited discrimination in the sale or rental of most housing—eventually covering nearly all the nation's housing. Housing was among the most controversial of discrimination issues because of deeply entrenched patterns of residential segregation across the United States.

Although it pronounced sweeping goals, the Fair Housing Act had little effect on housing segregation because its enforcement mechanisms were so weak. Individuals believing they had been discriminated against had to file suit themselves. The burden was on the individual to prove that housing discrimination had occurred, even though such discrimination is often subtle and difficult to document. Although local fair-housing groups emerged to assist individuals in their court claims, the procedures for proving discrimination proved a formidable barrier to effective change. These procedures were not altered until 1988, when Congress passed the Fair Housing Amendments Acts. This new law put more teeth in the enforcement procedures and allowed the Department of Housing and Urban Development

## TABLE 4.4

### Registration by Race and State in Southern States Covered by the 1965 Voting Rights Act (VRA)

| | BEFORE THE ACT* | | | AFTER THE ACT* 1971–72 | | |
|---|---|---|---|---|---|---|
| | WHITE | BLACK | GAP[†] | WHITE | BLACK | GAP[†] |
| Alabama | 69.2% | 19.3% | 49.9% | 80.7% | 57.1% | 23.6% |
| Georgia | 62.6 | 27.4 | 35.2 | 70.6 | 67.8 | 2.8 |
| Louisiana | 80.5 | 31.6 | 48.9 | 80.0 | 59.1 | 20.9 |
| Mississippi | 69.9 | 6.7 | 63.2 | 71.6 | 62.2 | 9.4 |
| North Carolina | 96.8 | 46.8 | 50.0 | 62.2 | 46.3 | 15.9 |
| South Carolina | 75.7 | 37.3 | 38.4 | 51.2 | 48.0 | 3.2 |
| Virginia | 61.1 | 38.3 | 22.8 | 61.2 | 54.0 | 7.2 |
| TOTAL | 73.4 | 29.3 | 44.1 | 67.8 | 56.6 | 11.2 |

*Available registration data as of March 1965 and 1971–72.
†The gap is the percentage point difference between white and black registration rates.
SOURCE: U.S. Commission on Civil Rights, *Political Participation* (1968), Appendix VII: "Voter Education Project, Attachment to Press Release," October 3, 1972.

(HUD) to initiate legal action in cases of discrimination. These provisions proved more successful than past efforts at combating housing discrimination.[74]

Even so, another kind of discrimination, related to discriminatory home mortgage–lending practices, remained significant. So-called "predatory lending"— offering loans well above market rates, including "subprime mortgages"—led to charges that such loans were offered to African Americans and Latinos, while whites with similar incomes were offered loans with lower rates. These charges received extensive national attention when the economic downturn of 2008–09 led to widespread mortgage defaults.[75]

## ● The Civil Rights Struggle Was Extended to Other Disadvantaged Groups

Even before equal employment laws began to have a positive effect on the economic situation of blacks, something far more dramatic began to happen: the universalization of civil rights. The right not to be discriminated against was being successfully claimed by the other groups listed in the 1964 Civil Rights Act—those defined by sex, religion, or national origin—and eventually by still other groups defined by age or sexual preference. This universalization of civil rights has become the new frontier of the civil rights struggle, and women have emerged with the greatest prominence in this new struggle. The effort to define and end gender discrimination in employment has led to the historic joining of women's rights to the civil rights cause.

### Women Fought Gender Discrimination

In many ways the Civil Rights Act fostered the growth of the women's movement. The first major campaign of the National Organization for Women (NOW) involved picketing the Equal Employment Opportunity Commission for its refusal to ban sex-segregated employment advertisements. NOW also sued the *New York Times* for continuing to publish such ads after the passage of the act. Another organization, the Women's Equity Action League (WEAL), pursued legal action on a wide range of sex discrimination issues, filing lawsuits against law schools and medical schools for discriminatory admission policies, for example.

Building on these victories and the growth of the women's movement, feminist activists sought an "Equal Rights Amendment" (ERA) to the Constitution. The proposed amendment was short; its substantive passage stated that "equality of rights under the law shall not be denied or abridged by the United States or by any State on account of sex." The amendment's supporters believed that such a sweeping guarantee of equal rights was a necessary tool for ending all discrimination against women and for making gender roles more equal. Opponents charged that it would be socially disruptive and would introduce changes—such as coed restrooms—that most Americans did not want. The amendment easily passed Congress in 1972 and won quick approval in many state legislatures, but it fell three states short of the thirty-eight needed to ratify the amendment by the 1982 deadline for its ratification.[76]

*Political equality did not end discrimination against women in the workplace or in society at large. African Americans' struggle for civil rights in the 1950s and 1960s spurred a parallel equal rights movement for women in the 1960s and 1970s.*

Despite the failure of the ERA, gender discrimination expanded dramatically as an area of civil rights law. In the 1970s, the conservative Burger Court (under Chief Justice Warren Burger) helped to establish gender discrimination as a major and highly visible civil rights issue. Although the Burger Court refused to treat gender discrimination as the equivalent of racial discrimination,[77] it did make it easier for plaintiffs to file and win suits on the basis of gender discrimination.

Courts began to find sexual harassment a form of sex discrimination during the late 1970s. Although sexual harassment law applies to education, most of the law of sexual harassment has been developed by courts through interpretation of Title VII of the Civil Rights Act of 1964. In 1986, the Supreme Court recognized two forms of sexual harassment: the quid pro quo type, which involves sexual extortion, and the hostile environment type, which involves sexual intimidation.[78]

Another major step was taken in 1992, when the Court decided in *Franklin v. Gwinnett County Public Schools* that violations of Title IX of the 1972 Education Act could be remedied with monetary damages.[79] Title IX forbade gender discrimination in education, but it initially sparked little litigation because of its weak enforcement provisions. The Court's 1992 ruling that monetary damages could be awarded for gender discrimination opened the door for more legal action in the area of education. The greatest impact has been in the areas of sexual harassment—the subject of the *Franklin* case—and in equal treatment of women's athletic programs. The potential for monetary damages has made universities and public schools take the problem of sexual harassment more seriously. Colleges and universities have also started to pay more attention to women's athletic programs.

In 1996, the Supreme Court made another important decision about gender and education by putting an end to all-male schools supported by public funds. It ruled that the policy of the Virginia Military Institute (VMI) not to admit women was unconstitutional.[80] Along with the Citadel, an all-male military college in South Carolina, VMI had never admitted women in its 157-year history. VMI argued that the unique educational experience it offered—including intense physical training and the harsh treatment of freshmen—would be destroyed if women students were admitted. The Court, however, ruled that the male-only policy denied "substantial equality" to women. Two days after the Court's ruling, the Citadel announced that it would accept women. VMI considered becoming a private institution in order to remain all-male, but in September 1996, the school board finally voted to admit women.

Women's rights suffered a setback in 2007, when the Supreme Court ruled against a claim of pay discrimination at work. The case, *Ledbetter v. Goodyear Tire and Rubber Co.*,[81] involved a female supervisor named Lilly Ledbetter who learned late in her career that she was being paid up to 40 percent less than male supervisors, including those with less seniority. Ledbetter filed a grievance with the Equal Employment Opportunity Commission charging sex discrimination. The Supreme Court denied her claim, ruling that according to the law, workers must file their grievance 180 days after the discrimination occurs. Many observers found the ruling unfair because workers often do not know about pay differentials until well after the initial decision to discriminate has been made. Justice Ruth Bader Ginsburg, the only female member of the Court, marked her disagreement by reading her dissent aloud, a rare occurrence. In 2009, Congress responded by enacting the Lilly Ledbetter Fair Pay Act, which became the first bill that President Obama signed into law. The new law gave workers expanded rights to sue in cases such as Ledbetter's, when an employee learns of discriminatory treatment well after it has started.

## Latinos and Asian Americans Fight for Rights

Although the Civil Rights Act of 1964 outlawed discrimination on the basis of national origin, limited English proficiency barred many Asian Americans and Latinos from full participation in American life. Two developments in the 1970s, however, established rights for language minorities. In 1974, the Supreme Court ruled in *Lau v. Nichols*, a suit filed on behalf of Chinese students in San Francisco, that school districts have to provide education for students whose English is limited.[82] It did not mandate bilingual education, but it established a duty to provide instruction that the students could understand. The 1970 amendments to the Voting Rights Act permanently outlawed literacy tests in all fifty states and mandated bilingual ballots or oral assistance for those who speak Spanish, Chinese, Japanese, Korean, Native American languages, or Eskimo languages.

Asian Americans and Latinos have also been concerned about the impact of immigration laws on their civil rights. Many Asian American and Latino organizations opposed the Immigration Reform and Control Act of 1986 because it imposed sanctions on employers who hire undocumented workers. Such sanctions, they feared, would lead employers to discriminate against Latinos and Asian Americans. These suspicions were confirmed in a 1990 report by the General Accounting Office

*Some states and cities have tried to address illegal immigration by enacting stricter laws than those under consideration by Congress. This worker protested one such law with a sign reading "I am a day laborer, not a criminal."*

that found employer sanctions had created a "widespread pattern of discrimination" against Latinos and others who appear foreign.[83] Latinos and Asian Americans have established organizations modeled on the NAACP's Legal Defense Fund, such as the Mexican American Legal Defense and Educational Fund (MALDEF) and the Asian Law Caucus, to monitor and challenge such discrimination. These groups have turned their attention to the rights of legal and illegal immigrants, as anti-immigrant sentiment has grown in recent years.

## Native Americans Have Sovereignty, but Still Lack Rights

As a language minority, Native Americans were affected by the 1975 amendments to the Voting Rights Act and the *Lau* decision. The *Lau* decision established the right of Native Americans to be taught in their own languages. This marked quite a change from the boarding schools once run by the Bureau of Indian Affairs, at which members of Indian tribes had been forbidden to speak their own languages. In addition to these language-related issues, Native Americans have sought to expand their rights on the basis of their sovereign status. Since the 1920s and 1930s, Native American tribes have sued the federal government for illegally seizing land, seeking monetary reparations and land as damages. Both types of damages have been awarded in such suits, but only in small amounts. Native American tribes have been more successful in winning federal recognition of their sovereignty. Sovereign status has, in turn, allowed them to exercise greater self-determination. Most significant economically was a 1987 Supreme Court decision that freed Native

American tribes from most state regulations prohibiting gambling. The establishment of casino gambling on Native American lands has brought a substantial flow of new income into some desperately poor reservations.

## Disabled Americans Won a Great Victory in 1990

The concept of rights for the disabled began to emerge in the 1970s as the civil rights model spread to other groups. The seed was planted in a little-noticed provision of the 1973 Rehabilitation Act, which outlawed discrimination against individuals on the basis of disabilities. As in many other cases, the law itself helped give rise to the movement demanding rights for the handicapped.[84] Modeling itself on the NAACP's Legal Defense Fund, the disability movement founded a Disability Rights Education and Defense Fund to press its legal claims. The movement achieved its greatest success with the passage of the Americans with Disabilities Act (ADA) of 1990, which guarantees equal employment rights and access to public businesses for the disabled. The Equal Opportunities Commission considers claims of discrimination in violation of this act. The impact of the law has been far-reaching, as businesses and public facilities have installed ramps, elevators, and other devices to meet the act's requirements.[85] In 1998, the Supreme Court interpreted the ADA to apply to people with HIV. Until then, ADA was interpreted as covering people with AIDS but not people with HIV. The case arose out of the refusal of a dentist to fill a cavity of a woman with HIV except in a hospital setting. The woman sued, and her complaint was that HIV had already disabled her because it was discouraging her from having children. (The act prohibits discrimination in employment, housing, and health care.)

In 2001, professional golfer Casey Martin, who suffers from a degenerative circulatory disorder that causes great pain and leg deterioration, won the legal right to ride in a golf cart on the Professional Golfers Association (PGA) Tour under the ADA's provision that owners of public accommodations must make "reasonable modifications" for the disabled. Despite the PGA's argument that walking golf courses during tour events was a necessary part of the game, the Supreme Court ruled in *PGA Tour v. Martin* that walking was "at best peripheral" to the game, thus upholding Martin's right to use a motorized golf cart. Justice Stevens, himself an amateur golfer, wrote in the Court's opinion that "from early on, the essence of the game has been shot-making."

## The Aged Are Protected under Law

Age discrimination in employment is illegal. The 1967 federal Age Discrimination in Employment Act (ADEA) makes age discrimination illegal when practiced by employers with at least twenty employees. Many states have added to the federal provisions with their own age discrimination laws, and some such state laws are stronger than the federal provisions. Age discrimination—especially in hiring—is widespread, and it is all the more pressing a problem because of Americans' significantly increased life expectancy. We are a much older population than we used to be. The idea of reduced psychological and physical capacity at age fifty, once perhaps reasonable, seems ridiculous today; and forcible retirement at sixty-five is looking sillier every year. Reasonable people will continue to disagree over the merits of laws against age discrimination. But it is clear that the major lobbyist for seniors, AARP, formerly the American Association of Retired Persons (see Chapter 7), with over 38 million members, will maintain its vigilance and its influence to keep these laws on the books and to make sure that they are vigorously implemented. Even so, rights for older workers received a setback in a 2009 Supreme Court decision.[86] The Court ruled that a fifty-four-year-old employee who had challenged his dismissal on the grounds of age discrimination would have to show that the dismissal was a direct result of discrimination. This was a major change in the law: in the past, the burden of proof was on employers to demonstrate that they had valid reasons other than age for demoting or terminating an employee.

## Gays and Lesbians Gained Significant Legal Ground

In less than thirty years, the gay and lesbian movement has become one of the largest civil rights movements in contemporary America. Beginning with street protests in the 1960s, the movement has grown into a well-financed and sophisticated lobby.

But until 1996, there was no Supreme Court ruling or national legislation explicitly protecting gays and lesbians from discrimination. The first gay rights case that the Court decided, *Bowers v. Hardwick* (1986), ruled against a right to privacy that would protect consensual homosexual activity.[87] After the *Bowers* decision, the gay and lesbian rights movement sought suitable legal cases to test the constitutionality of discrimination against gays and lesbians, much as the black Civil

*In 2008, California voters passed Proposition 8, which restricted marriage to couples consisting of a man and a woman. Opponents of the proposition argued that same-sex couples should be treated equally under the law and allowed the right to marry.*

Rights Movement did in the late 1940s and 1950s. As one advocate put it, "lesbians and gay men are looking for their *Brown v. Board of Education.*"[88] In 1996, the Supreme Court, in *Romer v. Evans,* explicitly extended fundamental civil rights protections to gays and lesbians, by declaring unconstitutional a 1992 amendment to the Colorado state constitution that prohibited local governments from passing ordinances to protect gay rights.[89] The decision's forceful language highlighted the connection between gay rights and civil rights as it declared discrimination against gay people unconstitutional.

Homosexuals won a major victory in the 2003 case of *Lawrence v. Texas,* in which the Supreme Court overturned *Bowers* and struck down a Texas law that made certain sexual conduct between consenting partners of the same sex illegal. Drawing lesbians and gay men under the right-to-privacy umbrella, the Court said that "petitioners are entitled to respect for their private lives. The State cannot demean their existence or control their destiny by making their private sexual conduct a crime."[90] While striking down laws that made homosexual acts a crime, the *Lawrence* ruling did not change various provisions in federal and state laws that deprive homosexuals of full civil rights, including the right to marry. The case did, however, embolden some local officials around the country, such as those in San Francisco and New Paltz, New York, to start performing gay marriages, despite state laws barring the practice. In 2004, the Massachusetts State Supreme Court ordered the state to recognize gay marriage under its state constitution, where it has been legal ever since. Subsequently, Connecticut, Iowa, New Hampshire, Vermont, and the District of Columbia also recognized gay marriage. California legalized gay marriage in 2008, but the law was overturned by state referendum that same year (gay marriages performed during this period were still considered valid). In 2010, a federal court ruled that the ban established by the referendum was unconstitutional and the matter seemed likely to eventually reach the Supreme Court. Maine recognized gay marriage in 2009, but a state referendum also overturned that law later that year.

Gay and lesbian Americans will continue to press their cases against the many laws they view as discriminatory. In response to the legalization of gay and lesbian marriage in some states, they are likely to push for observance of the *full faith and credit clause,* as discussed in Chapter 3. But because of the Defense of Marriage Act of 1996, declaring that states do not have to recognize same-sex marriage, and many state laws that bar same-sex marriage, the gay and lesbian struggle against discrimination will follow that of other minorities, using the federal equal protection clause.[91]

## ● Affirmative Action Attempts to Right Past Wrongs

Not only has the politics of rights spread to increasing numbers of groups in American society since the 1960s, it has also expanded its goal. The relatively narrow goal of equalizing opportunity by eliminating discriminatory barriers developed toward the far broader goal of **affirmative action**—government policies or programs that seek to redress past injustices against specified groups by making special efforts to provide members of these groups with access to educational and employment opportunities. An affirmative action policy uses two novel approaches: (1) positive or benign discrimination in which race or some other status is actually taken into account as a positive rather than negative factor; and (2) compensatory action to favor members of the disadvantaged group who themselves may never have been the victims of discrimination.

President Lyndon Johnson put the case emotionally in 1965: "You do not take a person who, for years, has been hobbled by chains . . . and then say you are free to compete with all the others, and still just believe that you have been completely fair."[92] Johnson attempted to inaugurate affirmative action through executive orders directing agency heads and personnel officers to pursue vigorously a policy of minority employment in the federal civil service and in companies doing business with the national government. But affirmative action did not become a prominent goal of the national government until the 1970s.

Affirmative action also took the form of efforts by the agencies in the Department of Health, Education, and Welfare to shift their focus from "desegregation" to "integration."[93] Federal agencies required school districts to present plans for busing children across district lines, for pairing schools, for closing certain schools, and for redistributing faculties as well as students, under pain of loss of grants-in-aid from the federal government. The guidelines issued for such plans literally constituted preferential treatment to compensate for past discrimination; without this legislatively assisted approach to integration orders, there would certainly not have been the dramatic increase in black children attending integrated classes.

Affirmative action was also initiated in the area of employment opportunity. The Equal Employment Opportunity Commission often has required plans whereby employers must attempt to increase the number of minority employees, and the office of Federal Contract Compliance in the Department of Labor has used the threat of contract revocation for the same purpose.

## The Supreme Court Shifts the Burden of Proof in Affirmative Action

Efforts by the executive, legislative, and judicial branches to shape the meaning of affirmative action today tend to center on a key issue: What is the appropriate level of review in affirmative action cases—that is, on whom should the burden of proof be placed, the plaintiff or the defendant? The Supreme Court formally addressed the issue of qualification versus minority preference in the case of Allan Bakke *(Regents of the University of California v. Bakke)*. Bakke, a white male, brought suit against the University of California at Davis Medical School on the grounds that in denying him admission the school had discriminated against him on the basis of his race (that year the school had reserved sixteen of one hundred available slots for minority applicants). He argued that his grades and test scores had ranked him well above many students who had been accepted at the school and that the only possible explanation for his rejection was that those others accepted were black or Latino whereas he was white. In 1978, Bakke won his case before the Supreme Court and was admitted to the medical school, but he did not succeed in getting affirmative action declared unconstitutional. The Court rejected the procedures at the University of California because its medical school had used both a quota and

# Civil Rights on Campus

Today there are many groups dedicated to advancing the cause of civil rights. For example, gay and lesbian groups argue that their civil rights are discriminated against on the basis of their sexuality.

Other groups advocating greater civil rights include undocumented immigrants and their supporters, who argue that despite their status as illegal citizens, they should still be afforded civil rights and legal protections because of the labor and financial contributions they make to society.

However, there is not always agreement that the civil rights of certain groups are being violated. For example, to many, the civil rights of women are not compromised by excluding them from certain combat positions in the military. For others this policy seems a clear civil rights violation.

Campuses often bring together diverse groups of people with different ideas regarding how society should function. The following ideas present ways that you can engage your fellow students on the issue of civil rights at your college or university.

- Identify whether your college or university practices affirmative action in recruiting and admissions. For example, are certain racial and ethnic groups recruited more heavily, and do they receive different considerations during the admissions process? What about the consideration that's given to students whose parents are alumni of the same college?

- Weigh in on what you think about your institution's affirmative action policies by writing a letter to the editor of your school newspaper; then see what kind of responses your letter generates. If your campus has a radio station, try using that as a venue for expressing your opinion about affirmative action at your college.

- Find out what kind of groups on campus organize students with similar backgrounds. For example, the National Council of La Raza often has campus chapters for Latino students; the LGBT (lesbian, gay, bisexual, and transgendered) community may have a student organization on your campus. If you find one that you can identify with, consider joining and exploring the activism that group is engaged in to advocate for civil rights on campus.

- Help organize a debate about civil rights on campus, perhaps through an organization such as those mentioned earlier. You can invite student panelists as well as representatives of interest groups on both sides of the issue that you'll be debating. The American Civil Liberties Union is one such group to contact for people who take a more liberal approach to civil rights issues. The American Conservative Union may be useful for putting you in touch with those who hold a conservative interpretation of civil rights.

a separate admissions system for minorities. The Court agreed with Bakke's argument that racial categorizations are suspect categories that place a severe burden of proof on those using them to show a "compelling public purpose." The Court went on to say that achieving "a diverse student body" was such a public purpose, but the method of a rigid quota of student slots assigned on the basis of race was incompatible with the equal protection clause. Thus, the Court permitted universities (and presumably other schools, training programs, and hiring authorities) to continue to take minority status into consideration, but limited severely the use of quotas to situations in which (1) previous discrimination had been shown, and (2) a quota was used more as a guideline for social diversity than as a mathematically defined ratio.[94]

In 1991, Congress enacted legislation designed to undo the effects of the decisions limiting affirmative action. The terms of the Civil Rights Act of 1991 shifted the burden of proof in employment discrimination cases back to employers. In addition, the act made it more difficult to mount later challenges to consent decrees in affirmative action cases. Despite Congress's actions, however, the federal judiciary continued to hear cases. In a 5–4 decision in 1993, the Supreme Court ruled that employees had to prove their employers intended discrimination, again placing the burden of proof on employees.[95]

In 1995, the Supreme Court's ruling in *Adarand Constructors v. Peña* further weakened affirmative action. This decision stated that race-based policies, such as preferences given by the government to minority contractors, must survive strict scrutiny, placing the burden on the government to show that such affirmative action programs serve a compelling government interest and are narrowly tailored to address identifiable past discrimination.[96]

In 2003, affirmative action again survived court challenge in two cases arising out of the University of Michigan. In *Grutter v. Bollinger*, the Court upheld the "holistic" and "individualized" affirmative action program used by Michigan's law school, finding it in keeping with the standard set in the *Bakke* case.[97] Michigan's undergraduate affirmative action program was declared unconstitutional, however, in *Gratz v. Bollinger* because it gave specific admissions points (20 out of 150) to African American, Hispanic, and Native American applicants.[98] This approach was barred for resembling too closely the specific numerical quota system struck down by *Bakke*.

In 2006, Michigan voters voted to outlaw affirmative action in public education, contracting, and employment. Modeled after California's Proposition 209—and championed by the California anti-affirmative activist Ward Connerly—Michigan's Proposition 2 amended the state constitution to prohibit affirmative action. Although University of Michigan officials declared that they would continue to use affirmative action criteria in the admissions process until all legal appeals were exhausted, in early 2007 the university announced that it would stop using affirmative action procedures in admissions. Buoyed by their success in Michigan, affirmative action opponents followed suit in other states.

# studyguide

## Practice Quiz

 Find a diagnostic Web Quiz with 40 additional questions on the StudySpace Web site: www.wwnorton.com/we-the-people

1. Which of the following rights were not included in the original Constitution? *(p. 93)*
   a) prohibition of bills of attainder
   b) prohibition of *ex post facto* laws
   c) guarantee of *habeas corpus*
   d) None—They were all included in the original Constitution.

2. The amendment that provided the basis for the modern understanding of the government's obligation to protect civil rights was the *(pp. 95–97)*
   a) First Amendment.
   b) Ninth Amendment.
   c) Fourteenth Amendment.
   d) Twenty-second Amendment.

3. The process by which some of the liberties in the Bill of Rights were applied to the states (or nationalized) is known as *(p. 95)*
   a) selective incorporation.
   b) judicial activism.
   c) civil liberties.
   d) establishment.

4. Which of the following provisions of the Bill of Rights was recently incorporated in 2010? *(p. 96)*
   a) the right to bear arms
   b) the right to counsel in any criminal trial
   c) the right against self-incrimination
   d) freedom from unnecessary searches and seizures

5. Which of the following protections are *not* contained in the First Amendment? *(pp. 97–106)*
   a) the establishment clause
   b) the free exercise clause
   c) freedom of the press
   d) All of the above are First Amendment protections.

6. In *Mapp v. Ohio*, the Supreme Court ruled that *(p. 109)*
   a) evidence obtained from an illegal search could not be introduced in a trial.
   b) a person cannot be tried twice for the same crime.
   c) persons under arrest must be informed prior to police interrogation of their rights to remain silent and to have the benefits of legal counsel.
   d) government has the right to take private property for public use if just compensation is provided.

7. Which civil rights case established the "separate but equal" rule? *(p. 115)*
   a) *Plessy v. Ferguson*
   b) *Brown v. Board of Education*
   c) *Regents of the University of California v. Bakke*
   d) *Adarand Constructors v. Peña*

8. Which of the following organizations established a Legal Defense Fund to challenge segregation? *(p. 116)*
   a) the Association of American Trial Lawyers
   b) the National Association for the Advancement of Colored People
   c) the Student Nonviolent Coordinating Committee
   d) the Southern Christian Leadership Council

9. Which of the following made discrimination by private employers and state governments illegal? *(p. 119)*
   a) the Fourteenth Amendment
   b) *Brown v. Board of Education*
   c) the 1964 Civil Rights Act
   d) *Regents of the University of California v. Bakke*

10. The Voting Rights Act of 1965 significantly extended and protected voting rights by doing which of the following? *(p. 120)*
    a) barring literacy tests as a condition for voting in six southern states
    b) setting criminal penalties for interference with voting efforts
    c) providing for the replacement of local registrars with federally appointed registrars in counties designated as resistant to registering blacks to vote
    d) all of the above

11. Which of the following is *not* an example of an area in which women have made progress since the 1970s in guaranteeing certain civil rights? *(pp. 122–24)*
    a) sexual harassment
    b) integration into all-male publicly supported universities
    c) more equal funding for college women's varsity athletic programs
    d) the passage of the Equal Rights Amendment

12. In what case did the Supreme Court find that rigid quotas are incompatible with the equal protection clause of the Fourteenth Amendment? *(p. 131)*
    a) *Bakke v. Board of Regents*
    b) *Brown v. Board of Education*
    c) *United States v. Nixon*
    d) *Immigration and Naturalization Service v. Chadha*

## Chapter Outline

Find a detailed Chapter Outline on the StudySpace Web site: www.wwnorton.com/we-the-people

## Key Terms

Find Flashcards to help you study these terms on the StudySpace Web site: www.wwnorton.com/we-the-people

**affirmative action** *(p. 128)* government policies or programs that seek to address past injustices against specified groups by making special efforts to provide members of these groups with access to educational and employment opportunities

**Bill of Rights** *(p. 91)* the first ten amendments to the Constitution, which guarantee certain rights and liberties to the people

**bills of attainder** *(p. 93)* laws that decree a person guilty of a crime without a trial

***Brown v. Board of Education*** *(p. 116)* the 1954 Supreme Court decision that struck down the "separate but equal" doctrine as fundamentally unequal. This case eliminated state power to use race as a criterion of discrimination in law and provided the national government with the power to intervene by exercising strict regulatory policies against discriminatory actions

**civil liberties** *(p. 91)* areas of personal freedom with which governments cannot interfere

**civil rights** *(p. 92)* legal or moral claims that citizens are entitled to make on government

**"clear and present danger" test** *(p. 101)* test to determine whether speech is protected or unprotected, based on its capacity to present a "clear and present danger" to society

***de facto*** *(p. 117)* literally, "by fact"; practices that occur even when there is no legal enforcement, such as school segregation in much of the United States today

**de jure** *(p. 117)* literally, "by law"; legally enforced practices, such as school segregation in the South before the 1960s

**double jeopardy** *(p. 110)* the Fifth Amendment right providing that a person cannot be tried twice for the same crime

**dual citizenship** *(p. 95)* the status of being governed by both the U.S. federal government and the individual's state government

**due process of law** *(p. 94)* the right of every citizen to be protected against arbitrary action by national or state governments

**eminent domain** *(p. 111)* the right of government to take private property for public use

**equal protection clause** *(p. 115)* provision of the Fourteenth Amendment guaranteeing citizens "the equal protection of the laws." This clause has served as the basis for the civil rights of African Americans, women, and other groups

**establishment clause** *(p. 97)* the First Amendment clause that says that "Congress shall make no law respecting an establishment of religion." This means that a "wall of separation" exists between church and state

**exclusionary rule** *(p. 109)* the ability of courts to exclude evidence obtained in violation of the Fourth Amendment

**ex post facto laws** *(p. 93)* laws that declare an action to be illegal after it has been committed

**Fifteenth Amendment** *(p. 115)* one of three Civil War amendments; guaranteed voting rights for African American men

**fighting words** *(p. 106)* speech that directly incites damaging conduct

**Fourteenth Amendment** *(p. 115)* one of three Civil War amendments; guaranteed equal protection and due process

**free exercise clause** *(p. 99)* the First Amendment clause that protects a citizen's right to believe and practice whatever religion he or she chooses

**grand jury** *(p. 110)* jury that determines whether sufficient evidence is available to

justify a trial; grand juries do not rule on the accused's guilt or innocence

**habeas corpus** *(p. 93)* a court order demanding that an individual in custody be brought into court and shown the cause for detention

**libel** *(p. 104)* a written statement, made in "reckless disregard of the truth," which is considered damaging to a victim because it is "malicious, scandalous, and defamatory"

**Miranda rule** *(p. 111)* the requirement, articulated by the Supreme Court in *Miranda v. Arizona* (1966), that persons under arrest must be informed prior to police interrogation of their rights to remain silent and to have the benefit of legal counsel

**preferred freedoms** *(p. 96)* certain protections in the Bill of Rights, such as free speech and free press, that are considered even more important than other freedoms

**prior restraint:** *(p. 103)* an effort by a governmental agency to block the publication of material it deems libelous or harmful in some other way; censorship. In the United States, the courts forbid prior restraint except under the most extraordinary circumstances

**right to privacy** *(p. 113)* the right to be left alone, which has been interpreted by the Supreme Court to entail free access to birth control and abortions

**selective incorporation** *(p. 95)* the process by which court decisions have required the states to follow parts of the Bill of Rights based on the use or application of the Fourteenth Amendment

**"separate but equal" rule** *(p. 115)* doctrine that public accommodations could be segregated by race but still be equal

**slander** *(p. 104)* an oral statement, made in "reckless disregard of the truth," which is considered damaging to the victim because it is "malicious, scandalous, and defamatory"

**speech plus** *(p. 103)* speech accompanied by conduct or physical activity such as sit-ins, picketing, and demonstrations; protection of this form of speech under the

First Amendment is conditional, and restrictions imposed by state or local authorities are acceptable if properly balanced by considerations of public order

**strict scrutiny** *(p. 100)* test, used by the Supreme Court in racial discrimination cases and other cases involving civil liberties and civil rights, which places the burden of proof on the government rather than on the challengers to show that the law in question is constitutional

**Thirteenth Amendment:** *(p. 115)* one of three Civil War amendments; abolished slavery

# For Further Reading

Abraham, Henry J. *Freedom and the Court: Civil Rights and Liberties in the United States.* 6th ed. New York: Oxford University Press, 1994.

Barendt, Eric. *Freedom of Speech.* 2nd ed. New York: Oxford University Press, 2007.

Chen, Anthony S. *The Fifth Freedom: Jobs, Politics, and Civil Rights in the United States, 1941–1972.* Princeton, NJ: Princeton University Press, 2009.

Cook, Byrne. *Reporting the War: Freedom of the Press from the American Revolution to the War on Terror.* New York: Palgrave Macmillan, 2007.

Dworkin, Ronald. *Justice in Robes.* Cambridge, MA: Belknap Press, 2006.

Friendly, Fred W. *Minnesota Rag: The Dramatic Story of the Landmark Supreme Court Case That Gave New Meaning to Freedom of the Press.* New York: Vintage, 1982.

Greenberg, Jack. *Crusades in the Courts: How a Dedicated Band of Lawyers Fought for the Civil Rights Revolution.* New York: Basic Books, 1994.

Hentoff, Nat. *The First Freedom: The Tumultuous History of Free Speech in America.* New York: Basic Books, 1994.

Lewis, Anthony. *Gideon's Trumpet.* New York: Random House, 1964.

Minow, Martha. *Making All the Difference: Inclusion, Exclusion, and American Law.* Ithaca, NY: Cornell University Press, 1990.

Nava, Michael. *Created Equal: Why Gay Rights Matter to America.* New York: St. Martin's, 1994.

Orth, John. *Due Process of Law: A Brief History.* Lawrence: University Press of Kansas, 2003.

Spitzer, Robert J. *The Right to Bear Arms.* Santa Barbara, CA: ABC-CLIO, 2001.

Spitzer, Robert J. *Saving the Constitution from Lawyers: How Legal Training and Law Reviews Distort Constitutional Meaning.* New York: Cambridge University Press, 2008.

Sundby, Scott. *A Life and Death Decision: A Jury Weighs the Death Penalty.* New York: Palgrave Macmillan, 2007.

Sunstein, Cass. *Radicals in Robes.* New York: Basic Books, 2005.

# Recommended Web Sites ───────────────────────

**ADA Home Page**
www.ada.gov
> The Americans with Disabilities Act (ADA), enacted in 1990, guarantees equal employment rights and access to public businesses for the physically disabled. The U.S. Department of Justice maintains this Web site, which offers general information on ADA standards, changes in regulation, and policy enforcement.

**American Civil Liberties Union (ACLU)**
www.aclu.org
> The ACLU is committed to protecting for all individuals the freedoms found in the Bill of Rights. This sometimes controversial organization continuously monitors the government for violations of liberty and encourages its members to take political action.

**Federal Bureau of Investigation**
www.fbi.gov/hq/cid/civilrights/hate.htm
> Civil rights violations fall under the jurisdiction of the Federal Bureau of Investigation. Find out what steps the FBI is taking to combat the problem of hate crimes and view some comprehensive statistical data.

**Freedom Forum**
www.freedomforum.org
> Freedom of speech and freedom of the press are considered critical in any democracy; however, only some kinds of speech are fully protected against restrictions. Freedom Forum is a nonpartisan agency that investigates and analyzes such First Amendment restrictions.

**Human Rights Campaign (HRC)**
www.hrc.org
**Gay and Lesbian Alliance Against Defamation (GLAAD)**
www.glaad.org
> These two prominent interest groups are dedicated to equal rights for gays and lesbians and ending gender discrimination.

**League of United Latin American Citizens (LULAC)**
www.lulac.org
> LULAC has worked to stem discrimination against Mexican Americans since World War II and is now the largest and oldest Hispanic organization in the United States. See what this group is doing to guarantee racial equality based on the Fourteenth Amendment's equal protection clause.

**NAACP**
www.naacp.org
> The NAACP is one of the oldest and largest civil rights organizations that is dedicated to equal rights and putting an end to racial discrimination. This group was particularly influential in the landmark case *Brown v. Board of Education,* which led to the desegregation of public schools.

**National Organization for Women**
www.now.org
**Feminist Majority Foundation**
www.feminist.org
> These leading women's rights groups continue to fight for gender equality and equal rights.

**Religious Freedom Page**
http://religiousfreedom.lib.virginia.edu

The establishment clause of the U.S. Constitution has been interpreted to mean a "wall of separation" between government and religion. On the Religious Freedom Page you can find information on a variety of issues pertaining to religious freedom in the United States and around the world.

**U.S. Commission on Civil Rights**
www.usccr.gov

The U.S. Commission on Civil Rights was created by Congress in the late 1950s and continues to investigate complaints of discrimination in American society.

**U.S. Supreme Court Media**
www.oyez.org

This Web site has a good search engine for finding information on such landmark civil rights and liberties cases as *Plessy v. Ferguson, Brown v. Board of Education, Lawrence v. Texas, United States v. Wong Kim Ark, Lemon v. Kurtzman, Miranda v. Arizona, Mapp v. Ohio,* and *New York Times v. Sullivan,* to name only a few.

How closely should the government follow public opinion? In 2010, public opinion was sharply divided over health care reform. Some Americans opposed any further government intervention into the health care industry.

# 5

# Public Opinion

**WHAT GOVERNMENT DOES AND WHY IT MATTERS** In a democracy, we expect the government to pay attention to **public opinion**, citizens' attitudes about political issues, leaders, institutions, and events. If the government's programs and policies do not seem consistent with popular preferences, we often begin to question the legitimacy of the government's actions. In 2007 and 2008, many Americans questioned why American forces remained in Iraq even though most Americans had concluded that it was time to bring the troops home. Americans also wonder why, on issues ranging from gun control through health care, the government never seems to be able to do what the public wants. Policy makers reply that the people often speak with many voices that are hard to reconcile and interpret. Sometimes, say public officials, their job is to do what's right even if it is unpopular. President George W. Bush, for example, once pointed to the fact that President Abraham Lincoln became quite unpopular as the Civil War dragged on. If Lincoln had allowed himself to be guided by public opinion, the United States might not exist today.

Another concern when we consider how closely government should follow public opinion is the fact that many Americans have very little knowledge about government. For example, 40 percent of the Americans responding to a recent survey did not know that every state has two senators; 71 percent could not name their own member of Congress; and a surprising 81 percent could not name both of their own state's senators.[1] Many Americans know even less about major policy issues, so their opinions on these issues may not be well informed.[2] Particularly troubling is that the opinions of the uninformed may be susceptible to manipulation by politicians, interest groups, and the government itself through public relations and advertising. Most Americans deny that they are affected by political advertising, but one study showed that many Americans' knowledge about politics is derived, in part, from biased (and sometimes inaccurate) information disseminated in political ads.[3]

## key concepts

- Americans' opinions are shaped by fundamental values and demographic background.

- Family, social groups, education, and political conditions all transmit political values and information.

- The ability of public opinion to influence government decisions depends on specific conditions and events.

## ● Fundamental Values Shape Our Opinions

Most Americans share a common set of values, including a belief in the principles—if not always the actual practice—of liberty, equality, and democracy. Equality of opportunity is a widely shared American ideal that all people should have the freedom to use whatever talents and wealth they have to reach their fullest potential. It has always been an important theme in American society. Americans believe that all individuals should be allowed to seek personal and material success. Moreover, Americans generally believe that such success should be linked to personal effort and ability, rather than to family connections or other forms of special privilege. Similarly, Americans have always voiced strong support for the principle of individual liberty, meaning freedom from government control. Americans typically support the notion that governmental interference with individuals' lives and property should be kept to the minimum consistent with the general welfare, although in recent years Americans have grown accustomed to greater levels of governmental intervention. And most Americans also believe in democracy, a system of rule where popular wishes and preferences regularly and systematically shape who controls the government and what the government does. Americans presume that every person should have the opportunity to take part in the nation's governmental and policy-making processes and to have some "say" in determining how they are governed.[4] Figure 5.1 offers some indication of this American consensus on fundamental values: 89 percent believe that gays should have equal employment rights (2008), 56 percent are worried about government monitoring of personal information (2007), and 69 percent agree that any group should be free to assemble (2007).

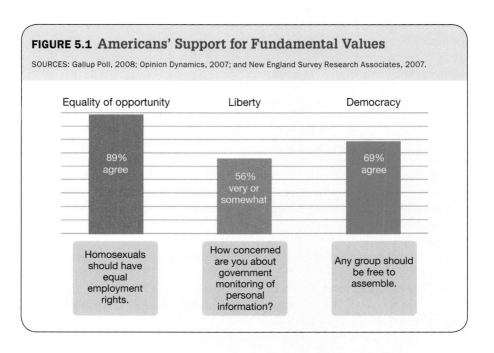

**FIGURE 5.1** **Americans' Support for Fundamental Values**

SOURCES: Gallup Poll, 2008; Opinion Dynamics, 2007; and New England Survey Research Associates, 2007.

Equality of opportunity     Liberty     Democracy

89% agree

56% very or somewhat

69% agree

Homosexuals should have equal employment rights.

How concerned are you about government monitoring of personal information?

Any group should be free to assemble.

*Even among Americans who supported health care reform in 2010, opinion was divided over the various plans that had been proposed.*

Obviously, the principles that Americans espouse have not always been put into practice. For two hundred years, Americans were able to believe in the principles of equality of opportunity and individual liberty while denying them in practice to generations of African Americans. Yet it is important to note that the strength of the principles ultimately helped to overcome practices that deviated from those principles. Proponents of slavery and, later, of segregation were defeated in the arena of public opinion because their practices differed so sharply from the fundamental principles accepted by most Americans.

## Political Values Come from Political Socialization

The attitudes that individuals hold about political issues and personalities tend to be shaped by their underlying political beliefs and values. For example, an individual who has basically negative feelings about government intervention in America's economy and society would probably oppose the development of new health care and social programs. Similarly, someone who distrusts the military would likely be suspicious of any call for the use of American troops. The process through which these underlying political beliefs and values are formed is called **political socialization.**

The process of political socialization is important. Probably no nation, and certainly no democracy, could survive if its citizens did not share some fundamental beliefs. For example, most Americans grumble about paying taxes. If the typical American is asked why he or she pays taxes, the first response is usually fear that the government will punish nonpayers. Yet if millions of Americans stopped paying taxes, the government could not possibly prosecute all of the lawbreakers. In fact, most Americans, when asked more closely, will admit that they pay taxes at least in part because they believe that government has a *right* to take part of their income (even though they may wish that the percent the government takes were smaller). This fundamental belief helps explain how and why socialization is so important. Four of the most important agents of socialization are the family, membership in social groups, education, and prevailing political conditions.

## Our Political Values Come from Family, Social Groups, Education, and Political Conditions

**The Family** Most people acquire their initial orientation to politics from their families. As might be expected, differences in family background tend to produce divergent political outlooks. Although relatively few parents spend much time teaching their children about politics, political conversations occur in many households and children tend to absorb these political views, perhaps without realizing it. Studies have suggested, for example, that party preferences are initially acquired at home. Children raised in households in which the primary caregivers are Democrats tend to become Democrats themselves, whereas children raised in homes where their caregivers are Republicans tend to favor the GOP (Grand Old Party, a traditional nickname for the Republican Party).[5] Obviously, not all children absorb their parents' political views. Two of former Republican president Ronald Reagan's four children, for instance, rejected their parents' conservative values and became active on behalf of Democratic candidates. Moreover, even those children whose views are initially shaped by parental values may change their minds as they mature and experience political life for themselves. Nevertheless, the family is an important initial source of political orientation for everyone.

**Social Groups** Another important source of divergent political orientations and values is the social group or groups to which individuals belong. Social groups include those to which individuals belong involuntarily—gender and racial groups, for example—as well as those to which people belong voluntarily—such as political parties, labor unions, and educational and occupational groups. Some social groups have both voluntary and involuntary attributes. For example, individuals are born with a particular social-class background, but as a result of their own efforts people may move up—or down—the class structure.

Membership in a particular group can give individuals important experiences and perspectives that shape their view of political and social life. In American society, for example, the experiences of blacks and whites can differ significantly. Blacks have been victims of persecution and discrimination throughout American history. Blacks and whites also have often had different educational and occupational opportunities, often live in separate communities, and may attend separate schools. Such differences tend to produce distinctive political outlooks (see Figure 5.2). For example, in 2009, 92 percent of black respondents but only 56 percent of white respondents approved of President Obama's handling of race relations since he became president.[6]

Blacks and whites differ considerably in their perceptions of the extent of racism in America. In a 2009 survey, 49 percent of white respondents thought racism was

## FIGURE 5.2 Disagreement among Blacks and Whites

SOURCES: CNN, www.cnn.com/2006/US/12/12/racism.poll/index.html; Gallup, Inc., www.gallup.com/poll/11686/
Race–Education–Years–After–Brown–Board–Education.aspx; and Pew Research Center Publications, http://
pewresearch.org/pubs/531/democratic-debate (accessed 4/1/08).

### RACE RELATIONS IN THE UNITED STATES

Racism is a very serious problem.

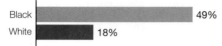

Black 49%
White 18%

Percentages who think only a few white people dislike blacks,
many white people dislike blacks, or just about all white people
dislike blacks.

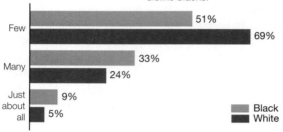

Few 51%
69%

Many 33%
24%

Just about all 9%
5%

Black
White

### EDUCATIONAL OPPORTUNITY

Do black children have as good a chance as white children
to get a good education?

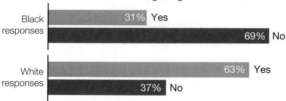

Black responses: 31% Yes / 69% No

White responses: 63% Yes / 37% No

### TREATMENT BLACKS RECEIVE

Discrimination against blacks is rare today.

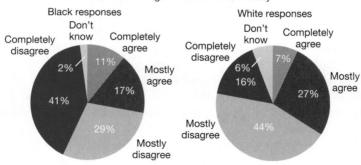

Black responses
- Don't know: 11%
- Completely agree
- Completely disagree: 2%
- Mostly agree: 17%
- 41%
- Mostly disagree: 29%

White responses
- Don't know: 6%
- Completely agree: 7%
- Completely disagree: 16%
- Mostly agree: 27%
- Mostly disagree: 44%

Percent who favor affirmative action programs.

Blacks 93%
Whites 65%

*Members of various social groups may see political issues in different ways. After a racially charged incident in 2009 involving Harvard professor Henry Louis Gates (second from left) and police officer James Crowley (second from right), President Obama tried to address the tensions surrounding the incident by bringing the two men together for a "beer summit" at the White House, along with Vice President Biden.*

rare in the United States while 47 percent thought it was fairly or very common. Among African Americans, on the other hand, 86 percent thought racism was common while 12 percent said it was rare.[7] Interestingly, Hispanic Americans, who have also been victims of racism in the United States, are less likely than African Americans to see America as a racist society. In response to a 2008 CBS News/New York Times survey, 52 percent of Hispanics and 55 percent of whites said race relations in the United States were generally good. Only 29 percent of blacks agreed.[8]

Men and women have important differences of opinion as well. Reflecting differences in social roles, political experience, and occupational patterns, women tend to be less militaristic than men on issues of war and peace, more likely than men to favor measures to protect the environment, and more supportive than men of government social and health care programs (see Table 5.1). Perhaps because of these differences on issues, women are more likely than men to vote for Democratic candidates. This tendency for men's and women's opinions to differ is called the *gender gap*.

In addition, social group membership can affect political beliefs through what might be called objective political interests. On many economic issues, for example, the interests of the rich and poor differ significantly. Struggles over tax policy, social security, medicare, welfare, and so forth are fueled by differences of interest between wealthier and poorer Americans. In a similar vein, objective differences of interest between "senior citizens" and younger Americans can lead to very different views on such diverse issues as health care policy, social security, and criminal justice.

**Differences in Education** A third important source of differences in political perspectives comes from a person's education. In some respects, of course, schooling is

## TABLE 5.1

## Disagreements among Men and Women on National Security Issues

| GOVERNMENT ACTION | PERCENTAGE APPROVING OF ACTION | |
| --- | --- | --- |
| | MEN | WOMEN |
| Agree that torture of terror suspects is acceptable | 50 | 31 |
| Agree NSA surveillance program is needed | 60 | 50 |
| Oppose sending more troops to Iraq | 52 | 69 |
| Favor cutting off funding for Iraq war | 48 | 57 |
| Believe U.S. should send more troops to Afghanistan | 49 | 36 |

SOURCES: ABC, 2009; *Ms*, 2006; UPI/Zogby, 2007; *USA Today*, 2007; *Washington Post*/ABC, 2007; CBS 2009.

a great equalizer. Governments use public education to try to teach all children a common set of civic values. It is mainly in school that Americans acquire their basic belief in liberty, equality, and democracy. In history classes, students are taught that the Founders fought for the principle of liberty. Through participation in class elections and student government, students are taught the virtues of democracy. In the course of studying such topics as the Constitution, the Civil War, and the civil rights movement, students are taught the importance of equality. These lessons are repeated in every grade in a variety of contexts. No wonder they are such an important element in Americans' beliefs.

At the same time, however, differences in educational attainment are strongly associated with differences in political outlook. In particular, those who attend college are often exposed to philosophies and modes of thought that will forever distinguish them from their friends and neighbors who do not pursue college diplomas. Table 5.2 outlines some general differences of opinion that are found between college graduates and other Americans.

A college education helps convince students of the importance of political participation and of their own ability to have an impact on politics and policy. Thus, one of the major differences between college graduates and Americans with less education can be seen in levels of political participation. College graduates are more likely to vote, write "letters to the editor," join campaigns, take part in protests, and, generally, make their voices heard.

**Political Conditions** A fourth set of factors that shapes political orientations and values is the conditions under which individuals and groups are recruited into and involved in political life. Although political beliefs are influenced by family background and group membership, the precise content and character of these views is, to a large extent, determined by political circumstances. For example, American white southerners were staunch members of the Democratic Party from the Civil

TABLE 5.2

## Education and Public Opinion

| ISSUES | EDUCATION | | | |
|---|---|---|---|---|
| | GRADE SCHOOL | HIGH SCHOOL | SOME COLLEGE | COLLEGE GRAD. |
| 1. Women and men should have equal roles. | 38% | 75% | 83% | 86% |
| 2. Abortion should never be allowed. | 21 | 10 | 7 | 4 |
| 3. The government should adopt national health insurance. | 35 | 47 | 42 | 49 |
| 4. The United States should not concern itself with other nations' problems. | 45 | 26 | 20 | 8 |
| 5. Government should see to fair treatment in jobs for African Americans. | 49 | 28 | 30 | 45 |
| 6. Government should provide fewer services to reduce government spending. | 8 | 17 | 19 | 27 |

NOTE: The figures show the percentage of respondents in each category agreeing with the statement.
SOURCE: The American National Election Studies, 2004 data, provided by the Inter-University Consortium for Political and Social Research, University of Michigan.

War through the 1960s. As members of this political group, they became key supporters of liberal New Deal and post–New Deal social programs that greatly expanded the size and power of the American national government. Since the 1960s, however, southern whites have shifted in large numbers to the Republican Party. Now they provide a major base of support for efforts to scale back social programs and to reduce sharply the size and power of the national government. The South's move from the Democratic to the Republican camp took place because of white southern opposition to the Democratic Party's racial policies and because of determined Republican efforts to win white southern support. It was not a change in the character of white southerners but a change in the political circumstances in which they found themselves that induced this major shift in political allegiances and outlooks in the South.

## The Two Main Ideologies in America Are Liberalism and Conservatism

As we have seen, people's beliefs about government can vary widely. But for some individuals, this set of beliefs can fit together into a coherent philosophy about government. This set of underlying orientations, ideas, and beliefs through which we come to understand and interpret politics is called a political ideology.

In America today, a variety of ideologies compete for attention and support. Libertarians, for example, argue that government is a wasteful and dangerous institution that should be limited to as few activities as possible. Socialists, on the other hand, argue that more government control is necessary to promote justice and reduce economic and political inequality. Environmentalists view global warming and other threats to the world's environment as the most important issues facing humanity today. While many subscribe to these and other ideas, most Americans describe themselves as either liberals or conservatives. Liberalism and conservatism are political ideologies that include beliefs about the role of the government, ideas about public policies, and notions about which groups in society should properly exercise power. These ideologies can be seen as the end result of the process of political socialization that was discussed in the preceding section.

Classically, a liberal was a person who favored individual initiative and was suspicious of the motives of governments and of their ability to manage economic and social affairs. Liberals saw government as the foe of freedom. The proponents of a larger and more active government called themselves "progressives." In the early twentieth century, though, many liberals and progressives coalesced around the doctrine of "social liberalism," which represented a recognition that government action might be needed to preserve individual liberty. Today's liberals are social liberals rather than classical liberals, so the term **liberal** now means support for political and social reform; extensive government intervention in the economy; support for federal social services; more vigorous efforts on behalf of the poor, minorities, and women; and greater concern for consumers and the environment. In social and cultural areas, liberals generally support abortion rights and stronger gun laws, are concerned with the rights of persons accused of crime, and oppose state involvement with religious institutions and religious expression. In international affairs, liberal positions are usually seen as including support for arms control, opposition to the development and testing of nuclear weapons, support for aid to poor nations, opposition to the use of American troops to influence the domestic affairs of developing nations, and support for international organizations such as the United Nations. Of course, all liberals do not have the same viewpoints on everything. For example, among individuals who view themselves as liberal, many support American military intervention when it is tied to a humanitarian purpose, as in the case of America's military action in Kosovo in 1998–99.

*One of the hallmarks of American democracy has been vigorous debate on important policy issues. During the 1960s and early 1970s, anti–Vietnam War protestors staged numerous demonstrations across the nation.*

By contrast, today's conservatives support the views of classical liberalism. Historically, conservatives were the defenders of monarchy and aristocracy— institutions that seem completely out of place today. The term **conservative** today is used to describe those who generally support the social and economic status quo and are suspicious of efforts to introduce new political formulae and economic arrangements. Conservatives believe strongly that a large and powerful government poses a threat to citizens' freedom. Thus, in the domestic arena, conservatives generally oppose the expansion of governmental activity, asserting that solutions to social and economic problems can be developed in the private sector. Conservatives particularly oppose efforts to impose government regulation on business, pointing out that such regulation is frequently economically inefficient and costly and can ultimately lower the entire nation's standard of living. As to social and cultural positions, many conservatives oppose abortion and gun control, support school prayer, are more concerned for the victims than the perpetrators of crimes, oppose school busing, and support traditional family arrangements. In international affairs, conservatism has come to mean support for the maintenance of American military power.

Of course, it is important to note that many people who call themselves liberals or conservatives accept only part of the liberal or conservative ideology. Many individuals who are liberal on social issues are conservative on economic issues. There is nothing illogical about these mixed positions. They simply indicate the relatively open and fluid character of American political debate. Stated differently, it has often been noted that most Americans are fairly pragmatic. As Figure 5.3 indicates, Americans are often apt to shift their ideological preferences.

## Political Knowledge Is Important in Shaping Public Opinion

As we have seen, general political beliefs can guide the formation of opinions on specific issues, but an individual's beliefs and opinions are not always consistent with one another. Studies of political opinion have shown that most people don't hold specific and clearly defined opinions on every political issue. As a result, they are easily influenced by others. The degree of consistency citizens show is shaped by knowledge and information about political issues. In general, knowledgeable citizens are better able to evaluate new information and determine whether it is relevant to and consistent with their beliefs and opinions. As a result, better-informed individuals can recognize their political interests and act consistently on behalf of them.

One of the most obvious and important examples of this proposition is voting. Despite the predisposition of voters to support their own party's candidates (see Chapter 7 for a discussion of party identification), millions of voters are affected by the information they receive about candidates during a campaign. During the 2008 presidential campaign, for instance, voters weighed the arguments of Barack Obama against those of John McCain about who was more qualified to oversee the U.S. economy. Many Republican voters turned to Obama because they held the GOP responsible for the nation's financial crisis and found Obama's economic proposals more credible than those put forward by John McCain. Thus citizens can use information and judgment to overcome their predispositions. Without some

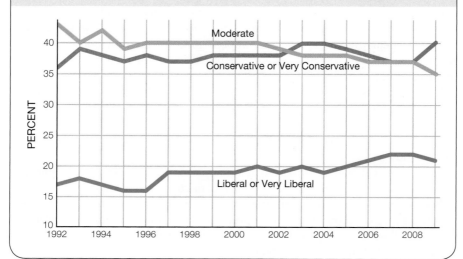

**FIGURE 5.3 Americans' Shifting Ideology, 1992–2009**

Over the past thirty years, the percentage of Americans claiming to be conservative or liberal has increased, whereas the percentage calling themselves moderates has not. Can you think of any reasons for this change? Would more moderates be better for democracy?

SOURCE: Gallup.com (accessed 8/5/10).

political knowledge, citizens would have a difficult time making sense of the complex political world in which they live.

This point brings up two questions, however. First, how much political knowledge is necessary for one to act as an effective citizen? And second, how is political knowledge distributed throughout the population? In an important study of political knowledge in the United States, the political scientists Michael X. Delli Carpini and Scott Keeter found that the average American exhibits little knowledge of political institutions, processes, leaders, and policy debates.[9] Many Americans cannot even name their own congressional representative. Does this ignorance of key political facts matter?

Another important concern is the character of those who possess and act on the political information that they acquire. Political knowledge is not evenly distributed throughout the population. Those with higher education, income, and occupational status and who are members of social or political organizations are more likely to know about and be active in politics. An interest in politics reinforces an individual's sense of **political efficacy**–the ability to influence government and politics–and provides more incentive to acquire additional knowledge and information about politics. Those who don't think they can have an effect on government tend not to be interested in learning about or participating in politics. As a result, individuals with a disproportionate share of income and education also have a disproportionate share of knowledge and influence and are better able to get what they want from government.

Because becoming truly knowledgeable about politics requires a substantial investment of time and energy, many Americans seek to acquire political information and to make political decisions "on the cheap," making use of shortcuts that seem to relieve them of having to engage in a lengthy process of information gathering and evaluation. One "inexpensive" way to become informed is to take cues from trusted others—the local minister, the television commentator or newspaper editorialist, an interest-group leader, friends and relatives.[10] Along the same lines, a common shortcut for political evaluation and decision making is to assess new issues and events through the lenses of one's more general beliefs and orientations. Thus, if a conservative learns of a plan to expand federal social programs, he or she might express opposition to the endeavor without spending too much time pondering the specific proposal. Similarly, if a liberal is told that Republican leaders are backing a major overhaul of the Social Security system, he or she will probably not need to read thousands of pages of economic projections before expressing disapproval of the GOP's efforts.

Neither of these shortcuts, however, is entirely reliable. As we saw above, general ideological orientations can be poor guides to decision making in concrete instances. And taking cues from others may lead individuals to accept positions they would not support if they had more information. For example, few Americans read the details of the health care reform proposals debated in the House and Senate in 2009 but, instead, took their cues from politicians whose views they assumed were similar to their own. Yet many liberals who took their cues from President Obama might have preferred no bill at all to a bill without the "public option" that the president agreed to drop. And many conservatives who took their cues from House and Senate Republican leaders might have found much to like in the legislation these politicians castigated.

Although understandable and, perhaps, inevitable, widespread inattentiveness to politics weakens American democracy in two ways. First, those who lack political information or resort to inadequate shortcuts to acquire and assess information cannot effectively defend their own political interests and can easily become victims or losers in political struggles. The presence, moreover, of large numbers of politically inattentive or ignorant individuals means that the political process can more easily be manipulated by the various institutions and forces that seek to shape public opinion.

## Political Leaders, Private Groups, and the Media All Influence Public Opinion

**Politicians Lead Opinion** Governmental leaders invariably attempt to influence, manipulate, or manage the opinions of the people. To some extent, this is the definition of a leader people admire. In the years leading up to World War II, for example, President Franklin Roosevelt came to believe that the United States should enter the war on the side of Britain and its allies against Nazi Germany and Imperial Japan, but there was strong sentiment in the United States that we should stay out of the war. Still, Roosevelt used his persuasive powers to move American

1778    1943

## AMERICANS
### will always fight for liberty

*Governments frequently attempt to influence public opinion. This 1943 poster was intended to build support for World War II by associating it with the American Revolution.*

opinion in favor of intervention. The debate came to an end when Japan attacked Pearl Harbor, which immediately rallied nearly all Americans to support going to war, showing also how a single dramatic event can sometimes help leaders move the country in a certain direction.

Political leaders pay close attention to public opinion even when the country does not face a crisis. For example, the Reagan and Clinton administrations regularly used techniques borrowed from election campaigns to bolster popular support for White House initiatives. President Clinton established a political "war room," similar to the one that operated in his campaign headquarters, where representatives from all departments met daily to discuss and coordinate the president's public relations efforts. Many of the same consultants and pollsters who directed the successful Clinton campaign were employed in the selling of the president's programs.[11]

Indeed, the Clinton White House made more sustained and systematic use of public opinion polling than any other administration. For example, during his presidency Clinton relied heavily on the polling firm of Penn & Schoen to help him decide which issues to emphasize and what strategies to adopt. During the 1995–96 budget battle with Congress, the White House commissioned polls almost every night to chart changes in public perceptions about the struggle. Poll data suggested to Clinton that he should present himself as struggling to save Medicare from Republican cuts. Clinton responded by launching a media attack against what he claimed were GOP efforts to hurt the elderly. This proved to be a successful strategy and helped Clinton defeat the Republican budget.[12] The administration, however, asserted that it used polls only as a check on its communications strategy.[13]

The Bush administration's efforts to mold public opinion were manifested during the 2003 Iraq war. Prior to the war, the administration invited more than 100 news correspondents and photographers to accompany American forces into battle. These "embedded" journalists rode in tanks and armored personnel carriers with the troops, sharing their hardships and dangers. As the administration anticipated, the embedded journalists developed considerable rapport with the soldiers and provided generally sympathetic war coverage, often beginning their accounts of military actions with the pronoun *we*. Despite these and other ploys, public support for the president's military policies faltered when the occupation of Iraq produced a steady stream of U.S. casualties and the president was unable to prove his allegations that Iraq possessed weapons of mass destruction. Like its predecessors, the Obama administration has sought to shape public opinion in the United States and abroad. President Obama is an excellent speaker, and the administration has relied on the power of the president's oratory to build support for its initiatives in domestic and foreign policy. When Obama visited China, the Chinese government, fearing that he would use his media presence to captivate the nation, drastically limited Obama's live media exposure in order to state off any popular democratic surge among the Chinese people against their own government.

**Private Groups Shape Opinion** As the discussion of opinion manipulation shows, the effort to sway public opinion sometimes goes beyond mere persuasion. Not surprisingly, private groups are very interested in shifting public opinion to their benefit. The ideas that become prominent in political life are often developed and spread by powerful economic and political groups searching for issues that will advance their causes. One example is the "right-to-life" issue that has inflamed American politics over the past forty years.

The notion of right-to-life, whose proponents seek to outlaw abortion and overturn the Supreme Court's *Roe v. Wade* decision, was developed and heavily promoted by conservative politicians who saw the issue of abortion as a means of uniting Catholic and Protestant conservatives and linking both groups to the Republican Party. These politicians convinced Catholic and evangelical Protestant leaders that they shared similar views on the question of abortion, and they worked with religious leaders to focus public attention on the negative issues in the abortion debate. To advance their cause, leaders of the movement sponsored well-publicized Senate hearings, where testimony, photographs, and other exhibits were presented to illustrate the violent effects of abortion procedures. At the same time, publicists for the movement produced leaflets, articles, books, and films such as *The Silent Scream* to highlight the agony and pain ostensibly felt by the "unborn" when they were being aborted. All this underscored the movement's claim that abortion was nothing more or less than the murder of millions of innocent human beings. Finally, Catholic and evangelical Protestant religious leaders were organized to denounce abortion from their church pulpits and, increasingly, from their electronic pulpits on the Christian Broadcasting Network (CBN) and the various other television forums available for religious programming. Religious leaders also organized demonstrations, pickets, and disruptions at abortion clinics throughout the nation.[14] Abortion rights remains a potent issue, even influencing the debate over health care reform in 2009 and 2010.

**The Media and Public Opinion** The communications media are among the most powerful forces operating in the marketplace of ideas. As we shall see in Chapter 7, the mass media are not simply neutral messengers for ideas developed by others. Instead, the media have an enormous impact on popular attitudes and opinions. Over time, the ways in which the mass media report political events help to shape

*Opponents and proponents of a woman's right to choose often clash with one another. Large, well-financed groups on both sides of the debate try to influence public opinion and government policy.*

the underlying attitudes and beliefs from which opinions emerge.[15] For example, for the past thirty years, the national news media have relentlessly investigated personal and official wrongdoing on the part of politicians and public officials. This continual media presentation of corruption in government and venality in politics has undoubtedly fostered the general attitude of cynicism and distrust that exists in the general public.

At the same time, the ways in which media coverage interprets or frames specific events can have a major impact on popular responses and opinions about these events.[16] Because media framing can be important, the Bush administration sought to persuade broadcasters to follow its lead in its coverage of terrorism and America's response to terrorism in the months following the September 11 attacks. Broadcasters, who found themselves targets of anthrax-contaminated letters apparently mailed by terrorists, needed little persuasion. For the most part, the media praised the president for his leadership and presented the administration's military campaign in Afghanistan and domestic antiterrorist efforts in a positive light. Even newspapers such as the *New York Times*, which had strongly opposed Bush in the 2000 election and questioned his fitness for the presidency, asserted that he had grown into the job. In the aftermath of the 2003 Iraq war, however, media coverage of the Bush administration became more critical. Formerly supportive media accused the president of failing both to anticipate the chaos and violence of postwar Iraq and to develop a strategy that would allow America to extricate itself from its involvement in Iraq. The president, for his part, accused the media of failing to present an accurate picture of his administration's successes in Iraq.

# Measuring Public Opinion Is Crucial to Understanding What It Is

It is no secret that politicians and public officials make extensive use of **public opinion polls**—scientific instruments for measuring public opinion—to help them decide whether to run for office, what policies to support, how to vote on important legislation, and what types of appeals to make in their campaigns. President Lyndon Johnson was famous for carrying the latest Gallup and Roper poll results in his pocket, and it is widely believed that he began to withdraw from politics because the polls reported losses in public support. All recent presidents and other major political figures have worked closely with polls and pollsters.

## Public Opinion Surveys Are Very Accurate If Done Properly

The population in which pollsters are interested is usually quite large. To conduct their polls they first choose a **sample** of the total population, meaning a small group selected by researchers to represent the most important characteristics of an entire population. The selection of this sample is important. Above all, it must be representative. To be reliable, the views of those in the sample must accurately and proportionately reflect the views of the whole (Table 5.3).

Modern polling is based on the principle of **random sampling,** meaning that even though a national poll sample may consist of only 500 to 1,500 people, it *can* be considered representative of the population as a whole, even though the sample seems very small, as long as each person in the population has an equal chance of being picked.

The most common techniques for choosing such a sample are probability sampling and random digit dialing. In the case of **probability sampling,** a method used by pollsters to select a sample in which every individual in the population has an equal probability of being selected as a respondent so that the correct weight can be given to all segments of the population, the pollster begins with a listing of the population to be surveyed. This listing is called the *sampling frame.* After the members of the population are assigned a number, a table of random numbers or a computerized random selection process is used to select those to be surveyed. This technique is appropriate where the entire population can be identified. For example, all students registered at Texas colleges and universities can be identified from college records and a sample easily drawn. Where the pollster is interested in a national sample of Americans, however, this technique is not feasible, since no complete list of Americans exists.[17] National samples are usually drawn using a technique called **random digit dialing.** A computer random number generator is used to produce a list of as many ten-digit numbers as the pollster deems to be necessary with every effort made to avoid bias in the construction of the sample. Since more than 95 percent of American households have telephones, this technique usually results in a random national sample.

The importance of sampling was brought home early in the history of political polling. A 1936 *Literary Digest* poll predicted that Republican presidential candidate,

## TABLE 5.3

## Two Pollsters and Their Records (1948–2008)

| | HARRIS | GALLUP | ACTUAL OUTCOME |
|---|---|---|---|
| **2008** | | | |
| McCain | 44% | 43% | 46% |
| Obama | 50 | 51 | 53 |
| **2004** | | | |
| Bush | 49% | 49% | 51% |
| Kerry | 48 | 49 | 48 |
| Nader | 1 | 1 | 0 |
| **2000** | | | |
| Bush | 47% | 48% | 48% |
| Gore | 47 | 46 | 49 |
| Nader | 5 | 4 | 3 |
| **1996** | | | |
| Clinton | 51% | 52% | 49% |
| Dole | 39 | 41 | 41 |
| Perot | 9 | 7 | 8 |
| **1992** | | | |
| Clinton | 44% | 44% | 43% |
| Bush | 38 | 37 | 38 |
| Perot | 17 | 14 | 19 |
| **1988** | | | |
| Bush | 51% | 53% | 54% |
| Dukakis | 47 | 42 | 46 |
| **1984** | | | |
| Reagan | 56% | 59% | 59% |
| Mondale | 44 | 41 | 41 |
| **1980** | | | |
| Reagan | 48% | 47% | 51% |
| Carter | 43 | 44 | 41 |
| Anderson | | 8 | |
| **1976** | | | |
| Carter | 48% | 48% | 51% |
| Ford | 45 | 49 | 48 |
| **1972** | | | |
| Nixon | 59% | 62% | 61% |
| McGovern | 35 | 38 | 38 |
| **1968** | | | |
| Nixon | 40% | 43% | 43% |
| Humphrey | 43 | 42 | 43 |
| Wallace | 13 | 15 | 14 |
| **1964** | | | |
| Johnson | 62% | 64% | 61% |
| Goldwater | 33 | 36 | 39 |

(Continued)

## TABLE 5.3

## Two Pollsters and Their Records (1948–2008) (*continued*)

|  | HARRIS | GALLUP | ACTUAL OUTCOME |
|---|---|---|---|
| **1960** | | | |
| Kennedy | 49% | 51% | 50% |
| Nixon | 41 | 49 | 49 |
| **1956** | | | |
| Eisenhower | NA | 60% | 58% |
| Stevenson | | 41 | 42 |
| **1952** | | | |
| Eisenhower | 47% | 51% | 55% |
| Stevenson | 42 | 49 | 44 |
| **1948** | | | |
| Truman | NA | 44.5% | 49.6% |
| Dewey | | 49.5 | 45.1 |

NOTE: All figures except those for 1948 are rounded. NA = Not asked.
SOURCES: Data from the Gallup Poll and the Harris Survey (New York: Chicago Tribune–New York News Syndicate, various press releases 1964–2004). Courtesy of the Gallup Organization and Louis Harris Associates.

Alf Landon, would defeat the incumbent, Democrat Franklin D. Roosevelt, in that year's presidential election. The actual election, of course, ended in a Roosevelt landslide. The main problem with the survey had been what is called **selection bias** in drawing the sample, a polling error that arises when the sample is not representative of the population being studied, which creates errors in overrepresenting or underrepresenting some opinions. The pollsters relied on telephone directories and automobile registration rosters to produce a sampling frame. During the Great Depression, only wealthier Americans owned telephones and cars. Thus, the millions of working-class Americans who constituted Roosevelt's principal base of support were excluded from the sample.

In recent years, the issue of selection bias has been further complicated by the fact that growing numbers of individuals refuse to answer pollsters' questions, or they use such devices as answering machines and caller ID to screen unwanted callers. If pollsters could be certain that those who responded to their surveys simply reflected the views of those who refused to respond, there would be no problem. Some studies, however, suggest that the views of respondents and non-respondents can differ, especially along social-class lines. Middle- and upper-middle-class individuals are more likely to be willing to respond to surveys than their working-class counterparts.[18] Adding further to pollsters' problems is the fact that increasing numbers of Americans rely solely on cellular phones, access to which is restricted. Polling organizations can obtain cell phone numbers from telephone database companies, but these lists do not include all cell phone numbers. In 2009, nearly a quarter of all households had no land lines. Cell phone–only users tend

*Though public opinion is important, it is not always easy to interpret, and polls often fail to predict accurately how Americans will vote. In 1948, election-night polls showed Thomas Dewey defeating Harry S. Truman for the presidency.*

to be young and male, whereas land line users tend to be older and female. These changing habits have the potential of undermining an accurate national sample.[19]

Even with reliable sampling procedures, **measurement error** (failure to iden-tify the true distribution of opinion within a population because of errors such as ambiguous or poorly worded questions) can occur. One frequent source of mea-surement error is the wording of survey questions. The validity of survey results can be adversely affected by poor question format, faulty ordering of questions, inappropriate vocabulary, ambiguous questions, or questions with built-in biases. Often, seemingly minor differences in the wording of a question can convey vastly different meanings to respondents and thus produce quite different response pat-terns. For example, for many years the University of Chicago's National Opinion Research Center has asked respondents whether they think the federal government is spending too much, too little, or about the right amount of money on "assistance for the poor." Answering the question posed this way, about two-thirds of all respon-dents seem to believe that the government is spending too little. However, the same survey also asks whether the government spends too much, too little, or about the right amount for "welfare." When the word "welfare" is substituted for "assistance for the poor," about half of all respondents indicate that too much is being spent.[20]

In recent years, a new form of bias has been introduced intentionally into surveys by the use of **push polling,** a polling technique in which the questions are designed to shape the respondent's opinion. This technique involves asking a respondent a

# Become a Savvy Consumer of Polls

How does one know when to trust a poll? If you were buying a new computer or car or MP3 player, you'd know something about its properties (or its manufacturer) in order to evaluate its worth. You can easily become a savvy consumer of polls as well. For the most part, it involves asking a few key questions, such as the ones listed below.

Topic: Crisis in Darfur

- *Who's behind the poll?* This means asking not just who paid for the poll but who actually conducted the interviews and published the results. Most news outlets include this information in their coverage, but if you find a reference to a poll in a candidate's promotional material or an interest group's solicitation, you may need to contact the campaign or group for more information.

- *Who participated in the poll?* This includes determining how many people were interviewed, if they were chosen scientifically (rather than by self-selection, for example), and if the respondents were representative of a larger population. Bigger samples aren't necessarily better—it is more important that the sample was selected through a scientific (usually random) method and that the characteristics of the respondents generally match those of the group they are supposed to represent. For example, are there more women than men in the sample? Are respondents balanced in terms of region, religion, and ethnicity? Should they be?

- *Is there a margin of error (also called sampling error) associated with the poll?* If this information is included in the description of the survey results, it is a good sign that the sample was drawn scientifically.

- *Is the wording or order of the questions suspicious?* Even a scientifically selected poll can be susceptible to other biases. For example, two questions about the same topic using similar but not exactly the same wording can elicit very different responses. Poll numbers can also be affected by the order in which questions were asked. Most polling organizations will include an exact copy of their questionnaire along with their analysis. Almost all online news outlets provide a link to the full set of questions.

- *Could this be considered a pseudopoll or a push poll?* Both of these types of polls are problematic, for different reasons. Pseudopolls, often found on Internet Web sites, are not accurate measures of public opinion because respondents simply decide for themselves that they want to participate, rather than being selected scientifically. Push polls are not really polls at all but an attempt to spread negative rumors or innuendos about a candidate for office under the guise of a poll.

loaded question about a political candidate designed to elicit the response sought by the pollster and, simultaneously, to build a negative image of the opponent. For example, in the 2000 election, the Bush campaign used push polling against John McCain. During the South Carolina primary, the Bush campaign asked voters in a survey whether they approved of McCain's "legislation that proposed the largest tax increase in U.S. history" and McCain's plan to "increase taxes on charitable contributions to churches, colleges, and charities by $20 billion."[21] The purpose of such polling is not simply to solicit opinions but to spread the view that McCain favored these obviously unpopular ideas, in hopes of "pushing" McCain voters away from him. To cite another example, during Mayor Michael Bloomberg's re-election race in 2005, New York City voters reported receiving phone calls from pollsters who asked a series of loaded questions about Republican Bloomberg's likely Democratic opponent, Fernando Ferrer. For example, voters were asked whether they would be more or less likely to vote for Ferrer for mayor if they knew that some of Ferrer's political supporters had been investigated for corruption. One woman reported receiving a phone call from someone claiming to be a pollster who said that Ferrer was running a "divisive campaign," whereas Bloomberg was "bringing people together." While no one could deny that this choice of wording was designed to cast Ferrer in a negative light and Bloomberg in a positive light rather than objectively determine people's opinions, the Bloomberg campaign denied having anything to do with these push polling tactics.[22] Bloomberg handily won his re-election bid. More than one hundred consulting firms across the nation now specialize in push polling.[23]

## ● Public Opinion Must Matter in a Democracy

In democratic nations, leaders should pay attention to public opinion, and the evidence suggests that indeed they do. There are many instances in which public policy and public opinion do not coincide, but in general the government's actions are consistent with citizens' preferences. One study, for example, found that between 1935 and 1979, in about two-thirds of all cases, significant changes in public opinion were followed within one year by changes in government policy consistent with the shift in the popular mood.[24] Other studies have come to similar conclusions about public opinion and government policy at the state level.[25] Some recent studies, however, have suggested that the responsiveness of government to public opinion has been declining. These findings imply that, contrary to popular beliefs, elected leaders don't always pander to the results of public opinion polls, but instead use polling to sell their policy proposals and shape the public's views.[26]

Several factors can contribute to a lack of consistency between opinion and governmental policy. First, the numerical majority on a particular issue may not be as intensely committed to its preference as the adherents of the minority viewpoint. An intensely committed minority may often be more willing to commit its time, energy, efforts, and resources to the affirmation of its opinions than an apathetic, even if large, majority. In the case of firearms, for example, although the proponents of gun control are by a wide margin the majority, most do not regard the issue as one of critical importance to themselves and are not willing to commit much effort to advancing their cause. The opponents of gun control, by contrast, are intensely committed, well organized, and well financed, and as a result are usually able to carry the day.

A second important reason that public policy and public opinion may not coincide has to do with the character and structure of the American system of government. The framers of the U.S. Constitution, as we saw in Chapter 2, sought to create a system of government that was based upon popular consent but that did not invariably and automatically translate shifting popular sentiments into public policies. As a result, the U.S. governmental process includes arrangements such as an appointed judiciary that can produce policy decisions that may run contrary to prevailing popular sentiment—at least for a time.

# studyguide

## Practice Quiz

 Find a diagnostic Web Quiz with 30 additional questions on the StudySpace Web site: www.wwnorton.com/we-the-people

1. The term *public opinion* is used to describe *(p. 139)*
   a) the collected speeches and writings made by a president during his or her term in office.
   b) the analysis of events broadcast by news reporters during the evening news.
   c) the beliefs and attitudes that people have about issues.
   d) decisions of the Supreme Court.

2. The process by which Americans learn political beliefs and values is called *(p. 142)*
   a) brainwashing.
   b) propaganda.
   c) indoctrination.
   d) political socialization.

3. Which of the following is an agency of socialization? *(p. 143)*
   a) the family
   b) social groups
   c) education
   d) all of the above

4. Variables such as income, education, race, gender, and ethnicity *(p. 143)*
   a) often create differences of political opinion in America.
   b) have consistently been a challenge to America's core political values.
   c) have little impact on political opinions.
   d) help explain why public opinion polls are so unreliable.

5. Members of a social group often have similar political beliefs because *(p. 143)*
   a) they share objective political interests.
   b) they often live in separate communities from people in other social groups.
   c) membership in a particular group can give individuals important experiences and perspectives that shape their view of political and social life.
   d) all of the above.

6. When men and women respond differently to issues of public policy, they are demonstrating an example of *(p. 145)*
   a) liberalism.
   b) educational differences.
   c) the gender gap.
   d) party politics.

7. A politician who opposes abortions, government regulation of business, and gay rights legislation would be best described as a *(p. 149)*
   a) liberal.
   b) conservative.
   c) libertarian.
   d) socialist.

8. Which of the following is (are) *not* an important external influence on how political opinions are formed? *(pp. 151–54)*
   a) the government and political leaders
   b) private interest groups
   c) the media
   d) the Constitution

9. Which of the following is the term used in public opinion polling to denote the small group representing the opinions of the whole population? *(p. 155)*
   a) control group
   b) sample
   c) micropopulation
   d) respondents

10. A poll that includes many poorly worded or ambiguous questions has a high degree of *(p. 158)*
    a) sampling error.
    b) measurement error.
    c) selection bias.
    d) validity error.

11. A push poll is a poll in which *(p. 158)*
    a) the questions are designed to shape the respondent's opinion rather than measure the respondent's opinion.
    b) the questions are designed to measure the respondent's opinion rather than shape the respondent's opinion.
    c) the questions are designed in order to reduce measurement error.
    d) none of the above.

12. Which of the following statements best characterizes the relationship between public opinion and public policy in the United States? *(p. 160)*
    a) They always coincide because the American system of government requires that politicians slavishly follow majority public opinion.
    b) They always coincide because the American public shifts their preferences to support whatever actions government takes.
    c) They never coincide because the American system of government was not designed to account for public opinion.
    d) They generally coincide but sometimes do not because the American system of government includes many arrangements, such as an appointed judiciary, that can produce policy decisions that may run contrary to prevailing popular sentiment.

## Chapter Outline

 Find a detailed Chapter Outline on the StudySpace Web site: www.wwnorton.com/we-the-people

# Key Terms

 Find Flashcards to help you study these terms on the StudySpace Web site: www.wwnorton.com/we-the-people

**conservative** *(p. 149)* today this term refers to those who generally support the social and economic status quo and are suspicious of efforts to introduce new political formulae and economic arrangements. Conservatives believe that a large and powerful government poses a threat to citizens' freedom

**liberal** *(p. 148)* today, one who generally supports political and social reform; extensive government intervention in the economy; the expansion of federal social services; more vigorous efforts on behalf of the poor, minorities, and women; and greater concern for consumers and the environment

**measurement error** *(p. 158)* failure to identify the true distribution of opinion within a population because of errors such as ambiguous or poorly worded questions

**political efficacy** *(p. 150)* the ability to influence government and politics

**political socialization** *(p. 142)* the process by which people learn political attitudes and beliefs

**probability sampling** *(p. 155)* a method used by pollsters to select a sample in which every individual in the population has an equal probability of being selected as a respondent so that the correct weight can be given to all segments of the population

**public opinion polls** *(p. 155)* scientific instruments for measuring public opinion

**push polling** *(p. 158)* a polling technique in which the questions are designed to shape the respondent's opinion

**random digit dialing** *(p. 155)* polls in which respondents are selected at random from a list of ten-digit telephone numbers, with every effort made to avoid bias in the construction of the sample

**random sampling** *(p. 155)* a method of measuring popular opinion whereby a small group of people, randomly selected from the population as a whole, may be considered representative, as long as every person had an equal chance of being picked

**sample** *(p. 155)* a small group selected by researchers to represent the most important characteristics of an entire population

**selection bias** *(p. 157)* polling error that arises when the sample is not representative of the population being studied, which creates errors in overrepresenting or underrepresenting some opinions

# For Further Reading

Ansolabehere, Stephen, and Shanto Iyengar. *Going Negative: How Attack Ads Shrink and Polarize the Electorate.* New York: Free Press, 1995.

Bartels, Larry. *Unequal Democracy.* Princeton, NJ: Princeton University Press, 2008.

Berinsky, Adam. *Silent Voices: Public Opinion and Political Participation in America.* Princeton, NJ: Princeton University Press, 2005.

Bishop, George. *The Illusion of Public Opinion.* New York: Rowman and Littlefield, 2004.

Clawson, Rosalee, and Zoe Oxley. *Public Opinion: Democratic Ideals and Democratic Practice.* Washington, DC: CQ Press, 2008.

Erikson, Robert, and Kent Tedin. *American Public Opinion,* 7th ed. New York: Longman, 2004.

Erikson, Robert S., Norman Luttbeg, and Kent Tedin. *American Public Opinion: Its Origins, Content and Impact,* 5th ed. Boston: Allyn Bacon, 1994.

Fiorina, Morris. *Culture War: The Myth of a Polarized America.* New York: Longman, 2005.

Gallup, George. *The Pulse of Democracy.* New York: Simon & Schuster, 1940.

Ginsberg, Benjamin. *The American Lie: Government By the People and Other Political Fables.* Boulder, CO: Paradigm, 2007.

Herbst, Susan. *Numbered Voices: How Opinion Polling Has Shaped American Politics.* Chicago: University of Chicago Press, 1993.

Jacobs, Lawrence R., and Robert Y. Shapiro. *Politicians Don't Pander: Political Manipulation and the Loss of Democratic Responsiveness.* Chicago: University of Chicago Press, 2000.

Key, V. O. *Public Opinion and American Democracy.* New York: Knopf, 1961.

Lee, Taeku. *Mobilizing Public Opinion.* Chicago: University of Chicago Press, 2002.

Lippmann, Walter. *Public Opinion.* New York: Harcourt, Brace, 1922.

Norrander, Barbara, and Clyde Wilcox. *Understanding Public Opinion.* Washington, DC: CQ Press, 2009.

Page, Benjamin I., and Robert Y. Shapiro. *The Rational Public: Fifty Years of Trends in Americans' Policy Preferences.* Chicago: University of Chicago Press, 1992.

Spitzer, Robert J., ed. *Media and Public Policy.* Westport, CT: Praeger, 1993.

# Recommended Web Sites

**American Association for Public Opinion Research**
**www.aapor.org**
This is one of the premier academic sites for public opinion data on a host of political and social topics.

**eTalkinghead**
**http://directory.etalkinghead.com**
Political blogs have become an increasingly popular way for Americans to express and discuss political opinions. This Web page provides a directory of political blogs by ideology and issue.

**Gallup**
**www.gallup.com**
The Gallup Organization has been involved in the scientific study of public opinion for over seventy years and is very highly regarded. This Web site contains public-opinion data archives, video archives, and international polls.

**The Political Compass**
**www.politicalcompass.org**
A political ideology is a cohesive set of beliefs that form a general philosophy about government; however, people are often unsure if they are liberal, moderate, or

conservative. Go to the Web site for The Political Compass and take the test to see if it helps you identify your ideology.

**Polling Report**
http://pollingreport.com

This independent, nonpartisan resource tracks trends in American public opinion. On this site you will find countless political opinion polls by all of the major media outlets, all in one place.

**ThisNation.com**
www.thisnation.com/socialization.html

The process through which underlying political beliefs and values are formed is called political socialization. This civic-minded Web page offers a brief discussion of political socialization with some related Web links.

The media play an essential role in American democracy. One function of the media is to communicate information about the government to the people. Here, House Speaker Nancy Pelosi holds a press conference to announce the Democrats' plan for withdrawing troops from Iraq.

# 6

# The Media

**WHAT GOVERNMENT DOES AND WHY IT MATTERS** One area in which our government's role is intended to be minimal is the realm of the news media. The Constitution's First Amendment guarantees freedom of the press, and most Americans believe that a free press is an essential condition for both liberty and democratic politics. Certainly, the press is usually ready to denounce any government action that smacks of censorship or news manipulation. Nevertheless, attempts to silence or discredit the opposition press have a long history in America. The infamous Alien and Sedition Acts were enacted by the Federalists in 1798 in an attempt to silence the Republican press. In more recent times, during the McCarthy era of the 1950s, right-wing politicians used charges of communist infiltration to intimidate the liberal news media. During President Richard Nixon's administration, the White House attacked its critics in the media by threatening to take action to bar the television networks from owning local affiliates, as well as by illegally wiretapping the phones of government officials suspected of leaking information to the press. During the early 1980s, conservative groups financed a series of libel suits against CBS News, *Time* magazine, and other media organizations in an attempt to discourage them from publicizing material critical of Reagan administration policies.[1] In 2004, an article by the investigative reporter Seymour Hersh in *The New Yorker,* along with a story on *60 Minutes II,* revealed that American soldiers had abused Iraqi prisoners in their custody. The story prompted a televised apology from President Bush, congressional hearings, and calls for the resignation of Defense Secretary Donald Rumsfeld. The Bush administration was furious but, like previous presidencies, could do little to silence its media critics.

In the 2008 presidential campaign, Republicans complained that the media were strongly anti-McCain and pro-Obama. Republican candidate John McCain normally had good relations with the press. During the course of the campaign, however, McCain began to attack the media regarding their alleged bias. Complaints from McCain and his advisers became especially sharp after the national media began to question his choice of Sarah Palin as the GOP's vice-presidential candidate. The media regarded Palin as unprepared and unqualified for the job and generally gave her negative coverage. During the 2008 vice-presidential debate, Palin made a point of expressing her gratitude to the debate's organizers for allowing her an opportunity to speak to the American people without the intervention of interviewers and commentators who, in her view, constantly distorted her comments to make her appear foolish and uninformed.

Public officials also sometimes accuse the media of presenting excessively negative coverage of political events and public affairs. But without the media's investigations and exposés, citizens would be forced to rely entirely on the information politicians and the government provide to them. This would hardly afford citizens a proper opportunity to evaluate issues and form reasoned opinions.

In the previous chapter, we examined the vital question of how public opinion is related to government actions and decisions. We turn now to the most important way in which Americans learn information about their government, which in turn shapes people's opinions. Because most Americans do not have the time, ability, or opportunity to find out directly what their government does on a day-to-day basis, they must rely on the media to inform them.

In this chapter, we will examine the media's role in the political process by studying some of the media's basic traits, government regulations of the media, patterns of media ownership, and factors that shape news coverage. We will also examine the extent to which the media do and do not shape people's opinions. The authors of the Bill of Rights (discussed in Chapter 4) included a very specific protection for the press when they wrote in the First Amendment that "Congress shall make no law . . . abridging the freedom . . . of the press." In the modern era, we therefore need to ask not only how free the press is today, but also whose interests does it reflect?

## ● The Media Must Matter in a Democracy

It is impossible to imagine democratic politics without a vigorous media. The public, and therefore public opinion, depends on the news media to publicize and assess the claims of political candidates. We depend on the media to examine government policies and programs and to reveal wrongdoing on the part of government agencies and public officials. Without the information provided by the media, the public could not possibly know enough to play any role in national politics. Freedom of the press definitely belongs in the First Amendment as one of the first principles of democratic government.

### Three Types of Media Dominate

Americans get their news from three main sources: broadcast media (radio and television), print media (newspapers and magazines), and, increasingly, the Internet (see Figure 6.1). Each of these sources has distinctive characteristics.

**Broadcast Media** Television news reaches more Americans than any other single news source. Tens of millions of individuals watch national and local news programs every day. Most television news, however, covers relatively few topics and provides little depth of coverage. Television news is more like a series of newspaper headlines connected to pictures. It serves the extremely important function of alerting viewers to issues and events, but, with exceptions like the Public Broadcasting System, provides little more than a series of "sound bites," brief quotes and short characterizations of the day's events. Because they are aware of the character of television news coverage, politicians and other news makers often seek to manipulate the news by providing the media with sound bites that will dominate news coverage for at least a few days. George H. W. Bush's famous 1988 sound bite, "Read my lips: no new taxes," received a great deal of media coverage. Two years later he was, in effect, bitten by his own sound bite when he signed legislation that included new taxes. The twenty-four-hour news stations such as Cable News Network (CNN), MSNBC, and Fox News, offer more detail and commentary than the networks' half-hour evening news shows. Even CNN and the others, however, offer more headlines than analysis, especially during their prime-time broadcasts.

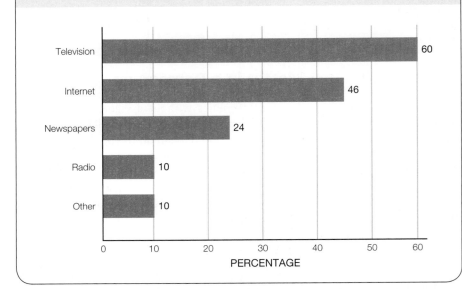

**FIGURE 6.1 Young Americans\* and Political News**

At one time, newspapers and then network news were the dominant news sources in the United States. However, this survey of young Americans about news sources during the 2008 elections indicates that television, including both network news and other types of programming, and the Internet have become more important than newspapers. What are some likely consequences of this shift?

\*Eighteen- to twenty-nine-year-olds.
SOURCE: Pew Internet and American Life Survey, 2008.

Politicians generally view the local broadcast news as a friendlier venue than the national news. National reporters are often inclined to criticize and question, whereas local reporters often accept the pronouncements of national leaders at face value. For this reason, presidents often introduce new proposals in a series of short visits to a number of cities—indeed, sometimes flying from airport to airport—in addition to or instead of making a national presentation. For example, in a nationally televised speech in 2009, President Barack Obama announced his plan to reduce violence in Afghanistan and then made a number of local speeches around the country promoting the same theme. National reports questioned the president's plans, but local news coverage was overwhelmingly positive.

Radio news is also essentially a headline service, but without pictures. In the short time—usually five minutes per hour—they devote to news, radio stations announce the day's major events without providing much detail. In major cities, all-news stations provide more coverage of major stories, but for the most part these stations fill the day with repetition rather than detail. All-news stations such as Washington, D.C.'s WTOP or New York's WCBS assume that most listeners are in their cars and that, as a result, the people in the audience change throughout the day as listeners reach their destinations. Thus, rather than use their time to flesh out a given set of stories, they repeat the same stories each hour to present them to new listeners. One notable exception is the noncommercial National Public Radio (NPR), which provides lengthy and detailed news coverage on a daily basis.

In recent years, radio talk shows have become important sources of commentary and opinion. A number of conservative radio hosts such as Rush Limbaugh and Sean Hannity have huge audiences and have helped to mobilize support for conservative political causes and candidates. Liberals have had less success in the world of talk radio. In 2003, however, a group of wealthy liberal political activists led by Anita Drobny, a major Democratic Party donor, launched a liberal talk-radio network, Air America, designed to combat conservative dominance of this important medium. One executive of the new network said, "There are so many right-wing talk shows, we think it's created a hole in the market you could drive a truck through." Despite liberals' expectations,[2] Air America went bankrupt and stopped broadcasting in 2010.

**Print Media** The most important source of news is still the old-fashioned newspaper. Newspapers remain critically important even though they are not the primary news source for most Americans. The print media are important for three reasons. First, as we shall see later in this chapter, the broadcast media rely on leading newspapers such as the *New York Times* and the *Washington Post* to set their news agenda. The broadcast media engage in relatively little original reporting; they primarily cover stories that have been "broken," or initially reported, by the print media. For example, sensational charges that President Bill Clinton had an affair with a White House intern were reported first in the mainstream media by the *Washington Post* and *Newsweek* before being trumpeted around the world by the broadcast media (the story first emerged on the Internet). In 2005, the *New York Times* broke the story that the Bush administration had authorized warrantless wiretaps of phone conversations in violation of the 1978 Foreign Intelligence Surveillance Act (FISA). It is only a slight exaggeration to observe that if an event is not covered in the *New York Times*, it is not likely to appear on the *CBS Evening News*. Second, the print media provide more detailed and complete information, offering a better context for analysis. They are able to do this because they usually employ more reporters, who are often the first to dig up stories that then spread to the Internet or to other media outlets, and because the newspaper format allows more space for information. Third, the print media are important because they are the prime source of news for educated and influential individuals. The nation's economic, social, and political elites rely on the detailed coverage provided by the print

*When President Obama announced his plan for increasing troop levels in Afghanistan in 2009, he knew that coverage of his speech in the news media would quickly reach tens of millions of Americans.*

media to inform and influence their views about important public matters. The print media may have a smaller audience than their cousins in broadcasting, but they have an audience that matters. Even so, falling revenues, declining circulation, and rising costs have placed increasing pressure on the ability of these traditional print outlets to retain their dominance.

**Internet** The Internet has been growing in importance as a news source. Every day, millions of Americans scan one of many news sites on the Internet for coverage of current events. Younger Americans are more likely to rely on the Internet than on almost any other news source (see Figure 6.1). One great advantage of the Internet is that it allows frequent updating. After the September 11, 2001, terrorists attacks, many Americans relied on the Internet for news about terrorism, bioterrorism, and the military campaign in Afghanistan. In September 2005, millions of Americans relied on the Internet for information about hurricanes Katrina and Rita, the powerful storms that devastated New Orleans and the Gulf Coast. News of widespread political unrest in Iran after allegations of rigged national elections in 2009 was spread to the outside world mostly by Internet-based forms of communication, including Internet video, blogs, and Twitter messages.

Political entrepreneurs have sought to organize online advocacy groups to raise money, make their positions known through e-mail and letter campaigns, and provide support for politicians who accepted their views. For example, Chris Hughes, one of the founders of the social networking site Facebook, helped the Obama presidential campaign establish a Facebook site that allowed Obama supporters to register as the senator's "friends." These friends, who numbered in the hundreds of thousands, could post photos of themselves along with other biographical

*In 2007, candidates for the Democratic and Republican presidential nominations participated in debates sponsored by YouTube and CNN. The questions for the candidates were submitted directly by voters, who posted videos of their questions on YouTube.*

information that was available to all registered users of the site. At the site's resource center, the senator's friends could download flyers, videos, and other campaign materials. In the site's "groups" section, the senator's friends could create or join online groups to share ideas and organize events and fund-raisers. Over 3 million people contributed money to Obama's 2008 campaign; most of those people gave through the Internet.

In addition, a growing number of readers turn to informal sources of Internet news and commentary called *Web logs*, or "blogs." Blogs are published online and generally feature personal opinion and commentary on national and world events. Some "bloggers," as the authors of blogs are called, achieve fame, or at least notoriety, among online readers for their political and social views. In 2002 and 2003, the Howard Dean presidential campaign relied on hundreds of friendly bloggers to publicize the candidate's views and tout his virtues. Bloggers also helped Dean raise tens of millions of dollars in small contributions to finance his unsuccessful presidential bid.[3] Dean's tactics were a direct precursor to Barack Obama's 2008 campaign, which raised hundreds of millions of dollars in contributions via the Internet.

A number of blogs such as the Daily Kos and the Drudge Report have thousands of regular readers who often comment on and critique stories presented by the print and broadcast media. In recent years, bloggers have uncovered a number of major factual errors in media reports and forced the networks and newspapers to broadcast and print corrections. In addition, a number of bloggers have proven adept at recognizing faked or Photoshop'd photographs in news stories. Sharp-eyed bloggers noticed that major news outlets, including the *New York Times*, the *Los Angeles Times*, Reuters, and the Associated Press, had presented doctored photos—a phenomenon known as fauxtography—in their reports from Iraq, Afghanistan, and the Israeli-Palestinian conflict. The fakes had been designed to create the appearance of criminal acts by American and Israeli troops.[4]

Although the Internet and the blogosphere are often seen as liberal and Democratic strongholds, conservatives have stepped up their efforts to make use of the new media. Over the past three years, conservative talk radio hosts and conservative bloggers have built an informal alliance to attack Democratic candidates and policies with which they disagree. In 2007, for example, conservative bloggers regularly posted material opposing the proposed immigration bill that would have given legal status to many illegal immigrants currently in the United States. Conservative talk-radio hosts relied on the bloggers to provide critical commentary that they could broadcast on their radio programs. This alliance also played a role in numerous attacks launched against Barack Obama in 2008, including the charge that Obama was closely associated with the 1960s radical William Ayers. Bloggers circulated claims that Obama and Ayers, a founder of the Weather Underground, had a long-standing relationship. Conservative commentators frequently used the bloggers' claims in their programs. During the early years of the Obama presidency, conservative blogs kept alive false allegations that Obama was not a native-born American (he was born in Hawaii in 1961) and was a Muslim (he's a Christian and a member of the United Church of Christ).

As the 2008 campaign proceeded, candidates or their supporters placed a number of ads on YouTube that were seen by millions of viewers. In one famous ad that ran during the Democratic primaries, Hillary Clinton is portrayed as an Orwellian "Big Brother." An unnamed female athlete is shown running from the riot police and then smashing a television screen on which Clinton's face appears. Reportedly, more than 4 million people viewed the video. During the general election, John McCain developed a series of YouTube ads mocking Barack Obama and comparing him to empty-headed media celebrities like Paris Hilton. In August 2008, Hilton responded with her own YouTube videos comparing McCain to the wizened *Stars Wars* character Yoda.

## Broadcast Media Are Regulated, but Not Print Media

In some countries, the government controls media content. In other countries, the government owns the broadcast media (e.g., the BBC in Britain) but does not tell the media what to say. In the United States, the government neither owns nor controls the communications networks, but it does regulate the content and ownership of the broadcast media.

In the United States, the print media are essentially free from government interference. The broadcast media, on the other hand, are subject to federal regulation. American radio and television are regulated by the Federal Communications Commission (FCC), an independent regulatory agency established in 1934. Radio and TV stations must have FCC licenses that must be renewed every five years. Licensing provides a mechanism for allocating radio and TV frequencies to prevent broadcasts from interfering with and garbling each other. License renewals are almost always granted automatically by the FCC. Indeed, renewal requests are now filed by postcard.

Through regulations prohibiting obscenity, indecency, and profanity, the FCC has also sought to prohibit radio and television stations from airing explicit sexual and excretory references between 6 A.M. and 10 P.M. These are the hours when children are most likely to be in the audience. The FCC has enforced these rules haphazardly. Since 1990, nearly half the $5 million in fines levied by the agency have involved Howard Stern, a "shock jock" whose programs are built around sexually explicit material. In 2004,

*Federal Communications Commission (FCC) regulations prohibit obscenity, indecency, and profanity in American television and radio broadcasts. The radio personality Howard Stern incurred millions of dollars in FCC fines before moving to satellite radio, which is not regulated by the FCC.*

after another set of FCC fines, Stern's program was dropped by a major outlet, Clear Channel Communications. Stern charged that the Bush administration had singled him out for censure because of his known opposition to the president. Stern subsequently moved to Sirius satellite radio. Because, under the law, satellite radio is not a broadcast medium, Sirius is not subject to FCC regulation. Generally speaking, FCC regulation applies only to the "over-the-air" broadcast media. It does not apply to cable television, the Internet, or satellite radio. As a result, explicit sexual content and graphic language that would fall afoul of the rules on broadcast television is regularly available on cable channels.

It is important to note a major difference between allowable government regulation of broadcast television and radio stations through government licensing and content regulation, and the print media—newspapers and magazines—which are not subject to either licensing or content regulation. Note that newspapers and magazines are not licensed by the government, and obscene language that is barred from broadcast can be legally printed. Government regulation of the broadcast media is allowed because of two distinctive traits of the broadcast media: first, the resource they use, radio and television frequency broadcast bands, is limited in number, a fact that encourages government regulation in order to ensure some degree of equitable access to this limited resource; second, the air through which broadcast waves pass is inherently public, which means that the government has an obligation to protect the public interest. While new technologies including cable television and satellite radio may ultimately render these principles obsolete, for now they continue to guide government policy.

For more than sixty years, the FCC also sought to regulate and promote competition in the broadcast industry, but in 1996 Congress passed the Telecommunications Act, a broad effort to do away with most regulations in effect since 1934. The act loosened restrictions on media ownership and allowed telephone companies, cable television providers, and broadcasters to compete with each other for telecommunication services. Following the passage of the act (thanks in large part to intense lobbying efforts by cable TV providers and communications companies), several mergers between telephone and cable companies and among different segments of the entertainment media produced an even greater concentration of media ownership.

The Telecommunications Act of 1996 also included an attempt to regulate the content of material transmitted over the Internet. This law, known as the Communications Decency Act, made it illegal to make "indecent" sexual material on the Internet accessible to those under eighteen years old. The act was immediately denounced by civil libertarians and challenged in court as an infringement of free speech. The case reached the Supreme Court in 1997, and the act was ruled an unconstitutional infringement of the First Amendment's right to freedom of speech (see Chapter 4).

Although the government's ability to regulate the content of the electronic media on the Internet has been questioned, the federal government has used its licensing power to impose several regulations that can affect the political content of radio and TV broadcasts. The first of these is the **equal time rule,** under which broadcasters must provide candidates for the same political office equal opportunities to communicate their messages to the public. If, for example, a television station sells commercial time to a state's Republican gubernatorial candidate, it may not refuse to sell time to the Democratic candidate for the same position.

The second regulation affecting the content of broadcasts is the **right of rebuttal,** which requires that individuals be given the opportunity to respond to personal attacks made on a radio or television broadcast. In the 1969 case of *Red Lion Broadcasting Company v. FCC,* for example, the U.S. Supreme Court upheld the FCC's determination that a radio station was required to provide a liberal author with an opportunity to respond to a conservative commentator's attack that the station had aired.[5]

For many years, a third important federal regulation was the **fairness doctrine.** Under this doctrine, broadcasters who aired programs on controversial issues were required to provide time for opposing views. In 1985, however, the FCC stopped enforcing the fairness doctrine on the grounds that there were so many radio and television stations—to say nothing of newspapers and newsmagazines—that in all likelihood many different viewpoints were already being presented without each station's being required to try to present all sides of an argument. Critics of this FCC decision charge that in many media markets the number of competing viewpoints is small. Efforts to revive the fairness doctrine by some Democrats have failed.

## More Media Outlets Are Owned by Fewer Companies

The United States boasts nearly 2,000 television stations, approximately 1,400 daily newspapers, and more than 13,000 radio stations (20 percent of which are devoted to news, talk, or public affairs).[6]

Even though the number of TV and radio stations and daily newspapers reporting news in the United States is enormous, the number of sources of national news is actually quite small—several wire services, four broadcast networks, public radio (NPR) and television (PBS), a few elite newspapers and newsmagazines, and a scattering of other sources such as the national correspondents of a few large local papers and the small independent radio networks. More than three-fourths of the daily newspapers in the United States are owned by large media conglomerates such as the Hearst, McClatchy, or Gannett corporations; thus the diversity of coverage and editorial opinion in American newspapers is not as broad as it might seem. Much of the national news that is published by local newspapers is provided by one wire service, the Associated Press, while additional coverage is provided by services run by several major newspapers such as the *New York Times* and the *Chicago Tribune.* More than five hundred of the nation's television stations are affiliated with one of the four networks and carry that network's evening news reports. Dozens of others carry PBS (Public Broadcasting System) news. Several hundred local radio stations also carry network news or National Public Radio news broadcasts. At the same time, although there are only three truly national newspapers, the *Wall Street Journal,* the *Christian Science Monitor,* and *USA Today,* two other papers, the *New York Times* and the *Washington Post,* are read by political leaders and other influential Americans throughout the nation. Such is the influence of these two "elite" newspapers that their news coverage sets the standard for virtually all other news outlets. Stories carried in the *New York Times* or the *Washington Post* influence the content of many other papers as well as of the network news. Note how often this book, like most others, relies on *New York Times* and *Washington Post* stories as sources for contemporary events. National news is also carried to millions of Americans by two major newsmagazines—*Time* and *Newsweek*, although both face declining circulation. Beginning in the late 1980s, CNN became another major news source for Americans, especially after its spectacular coverage of the Persian Gulf war in 1991. At one point, CNN was able to provide live reports of American bombing raids on Baghdad, Iraq, after the major networks' correspondents had been forced to flee to bomb shelters. However, the number of news sources has remained essentially the same. Even the availability of new electronic media on the Internet has failed to expand the number of news sources. Most national news available on the Web, for example, consists of electronic versions of the conventional print or broadcast media.

The trend toward the homogenization of national news has been hastened by dramatic changes in media ownership, which became possible in large part due to the relaxation of government regulations in the 1980s and 1990s. The enactment of the 1996 Telecommunications Act opened the way for further consolidation in the media industry, and a wave of mergers and consolidations has further reduced the field of independent media across the country. Since that time, among the major news networks, ABC was bought by the Walt Disney corporation; CBS was bought by Westinghouse Electric and later merged with Viacom, the owner of MTV and Paramount Studios; and CNN was bought by Time Warner. General Electric has owned NBC since 1986, and a $30 billion deal between GE and Comcast, announced in 2009, gave corporate giant Comcast majority control of NBC. The Australian press baron Rupert Murdoch owns the Fox network plus a host of radio, television, and newspaper properties around the world, including the important *Wall Street Journal*, which he acquired in 2007. A small number of giant corporations now controls a wide swath of media holdings, including television networks, movie studios, record companies, cable channels and local cable providers, book publishers, magazines, and newspapers. These developments have prompted questions about whether enough competition exists among the media to produce a diverse set of views on political and corporate matters or whether the United States has become the prisoner of media monopolies.[7]

As major newspapers, television stations, and radio networks fall into fewer and fewer hands, the risk increases that less popular or minority viewpoints and the politicians who express them will have difficulty finding a public forum in which to disseminate their ideas. Increasingly, such individuals turn to the Internet and its numerous blogs and other Web sites to express their views. The problem, however, is that ideas presented on the Internet tend to be very fragmented and read mainly by those who already agree with them. The Internet can be an important mechanism for linking communities of adherents and for pushing news into the rest of the media, but most primary news gathering is still done by traditional news organizations. Hence, growing concentration and consolidation in the print and broadcast industries are important policy problems.

# News Reporting Has Become Nationalized

In general, the national news media cover more or less the same sets of events, present similar information, and emphasize similar issues and problems. Indeed, the national news services watch each other quite carefully. It is very likely that a major story carried by one service will quickly find its way into the pages or programming of the others. As a result, in the United States a rather centralized national news has developed, through which a relatively similar picture of events, issues, and problems is presented to the entire nation.[8] The nationalization of the news began in the early 1900s, was accelerated by the development of radio networks in the 1920s and 1930s and by the creation of the television networks after the 1950s, and has been further strengthened by the recent trends toward concentrated media ownership. This nationalization of news content has very important consequences for the American political system.

Nationalization of the news has contributed greatly to the nationalization of politics and of political perspectives in the United States. Prior to the development of the national media and the nationalization of news coverage, news traveled very slowly. Every region and city saw national issues and problems primarily through a local lens. Concerns and perspectives varied greatly from region to region, city to city, and village to village. Today, in large measure as a result of the nationalization of the media, residents of all parts of the country share similar pictures of the day's events.[9] They may not agree on everything, but most see the world in similar ways.

The exception to this pattern can be found with those Americans whose chief source of news is something other than the "mainstream" national media. Despite the nationalization and homogenization of the news, in some American cities, alternative news coverage is available. Such media markets are known as **news enclaves** (groups seeking specialized information not provided by the mainstream media). For example, some African Americans rely on newspapers and radio stations that aim their coverage primarily at black audiences. This general strategy is known as "narrowcasting" (to distinguish it from broadcasting). As a result, these individuals may interpret events differently from white Americans and even other blacks.[10] The existence of black-focused media helps to explain why many African Americans and white Americans reacted differently to the 1995 trial of O. J. Simpson in Los Angeles. While national media outlets generally portrayed Simpson as guilty of the murder of his former wife, African American media outlets depicted Simpson as a victim of a racist criminal-justice system. This latter view came to be held by a large number of African Americans.

In a similar vein, some radio stations and print media are aimed exclusively at religious and social conservatives. These individuals are also likely to develop and retain a perception of the news that is quite different from that of "mainstream" America. For example, the rural midwesterners who rely on the ultraconservative People's Radio Network for their news coverage may become concerned about the alleged efforts of the United Nations to subordinate the United States in a world government, a viewpoint unfamiliar to most Americans.

Internet newsgroups are another form of news enclave. Newsgroups are informal and tend to develop around the discussion of a particular set of issues. Individuals post their views for others to read; comments are also posted. Users tend to seek out and exchange postings with those who share their opinions. Perhaps the long-term significance of the Internet is that it will increasingly allow contacts among individuals with unconventional viewpoints who are geographically dispersed and might otherwise be unaware of the existence of others who share their views.

The same principle seems to hold for another form of discussion on the Internet, known as a chat room. Chat rooms are online forums in which individuals form groups spontaneously and converse with each other. The topics change often as participants leave and are replaced by newcomers. Like newsgroups, chat rooms often function as opinion enclaves where like-minded individuals from across the nation can congregate and reinforce each other's view.

## News Coverage Matters Because People Rely on It

Because of the important role the media can play in national politics, it is vitally important to understand the factors that affect media coverage.[11] What accounts for the media's agenda of issues and topics? What explains the character of coverage—why does a politician receive good or bad press? What factors determine the interpretation or "spin" that a particular story will receive? Although a host of

LIVE

DAVID BLOOM
WITH THE THIRD INFANTRY DIVISION
IN IRAQ
LITY 📷 NOW ON MSNBC.COM: U.S. STEPS UP MEC.

*Prior to the Iraq war, the Bush administration invited more than one hundred news correspondents and photographers to accompany American forces into battle. These "embedded" journalists developed considerable rapport with the soldiers and provided generally sympathetic war coverage.*

*In 2009, shortly after President Obama announced a "surge" of 30,000 additional troops in Afghanistan, Secretary of Defense Robert Gates visited Afghanistan and made the administration's case for the surge in a series of interviews.*

minor factors plays a role, three major factors are important: (1) the journalists and others who produce the news; (2) the subjects or topics of the news; and (3) the audience for the news.

## Journalists Can Shape the News

Media content and news coverage are inevitably affected by the views, ideals, and interests of those who seek out, write, and produce news and other stories. At one time, newspaper publishers exercised a great deal of influence over their papers' news content. Publishers such as William Randolph Hearst and Joseph Pulitzer became political powers through their manipulation of news coverage. Hearst, for example, almost single-handedly pushed the United States into war with Spain in 1898 through his newspapers' relentless coverage of the alleged brutality employed by Spain in its efforts to suppress a rebellion in Cuba, at that time a Spanish colony. The sinking of the American battleship *Maine* in Havana Harbor under mysterious circumstances gave Hearst the ammunition he needed to force a reluctant President McKinley to lead the nation into war.

More important than publishers, for the most part, are the reporters. Those who cover the news for the national media generally have a good deal of freedom to interpret stories and, as a result, have an opportunity to interject their views and ideals into news stories. For example, the friendship and respect that some reporters felt for Franklin Roosevelt or John Kennedy helped to generate more favorable news coverage for these presidents. Likewise, the dislike and distrust many reporters felt for Richard Nixon and Ronald Reagan were also communicated to the public.

## News Subjects Can Shape the News

News coverage is also influenced by the individuals or groups who are subjects of the news or whose interests and activities are actual or potential news topics. All politicians seek to shape or manipulate their media images by cultivating good relations with reporters as well as through news leaks and staged news events. A *leak* is the disclosure of confidential information to the news media. Most leaks originate with senior government officials and prominent politicians and political activists. These individuals cultivate long-term relationships with journalists to whom they regularly leak confidential information, knowing that it is likely to be published on a priority basis in a form acceptable to them. Their confidence is based on the fact that journalists are likely to regard high-level sources of confidential information as valuable assets whose favor must be retained.

*During the late 1990s, President Bill Clinton was nearly driven from office by media revelations of his sexual misconduct with White House intern Monica Lewinsky. The media relentlessly pursued Clinton's evasions, lies, and indiscretions, and provided fuel for a congressional effort to impeach the president.*

However, the capacity of news subjects to influence the news is hardly unlimited. Media consultants and issues managers may shape the news for a time, but it is generally not difficult for the media to penetrate the smoke screens thrown up by news sources, if they have a reason to do so. Thus, for example, despite the administration's media management, media accounts of continuing U.S. casualties in Afghanistan, coupled with stories about the corruption and incompetence of the Afghan government, forced the Obama administration to declare in 2009 that America's commitment to Afghanistan was not open-ended and to indicate that there would be a timetable for the removal of American forces.

Occasionally, a politician proves incredibly adept at surviving repeated media attacks. Clinton, for example, was able to survive repeated revelations of sexual improprieties, financial irregularities, lying to the public, and illegal campaign fundraising activities. Clinton and his advisors crafted what the *Washington Post* called a "toolkit" for dealing with potentially damaging media revelations. This toolkit includes techniques such as chiding the press, browbeating reporters, referring inquiries quickly to lawyers who will not comment, and acting quickly to change the agenda. These techniques helped Clinton maintain a favorable public image despite the Lewinsky scandal and even the humiliation of a formal impeachment and trial.

## Consumers Can Influence News Content

The print and broadcast media are businesses that, in general, seek to show a profit. This means that like any other business, they must cater to the preferences of consumers. This has very important consequences for the content and character of the news media.

**Catering to the Upscale Audience** The print and broadcast media and the publishing industry are responsive not only to the interests of consumers generally, but also in particular to the interests and views of the more "upscale" segments of their audience. The preferences of these audience segments have a profound effect on the content and orientation of the press, of radio and television programming, and of books, especially in the areas of news and public affairs.[12]

Newspapers, magazines, and the broadcast media depend primarily on advertising revenues for their profits. These revenues, in turn, depend on the character and size of the audience that they are able to provide to advertisers for their product displays and promotional efforts. From the perspective of most advertisers and especially those whose products are relatively expensive, the most desirable audiences for their ads and commercials consist of younger, upscale consumers. What makes these individuals an especially desirable consumer audience is, of course, their affluence and their spending habits. Although they represent only a small percentage of the population, individuals under the age of fifty whose family income is in the top 20 percent account for nearly 50 percent of the retail dollars spent on consumer goods in the United States. To reach this audience, advertisers are particularly anxious to promote their products in the periodicals and newspapers and on the radio and television broadcasts that are known or believed to attract upscale patronage.

**The Media and Conflict** While the media respond most to the upscale audience, groups who cannot afford the services of media consultants and issues managers can publicize their views and interests through protest. Frequently, the media are accused of encouraging conflict and even violence as a result of the fact that they are instantly available to cover it, providing protesters with the publicity they crave. Clearly, conflict and even violence can be important vehicles for attracting the attention and interest of the media, and thus may provide an opportunity for media attention to groups otherwise lacking the financial or organizational resources to broadcast their views. During the 1960s, for example, the media coverage given to civil rights demonstrators and particularly to the violence that southern law enforcement officers in cities such as Selma and Birmingham directed against peaceful black demonstrators dramatically increased white sympathy for the civil rights cause. This was, of course, one of the chief aims of Dr. Martin Luther King's strategy of nonviolence.[13] In subsequent years, the media turned their attention to antiwar demonstrations and, more recently, to anti-abortion demonstrations, antinuclear demonstrations, and even to acts of international terrorism designed specifically to induce the Western media to publicize the terrorists' causes. In 2009 anti-tax activists who called themselves the "Tea Party" movement were able to garner enormous media coverage, which helped them play a major role in the 2010 Republican primaries and general election. "Tea Party" was a name designed to refer to America's original anti-tax rebels.

# The Media Affect Power Relations in American Politics

The content and character of news and public affairs programming—what the media choose to present and how they present it—can have far-reaching political consequences. Media disclosures can greatly enhance—or fatally damage—the careers of public officials. Media coverage can rally support for—or intensify opposition to—national policies. The media can shape and modify public perceptions of events, issues, and institutions.

## The Media Influence Public Opinion through Agenda Setting, Priming, and Framing

Many people wrongly assume that the American media have an almost dictatorial power over public opinion—that people believe anything and everything presented in the media. This is obviously false, not only because people get information from many sources, but because people are typically skeptical about what is portrayed in the media. The media do have an effect on opinion, but this occurs through agenda setting, framing, and priming.

**Agenda Setting** The media almost never tell people what to think; however, they can shape what people think *about*. This is called **agenda setting,** referring to the power of the media to bring public attention to particular issues and problems. When the media focus primary attention on a single story, especially when it appears on the front pages of newspapers and as the lead story on network news broadcasts, the public turns more attention to it, thereby elevating its importance, and making it more likely that the government will act. For example, in October 1987, NBC News aired an extensive report on a devastating famine in Ethiopia. Suddenly, major relief efforts were launched, polls showed that African famine relief was now on the minds of many citizens, and political leaders urged that action be taken. As a news producer noted about this sudden outpouring of attention, "This famine has been going on for a long time and nobody cared. Now it's on TV and everybody cares. I guess a picture is worth many words."[14] A similar pattern unfolded after the island nation of Haiti suffered a devastating earthquake in 2010. Pictures of widespread destruction prompted an outpouring of money and relief efforts.

**Framing** Framing is the media's ability to influence how the American people interpret political events and results. For example, in 2009 by always referring to the Obama administration's health care initiative as "reform," the media was tacitly framing the legislation in a positive way. Americans generally approve of the idea of "reform" and are likely to support ideas labeled as reforms. Had the media framed the initiative as "health care rationing," which some Republicans called it, the proposal would easily have been defeated.

Media frames were quite important during the 2008 election. From the perspective of the national media, one of the most important aspects of the 2008 election was that for the first time in American history an African American was

*This famous photograph of the aftermath of a napalm attack was one of many media images that shaped the American public's views on the Vietnam War. Media accounts critical of the war helped to turn public opinion against it and hastened the withdrawal of American troops.*

making a serious bid for the presidency of the United States. The media appeared to regard this aspect of the campaign as more significant than Hillary Clinton's bid to become the first woman to serve as president. Partly because they regarded the fact that Obama was America's first significant black presidential candidate as supremely important, the media gave Obama much more attention and scrutiny than they afforded other candidates. This extra attention frequently allowed Obama to dominate the news and led his opponents constantly to charge that the media were biased in his favor. It may be true that many reporters and commentators supported Obama. Nevertheless, if he had been an inept candidate, the extra coverage he received would only have amplified his weakness. Obama, however, was able to take full advantage of the extra media attention he was given to generate popular enthusiasm for his campaign and raise tens of millions of dollars in small contributions via the Internet. By devoting enormous quantities of ink and air time to Obama, the media were not so much exhibiting bias as reflecting what they saw as the historic importance of the story. Extra media coverage, in turn, gave Obama an extra opportunity—which he seized—to display his intelligence and ability to the electorate.

In terms of media coverage, Sarah Palin's candidacy was almost the opposite of Obama's experience. One reason that John McCain chose Palin as his vice-presidential running mate was a calculation that the media would find Palin sufficiently new and interesting to divert their attention from Obama. Palin's acceptance speech at the Republican convention in which she described herself as a simple "hockey mom," and declared that the difference between a hockey mom and a pit bull was "lipstick," captured the media's interest and briefly gave the GOP a stage to rival Obama's. Palin, however, was not able to put her extra media exposure to good use. After two disastrous network interviews in which Palin appeared unable to answer the simplest questions, the media generally dismissed the Alaska governor as inept and uninformed, and resumed their focus on Obama.

**Priming** A third source of media influence over opinion is **priming**. This occurs when media coverage affects the way the public evaluates political leaders, issues, and events. For example, nearly unanimous media praise for President Bush's speeches to the nation in the wake of the September 11 terrorist attacks prepared, or *primed*, the public to view Bush's subsequent response to terrorism in an extremely positive light, even though some aspects of the administration's efforts, most notably those in the realm of bioterrorism, were quite problematic.

In the case of political candidates, the media have considerable influence over whether a particular individual will receive public attention, whether a particular individual will be taken seriously as a viable contender, and whether the public will evaluate a candidate's performance favorably. Thus, if the media find a candidate interesting, they may treat him or her as a serious contender even though the facts of the matter seem to suggest otherwise. In a similar vein, the media may declare that a candidate has "momentum," a mythical property that the media confer on candidates if they happen to exceed the media's expectations. Midway through the 2008 Democratic primaries, the media declared that Barack Obama had momentum, as his fund-raising and poll numbers exceeded early expectations. Nothing Hillary Clinton was able to do seemed to deprive Obama of the coveted momentum the media had granted him.

Typically, media coverage of election campaigns focuses on the "horse race" (that is, who is ahead and by how much) to the detriment of attention to issues and candidate records. In the year preceding the 2008 national elections, several candidates fought for the Democratic and Republican presidential nominations. From the outset, it appeared that Senator Hillary Clinton was nearly certain to become the Democratic nominee. Looking for a horse race, however, the national media gave enormous publicity to Senator Barack Obama. Newspapers and magazines ran hundreds of positive profiles of Obama, touting him as the first serious African American presidential contender. Hardly a negative word about Obama was uttered on the air or in print. Obama was even allowed to appear in a *Saturday Night Live* Halloween skit poking fun at Clinton, who was portrayed as a witch.[15] Months of positive coverage helped transform Obama into a serious presidential contender.

The media's power to influence people's evaluation of public figures is not absolute. Throughout the last decade, politicians implemented new techniques for

*In an effort to avoid tough questions from interviewers on traditional news programs, politicians increasingly seek out opportunities to reach the public through entertainment or "soft news" programs. Bill Clinton played his saxophone on* The Arsenio Hall Show *and discussed his choice of underwear with a teenage interviewer on MTV. George W. Bush also made good use of appearances on entertainment programs, appearing on* The Tonight Show with Jay Leno *and other programs.*

communicating with the public and shaping their own images. For instance, Bill Clinton pioneered the use of town meetings and television entertainment programs as a means of communicating directly with voters in the 1992 election. During the 2000 presidential race between Bush and Gore, both candidates made use of town meetings, as well as talk shows and entertainment programs such as *The Oprah Winfrey Show, The Tonight Show with Jay Leno,* and *Saturday Night Live,* to reach mass audiences. During a town meeting, talk show, or entertainment program, politicians are free to craft their own images without interference from journalists.

In 2008, the McCain campaign quickly determined that Sarah Palin, the vice-presidential nominee, was not quite ready for prime-time media exposure. Palin had little experience outside her own state and was not conversant with most national political issues. Accordingly, GOP strategists sought to limit Palin's media exposure to situations in which she would not be subjected to the sort of intensive questioning that might reveal her limitations.

## Media Bias Can Be Ideological or Institutional

Charges that the media are biased for or against public officials, candidates, or issues are commonplace. While bias certainly exists, many of these claims disguise the simple fact that people do not like some of the news they hear. For example, many who oppose gun control argue that the media are pro–gun control. According to conservative media critic Jonah Goldberg, "There are few things they [reporters] hate more than guns." This attitude is "so prevalent and so obvious," according to Goldberg, that the media are simply incapable of being objective on the issue.[16] Yet another media critic, Jeff Cohen, has argued exactly the opposite—that the "gun lobby," dominated by the National Rifle Association, has "dominated the terms of the media debate on gun control." To Cohen, the media has shown "bias toward the NRA's view of the Second Amendment," even though the courts did not support

**TABLE 6.1**

## Learning while Laughing

| LEARN ABOUT 2008 CAMPAIGN FROM . . . | 18–29 % | 30–49 % | 50–64 % | 65+ % |
|---|---|---|---|---|
| **Comedy Shows\*** | | | | |
| Regularly | 21 | 6 | 5 | 2 |
| Sometimes | 29 | 21 | 9 | 9 |
| **Late Night TV\*\*** | | | | |
| Regularly | 13 | 7 | 7 | 9 |
| Sometimes | 31 | 20 | 8 | 14 |
| Number of Cases | (276) | (596) | (343) | (278) |

\*Like *Saturday Night Live* or *The Daily Show*.
\*\*Like *The Tonight Show with Jay Leno* or *The Late Show with David Letterman*.
SOURCE: Pew Research Center, *Cable and Internet Loom Large in Fragmented Political News Universe*, January 11, 2004, p. 8.

the NRA view that the "right to bear arms" supports individual gun ownership until 2008.[17]

Regardless of whether the media are biased for or against gun control, it is certainly true that much of the reporting on gun issues has resulted from sensational crimes involving guns, such as the shooting at Columbine High School in Colorado in 1999, when fourteen students and one teacher died in a shooting spree, or the 2009 shooting at Fort Hood, Texas, where a troubled Army psychiatrist used two handguns to shoot and kill 12 people and wound 31 others. By the very nature of the story, it is inevitable that many will consider guns to be part of the problem, no matter what kind of "bias" the reporters do or do not have.

**The Institutional Bias of the Media** Some analysts have argued that the biggest bias in reporting is not liberal or conservative at all, but rather is either for or against the institutions of government. The charge of bias in favor of the government argues that reporters rely for most of their information on government sources, which are naturally self-serving. During the Persian Gulf War of 1990–91, for example, most stories of the war came from the government's military sources, which gave a far more rosy and sanitized picture of the conflict than what emerged later. According to media expert Doris Graber, successful military actions were shown, but not the mistakes and failures, and not pictures of the dead and wounded.[18] The American military told the press that all Iraqi airfields had been destroyed; ten days later, it was revealed that 65 percent of them were still working. The military bragged that American Patriot missiles had shot down many Iraqi Scud missiles; ultimately, the Pentagon was unable to confirm a single instance when a Patriot actually hit a Scud.[19] This pattern has been true in every modern war, even Vietnam. The same criticisms were leveled against media coverage of the 2003 Iraq war; critics charged that Americans were not informed of the deteriorating conditions there until a succession of adverse stories in 2005 and 2006 led to increased scrutiny. In times of war, the government generally succeeds in controlling the flow, management, and content of news.

War aside, government reports, presidential and congressional statements, and other government actions compose the bulk of daily domestic and foreign policy reporting. This adds up to a bias in favor of whoever is running the government, as does the huge effort made by every modern president, and other top governmental leaders, to provide a positive public relations "spin" on what they do.[20] In addition, the broadcast media—radio and television—are regulated by the Federal Communications Commission (FCC), an independent regulatory agency established in 1934 to license and regulate all broadcasting. While the FCC is not a "Big Brother" agency monitoring every transmission, it does have the power to withdraw the operating licenses of broadcasters as a form of "performance control."[21]

In opposition to this is the view that the press is biased against the government. From the muckraking tradition during the Progressive Era in the early 1900s, to critical coverage of the Vietnam War in the late 1960s, to the *Washington Post*'s investigation of the Watergate scandal in the early 1970s, to the subsequent rise of more aggressive, adversarial journalism (an aggressive form of investigative journalism that attempts to expose and antagonize the status quo) and investigative reporting, as seen in such popular investigative TV programs as *60 Minutes*, reporters seem to relish finding scandal and wrongdoing in government.

The national media's aggressive use of the techniques of investigation, publicity, and exposure allowed them to enhance their autonomy and carve out a prominent place for themselves in American government and politics. The power derived by the press from adversarial journalism is one of the reasons that the media seem to relish opportunities to attack political institutions and to publish damaging information about important public officials. Increasingly, media coverage has come to influence politicians' careers, the mobilization of political constituencies, and the fate of issues and causes.

Adversarial, or "attack," journalism has become commonplace in America, and some critics have suggested that the media have contributed to popular cynicism and the low levels of citizen participation that characterize contemporary American political processes. But before we begin to think about means of compelling the media to adopt a more positive view of politicians and political issues, we should consider the possibility that media criticism is one of the major mechanisms of political accountability in the American political process. Without aggressive media coverage would we have known of Bill Clinton's misdeeds or, for that matter, those of Richard Nixon? Without aggressive media coverage, would important questions be raised about the conduct of American foreign and domestic policy? It is easy to criticize the media for their aggressive tactics, but would our democracy function effectively without the critical role of the press? Vigorous and critical media are needed as the "watchdogs" of American politics. Of course, in October 2001, the adversarial relationship between the government and the media was at least temporarily transformed into a much more supportive association as the media helped rally the American people for the fight against terrorism, after the 9/11 attacks the month before.

# Become an Informed and Vocal News Critic

Americans today are less trusting of major news outlets than they were in the not too distant past, and many of the traditional sources of news and information— newspapers and the nightly news on television—have seen reductions in their audiences. Although dissatisfaction with the media is on the rise across all age groups, young people are among the most likely to have negative things to say about the news media.

If you're interested in digging a little deeper into the mass media's news coverage, here are some things that you can do to become a more informed consumer of news and information:

- People often complain that the news media seem biased. Rather than adhering to norms of objectivity, the news is often reported from a liberal or conservative perspective. Instead of accepting this complaint at face value, try a little experiment yourself. Spend some time watching, reading, and listening to news from two sources, one that is considered "conservative" and the other "liberal" (for example, Fox News and NPR, or the editorial pages of the *Wall Street Journal* and *New York Times*). Do you agree with the characterization of these organizations as biased?

- Make your voice heard if you have concerns about news that's presented in a partisan fashion. Let the editors, hosts, writers, and owners of the broadcast or print media know that you expect more objectivity in the news that's being presented. Most major news sources have sections on their Web sites where comments can be submitted. You can also send a letter to the editor via e-mail or regular mail.

- Spend some time checking out "new" and "alternative" media. Many blogs provide readers with a portal to information across a variety of sources, often with commentary. A few to consider are: the Huffington Post (www.huffington post.com), the Drudge Report (www.drudgereport.com), the Daily Dish (andrew sullivan.theatlantic.com), and the Daily Kos: State of the Nation (www.dailykos .com).

- If none of the above interests you, simply do an Internet search for "political blog" or "news blogs." Compare the blogss content with what's covered in national newspapers and broadcasts. Do the blogs provide better, more comprehensive, or more up-to-date information than what you'd get from traditional news sources? Are they more objective or less objective?

The adversarial relationship between the government and segments of the press, however, resumed in the wake of the 2003 Iraq war. Such newspapers as the *Washington Post* and the *New York Times* castigated President Bush for going to war without the support of some of America's major allies. When American forces failed to uncover evidence that Iraq possessed weapons of mass destruction—a major reason cited by the administration for launching the war—these newspapers intimated that the war had been based on intelligence failures, if not outright presidential deceptions. The president denounced the media for distorting his record. Thus, after a brief interlude of post–September 11 harmony, the customary hostilities between politicians and the press resumed.

## ● The Media Are More Partisan Than Ever

The free media are an institution absolutely essential to democratic government. Ordinary citizens depend on the media to investigate wrongdoing, to publicize and explain governmental actions, to evaluate programs and politicians, and to bring to light matters that might otherwise be known to only a handful of governmental insiders. In short, without free and active media, popular government would be virtually impossible. Citizens would have few means through which to know or assess the government's actions—other than the claims or pronouncements of the government itself. Moreover, without active—indeed, aggressive—media, citizens would be hard pressed to make informed choices among competing candidates at the polls. Of course, by continually emphasizing deceptions and wrongdoing by political figures, the media encourage the public to become cynical and distrustful, not only of the people in office, but of the government and the political process. A widespread sense that all politics is corrupt or deceptive can easily lead to a sense that nothing can be done. In this way, the media's adversarial posture may contribute to the low levels of political participation seen in America today.

Today's media are not only adversarial but also increasingly partisan. Debates about the liberalism and conservatism of the mass media point up the fact that many readers and viewers perceive a growing bias in newspapers, radio, and television. Blogs and other Internet outlets, of course, are often unabashedly partisan. To some extent, increasing ideological and partisan stridency is an inevitable result of the expansion and proliferation of news sources. When the news was dominated by three networks and a handful of national papers, each sought to appeal to the entire national audience. This required a moderate and balanced tone so that consumers would not be offended and jump ship to a rival network or newspaper. Today, there are so many news sources that few can aim for a national audience. Instead, many target a partisan or ideological niche and aim to develop a strong relationship with consumers in that audience segment by catering to their biases and predispositions. The end result may be to encourage greater division and disharmony among Americans.

In addition, politicians are ever more dependent on favorable media coverage. National political leaders and journalists have had symbiotic relationships, at least since FDR's presidency, but initially politicians were the senior partners. They benefited from media publicity, but they were not totally dependent on it as long as they could still rely on party organizations to mobilize votes. Journalists, on the other hand, depended on their relationships with politicians for access to information and would hesitate to report stories that might antagonize valuable sources for fear of being excluded from the flow of information in retaliation.

With the decline of traditional party organizations, journalists have less fear that their access to information can be restricted in retaliation for negative coverage. Such freedom gives the media enormous power. The media can make or break reputations, help to launch or to destroy political careers, and build support for or rally opposition to programs and institutions.[22] Wherever there is so much power, at least the potential exists for its abuse or overly zealous use.

Finally, it is important to rely on more than one source of news. The best approach is to make use of news sources with disparate ideological perspectives. For example, residents of Washington D.C. sometimes read both the liberal *Washington Post* and the conservative *Washington Times*. Anyone can subscribe to both a liberal magazine, such as *The Public Interest*, and a conservative one, such as the *Weekly Standard*, that often cover the same topics. The value of using such disparate news sources is to obtain different perspectives on the same events. This, in turn, will help you see more than one possibility and, ultimately, to make up your own mind.[23]

# studyguide

## Practice Quiz

 Find a diagnostic Web Quiz with 33 additional questions on the StudySpace Web site: www.wwnorton.com/we-the-people

1. Which of the following is *not* one of the main sources of news in America? *(p. 169)*
   a) the Internet
   b) broadcast media
   c) adversarial journalism
   d) print media

2. Which of the following statements is *not* true about old-fashioned newspapers? *(p. 171)*
   a) They typically offer readers a better context for analysis by providing more detailed and complete information than other forms of media.
   b) They are the read on a daily basis by almost all Americans.

   c) They serve as the primary source of news for the nation's social and political elites.
   d) Broadcast media organizations rely heavily on newspapers to set their news agenda.

3. In general, FCC regulations apply only to *(p. 174)*
   a) Cable television.
   b) Internet Web sites.
   c) over-the-air broadcast media.
   d) satellite radio.

4. The now defunct requirement that broadcasters provide time for opposing views when they air programs on controversial issues was called *(p. 175)*
   a) the equal time rule.
   b) the fairness doctrine.
   c) the right of rebuttal.
   d) the response rule.

5. Which of the following best describes national news in the United States? *(pp. 176–77)*
   a) fragmented and localized
   b) nationalized and centralized
   c) centralized but still localized
   d) none of the above

6. Which of the following can be considered an example of a news enclave? *(pp. 178–79)*
   a) people who participate in Internet chat rooms
   b) letters to the editor
   c) readers of the *New York Times*
   d) people who watch CNN

7. Which of the following have an impact on the nature of media coverage of politics? *(p. 180)*
   a) reporters
   b) political actors
   c) news consumers
   d) all of the above

8. The newspaper publisher William Randolph Hearst was responsible for encouraging U.S. involvement in which war? *(p. 180)*
   a) the Spanish-American War
   b) the Vietnam War
   c) the U.S. war with Mexico
   d) the Gulf War

9. Which of the following is a strategy available to poor people to increase their coverage by the news media? *(p. 182)*
   a) protest
   b) media consultants
   c) television advertising
   d) newspaper advertising "time sharing"

10. The media's powers to determine what becomes a part of the political discussion and to shape how political events are interpreted by the American people are known as *(pp. 183–84)*
    a) issue definition and protest power.
    b) agenda setting and framing.
    c) the illusion of saliency and the bandwagon effect.
    d) the equal time rule and the right of rebuttal.

11. Which of the following has *not* been a consequence of the emergence of adversarial (or "attack") journalism? *(p. 188)*
    a) It has led the media to adopt a more positive view of politicians and political issues.
    b) It has enhanced the media's autonomy from politicians and allowed them to carve out a prominent place for themselves in the political process.
    c) It has increased the likelihood that the media will act as the much-needed "watchdog" of American politics.
    d) It has led to accusations that the media is creating popular cynicism and depressing levels of political participation.

12. The declining power of party organizations has had which of the following effects on the power of the media in the United States? *(p. 191)*
    a) The media is less powerful because politicians are no longer forced to follow the fairness doctrine.
    b) The media is more powerful because politicians must now rely on the media to mobilize votes.
    c) The media is more powerful because politicians can no longer raise money through campaign contributions.
    d) It has had no effect on the power of the media.

# Chapter Outline

 Find a detailed Chapter Outline on the StudySpace Web site:
www.wwnorton.com/we-the-people

# Key Terms

 Find Flashcards to help you study these terms on the
StudySpace Web site: www.wwnorton.com/we-the-people

**agenda setting** *(p. 183)* the power of the media to bring public attention to particular issues and problems

**equal time rule** *(p. 175)* the requirement that broadcasters provide candidates for the same political office equal opportunities to communicate their messages to the public

**fairness doctrine** *(p. 176)* a Federal Communications Commission requirement for broadcasters who air programs on controversial issues to provide time for opposing views. The FCC ceased enforcing this doctrine in 1985

**framing** *(p. 183)* the power of the media to influence how events and issues are interpreted

**news enclave** *(p. 178)* a group seeking specialized information not provided by the mainstream media

**priming** *(p. 185)* preparing the public to take a particular view of an event or political actor

**right of rebuttal** *(p. 176)* a Federal Communications Commission regulation giving individuals the right to have the opportunity to respond to personal attacks made on a radio or television broadcast

# For Further Reading

Ansolabehere, Stephen, and Shanto Iyengar. *Going Negative: How Attack Ads Shrink and Polarize the Electorate*. New York: Free Press, 1995.

Bagdikian, Ben. *The Media Monopoly*. Boston: Beacon, 2004.

Campbell, Richard, Christopher Martin, and Bettina Fabos. *Media and Culture*. New York: St. Martins Press, 2009.

Cook, Timothy. *Governing with the News: The News Media as a Political Institution*. Chicago: University of Chicago Press, 1997.

de Zengotita, Thomas. *Mediated: How the Media Shapes Our World and the Way We Live in It*. New York: Bloomsbury, 2006.

Fenton, Tom. *Bad News: The Decline of Reporting, the Business of News, and the Danger to Us All*. New York: HarperCollins, 2005.

Graber, Doris. *Mass Media and American Politics,* 7th ed. Washington, DC: Congressional Quarterly Press, 2005.

Graber, Doris, et al. *The Politics of News, The News of Politics.* Washington, DC: Congressional Quarterly Press, 1998.

Hallin, Daniel C. *The Uncensored War.* Berkeley and Los Angeles: University of California Press, 1986.

Hamilton, James T. *All the News That's Fit to Sell.* Princeton, NJ: Princeton University Press, 2004.

Hart, Roderick. *Seducing America: How Television Charms the Modern Voter.* New York: Oxford University Press, 1994.

Jenkins, Henry. *Convergence Culture: Where Old and New Media Collide.* New York: New York University Press, 2008.

Kellner, Douglas. *Media Spectacle and the Crisis of Democracy.* Boulder, CO: Paradigm, 2005.

Kurtz, Howard. *Reality Show: Inside the Last Great Television News War.* New York: Free Press, 2007.

MacArthur, John. *Second Front: Censorship and Propaganda in the 1991 Gulf War.* Berkeley and Los Angeles: University of California Press, 2004.

Rutherford, Paul. *Weapons of Mass Persuasion.* Toronto: University of Toronto Press, 2004.

Sparrow, Bartholomew H. *Uncertain Guardians: The News Media as a Political Institution.* Baltimore, MD: Johns Hopkins University Press, 1998.

Spitzer, Robert J., ed. *Media and Public Policy.* Westport, CT: Praeger, 1993.

West, Darrell M. *Air Wars: Television Advertising in Election Campaigns, 1952–2008.* Washington, DC: Congressional Quarterly Press, 2010.

# Recommended Web Sites

**Accuracy in Media**
**www.aim.org**
> This nonprofit, watchdog group attempts to ensure accuracy in media reporting by identifying botched or slanted stories and then "setting the record straight." Check out the media monitor, special reports, and press releases to see what current stories may be cause for concern.

**Drudge Report**
**www.drudgereport.com**
> The site for the Drudge Report is a great source page for all the world's breaking news and most recent columns. Any consumer of the news will appreciate this handy guide to specific columnists and opinion pages of major publications.

**Federal Communications Commission**
**www.fcc.gov**
> The FCC is an independent regulatory agency established by the U.S. government in 1934 to regulate the broadcast media. On the official FCC Web site you can read about the rules and regulations that affect the media, along with other current topics of interest.

FOX News.com
www.foxnews.com/politics
CNN Politics.com
www.cnn.com/POLITICS
*The New York Times*
www.nytimes.com/pages/politics/index.html

Political news sites provide a good variety of perspectives on the news from conservative to liberal.

Journalism.org
www.journalism.org

This nonprofit, nonpolitical site, sponsored by the Project for Excellence in Journalism, examines the overall performance of the press as providers of information. Its aim is to help both consumers and producers of the news understand what the press is delivering and make it better.

National Newspaper Association
www.nnaweb.org

The NNA is one of the oldest and largest professional associations in the print media today. As ownership of major newspapers fall into fewer and fewer hands, the NNA is trying to protect, promote, and enhance America's community newspapers.

Newseum
www.newseum.org

Newseum is the Web page for an interactive museum of news journalism. On this site you can browse the front pages of over 500 daily national and international newspapers and explore the galleries and theaters of the news museum in Washington, D.C.

The Pew Research Center for the People and the Press
http://people-press.org

This independent survey research organization studies attitudes toward the press and numerous political issues.

llowing the 2010 election, the
epublican Party reclaimed some
the power it had lost in the 2008
ections. A new Republican major-
y took control of the House of Rep-
esentatives, led by Representative
ohn Boehner.

# Political Parties and Elections

**WHAT GOVERNMENT DOES AND WHY IT MATTERS** In November 2008, Americans chose Democrat Barack Obama to be their forty-fourth president. Obama defeated Republican senator John McCain by a margin of more than 7 million votes out of some 120 million votes cast, posting 53 percent of the popular vote to McCain's 46 percent. Little more than a half century after the enactment of the 1965 Voting Rights Act enfranchised millions of black voters, Obama became America's first nonwhite president. Americans also elected an overwhelmingly Democratic Congress in 2008. By 2010, however, many voters had become disenchanted with the performance of the administration and the Democratic Congress. Many liberal Democrats thought the president had not done enough to end America's military involvement in the Middle East or to advance a progressive social agenda. Republican conservatives, on the other hand, blamed the president and Congress for the failure of the economy to fully recover from the 2008–09 recession and were concerned with the long-term costs and consequences of Democraric social and economic programs. As a result, the Democrats suffered heavy losses in the 2010 midterm elections and the president saw his agenda threatened by a newly assertive GOP.

Political parties and elections are all about who controls the government. Social forces work through the parties to gain control over government personnel (meaning those who run the government) and policies. Yet political parties and elections serve another purpose: parties are also a means by which those in government try to influence important groups in society.

The importance of parties in organizing congressional debate and mobilizing citizens was evident in the 2009 debate over health care. Democratic party leaders in the House of Representatives and in the Senate worked to build support among their members for a bill, forging compromises and applying pressure where necessary. This was no easy task: in such a complex policy area, winning party unity required that the bill omit features that some party members supported and include provisions that others disliked. In the House of Representatives, 84 percent of Democrats supported the bill. In the Senate, where it was necessary to win 60 votes in order to overcome the threat of a filibuster, the initial version of the health care bill passed by exactly 60 votes, with all 60 Democrats voting for the bill. The role of parties was also evident in the near-unanimous opposition of the Republican party to the health bill. Republican opposition stemmed from both policy and political concerns. Most Republicans preferred policy approaches that would require less government regulation of the market and less public spending. As the opposition party, however, Republicans were also aware that a major policy win would likely strengthen Democrats. Republican party leaders mobilized staunch opposition to the Democratic health reform proposals in both the House and the Senate. In the end, only one Republican in the House voted for health reform. In the Senate, the death of Massachusetts Democratic Senator Edward Kennedy reduced the Democrats' majority to 59 (a Republican won the special election in 2010 to replace Kennedy). But because the Senate had approved the initial health care bill in 2009, Senate leaders relied on a procedure called "reconciliation" that allowed them to approve the final bill by a simple majority vote, thereby bypassing the possibility of a filibuster.

In Chapter 5, we examined the direct links between the public's preferences as expressed through public opinion and government action, finding that the link was strong at times, but weak, or even nonexistent, at others. Chapter 6 on the nation's media examined how government leaders and private interests often use the media to shape and direct public opinion. Both chapters examined the impact and limits of direct popular influence. This chapter brings these themes together in the examination of political parties and elections—mechanisms that can help citizens change their government at times, but that may also help leaders consolidate or extend power at other times.

# Parties and Elections Have Been Vital to American Politics and Government

**Political parties,** like interest groups, are organizations seeking to influence the government by electing their members to important government offices. Ordinarily, they can be distinguished from interest groups on the basis of their orientation. A party seeks to control the entire government by electing its members to office and thereby controlling the government's personnel. Interest groups usually accept government and its personnel as a given and try to influence government policies through them.

In the United States today, the relationship between parties and government is more complex than this basic definition suggests.

## Political Parties Arose from the Electoral Process

Political parties as they are known today developed along with the expansion of suffrage and can be understood only in the context of elections. The two are so intertwined that American parties actually take their structure from the electoral process. The shape of party organization in the United States has followed a simple rule: For every district where an election is held, there should be some kind of party unit. Republicans failed to maintain units in most counties of the southern states between 1900 and 1952; Democrats were similarly unsuccessful in many areas of New England. But for most of the history of the United States, two major parties have had enough of an organized presence to oppose each other in elections in most of the nation's towns, cities, and counties. This makes the American party system one of the oldest political institutions in the history of democracy.

Political parties play a traditionally important role in elections. They recruit candidates to run for office, get their loyal party members out to vote, and work in a variety of ways to promote the causes and issues of the party. In earlier times, the parties had near monopoly control over the electoral process. In recent decades, however, they have lost their monopoly to candidates who decide not to work within the party, to **political action committees (PACs)** that generate millions of dollars for candidates, and to direct appeals through the media.

*The Democratic Party of the United States is the world's oldest political party. It can trace its history back to Thomas Jefferson's Jeffersonian Republicans and, later, to Andrew Jackson's Jacksonian Democrats. The Jacksonians expanded voter participation and ushered in the political era of the common person, as shown in this image of Jackson's inauguration celebration.*

## Parties Recruit Candidates

One of the most important but least noticed party activities is the recruitment of candidates for local, state, and national office. Each election year, candidates must be found for thousands of state and local offices as well as congressional seats. Where they do not have an incumbent running for re-election, party leaders attempt to identify strong candidates and to interest them in entering the campaign.

An ideal candidate will have an unblemished record and the capacity to raise enough money to mount a serious campaign. Party leaders are usually not willing to provide financial backing to candidates who are unable to raise substantial funds on their own. For a House seat, this can mean several hundred thousand dollars; for a Senate seat, a serious candidate must be able to raise several million dollars. Often, party leaders have difficulty finding attractive candidates and persuading them to run. Candidate recruitment has become particularly difficult in an era in which **incumbents** (candidates running for positions that they already hold) are so hard to beat, when lengthy political campaigns often involve mudslinging, and when candidates must assume that their personal lives will be intensely scrutinized in the press.[1]

## Parties Organize Nominations

Article I, Section 4, of the Constitution makes only a few provisions for elections. It delegates to the states the power to set the "times, places, and manner" of holding elections, even for U.S. senators and representatives. It does, however, reserve to Congress the power to make such laws if it chooses to do so. The Constitution has been amended from time to time to expand the right to participate in elections. Congress has also occasionally passed laws about elections, congressional districting, and campaign practices. But the Constitution and the laws are almost completely silent on nominations, setting only citizenship and age requirements for candidates. The president must be at least thirty-five years of age, a natural-born citizen, and a resident of the United States for fourteen years. A senator must be at least thirty, a U.S. citizen for at least nine years, and a resident of the state he or she represents. A member of the House must be at least twenty-five, a U.S. citizen for seven years, and a resident of the state he or she represents.

**Nomination** is the process by which political parties select their candidates for election to public office. The nominating process can precede the election by many months, as it does when the many candidates for the presidency are eliminated from consideration through a grueling series of debates and state primaries until there is only one survivor in each party—the party's nominee.

Nomination is the parties' most serious and difficult business. When more than one person aspires to an office, the choice can divide friends and associates. In comparison to such an internal dispute, the electoral campaign against the opposition is almost fun, because there the fight is against the declared adversaries.

## Parties Help Get Out the Vote

The actual election period begins immediately after the nominations. Historically, this has been a time of glory for the political parties, whose popular base of support is fully displayed. All the paraphernalia of party committees and all the committee members are activated into local party workforces.

The first step in the electoral process involves voter registration. This aspect of the process takes place all year round. There was a time when party workers were responsible for virtually all of this kind of electoral activity, but they have been supplemented (and in many states virtually replaced) by groups such as the League of Women Voters, unions, and chambers of commerce.

Registered voters then have to decide on Election Day whether to go to the polling place, stand in line, and actually vote for the various candidates and referenda on the ballot. If they are planning to vote by mail in one of the states that allows this, they have to request the ballot, fill it out and return it. Political parties, candidates, and campaigning can make a big difference in convincing voters to vote. In recent years, each of the two parties has developed extensive data files on hundreds of millions of potential voters. The GOP has called its archive "Voter Vault," while the Democratic file designated "Demzilla" and later "VoteBuilder" was created by a private software company called Voter Activation Network. In around 2005, the Democratic National Committee began to use this state-of-the-art Web-based system for collecting and sharing voter information in a bid to compete with the technologically sophisticated Republicans. In the 2008 election, the DNC made the voter file available to state parties, and this technology became one of the keys to the successful mobilization and get-out-the-vote activities of the Democrats. These elaborate data files allow the two parties to bring their search for votes, contributions, and campaign help down to named individuals. Voter mobilization, once an art, has now become a science.

## Parties Facilitate Voter Choice

On any general election ballot, there are likely to be only two or three candidacies where the nature of the office and the characteristics and positions of the candidates are well known to voters. But what about the choices for judges, the state comptroller, the state attorney general, and many other elective positions about which voters have little information or awareness? And what about states that hold votes on ballot initiatives, where policy measures are determined directly by voters instead of by state legislatures, or referenda, where voters can state laws enacted by state legislatures? In both instances, these measures can be put on the ballot by gathering petition signatures; both are ways by which voters can change state law or state constitution provisions by direct vote. Initiatives and referenda are often hailed as effective means of direct democracy, where the people can vote directly on a proposed law instead of leaving the decisions to their state legislature. In the case of hot-button issues like affirmative action and gay marriage, most voters have a good idea of where they stand and therefore know how they wish to vote. But most ballot measures involve obscure subjects about which voters have little information, and vote outcomes are often swayed by heavy interest group spending. When voters face ballot choices about which they have little information, political parties can play a critical role by providing them with information and "cues."

## Parties Organize Power in Congress

The ultimate test of the party system is its relationship to and influence on the institutions of government. Congress, in particular, depends more on the party system than is generally recognized. For one thing, power in Congress is organized along party lines. Specifically, the speakership of the House is essentially a party office. All the members of the House take part in the election of the speaker. But the actual selection is made by the **majority party,** that is, the party that holds a majority of seats in the House or Senate. (The other party is known as the **minority party,** meaning that it holds a minority of legislative seats in either the House or the Senate.) When the majority party caucus presents a nominee to the entire House, its choice is then invariably ratified in a straight vote along party lines.

The committee system of both houses of Congress is also a product of the two-party system. Although the rules organizing committees and the rules defining the jurisdiction of each are adopted like ordinary legislation by the whole membership, parties shape all other features of the committees.

The assignment of individual members to committees is a party decision. Each party has a "committee on committees" to make such decisions. Permission to transfer to another committee is also a party decision. Moreover, advancement up the committee ladder toward the chair is a party decision. Since the late nineteenth century, most advancements have been automatic—based upon the length of continual service on the committee. This seniority system has existed only because of the support of the two parties, however, and either party can deviate from it—that is, pick someone with less seniority to chair a committee—by a simple vote.

## Presidents Need Political Parties

The party that wins the White House is always led, in title anyway, by the president. The president normally depends on fellow party members in Congress to support legislative initiatives. At the same time, members of the party in Congress hope that the president's programs and personal prestige will help them raise campaign funds and secure re-election.

# America Is One of the Few Nations with a Two-Party System

Although George Washington and many other leaders of his time deplored partisan politics, the **two-party system**—a political system in which only two parties have a realistic opportunity to compete effectively for control of the government—emerged early in the history of the new Republic. Beginning with the Federalists and the Jeffersonian Republicans in the 1790s, two major parties would dominate national politics, although which particular two parties they were would change with the times and issues. This two-party system has culminated, after a series of historical collisions, in today's Democrats and Republicans (see Figure 7.1). Each has had an important place in U.S. history.

## Electoral Realignments Define Party Systems in American History

American party history has followed a fascinating and very regular pattern (see Figure 7.2). Typically, the national electoral arena has been dominated by one party for a period of roughly thirty years. At the conclusion of this period, the dominant party has been replaced by a new party in what political scientists call an **electoral realignment** (the point in history when a new party supplants the ruling party, becoming in turn the dominant political force). The realignment is typically followed by a long period in which the new party is the dominant political force in the United States—not necessarily winning every election but generally maintaining control of the Congress and usually of the White House as well.[2] Each of these periods is referred to as a "party system."

Although there are some disputes among scholars about the precise timing of these critical realignments, there is general agreement that at least five have occurred since the Founding. The first took place around 1800 when the Jeffersonian Republicans defeated the Federalists and became the dominant force in American politics. The second realignment occurred in about 1828, when the Jacksonian Democrats took control of the White House and the Congress. The third period of realignment centered on 1860. During this period, the newly founded Republican Party led by Abraham Lincoln won power, in the process destroying the Whig

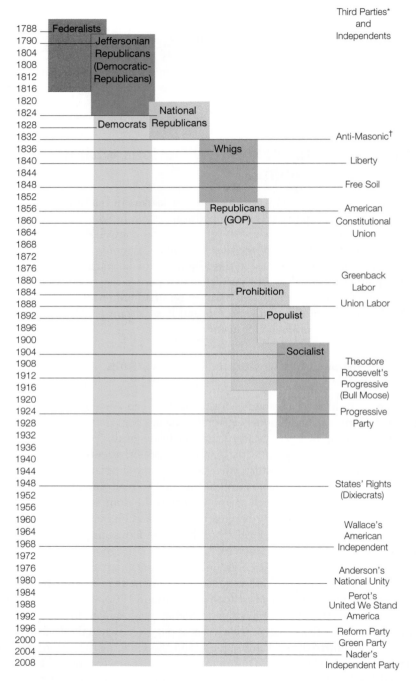

**FIGURE 7.1 How the Party System Evolved**

| | | | Third Parties* and Independents |
|---|---|---|---|
| 1788 | Federalists | | |
| 1790 | Jeffersonian | | |
| 1804 | Republicans | | |
| 1808 | (Democratic- | | |
| 1812 | Republicans) | | |
| 1816 | | | |
| 1820 | | | |
| 1824 | | National | |
| 1828 | Democrats | Republicans | |
| 1832 | | | Anti-Masonic† |
| 1836 | | Whigs | |
| 1840 | | | Liberty |
| 1844 | | | |
| 1848 | | | Free Soil |
| 1852 | | | |
| 1856 | | Republicans | American |
| 1860 | | (GOP) | Constitutional |
| 1864 | | | Union |
| 1868 | | | |
| 1872 | | | |
| 1876 | | | |
| 1880 | | | Greenback |
| 1884 | | Prohibition | Labor |
| 1888 | | | Union Labor |
| 1892 | | Populist | |
| 1896 | | | |
| 1900 | | | |
| 1904 | | Socialist | |
| 1908 | | | Theodore |
| 1912 | | | Roosevelt's |
| 1916 | | | Progressive |
| 1920 | | | (Bull Moose) |
| 1924 | | | Progressive |
| 1928 | | | Party |
| 1932 | | | |
| 1936 | | | |
| 1940 | | | |
| 1944 | | | |
| 1948 | | | States' Rights |
| 1952 | | | (Dixiecrats) |
| 1956 | | | |
| 1960 | | | Wallace's |
| 1964 | | | American |
| 1968 | | | Independent |
| 1972 | | | |
| 1976 | | | Anderson's |
| 1980 | | | National Unity |
| 1984 | | | Perot's |
| 1988 | | | United We Stand |
| 1992 | | | America |
| 1996 | | | Reform Party |
| 2000 | | | Green Party |
| 2004 | | | Nader's |
| 2008 | | | Independent Party |

*Or in some cases, fourth parties; most of these parties lasted through only one term.
†The Anti-Masonics had the distinction of being not only the first third party, but also the first party to hold a national nominating convention and the first to announce a party platform.

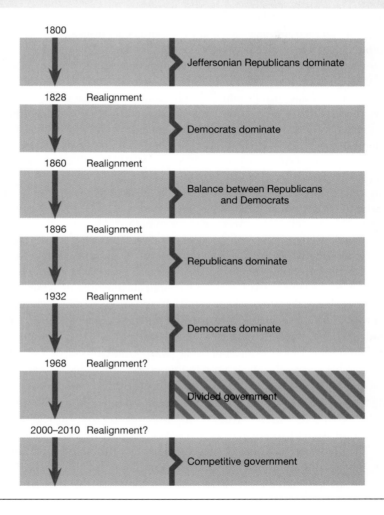

**FIGURE 7.2 Electoral Realignments**

Political scientists disagree over whether an electoral alignment occurred in 1968, because no one party clearly dominated the national government after that election. Although Republicans dominated the federal government between 2000 and 2006, their control fell short of a full-fledged realignment: Republicans never gained a majority of party identifiers, they failed to enact many of their key policy goals, and elections remained extremely close.

1800

Jeffersonian Republicans dominate

1828    Realignment

Democrats dominate

1860    Realignment

Balance between Republicans and Democrats

1896    Realignment

Republicans dominate

1932    Realignment

Democrats dominate

1968    Realignment?

Divided government

2000–2010   Realignment?

Competitive government

Party, which had been one of the nation's two major parties since the 1830s. During the fourth critical period, centered on the election of 1896, the Republicans reasserted their dominance of the national government, which had been weakening since the 1880s. The fifth realignment took place during the period 1932–36, when the Democrats, led by Franklin Delano Roosevelt, took control of the White House and Congress and, despite sporadic interruptions, maintained control of both through the 1960s. Since that time, American party politics has been characterized primarily by **divided government,** wherein the presidency is controlled by one party while the other party controls one or both houses of Congress.

Historically, realignments occur when new issues combined with economic or political crises mobilize new voters and persuade large numbers of voters to reexamine their traditional partisan loyalties and permanently shift their support from one party to another. Each period of realignment represents a turning point in American politics.[3]

**The First Party System: Federalists and Jeffersonian Republicans** The first party system emerged in the 1790s and pitted the Federalists against the Jeffersonian Republicans. The Federalists spoke mainly for New England merchants and supported a program of protective tariffs to encourage manufacturing, assumption of the states' Revolutionary War debts, the creation of a national bank, and resumption of commercial ties with Britain. The Jeffersonians, led by southern agricultural interests, opposed these policies and instead favored free trade, the promotion of agricultural over commercial interests, and friendship with France. Over the years, the Federalists gradually weakened and disappeared altogether after the pro-British sympathies of some Federalist leaders during the War of 1812 led to charges of treason against the party.

From the collapse of the Federalists until the 1830s, America had only one political party, the Jeffersonian Republicans, who gradually came to be known as the Democrats. This period of one-party politics is sometimes known as the Era of Good Feelings to indicate the absence of party competition. Throughout this period, however, there was intense factional conflict within the Democratic Party, particularly between the supporters and opponents of General Andrew Jackson, America's great military hero of the War of 1812. Jackson's opponents united to deny him the presidency in 1824, but Jackson won election in 1828 and again in 1832. Jackson's base of support was in the South and the West, and he generally espoused a program of free trade and policies that would make it easier to borrow money that appealed to those regions. During the 1830s, groups opposing Jackson united to form a new political force—the Whig Party—thus giving rise to the second American party system.

**The Second Party System: Democrats and Whigs** During the 1830s and 1840s, the Democrats and the Whigs built party organizations throughout the nation; they both sought to enlarge their bases of support by expanding the right to vote. They increased the number of eligible voters through the elimination of property restrictions and other barriers to voting—at least voting by white males. Support for the new Whig Party was stronger in the Northeast than in the South and West and stronger among merchants than among small farmers. Hence, in some measure, the Whigs were the successors of the Federalists. Yet conflict between the two parties revolved more around personalities than policies. The Whigs were a diverse group united more by opposition to the Democrats than by agreement on programs. In 1840, the Whigs won their first presidential election under the leadership of General William Henry Harrison, a military hero known as "Old Tippecanoe." The Whig campaign carefully avoided issues—since the party could agree on almost none—and emphasized the personal qualities and heroism of the candidate. The Whigs also invested heavily in campaign rallies and entertainment to win the hearts, if not exactly the minds, of the voters. The 1840 campaign came to be called the "hard cider" campaign because of the practice of using food and especially drink to win votes.

During the late 1840s and early 1850s, conflicts over slavery produced sharp divisions within both the Whig and the Democratic parties despite the efforts of party leaders to develop compromises. By 1856, the Whig Party had all but disintegrated under the strain, and many Whig politicians and voters, along with antislavery Democrats, joined the new Republican Party, which pledged to ban slavery from the western territories. In 1860, the Republicans nominated Abraham Lincoln for the presidency. Lincoln's victory strengthened southern calls for secession from the Union and, soon thereafter, for all-out civil war.

### The Civil War and Post–Civil War Party System: Republicans and Democrats

The secession of the South had stripped the Democratic Party of many of its leaders and supporters, but the Democrats remained politically competitive throughout the war and nearly won the 1864 presidential election against Republican Lincoln because of war weariness on the part of the northern public. With the defeat of the Confederacy in 1865, some congressional Republicans sought to convert the South into a Republican bastion through a program of Reconstruction that enfranchised newly freed slaves. This Reconstruction program collapsed in the 1870s as a result of disagreement within the Republican Party in Congress and violent resistance to Reconstruction by southern whites. With the end of Reconstruction, the former Confederate states regained full membership in the Union and full control of their

*The Republican Party was formed during the 1850s as a coalition of antislavery and other forces. The party's nomination of Abraham Lincoln for the presidency at the 1860 convention sparked the secession of the South and of the Civil War.*

internal affairs. Throughout the South, African Americans were deprived of political rights, including the right to vote, despite post–Civil War constitutional guarantees to the contrary. The post–Civil War South was solidly Democratic in its political affiliation, and with a firm Southern base, the national Democratic Party was able to confront the Republicans on a more or less equal basis. From the end of the Civil War to the 1890s, the Republican Party remained the party of the North, with strong business and middle-class support, while the Democrats were the party of the South, with support also from Northern working-class and immigrant groups.

**The System of 1896: Republicans and Democrats** During the 1890s, profound and rapid social and economic changes led to the emergence of a variety of protest parties, including the Populist Party, which appealed mainly to small farmers but also attracted western mining interests and urban workers as well. In the 1892 presidential election, the Populist Party carried four states and elected governors in eight. In 1896, the Populist Party effectively merged with the Democrats, who nominated William Jennings Bryan, a Democratic senator with pronounced Populist sympathies, for the presidency. The Republicans nominated the conservative senator William McKinley. In the ensuing campaign, northern and midwestern businesses made an all-out effort to defeat what they saw as a radical threat from the Populist-Democratic alliance. When the dust settled, the Republicans had won a resounding victory and confined the Democrats to their smaller bases of support in the South and far West. For the next thirty-six years, the Republicans were the nation's majority party, carrying seven of nine presidential elections and controlling both houses of Congress in fifteen of eighteen contests. The Republican Party of this era was very much the party of American business, advocating low taxes, high tariffs on imports, and a minimum of government regulation. The Democrats were far too weak to offer much opposition.

**The New Deal Party System: Reversal of Fortune** Soon after the Republican presidential candidate Herbert Hoover won the 1928 presidential election, the nation's economy collapsed. The Great Depression, which produced unprecedented economic hardship, stemmed from a variety of causes, but from the perspective of millions of Americans the Republican Party did not do enough to promote economic recovery. In 1932, Americans elected Franklin Delano Roosevelt (FDR) and a solidly Democratic Congress. FDR developed a program for economic recovery that he dubbed the "New Deal." Under the auspices of the New Deal, the size and reach of America's national government increased substantially. The federal government took responsibility for economic management and social welfare to an extent that was unprecedented in American history. Roosevelt designed many of his programs specifically to expand the political base of the Democratic Party. He rebuilt the party around a nucleus of unionized workers, upper-middle-class intellectuals and professionals, southern farmers, Jews, Catholics, and African Americans that revitalized the Democrats. This so-called New Deal coalition made the Democrats the nation's majority party for the next thirty-six years. Republicans groped for a response to the New Deal and often wound up supporting popular New Deal programs such as Social Security in what was sometimes derided as "me too" Republicanism.

The New Deal coalition was severely strained during the 1960s by conflicts over civil rights and the Vietnam War. The struggle over civil rights initially divided northern Democrats who supported the civil rights cause from white southern Democrats who defended the system of racial segregation. The struggle over the Vietnam War further divided the Democrats, with upper-income liberal Democrats strongly opposing the Johnson administration's decision to send U.S. forces to fight in Southeast Asia. These schisms within the Democratic Party provided an opportunity for the GOP, which returned to power in 1968 under the leadership of Richard Nixon.

**The Contemporary American Party System** In the 1960s, conservative Republicans argued that "me-tooism" was a recipe for continual failure and sought to reposition the GOP as a genuine alternative to the Democrats. In 1964, for example, the conservative Republican presidential candidate Barry Goldwater argued in favor of substantially reduced levels of taxation and spending, less government regulation of the economy, and the elimination of many federal social programs. Though Goldwater was defeated by Lyndon Johnson, the ideas he espoused continued to be major themes for the Republican Party. It took Richard Nixon's "southern strategy" to give the GOP the votes it needed to end Democratic dominance of the political process. Nixon appealed strongly to disaffected white southerners, and with the help of the independent candidate and former Alabama governor George Wallace, he sparked the shift of voters that eventually gave the once-hated "party of Lincoln" a strong position in all the states of the former Confederacy. During the 1980s, under the leadership of Ronald Reagan, Republicans added two additional important groups to their coalition. The first were religious conservatives who were offended by Democratic support for abortion and gay rights as well as alleged Democratic disdain for traditional cultural and religious values. The second were working-class whites who were drawn to Reagan's tough approach to foreign policy as well as his positions against affirmative action.

While Republicans built a political base around economic and social conservatives and white southerners, the Democratic Party maintained its support among a majority of unionized workers and upper-middle-class intellectuals and professionals. Democrats also appealed strongly to racial minorities. The 1965 Voting Rights Act had greatly increased black voter participation in the South and helped the Democratic Party retain some House and Senate seats in southern states. And whereas the GOP appealed to social conservatives, the Democrats appealed strongly to Americans concerned with abortion rights, gay rights, feminism, environmentalism, and other progressive social causes.

In 2008, Democrats sought to reach beyond their base by appealing to moderate voters in states that had once been Republican strongholds. After the 2008 elections, Democrats controlled the Congress as well as the presidency for the first time since 1995. Obama's post-partisan rhetoric of "one America" signaled the party's efforts to move beyond the social cleavages that had dominated politics since the 1960s. However, ongoing partisan differences in Congress signaled that intense party conflict would continue to characterize American politics.

## American Third Parties Have Altered the Shape of the Major Parties

Although the United States is said to possess a two-party system, the country has always had more than two parties. Typically, **third parties** in the United States (parties that organize to compete against the two major American political parties) have represented social and economic interests that, for one reason or another, were not given voice by the two major parties (see Figure 7.1).[4] Such parties have had a good deal of influence on ideas and elections in the United States. The Populists, a party centered in the rural areas of the West and Midwest, and the Progressives, spokespeople for the urban middle classes in the late nineteenth and early twentieth centuries, are the most important examples in the past hundred years. More recently, Ross Perot, who ran in 1992 as an independent and in 1996 as the Reform Party's nominee, impressed voters with his folksy style; he garnered almost 19 percent of the votes cast in the 1992 presidential election. Table 7.1 lists the top presidential candidates in 2008, including the top independent and third-party candidates. The third-party and independent candidates gained no electoral votes for president, and most of them disappeared immediately after the election.

Although the Republican Party was only the third American political party ever to make itself permanent (by replacing the Whigs), other third parties have enjoyed an influence far beyond their electoral size. This was because large parts of their programs were adopted by one or both of the major parties, who sought to appeal to the voters mobilized by the new party and so to expand their own electoral strength. The Democratic Party, for example, became a great deal more liberal when it adopted most of the Progressive program early in the twentieth

### TABLE 7.1

## Parties and Candidates in 2008

In the 2008 presidential election, in addition to the Democratic and Republican nominees, several candidates appeared on the ballot in one or more states.

| CANDIDATE | PARTY | VOTE TOTAL* | PERCENTAGE OF VOTE* |
|---|---|---|---|
| Barack Obama | Democratic | 64,629,649 | 53% |
| John McCain | Republican | 56,887,996 | 46% |
| Ralph Nader | Independent | 667,045 | 0.5% |
| Robert L. Barr, Jr. | Libertarian | 493,987 | 0.4% |
| Charles O. Baldwin | Independent | 177,690 | 0.1% |
| Alan Keyes | Independent | 35,299 | 0% |

*With 99 percent of votes tallied.
SOURCE: http://elections.foxnews.com/tracker.html (accessed 11/6/08).

century. Many socialists felt that President Franklin Roosevelt's New Deal had adopted most of their party's program, including old-age pensions, unemployment compensation, an agricultural marketing program, and laws guaranteeing workers the right to organize into unions.

As many scholars have pointed out, third-party prospects for winning elections are hampered by America's **single-member-district** (an electorate that is allowed to select only one representative from each district; the normal method of representation in the United States) plurality election system. In many other nations, several individuals can be elected to represent each legislative district. This is called a system of **multiple-member districts** (when an electorate selects all candidates at large from the whole district; each voter is given the number of votes equivalent to the number of seats to be filled). With this type of system, the candidates of weaker parties have a better chance of winning at least some seats. For their part, voters are less concerned about wasting ballots and usually more willing to support minor-party candidates.

Reinforcing the effects of the single-member district, the **plurality system** of voting (a type of electoral system in which, to win a seat in the parliament or other representative body, a candidate need only receive the most votes in the election, not necessarily a majority of the votes cast) generally has the effect of setting what could be called a high threshold for victory. To win a plurality race, candidates usually must secure many more votes than they would need under most European systems of **proportional representation** (a multiple-member district system that allows each political party representation in proportion to its percentage of the total vote). For example, to win an American plurality election in a single-member district where there are only two candidates, a politician must win more than 50 percent of the votes cast. To win a seat from a European multiple-member district under proportional rules, a candidate may need to win only 15 or 20 percent of the votes cast because seats are apportioned according to the percentage of votes received, meaning that a party's candidates need not come in first to win seats. This high American threshold (meaning that candidates in American elections must come in first to win elections) discourages minor parties and encourages the various political factions that might otherwise form minor parties to minimize their differences and remain within the major-party coalitions.[5]

## Group Affiliations Are Based on Voters' Psychological Ties to One of the Parties

The Democratic and Republican parties are America's only national parties made up of millions of rank-and-file members who develop **party identification** (an individual voter's psychological ties to one party or another) with one of the political parties. An examination of changes in party loyalty among voters, as seen in Figure 7.3, would seem to show that Americans, on the whole, are less loyal to a political party today, whether Republican or Democrat, than they were in the 1950s and 1960s. The trends reflected in this graph help explain why many believe that party loyalties, and political parties themselves, have suffered a "decline" since the 1970s. In a formal sense, this would seem to be true; however, it is still true that more Americans at present admit to a party loyalty than identify them-

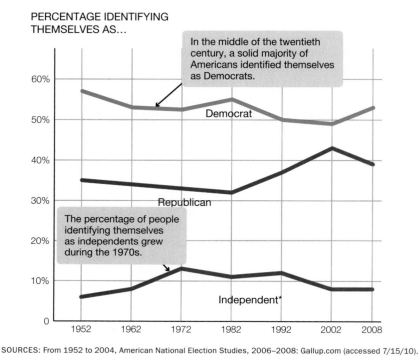

**FIGURE 7.3** Americans' Party Identification, 1952–2008

Over time, the Democrats lost strength as more Americans identiied themselves as Republicans and independents. However, the percent identifying as Democrats has grown in recent years. Why do you think the percentage of people identifying them-selves as independents grew during the 1970s?

PERCENTAGE IDENTIFYING THEMSELVES AS...

In the middle of the twentieth century, a solid majority of Americans identified themselves as Democrats.

Democrat

Republican

The percentage of people identifying themselves as independents grew during the 1970s.

Independent*

1952    1962    1972    1982    1992    2002    2008

SOURCES: From 1952 to 2004, American National Election Studies, 2006–2008: Gallup.com (accessed 7/15/10).

selves as independent. More important, though, is the fact that many people who now identify themselves as independents actually vote pretty consistently with one political party or the other (something that was less true decades ago). And as this chapter discusses, political parties continue to be essential to the electoral process. Moreover, those who support one party or the other consist of different "coalitions," meaning that they have different group characteristics, including race and ethnicity, gender, religion, class, ideology, region, and age.

Figure 7.4 indicates the relationship between party identification and a number of social criteria. Race, religion, and income seem to have the greatest influence on Americans' party affiliations. But note that these are trends, not absolutes. There are black Republicans, southern white Democrats, Jewish Republicans, and even some conservative Democrats. The general party identifications just discussed are

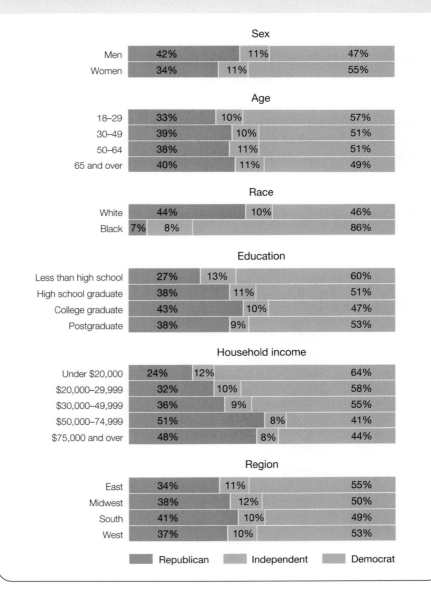

**FIGURE 7.4 Party Identification by Social Groups, 2008**

Party identification varies sharply by income, ideology, and race. Republicans are strongest among whites, higher-income voters, and those who identify themselves a conservatives. Democrats are strongest among those who identify themselves as liberals, lower-income voters and black people. Women are substantially more likely to identify as Democrats than are men. How do younger people differ from older people in their party identification? How does education affect party identification? Are there regional differences in the strength of the two parties?

NOTE: Group percentages are rounded and may equal more than 100 percent in this graph.
SOURCE: Harold W. Stanley and Richard G. Niemi, *Vital Statistics on American Politics*, 2009–2010, 5th ed. (Washington, DC: Congressional Quarterly Press, 2009), p. 108–109.

**Sex**

| | Republican | Independent | Democrat |
|---|---|---|---|
| Men | 42% | 11% | 47% |
| Women | 34% | 11% | 55% |

**Age**

| | Republican | Independent | Democrat |
|---|---|---|---|
| 18–29 | 33% | 10% | 57% |
| 30–49 | 39% | 10% | 51% |
| 50–64 | 38% | 11% | 51% |
| 65 and over | 40% | 11% | 49% |

**Race**

| | Republican | Independent | Democrat |
|---|---|---|---|
| White | 44% | 10% | 46% |
| Black | 7% | 8% | 86% |

**Education**

| | Republican | Independent | Democrat |
|---|---|---|---|
| Less than high school | 27% | 13% | 60% |
| High school graduate | 38% | 11% | 51% |
| College graduate | 43% | 10% | 47% |
| Postgraduate | 38% | 9% | 53% |

**Household income**

| | Republican | Independent | Democrat |
|---|---|---|---|
| Under $20,000 | 24% | 12% | 64% |
| $20,000–29,999 | 32% | 10% | 58% |
| $30,000–49,999 | 36% | 9% | 55% |
| $50,000–74,999 | 51% | 8% | 41% |
| $75,000 and over | 48% | 8% | 44% |

**Region**

| | Republican | Independent | Democrat |
|---|---|---|---|
| East | 34% | 11% | 55% |
| Midwest | 38% | 12% | 50% |
| South | 41% | 10% | 49% |
| West | 37% | 10% | 53% |

Republican   Independent   Democrat

broad tendencies that both reflect and reinforce the issue and policy positions the two parties take in the national and local political arenas.

## ● Voters Decide Based on Party, Issues, and Candidate

Three key factors influence voters' decisions at the polls: party loyalty, issue and policy concerns, and candidate characteristics. The prominence of these three bases of electoral choice varies from contest to contest and from voter to voter.

### Party Loyalty Is Important

Most voters feel a certain sense of identification or kinship with the Democratic or Republican party. This sense of identification is often handed down from parents to children and is reinforced by social and cultural ties. Partisan identification predisposes voters in favor of their party's candidates and against those of the opposing party (see Figure 7.5). At the level of the presidential contest, issues and candidate personalities may become very important, although even here many Americans support presidential candidates only because of party loyalty. But partisanship is more likely to be a factor in the less-visible races, where issues and the candidates

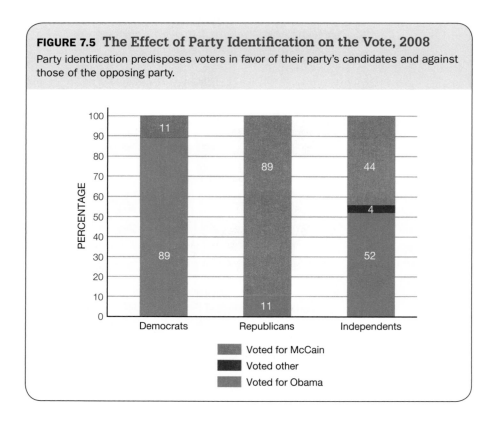

**FIGURE 7.5** The Effect of Party Identification on the Vote, 2008

Party identification predisposes voters in favor of their party's candidates and against those of the opposing party.

are not as well known. State legislative races, for example, are often decided by voters' party ties. Once formed, voters' partisan loyalties seldom change. Voters tend to keep their party affiliations unless some crisis causes them to reexamine the bases of their loyalties and to decide to support a different party. During these relatively infrequent periods of electoral change (see earlier discussion of realignments), millions of voters can change their party ties. For example, at the beginning of the New Deal era, between 1932 and 1936, millions of former Republicans transferred their allegiance to Franklin Roosevelt and the Democrats.

As discussed earlier, after the 1960s, many analysts expressed concern that American parties had become too weak to play their role in organizing political conflict, promoting participation, and developing coherent policy proposals and enacting them into government programs. One prominent scholar even proclaimed in 1969 that we had seen "the end of American party politics."[6] Among the trends that these scholars noted was a decline of partisan attachment within the electorate, a growth in the number of voters identifying as independents, and a rise in so-called split-ticket voting. This trend, sometimes termed "dealignment," seemed to emerge in the late 1960s; it was seen as a product of growing social diversity and educational attainment, factors that made voters less reliant on parties to guide their political decision making. The growth of the mass media, particularly television, also seemed to reduce the role of parties in elections, as television tends to focus on the personalities of individual candidates rather than the "institution" of the party. This period also saw a massive increase in the number and influence of interest groups that, in many ways, seemed to be doing the job that traditional party organizations once fulfilled, such as mobilizing voters and raising money.

Parties also seemed to be becoming increasingly detached from their own candidates and officeholders. The introduction of primaries and open **caucuses** (face to face meetings of voters enrolled in a party who meet to choose a nominee), first for congressional candidates and later, in 1972, for presidential nominations, excluded the party elites that had previously selected candidates. In the view of many, there was now very little the party could do to influence campaigns. Unsurprisingly, once candidates were in office, it seemed that political parties had little influence over their members.

More recently, parties appear to have grown stronger. There is solid evidence suggesting a high level of ideological polarization along party lines in Congress, with growing levels of party unity in roll-call voting. Since the mid-1970s, the power of the party leadership within Congress has also grown significantly, with party leaders now more able to remove "wayward" committee chairs and members. In elections, parties have become more active again and are taking on a new, important role in recruiting candidates, coordinating campaigns, mobilizing voters, and raising money.[7] While many ordinary voters have not polarized as much as have members of Congress, a large number of the most active voters have developed stronger partisan attachments.[8]

There is an old saying that politics is the art of compromise, but politics is more than that. It is also the challenge of making choices. Parties help to crystallize a world of possible government actions into a set of distinct choices. In so doing, they make it easier for ordinary citizens to understand politics, evaluate candidates, and make their own choices.

## Issues Can Shape an Election

Issues and policy preferences are a second factor influencing voters' choices at the polls. Voters may cast their ballots for the candidate whose position on economic issues they believe to be closest to their own. Similarly, they may select the candidate who has what they believe to be the best record on foreign policy. Issues are more important in some races than others. If candidates actually "take issue" with one another—that is, articulate and publicize very different positions on important public questions—then voters are more likely to be able to identify and act on whatever policy preferences they may have. The 2008 presidential race proved to be one where issues played an important role, and the candidates differed significantly in their issue stands. Republican nominee John McCain sought to portray himself as a "maverick" who had disagreed with President George Bush on a variety of issues. For his part, Democrat Barack Obama sought to portray himself as offering alternatives on issues including the war in Iraq, the economy, health care, immigration, civil liberties, the environment, and global climate change. In the end, voters expressed their unhappiness with the state of the economy in 2008 by supporting the Democratic nominee. In 2010, the economy was again a focal issue, which this time led more voters to support Republicans, turning dozens of Democrats out of office.

The ability of voters to make choices on the basis of issue or policy preferences is diminished, however, if competing candidates do not differ substantially or do not focus their campaigns on policy matters. Very often, candidates deliberately take the safe course and emphasize issues that will not be offensive to any voters. Thus, candidates often stress their opposition to corruption, crime, and inflation, since few voters favor these things.

## Candidate Characteristics Are More Important in the Media Age

Candidates' personal attributes always influence voters' decisions. The more important candidate characteristics that affect voters' choices include race, ethnicity, religion, gender, geography, and social background. In general, voters prefer candidates who are closer to themselves in terms of these categories; voters presume that such candidates are likely to have views and perspectives close to their own. This is why, for many years, politicians sought to "balance the ticket," making certain that their party's ticket included members of as many important groups as possible.

Just as candidates' personal characteristics may attract some voters, they may repel others. Many voters are prejudiced against candidates of certain ethnic, racial, or religious groups. And for many years voters were reluctant to support the candidacies of women, although this appears to be changing. Indeed, the fact that in 2008 the Democratic candidate was a black man and the Republican vice-presidential candidate a woman indicates the ongoing collapse of previously rigid political barriers.

Voters also pay attention to candidates' personality characteristics, such as "decisiveness," "honesty," and "vigor." In recent years, integrity has become a key election issue. In 2008, Republicans frequently questioned Barack Obama's character, pointing to his association with 1960s radical William Ayers and with the outspoken black minister Jeremiah Wright. Democrats, for their part, attacked

Republican vice-presidential candidate Sarah Palin for alleged abuses of power in Alaska. However, voters seemed less concerned with these matters than with the ability of the candidates to deal with the nation's economic woes. In hard times, the electorate tends to become impatient with partisan mudslinging.

## Voter Turnout in America Is Low

The right to vote, or **suffrage** (also called franchise), can serve as an important source of protection for groups in American society. The passage of the 1965 Voting Rights Act, for example, enfranchised millions of African Americans in the South, paving the way for election of thousands of new black public officials at the local, state, and national levels and ensuring that white politicians could no longer ignore the views and needs of African Americans. It is therefore ironic that many Americans choose not to vote.

Although the United States has developed a system of universal suffrage, the percentage of eligible individuals who actually vote in America, or **turnout,** is very low. For example, in the 1996 presidential election only 49 percent of eligible voters cast ballots, the lowest percentage of voter participation in a presidential election in more than seventy years. In 2004 and 2008, massive efforts to bring out the vote caused voter turnout to rise to about 60 percent in 2004 and nearly 62 percent in 2008 (see Figure 7.6). Turnout in state and local races that do not coincide with national contests is typically even lower. In European countries, by contrast, national voter turnout is usually between 70 and 90 percent.[9]

The difference between American and European levels of turnout has much to do with complex election regulations, including registration rules, and party strength (see Figure 7.7). In the United States, individuals who are eligible to vote must register with the state election board before they are actually allowed to vote. Registration requirements particularly depress the participation of those with little education and low incomes because registration requires a greater degree of political involvement and interest than does the act of voting itself. To vote, a person need be concerned only with the particular election campaign at hand. Requiring individuals to register before the next election forces them to make a decision to participate on the basis of an abstract interest in the electoral process rather than a simple concern with a specific campaign. Such an abstract interest in electoral politics is largely a product of education and age. Those with relatively little education may become interested in political events once the issues of a particular campaign become salient, but by that time it may be too late to register. Young people tend to assign a low priority to registration even if they are well educated. As a result, personal registration requirements not only diminish the size of the electorate but also tend to create an electorate that is, on average, better educated, higher in income and social status, and composed of fewer young people, African Americans, and other minorities than the citizenry as a whole.

Over the years, voter registration restrictions have been relaxed some to make registration easier. In most states, an eligible individual may register to vote simply by mailing a postcard to the state election board. In 1993, Congress approved and President Clinton signed the Motor Voter bill to ease voter registration by allowing individuals to register when they apply for driver's licenses, as well as in public

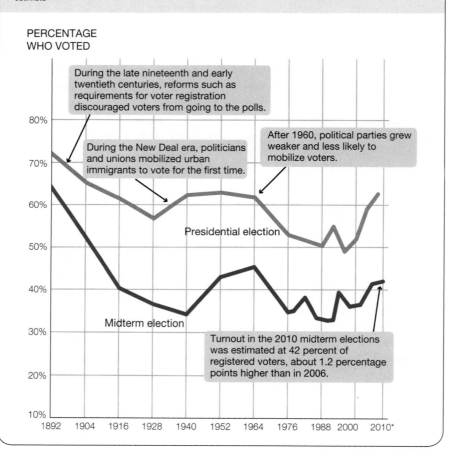

**FIGURE 7.6 Voter Turnout in Presidential and Midterm Elections, 1892–2010**

Since the 1800s, participation in elections has declined substantially. One pattern is consistent across time: more Americans tend to vote in presidential election years than in years when only congressional and local elections are held. What are some of the reasons that participation rose and fell during the last century?

SOURCES: Erik Austin and Jerome Clubb, *Political Facts of the United States since 1789* (Columbia University Press, 1986), pp. 378–79; U.S. Census Bureau, www.census.gov/compendia/statab/tables/08s0404.pdf (accessed 4/7/08); Mathew Daly, "Voter turnout increases from last midterm in 2006," *Washington Post*, 11/3/10.
*estimate

PERCENTAGE WHO VOTED

During the late nineteenth and early twentieth centuries, reforms such as requirements for voter registration discouraged voters from going to the polls.

During the New Deal era, politicians and unions mobilized urban immigrants to vote for the first time.

After 1960, political parties grew weaker and less likely to mobilize voters.

Presidential election

Midterm election

Turnout in the 2010 midterm elections was estimated at 42 percent of registered voters, about 1.2 percentage points higher than in 2006.

assistance and military recruitment offices.[10] In most democratic nations, there is typically no registration burden on the individual voter; the government handles voter registration automatically.

In addition to registration, other election regulations that Americans take for granted have an impact on turnout at well. For example, America holds elections during the work week, whereas most other nations hold them on weekends (and election days are treated as holidays), when most people are not working. Many states maintain residency requirements that result in citizens losing their

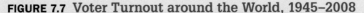

## FIGURE 7.7 Voter Turnout around the World, 1945–2008

Although the United States is the oldest mass democracy, rates of voter turnout are substantially higher in other countries. In many of these countries, election days are holidays and voting is compulsory. Do you think that either of these reforms would increase voting in the United States?

NOTE: Average between 1945 and 2008.
SOURCE: International Institute of Democracy and Electoral Assistance.

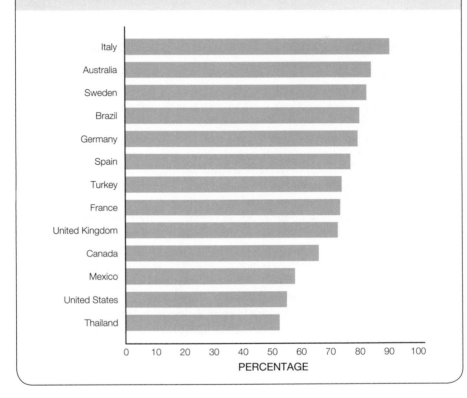

registration if they move their residences even short distances. Most states purge their voter registration rolls of voters who fail to vote for a given period of time. Americans hold many different elections, often at staggered times, such as primary elections and elections for local offices and school budget votes, rather than consolidating elections at a single time. Finally, some have charged that campaign tactics aimed at suppressing voter turnout among voters likely to vote for an opposing candidate or party (tactics said to be aimed at especially vulnerable groups like students, minority communities, and senior citizens) have driven down overall voter participation. While such tactics have been employed in recent elections, it is unclear whether they have produced measurable drops in turnout.

The second factor explaining low rates of voter turnout in the United States is the weakness of the American party system. During the nineteenth century, American political party machines employed hundreds of thousands of workers to organize and mobilize voters and bring them to the polls. The result was an extremely high rate of turnout, typically more than 90 percent of eligible voters.[11] But political party machines began to decline in strength in the early twentieth century and have now largely disappeared. Without party workers to encourage them to go to the polls and even to bring them there if necessary, many eligible voters will not participate. In the absence of strong parties, participation rates drop the most among poorer and less-educated citizens.

## ● The Electoral Process Has Many Levels and Rules

These types of elections are held broadly in the United States: primary elections, general elections, and runoff elections.

**Primary elections** are elections used to select each party's candidates for the general election. In the case of local and statewide offices, the winners of primary elections face one another as their parties' nominees in the general election. At the presidential level, however, primary elections are indirect because they are used to select state delegates to the national nominating conventions, at which the major party presidential candidates are chosen (see Figure 7.8 for a timeline of this process). The United States is one of the only nations in the world to use primary elections. In most countries, nominations are controlled by party officials, as they once were here. The primary system was introduced at the turn of the century by Progressive reformers who hoped to weaken the power of party leaders by taking candidate nominations out of their hands.

Under the law of most states, only registered members of a political party may vote in a primary election to select that party's candidates. This is called a **closed primary.** Other states allow all registered voters to decide on the day of the primary in which party's primary they will participate. This is called an **open primary.**

The primary is followed by the general election—the decisive electoral contest. The winner of the general election is elected to office for a specified term. In some states, however, mainly in the Southeast, if no candidate wins an absolute majority in the primary, a runoff election is held before the general election. This situation is most likely to arise if there are more than two candidates, none of whom receives a majority of the votes cast. A runoff election is held between the two candidates who received the largest number of votes.

Twenty-four states also provide for referendum voting. The **referendum** process is the practice of referring a measure proposed or passed by a legislature to the vote of the electorate for approval or rejection. In recent years, voters in several states have voted to set limits on tax rates, to block state and local spending proposals, and to prohibit social services for illegal immigrants. Unlike an election between candidates running for office, the referendum is an institution of direct democracy; it allows voters to govern directly without intervention by government officials. The validity of referenda results, however, is subject to judicial action. If a court finds that a referendum outcome violates the state or national constitution, it can overturn the result. This happened in the case of a 1995 California referendum curtailing social services to illegal aliens.[12]

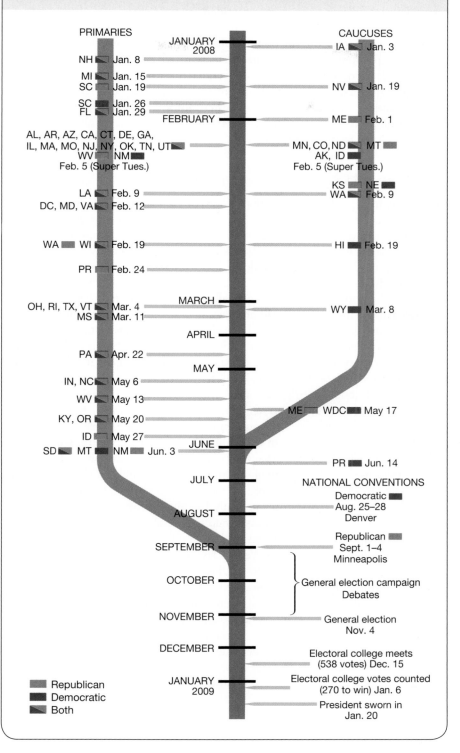

**FIGURE 7.8** The 2008 Presidential Election Season

The presidential election season is a marathon for the candidates.

PRIMARIES

CAUCUSES

JANUARY 2008

IA — Jan. 3

NH — Jan. 8

MI — Jan. 15
SC — Jan. 19

NV — Jan. 19

SC — Jan. 26
FL — Jan. 29

FEBRUARY

ME — Feb. 1

AL, AR, AZ, CA, CT, DE, GA,
IL, MA, MO, NJ, NY, OK, TN, UT
WV   NM
Feb. 5 (Super Tues.)

MN, CO, ND   MT
AK, ID
Feb. 5 (Super Tues.)

KS   NE
WA   Feb. 9

LA — Feb. 9
DC, MD, VA — Feb. 12

WA   WI — Feb. 19

HI — Feb. 19

PR — Feb. 24

MARCH

OH, RI, TX, VT — Mar. 4
MS — Mar. 11

WY — Mar. 8

APRIL

PA — Apr. 22

MAY

IN, NC — May 6

WV — May 13

KY, OR — May 20

ID — May 27

ME   WDC — May 17

SD   MT   NM — Jun. 3

JUNE

PR — Jun. 14

JULY

NATIONAL CONVENTIONS

Democratic
Aug. 25–28
Denver

AUGUST

Republican
Sept. 1–4
Minneapolis

SEPTEMBER

General election campaign
Debates

OCTOBER

NOVEMBER

General election
Nov. 4

DECEMBER

Electoral college meets
(538 votes) Dec. 15

JANUARY 2009

Electoral college votes counted
(270 to win) Jan. 6

President sworn in
Jan. 20

Republican
Democratic
Both

Eighteen states also have legal provisions for **recall** elections. The recall is an electoral device introduced by turn-of-the-century Populists that allows voters to remove public officials from office by popular vote prior to the expiration of their terms. Federal officials, such as the president and members of Congress, are not subject to recall. Generally, a recall effort begins with a petition campaign. For example, in California, the site of a tumultuous recall battle in 2003, if 12 percent of those who voted in the last general election sign petitions demanding a special recall election, the state board of elections must schedule one. Such petition campaigns are relatively common, but most fail to garner enough signatures to bring the matter to a statewide vote. In the California case, however, a conservative Republican member of Congress, Darrell Issa, led a successful effort to recall Governor Gray Davis, a Democrat.

## The Electoral College Still Organizes Presidential Elections

In the early history of popular voting, nations often made use of indirect elections. In these elections, voters would choose the members of an intermediate body. These members would, in turn, select public officials. The assumption underlying such processes was that ordinary citizens were not really qualified to choose their leaders and could not be trusted to do so directly. The last vestige of this procedure in America is the **electoral college,** the presidential electors from each state who meet after the popular election to cast ballots for president and vice president.

When Americans go to the polls on Election Day, they are technically not voting directly for presidential candidates. Instead, voters within each state are choosing among slates of electors selected by each state's party leadership and pledged, if elected, to support that party's presidential candidate. In each state except Maine and Nebraska, the slate that wins casts all the state's electoral votes for its party's candidate. Each state is entitled to a number of electoral votes equal to the number of the state's senators and representatives combined (although the members of Congress are barred from serving as electors), for a total of 538 electoral votes for the fifty states plus the District of Columbia. Occasionally, an elector will break his or her pledge and vote for the other party's candidate. For example, in 1976, when the Republicans carried the State of Washington, one Republican elector from that state refused to vote for Gerald Ford, the Republican presidential nominee. Many states have now enacted statutes formally binding electors to their pledges, but some constitutional authorities doubt whether such statutes are enforceable.

In each state, the electors whose slate has won proceed to the state's capital on the Monday following the second Wednesday in December and formally cast their ballots. These are sent to Washington, tallied by the Congress in January, and the name of the winner is formally announced. If no candidate were to receive a majority of all electoral votes, the names of the top three candidates would be submitted to the House, where each state would be able to cast one vote. Whether a state's vote would be decided by a majority, plurality, or some other fraction of the state's delegates would be determined under rules established by the House.

In 1800 and 1824, the electoral college failed to produce a majority for any candidate. In the election of 1800, Thomas Jefferson was chosen by the House.

In 1824, John Quincy Adams was selected over Andrew Jackson. Four years later, Jackson came back and soundly defeated Adams.

On all but three occasions since 1824, the electoral vote has simply ratified the nationwide popular vote. Since electoral votes are won on a state-by-state basis, it is mathematically possible for a candidate who receives a nationwide popular plurality to fail to carry states whose electoral votes would add up to a majority. Thus, in 1876, Rutherford B. Hayes was the winner in the electoral college despite receiving fewer popular votes than his rival, Samuel Tilden. In 1888, Grover Cleveland received more popular votes than Benjamin Harrison, but received fewer electoral votes. And in 2000, Al Gore received 540,000 more popular votes nationwide than his opponent, George W. Bush but narrowly lost the electoral college by a mere four electoral votes.

# ● The 2008 and 2010 Elections

The 2008 presidential election was in some ways predictable—voters wanted a change from a very unpopular Republican administration—but in many ways the 2008 race was a groundbreaking departure from politics as usual. In 2008, for the first time in the nation's history, Americans elected an African American to the White House as Senator Barack Obama Illinois led the Democratic Party to a solid electoral victory, securing 53 percent of the popular vote versus Republican candidate Senator John McCain's 46 percent. Obama won a 365–173 majority in the Electoral College (see Figure 7.9).

The Democrats also increased their strength in both houses of Congress in 2008, adding eight seats in the Senate. Democrats gained twenty-five seats in the House of Representatives to win a 256–178 majority in the lower chamber. Because of enormous interest in the campaign, the increasing use of absentee and pre–Election Day voting, and well-financed voter registration drives conducted mainly by Democrats, more than 120 million Americans cast ballots in 2008, a number comparable to the level of turnout reached in 2004. In the 2010 midterm elections, however, the GOP was able to recover much of the ground it had ceded to the Democrats in 2008.

## The 2008 Primaries

The 2008 Democratic and Republican primaries and caucuses to select the parties' candidates for the presidency began January 3 with the Iowa Democratic caucuses. The actual campaigns, of course, began early in 2007 as ambitious politicians started the long process of raising the tens of millions of dollars required to launch a presidential candidacy. On the Republican side, the front-runner was Senator John McCain. Traditional business-oriented Republicans might have preferred Mitt Romney, a successful businessperson and former governor of Massachusetts. Social conservatives supported former Arkansas governor and evangelical minister Mike Huckabee, an articulate politician whose sense of humor made him a successful guest on *Saturday Night Live*. After losing the Iowa caucuses to Huckabee and struggling to

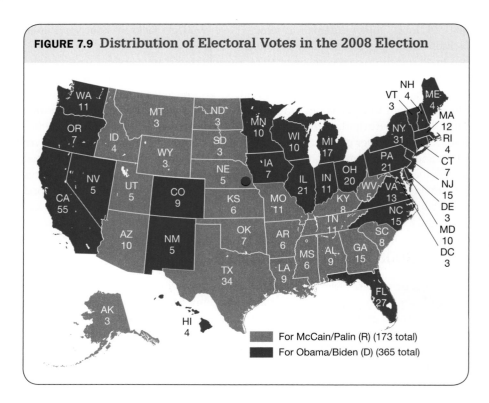

**FIGURE 7.9** Distribution of Electoral Votes in the 2008 Election

For McCain/Palin (R) (173 total)
For Obama/Biden (D) (365 total)

raise money, McCain regained his political and financial footing and had effectively secured the Republican nomination by the beginning of March.

On the Democratic side, the early front-runner for the presidential nomination was New York senator and former first lady Hillary Rodham Clinton. Senator Clinton was famous, her husband was extraordinarily popular among Democrats, and her contacts and position as one of New York's senators meant that she would be able to count on tens of millions of dollars in campaign contributions. Most pundits predicted an easy Clinton victory. Other Democratic contenders included former North Carolina senator and 2004 vice-presidential candidate John Edwards, former New Mexico governor Bill Richardson, Congressman Dennis Kucinich, former Alaska senator Mike Gravel, and senators Joe Biden, Chris Dodd, and Barack Obama. The surprise of the Democratic primary contest was, of course, Senator Barack Obama of Illinois.

Obama was a first-term senator, having arrived in Washington in 2004. Many Democrats' first opportunity to see Obama as a serious contender came in the Democratic debates. Throughout the primaries, Clinton and Obama battled furiously in state after state.

By late spring, it became clear that Obama would be the Democratic presidential nominee. The result was close. Under Democratic rules, 2,118 delegates were needed to win the nomination. In the various primaries and caucuses, Obama had won 1,763 delegates to Clinton's 1,640. This effectively left the decision to the party's 796 "superdelegates," party officials and notables chosen to attend the convention. At the outset, most superdelegates had backed Clinton. As the race wore on, however, sentiment shifted toward Obama. With 438 superdelegates supporting Obama, he could count on 2,201 votes. On June 3, Clinton withdrew and announced that she and her husband would staunchly support Obama in the general election.

## The 2008 General Election

At the August 2008 Democratic national convention, Obama chose Senator Joseph Biden of Delaware as his vice-presidential running mate. Biden, chair of the Senate Foreign Relations Committee, was selected at least partly in response to questions about Obama's scant foreign policy experience. In addition, Biden had working-class roots in Pennsylvania. Democrats hoped that Biden would appeal to the so-called "Joe Six-Pack" voters, blue-collar workers whom the Democrats needed in such battleground states as Ohio and Pennsylvania.

The Republican convention, which opened a few days after the Democratic convention ended, began without much fanfare. Although John McCain won the primary battle, he was not an especially beloved figure among rank-and-file Republicans. Nevertheless, McCain energized Republicans when he chose Sarah Palin, the little-known governor of Alaska, as his vice-presidential running mate and "introduced" her to the GOP base at the convention. Palin, a religious conservative who opposed abortion, excited many Republicans who had been cool toward McCain.

Despite the brief surge of enthusiasm generated by the selection of Palin, the McCain ticket struggled throughout the campaign. McCain had decided to accept public funding for the general election. This would give his campaign some $84 million to spend on organizing, advertising, and voter registration. Obama, on the other hand, decided to forgo general election public funding and was able to step up his Internet and conventional fund-raising, which eventually produced for his primary and general election campaigns about $700 million, giving Obama and the Democrats some $200 million more to spend than was available to McCain and the Republicans. Lack of money was not McCain's only problem. In September 2008, the nation experienced a serious financial crisis that began with a decline in home sales and a wave of mortgage foreclosures. Toward the end of September, the stock market lost more than a third of its value, wiping out trillions of dollars in investments. Since all these events took place while the Republicans controlled the White House, the Democrats were quick to blame the Bush administration's economic policies for the crisis.

Throughout October, Obama led consistently in the national polls, but by single-digit margins. Given the faltering economy, an unpopular president, and the Democrats' enormous financial advantage, the GOP should have been heading for a train wreck of epic proportions, and yet, until late October when Obama's lead increased, McCain trailed only by three- to five-point margins in the polls. Some analysts of opinion data thought the problem was race. These analysts pointed to the so-called Bradley effect, a phantom lead in the polls produced when white voters, reluctant to display overt signs of racism, lie to pollsters about their intentions. In the end, though, racial antipathy did not determine the outcome of the 2008 presidential election. But the election of a black president does not mean the end of racism in America.

# The 2010 Elections

In 2010, after nearly two years in office, President Obama and his Democratic allies in Congress could point to an impressive set of accomplishments, led by a major overhaul of the nation's health care system. Under what came to be known in the press as "Obamacare," tens of millions of previously uninsured Americans would now be eligible for health insurance. Obama and congressional Democrats also overhauled banking regulations aimed at protecting the nation's financial system from a future crisis like the one that nearly brought about a global financial catastrophe in 2008–09. Congress enacted laws to bail out troubled financial institutions, to help impoverished children obtain health insurance, to make it easier for women to sue their employers for wage discrimination, and to reform the Pentagon's weapons procurement policies.

Despite these accomplishments, public opinion polls indicated that the Democrats were likely to lose a large number of congressional seats in the November 2010 midterm elections. The nation's economy remained sluggish. Many Democrats were unsatisfied with Obama's initiatives, feeling that they did not go far enough. Many Republicans were outraged by the Obama agenda, especially the health insurance plan.

The most visible manifestation of conservative Republicans' anger was the Tea Party movement that arose in 2009. Tea Party activists held demonstrations to protest the administration's policies and campaigned vigorously in the 2010 Republican primaries, supporting conservative insurgents who often defeated more established mainstream Republicans. For the first time since the 1930s, more Republicans voted in primaries across the country than Democrats.

Republicans also benefitted from the effects of the Supreme Court's 2010 decision in the case of *Citizens United v. Federal Election Commission*, which opened the way for unlimited corporate funding of political broadcasts calling for the election or defeat or particular candidates.[13] Republicans took the lead in super-PAC fund-raising, forming such groups as American Crossroads. The U.S. Chamber of Commerce also spent heavily on behalf of Republican candidates.[14] This spending allowed Republican challengers to offset the fund-raising advantage that would otherwise have been enjoyed by their incumbent Democratic foes.[15]

On November 2, 2010, America went to the polls and handed the GOP a solid victory. Republicans added over sixty seats in the House of Representatives, taking control of that chamber from the Democrats. In the Senate, Republicans picked up six seats, falling short of the ten needed to take control from the Democrats. Republicans also fared well in elections for state offices, gaining majorities in nineteen state legislative chambers and winning ten gubernatorial seats.

What accounted for the drubbing suffered by the Democrats in 2010? Consistent with the usual pattern seen in midterm elections, many of the voters who had been drawn to the polls by Obama in the 2008 presidential election stayed home in 2010.[16] In addition to the factors mentioned above, Democrats were also defeated by the struggling economy and the perception that their economic policies were not solving the nation's problems.

# ● Money Is the Mother's Milk of Politics

Modern national political campaigns are fueled by enormous amounts of money. In 2008, incumbent candidates in competitive races for the House of Representatives typically spent close to $2 million to hold on to their seats. In Senate races, the average winner spent more than $4 million. In recent years, some Senate contests have cost $25 million or more. In 2010, California Republican gubernatorial candidate Meg Whitman spent more than $160 million, including $140 million of her own money in an ultimately unsuccessful bid for office.

## Campaign Funds Come from Direct Mail, the Rich, PACs, and Parties

In 2008, according to the Center for Responsive Politics, roughly $3 billion was spent by candidates for federal offices. About 10 percent of this total came from political action committees (PACs), and the remainder from individual donors. One of the sources of Barack Obama's fund-raising advantage in the 2008 campaign was his ability to generate 3 million small- and medium-size contributions to his campaign.[17] Another $500 million in 2008 was raised and spent by individuals and advocacy groups—the so-called 527 and 501(c)(4) groups operating outside the structure of the Democratic and Republican campaigns. According to early estimates, as mush as $4 billion was spent by candidates and their supporters during the 2010 midterm elections in the wake of federal court decisions which eliminated many of the previous limits on campaign spending.

*Fund-raising is a major part of political campaigns. Candidates and parties meet with individual donors and leaders of important groups in an effort to amass campaign funds. Here, Governor Mitch Daniels of Indiana speaks at a fund-raiser for the Republican Party.*

**Individual Donors** Politicians spend a great deal of time asking people for money. Money is solicited via direct mail, through the Internet, over the phone, and in numerous face-to-face meetings. Under federal law, individual donors may donate as much as $2,300 per candidate per election, $5,000 per PAC per calendar year (to a maximum of $65,500), $28,500 per national party committee per calendar year, and $10,000 to state and local committees per calendar year (to a maximum of $42,700). Federal rules also impose an overall limit on individual contributors of $108,200 per election cycle. Individuals may also contribute freely to **527 committees** and to 501(c)(4) groups. Donations to 527 groups are a matter of public record, but 501(c)(4)s are not required to disclose their donor lists. Individuals may also attempt to enhance their influence by raising and "bundling" their contributions with those of friends and associates. Many Washington lobbyists curry favor with politicians through vigorous bundling efforts.

**Political Action Committees** Political action committees (PACs) are organizations established by corporations, labor unions, or interest groups to channel the contributions of their members into political campaigns. Under the terms of the 1971 Federal Elections Campaign Act, which governs campaign finance in the United States, PACs are permitted to make larger contributions to any given candidate than individuals are allowed to make. As noted above, individuals cannot donate more than $2,300 to any single candidate, but a PAC may donate as much as $5,000 to each candidate. Moreover, allied or related PACs often coordinate their campaign contributions, greatly increasing the amount of money a candidate actually receives from the same interest group. More than 4,500 PACs are registered with the Federal Election Commission, which oversees campaign finance practices in the United States. Nearly two-thirds of all PACs represent corporations, trade associations, and other business and professional groups. Alliances of bankers, lawyers, doctors, and merchants all sponsor PACs. One example of a PAC is the National Beer Wholesalers' Association PAC, which for many years was known as "SixPAC." Labor unions also sponsor PACs, as do ideological, public interest, and nonprofit groups. The National Rifle Association sponsors a PAC, as does the Sierra Club. Many congressional and party leaders have established PACs, known as leadership PACs, to provide funding for their political allies.

**The Candidates** On the basis of the Supreme Court's 1976 decision in *Buckley v. Valeo*, the right of individuals to spend their *own* money to campaign for office is a constitutionally protected matter of free speech and is not subject to limitation.[18] Thus, extremely wealthy candidates often contribute millions of dollars to their own campaigns. Jon Corzine, for example, spent approximately $60 million of his own funds in a successful bid for the U.S. Senate from New Jersey in 2000. New York City mayor and billionaire businessman Michael Bloomberg spent over $75 million in each of his three successful elections, in 2001, 2005, and 2009.

**Independent Spending—527, 501(c)(4), and Super PAC Committees** Committees known as 527s and 501(c)(4)s are independent groups that are not covered by the campaign-spending restrictions imposed in 2002 by the Bipartisan Campaign Reform Act (BCRA). These groups, named for the sections of the tax code under which they are organized, can raise and spend unlimited amounts on political advocacy so long as their efforts are not coordinated with those of any candidate's campaign. A 527 is a group established specifically for the purpose of political advocacy, whereas a 501(c)(4) is a nonprofit group such as an environmental or other public interest group that also engages in advocacy. A 501(c)(4) may not spend more than half its revenues for political purposes, but many political activists favor this mode of organization. Unlike a 527, a 501(c)(4) is not required to disclose where it gets its funds or exactly what it does with them. As a result, it has become a common practice for wealthy and corporate donors to route campaign contributions far in excess of the legal limits through 501s. The donor makes a legal contribution to the 501, which keeps a cut and donates the remainder of the money to a designated "grassroots" campaign on behalf of the politician. In the 2008 national elections the top 527s were mainly, but not exclusively, supportive of the Democrats. These included the Service Employees International Union, America Votes, EMILY's List, and Citizens United. A new form of independent group, the independent expenditure committee or "Super PAC", came about as a result of an FEC ruling that the Supreme Court's decision in *Citizens United v. FEC* permitted individuals and organizations to form committees that could raise unlimited amounts of money to run advertising for and against candidates so long as their efforts were not coordinated with those of the candidates. Super PACs played an important role in the 2010 midterm elections.

**Public Funding** The Federal Election Campaign Act also provides for public funding of presidential campaigns. As they seek a major party presidential nomination, candidates become eligible for public funds by raising at least $5,000 in individual contributions of $250 or less in each of twenty states. Candidates who reach this threshold may apply for federal funds to match, on a dollar-for-dollar basis, all individual contributions of $250 or less that they receive. Currently, candidates who accept matching funds may spend no more than $42 million, including matching funds, in their presidential primary campaigns. The funds are drawn from the Presidential Election Campaign Fund. Taxpayers can contribute $3 to this fund, at no additional cost to themselves, by checking a box on the first page of their federal income tax returns. Major party presidential candidates receive a lump sum (currently nearly $85 million) during the summer prior to the general election. They must meet all their general expenses from this money. Third-party candidates are eligible for public funding only if they received at least 5 percent of the vote in the previous presidential race. This stipulation effectively blocks preelection funding for third-party or independent candidates, although a third party that wins more than 5 percent of the vote can receive public funding after the election. Under current law, no candidate is required to accept public funding for either the nominating races or the general presidential election. Candidates who do not accept public funding are not affect by any expenditure limits. In 2008, John McCain accepted public funding for the general election campaign, receiving $84 million, but Barack Obama declined, choosing to rely on his own fund-raising prowess. Obama was ultimately able to outspend McCain by a wide margin. As a result, many observers believe that the 2008 race may be the last time that a major-party candidate will forgo his or her own fund-raising in favor of public funding. Candidates who

# Become a Voter and More

If you are a citizen and eighteen years old, you are eligible to vote in all federal, state, and local elections. In most states, however, you must register to vote approximately thirty days before Election Day. A growing number of states, including Maine, Minnesota, Wisconsin, Idaho, New Hampshire, Wyoming, Iowa, and Montana, allow for Election Day registration. This means you can show up at the polls and register on the spot. In general, registration is fairly simple, but it does require a bit of time and effort.

- Register. The easiest method is to use several online resources to get you started. Various organizations such as the League of Women Voters (www.lwv.org), Rock the Vote (www.rockthevote.org), or the National Association of Secretaries of State (www.canivote.org) allow you to see the voter registration guidelines particular to your state. Most states require individuals to print out and complete a voter registration form that you must then mail to your local registrar's office, although some states ask that you complete a request for an official voter registration form that they mail to you.

- Request an absentee ballot. If you go to college away from home, you can choose to register to vote at school or at your "home" address. If you choose to register at your home address, you will most likely have to vote absentee, which will require an additional request for an absentee ballot. The League of Women Voters and the National Association of Secretaries of States Web sites cited above can help you find the right paperwork for your state.

- Know where and when to vote. Once you're registered to vote, you'll want to make sure you know where to go, when the polls are open, and what kind of identification is required of you. The League of Women Voters Web site can answer all of these questions for you.

- Sign up to be an election judge. Local election officials are often desperate for young poll workers to help monitor and manage polling places on Election Day. (The average age of a poll worker is seventy-two!) With a little bit of training, you can participate in this process—and get paid for your work. There is no national program, but the National Association of Secretaries of State Web site has a link that will connect you to your local offices.

- Learn about the candidates and issues. Deciding whom to vote for can be difficult especially when it comes to less publicized state and local races, initiatives and referendums, and the retention of judges. However, with a little time on the Internet, you can learn a lot about the candidates and the ballot questions. Some election offices will send out sample ballots that will allow you to see ahead of time what you will be asked to vote on, including the names of various candidates. Other organizations (such as those listed in the first point above) provide information about candidates' stands on various issues. Or, armed with the candidates' names, you can check out their own Web sites. Often, local newspapers will publish a list of endorsements just prior to the election.

accept public funding may not engage in fund-raising for their own campaigns with one exception: Publicly funded candidates may raise money to meet the costs of complying with federal campaign laws and other legal and accounting costs, up to a total of 5 percent of their campaign expenditures. Hence in 2008, John McCain raised more than $4 million for the "McCain-Palin Compliance Fund."

## The Current System Has Negative Implications for Democracy

The important role played by private funds in American politics affects the balance of power among contending social groups. Politicians need large amounts of money to campaign successfully for major offices. This fact inevitably ties their interests to the interests of the groups and forces that can provide this money. In a nation as large and diverse as the United States, to be sure, campaign contributors represent many different groups and often represent clashing interests. Business groups, labor groups, environmental groups, and pro-choice and right-to-life forces all contribute millions of dollars to political campaigns. Through such PACs as List, women's groups contribute millions of dollars to women running for political office. One set of trade associations may contribute millions to win politicians' support for telecommunications reform, while another set may contribute just as much to block the same reform efforts. Insurance companies may contribute millions of dollars to Democrats to win their support for changes in the health care system, while physicians may contribute equal amounts to prevent the same changes from becoming law.

Despite this diversity of contributors, however, not all interests play a role in financing political campaigns. Only those interests that have a good deal of money to spend can make their interests known in this way. These interests are not monolithic, but they do not completely reflect the diversity of American society. The poor, the destitute, and the downtrodden also live in America and have an interest in the outcome of political campaigns. Who is to speak for them?

# studyguide

## Practice Quiz

 Find a diagnostic Web Quiz with 38 additional questions on the StudySpace Web site: www.wwnorton.com/we-the-people

1. A political party is different from an interest group in that a political party (p. 199)
   a) seeks to control the entire government by electing its members to office and thereby controlling the government's personnel.
   b) seeks to control only limited, very specific functions of government.
   c) is entirely nonprofit.
   d) has a much smaller membership.

2. Which of the following features of the committee system are determined by the whole membership of each house of Congress rather than by decisions within each party? *(p. 202)*
   a) the assignments of individual members to particular committees
   b) the rules defining the jurisdiction of each committee
   c) the ability of individual members to transfer from one committee to another
   d) the use of the seniority system for determining committee chairs

3. The periodic episodes in American history in which an "old" dominant political party is replaced by a "new" dominant political party are called *(p. 203)*
   a) constitutional revolutions.
   b) party turnovers.
   c) presidential elections.
   d) electoral realignments.

4. Historically, when do realignments occur? *(p. 203)*
   a) typically, every twenty years
   b) whenever a minority party takes over Congress
   c) when large numbers of voters permanently shift their support from one party to another
   d) in odd-numbered years

5. Which party was founded as a political expression of the antislavery movement? *(p. 208)*
   a) American Independent
   b) Prohibition
   c) Republican
   d) Democratic

6. A proportional representation electoral system is *(p. 211)*
   a) a multiple-member district system that gives each political party representation in proportion to its percentage of the total vote.
   b) a single-member district system that gives each political party representation in proportion to its percentage of the total vote.
   c) a multiple-member district system where the candidate with the most votes wins the election.

   d) a single-member district system where the candidate with the most votes wins the election.

7. Which of the following best describes the changes in Americans' party identification since 1952? *(p. 212)*
   a) The number of Democrats has declined and been surpassed by the number of Republicans.
   b) The number of Democrats has declined but remained larger than the number of Republicans.
   c) The number of Democrats and Republicans has always been roughly the same.
   d) The number of independents has always been larger than the number of Republicans and Democrats combined.

8. Party loyalty *(p. 214)*
   a) is often handed down from parents to children.
   b) changes frequently.
   c) has little impact on electoral choice.
   d) is mandated in states with closed primaries.

9. An election to nominate a presidential candidate that is open only to registered party members is called *(p. 220)*
   a) a recall.
   b) a referendum.
   c) an open primary.
   d) a closed primary.

10. Which of the following is not an organizer of political action committees (PACs)? *(p. 228)*
    a) corporations
    b) political parties
    c) interest groups
    d) labour unions

11. In *Buckley v. Valeo*, the Supreme Court ruled that *(p. 228)*
    a) PAC donations to campaigns are constitutionally protected.
    b) the right of individuals to spend their own money to campaign is constitutionally protected.
    c) the political system is corrupt.
    d) the Federal Elections Campaign Act is unconstitutional.

12. What is the total amount of money 527s and 501(c)(4)s are allowed to raise and spend on political advocacy? *(p. 229)*
    a) $10,000
    b) $50,000
    c) $100,000
    d) They have no contribution limits.

## Chapter Outline

Find a detailed Chapter Outline on the StudySpace Web site: www.wwnorton.com/we-the-people

## Key Terms

Find Flashcards to help you study these terms on the StudySpace Web site: www.wwnorton.com/we-the-people

**caucus** *(p. 215)* face-to-face meetings of voters enrolled in a party who meet to choose a nominee

**closed primary** *(p. 220)* a primary election in which only registered members of a political party may vote

**divided government** *(p. 206)* the condition in American government wherein the presidency is controlled by one party while the opposing party controls one or both houses of Congress

**electoral college** *(p. 222)* the presidential electors from each state who meet after the popular election to cast ballots for president and vice president

**electoral realignment** *(p. 203)* the point in history when a new party supplants the ruling party, becoming in turn the dominant political force. In the United States, this has tended to occur roughly every thirty years

**527 committee** *(p. 228)* nonprofit independent groups that receive and disburse funds to influence the nomination, election, or defeat of candidates. Named after Section 527 of the Internal Revenue Code, which defines and provides tax-exempt status for nonprofit advocacy groups

**incumbent** *(p. 200)* a candidate running for a position that he or she already holds

**majority party** *(p. 202)* the party that holds the majority of legislative seats in either the House or the Senate

**minority party** *(p. 202)* the party that holds a minority of legislative seats in either the House or the Senate

**multiple-member district** *(p. 211)* an electorate that selects all candidates at large from the whole district; each voter is given the number of votes equivalent to the number of seats to be filled

**nomination** *(p. 201)* the process through which political parties select their candidates for election to public office

**open primary** *(p. 220)* a primary election in which registered voters decide on the day of the primary in which party's primary they will participate

**party identification** *(p. 211)* an individual voter's psychological ties to one party or another

**plurality system** *(p. 211)* a type of electoral system in which, to win a seat in the parliament or other representative body, a candidate need only receive the most votes in the election, not necessarily a majority of the votes cast

**political action committee (PAC)** *(p. 199)* a private group that raises and distributes funds for use in election campaigns

**political parties** *(p. 199)* organized groups that attempt to influence the government by electing their members to important government offices

**primary elections** *(p. 220)* elections used to select a party's candidate for the general election

**proportional representation** *(p. 211)* a multiple-member district system that allows each political party representation in proportion to its percentage of the total vote

**recall** *(p. 222)* removal of a public official by popular vote

**referendum** *(p. 220)* the practice of referring a measure proposed or passed by a legislature to the vote of the electorate for approval or rejection

**single-member district** *(p. 211)* an electorate that is allowed to select only one representative from each district; the normal method of representation in the United States

**suffrage** *(p. 217)* the right to vote; also called franchise

**third parties** *(p. 210)* parties that organize to compete against the two major American political parties

**turnout** *(p. 217)* the percentage of eligible individuals who actually vote

**two-party system** *(p. 203)* a political system in which only two parties have a realistic opportunity to compete effectively for control of the government

# For Further Reading

Abramson Paul, John, Aldrich, and David Rohde. *Change and Continuity in the 2008 Elections.* Washington, D.C.: Congressional Quarterly Press, 2009

Aldrich, John W. *Why Parties? The Origin and Transformation of Political Parties in America.* Chicago: University of Chicago Press, 1995.

Crotty, William J., ed. *Winning the Presidency 2008.* Boulder, CO: Paradigm Publishers, 2009.

Edsall, Thomas Byrne, and Mary D. Edsall. *Chain Reaction: The Impact of Race, Rights, and Taxes on American Politics.* New York: Norton, 1993.

Galvin, Daniel J., *Presidential Party Building: Dwight D. Eisenhower to George W. Bush.* Princeton, NJ: Princeton University Press, 2009.

Ginsberg, Benjamin, and Martin Shefter. *Politics by Other Means: Institutional Conflict and the Declining Significance of Elections in America.* New York: Norton, 1999.

Heilemann, John, and Mark Halperin. *Game Change: Obama and the Clintons, McCain and Palin, and the Race of a Lifetime.* New York: Harper, 2010.

Karol, David. *Party Position Change in American Politics: Coalition Management.* New York: Cambridge University Press, 2009.

Maisel, L. Sandy. *Political Parties and Elections: A Very Short Introduction.* New York: Oxford University Press, 2007.

McCarty, Nolan, Keith Poole, and Howard Rosenthal. *Polarized America: The Dance of Ideology and Unequal Riches.* Cambridge, MA: MIT Press, 2006.

Milkis, Sidney. *Political Parties and Constitutional Government: Remaking American Democracy.* Baltimore, MD: Johns Hopkins Press, 1999.

Milkis, Sidney. *The President and the Parties: The Transformation of the American Party System since the New Deal.* New York: Oxford University Press, 1993.

Patterson, Thomas E. *The Vanishing Voter: Public Involvement in an Age of Uncertainty.* New York: Vintage Books, 2003.

Shefter, Martin. *Political Parties and the State: The American Historical Experience.* Princeton, NJ: Princeton University Press, 1994.

Wayne, Stephen. *Is This Any Way to Run A Democratic Election?* 3rd ed. Washington, D.C.: Congressional Quarterly Press, 2007.

# Recommended Web Sites

**Center for Voting and Democracy**
www.fairvote.org

The Center for Voting and Democracy is dedicated to open access to voting, equal representation, and a voice for all Americans. Read about some of their electoral reform proposals such as runoff elections, proportional representation, and alternatives to the electoral college.

**Democratic Party**
www.dnc.org
**Republican Party**
GOP.com, www.rnc.org

These are the official Web sites for the Democrats and Republicans. Compare the platforms of the two main U.S. parties and see if there's "not a dime's worth of difference" between the two of them.

**Federal Election Commission**
www.fec.gov

The Federal Election Commission (FEC) is an independent government agency that was created in 1975 to administer and enforce the Federal Election Campaign Act (FECA). At the official FEC Web site you can read about the rules and regulations that govern the financing of federal elections and other topics of interest.

**Green Party**
www.gp.org
**Libertarian Party**
www.lp.org
**Reform Party National Committee**
http://reformparty.org

The Green Party, Libertarian Party, and Reform Party are three of the largest and most successful parties in recent years. Find out what these parties are trying to accomplish and why their candidates run when they have little or no chance of winning.

**National Annenberg Election Survey**
http://dev.annenbergpublicpolicycenter.org/ProjectDetails.aspx?myId=1

Individual voters tend to develop psychological ties to one party or another. The National Annenberg Election Survey (NAES) uses survey data to track party identification by state every two years. Find out if your state has more Democratic or Republican identifiers.

**National Archives and Records Adminstration**
www.archives.gov/federal-register/electoral-college/index.html

The U.S. National Archives and Records Administration's Electoral College page is an excellent resource on presidential elections. Find answers to frequently asked questions about our electoral system, read about how electors vote, or try predicting who will win the next presidential election with the electoral college calculator.

**Project Vote Smart**
www.votesmart.org

Project Vote Smart is a nonpartisan site dedicated to providing citizens with information on political candidates and elected officials. Here you can easily view a candidate's biographical information, positions on issues, and voting record, so that you can make an informed choice on Election Day.

Many organized groups, including business groups, try to influence the government. When Congress considered various forms of health care legislation in 2009 and 2010, the health insurance and pharmaceutical industries lobbied for laws that would benefit them. Here, Angela Braly, the CEO of the health insurance company WellPoint, testifies before Congress.

MS. BRALY

# 8

# Interest Groups

**WHAT GOVERNMENT DOES AND WHY IT MATTERS** In 2009 and early 2010, the major item on the congressional agenda was health care reform. President Obama had made health care his main legislative priority, and congressional Democrats promised to craft legislation that would increase the availability and affordability of health care for all Americans. The health care industry is among America's largest and includes insurance companies, hospitals, physicians, pharmaceutical companies, medical device manufacturers, and a host of other people and institutions. Each of these interests was, of course, determined to make certain that it was not hurt by and, indeed, would benefit from the law that might be enacted. To promote their interests, more than three hundred industry groups deployed hundreds of lobbyists and spent over $1 billion on lobbying and campaign contributions in 2009 and 2010. Many of the lobbyists employed by health care groups were former members of Congress and former congressional staffers with close ties to key lawmakers. Indeed, over 350 individuals who had previously worked in congressional leadership offices or for key members of committees involved in writing health legislation, including former members of Congress, lobbied for health care clients in 2008 and 2009.[1]

One important consequence of this lobbying effort was that the health insurance industry was able to secure language in the Senate's 2009 health care bill that would require 30 million Americans to buy health insurance, while blocking a "public option" or expansion of Medicare that might compete with the private insurance companies. Polls suggested that most Americans favored a publicly financed health care option or an expansion of Medicare, but, of course, most Americans do not employ lobbyists.

The case of the health care bill exemplifies the power of interest groups in action. Tens of thousands of organized groups have formed in the United States, ranging from civic associations to huge nationwide groups such as the National Rifle Association (NRA), whose chief cause is opposition to restrictions on gun ownership, or Common Cause, a public-interest group that advocates a variety of liberal political reforms. Despite the array of interest groups in American politics, however, we cannot be sure that all interests are represented equally nor that the results of this group competition are consistent with the common good. The preceding chapter, on political parties and elections, examined another way in which citizens can influence the government. Yet the interest-group process, as we will see, is both more selective and more dynamic: selective because society's "elites"—those with more money, education, and other resources—are better able to exploit the interest-group process to their advantage; more dynamic because of the explosive growth in the sheer number and diversity of interest groups that have proliferated in the last four decades. In this chapter, we will examine the nature and consequences of interest-group politics in the United States.

## key concepts

- Interest groups have become the most vital and effective form of political expression for citizens trying to shape government decisions.

- Interest-group activity does not necessarily equal democracy, since those with more time, information, and resources are more likely to succeed through group action.

- The growth of government programs has spurred the growth of groups.

- Interest groups follow many strategies aside from lobbying to shape government decisions.

# Pluralist and Elitist Views Both Explain the Group Process

The framers of the U.S. Constitution feared the power that could be wielded by organized interests. Yet they believed that interest groups thrived because of liberty—the freedom that all Americans enjoyed to organize and express their views. If the government were given the power to regulate or in any way to forbid efforts by organized interests to interfere in the political process, the government would in effect have the power to suppress liberty. The solution to this dilemma was presented by James Madison:

> Take in a greater variety of parties and interest [and] you make it less probable that a majority of the whole will have a common motive to invade the rights of other citizens . . . . [Hence the advantage] enjoyed by a large over a small republic.[2]

According to the Madisonian theory, a good constitution encourages multitudes of interests so that no single interest, which Madison called a "faction," can ever tyrannize the others. The basic assumption is that competition among interests will produce balance, with all the interests regulating each other.[3] Today, this Madisonian principle of regulation is called **pluralism.** According to pluralist theory, all interests are and should be free to compete for influence in the United States. Moreover, according to a pluralist doctrine, the outcome of this competition is compromise and moderation, since no group is likely to be able to achieve any of its goals without accommodating itself to some of the views of its many competitors.[4]

One criticism of interest-group politics is its class bias in favor of those with greater financial resources. As one critic put it, "The flaw in the pluralist heaven is that the heavenly chorus sings with a strong upper-class accent."[5] When interest-group politics is dominated by the rich and the socially well-positioned, such as top business or government officials, it may take an elitist orientation.

Another assumption of pluralism is that all groups have equal access to the political process and that achieving an outcome favorable to a particular group depends only upon that group's strength and resources, not upon biases inherent in the political system. But, as we shall see, group politics is a political format that has worked and continues to work more to the advantage of some types of interests than others.

# Interest Groups Represent Different Interests but Have Similar Organizations and Membership

An **interest group** is a group of people organized to pursue a common interest or interests, through political participation, toward the ultimate goal of getting favorable public policy decisions from government. This definition of interest groups includes membership organizations but also businesses, corporations, universities,

As long as there is government, there will be interests trying to influence it. During the late 1890s, for instance, business interests fought for protective tariffs from Congress and President McKinley. This 1897 cartoon satirizes their success in capturing Congress.

and other institutions that do not accept members. Individuals form groups in order to increase the chance that their views will be heard and their interests treated favorably by the government. Interest groups are organized to influence governmental decisions.

Interest groups are sometimes referred to as "lobbies." They are also sometimes confused with political action committees. PACs are actually interest groups that focus on influencing elections rather than trying to influence the elected. One final distinction that we should make is that interest groups are also different from political parties: Interest groups tend to concern themselves with the *policies* of government; parties tend to concern themselves with the *personnel* of government.

## What Interests Are Represented?

**Business and Agricultural Groups** Interest groups come in as many shapes and sizes as the interests they represent. When most people think about interest groups, they immediately think of groups with a direct economic interest in governmental actions. These groups are generally supported by groups of producers or manufacturers in a particular economic sector. Examples of this type of group include the National Petroleum Refiners Association and the American Farm Bureau Federation. At the same time that broadly representative groups such as these are active in Washington, specific companies, such as Shell Oil, IBM, and General Motors, may be active on certain issues that are of particular concern to them.

**Labor Groups** Labor organizations are equally active lobbyists. The AFL-CIO, the United Mine Workers, and the Teamsters are all groups that lobby on behalf of organized labor. In recent years, groups have arisen to further the interests of public employees, the most significant among these being the American Federation of State, County, and Municipal Employees (AFSCME).

**Professional Associations** Professional lobbies like the American Bar Association and the American Medical Association have been particularly successful in furthering their members' interests in state and federal legislatures. Financial institutions, represented by organizations such as the American Bankers Association and the National Savings & Loan League, although often less visible than other lobbies, also play an important role in shaping legislative policy.

**Public Interest Groups** Recent years have witnessed the growth of a powerful "public interest" lobby, purporting to represent interests whose concerns are not addressed by traditional lobbies. These groups have been most visible in the consumer protection and environmental policy areas, although public interest groups cover a broad range of issues. The National Resources Defense Council, the Sierra Club, the Union of Concerned Scientists, and Common Cause are all examples of public interest groups.

**Ideological Groups** Closely related to and overlapping public interest groups are ideological groups, organized in support of a particular political or philosophical perspective. People for the American Way, for example, promotes liberal values, whereas the Christian Coalition focuses on conservative social goals, and the National Taxpayers Union campaigns to reduce the size of the federal government.

**Public-Sector Groups** The perceived need for representation on Capitol Hill has generated a public-sector lobby in the past several years, including the National League of Cities and the "research" lobby. The latter group includes think tanks and universities that have an interest in obtaining government funds for research and support, and also includes such institutions as Harvard University, the Brookings Institution, and the American Enterprise Institute. Indeed, universities have expanded their lobbying efforts even as they have reduced faculty positions and course offerings.[6]

## The Organizational Components of Groups Include Money, Offices, and Members

Although there are many interest groups, most share certain key organizational components. These include leadership, money, an agency or office, and members.

First, every group must have a leadership and decision-making structure. For some groups, this structure is very simple. For others, it can be quite elaborate and involve hundreds of local chapters that are melded into a national apparatus. Interest group leadership is, in some respects, analogous to business leadership. Just as in the business world, successful groups often become bureaucratized; the initial entrepreneurial leadership is replaced by a paid professional staff. In the 1960s, for example, Ralph Nader led a loosely organized band of consumer advocates ("Nader's Raiders") in a crusade for product safety that resulted in the enactment of a number of pieces of legislation and numerous regulations, such as the require-

*Public interest groups often advocate for interests that are not addressed by traditional lobbies. For example, in addition to many other activities, the Public Interest Research Group (PIRG) publishes an annual toy safety report to help protect consumers and to encourage policymakers to address problems in this area.*

ment that all new cars be equipped with seat belts. Today, Nader's ragtag band of raiders has been transformed into a well-organized and well-financed phalanx of interlocked groups led by professional staffs.

Second, every interest group must build a financial structure capable of sustaining an organization and funding the group's activities. Most interest groups rely on membership dues and voluntary contributions from sympathizers. Many also sell some ancillary services to members, such as insurance and vacation tours. Third, most groups establish an agency that carries out the group's tasks. This may be a research organization, a public relations office, or a lobbying office in Washington or a state capital.

Finally, all interest groups must attract and keep members. Somehow, groups must persuade individuals to invest the money, time, energy, or effort required to take part in the group's activities. Members play a larger role in some groups than in others. In **membership associations**, group members actually play a substantial role, serving on committees and engaging in projects. In the case of labor unions, members may march on picket lines, and in the case of political or ideological groups, members may participate in demonstrations and protests. In another set of groups, **staff organizations**, a professional staff conducts most of the group's activities; members are called upon only to pay dues and make other contributions. Among well-known public interest groups, some, such as the National Organization for Women (NOW), are membership groups, whereas others, such as Defenders of Wildlife and the Children's Defense Fund, are staff organizations.

**The "Free Rider" Problem** Whether they need individuals to volunteer or merely to write checks, both types of groups need to recruit and retain members. Yet many groups find this task difficult, even when it comes to recruiting members who agree strongly with the group's goals. Why? As economist Mancur Olson explains, the benefits of a group's success are often broadly available and cannot be denied to nonmembers.[7] Such benefits can be called **collective goods.** Following Olson's own example, suppose a number of private property owners live near a mosquito-infested swamp. Each owner wants this swamp cleared. But if one or a few of the owners were to clear the swamp alone, their actions would benefit all the other owners as well, without any effort on the part of those other owners. Each of the inactive owners would be a **free rider** on the efforts of the ones who cleared the swamp, meaning that they enjoy the benefits of collective goods but did not participate in acquiring them. Thus, there is a disincentive for any of the owners to undertake the job alone.

Since the number of concerned owners is small in this particular case, they might eventually be able to organize themselves to share the costs as well as enjoy the benefits of clearing the swamp. But suppose the number of interested people increases. Suppose the common concern is not the neighborhood swamp but polluted air or groundwater involving thousands of residents in a region, or in fact millions of residents in a whole nation. National defense is the most obvious collective good whose benefits are shared by every resident, regardless of the taxes they pay or the support they provide. As the number of involved persons increases, or as the size of the group increases, the free rider phenomenon becomes more of a problem. Individuals do not have much incentive to become active members and supporters of a group that is already working more or less on their behalf.

**Why Join?** Despite the free rider problem, interest groups offer numerous incentives to join. Most importantly, they make various "selective benefits" available only to group members. These benefits can be information-related, material, solidary, or purposive. Table 8.1 gives some examples of the range of benefits in each of these categories.

**Informational benefits** are the most widespread and important category of selective benefits offered to group members. Information is provided through conferences, training programs, and newsletters and other periodicals sent automatically to those who have paid membership dues.

**Material benefits** include anything that can be measured monetarily, such as special services, goods, and even money, provided to members of groups to entice others to join. A broad range of material benefits can be offered by groups to attract members. These benefits often include discount purchasing, shared advertising, and, perhaps most valuable of all, health and retirement insurance.

Another option identified on Table 8.1 is that of **solidary benefits.** These are benefits of an emotional nature that include friendship, "networking" opportunities, and consciousness raising. Many businesspeople join their local chapters of Rotary International, a service organization, in order to meet and develop contacts with other businesspeople in their communities. Another benefit that has become extremely important to many of the newer nonprofit and citizen groups is what has come to be called "consciousness raising." One example of this can be seen in the claims of many women's organizations that active participation conveys to each female member of the organization an enhanced sense of her own value and a stronger ability to advance individual as well as collective rights.

A fourth type of benefit involves the appeal of the purpose of an interest group. These **purposive benefits** emphasize the purpose and accomplishments of the group. For example, people join religious consumer, environmental, or other civic groups to pursue goals important to them.

**TABLE 8.1**

## Selective Benefits of Interest Group Membership

| CATEGORY | BENEFITS |
| --- | --- |
| Informational benefits | Conferences<br>Professional contacts<br>Training programs<br>Publications |
| | Coordination among organizations<br>Research |
| | Legal help<br>Professional codes<br>Collective bargaining |
| Material benefits | Travel packages<br>Insurance<br>Discounts on consumer goods |
| Solidary benefits | Friendship<br>Networking opportunities |
| Purposive benefits | Advocacy<br>Representation before government<br>Participation in public affairs |

SOURCE: Adapted from Jack Walker, Jr., *Mobilizing Interest Groups in America: Patrons, Professions, and Social Movements* (Ann Arbor: University of Michigan Press, 1991), p. 86.

Many of the most successful interest groups of the past twenty years have been citizen groups or public interest groups, whose members are brought together largely around shared ideological goals, including government reform, election and campaign reform, civil rights, economic equality, "family values," or even opposition to government itself.

**AARP and the Benefits of Membership** One group that has been extremely successful in recruiting members and mobilizing them for political action is AARP (formerly called the American Association of Retired Persons). AARP was founded in 1958 as a result of the efforts of a retired California high school principal, Ethel Percy Andrus, to find affordable health insurance for herself and for the thousands of members of the National Retired Teachers Association (NRTA).

Today, AARP is a large and powerful organization with 38 million members and an annual income of $900 million. In addition, the organization receives $90 million in federal grants. Its national headquarters in Washington, D.C., staffed by nearly 3,000 full-time employees, is so large that it has its own zip code. Its monthly periodical, *AARP The Magazine* (formerly called *Modern Maturity*), has a circulation larger than the combined circulations of *Time*, *Newsweek*, and *U.S. News & World Report*.

How did this large organization overcome the free-rider problem and recruit 38 million older people as members? First, no other organization on earth has ever provided more successfully the selective benefits necessary to overcome the free-rider problem. It helps that AARP began as an organization to provide affordable health insurance for aging members rather than as an organization to influence public policy. But that fact only strengthens the argument that members need short-term individual benefits if they are to invest effort in a longer-term and less concrete set of benefits. As AARP evolved into a political interest group, its leadership added more selective benefits for individual members. They provided guidance against consumer fraud, offered low-interest credit cards, evaluated and endorsed products that were deemed of best value to members, and provided auto insurance and a discounted mail-order pharmacy.

## Group Membership Has a Bias

Membership in interest groups is not randomly distributed in the population. People with higher incomes, higher levels of education, and management or professional occupations are much more likely to become members of groups than those who occupy the lower rungs on the socio-economic ladder.[9] Well-educated, upper-income business and professional people are more likely to have the time and the money and to have acquired through the educational process the concerns and skills needed to play a role in a group or association. Moreover, for business and professional people, group membership may provide personal contacts and access to information that can help advance their careers. At the same time, of course, corporate entities—businesses and the like—usually have ample resources to form or participate in groups that seek to advance their causes.

*During the 2003 national debate over Medicare reform and prescription drug pricing, it was the support of senior citizen groups for a new Medicare bill that ultimately allowed the bill to prevail in Congress.*

The result of this elitist tendency is that interest-group politics in the United States tends to have a very pronounced class bias. Certainly, there are many interest groups and political associations that have a working-class or lower-class membership—labor organizations or welfare–rights organizations, for example—but the great majority of interest groups and their members are drawn from the middle and upper-middle classes. In general, the "interests" served by interest groups are the interests of society's "haves." Even when interest groups take opposing positions on issues and policies, the conflicting positions they espouse usually reflect divisions among upper-income strata rather than conflicts between the upper and lower classes.

# ● The Number of Groups Has Increased in the Last Forty Years

Over the past forty years, there has been an enormous increase both in the number of interest groups seeking to play a role in the American political process and in the extent of their influence over that process. This explosion of interest-group activity has three basic origins: first, the expansion of the role of government during this period; second, the coming of age of a new dynamic set of political forces in the United States—forces that have relied heavily on public interest groups to advance their causes; and third, an explosion in the number and political vitality of grassroots and conservative groups.

## The Expansion of Government Has Spurred the Growth of Groups

Modern governments' extensive economic and social programs have powerful politicizing effects, often sparking the organization of new groups and interests. In other words, interest groups often form as the result of, or in response to, government actions, rather than groups pressing the government to take on new responsibilities. Even when national policies are initially responses to the appeals of pressure groups, government involvement in any area can be a powerful stimulus for political organization and action by those whose interests are affected. For example, during the 1970s, expanded federal regulation of the automobile, oil, gas, education, and health care industries impelled each of these interests to increase substantially its efforts to influence the government's behavior. These efforts, in turn, spurred the organization of other groups to either support or oppose the activities of the first.[10] Similarly, federal social programs have occasionally sparked political organization and action on the part of clientele groups seeking to influence the distribution of benefits and, in turn, the organization of groups opposed to the programs or their cost. For example, federal programs and court decisions in such areas as abortion and school prayer were the stimuli for new political action and organization by fundamentalist religious groups. Thus, the expansion of government in recent decades has also stimulated increased group activity and organization.

## The New Politics Movement Focuses on Public Interest Groups

The second factor accounting for the explosion of interest-group activity in recent years has been the emergence of a new set of forces in American politics that can collectively be called the "New Politics" movement.

The **New Politics movement** is made up of upper-middle-class professionals and intellectuals for whom the civil rights and anti–Vietnam War movements of the 1960s were formative experiences, just as the Great Depression and World War II had been for their parents in the 1930s and 1940s. The crusade against racial discrimination and the Vietnam War led these young men and women to see themselves as a political force in opposition to the public policies and politicians associated with the nation's postwar regime. The forces of New Politics strengthened public-interest groups and the years that followed focused their attention on such issues as environmental protection, women's rights, and nuclear disarmament.

Members of the New Politics movement constructed or strengthened public interest groups such as Common Cause, the Sierra Club, the Environmental Defense Fund, Physicians for Social Responsibility, the National Organization for Women, and the various organizations formed by consumer activist Ralph Nader. Through these groups, New Politics forces were able to influence the media, Congress, and even the judiciary and enjoyed a remarkable degree of success during the late 1960s and early 1970s in securing the enactment of policies they favored. New Politics activists also played a major role in securing the enactment of environmental, consumer, and occupational health and safety legislation.

# ● Interest Groups Use Different Strategies to Gain Influence

As we have seen, interest groups work to improve the probability that they and their interests will be heard and treated favorably by the government. The quest for political influence or power takes many forms, but among the most frequently used strategies are lobbying, gaining access to key decision makers, using the courts, mobilizing public opinion, and using electoral politics. These "tactics of influence" do not exhaust all the possibilities, but they paint a broad picture of groups competing for power through the maximum utilization of their resources (see Figure 8.1).

Many groups employ a mix of strategies. For example, environmental groups such as the Sierra Club lobby members of Congress and key congressional staff members, participate in bureaucratic rule making by offering comments and suggestions to agencies on new environmental rules, and bring lawsuits under various environmental acts such as the Endangered Species Act, which authorizes groups and citizens to come to court if they believe the act is being violated. At the same time, the Sierra Club attempts to influence public opinion through media campaigns and to influence electoral politics by supporting candidates who they believe share their environmental views and opposing candidates whom they view as foes of environmentalism.

## Direct Lobbying Combines Education, Persuasion, and Pressure

**Lobbying** is a strategy by which organized interests seek to influence the passage of legislation or other public policy by exerting direct pressure on members of the legislature or others in government. Most Americans tend to think that interest groups exert their influence through direct contact with members of Congress, but lobbying encompasses a wide range of activities that groups engage in with all sorts of government officials and the public as a whole.

Lobbying involves a great deal of activity on the part of someone speaking for an interest. Lobbyists badger and buttonhole legislators, administrators, and committee staff members and bring to their attention facts about pertinent issues and

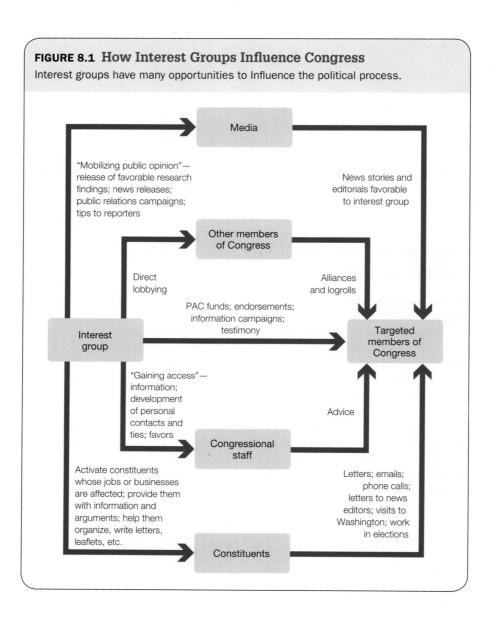

**FIGURE 8.1 How Interest Groups Influence Congress**

Interest groups have many opportunities to Influence the political process.

Media

"Mobilizing public opinion"—release of favorable research findings; news releases; public relations campaigns; tips to reporters

News stories and editorials favorable to interest group

Other members of Congress

Direct lobbying

Alliances and logrolls

PAC funds; endorsements; information campaigns; testimony

Interest group

Targeted members of Congress

"Gaining access"—information; development of personal contacts and ties; favors

Advice

Congressional staff

Activate constituents whose jobs or businesses are affected; provide them with information and arguments; help them organize, write letters, leaflets, etc.

Letters; emails; phone calls; letters to news editors; visits to Washington; work in elections

Constituents

facts or claims about public support of certain issues.[11] Lobbyists can serve a useful purpose in the legislative and administrative processes by providing this kind of information. In 1978, during debate on a bill to expand the requirement for lobbying disclosures, Democratic senators Edward Kennedy of Massachusetts and Dick Clark of Iowa joined with Republican senator Robert Stafford of Vermont to issue the following statement: "Government without lobbying could not function. The flow of information to Congress and to every federal agency is a vital part of our democratic system."[12]

Groups often select lobbyists with a considerable amount of Washington experience. In the days following the September 11, 2001, terrorist attacks, the airline industry mounted a furious lobbying effort to win a multibillion-dollar aid package to rescue the industry. Among the most important lobbyists was Linda Daschle, a lobbyist for American Airlines and wife of the Senate Democratic leader Tom Daschle. In less than two weeks after the attacks, Congress had given the airlines a $15-billion aid package, including $5 billion in direct grants and $10 billion in loan guarantees (to support airline loans from private banks, so that if any airline were unable to pay back a loan, the government would cover it). According to Illinois senator Peter Fitzgerald, the lobbying by the airlines "was masterful. The airline industry made a full-court press to convince Congress that giving them billions in taxpayer cash was the only way to save the republic."[13] A study by the Center for Responsive Politics concluded in 1999 that 129 former members of Congress lobbied the institution where they once worked. Some estimates run even higher. Many former members of the executive branch also pursue lobbying careers, underscoring the value of well-connected and well-financed efforts to influence public policy.

Even when an interest group succeeds at getting its bill passed by Congress and signed by the president, the prospect of full and faithful implementation of that law is not guaranteed. Often, a group and its allies do not pack up and go home as soon as the president turns their lobbied-for new law over to the appropriate agency. On average, 40 percent of interest-group representatives regularly contact both legislative and executive branch organizations, while 13 percent contact only the legislature and 16 percent only the executive branch.[14]

*Interest groups may also try to influence the president's decisions. In 2009, President Obama met with business leaders to discuss how a new health care policy would affect their employees' health insurance plans.*

## Cultivating Access Means Getting the Attention of Decision Makers

Exerting influence on Congress or government agencies by providing them with information about issues, support, and even threats of retaliation requires easy and constant access to decision makers. Lobbyists' extensive access to members of Congress has led to repeated calls for reform. In 2007, congressional Democrats secured the enactment of a new package of ethics rules designed to fulfill their 2006 campaign promise to bring an end to lobbying abuses. The new rules prohibited lobbyists from paying for most meals, trips, parties, and gifts for members of Congress. Lobbyists were also required to disclose the amounts and sources of small campaign contributions they collected from clients and "bundled" into large contributions. And interest groups were required to disclose the funds they used to rally voters to support or oppose legislative proposals. According to the *Washington Post*, however, within a few weeks lobbyists had learned how to circumvent many of the new rules and lobbying firms were as busy as ever.[15]

After the Abramoff scandal, in which a prominent lobbyist pleaded guilty to conspiring to bribe members of Congress, both parties called for reform of the lobbying process. In 2007, Democrats in the House of Representatives passed new ethics rules designed to end lobbying abuses.

Figure 8.2 illustrates an example of one of the most important access patterns in recent American political history: that of the defense industry. Each such pattern, or **iron triangle** (a stable, cooperative relationship that often develops between a congressional committee, an administrative agency, and one or more supportive interest groups), is almost literally a triangular shape, with one point in an executive branch program, another point in a Senate or House legislative committee or subcommittee, and a third point in some highly stable and well-organized interest group. The points in the triangular relationship are mutually supporting; they count as access only if they last over a long period of time. For example, access to a legislative committee or subcommittee requires that at least one of its members supports the interest group in question. This member also must have built up considerable seniority in Congress. An interest cannot feel comfortable about its access to Congress until it has one or more of its "own" people with ten or more years of continuous service on the relevant committee or subcommittee.[16] Similar relationships with more than the three parts found in iron triangles exist, but the iron triangle is the most typical.

## Using the Courts (Litigation) Can Be Highly Effective

Most people think of lobbying as the chief, or only, way interest groups attempt to influence politics. Yet interest groups often turn to lawsuits as a way to change policy, government agency behavior, and the actions of other groups they oppose.

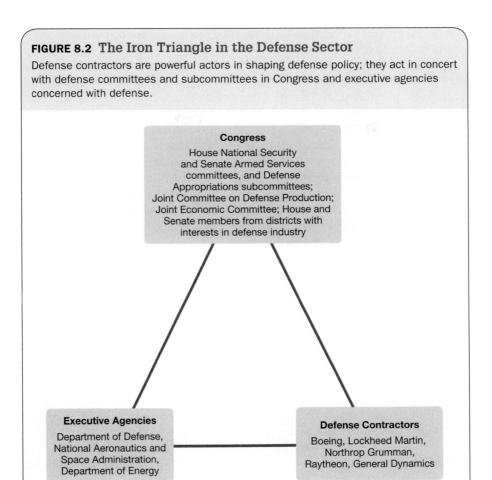

**FIGURE 8.2 The Iron Triangle in the Defense Sector**

Defense contractors are powerful actors in shaping defense policy; they act in concert with defense committees and subcommittees in Congress and executive agencies concerned with defense.

**Congress**

House National Security and Senate Armed Services committees, and Defense Appropriations subcommittees; Joint Committee on Defense Production; Joint Economic Committee; House and Senate members from districts with interests in defense industry

**Executive Agencies**

Department of Defense, National Aeronautics and Space Administration, Department of Energy

**Defense Contractors**

Boeing, Lockheed Martin, Northrop Grumman, Raytheon, General Dynamics

Interest groups can use the courts to affect public policy in at least three ways: (1) by bringing suit directly on behalf of the group itself, (2) by financing suits brought by individuals, and (3) by filing a companion brief as "*amicus curiae*" (literally "friend of the court") to an existing court case.

Among the most significant modern illustrations of the use of the courts as a strategy for political influence are those that accompanied the "sexual revolution" of the 1960s and the emergence of the movement for women's rights.

The 1973 Supreme Court case of *Roe v. Wade*, which made it illegal for states to ban abortions, sparked a controversy that brought conservatives to the fore on a national level.[17] Conservative groups made extensive use of the courts to whittle away the scope of the privacy doctrine. They obtained rulings, for example, that prohibit the use of federal funds to pay for voluntary abortions. And in 1989, right-to-life groups were able to use a strategy of litigation that significantly undermined the *Roe v. Wade* decision, namely in the case of *Webster v. Reproductive Health Services*, which restored the right of states to place restrictions on abortion.[18] The

*Webster* case brought more than three hundred interest groups on both sides of the abortion issue to the Supreme Court's door.

Another extremely significant use of the courts as a strategy for political influence is found in the history of the National Association for the Advancement of Colored People (NAACP). The most important of such court case was, of course, *Brown v. Board of Education of Topeka, Kansas* (1954), in which the U.S. Supreme Court held that legal segregation of the schools was unconstitutional.[19]

Business groups are also frequent users of the courts because of the number of government programs applied to them. Litigation involving large businesses is most mountainous in such areas as taxation, antitrust, interstate transportation, patents, and product quality and standardization. Often a business is brought to litigation against its will by virtue of initiatives taken against it by other businesses or by government agencies. But many individual businesses bring suit themselves in order to influence government policy.

New Politics forces made significant use of the courts during the 1970s and 1980s, and judicial decisions were instrumental in advancing their goals. Facilitated by changes in the rules governing access to the courts, the New Politics agenda was clearly visible in court decisions handed down in several key policy areas. In the environmental policy area, New Politics groups were able to force federal agencies to pay attention to environmental issues, even when the agency was not directly involved in activities related to environmental quality. For example, the Federal Trade Commission (FTC) became very responsive to the demands of New Politics activists during the 1970s and 1980s. The FTC stepped up its activities considerably, litigating a series of claims arising under regulations prohibiting deceptive advertising in cases ranging from false claims for over-the-counter drugs to inflated claims about the nutritional value of children's cereal.

And while feminists and equal rights activists enjoyed enormous success in litigating discrimination claims under the Civil Rights Act of 1964, anti-nuclear power activists succeeded in virtually shutting down the nuclear power industry. Despite significant defeats, challenges to power plant siting and licensing regulations were instrumental in discouraging energy companies from pursuing nuclear projects over the long term.[20]

## Mobilizing Public Opinion Brings Wider Attention to an Issue

Going public is a strategy that attempts to mobilize the widest and most favorable climate of opinion. Many groups consider it imperative to maintain this climate at all times, even when they have no issue to fight about. An increased use of this kind of strategy is usually associated with modern advertising. As early as the 1930s, political analysts were distinguishing between the "old lobby" of direct group representation before Congress and the "new lobby" of public relations professionals addressing the public at large to reach Congress.[21]

**Institutional Advertising** One of the best known ways of going public is the use of **institutional advertising,** which is advertising designed to create a positive image of an organization. A casual scanning of important mass circulation magazines and newspapers provides numerous examples of expensive and well-designed ads by the major oil companies, automobile and steel companies, other large corporations, and trade associations. The ads show how much these organizations are doing for the country, for the protection of the environment, or for the defense of the American way of life. Their purpose is to create and maintain a strongly positive association between the organization and the community at large, in the hope that these favorable feelings can be drawn on as needed for specific political campaigns later on. One increasingly common way that corporations and interest groups have sought to help themselves politically is by adopting aliases in their advertising efforts. For example, the "Partnership to Protect Consumer Credit" is an alias used by a coalition of credit card companies seeking higher interest rates. "Americans for Balanced Energy Choices" is an alias for a coal industry trade group. As is often the case, the names chosen imply that these organizations are citizen-based, grassroots groups instead of front groups for large corporations. A bill rejected by the Senate in 2006 would have required lobby groups to disclose their actual identities, but it was attacked by the industry as a threat to free speech.

**Protests and Demonstrations** Going public is not limited to businesses or to groups of upper-income professionals. Many groups resort to it because they lack the resources, the contacts, or the experience to use other political strategies. The sponsorship of boycotts, sit-ins, mass rallies, and marches by Martin Luther King's Southern Christian Leadership Conference (SCLC) and related organizations in the 1950s and 1960s is one of the most significant and successful cases of going public to create a more favorable climate of opinion by calling attention to abuses. The success of these events inspired similar efforts on the part of women. Organizations such as the National Organization for Women (NOW) used public strategies in their drive for legislation and in their efforts to gain ratification of the Equal Rights Amendment. In 2009, gay rights groups organized mass rallies as part of their effort to eliminate restrictions on military's service and other forms of discrimination based on individuals' sexual preferences. President Obama spoke before gay rights groups to affirm his desire to eliminate the military's "don't ask, don't tell" policy, which discharged military personnel if their sexual orientation became known.

**Grassroots Mobilization** Another form of going public is **grassroots mobilization.** In such a campaign, a lobby group mobilizes its members and their families throughout the country to contact government officials in support of the group's position.

Among the most effective users of the grassroots lobby effort in contemporary American politics is the religious right. Networks of evangelical churches have the capacity to generate hundreds of thousands of letters and phone calls to Congress and the White House. For example, the religious right was outraged when President Clinton announced soon after taking office that he planned to end the military's ban on gay and lesbian soldiers. The Rev. Jerry Falwell, an evangelical leader, called upon viewers of his television program to dial a telephone number that would add their names to a petition urging Clinton to retain the ban on gays in the military. Within a few hours, twenty-four thousand people had called to support the petition.[22] In 2007, a grassroots firm called Grassfire.org led the drive to kill the immigration reform bill supported by President Bush and a number of congressional Democrats that would have legalized the status of many illegal immigrants. Grassfire.org used the Internet and talk radio programs to generate a campaign that yielded 700,000 signatures on petitions opposing the bill. The petitions, along with tens of thousands of phone calls, letters, and emails generated by Grassfire and several other groups, led to the bill's defeat in the U.S. Senate.[23]

Has grassroots campaigning been cynically exploited? More and more people, including leading members of Congress, are becoming quite skeptical of such methods, charging that these are not genuine grassroots campaigns but instead represent "Astroturf lobbying" (a play on the name of an artificial grass used on many sports fields). Such Astroturf campaigns have increased in frequency in recent years as members of Congress have grown more and more skeptical of Washington lobbyists and far more concerned about demonstrations of support for a particular issue by their constituents.

## Groups Often Use Electoral Politics

In addition to attempting to influence members of Congress and other government officials, interest groups also seek to use the electoral process to elect the right legislators in the first place and to ensure that those who are elected will owe them a debt of gratitude for their support. To put matters in perspective, groups invest far more resources in lobbying than in electoral politics. Nevertheless, financial support and campaign activism can be important tools for organized interests.

**Political Action Committees** By far the most common electoral strategy employed by interest groups is that of giving financial support to the parties or to particular candidates. But such support can easily cross the threshold into outright bribery. Therefore, Congress has occasionally made an effort to regulate this strategy. Congress's most recent effort was the Federal Election Campaign Act of 1971 (amended in 1974). This act limits campaign contributions and requires that each candidate or campaign committee itemize the full name and address, occupation, and principal business of each person who contributes more than $200. These provisions have been effective up to a point, considering the rather large number of embarrassments, indictments, resignations, and criminal convictions in the aftermath of the Watergate scandal of the early 1970s.

Reaction to Watergate produced further legislation on campaign finance in 1974 and 1976, but the effect has been to restrict individual rather than interest-group campaign activity. Individuals may now contribute no more than $2,300 (as of 2008) to any candidate for federal office in any primary or general election. A **political action committee** (PAC—a private group that raises and distributes funds for use in election campaigns), however, can contribute $5,000, provided it contributes to at least five different federal candidates each year. Beyond this, the laws permit corporations, unions, and other interest groups to form PACs and to pay the costs of soliciting funds from private citizens for the PACs. In other words, PACs are interest groups, trade associations, unions, corporations, and even some wealthy individuals operating in the electoral system rather than in the interest-group system.

Electoral spending by interest groups has been increasing steadily despite the flurry of reform following Watergate. Table 8.2 presents a dramatic picture of the growth of PACs as the source of campaign contributions. The dollar amounts for each year reveal the growth in electoral spending. The number of PACs has also increased significantly—from 480 in 1972 to more than 5,000 in 2008 (see Figure 8.3). Although the reform legislation of the early and mid-1970s attempted to reduce the influence that special interests have over elections, the effect has been almost the exact opposite. Opportunities for legally influencing campaigns are now widespread.

Given the enormous costs of television commercials, polls, computers, and other elements of the new political technology, most politicians are eager to receive PAC contributions and are at least willing to give a friendly hearing to the needs and interests of contributors. It is probably not the case that most politicians simply sell their votes to the interests that fund their campaigns. But there is considerable evidence to support the contention that interest groups' campaign contributions do influence the overall pattern of political behavior in Congress and in the state legislatures.

Indeed, PACs and campaign contributions provide organized interests with such a useful tool for gaining access to the political process that

## TABLE 8.2

### PAC Spending, 1977–2008

Campaign spending by political action committees has increased tenfold since the late 1970s. Why do interest groups form PACs? Should PAC spending be restricted or would restrictions prevent opposing groups and forces from making their views known in the political arena?

| YEARS | CONTRIBUTIONS |
| --- | --- |
| 1977–78 (est.) | $77,800,000 |
| 1979–80 | 131,153,384 |
| 1981–82 | 190,173,539 |
| 1983–84 | 266,822,476 |
| 1985–86 | 339,954,416 |
| 1987–88 | 364,201,275 |
| 1989–90 | 357,648,557 |
| 1991–92 | 394,785,896 |
| 1993–94 | 388,102,643 |
| 1995–96 | 429,887,819 |
| 1997–98 | 470,830,847 |
| 1999–2000 | 579,358,330 |
| 2001–02 | 685,305,553 |
| 2003–04 | 915,700,000 |
| 2005–06 | 1,086,000,000 |
| 2007–08 | 1,117,000,000 |

SOURCE: Federal Election Commission, www.fec.gov.

calls to abolish PACs have been quite frequent among political reformers. Concern about PACs grew through the 1980s and 1990s, creating a constant drumbeat for reform of federal election laws. Proposals were introduced in Congress on many occasions, perhaps the most celebrated being the McCain-Feingold bill. When it was originally proposed in 1996, the bill was aimed at reducing or eliminating PACs. But, in a stunning about-face, when campaign finance reform was adopted in 2002, it did not restrict PACs in any significant way. Rather, it eliminated unrestricted soft money donations to the national political parties. One consequence of this reform was the creation of a host of new organizations, often directed by former party officials but nominally unaffiliated with the two parties. These organizations are free to raise and spend as much money as they are able. Thus, contemporary reforms may have weakened political parties and strengthened interest groups.

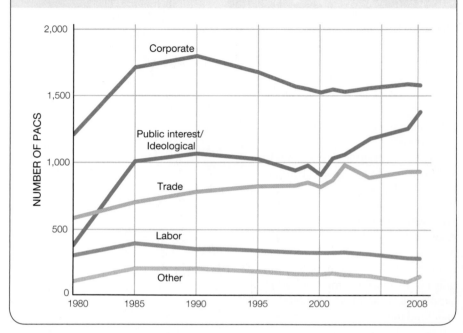

**FIGURE 8.3** Growth of Political Action Committees, 1980–2008

The majority of political action committees represent corporations or trade associations. What accounts for business dominance of PACs? Would America be better off without PACs?

SOURCE: Federal Election Commission, www.fec.gov.

**Campaign Activism** Financial support is not the only way that organized groups seek influence through electoral politics. Sometimes activism can be even more important than campaign contributions. Campaign activism on the part of conservative groups played a very important role in bringing about the Republican capture of both houses of Congress in the 1994 congressional elections. For example, Christian Coalition activists played a role in many races, including ones in which Republican candidates were not overly identified with the religious right. One post-election study suggested that more than 60 percent of the more than six hundred candidates supported by the Christian right were successful in state, local, and congressional races in 1994.[24] The efforts of conservative Republican activists to bring voters to the polls in 1994 is one major reason that turnout among Republicans exceeded Democratic turnout in a midterm election for the first time since 1970. This increased turnout was especially marked in the South, where the Christian Coalition was most active.

**The Initiative** Another political tactic sometimes used by interest groups is sponsorship of ballot initiatives at the state level. The initiative, a device adopted by a number of states around 1900, allows proposed laws to be placed on the general election ballot and submitted directly to the state's voters. This procedure bypasses the state

# GET INVOLVED

# Take an Interest In Interest Groups

The words "interest group" often conjure up images of powerful lobbyists working on behalf of people far removed from yourself and your peers. However, as easy as it is to buy into the conventional wisdom that interest groups are a political force used only by people older and wealthier than you, it's simply not the case.

The following ideas for getting involved will help you think through issues like interest group representation and influence. You don't necessarily need to become an activist yourself to gain a better understanding of what interest groups actually do in our democracy.

- Identify the issues you care the most about in politics today and find out if there are any interest groups out there who advocate on behalf of those issues. You might consider joining one or two in order to show your support. An easy way to learn about relevant issues of the day is to visit the Web site for Campus Activism (www. campusactivism.org) and check out their list of issues and campaigns that are going on around the country to help address them.

- If you find a group for which you feel a close affinity, consider forming a campus chapter. There are a lot of groups that will gladly help students start campus chapters. Some that come to mind include AAUW, formerly the American Association of University Women, (www.aauw. org) and Amnesty International (www. amnesty.org).

- Find out how those who represent you in Congress measure up according to

interest groups. As you'll see when you visit the link to interest group ratings on the Project Vote Smart Web site (www. votesmart.org), interest groups assess how consistently elected officials vote for legislation that's supportive of group interests. You may find a few surprising scores tied to those who represent you in Congress.

- Interest groups often get a bad rap in American politics, mainly because people think they have too much influence over elected officials who end up responding to them more than average voters. These concerns are especially heightened during an election year because people believe that candidates are "bought and sold" by campaign donations from interest groups. Look up the McCain-Feingold Act, which was intended to reduce the influence of interest groups' money in elections. If you are still concerned about the influence of interest groups and think further reform is needed, email your member of Congress, using the contact information at www.house.gov or www. senate.gov.

legislature and governor. The initiative was originally promoted by late-nineteenth-century Populists as a mechanism that would allow the people to govern directly. Populists saw the initiative as an antidote to interest-group influence in the legislative process.

Ironically, many studies have suggested that most initiative campaigns today are actually sponsored by interest groups seeking to circumvent legislative opposition to their goals. In recent years, for example, initiative campaigns have been sponsored by the insurance industry, trial lawyers associations, and tobacco companies.[25] The role of interest groups in initiative campaigns should come as no surprise, since such campaigns can cost millions of dollars.

## ● Interest Groups Both Help and Hurt Democracy

There is considerable competition among organized groups in the United States. Although the weak and poor do occasionally become organized to assert their rights, interest-group politics is generally a form of political competition in which the wealthy and powerful are best able to engage. In the realm of group politics, liberty seems inconsistent with equality.

Moreover, although groups sometimes organize to promote broad public concerns, interest groups more often represent relatively narrow, selfish interests. Small, self-interested groups can be organized much more easily than large and more diffuse collectives. For one thing, the members of a relatively small group—say, bankers or hunting enthusiasts—are usually able to recognize their shared interests and the need to pursue them in the political arena. Members of large and more diffuse groups—say, consumers or potential victims of firearms—often find it difficult to recognize their shared interests or the need to engage in collective action to achieve their common goals.[26] This is why causes presented as public interests by their proponents often turn out, upon examination, to be private interests wrapped in a public mantle. Thus the elitist quality of group politics often appears to be inconsistent with democracy.

# studyguide

## Practice Quiz

 Find a diagnostic Web Quiz with 33 additional questions on the StudySpace Web site: www.wwnorton.com/we-the-people

1. The theory that competition among organized interests will produce balance with all the interests regulating one another is *(p. 239)*
   a) pluralism.
   b) elite power politics.
   c) democracy.
   d) socialism.

2. Groups that have an interest in obtaining government funds for research, such as Harvard University, the Brookings Institution and the American Enterprise Institute, are referred to as *(pp. 240–41)*
   a) public-sector groups.
   b) public-interest groups.
   c) professional associations.
   d) ideological groups.

3. To overcome the free-rider problem, groups *(pp. 242–43)*
   a) provide general benefits.
   b) litigate.
   c) go public.
   d) provide selective benefits.

4. Politically organized religious groups often make use of *(p. 243)*
   a) material benefits.
   b) solidary benefits.
   c) purposive benefits.
   d) none of the above.

5. Which of the following best describes AARP today? *(p. 244)*
   a) a group that is successful in recruiting members and mobilizing them for political action
   b) a group that is supported and well liked by all political forces

   c) a group that has failed to provide selective benefits
   d) a group struggling to overcome the free-rider problem

6. Which of the following is an important reason for the enormous increase in the number of groups seeking to influence the American political system? *(pp. 246–47)*
   a) the decrease in the size and activity of government during the last few decades
   b) the increase in the size and activity of government during the last few decades
   c) the increase in the number of people identifying themselves as an independent in recent decades
   d) the increase in the amount of soft money in election campaigns in recent decades

7. Which types of interest groups are most often associated with the New Politics movement? *(p. 246)*
   a) public-interest groups
   b) professional associations
   c) government groups
   d) labor groups

8. Access politics, exemplified by defense contractors acting in concert with congressional committees and executive agencies, is an example of *(pp. 250–51)*
   a) campaign activism.
   b) public-interest politics.
   c) an iron triangle.
   d) the role of conservative interest groups.

9. In which of the following ways do interest groups use the courts to affect public policy? *(p. 251)*
   a) filing *amicus* briefs
   b) bringing lawsuits
   c) financing those bringing suit
   d) all of the above

10. Which of the following is *not* a way for an interest group to use a "going public" strategy? *(pp. 252–53)*
    a) institutional advertising
    b) grassroots mobilization
    c) protests and demonstrations
    d) lobbying the executive branch

11. According to this text, what is the limit a PAC can contribute to a candidate in a primary or general election campaign? *(p. 254)*
    a) $1,000
    b) $5,000
    c) $10,000
    d) $50,000

12. Which of the following statements is true about the kinds of groups that are likely to organize? *(p. 256)*
    a) Small, self-interested groups can be organized more easily than large and diffuse groups.
    b) Small, self-interested groups can be organized less easily than large and diffuse groups.
    c) Small, self-interested groups are just as easy to organize as large and diffuse groups.
    d) Small, self-interested groups are only easy to organize when large and diffuse groups have already organized.

## Chapter Outline

 Find a detailed Chapter Outline on the StudySpace Web site: www.wwnorton.com/we-the-people

## Key Terms

 Find Flashcards to help you study these terms on the studyspace Web site: www.wwnorton.com/we-the-people

**collective goods** *(p. 242)* benefits, sought by groups, that are broadly available and cannot be denied to nonmembers

**free riders** *(p. 243)* those who enjoy the benefits of collective goods but did not participate in acquiring them

**grassroots mobilization** *(p. 253)* a lobbying campaign in which a group mobilizes its membership to contact government officials in support of the group's position

**informational benefits** *(p. 243)* special newsletters, periodicals, training programs, conferences, and other information provided to members of groups to entice others to join

**institutional advertising** *(p. 252)* advertising designed to create a positive image of an organization

**interest group** *(p. 239)* a voluntary membership association organized to pursue a common interest or interests, through political participation, toward the ultimate goal of getting favorable public policy decisions from government

**iron triangle** *(p. 250)* the stable, cooperative relationships that often develop among a congressional committee, an administrative agency, and one or more supportive interest groups. Similar relationships with more than three parties exist, but the iron triangle is the most typical

**lobbying** *(p. 247)* a strategy by which organized interests seek to influence the passage of legislation or other public policy by exerting direct pressure on members of the legislature or others in government

**material benefits** *(p. 243)* special goods, services, or money provided to members of groups to entice others to join

**membership association** *(p. 242)* an organized group in which members actually play a substantial role, sitting on committees and engaging in group projects

**New Politics movement** *(p. 246)* a political movement that began in the 1960s and 1970s, made up of professionals and intellectuals for whom the civil rights and antiwar movements were formative experiences. The New Politics movement strengthened public-interest groups

**pluralism** *(p. 239)* the theory that all interests are and should be free to compete for influence in the government. The outcome of this competition is compromise and moderation

**political action committee (PAC)** *(p. 254)* a private group that raises and distributes funds for use in election campaigns

**purposive benefits** *(p. 243)* selective benefits of group membership that emphasize the purpose and accomplishments of the group

**solidary benefits** *(p. 243)* selective benefits of a group membership of an emotional nature that include friendship, networking, and consciousness raising

**staff organization** *(p. 242)* type of membership group in which a professional staff conducts most of the group's activities

# For Further Reading

Ainsworth, Scott. *Analyzing Interest Groups.* New York: Norton, 2002.

Baumgartner, Frank, Jeffrey M. Berry, Beth L. Leech, David C. Kimball, and Marie Hojnacki. *Lobbying and Policy Change: Who Wins, Who Loses, and Why.* Chicago: University of Chicago Press, 2009.

Berry, Jeffrey. *Interest Group Society,* 5th ed. New York: Longman, 2008.

Cigler, Allan J., and Burdett A. Loomis, eds. *Interest Group Politics.* Washington, DC: Congressional Quarterly Press, 2007.

Goldstein, Kenneth. *Interest Groups, Lobbying, and Participation in America.* New York: Cambridge University Press, 2008.

Goss, Kristin A. *Disarmed: The Missing Movement for Gun Control in America.* Princeton, NJ: Princeton University Press, 2006.

Kaiser, Robert. *So Damn Much Money: The Triumph of Lobbying and the Corrosion of American Government.* New York: Vintage, 2010.

Lowi, Theodore J. *The End of Liberalism.* New York: Norton, 1979.

Olson, Mancur, Jr. *The Logic of Collective Action: Public Goods and the Theory of Groups.* Cambridge, MA: Harvard University Press, 1971.

Scholzman, Kay Lehman, and John T. Tierney. *Organized Interests and American Democracy.* New York: Harper & Row, 1986.

Skinner, Richard. *More Than Money.* New York: Rowman and Littlefield, 2006.

Spitzer, Robert J. *The Politics of Gun Control.* Washington, DC: Congressional Quarterly Press, 2008.

Strolovitch, Dara. *Affirmative Advocacy: Race, Class, and Gender in Interest Group Politics.* Chicago: University of Chicago Press, 2007.

Truman, David B. *The Governmental Process: Political Interests and Public Opinion.* New York: Knopf, 1951.

# Recommended Web Sites

**AARP**
www.aarp.org
AARP (formerly the American Association of Retired Persons) is one of the largest and most significant interest groups in the United States. Read about the history of this organization, its group benefits, and how it is affecting political issues and elections.

**AFL-CIO Legislative Alert Center**
www.aflcio.org/issues/legislativealert/
Created in 1955, the AFL-CIO represents over 10 million working men and women. See how this influential labor group is active and involved in political issues.

**American Civil Liberties Union**
www.aclu.org
**American Conservative Union**
www.conservative.org
The American Civil Liberties Union and the American Conservative Union are two of the nation's largest and most influential ideological interest groups. See what these opposing groups have to say about our government and current political issues.

**American Israel Public Affairs Committee (AIPAC)**
www.aipac.org
Due to globalization, interest groups cannot limit their activities to only one country. Decisions made in Washington, D.C., can affect countries around the world. The American Israel Public Affairs Committee (AIPAC) works with Republicans and Democrats to maintain a strong relationship between the United States and Israel.

**MoveOn**
www.moveon.org
This progressive interest group is dedicated to bringing ordinary citizens back into the political process and electing liberal members of government. See how this group uses electoral politics, via political action committees and campaign activism, to achieve its agenda.

**National Rifle Association**
www.nra.org
**Coalition to Stop Gun Violence**
www.csgv.org
**Brady Campaign to Prevent Gun Violence**
www.bradycampaign.org

Lobbying is an attempt by a group to influence the policy process by persuading government officials. These three groups employ a variety of lobbying techniques on the issue of gun control.

**Political Advocacy Groups: A Directory of United States Lobbyists**
www.csuchico.edu/~kfountain/

Kathi Fountain at California State University, Chico, maintains this site, which lists political advocacy groups. This directory is a great place to find interest groups and lobbyists on most political issues.

**U.S. PIRG (United States Public Interest Research Group)**
www.uspirg.org

This public interest group stands up for ordinary citizens. Its special emphasis is on consumer rights and the environment. U.S. PIRG mobilizes public opinion via institutional advertising, social movements, and grassroots efforts. PIRG chapters can be found in most states and at many colleges and universities.

**World Wildlife Fund**
www.wwf.org

The World Wildlife Fund is dedicated to protecting nature. It provides information to policy makers about conservation and advocates policies to help preserve the natural environment.

In addition to its lawmaking powers, Congress plays a critical role in American democracy as a representative institution. The members of Congress—100 senators and 435 representatives—represent the voice of the people across America. Yet some observers worry that Congress does not equally represent all voices.

# Congress

**WHAT GOVERNMENT DOES AND WHY IT MATTERS** Congress has vast authority over most aspects of American life. Laws related to federal spending, taxing, and regulation all pass through Congress. While the debates over these laws are often hard to follow because they are complex and technical or heated and partisan, it is important for the American people to learn about what Congress is doing. Actions taken—or not taken—in Congress affect the everyday choices that people face and the opportunities they can expect in life. With so much information about Congress available on the Internet, it is not hard to get beyond the heated rhetoric and simplistic headlines and ask your own questions about a proposed law. How will it affect my life and the lives of people I care about? What is the impact on our country? Making laws is often compared to making sausage because it is such a complex—and often ugly—process. Even so, it is vital for citizens to monitor what Congress does because the laws it passes are so central to our lives.

In the realm of foreign policy, Congress has the power to declare war, deal with piracy, regulate foreign commerce, and raise and regulate the armed forces and military installations. These powers over war and the military are supreme—even the president, as commander in chief of the military, must obey the laws and orders of Congress if Congress chooses to assert its constitutional authority. (In the past century, Congress has usually surrendered this authority to the president.) Congress could end our military engagement in foreign countries by cutting off funds for wars; it can also spread the burden of military engagement more broadly by reinstituting the draft. Further, the Senate has the power to approve treaties (by a two-thirds vote) and to approve the appointment of ambassadors. Capping these powers, Congress is charged to make laws that determine exactly how these powers—and all other powers of the government—will actually be implemented. This impressive array of powers reflects the founders' purpose of establishing legislative supremacy rather than three purely equal branches.[1]

If it seems that many of these powers belong to the president, from war power to spending power, that is because modern presidents do exercise great authority in these areas. The modern presidency is a more powerful institution than it was 200 years ago, and much of that power has come from Congress, either because Congress has delegated the power to the president by law, or because Congress has simply allowed, or even urged, presidents to be more active in these areas. This also helps explain why the executive branch often seems like a more important branch of government today than Congress. Still, the constitutional powers of Congress remain intact in the document.

In addition to its lawmaking powers, Congress plays a critical role in American democracy as a representative institution. This is because Congress represents in Washington the voice of the people across America. Yet some worry today that Congress does not represent all voices equally. Less political participation among lower-income voters and the growing importance of money in politics may make Congress more responsive to higher-income voters and resource-rich interest groups.

As discussed in the last chapter, interest groups are a primary means by which the "resource-rich" are able to advance their objectives through the various techniques we examined. Even though Congress has, in certain respects, been pushed to the side in some areas of national governance, it nevertheless continues to play a central role in governance because of its power to make the nation's laws.

## Congress Represents the American People

Congress is the most important representative institution in American government. Each member's primary responsibility is to the district, to his or her **constituency** (the people in the district from which an official is elected), not to the congressional leadership, a party, or even Congress itself. Yet the task of representation is not a simple one. Views about what constitutes fair and effective representation differ and constituents can make very different kinds of demands on their representatives. Members of Congress must consider these diverse views and demands as they represent their districts.

### The House and Senate Offer Differences in Representation

The framers of the Constitution provided for a **bicameral** legislature—that is, a legislative body consisting of two chambers or houses. The 435 members of the House are elected from districts apportioned according to population; the 100 members of the Senate are elected by state, with 2 senators from each. Senators have much longer terms in office and usually represent much larger and more diverse constituencies than do their counterparts in the House (see Table 9.1).

Both formal and informal factors contribute to differences between the two chambers of Congress. Differences in the length of terms and requirements for holding office specified by the Constitution in turn generate differences in how members of each body develop their constituencies and exercise their powers of office. The result is that members of the House most effectively and frequently serve as the agents of well-organized local interests with specific legislative agendas—for instance, used-car dealers seeking relief from regulation, labor unions seeking more favorable legislation, or farmers looking for higher subsidies. The small size and relative homogeneity of their constituencies and the frequency with which they must seek re-election make House members more attuned to the legislative needs of local interest groups.

**TABLE 9.1**

## Differences between the House and the Senate

|  | HOUSE | SENATE |
|---|---|---|
| Minimum age of member | 25 years | 30 years |
| U.S. citizenship | At least 7 years | At least 9 years |
| Length of term | 2 years | 6 years |
| Number representing each state | 1–53 (depends on population: 1 per 30,000 in 1789; now 1 per 650,000) | 2 per state |
| Constituency | Tends to be local | Both state and national |

Senators, on the other hand, serve larger and more heterogeneous constituencies. As a result, they are somewhat better able than members of the House to serve as the agents for groups and interests organized on a statewide or national basis. Moreover, with longer terms in office, senators have the luxury of considering "new ideas" or seeking to bring together new coalitions of interests rather than simply serving existing ones.

## Representation Can Be Sociological or Agency

We have become so accustomed to the idea of representative government that we tend to forget what a peculiar concept representation really is. A representative claims to act or speak for some other person or group. But how can one person be trusted to speak for another? How do we know that those who call themselves our representatives are actually speaking on our behalf rather than simply pursuing their own interests?

There are two circumstances under which one person reasonably might be trusted to speak for another. The first of these occurs if the two individuals are so similar in background, character, interests, and perspectives that anything said by one would very likely reflect the views of the other as well. This principle is at the heart of what is sometimes called **sociological representation**—the sort of representation that takes place when representatives have the same racial, ethnic, religious, or educational backgrounds as their constituents. The assumption is that sociological similarity helps to promote good representation; thus, the composition of a properly constituted representative assembly should mirror the composition of society.

The second circumstance under which one person might be trusted to speak for another occurs if the two are formally bound together so that the representative is in some way accountable to those he or she purports to represent. If representatives can somehow be punished or held to account for failing to represent their constituents properly, then they have incentive to provide good representation even if their own personal backgrounds, views, and interests differ from those of the people they represent. This principle is called **agency representation**—the sort of representation that takes place when constituents have the power to hire and fire their representatives.

Both sociological and agency representation play a role in the relationship between members of Congress and their constituencies.

**The Social Composition of the U.S. Congress** The extent to which the U.S. Congress is representative of the American people in a sociological sense can be seen by examining the distribution of important social characteristics in the House and Senate today.

African Americans, women, Hispanic Americans, and Asian Americans have increased their congressional representation somewhat in the past two decades (see Figure 9.1). In 2010, seventy-eight women served in the House of Representatives (up from only twenty-nine in 1990). Most notably, California Democrat Nancy Pelosi became the first woman Speaker of the House of Representatives

*The increase in the number of African Americans in Congress in the last forty years is shown by the membership of the Congressional Black Caucus, which had forty-three members in 2008. Caucus members are shown here at a press conference about the government's response to Hurricane Katrina, which was especially devastating to the African American community in the Gulf states.*

in 2007 after the Democrats won control of the House in the 2006 elections. She held that position through 2010. Also in 2010, seventeen women served in the Senate. However, the representation of women and minorities in Congress is still not comparable to their proportions in the general population. Since many important contemporary national issues do cut along racial and gender lines, a considerable amount of clamor for reform in the representative process is likely to continue until these groups are fully represented.

The occupational backgrounds of members of Congress have always been a matter of interest because so many issues cut along economic lines that are relevant to occupations and industries. The legal profession is the dominant career of most members of Congress prior to their election. Public service or politics is also a significant background. In addition, many members of Congress also have important ties to business and industry.[2] One composite portrait of a typical member of Congress has been that of "a middle-aged male lawyer whose father was of the professional or managerial class; a native-born 'white,' or—if he cannot avoid being an immigrant—a product of northwestern or central Europe or Canada, rather than of eastern or southern Europe, Latin America, Africa or Asia."[3] This is not a portrait of the U.S. population.

Is Congress still able to legislate fairly or to take account of a diversity of views and interests if it is not a sociologically representative assembly? The task is

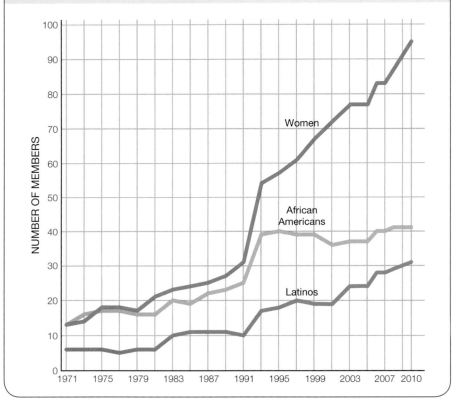

**FIGURE 9.1** Women, African Americans, and Latinos in the U.S. Congress, 1971–2010

Congress has become much more socially diverse since the 1970s. After a gradual increase from 1971 to 1990, the number of women and African American members grew quickly during the first half of the 1990s. How does the pattern of growth for Latino representatives compare with that of women and African Americans?

SOURCES: Harold W. Stanley and Richard G. Niemi, eds., *Vital Statistics on American Politics 2003–2004* (Washington, DC: Congressional Quarterly Press, 2003), p. 207, Table 5-2; CRS Report for Congress, http://assets.opencrs.com (accessed 3/3/08); Mildred Amer and Jennifer E. Manning, *Membership of the 111th Congress: A Profile*, Congressional Research Service 7-5700, December 31, 2008; http://assets .opencrs.com (accessed 1/31/10).

certainly much more difficult. Yet there is reason to believe it can. Representatives can serve as the agents of their constituents, even if they do not precisely mirror their sociological attributes.

**Representatives as Agents** A good deal of evidence indicates that whether or not members of Congress share their constituents' sociological characteristics, they do work very hard to speak for their constituents' views and serve their constituents' interests in the governmental process. The idea of representative as agent is similar to the relationship of lawyer and client. True, the relationship between the member of Congress and as many as 660,000 "clients" in the district, or the senator and millions of "clients" in the state, is very different from that of the lawyer and client. But the criteria of performance are comparable. One expects at the very least that each representative will constantly be seeking to discover the interests of the constituency and will be speaking for those interests in Congress and in other centers of government.[4]

There is constant communication between constituents and congressional offices. For example, in 2006 House and Senate offices received 20 million pieces of mail delivered by the postal service, and 313 million e-mail communications. Also in 2006, they sent 116 million pieces of mail.[5] Congressional offices have Web sites to describe their accomplishments and give others ready access to additional information about their offices and Congress. Many offices also send out regular e-newsletters, have created their own blogs, and use Twitter accounts.

The seriousness with which members of the House attempt to behave as representatives can be seen in the amount of time spent on behalf of their constituents. Well over a quarter of their time and nearly two-thirds of the time of their staff members is devoted to constituency service (called "case work"). This service is not merely a matter of writing and mailing letters. It includes talking to constituents, providing them with minor services, presenting special bills for them, and attempting to influence decisions by regulatory commissions on their behalf.[6]

Although no members of Congress are above constituency pressures (and they would not want to be), on many issues constituents do not have very strong views, so representatives are free to act as they think best. Foreign policy issues often fall into this category. (An exception to this is the Iraq war, as this issue aroused strong feelings among voters.) But in many districts there are two or three issues on which constituents have such pronounced opinions that representatives feel they have little freedom of choice. For example, representatives from districts that grow wheat, cotton, or tobacco probably will not want to exercise a great deal of independence on relevant agricultural legislation. In oil-rich states such as Oklahoma, Texas, and California, senators and members of the House are likely to be leading advocates of oil interests. For one thing, representatives are probably fearful of voting against their district interests; for another, the districts are unlikely to have elected representatives who would *want* to vote against them.

The influence of constituencies is so pervasive that both parties have strongly embraced the informal rule that nothing should be done to endanger the reelection chances of any member. Party leaders obey this rule fairly consistently by not asking any member to vote in a way that might conflict with a district interest.

## The Electoral Connection Hinges on Incumbency

The sociological composition of Congress and the activities of representatives once they are in office are very much influenced by electoral considerations. Two factors related to the U.S. electoral system affect who gets elected and what they do once in office. The first issue is that of incumbency advantage. Second, the way congressional district lines are drawn can greatly affect the outcome of an election. Let us examine more closely the impact that these considerations have on representation.

**Incumbency**—the ability to hold a political office election after election— plays a very important role in the American electoral system and in the kind of representation citizens get in Washington. Once in office, members of Congress possess an array of tools that they can use to stack the deck in favor of their re-election. The most important of these is constituency service—taking care of the problems and requests of individual voters. Congressional offices will intervene on behalf of constituents when they have problems with federal programs or agencies, such as Social Security benefits, veterans benefits, obtaining passports, and so on. When congressional offices contact federal agencies dealing with such matters, the offices usually respond with extra speed, knowing that members of Congress can embarrass or penalize an agency that doesn't do its job properly. Through such services and through regular newsletter mailings, the incumbent seeks to establish a "personal" relationship with his or her constituents. The success of this strategy is evident in the high rates of re-election for congressional incumbents, which is as high as 98.5 percent for House members and 96 percent for members of the Senate in recent years (see Figure 9.2). It is also evident in what is called "sophomore surge"—the tendency for candidates to win a higher percentage of the vote when seeking future terms in office.

Incumbency re-election dipped some in the 2006 elections, when 94 percent of House incumbents and 79 percent of Senate incumbents were re-elected. This

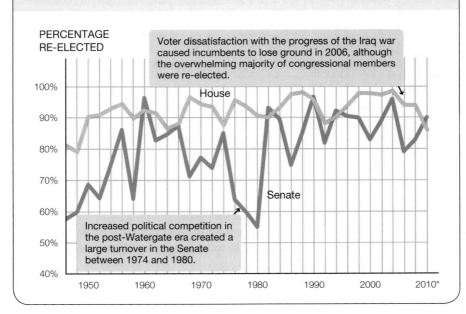

**FIGURE 9.2 The Power of Incumbency**

Members of Congress who run for re-election have a good chance of winning. Senators have at times found it difficult to use the power of incumbency to protect their seats, as the decline in Senate incumbency rates between 1974 and 1980 indicates. Has the incumbency advantage generally been greater in the House or Senate?

SOURCES: Norman J. Ornstein et al., eds., *Vital Statistics on Congress, 1997–2000* (Washington, DC: AEI Press, 2000), pp. 57–58; and authors' updates.
*estimate

PERCENTAGE RE-ELECTED

Voter dissatisfaction with the progress of the Iraq war caused incumbents to lose ground in 2006, although the overwhelming majority of congressional members were re-elected.

House

Senate

Increased political competition in the post-Watergate era created a large turnover in the Senate between 1974 and 1980.

relative drop was caused by voter dissatisfaction with Republican rule, the unpopularity of President Bush, and widespread dissatisfaction with the Iraq war. As a result, the Democrats won control of both houses for the first time since 1994. Every incumbent defeated in 2006 was a Republican. Based on early estimates of the 2010 elections, approximately 86 percent of incumbents were re-elected in the House and roughly 90 percent in the Senate.

Incumbency can also help a candidate by scaring off potential challengers. In many races, potential candidates may decide not to run because they fear that the incumbent simply has too much money or is too well liked or too well known. Potentially strong challengers may also decide that a district's partisan leanings are too unfavorable. The efforts of incumbents to raise funds to ward off potential challengers start early. Connecticut Democratic House member Joe Courtney earned the nickname "Landslide Joe" because of his 91-vote margin of victory in 2006. He began fund-raising for the 2008 election even before he was sworn in for his first term. In addition, the Democratic Congressional Campaign Committee placed him on its Frontline team, a group of the twenty-nine most vulnerable Democrats—these representatives were given high-profile speaking assignments and important committee appointments to elevate their profiles. In 2008, Courtney was re-elected by a 2–1 margin over his opponent, and he was easily re-elected in 2010.

The advantage of incumbency thus tends to preserve the status quo in Congress. This fact has implications for the social composition of Congress. For example, incumbency advantage makes it harder for women to increase their numbers in Congress because most incumbents are men. Women who run for open seats (for which there are no incumbents) are just as likely to win as male candidates.[7] Supporters of **term limits** (legally set limits on the number of terms an elected official can serve) argue that such limits are the only way to get new faces into Congress. They believe that because of incumbency advantage and the tendency of many legislators to view politics as a career, very little turnover will occur in Congress unless limits are imposed on the number of terms a legislator can serve.

Another major factor that affects who wins a seat in Congress is the way congressional districts are drawn. Every ten years, state legislatures must redraw congressional districts to reflect population changes or in response to legal challenges to existing districts. This is a highly political process: Districts are shaped to create an advantage for the majority party in the state legislature, which controls the **redistricting** process. In this complex process, those charged with drawing districts use sophisticated computer technologies to come up with the most favorable district boundaries. Redistricting can create open seats and pit incumbents of the same party against one another, ensuring that one of them will lose. Redistricting can also give an advantage to one party by clustering voters with some ideological or sociological characteristics in a single district, or diluting the influence of voters blocs by separating those voters into two or more districts. This process of redrawing legislative district boundary lines to provide political advantage or disadvantage is known as **gerrymandering.**

Since the passage of the 1982 amendments to the 1964 Civil Rights Act, race has become a major—and controversial—consideration in drawing voting districts. These amendments, which encouraged the creation of districts in which members of racial minorities have decisive majorities, have greatly increased the number of minority representatives in Congress. After the 1991–92 redistricting, the number of predominantly minority districts doubled, rising from twenty-six to fifty-two. Among the most fervent supporters of the new minority districts were white Republicans, who used the opportunity to create more districts dominated by white Republican voters. These developments raise thorny questions about representation. Some analysts argue that the system may grant minorities greater sociological representation, but it has made it more difficult for minorities to win substantive policy goals. This was a common argument after the sweeping Republican victories in the 1994 congressional elections. Others dispute this argument, noting that the strong surge of Republican voters was more significant than any losses due to racial redistricting.[8]

In 1995, the Supreme Court limited racial redistricting in *Miller v. Johnson*, in which the Court stated that race could not be the predominant factor in creating electoral districts.[9] Yet concerns about redistricting and representation have not disappeared. The distinction between race being a "predominant" factor and its being one factor among many is very hazy. Because the drawing of district boundaries affects incumbents as well as the field of candidates who decide to run for office, it continues to be a key battleground on which political parties fight about the meaning of representation (Figure 9.3).

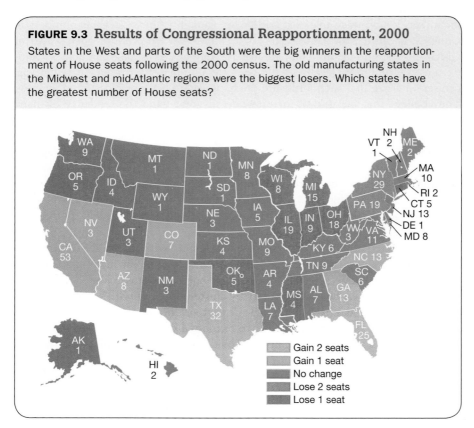

**FIGURE 9.3 Results of Congressional Reapportionment, 2000**
States in the West and parts of the South were the big winners in the reapportionment of House seats following the 2000 census. The old manufacturing states in the Midwest and mid-Atlantic regions were the biggest losers. Which states have the greatest number of House seats?

WA 9
OR 5
MT 1
ND 1
MN 8
WI 8
MI 15
VT 1
NH 2
ME 2
NY 29
MA 10
RI 2
CT 5
NJ 13
DE 1
MD 8
ID 4
WY 1
SD 1
IA 5
IL 19
IN 9
OH 18
PA 19
WV 3
VA 11
NV 3
UT 3
CO 7
NE 3
KS 4
MO 9
KY 6
NC 13
CA 53
AZ 8
NM 3
OK 5
AR 4
TN 9
SC 6
TX 32
LA 7
MS 4
AL 7
GA 13
FL 25
AK 1
HI 2

Gain 2 seats
Gain 1 seat
No change
Lose 2 seats
Lose 1 seat

## Direct Patronage Means Bringing Home the Bacon

Members of Congress often have an opportunity to provide direct benefits, or **patronage,** for their constituents. Patronage resources are available to higher officials, and include making partisan appointments to offices and conferring grants, licenses, or special favors to supporters. The most important of these opportunities for direct patronage is in legislation that has been described half-jokingly as the **pork barrel**—appropriations made by legislative bodies for local projects that are often not needed but that are created to help local representatives win re-election in their home districts. This type of legislation specifies a project to be funded, as well as the location of the project within a particular district. Many observers of Congress argue that pork-barrel bills are the only ones that some members are serious about moving toward actual passage, because they are seen as so important to members' re-election bids.

A common form of pork barreling is the "earmark," the practice through which members of Congress insert into bills language that provides special benefits for their own constituents. Highway bills are a favorite vehicle for congressional pork-barrel spending. The 2005 highway bill was full of such items, containing more than three thousand projects earmarked for specific congressional districts. Among them were such projects as $3.5 million for horse trails in Virginia and $5 million for a parking garage in downtown Bozeman, Montana. These measures often have little to do with transportation needs, instead serving as evidence that congressional members can bring federal dollars back home. Perhaps the most extravagant—and least needed for transportation—item in the 2005 bill was a bridge in Alaska designed to connect a barely populated island to the town of Ketchikan, whose population is just short of eight thousand. At a cost that could have soared to $2 billion, the bridge would have replaced an existing five-minute ferry ride. Representative Don Young, an influential Alaska Republican, proudly claimed credit for such pork-barrel projects. At the suggestion that Alaska's senior senator Ted Stevens, Republican chair of the Senate Appropriations Committee, might be the reason Alaska won these projects, Young pretended to be offended, saying, "If he's the chief porker, I'm upset."[10] In the face of fierce criticism, the project was dropped in 2007.

When Democrats took over Congress in 2007, they vowed to limit the use of earmarks, which had grown from 1,439 per year in 1995 to 15,268 in 2006. More troubling, earmarks were connected to congressional scandals. For example, Republican House member Randy "Duke" Cunningham (R-Calif.) was sent to jail in 2005 for accepting bribes by companies hoping to receive earmarks in return.[11] The House passed a new rule requiring that those representatives supporting each earmark identify themselves and guarantee that they had no personal financial stake in the requested project. A new ethics law applies similar provisions to the Senate. The new requirements appear to have had some impact: the 2007 military bill, for example, cut in half the value of earmarks contained in the military bill passed in 2006. But in the midst of the sharp economic downturn in 2009, Congress passed a bill designed to stimulate the economy, which contained more than 8,000 earmarks. In many cases, Republicans and some Democrats who voted against the bill later were happy to take credit from their constituents for the earmarks they had placed in it. In his 2010 State of the Union address, President Obama called for Congress to publish a list of all earmark requests on a single website. Reformers hope that such transparency will cause members of Congress to think twice before they request an earmark.[12]

A limited amount of other direct patronage also exists (see Figure 9.4). One important form of constituency service is intervention with federal administrative agencies on behalf of constituents. Members of the House and Senate and their staff members spend a great deal of time on the telephone and in administrative offices seeking to secure favorable treatment for constituents and supporters. Among the kind of services that members of Congress offer to constituents is assistance for senior citizens who are having Social Security or Medicare benefit eligibility problems. They may also help constituents find federal grants for which they may be eligible to apply. As Representative Pete Stark (D-Calif.) puts it on his Web site, "We cannot make the decision for a federal agency on such matters, but we can make sure that you get a fair shake."[13] A small but related form of patronage is getting an appointment to one of the military academies for the child of a constituent. Traditionally, these appointments are allocated one to a district.

A different form of patronage is the **private bill**—a bill to grant some kind of relief, special privilege, or exemption to the person named in the bill, such as a special exemption from immigration quotas. The private bill is a type of legislation, but it is distinguished from a public bill, which is supposed to deal with general rules and categories of behavior, people, and institutions. As many as 75 percent

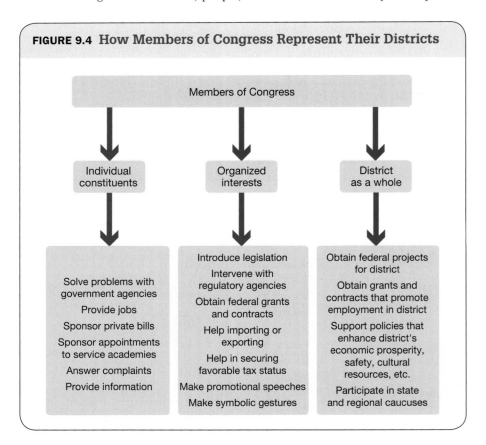

**FIGURE 9.4  How Members of Congress Represent Their Districts**

Members of Congress

Individual constituents

Organized interests

District as a whole

Solve problems with government agencies

Provide jobs

Sponsor private bills

Sponsor appointments to service academies

Answer complaints

Provide information

Introduce legislation

Intervene with regulatory agencies

Obtain federal grants and contracts

Help importing or exporting

Help in securing favorable tax status

Make promotional speeches

Make symbolic gestures

Obtain federal projects for district

Obtain grants and contracts that promote employment in district

Support policies that enhance district's economic prosperity, safety, cultural resources, etc.

Participate in state and regional caucuses

of all private bills introduced (and one-third of the ones that pass) are concerned with providing relief for foreign nationals who cannot get permanent visas to the United States because the immigration quota for their country is filled or because of something unusual about their particular situation.[14] For example, in 2007 Gene Green (D-Tex.) sponsored a private bill to obtain legal status for an undocumented couple in danger of being deported but whose son had died as a marine in Iraq.[15]

## The Organization of Congress Is Shaped by Party

The United States Congress is not only a representative assembly. It is also a legislative body. For Americans, representation and legislation go hand in hand; however, many parliamentary bodies in other countries are representative without the power to legislate. It is no small achievement that the U.S. Congress both represents *and* governs.

Because of the many interests represented by the 535 members of Congress, it is typically difficult for Congress to get things done. For this reason, presidents have come to play a vital role in leading Congress. In fact, members of Congress often complain when the president fails to provide leadership on important issues, even when the party controlling Congress is different from that of the president.

### Party Leadership in the House and the Senate Organizes Power

Every two years, at the beginning of a new Congress, the members of each party in the House of Representatives gather to elect their leaders. This gathering is traditionally called the **conference** (House Democrats call theirs the caucus). The elected leader of the majority party is later proposed to the whole House and is automatically elected to the position of **Speaker of the House,** with voting along straight party lines. The Speaker is the most important party and House leader and can influence the legislative agenda, the fate of individual pieces of legislation, and members' positions within the House. The House majority conference or caucus then also elects a **majority leader,** the elected leader of the majority party in the House of Representatives or in the Senate (in the House, the majority leader is subordinate in the party hierarchy to the Speaker of the House). The minority party goes through the same process and selects the **minority leader,** who is the elected leader of the minority

*In 2006, Nancy Pelosi (D-CA) became the first woman Speaker of the House of Representatives. Minority leader John Boehner (R-OH), who handed her the gavel that year, took over as Speaker in 2011 after Republicans won a majority in the House in the 2010 elections.*

party in the House or Senate. Both parties also elect assistants to their party leaders, called **whips** who are responsible for coordinating the party's legislative strategy, building support for key issues, and counting votes.

Next in line of importance for each party after the Speaker and majority or minority leader is its Committee on Committees (called the Steering and Policy Committee by the Democrats), whose tasks are to assign new legislators to committees and to deal with the requests of incumbent members for transfers from one committee to another.

Generally, members of Congress seek assignments that will allow them to influence decisions of special importance to their districts. Representatives from farm districts, for example, may request seats on the Agriculture Committee.[16] Seats on powerful committees such as Ways and Means, which is responsible for tax legislation, and Appropriations are especially popular.

Within the Senate, the president pro tempore exercises primarily ceremonial leadership. Usually, the majority party designates a member with the greatest seniority to serve in this capacity. Real power is in the hands of the majority leader and minority leader, each elected by party conference. Together they control the Senate's calendar, or agenda for legislation. In addition, the senators from each party elect a whip. Each party also elects a Policy Committee, which advises the leadership on legislative priorities. The structure of majority party leadership in the House and the Senate is shown in Figures 9.5 and 9.6.

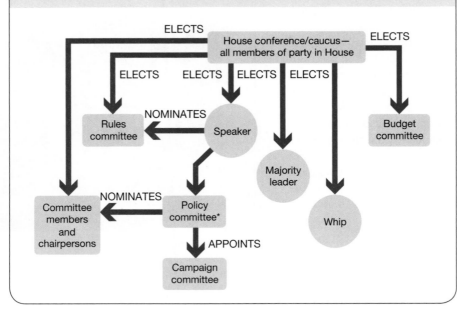

**FIGURE 9.5 Majority Party Structure in the House of Representatives**

Includes the Speaker, majority leader chief and deputy whips, caucus chair, chairs of live major committees, members elected by regional caucuses, members elected by recently elected representatives, and at large members appointed by the Speaker.

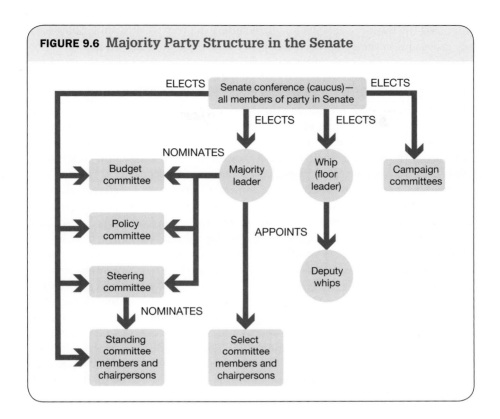

**FIGURE 9.6 Majority Party Structure in the Senate**

In addition to these tasks of organization, congressional party leaders may also seek to establish a legislative agenda. Since the New Deal, presidents have taken the lead in creating legislative agendas (this trend will be discussed in the next chapter). When congressional leaders have been faced with a White House controlled by the opposing party, they have attempted to devise their own agendas. Democratic leaders of Congress sought to create a common Democratic perspective in 1981 when Ronald Reagan became president. The Republican Congress elected in 1994 expanded on this idea, calling its agenda the "Contract with America."

In 2007, when Democrats took over Congress, Democratic House Speaker Nancy Pelosi sought to promote party unity with a plan to pass six key pieces of legislation in the first hundred hours of Democratic congressional control. Although the House succeeded in passing the six measures, most of them died in the Senate, where the frequent threat of a filibuster by opponents means that at least sixty votes is required to enact legislation instead of a simple majority of fifty-one.[17] The pattern of the Democratic House passing legislation that then became bottled up in the Senate continued into 2009–10. Because a Senate minority of 41 can block legislation by using the filibuster, the Democratic leadership found it difficult to enact legislation with a cohesive Republican minority. It meant that the Democratic leadership had to keep every Senate Democrat (and two independents who voted with the Democrats) on board to enact legislation. As the Republicans prepared to take over the House in 2010, they stressed reducing the deficit, extending the Bush-era tax cuts for all, including the very wealthy, and rolling back key provisions in the comprehensive health care legislation enacted in 2010.

## The Committee System Is the Core of Congress

The committee system is central to the operation of Congress. At each stage of the legislative process, Congress relies on committees and subcommittees to do the hard work of sorting through alternatives and writing legislation. There are several different kinds of congressional committees; these include standing committees, select committees, joint committees, and conference committees.

**Standing committees** are the most important arenas of congressional policy making. These permanent committees continue in existence from congress to congress; they have the power to propose and write legislation. The jurisdiction of each standing committee covers a particular subject matter, such as finance or appropriations, which in most cases parallels the major departments or agencies in the executive branch (see Table 9.2). Among the most important standing committees are those in charge of finances. The House Ways and Means Committee and the Senate Finance Committee are powerful because of their jurisdiction over taxes, trade, and expensive entitlement programs such as Social Security and Medicare. The Senate and House Appropriations committees also play important ongoing roles because they decide how much funding various programs will actually receive; they also determine exactly how the money will be spent. A seat on the Appropriations Committee allows a member the opportunity to direct funds to a favored program—perhaps one in his or her home district.

Except for the House Rules Committee, all standing committees receive proposals for legislation and process them into official bills. The House Rules Committee decides the order in which bills come up for a vote on the House floor and determines the specific rules that govern the length of debate and opportunity for amendments. The Senate, which has less formal organization and fewer rules, does not have a rules committee.

**Select committees** are usually temporary and normally do not have the power to report legislation, but rather are set up to highlight or investigate a particular issue or address an issue not within the jurisdiction of existing committees. (The House and Senate Select Intelligence committees are permanent, however, and do have the power to report legislation.) These committees may hold hearings and serve as focal points for the issues they are

*After the 2010 Gulf oil spill, the Senate Environment and Public Works Committee held hearings on the disaster. Executives from BP America, Transocean Limited, and Halliburton were called to testify on their companies' roles in the spill.*

## TABLE 9.2

## Permanent Committees of Congress

### HOUSE COMMITTEES

| | |
|---|---|
| Agriculture | Oversight and Government Reform |
| Appropriations | Permanent Select Committee on Intelligence |
| Armed Services | Rules |
| Budget | Science and Technology |
| Education and Labor | Select Committee on Energy Independence and Global Warming |
| Energy and Commerce | Small Business |
| Financial Services | Standards of Official Conduct |
| Foreign Affairs | Transportation and Infrastructure |
| Homeland Security | Veterans' Affairs |
| House Administration | Ways and Means |
| Judiciary | |
| Natural Resources | |

### SENATE COMMITTEES

| | |
|---|---|
| Agriculture, Nutrition, and Forestry | Foreign Relations |
| Approprations | Health, Education, Labor, and Pensions |
| Armed Services | Homeland Security and Governmental Affairs |
| Banking, Housing, and Urban Affairs | Judiciary |
| Budget | Rules and Administration |
| Commerce, Science, and Transportation | Select Intelligence |
| Energy and Natural Resources | Small Business and Entrepreneurship |
| Environment and Public Works | Veterans'Affairs |
| Finance | |

charged with considering. Congressional leaders form select committees when they want to take up issues that fall between the jurisdictions of existing committees, to highlight an issue, or to investigate a particular problem. Examples of select committees investigating political scandals include the Senate Watergate Committee of 1973, the committees set up in 1987 to investigate the Iran-Contra affair, and the Whitewater Committee of 1995–96. In 2003, Congress created the Select Homeland Security Committee to oversee the new cabinet department, Homeland Security. This committee also has the power to report legislation and is now permanent.

**Joint committees** are formed of members from both the Senate and the House. There are four such committees: economic, taxation, library, and printing. These joint committees are permanent, but they do not have the power to report legislation. The Joint Economic Committee and the Joint Taxation Committee have often played important roles in collecting information and holding hearings on economic and financial issues.

Finally, **conference committees** are temporary joint committees whose members are appointed by the Speaker of the House and the presiding officer of the Senate. These committees are charged with reaching a compromise on legislation that has been passed by the House and the Senate, but in different versions. Conference committees play an extremely important role in determining what laws are actually passed, because they must reconcile any differences in the legislation passed by the House and Senate. In recent years, however, House and Senate leaders have at times bypassed conference committees. Instead, leaders have negotiated directly to seek legislative compromise on some major bills and then presented them directly to their chambers for up-or-down votes. The rise of this practice reflects the desire of leaders to control key bills and to exert partisan muscle.

Within each committee, hierarchy is based on seniority. **Seniority** is the priority or status ranking determined by years of continuous service on a particular committee, not years of service in the House or Senate. In general, each committee is chaired by the most senior member of the majority party. But the principle of seniority is not absolute. Both Democrats and Republicans have violated it on occasion. But in 1995, when the Republicans won control of the House, then-Speaker Newt Gingrich instituted a new practice of frequent seniority violations, often selecting committee chairs based on loyalty or fund-raising abilities, a practice that subsequent Republican leaders have maintained. In 2007, the Democrats returned to the seniority principle to select committee chairs.

## The Staff System Is the Power behind the Power

A congressional institution second in importance only to the committee system is the staff system. Every member of Congress employs a large number of staff members, whose tasks include handling constituency requests and, to a large and growing extent, dealing with legislative details and the activities of administrative agencies. Increasingly, staffers bear the primary responsibility for formulating and drafting proposals, organizing hearings, dealing with administrative agencies, and negotiating with lobbyists. Indeed, legislators typically deal with one another through staff rather than through direct, personal contact. Representatives and senators together employ 11,500 staffers in their Washington and home offices. Today, staffers develop policy ideas, draft legislation, and have a good deal of influence over the legislative process.

In addition to the personal staffs of individual senators and representatives, Congress also employs roughly two thousand committee staffers. These individuals make up the permanent staff, who stay attached to every House and Senate committee regardless of turnover in Congress and who are responsible for organizing and administering the committee's work, including researching, scheduling, organizing hearings, and drafting legislation. Committee staffers also play key roles in the legislative process.

# Rules of Lawmaking Explain How a Bill Becomes a Law

The institutional structure of Congress is one key factor that helps to shape the legislative process. A second and equally important set of factors is the rules of congressional procedure. These rules govern everything from the introduction of a **bill** (a proposed law that has been sponsored by a member of Congress and submitted to the clerk of the House or Senate) through its submission to the president for signing (see Figure 9.7). Not only do these regulations influence the fate of each and every bill, they also help to determine the distribution of power in the Congress.

## The First Step Is Committee Deliberation

Even if a member of Congress, the White House, or a federal agency has spent months developing and drafting a piece of legislation, it does not become a bill until it is submitted officially by a senator or representative to the clerk of the House or Senate and referred to the appropriate committee for deliberation. No floor action on any bill can take place until the committee with jurisdiction over it has taken all the time it needs to deliberate. During the course of its deliberations, the committee typically refers the bill to one of its subcommittees, which may hold hearings, listen to expert testimony, and amend the proposed legislation before referring it to the full committee for consideration. The full committee may accept the recommendation of the subcommittee or hold its own hearings and prepare its own amendments. Or, even more frequently, the committee and subcommittee may do little or nothing with a bill that has been submitted to them. Many bills are simply allowed to "die in committee" with little or no serious consideration given to them. In a typical congressional session, 95 percent of the roughly eight thousand bills introduced die in committee—an indication of the power of the congressional committee system.

The relative handful of bills that are reported out of committee must, in the House, pass one additional hurdle within the committee system: the Rules Committee. This powerful committee determines the rules that will govern action on the bill on the House floor. In particular, the Rules Committee allots the time for debate and decides to what extent amendments to the bill can be proposed from the floor. Except under unusual circumstances, a bill cannot reach the floor of the House unless it is given a rule from the Rules Committee.

## Debate Is Less Restricted in the Senate Than in the House

In the House, virtually all of the time allotted for debate on a given bill is controlled by the bill's sponsor and by its leading opponent. In almost every case, these two people are the committee chair and the ranking minority member of the committee that processed the bill—or those they designate. These two participants are, by rule and tradition, granted the power to allocate most of the debate time in small amounts to members who are seeking to speak for or against the measure. Preference in the allocation of time goes to the members of the committee whose jurisdiction covers the bill.

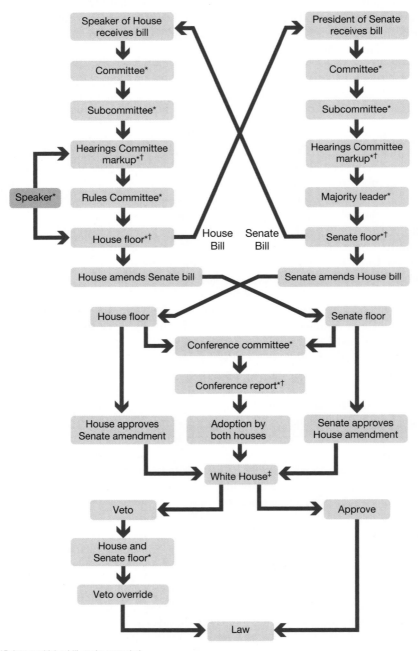

**FIGURE 9.7 How a Bill-Becomes a Law**

There are many points where a bill can be stopped.

Speaker of House receives bill

Committee*

Subcommittee*

Hearings Committee markup*†

Speaker*

Rules Committee*

House floor*†

House Bill

President of Senate receives bill

Committee*

Subcommittee*

Hearings Committee markup*†

Majority leader*

Senate floor*†

Senate Bill

House amends Senate bill

Senate amends House bill

House floor

Senate floor

Conference committee*

Conference report*†

House approves Senate amendment

Adoption by both houses

Senate approves House amendment

White House‡

Veto

Approve

House and Senate floor*

Veto override

Law

*Points at which a bill can be amended.
†Points at which a bill can die.
‡If the president neither signs nor vetoes a bill within ten days, it automatically becomes law.

In the Senate, the leadership has much less control over floor debate. Indeed, the Senate is unique among the world's legislative bodies for its commitment to unlimited debate. Once given the floor, a senator may speak as long as he or she wishes. On a number of memorable occasions, senators have used the right to talk without interruption for as long as they want to prevent action on legislation that they opposed. Through this tactic, called the **filibuster,** members of the Senate can prevent action on legislation they oppose by continuously holding the floor and speaking until the majority backs down. Once given the floor, senators have unlimited time to speak, and it requires a vote of three-fifths of the Senate to end a filibuster. During the 1950s and 1960s, for example, opponents of civil rights legislation often sought to block its passage by staging filibusters. Democrats used the threat of a filibuster to block some of President George W. Bush's judicial nominees, much as Republicans used the same tactic to derail Clinton nominees. In 2003, Senate Republicans staged a thirty-hour marathon, bringing cots and sleeping bags into the Senate to protest Democratic use of the tactic. Senate Democrats staged a similar marathon session, cots and all, when they held the Senate majority in 2007. The votes of three-fifths of the Senate, or sixty votes, are needed to end a filibuster. This procedure is called **cloture.**

For much of American history, senators used the filibuster only rarely. In the last twenty years, however, the filibuster has become so common that observers routinely note that it takes 60 votes (instead of a simple majority of 51) to pass anything in the Senate. The 110th Congress (2007–08) set a new record, with 134 cloture votes (the vote to end a filibuster). Yet that record would be eclipsed in the

*After a senator or representative proposes a new bill, it is referred to the appropriate committee for deliberation. Here, the Senate Foreign Relations Committee hears testimony from the U.S. ambassador in Baghdad via teleconference as they consider numerous proposals to address the ongoing conflict in Iraq.*

111th Congress (2009–10), when 112 cloture votes were held in 2009 alone, with 40 more in just the first two months of 2010.[18] Despite Democrats' frustration, the filibuster is a tool that both parties have used and, with a 67-vote majority required to change Senate filibuster (or other) rules, the filibuster is likely to remain a prominent feature of the Senate for the foreseeable future.

Once debate is concluded on the floor of the House and the Senate, the leaders schedule it for a vote on the floor of each chamber. By this time, congressional leaders know what the vote will be; leaders do not bring legislation to the floor unless they are fairly certain it is going to pass. As a consequence, it is unusual for the leadership to lose a bill on the floor. On rare occasions, the last moments of the floor vote can be very dramatic, as each party's leadership puts its whip organization into action to make sure that wavering members vote with the party. The passage of Medicare reform in 2003 was one such occasion. Republican party leaders took the unprecedented step of keeping the vote open for two hours and fifty-one minutes while they looked high and low for the remaining votes they needed to pass the law. It was nearly 6 A.M. by the time the bill passed.

## Conference Committees Reconcile House and Senate Versions of Legislation

Getting a bill out of committee and through one of the houses of Congress is no guarantee that a bill will be enacted into law. Before a bill can be sent to the president, both houses must pass it in the identical form. Frequently, bills that began with similar provisions in both chambers emerge with little resemblance to each other. Alternatively, a bill may be passed by one chamber but undergo substantial revision in the other chamber. In such cases, a conference committee composed of the senior members of the committees or subcommittees that initiated the bills may be convened to iron out differences between the two pieces of legislation.

When a bill comes out of conference, it faces one more hurdle. Before a bill can be sent to the president for signing, the House-Senate conference committee's version of the bill must be approved on the floor of each chamber. Usually such approval is given quickly. Occasionally, however, a bill's opponents use this round of approval as one last opportunity to defeat a piece of legislation.

## The President's Veto Controls the Flow of Legislation

Once adopted by the House and Senate, a bill goes to the president, who may choose to sign the bill into law or **veto** it. The veto is the president's constitutional power to prevent a bill from becoming a law. To veto a bill, the president returns it unsigned within ten days to the house of Congress in which it originated. If Congress adjourns during the ten-day period, such that congressional adjournment prevents the president from returning the bill to Congress, the bill is also considered to be vetoed. This latter method is known as the **pocket veto.** The possibility of a presidential veto affects how willing members of Congress are to push for different pieces of legislation at different times. If they think a proposal is likely to be vetoed, they might shelve it for a later time.

A presidential veto may be overridden by a two-thirds vote in both the House and the Senate. A veto override says much about the support that a president can expect from Congress, and a successful override can deliver a stinging blow to the executive branch.

# ● Several Factors Influence How Congress Decides

What determines the kinds of legislation that Congress ultimately produces? According to the simplest theories of representation, members of Congress would respond to the views of their constituents. In fact, creating a legislative agenda, drawing up a list of possible measures, and deciding among them is a complex process in which a variety of influences from inside and outside government play important roles. External influences include a legislator's constituency and various interest groups. Influences from inside government include party leadership, congressional colleagues, and the president. Let us examine each of these influences individually and then consider how they interact to produce congressional policy decisions.

## Constituents Matter

Because members of Congress, for the most part, want to be re-elected, we would expect the views of their constituents to be a primary influence on the decisions that legislators make. Yet most constituents do not even know what policies their representatives support. The number of citizens who *do* pay attention to such matters—the attentive public—is usually very small. Nonetheless, members of Congress spend a lot of time worrying about what their constituents think, because these representatives realize that the choices they make may be scrutinized in a future election and used as ammunition by an opposing candidate. Because of this possibility, members of Congress try to anticipate their constituents' policy views.[19]

## Interest Groups Influence Constituents and Congress

Interest groups are another important external influence on the policies that Congress produces. When members of Congress are making voting decisions, those interest groups that have some connection to constituents in particular members' districts are most likely to be influential. For this reason, interest groups with the ability to mobilize followers in many congressional districts may be especially influential in Congress.

Interest groups also have substantial influence in setting the legislative agenda and in helping to craft specific language in legislation. Today, sophisticated lobbyists win influence by providing information about policies to busy members of Congress. In the 2009–2010 health reform effort, the biotechnology firm Genentech ghostwrote statements that more than a dozen members of Congress placed into the Congressional Record. Genentech's role came to light when it became evident that members had used the exact same language in their entries.[20] In recent years, interest groups have also begun to build broader coalitions and comprehensive campaigns around particular policy issues. These coalitions do not rise from the grass roots but instead are put together by Washington lobbyists who launch comprehensive lobbying campaigns that combine simulated grassroots activity with information and campaign funding for members of Congress.

Concerns that special interests exerted too much influence led Congress to enact new ethics legislation in 2007. The new law set new restrictions on the gifts lobbyists can bestow on lawmakers and limited privately funded travel. The law also prohibited members of Congress from lobbying for two years after they retire (it had been one year) and required lawmakers to identify the earmarks they insert in legislation. It also aimed to shine light on the practice of "bundling," in which lobbyists assemble money from a number of clients to make a single political donation. Now lobbyists will be required to disclose the names of the individual contributors to these political donations. Although the new law provides additional transparency, allowing the public to learn more about the relationship between lobbyists and members of Congress, it does not fundamentally alter the fact that wealthy interest groups continue to exercise tremendous influence in Congress.

*Members often spend a great deal of time in their electoral districts meeting with constituents. Congressman Elijah E. Commings of Maryland is shown here greeting constituents at an event in Baltimore.*

## Party Leaders Rely on Party Discipline

In both the House and the Senate, party leaders have a good deal of influence over the behavior of their party members. This influence, sometimes called "party discipline," was once so powerful that it dominated the lawmaking process. At the turn of the century, party leaders could often command the allegiance of more than 90 percent of their members. A vote in which 50 percent or more of the members of one party take one position while at least 50 percent of the members of the other party take the opposing position is called a **party unity vote.** At the beginning of the twentieth century, nearly half of all **roll-call votes** (a vote in which each legislator's yes or no vote is recorded as the clerk calls the names of the members alphabetically) in the House of Representatives were party votes. While party voting is rarer today than a century ago, in the last decade it has been fairly common to find at least a majority of the Democrats opposing a majority of the Republicans on any given issue.

Typically, party unity is greater in the House than in the Senate. House rules give more power to the majority party leaders, which gives them more influence over House members. In the Senate, however, the leadership has few controls over its members. Former Senate majority leader Tom Daschle once observed that a

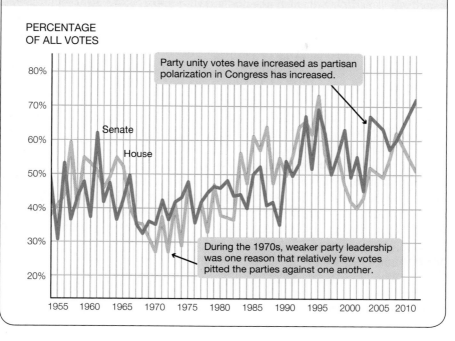

**FIGURE 9.8 Party Unity Votes by Chamber**

Party unity votes are roll-call votes in which a majority of one party lines up against a majority of the other party. Party unity votes increase when the parties are polarized and when the party leadership can enforce discipline. Why did the percentage of party unity votes decline in the 1970s? Why has it risen in recent years?

SOURCE: Richard Rubin, "Party Unity: An Ever Thicker Dividing Line," *CQ Weekly Online* (January 11, 2010): 122–31. http://library.cqpress.com (accessed 2/5/10).

Former Senate leader seeking to influence other senators has as incentives "a bushel full of carrots and a few twigs."[21]

Party unity has been on the rise in recent years because the divisions between the parties have deepened on many high-profile issues such as abortion, affirmative action, the minimum wage, and school vouchers (see Figure 9.8), and because the majority-minority party difference has been small in recent years. Party unity scores rise when congressional leaders try to put a partisan stamp on legislation. For example, in 1995, then-Speaker Newt Gingrich sought to enact a Republican Contract with America that few Democrats supported. The result was more party unity in the House than in any year since 1954. Since then, the polarization of political parties has shown up in very high party unity scores. In 2009, House Democrats voted with the majority 91 percent of the time, close to their all-time high of 92 percent in 2007 and 2008. In 2009, Senate Democrats set a record for party unity by voting with their caucus 91 percent of the time. Republicans were also very united, althought at slightly lower levels. In 2009, House Republicans voted with their party 87 percent of the time; Senate Republicans voted with their party 85 percent of the time.

Although party organization has weakened since the turn of the twentieth century, today's party leaders still have some resources at their disposal: (1) leadership PACs, (2) committee assignments, (3) access to the floor, (4) the whip system, (5) logrolling, and (6) the presidency. These resources are regularly used and are often effective in securing the support of party members.

**Leadership Pacs** Leaders have increased their influence over members in recent years with aggressive use of leadership political action committees. Leadership PACs are organizations that members of Congress use to raise funds that they then distribute to other members of their party running for election. Republican congressional leaders pioneered the aggressive use of leadership PACs to win their congressional majority in 1995, and the practice has spread widely since that time. Money from leadership PACs can be directed to the most vulnerable candidates or to candidates who are having trouble raising money. The PACs enhance the power of the party and create a bond between the leaders and the members who receive their help.[22]

**Committee Assignments** Leaders can create debts among members by helping them get favorable committee assignments. These assignments are made early in the congressional careers of most members and cannot be taken from them if they later go against party discipline. Nevertheless, if the leadership goes out of its way to get the right assignment for a member, this effort is likely to create a bond of obligation that can be called upon without any other payments or favors. This is one reason the Republican leadership gave freshmen favorable assignments when the Republicans took over Congress in 1995. When the Democrats won control of Congress in 2007, House Speaker Nancy Pelosi gave desirable and prestigious committee assignments to Democratic House members who faced competitive re-election races to assist them in their home districts.

**Access to the Floor** The most important everyday resource available to the parties is control over access to the floor. With thousands of bills awaiting passage and most members clamoring for access in order to influence a bill or to publicize themselves, floor time is precious. In the Senate, the leadership allows ranking committee members to influence the allocation of floor time—who will speak for how long; in the House, the Speaker, as head of the majority party (in consultation with the minority leader), allocates large blocks of floor time. Thus, floor time is allocated in both houses of Congress by the majority and minority leaders. More importantly, the Speaker of the House and the majority leader in the Senate possess the power of recognition—that is, they decide who may and may not speak on the floor. Although this power may not appear to be substantial, it is a formidable authority and can be used to stymie a piece of legislation completely or to frustrate a member's attempts to speak on a particular issue. Because the power is significant, members of Congress usually attempt to stay on good terms with the Speaker and the majority leader in order to ensure that they will continue to be recognized.

**The Whip System** Some influence accrues to party leaders through the whip system within each party in Congress, which is primarily a communications network in each house of Congress; whips take polls of the membership in order to learn their intentions on specific legislative issues and to assist the majority and minority leaders in various tasks. Between twelve and twenty assistant and regional whips are selected to operate at the direction of the majority or minority leader and the whip. They take polls of all the members in order to learn their intentions on specific bills. This enables the leaders to know if they have enough support to allow a vote as well as whether the vote is so close that they need to put pressure on a few undecided members. Leaders also use the whip system to convey their wishes and plans to the members, but only in very close votes do they actually exert pressure on a member.

The whip system helps maintain party unity in both houses of Congress, but it is particularly critical in the House of Representatives because of the large number of legislators whose positions and votes must be accounted for. The majority and minority whips and their assistants must be adept at inducing compromise among legislators who hold widely differing viewpoints.

As Republican House whip from 1995 to 2002, Tom DeLay (R-Tex.) established a reputation as an effective vote counter and a tough leader, earning the nickname "the hammer." DeLay also expanded the reach of the whip, building alliances with Republican allies outside of Congress in ideological and business-oriented groups. Under DeLay's leadership, these lobbyists effectively worked as part of the whip operation. As whip, DeLay also began a campaign to pressure trade associations to hire Republicans as their lobbyists, which has since been continued by his successor, Roy Blunt (R-Mo.). These relationships led to accusations of corruption, leading to DeLay's resignation from Congress in 2006. Under the Democrats, the whip system returned to its former status as an instrument of the Speaker.

*As Speaker of the House, Nancy Pelosi ensured that freshmen Democrats—such as Steve Driehaus of Ohio, pictured here—had opportunities to speak on the floor. Despite this increased visibility, many Democratic freshmen, including Driehaus, lost their bids for re-election in 2010.*

**Logrolling** A legislative practice wherein agreements are made between legislators in voting for or against a bill is called **logrolling.** Unlike bargaining, parties to logrolling have nothing in common but their desire to exchange support. The agreement states, in effect, "You support me on bill X and I'll support you on bill Y." Since party leaders are the center of the communications networks in the two chambers, they can help members create large logrolling coalitions. Hundreds of logrolling deals are made each year, and although there are no official record-keeping books, it would be a poor party leader whose whips did not know who owed what to whom.

**The Presidency** Of all the influences that maintain the clarity of party lines in Congress, the influence of the presidency is probably the most important. Indeed, the office is a touchstone of party discipline in Congress. Since the late 1940s, under President Harry Truman, presidents each year have identified a number of bills to be considered part of their administration's program. By the mid-1950s, both parties in Congress began to look to the president for these proposals, which became the most significant part of Congress's agenda. The president's support is an important criterion for party loyalty, and party leaders are able to use it to rally some members.

## ● Much Congressional Energy Goes to Tasks Other Than Lawmaking

In addition to the power to make the law, Congress has at its disposal an array of other instruments through which to influence the process of government. The Constitution gives the Senate the power to approve treaties and appointments. And Congress has a number of other powers through which it can influence the other branches of government.

### Congress Oversees How Legislation Is Implemented

**Oversight** refers to the effort by Congress, through hearings, investigations, and other techniques, to exercise control over the activities of executive agencies by overseeing or supervising how legislation is carried out by the executive branch. Oversight is carried out by committees or subcommittees of the Senate or the House, which conduct hearings and investigations in order to analyze and evaluate bureaucratic agencies and the effectiveness of their programs. Their purpose may be to locate inefficiencies or abuses of power, to explore the relationship between what an agency does and what a law intended, or to change or abolish a program. Most programs and agencies are subject to some oversight every year during the course of hearings on **appropriations,** that is, the amounts of money approved by Congress in statutes (bills) that each unit or agency of government can spend.

Committees or subcommittees have the power to subpoena witnesses, take oaths, cross-examine, compel testimony, and bring criminal charges for contempt (refusing to cooperate) and perjury (lying). Hearings and investigations resemble each other in many ways, but they differ on one fundamental point. A hearing is usually held on a specific bill, and the questions asked there are usually intended to build a record with regard to that bill. In an investigation, the committee or subcommittee does not begin with a particular bill, but examines a broad area or problem and then concludes its investigation with one or more proposed bills. One example of an investigation is the Senate hearings on the abuse of prisoners in Iraq's Abu Ghraib prison. Many Democrats and some Republicans complained that congressional oversight of the entire Iraq war had been lax. Reflecting on the prison abuse scandal, Representative Christopher Shays (R-Conn.) stated, "I believe our failure to do proper oversight has hurt our country and the administration. Maybe they wouldn't have gotten into some of this trouble if our oversight had been better."[23]

When Democrats took control of Congress in 2007, the congressional oversight role increased dramatically. To highlight the importance of the oversight, Democrats renamed the House Government Reform Committee as the House Oversight and Government Reform Committee and added four new subcommittees dedicated to oversight. They also hired over two hundred new investigative staffers.[24] Armed with these resources, Congress stepped up the number of oversight hearings: during its first six months in power, the Democratic Congress held 942 oversight hearings, compared to 579 for the same period when Republicans controlled the Congress in 2005.[25] The hearings dealt with a wide range of issues, including inquiries into government contracting, the activities of the private contractor Blackwater in Iraq, the revelation of the identity of CIA officer Valerie Plame, and the firing of nine U.S. attorneys. Many of the hearings created high drama as once-powerful former administration officials, such as former Secretary of Defense Donald Rumsfeld and Attorney General Alberto Gonzales, were called to account for their actions in office. Congress also held hearings on the financial crisis in 2008, sharply questioning the fallen titans of Wall Street. Members wanted to know whether the executives withheld information from their shareholders or protected their own salaries at the expense of their employees. Congress has been especially vigilant in using its oversight powers to investigate the financial crisis. Under the legislation passed in 2008, Congress appointed an oversight panel to help it monitor the Treasury Department's implementation of the $700 billion Troubled Asset Relief Program (TARP, otherwise known as "the bank bailout"). That panel, headed by Harvard law professor Elizabeth Warren, submitted monthly reports to Congress throughout 2009 and held multiple public meetings across the country. Congress also enacted a law that created the Financial Crisis Inquiry Commission, a ten-member commission charged with holding hearings to establish the causes of the 2008 financial collapse.[26]

## Special Senate Powers Include Advice and Consent

The Constitution has given the Senate a special power, one that is not based on lawmaking. The president has the power to make treaties and to appoint top executive officers, ambassadors, and federal judges—but only "with the Advice and Consent of the Senate" (Article II, Section 2). For treaties, two-thirds of senators present must concur; for appointments, a simple majority is required.

# Get Your Representatives in Congress Working for You

Most college students receive federal financial assistance in the form of Pell grants or subsidized loans. Many students view such assistance as absolutely essential to their ability to stay in school. Members of Congress are well aware of these concerns, thanks in part to the letters, emails, and personal visits from many young people who have contacted them. In 2007, Congress responded by passing the College Cost Reduction and Access Act, which overhauls the federal student aid program and raises the level of grants. Voicing your opinion on this issue—or the countless others that Congress takes up each session—may seem difficult, but it is actually relatively easy.

- You first need to know who is representing you in the House and Senate. To locate your senators, go to the U.S. Senate Web site (www.senate.gov) and use the drop-down menu to enter your state. You can find out who your representative is by visiting the U.S. House of Representatives Web site (www.house.gov) and entering your zip code.

- Follow the links to your representatives' Web sites, where you can read their biographies, learn about their committee assignments, and find out what legislation they have sponsored.

- *Learn about past votes.* You can also use the Web sites of the two chambers to look up how your member may have voted in the past.

- *Follow current policymaking.* Both the House and the Senate Web sites have links to allow you to check what legislation is currently on the floor or in committee. You can also use the Library of Congress's Web site (thomas.loc.gov) to search for bills.

- *Contact Congress directly.* You can phone Congress by calling the U.S. Capitol Switchboard at (202) 224-3121 and ask to be connected to your senators or your representative. You can send them emails through links on their home Web sites. Or you can send a letter to their Washington, D.C., office (the address is on their Web site).

- *See your representative or senator in person.* Members of Congress spend a lot of time in their home districts and states, holding town hall meetings and listening to the concerns of their constituents. You can find out their schedules by emailing or calling their office, and then simply show up at a local event.

- *Follow the money.* You can find out who is donating money to your representative and senators by visiting www.opensecrets.org and clicking on "Politicians and Elections."

- *Apply for an internship.* Most members of Congress have internships that run either for a school term or for the summer. Your university's internship coordinator (and sometimes even the political science department) has probably worked with local congressional offices in the past and can help facilitate your application.

The power to approve or reject presidential requests also involves the power to set conditions. The Senate only occasionally exercises its power to reject treaties and appointments, and usually that is when opposite parties control the Senate and the White House. For example, only nine judicial nominees have been rejected by the Senate during the past century, whereas hundreds have been approved.

## Impeachment Is the Power to Remove Top Officials

The Constitution also grants Congress the power of **impeachment** over the president, vice president, top executive branch officials, and judicial officials. To impeach means the House of Representatives charges a government official (president or otherwise) with "Treason, Bribery, or other high Crimes and Misdemeanors" and brings that person before Congress to determine guilt. Impeachment is thus like a criminal indictment in which the House of Representatives acts like a grand jury, voting (by simple majority) on whether the accused ought to be impeached. If a majority of the House votes to impeach, an impeachment trial is conducted in and by the Senate, which acts like a trial jury by voting whether or not to convict and forcibly remove the person from office (this vote requires a two-thirds majority of the Senate).

Controversy over Congress's impeachment power has arisen over the grounds for impeachment, especially the meaning of "high Crimes and Misdemeanors." The most widely accepted legal view says that an impeachable offense would include a serious crime committed by the president, such as murder, but not all crimes. Obviously, no one would impeach a president for, say, a traffic violation. In addition, an impeachable offense could include an action that is legal, such as a president deserting his office and presidential responsibilities to, say, lie on a beach in Brazil for six months. Any serious abuse of presidential powers and responsibilities would also be impeachable.[27] Politically speaking, the ambiguity of the definition of impeachment also means that "an impeachable offense is whatever the majority of the House of Representatives considers it to be at a given moment in history."[28] In other words, impeachment, especially impeachment of a president, is a political decision.

Two presidents have been subjected to impeachment trials. In 1867, President Andrew Johnson, a southern Democrat who had battled a congressional Republican majority over Reconstruction, was impeached by the House but saved from conviction by one vote in the Senate. On December 19, 1998, the House of Representatives approved two articles of impeachment against President Bill Clinton, accusing him of lying under oath and obstructing justice in the investigation of his affair with White House intern Monica Lewinsky. The articles were approved on a nearly straight line party vote, and Clinton's defenders argued that the impeachment effort was politically motivated and that while Clinton had made mistakes in attempting to hide his affair with Lewinsky, nothing he did constituted an impeachable offense. After a Senate trial, Clinton was acquitted on February 12, 1999. Neither of the two articles of impeachment garnered even a majority of Senate votes. Within days of the end of the impeachment saga, Clinton moved to resume constructive relations with Congress.

# studyguide

## Practice Quiz

 Find a diagnostic Web Quiz with 35 additional questions on the StudySpace Web site: www.wwnorton.com/we-the-people

1. Because they have larger and more heterogeneous constituencies, senators *(p. 268)*
   a) are more attuned to the needs of localized interest groups.
   b) care more about re-election than House members.
   c) can better represent the national interest.
   d) face less competition in elections than House members.

2. What type of representation is described when constituents have the power to hire and fire their representative? *(p. 269)*
   a) agency representation
   b) sociological representation
   c) democratic representation
   d) trustee representation

3. Which is *not* an advantage congressional incumbents have in winning re-election? *(p. 272)*
   a) their ability to provide constituency service
   b) their ability to raise money and their strong public recognition scaring off potentially strong challengers
   c) their legislative ability to redistrict
   d) the support of their party's congressional campaign committees

4. Some have argued that the creation of minority congressional districts has *(p. 274)*
   a) lessened the sociological representation of minorities in Congress.
   b) made it more difficult for minorities to win substantive policy goals.
   c) been a result of the media's impact on state legislative politics.
   d) lessened the problem of "pork-barrel" politics.

5. Members of Congress can work as agents of their constituents by *(pp. 275–76)*
   a) providing direct patronage.
   b) taking part in a party vote.
   c) joining a caucus.
   d) supporting term limits.

6. Which of the following types of committees does *not* include members of both the House and the Senate? *(pp. 280–82)*
   a) standing committee
   b) joint committee
   c) conference committee
   d) No committees include both House members and senators.

7. Which of the following is a technique that can be used to block debate about a bill in the Senate? *(pp. 283–86)*
   a) floor vote
   b) the introduction of new amendments
   c) veto
   d) fillibuster

8. Which of the following is *not* an important influence on how members of Congress vote on legislation? *(pp. 287–89)*
   a) the media
   b) constituency
   c) interest groups
   d) party leaders

9. Which of the following is *not* a resource that party leaders in Congress use to create party discipline? *(pp. 290–92)*
   a) committee assignments
   b) access to the floor
   c) the whip system
   d) roll-call votes

10. An agreement between members of Congress to trade support for each other's bill is known as *(p. 292)*
    a) oversight.
    b) filibuster.
    c) logrolling.
    d) patronage.

11. When Congress conducts an investigation to explore the relationship between what a law intended and what an executive agency has done, it is engaged in *(p. 292)*
    a) advice and consent.
    b) oversight.
    c) executive agreement.
    d) direct patronage.

12. Which of the following statements about impeachment is *not* true? *(p. 295)*
    a) The president is the only official who can be impeached by Congress.
    b) The House of Representatives decides by simple majority vote whether the accused ought to be impeached.
    c) The Senate decides whether to convict and remove the person from office.
    d) There have only been two instances of impeachment in American history.

## Chapter Outline

Find a detailed Chapter Outline on the StudySpace Web site: www.wwnorton.com/we-the-people

## Key Terms

Find Flashcards to help you study these terms on the StudySpace Web site: www.wwnorton.com/we-the-people

**agency representation** *(p. 269)* the type of representation by which representatives are held accountable to their constituency if they fail to represent that constituency properly. This is the incentive for good representation when the personal backgrounds, views, and interests of the representative differ from those of his or her constituency

**appropriations** *(p. 292)* the amounts of money approved by Congress in statutes (bills) that each unit or agency of government can spend

**bicameral** *(p. 267)* a two-chambered legislature; opposite of unicameral

**bill** *(p. 283)* a proposed law that has been sponsored by a member of Congress and submitted to the clerk of the House or Senate

**cloture** *(p. 285)* a rule allowing three-fifths of the members in the U.S. Senate to set a time limit on debate over a given bill

**conference** *(p. 277)* a gathering of House Republicans every two years to elect their House leaders. Democrats call their gathering the caucus

**conference committee** *(p. 282)* a joint committee created to work out a compromise on House and Senate versions of a piece of legislation

**constituency** *(p. 267)* the people in the district from which an official is elected

**filibuster** *(p. 285)* a tactic used by members of the Senate to prevent action on legislation they oppose by continuously holding the floor and speaking until the majority backs down. Once given the floor, senators have unlimited time to speak, and it requires a vote of three-fifths of the Senate to end a filibuster

**gerrymandering** *(p. 273)* the process of re-drawing legislative district boundary lines to provide political advantage or disadvantage

**impeachment** *(p. 295)* the formal charge by the House of Representatives that a government official has committed "Treason, Bribery, or other high Crimes and Misdemeanors"

**incumbency** *(p. 271)* holding a political office for which one is running election after election

**joint committee** *(p. 281)* a legislative committee formed of members of both the House and the Senate

**logrolling** *(p. 292)* a legislative practice wherein agreements are made between legislators in voting for or against a bill; vote trading

**majority leader** *(p. 277)* the elected leader of the majority party in the House of Representatives or in the Senate. In the House, the majority leader is subordinate in the party hierarchy to the Speaker of the House

**minority leader** *(p. 277)* the elected leader of the minority party in the House or Senate

**oversight** *(p. 292)* the effort by Congress, through hearings, investigations, and other techniques, to exercise control over the activities of executive agencies by overseeing or supervising how legislation is carried out by the executive branch

**party unity vote** *(p. 288)* a roll-call vote in the House or Senate in which at least 50 percent of the members of one party take a particular position and are opposed by at least 50 percent of the members of the other party. Party votes are rare today, although they were fairly common in the nineteenth century

**patronage** *(p. 275)* the resources available to higher officials, including making partisan appointments to offices and conferring grants, licenses, or special favors to supporters

**pocket veto** *(p. 286)* a veto that occurs when the president does not sign a passed bill within ten days of receiving it, and Congress adjourned

**pork barrel (or pork)** *(p. 275)* appropriations made by legislative bodies for local projects that are often not needed but that are created to help local representatives win re-election in their home districts

**private bill** *(p. 276)* a proposal in Congress to provide a specific person with some kind of relief, such as a special exemption from immigration quotas

**redistricting** *(p. 273)* the process of redrawing election districts and redistributing legislative representatives. This happens every ten years to reflect shifts in population or in response to legal challenges to existing districts

**roll-call vote** *(p. 288)* a vote in which each legislator's yes or no vote is recorded as the clerk calls the names of the members alphabetically

**select committee** *(p. 280)* a (usually) temporary legislative committee set up to highlight or investigate a particular issue or address an issue not within the jurisdiction of existing committees

**seniority** *(p. 282)* priority or status ranking given to an individual on the basis of length of continuous service on a committee in Congress

**sociological representation** *(p. 268)* a type of representation in which representatives have the same racial, ethnic, religious, or educational backgrounds as their constituents. It is based on the principle that if two individuals are similar in background, character, interests, and perspectives, then one could represent the other's views

**Speaker of the House** *(p. 277)* the chief presiding officer of the House of Representatives. The Speaker is elected at the beginning of every Congress on a straight party vote. The Speaker is the most important party and House leader and can influence the legislative agenda, the fate of individual pieces of legislation, and members' positions within the House

**standing committee** *(p. 280)* a permanent committee with the power to propose and write legislation that covers a particular subject, such as finance or appropriations

**term limits** *(p. 273)* legally set limits on the number of terms an elected official can serve

**veto** *(p. 286)* the president's constitutional power to turn down law. A presidential veto may be overridden by a two-thirds vote of each house of Congress

**whips** *(p. 278)* party members in the House or Senate who are responsible for coordinating the party's legislative strategy, building support for key issues, and counting votes

# For Further Reading

Berg, John C. *Class, Gender, Race, and Power in the U.S. Congress.* Boulder, CO: Westview, 1994.

Burrell, Barbara C. *A Woman's Place Is in the House: Campaigning for Congress in the Feminist Era.* Ann Arbor: University of Michigan Press, 1994.

Davidson, Roger H., ed. *The Postreform Congress.* New York: St. Martin's, 1991.

Dodd, Lawrence, and Bruce I. Oppenheimer, eds. *Congress Reconsidered,* 9th ed. Washington, DC: Congressional Quarterly Press, 2008.

Dodson, Debra L. *The Impact of Women in Congress.* New York: Oxford University Press, 2006.

Fenno, Richard F. *Homestyle: House Members in Their Districts.* Boston: Little, Brown, 1978.

Fiorina, Morris. *Congress: Keystone of the Washington Establishment,* 2nd ed. New Haven, CT: Yale University Press, 1989.

Fowler, Linda, and Robert McClure. *Political Ambition: Who Decides to Run for Congress?* New Haven, CT: Yale University Press, 1989.

Koger, Gregory. *Filibustering: A Political History of Obstruction in the House and Senate.* Chicago: University of Chicago Press, 2010.

Mann, Thomas E., and Norman J. Ornstein. *The Broken Branch: How Congress Is Failing America and How to Get It Back on Track.* New York: Oxford University Press, 2006.

Mayhew, David R. *Congress: The Electoral Connection.* New Haven, CT: Yale University Press, 1974.

Palmer, Barbara, and Denise Simon. *Breaking the Political Glass Ceiling: Women and Congressional Elections*, 2nd ed. New York: Routledge, 2008.

Sinclair, Barbara. *Unorthodox Lawmaking,* 3rd ed. Washington, DC: Congressional Quarterly Press, 2007.

Smith, Steven S., and Christopher Deering. *Committees in Congress,* 3rd ed. Washington, DC: Congressional Quarterly Press, 1997.

Spitzer, Robert J. *President and Congress.* New York: McGraw-Hill, 1993.

# Recommended Web Sites

**Capitol Hearings**
www.capitolhearings.org
> Congressional committees are essential to the lawmaking process. They do most of the legislative work by gathering information and writing bills. Read about congressional committees at C-SPAN's Capitol Hearings page.

**Cook Political Report**
www.cookpolitical.com
> The Cook Political Report, by Charlie Cook, is a nonpartisan analysis of electoral politics. Check out current House and Senate races for an in-depth analysis of past elections and previews of congressional elections.

**Library of Congress: Thomas**
http://thomas.loc.gov
> The Library of Congress's "Thomas" website is a superb place to find roll-call votes, current legislation, and the full text of the *Congressional Record* and committee reports.

**National Committee for an Effective Congress**
www.ourcampaigns.com
> Congressional redistricting is the process of redrawing House districts every ten years to account for shifts in population. For information about redistricting in your state, log on to the Redistricting Resource Center, provided by the National Committee for an Effective Congress.

**Roll Call**
www.rollcall.com
> *Roll Call*, the newspaper of Capitol Hill, provides daily coverage on the members, legislation, and events taking place in and around the U.S. legislature.

**The Sunlight Foundation and Taxpayers for Common Sense**
http://earmarkwatch.org
> Earmarks are language that members of Congress put into legislation that dedicates funds for specific uses, many whose broad benefits can be questioned. The Sunlight Foundation and Taxpayers for Common Sense are two watchdog groups that have joined forces to publish a database of congressional earmarks. Earmarks can be searched by state, congressional sponsor, recipient, and description of the project.

**U.S. House of Representatives**
**www.house.gov**
**U.S. Senate**
**www.senate.gov**

These are the official websites for the U.S. House of Representatives and the U.S. Senate. Here you can find information on your members of Congress, key congressional leaders, bills currently under consideration, and legislative committees.

Shortly after taking office in 2009, President Barack Obama signed the American Recovery and Reinvestment Act Bill, which provided $787 billion to help stimulate the economy. As a new president, Obama inherited numerous challenges—like the economic recession—as well as vast powers.

# 10

# The Presidency

**WHAT GOVERNMENT DOES AND WHY IT MATTERS** When the Obama administration took office in 2008, it inherited a host of problems from its predecessor, including the ongoing wars in Iraq and Afghanistan, continuing fears of terrorism, and an ongoing financial crisis. During the campaign, all the candidates had pledged to find new solutions to the global challenges facing America. Yet in his first years in office, President Obama found the nation's problems to be difficult to solve. Despite a massive economic stimulus package, levels of unemployment remained high and the health of the nation's financial and housing markets remained in doubt. The war in Afghanistan ground on, with the administration searching for a strategy that might bring an end to the conflict. And, as Americans were reminded by an attempt to smuggle powerful bombs onto two airplanes in October, 2010, the threat of terrorism had not been ended.

The new president also inherited a presidency vastly more powerful than the institution imagined by the framers of the U.S. Constitution. Ironically, the same wars that presented such an enormous challenge to the new administration also had the potential to enhance its power.

Presidential power increases during times of war. For example, President Abraham Lincoln's 1862 declaration of martial law and Congress's 1863 legislation giving the president the power to make arrests and imprisonments through military tribunals amounted to a "constitutional dictatorship" that lasted through the war. During World War II, Franklin D. Roosevelt brought the United States into an undeclared naval war against Germany a year before Pearl Harbor, and he ordered the unauthorized use of wiretaps and other surveillance as well as the investigation of suspicious persons for reasons not clearly specified. The most egregious of these actions was his segregation and confinement of 120,000 individuals of Japanese descent, many of whom were American citizens. The Supreme Court validated Roosevelt's treatment of the Japanese, citing military necessity. One dissenter on the Court called the president's assumption of emergency powers "a loaded weapon ready for the hand of any authority that can bring forward a plausible claim of an urgent need."

The "loaded weapon" was seized again on September 14, 2001, when Congress defined the World Trade Center and Pentagon attacks as an act of war and proceeded to adopt a joint resolution authorizing the president to use "all necessary and appropriate force against those nations, organizations or persons he determines planned, authorized, committed or aided the terrorist attacks that occurred on September 11, 2001, or harbored such organizations or persons. . . ." On the basis of this authorization, President Bush ordered the invasion of Afghanistan and began the reorganization of the nation's "homeland security." President Obama rescinded some Bush-era policies, but disappointed many civil libertarians as he continued Bush's policy of vigorously asserting national security needs and government secrecy claims to block lawsuits and press access to information regarding the treatment of terror suspects.[1]

In this chapter, we will examine the foundations of the American presidency and the character of presidential power in the twenty-first century. National emergencies are one source of presidential power, but presidents are also empowered by democratic political processes and, increasingly, by their ability to control and expand the institutional resources of the office. We saw in the last chapter that Congress's power is built on the Constitution, but that the legislative branch has changed in many ways since 1789. The same can be said of the presidency, yet the two institutions have taken very different paths. Whereas Congress is less assertive of its constitutional powers, modern presidents claim even greater powers, both from the Constitution and from their often superior political position. Congress's constitutional powers are many; those of the presidency are few, by comparison. Yet today, presidents behave as though it were the reverse.

# Presidential Power Is Rooted in the Constitution

The presidency was established by Article II of the Constitution. Article II begins by asserting, "The executive power shall be vested in a President of the United States of America." It goes on to describe the manner in which the president is to be chosen and defines the basic powers of the presidency. By vesting the executive power in a single president, the framers were emphatically rejecting proposals for various forms of collective leadership.

The presidential selection process defined by Article II resulted from a struggle between those delegates who wanted the president to be selected by, and thus responsible to, Congress and those delegates who preferred that the president be elected directly by the people. Direct popular election would create a more independent and more powerful presidency. With the adoption of a scheme of indirect election through an electoral college in which the electors would be selected by the state legislatures (and close elections would be resolved in the House of Representatives), the framers hoped to achieve a "republican" solution: a strong president responsible to state and national legislators rather than directly to the electorate. This indirect method of electing the president probably did dampen the power of most presidents in the nineteenth century. This conclusion is supported by the fact that, as we shall see later in this chapter, presidential power increased as the president developed a closer and more direct relationship with a mass electorate.

While Section 1 of Article II explains how the president is to be chosen, Sections 2 and 3 outline the powers and duties of the president. These two sections identify two sources of presidential power. Some presidential powers are specifically established by the language of the Constitution. For example, the Constitution authorizes the president to make treaties, grant pardons, and nominate judges and other public officials. These specifically defined powers granted to the president in the Constitution are called the **expressed powers** of the office and cannot be revoked by the Congress or any other agency without an amendment to the Constitution. Other expressed powers include the power to receive ambassadors and command of the military forces of the United States.

In addition to the president's expressed powers, Article II declares that the president "shall take Care that the Laws be faithfully executed." Since the laws are enacted

*The framers of the Constitution wanted an "energetic" presidency, capable of quick, decisive action. However, when George Washington was sworn in as the first president in 1789, the presidency was a less powerful office than it is today.*

by Congress, this language implies that Congress is to delegate to the president the power to implement or execute its will. Powers given to the president by Congress are called **delegated powers** (constitutional powers that are assigned to one governmental agency but that are exercised by another agency with the express permission of the first). In principle, Congress delegates to the president only the power to identify or develop the means through which to carry out its decisions. So, for example, if Congress determines that air quality should be improved, it might delegate to the executive the power to identify the best means of bringing about such an improvement as well as the power to implement the cleanup process. In practice, of course, decisions about how to clean the air are likely to have an enormous impact on businesses, organizations, and individuals throughout the nation. As it delegates power to the executive, Congress substantially enhances the importance of the presidency and the executive branch. In most cases, Congress delegates power to executive agencies rather than to the president. As we shall see, however, contemporary presidents have found ways to capture a good deal of this delegated power for themselves.

Presidents have claimed a third source of power beyond expressed and delegated powers. These are powers not specified in the Constitution or the law but said to stem from "the rights, duties and obligations of the presidency."[2] These powers claimed by a president that are not expressed in the Constitution, but are inferred from it, are referred to as the **inherent powers** of the presidency and are most often asserted by presidents in times of war or national emergency. For example, after the fall of Fort Sumter and the outbreak of the Civil War, President Abraham Lincoln issued a series of executive orders for which he had no clear legal basis. Without even calling Congress into session, Lincoln combined the state militias into a ninety-day national volunteer force, called for forty thousand new volunteers, enlarged the regular army and navy, diverted $2 million in unspent appropriations to military needs, instituted censorship of the U.S. mails, ordered a blockade of southern ports, suspended the writ of *habeas corpus* in the border states, and ordered the arrest by military police of individuals whom he deemed to be guilty of engaging in or even contemplating treasonous actions.[3] Lincoln asserted that these extraordinary measures were justified by the president's inherent power to protect the nation.[4] Subsequent presidents, including Franklin D. Roosevelt and George W. Bush, have had similar views.

## Expressed Powers Come Directly from the Words of the Constitution

The president's expressed powers, as defined by Sections 2 and 3 of Article II, fall into several categories:

1. *Military.* Article II, Section 2, provides for the power as "Commander in Chief of the Army and Navy of the United States, and of the Militia of the several States, when called into the actual Service of the United States."

2. *Judicial.* Article II, Section 2, also provides the power to "grant Reprieves and Pardons for Offenses against the United States, except in Cases of Impeachment."

3. *Diplomatic.* Article II, Section 2, also provides the power "by and with the Advice and Consent of the Senate, to make Treaties." Article II, Section 3, provides the power to "receive Ambassadors and other public Ministers."

4. *Executive.* Article II, Section 3, authorizes the president to see to it that all the laws are faithfully executed; Section 2 gives the chief executive the power to appoint, remove, and supervise all executive officers and to appoint all federal judges.

5. *Legislative.* Article I, Section 7, and Article II, Section 3, give the president the power to participate authoritatively in the legislative process.

**Military** The president's military powers are among the most important exercised by the chief executive. The position of **commander in chief** (the power of the president as commander of the national military and the state national guard units when called into service) makes the president the highest military authority in the executive branch. Final authority over military matters rests with Congress, which may direct the commander in chief as it chooses. In the nineteenth century, Congress normally directed the president's military actions and decisions. In the twentieth century, however, presidents have engaged the country in many military campaigns abroad without congressional approval. Congress has not declared war since December 1941, and yet since then American military forces have engaged in numerous campaigns throughout the world under orders of the president. When North Korean forces invaded South Korea in June 1950, Congress was actually prepared to declare war, but President Harry S. Truman decided not to ask for congressional action. Instead, Truman asserted the principle that the president and not Congress could decide when and where to deploy America's military might. Truman dispatched American forces to Korea without a congressional declaration, and in the face of the emergency, Congress felt it had to acquiesce. Congress passed a resolution approving the president's actions, and this became the pattern for future congressional-executive relations in the military realm. The wars in Vietnam, Bosnia, Afghanistan, Iraq, and a host of lesser conflicts—all were fought without declarations of war.

In 1973, Congress responded to presidential unilateralism by passing the **War Powers Resolution** over President Richard Nixon's veto. This law states that the president can send troops into action abroad only by authorization of Congress, or if American troops are already under attack or serious threat. It reasserted the principle of congressional war power, required the president to inform Congress of any planned military campaign, and stipulated that forces must be withdrawn within sixty days in the absence of a specific congressional authorization for their continued deployment. Presidents, however, have generally ignored the War Powers Resolution, claiming inherent executive power to defend the nation.

President George W. Bush responded to the 2001 attacks by Islamic terrorists by organizing a major military campaign to overthrow the Taliban regime in Afghanistan, which had sheltered the terrorists. In 2003, Bush ordered a major American campaign against Iraq, which he accused of posing a threat to the United States. U.S. forces overthrew the government of the Iraqi dictator, Saddam Hussein, and occupied the country. In both instances, Congress passed resolutions approving the president's actions beforehand, but the president was careful to assert that he did not need congressional authorization. The War Powers Resolution was cited in both the terror attack and Iraq resolutions but was ignored by the White House.

Within the executive branch, the president directs the secretary of defense, who heads the vast Defense Department, encompassing all the military branches of service. The president also directs the nation's intelligence network, which includes not only the Central Intelligence Agency (CIA) but also the National Security Council (NSC), the National Security Agency (NSA), the Federal Bureau of Investigation (FBI), and a host of less well-known but very powerful international and domestic security agencies.

**Military Sources of Domestic Power** The president's military powers extend into the domestic sphere. Article IV, Section 4, provides that the "United States shall [protect] every State . . . against Invasion . . . and . . . domestic Violence," and Congress has made this an explicit presidential power through statutes directing the president as commander in chief to discharge these obligations.[5] The Constitution restrains the president's use of domestic force by providing that a state legislature (or governor when the legislature is not in session) must request federal troops before the president can send them into the state to provide public order. Yet this proviso is not absolute. First, presidents are not obligated to deploy national troops merely because the state legislature or governor makes such a request. And more important, the president may deploy troops in a state or city without a specific request from the state legislature or governor if the president considers it necessary to maintain an essential national service during an emergency, to enforce a federal judicial order, or to protect federally guaranteed civil rights.

One historic example of the unilateral use of presidential emergency power to protect the states against domestic disorder, even when the states don't request it, was the decision by President Dwight Eisenhower in 1957 to send troops into Little

*In 2010, President Obama visited American troops in Afghanistan. A few months earlier, Obama ordered a "surge" of 30,000 reinforcements to be sent to Afghanistan. Although the strategy was controversial, even among Obama's own party, Congress approved funding for the increase in troops.*

Rock, Arkansas, literally against the wishes of the state of Arkansas, to enforce court orders to integrate Little Rock's Central High School. The governor of Arkansas, Orval Faubus, had actually posted the Arkansas National Guard at the entrance of Central High School to prevent the court-ordered admission of nine black students. After an effort to negotiate with Governor Faubus failed, President Eisenhower reluctantly sent a thousand paratroopers to Little Rock, who stood watch while the black students took their places in the all-white classrooms. This case makes it quite clear that the president does not have to wait for a request by a state legislature or governor before acting as a domestic commander in chief.[6]

Military emergencies have typically also led to expansion of the domestic powers of the executive branch. This was true during the First and Second World Wars and has been true in the wake of the war on terrorism as well. Within a month of the 9/11 attacks, the White House had drafted and Congress had enacted the USA PATRIOT Act, expanding the power of government agencies to engage in domestic surveillance activities, including electronic surveillance, and restricting judicial review of such efforts. The act also gave the attorney general greater authority to detain and deport aliens suspected of having terrorist affiliations. The following year, Congress created the Department of Homeland Security, combining offices from twenty-two federal agencies into one huge new cabinet department responsible for protecting the nation from attack and responding to other emergencies. The new agency included the Coast Guard, Transportation Safety Administration, Federal Emergency Management Administration, Immigration and Naturalization Service, and offices from the departments of Agriculture, Energy, Transportation, Justice, Health and Human

Services, Commerce, and the General Services Administration. The White House drafted the actual reorganization plan, but Congress weighed in to make certain that the new agency's workers had civil service and union protections.

**Judicial** The presidential power to grant reprieves, pardons, and amnesties involves the power of life and death over all individuals who may be a threat to the security of the United States. Presidents may use this power on behalf of a particular individual, as did Gerald Ford when he pardoned Richard Nixon in 1974 "for all offenses against the United States which he . . . has committed or may have committed." Or they may use it on a large scale, as did President Andrew Johnson in 1868, when he gave full amnesty to all southerners who had participated in the "Late Rebellion," and President Carter in 1977, when he declared an amnesty for all the draft evaders of the Vietnam War. President Clinton created great controversy with a large number of last-minute pardons issued in the final days of his presidency in 2000. President George W. Bush, on the other hand, issued fewer pardons than any president in modern times.[7]

**Diplomatic** The president is America's "head of state"—its chief representative in dealings with other nations. As head of state, the president has the power to make treaties for the United States (with the advice and consent of the Senate). And when President Washington received Edmond Genêt ("Citizen Genêt") as the formal emissary of the revolutionary government of France in 1793 and had his cabinet officers and Congress back his decision, he established a greatly expanded interpretation of the power to "receive Ambassadors and other public Ministers," extending it to the power to "recognize" other countries. That power gives the president the almost unconditional authority to review the claims of any new ruling groups to determine if they indeed control the territory and population of their country, so that they can commit it to treaties and other agreements.

In recent years, presidents have expanded the practice of using executive agreements instead of treaties to establish relations with other countries.[8] An **executive agreement** is exactly like a treaty because it is a contract between two countries that has the force of a treaty but does not require the Senate's "advice and consent." Ordinarily, executive agreements are used to carry out commitments already made in treaties or laws, or to arrange for matters well below the level of policy. But when presidents have found it expedient to use an executive agreement in place of a treaty, Congress has typically acquiesced.

**Executive Power** The most important basis of the president's power as chief executive is to be found in Article II, Section 3, which stipulates that the president must see that all the laws are faithfully executed, and Section 2, which provides that the president will appoint, remove, and supervise all executive officers, and appoint all federal judges (with Senate approval). The power to appoint the principal executive officers and to require each of them to report to the president on subjects relating to the duties of their departments makes the president the true chief executive officer (CEO) of the nation. In this manner, the Constitution focuses executive power and legal responsibility on the president. The famous sign on President Truman's desk, "The buck stops here," was not merely an assertion of Truman's personal sense of responsibility but was in fact recognition by him of the legal and constitutional responsibility of the president. The president is subject to some limitations, because the appointment of all such officers, including ambassadors, ministers, and federal judges, is subject to a majority approval by the Senate. But these appointments are at the discretion of the president, and the loyalty and the responsibility of each appointee are presumed to be directed toward the president.

**The President's Legislative Power** The president plays a role not only in the administration of government but also in the legislative process. Two constitutional provisions are the primary sources of the president's power in the legislative arena. The first of these is the provision in Article II, Section 3, providing that the president "shall from time to time give to the Congress Information of the State of the Union, and recommend to their Consideration such Measures as he shall judge necessary and expedient." The second of the president's legislative powers is of course the veto power assigned by Article I, Section 7.[9]

Delivering a "State of the Union" address does not at first appear to be of any great import. It is a mere obligation on the part of the president to make recommendations for Congress's consideration. But as political and social conditions began to favor an increasingly prominent role for presidents, each president, especially since Franklin Delano Roosevelt, began to rely on this provision to become the primary initiator of proposals for legislative action in Congress and the principal source for public awareness of national issues, as well as the most important single individual participant in legislative decisions. Few today doubt that the president and the executive branch together are the primary source for many important congressional actions.[10]

The **veto** power is the president's constitutional power to prevent a bill from becoming a law (see Figure 10.1). It makes the president the most important single legislative leader.[11] No bill vetoed by the president can become law unless both the House and the Senate override the veto by a two-thirds vote. In the case of a **pocket veto,** Congress does not have the option of overriding the veto but must reintroduce the bill in the next session. A pocket veto can occur if the president does not act on a given piece of legislation passed during the final ten days of a legislative session. Usually, if a president does not sign a bill within ten days, it automatically becomes law. But this is true only while Congress is in session. If a president chooses not to sign a bill presented within the last ten days of a legislative session, then Congress is out of session when the ten-day limit expires, and instead of becoming law, the bill is vetoed.

Use of the veto varies according to the political situation that each president confronts. President Bush vetoed only twelve bills in his eight-year presidency, the lowest per year average of any president since the nineteenth century. Eleven of those vetoes came during his last two years in office, when the Democratic Party controlled both houses of Congress. President Obama vetoed only one bill during his first two years in office: a minor bill having to do with stopgap (short-term) spending.

Although not explicitly stated, the Constitution implies that the president has the power of **legislative initiative**—the president's inherent power to bring a legislative agenda before Congress. To "initiate" means to originate, and in government that can mean power. Initiative obviously implies the ability to formulate proposals for important policies, and the president, as an individual with a great deal of staff

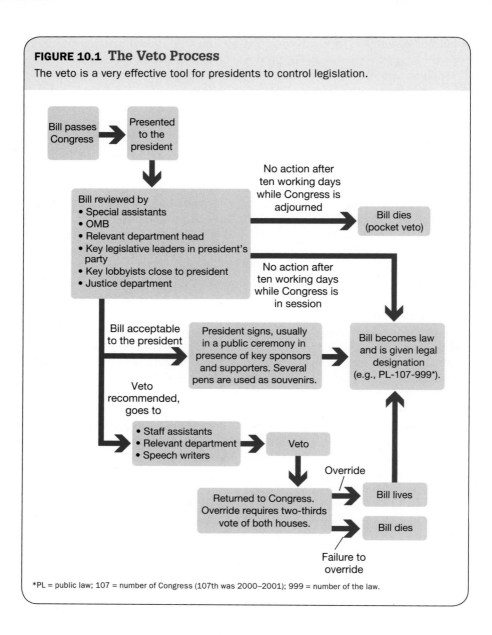

**FIGURE 10.1 The Veto Process**

The veto is a very effective tool for presidents to control legislation.

Bill passes Congress → Presented to the president

Bill reviewed by
- Special assistants
- OMB
- Relevant department head
- Key legislative leaders in president's party
- Key lobbyists close to president
- Justice department

No action after ten working days while Congress is adjourned → Bill dies (pocket veto)

No action after ten working days while Congress is in session → Bill becomes law and is given legal designation (e.g., PL-107-999*).

Bill acceptable to the president → President signs, usually in a public ceremony in presence of key sponsors and supporters. Several pens are used as souvenirs. → Bill becomes law and is given legal designation (e.g., PL-107-999*).

Veto recommended, goes to
- Staff assistants
- Relevant department
- Speech writers
→ Veto → Returned to Congress. Override requires two-thirds vote of both houses.
→ Override → Bill lives
→ Failure to override → Bill dies

*PL = public law; 107 = number of Congress (107th was 2000–2001); 999 = number of the law.

assistance, is able to initiate decisive action more frequently than Congress, with its large assemblies that have to deliberate and debate before taking action. With some important exceptions, Congress banks on the president to set the agenda of public policy. For example, during the weeks following September 11, 2001, George W. Bush took many presidential initiatives to Congress, and each was given nearly unanimous support—from commitments to pursue al Qaeda and the Taliban in Afghanistan, to a proposal to reconstitute the Afghan regime and a request for nearly unlimited power to mobilize American military force and impose greater restrictions on American civil liberties. In a similar vein, President Obama moved quickly after his election to deal with the nation's financial emergency and to overhaul America's health care system. Congress rapidly enacted the $787 billion financial stimulus package proposed by the president. On the matter of health care, political conflicts broke out between congressional advocates of a variety of competing approaches. Congressional leaders and Obama administration officials labored for almost a year to craft a health care plan that would pass muster in Congress. Nearly a year after the initiative was introduced, and after tumultuous political conflict, President Obama logged a major victory when he signed a sweeping health care reform bill. Obama's assertion that health care would be his top priority during his first year in office meant that it dominated Congress's attention as well.

The president's initiative does not end with policy making involving Congress and the making of laws in the ordinary sense of the term. The president has still another legislative role (in all but name) within the executive branch. This is designated as the power to issue **executive orders**. The executive order is a rule or regulation issued by the president that has the effect and formal status of legislation. It is first and foremost simply a normal tool of management, a power possessed by virtually any CEO to make rules setting procedures, etiquette, chains of command, functional responsibilities, and so on—"company policy." But evolving out of this normal management practice is a recognized presidential power to promulgate rules that have the effect and the formal status of legislation. Most of the executive orders of the president provide for the reorganization of structures and procedures or otherwise direct the affairs of the executive branch—either to be applied across the board to all agencies or applied in some important respect to a single agency or department. One of the most important examples is Executive Order No. 8248, September 8, 1939, establishing the divisions of the Executive Office of the President. Another one of equal importance is President Nixon's executive order establishing the Environmental Protection Agency in 1970–71.

## Delegated Powers Come from Congress

Many of the powers exercised by the president and the executive branch are not found in the Constitution but are the products of congressional statutes and resolutions. Over the past three-quarters of a century, Congress has voluntarily delegated a great deal of its own legislative authority to the executive branch. To some extent, this delegation of power has been an almost inescapable consequence of the expansion of government activity in the United States since the New Deal. Given the vast range of the federal government's responsibilities, Congress cannot execute and administer all the programs it creates and the laws it enacts. Inevitably, Congress must turn to the hundreds of departments and agencies in the executive branch or, when necessary, create new agencies to implement its goals. Thus, for example, in 2002, when Congress sought to protect America from terrorist attacks, it established a Department of Homeland Security and gave it broad powers in the realms of law enforcement, public health, and immigration. Similarly, in 1970, when Congress enacted legislation designed to improve the nation's air and water quality, it assigned the task of implementing its goals to the Environmental Protection Agency (EPA), which President Nixon created by an executive order. Congress gave the EPA substantial power to set and enforce air and water quality standards.

# Institutional Resources of Presidential Power Are Numerous

Constitutional sources of power are not the only resources available to the president. Presidents have at their disposal a variety of other formal and informal resources that have important implications for their ability to govern (see Figure 10.2). Indeed, without these other resources, presidents would lack the ability—the tools of management and public mobilization—to make much use of the power and responsibility given to them by Congress. Let us first consider the president's formal institutional resources and then, in the section following, turn to the more informal political resources that affect a president's capacity to govern, in particular the president's base of popular support.

## The Cabinet Departments

| DEPARTMENT CREATED | YEAR |
| --- | --- |
| State | 1789 |
| Treasury | 1789 |
| Defense* | 1947 |
| Justice | 1789 |
| Interior† | 1862 |
| Agriculture | 1889 |
| Commerce | 1913 |
| Labor | 1913 |
| Health and Human Services† | 1953 |
| Housing and Urban Development | 1965 |
| Transportation | 1966 |
| Energy | 1977 |
| Education | 1979 |
| Veterans Affairs | 1989 |
| Homeland Security | 2002 |

*Formerly the War and Navy Departments, created in 1789 and 1798, respectively.
†Created in 1862; made part of Cabinet in 1889.
†Formerly Health, Education, and Welfare; reorganized in 1979 (when separate Department of Education was created).

## The Cabinet Is Often Distant from the President

In the American system of government, the **Cabinet** is the traditional but informal designation for the heads (secretaries, or chief administrators), of all the major federal government departments. Cabinet secretaries are appointed by the president with the consent of the Senate. The Cabinet has no constitutional status. Unlike in England and many other parliamentary countries, where the cabinet *is* the government, the American Cabinet meets but it makes no decisions as a group. The Senate must approve each appointment, but Cabinet members are not responsible to the Senate or to Congress at large. Cabinet appointments help build party and popular support, but the Cabinet is not a party organ. The Cabinet is made up of directors but is not a true board of directors.

Aware of this fact, the president tends to (1) develop a burning impatience with and a mild distrust of Cabinet members; (2) make the Cabinet a rubber stamp for actions already decided on; and (3) demand results, or the appearance of results, more immediately and more frequently than most department heads can provide them. Since Cabinet appointees generally have not shared political careers with the president or with each other, and since they may meet literally for the first time after their selection, the formation of an effective governing group out of this diverse collection of appointments is unlikely.

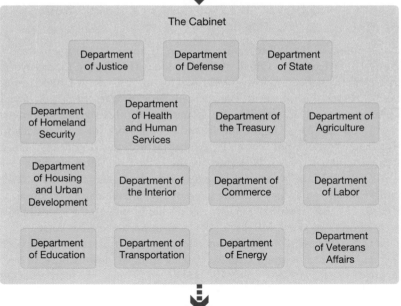

**FIGURE 10.2** The Institutional Presidency

Many offices and departments serve the modern president.

SOURCE: Office of the Federal Register, National Archives and Records Administration. *The United States Government Manual, 1995–96* (Washington, DC: Government Printing Office, 1995), p. 22.

The President

⬇

The White House Staff

⬇

**Executive Office of the President**

White House Office
Office of Management and Budget
Council of Economic Advisers
National Security Council
Office of National Drug Control Policy

Office of the U.S. Trade Representative
Council on Environmental Quality
Office of Science and Technology Policy
Office of Policy Development
Office of Administration
Vice President

⬇

**The Cabinet**

| | | |
|---|---|---|
| Department of Justice | Department of Defense | Department of State |

| | | | |
|---|---|---|---|
| Department of Homeland Security | Department of Health and Human Services | Department of the Treasury | Department of Agriculture |
| Department of Housing and Urban Development | Department of the Interior | Department of Commerce | Department of Labor |
| Department of Education | Department of Transportation | Department of Energy | Department of Veterans Affairs |

⬇

Independent Establishments and Government Corporations

## The White House Staff Constitutes the President's Eyes and Ears

The **White House staff** is composed mainly of analysts and advisers who are closest to, and most responsive to, the president's needs and preferences.[12] Although many of the top White House staff members are given the title "special assistant" for a particular task or sector, the types of judgments they are expected to make and the kinds of advice they are supposed to give are a good deal broader and more generally political than those coming from the Executive Office of the President or from the cabinet departments. The members of the White House staff also tend to be more closely associated with the president than other presidentially appointed officials.

From an informal group of fewer than a dozen people (popularly called the **Kitchen Cabinet**—advisers to whom the president turns for counsel and guidance; members of the official Cabinet may or may not also be members of the Kitchen Cabinet), and no more than four dozen domestic advisors at its height during the Roosevelt presidency in 1937, the White House staff has grown substantially with each successive president.[13] Nixon employed 550 people in 1972. President Carter, who found so many of the requirements of presidential power distasteful, and who publicly vowed to keep his staff small and decentralized, built an even larger and more centralized staff. President Clinton reduced the White House staff by 20 percent, but a large White House staff has become essential.

## The Executive Office of the President Is a Visible Sign of the Modern Strong Presidency

The development of the White House staff can be appreciated only in its relation to the still-larger **Executive Office of the President (EOP),** the permanent agencies that perform defined management tasks for the president. Created in 1939, the EOP includes the Office of Management and Budget, the Council of Economic Advisers, the National Security Council, and other agencies. Somewhere between 1,500 and 2,000 highly specialized people work for EOP agencies. The EOP is a major part of what is often called the "institutional presidency." The most important and the largest EOP agency is the Office of Management and Budget (OMB). Its roles in preparing the national budget, designing the president's program, reporting on agency activities, and overseeing regulatory proposals make OMB personnel part of virtually every conceivable presidential responsibility. The status and power of the OMB have grown in importance with each successive president. The process of budgeting at one time was a "bottom-up" procedure, with expenditure and program requests passing from the lowest bureaus through the departments to "clearance" in OMB and hence to Congress, where each agency could be called in to reveal what its "original request" had been before OMB revised it. Now the budgeting process is "top-down"; OMB sets priorities for agencies as well as for Congress. The director of OMB is now one of the most powerful officials in Washington.

The staff of the Council of Economic Advisers (CEA) constantly analyzes the economy and economic trends and attempts to give the president the ability to anticipate events rather than waiting and reacting to events. The Council on Environmental Quality was designed to do for environmental issues what the CEA does for economic issues. The National Security Council (NSC) is composed of designated Cabinet officials who meet regularly with the president to give advice on the large national security picture. The staff of the NSC assimilates and analyzes data from all intelligence-gathering agencies (CIA, etc). Other EOP agencies perform more specialized tasks.

## The Vice Presidency Has Become More Important since the 1970s

The vice presidency is a constitutional anomaly even though the Constitution created the office along with the presidency. The vice president exists for two purposes only: to succeed the president in case of death, resignation, or incapacitation and to preside over the Senate, casting a tie-breaking vote when necessary.[14]

The main value of the vice presidency as a political resource for the president is electoral. Traditionally, a presidential candidate's most important rule for the choice of a running mate is that he or she bring the support of at least one state (preferably a large one) not otherwise likely to support the ticket. Another rule holds that the vice presidential nominee should provide some regional balance and, wherever possible, some balance among various ideological or ethnic subsections of the party. It is very doubtful that John Kennedy would have won in 1960 without his vice presidential candidate, Lyndon Johnson, and the contribution Johnson made to winning in Texas. In 2008, Barack Obama chose Senator Joseph Biden of Delaware to be his running mate for a number of reasons. To begin with, Biden is Catholic and has blue-collar origins. Obama believed correctly that Biden would appeal to these important groups in such must-win states as Pennsylvania and Ohio. Perhaps even more important, Biden possessed enormous foreign policy experience and chaired the Senate Foreign Relations Committee. The Republicans had often pointed to Obama's lack of experience in the international realm as indicating that he was not ready to be president. Democrats hoped that Biden's presence on the ticket would put the "experience" issue to rest. Indeed, after John McCain designated Sarah Palin to be his vice presidential running mate in 2008, Republicans found it difficult to claim that their ticket was more experienced than that of the Democrats.

*Vice President Joseph Biden had thirty-five years' experience in the Senate before Barack Obama selected him as his running mate. In particular, Biden's foreign policy experience was seen as an important strength in the campaign and the Obama administration.*

Throughout history, presidential spouses have played an important role in White House initiatives. Eleanor Roosevelt was the first first lady to hold regular press conferences; she served as the administration's spokesperson on matters pertaining to race relations and human rights.

Presidents have often promised to give their vice presidents more responsibility, but this has only happened with recent presidents. Jimmy Carter involved his vice president, Walter Mondale, in important administrative decisions. Under President Reagan, Vice President George H. W. Bush was "kept within the loop" of decision making because Reagan delegated much of his power. President Clinton gave Vice President Al Gore major responsibility over such areas as administrative reform, technology, and environmental issues. Gore also became one of Clinton's closest, and most trusted, advisers.[15] The presidency of George W. Bush resulted in unprecedented power and responsibility for his vice president, Dick Cheney. At the start of his presidency, Bush gave Cheney unlimited access to, and control over, the political and policy apparatus of his presidency. Cheney used his position to exercise primary control over what he called "the iron issues"—the economy, national security, and energy. In late 2001, for example, Cheney obtained Bush's assent to order that foreign terrorism suspects held in the United States be denied access to the courts and that they could be detained indefinitely. This order was significant not only for its sweeping assertion of power but because the administration's foreign policy heads who would normally play a key role in such a policy—Secretary of State Colin Powell and National Security Adviser Condoleezza Rice—were neither informed about the decision nor consulted beforehand. Powell and Rice only learned of the decision when they heard about it on CNN.[16] In the Obama White House, Vice President Joe Biden is said to be regarded as the "skeptic-in-chief."[17] Biden's role is to question and criticize policy recommendations made to the president until, of course, the president makes a decision and the vice president falls loyally in step.

## The First Spouse Has Become Important to Policy

The president serves as both chief executive and chief of state—the equivalent of Great Britain's prime minister and monarch rolled into one, simultaneously leading the government and serving as a symbol of the nation at official ceremonies and functions. Traditionally, most first ladies (all presidents so far have been men, and only one president, James Buchanan, was a bachelor) limit their activities to the ceremonial portion of the presidency. First ladies greet foreign dignitaries, visit other countries, and attend important national ceremonies.

Because they are generally associated with the head-of-state aspect of America's presidency, presidential spouses are usually not subject to the same degree of media scrutiny or partisan attack as the president. Yet this has changed in recent times as first spouses have begun to exert more influence over policy. Franklin Roosevelt's wife, Eleanor, was widely popular, but also widely criticized, for her active role in many elements of her husband's presidency. Hillary Clinton played a major political and policy role in Bill Clinton's presidency. During the 1992 campaign, Bill Clinton often implied that she would be active in the administration by joking that voters would get "two for the price of one." After the election, Hillary took a leading role in many policy areas, most notably heading the administration's health care reform effort. She also became the first first lady to seek public office on her own when she ran for and won a seat in the U.S. Senate from New York in 2000, ran for the presidency in 2008, and was appointed Secretary of State by Obama in 2009. Barack Obama's wife, Michelle, is an attorney and served for a number of years as a senior administrator at the University of Chicago's Pritzker School of Medicine. Despite her legal and policy background, Michelle Obama played a mainly behind-the-scenes role in the first year, but became more visible and active thereafter, launching, for example, an anti-childhood-obesity campaign in 2010.

## ● Party, Popular Mobilization, and Administration Make Presidents Stronger

During the nineteenth century, Congress was America's dominant institution of government, and members of Congress sometimes treated the president with disdain. Today, however, no one would assert that the presidency is an unimportant institution. Presidents seek to dominate the policy-making process and claim the inherent power to lead the nation in time of war. The expansion of presidential power over the course of the past century has not come about by accident but as the result of an ongoing effort by successive presidents to enlarge the powers of the office. Some of these efforts have succeeded and others have failed. As the framers of the Constitution predicted, presidential *ambition* has been a powerful and unrelenting force in American politics.

Generally, presidents can expand their power in three ways: party, popular mobilization, and administration. In the first instance, presidents may construct or strengthen national partisan institutions with which to exert influence in the legislative process and through which to implement their programs. Second, presidents may use popular appeals to create a mass base of support that will allow them to subordinate their political foes. This tactic is called "going public."[18] Third, presidents may seek to bolster their control of established executive agencies or to create new administrative institutions and procedures that will reduce their dependence on Congress and give them a more independent governing and policy-making capability. Presidents' use of executive orders to achieve their policy goals in lieu of seeking to persuade Congress to enact legislation is, perhaps, the most obvious example.

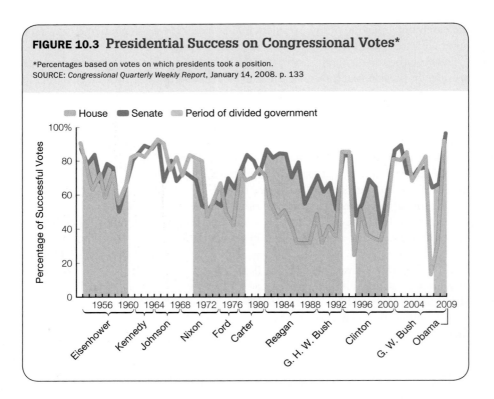

**FIGURE 10.3** Presidential Success on Congressional Votes*

*Percentages based on votes on which presidents took a position.
SOURCE: *Congressional Quarterly Weekly Report*, January 14, 2008. p. 133

House ■ Senate ■ Period of divided government

Percentage of Successful Votes

100%
80
60
40
20
0

1956 1960 1964 1968 1972 1976 1980 1984 1988 1992 1996 2000 2004 2009

Eisenhower  Kennedy  Johnson  Nixon  Ford  Carter  Reagan  G. H. W. Bush  Clinton  G. W. Bush  Obama

## Party Is a Source of Power

All presidents have relied on the members and leaders of their own party to implement their legislative agendas. President George W. Bush, for example, worked
closely with congressional GOP leaders on such matters as energy policy and Medicare reform. President Obama relied heavily on Democratic leaders in Congress to
advance health care reform. But the president does not control his own party.
Moreover, in America's system of separated powers, the president's party may be in
the minority in Congress and unable to do much for the chief executive's programs
(see Figure 10.3). Consequently, although their party is valuable to chief executives, it has not been a fully reliable presidential tool. As a result, contemporary
presidents are more likely to use two other methods—popular mobilization and
executive administration—to achieve their political goals.

## Going Public Tries to Whip Up the People

Popular mobilization as a technique of presidential power has its historial roots
in the presidencies of Theodore Roosevelt and Woodrow Wilson and has, subsequently, become a weapon in the political arsenals of most presidents since the
mid-twentieth century. During the nineteenth century, it was considered inappropriate for presidents to engage in personal campaigning on their own behalf or in
support of programs and policies. When Andrew Johnson broke this unwritten rule

and made a series of speeches vehemently seeking public support for his Reconstruction program, even some of Johnson's most ardent supporters were shocked at what they saw as his lack of decorum and dignity. The president's opponents cited his "inflammatory" speeches in one of the articles of impeachment drafted by the Congress pursuant to the first impeachment trial of a president in history.[19]

The first presidents to make systematic use of appeals to the public were Theodore Roosevelt and Woodrow Wilson, but the president who used public appeals most effectively was Franklin Delano Roosevelt. The political scientist Sydney Milkis observes that FDR was "firmly persuaded of the need to form a direct link between the executive office and the public.[20] Roosevelt developed a number of tactics aimed at forging such a link. FDR made important use of the new electronic

*President Franklin Delano Roosevelt's direct appeals to the American people allowed FDR to "reach over the heads" of congressional opponents and force them to follow his lead because their constituents demanded it.*

medium, the radio, to reach millions of Americans. In his famous "fireside chats," the president, or at least his voice, came into every living room in the country to discuss programs and policies and generally to assure Americans that Franklin Delano Roosevelt was aware of their difficulties and working diligently toward solutions.

Roosevelt was also an innovator in the realm of what is now called press relations. When he entered the White House, FDR faced a mainly hostile press typically controlled by conservative members of the business establishment. As the president wrote, "All the fat-cat newspapers—85 percent of the whole—have been utterly opposed to everything the Administration is seeking."[21] Roosevelt hoped use the press to mold public opinion, but to do so he needed to circumvent the editors and publishers who were generally unsympathetic to his goals. To this end, the president worked to cultivate the reporters who covered the White House. Roosevelt made himself available for biweekly press conferences where he offered candid answers to reporters' questions and made certain to make important policy announcements that would provide the reporters with significant stories to file with their papers.[22]

Every president since FDR has sought to craft a public-relations strategy that would emphasize the incumbent's strengths and maximize his popular appeal. For John F. Kennedy, handsome and quick-witted, the televised press conference was an excellent public-relations vehicle. Johnson and Nixon lacked Kennedy's charisma, but both were effective television speakers, usually reading from a prepared text. Bill Clinton made extensive use of televised town meetings—carefully staged events in which the president would not be asked the sorts of pointed questions preferred by reporters and which gave the president an opportunity to appear to consult with rank-and-file citizens about his goals and policies. President Obama is a talented and effective speaker who often relies on his own speaking abilities rather than material crafted by the Communications Office.

**The Limits of Going Public** Some presidents have been able to make effective use of popular appeals to overcome congressional opposition. Popular support, though, has not been a firm foundation for presidential power. The public is notoriously fickle. President George W. Bush maintained an approval rating of over 70 percent for more than a year following the September 11 terrorist attacks. By the end of 2005, however, President Bush's approval rating had dropped to 39 percent as a result of the growing unpopularity of the Iraq war, the administration's inept handling of hurricane relief, and several White House scandals, including the conviction of Vice President Cheney's chief of staff on charges of lying to a federal grand jury. After America's triumph in the 1990 Persian Gulf War, President George H. W. Bush scored a remarkable 90 percent approval rating in the polls. Two years later, however, after the 1991 budget crisis, Bush's support plummeted and the president was defeated in his bid for re-election. Such declines in popular approval during a president's term in office are nearly inevitable and follow a predictable pattern (see Figure 10.4).[23] Presidents generate popular support by promising to undertake important programs that will contribute directly to the well-being of large numbers of Americans. Almost inevitably, presidential performance falls short of promises and popular expectations, leading to a sharp decline in public support and the ensuing collapse of presidential influence.[24] President Obama managed to maintain high personal approval, even as the public became more doubtful about some of his policy proposals.

## The Administrative State

Contemporary presidents have increased the administrative capabilities of their office in four ways. First, they have enhanced the reach and power of the Executive Office of the President (EOP). Second, they have sought to increase White House control over the federal bureaucracy. Third, they have expanded the role of executive orders and other instruments of direct presidential governance. Fourth, presidents have used signing statements to negate congressional actions to which they object. Taken together, these four components of what might be called the White House "administrative strategy" have given presidents a capacity to achieve their programmatic and policy goals even when they are unable to secure congressional approval. Indeed, some recent presidents have been able to accomplish quite a bit without much congressional, partisan, or even public support.

**The Executive Office of the President** The Executive Office of the President has grown from six administrative assistants in 1939 to today's 400 employees working directly for the president in the White House office along with some 1,400 individuals staffing the divisions of the Executive Office.[25] The creation and growth of the White House staff gives the president an enormously enhanced capacity to gather information, plan programs and strategies, communicate with constituencies, and exercise supervision over the executive branch. The staff multiplies the president's eyes, ears, and arms, becoming a critical instrument of presidential power.[26]

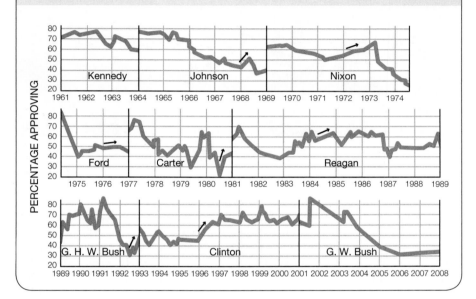

In particular, the Office of Management and Budget (OMB) serves as a potential instrument of presidential control over federal spending and hence a mechanism through which the White House has greatly expanded its power. In addition
to its power over the federal budget process (discussed earlier), the OMB has
the capacity to analyze and approve all legislative proposals, not only budgetary
requests, emanating from all federal agencies before being submitted to Congress.
This procedure, now a matter of routine, greatly enhances the president's control
over the entire executive branch. All legislation emanating from the White House
as well as all executive orders also go through the OMB.[27] Thus, through one White
House agency, the president has the means to exert major influence over the flow
of money as well as the shape and content of national legislation.

**Regulatory Review** A second tactic that presidents have used to increase their
power and reach is the process of regulatory review, through which presidents
have sought to seize control of rule making by the agencies of the executive branch
implementation (see also Chapter 11). Whenever Congress enacts a statute, its

*President Bill Clinton was a master of the televised town meeting, in which the president gives the appearance of consulting average citizens on important policy issues. Clinton's technique illustrated how campaign-style events could become tools to shape and sell national policy.*

actual implementation requires the promulgation of hundreds of rules by the agency charged with administering the law and giving effect to the will of Congress. Some congressional statutes are quite detailed and leave agencies with relatively little discretion. Typically, however, Congress enacts a relatively broad statement of legislative intent and delegates to the appropriate administrative agency the power to fill in many important details.[28] In other words, Congress typically says to an administrative agency, "Here is the problem: deal with it."[29]

The discretion Congress delegates to administrative agencies has provided recent presidents with an important avenue for expanding their own power. For example, President Clinton believed the president had full authority to order agencies of the executive branch to adopt such rules as the president thought appropriate. During the course of his presidency, Clinton issued 107 directives to administrators ordering them to propose specific rules and regulations. In some instances, the language of the rule to be proposed was drafted by the White House staff; in other cases, the president asserted a priority but left it to the agency to draft the precise language of the proposal. President George W. Bush continued the Clinton-era practice of issuing presidential directives to agencies to spur them to issue new rules and regulations. In January 2009, President Obama affirmed the importance of regulatory review but said his administration would review the process to make certain that federal agency guidance by the president would be fair and would involve public participation.[30]

**Governing by Decree: Executive Orders** Another mechanism through which contemporary presidents have sought to enhance their power to govern unilaterally is through the use of executive orders and other forms of presidential decrees, including executive agreements, national security findings and directives rectives, proclamations, reorganization plans, the signing of statements, and a host of others.[31] Executive orders have a long history in the United States and have been the vehicles for a number of important government policies, including the purchase of Louisiana, the annexation of Texas, the emancipation of the slaves, the internment of people of Japanese descent, the desegregation of the military, the initiation of affirmative action, and the creation of important federal agencies, among them the EPA, the FDA, and the Peace Corps.[32]

Presidents may not use executive orders to issue whatever commands they please. The use of such decrees is bound by law. If a president issues an executive order, proclamation, directive, or the like, in principle he does so pursuant to the powers granted to him by the Constitution or delegated to him by Congress, usually through a statute. When presidents issue such orders, they generally state the constitutional or statutory basis for their actions. For example, when President Truman ordered the desegregation of the armed services, he did so pursuant to his constitutional powers as commander in chief. In a similar vein, when President Johnson issued Executive Order No. 11246, he asserted that the order was designed to implement the 1964 Civil Rights Act, which prohibited employment discrimination. Where an executive order has no statutory or constitutional basis, the courts have held it to be void.[33]

President Clinton issued numerous orders designed to promote a coherent set of policy goals: protecting the environment, strengthening federal regulatory power, shifting America's foreign policy from a unilateral to a multilateral focus, expanding affirmative action programs, and helping organized labor in its struggles with employers.[34] President George W. Bush also did not hesitate to use executive orders, issuing nearly 300 during his two terms. During his first months in office, Bush issued orders prohibiting the use of federal funds to support international family-planning groups that provided abortion-counseling services and placing limits on the use of embryonic stem cells in federally funded research projects. Throughout his administration, Bush made very aggressive use of executive orders in response to the threat of terrorism. In November 2001, for example, Bush issued a directive authorizing the creation of military tribunals to try noncitizens accused of involvement in acts of terrorism against the United States. In 2007, Bush issued controversial national security directives that gave the president sole responsibility for determining when and how constitutional government could be reestablished in the event of a catastrophic attack on the United States. President Obama issued thirty-eight executive orders in his first year in office, using some of them to reverse executive orders of his predecessor (just as Bush reversed some of those of the Clinton years). Obama executive orders authorized stem cell research, restored funding for international family-planning organizations, opened access to presidential papers, and barred improper interrogation methods of detainees captured by the United States.

**Signing Statements** To negate congressional actions to which they object, recent presidents have made frequent and calculated use of presidential **signing statements**.[35] The signing statement is an announcement made by the president at the time of signing a congressional enactment into law, often presenting the president's interpretation of the law in addition to the usually innocuous remarks about the many benefits the law will bring the nation. Occasionally, presidents have used signing statements to point to sections of the law they deemed improper or even unconstitutional and to instruct executive branch agencies how to execute the law.[36] President Harry Truman, for example, accompanied his approval of the 1946 Hobbs Anti-Racketeering Act with a message offering his interpretation of ambiguous sections of the statute and indicating how the federal government would implement the law.[37]

Presidents have made signing statements throughout American history, though many were not recorded and did not become part of the official legislative record. Ronald Reagan's attorney general, Edwin Meese, is generally credited with transforming the signing statement into a significant tool of presidential direct action.[38]

With the way paved, Reagan, followed by G. H. W. Bush, Clinton, and G. W. Bush proceeded to use detailed and artfully designed signing statements—prepared by the Department of Justice—to attempt to actually reinterpret congressional enactments. For example, when signing the Safe Drinking Water Act Amendments of 1986, President Reagan issued a statement that interpreted sections of the act to allow discretionary enforcement when the Congress seemed to call for mandatory enforcement.[39] Reagan hoped the courts would accept his version of the statute when examining subsequent enforcement decisions. In other cases, Reagan used his signing statements to attempt to nullify portions of statutes. George W. Bush issued over 1,200 signing statements (twice as many as all previous presidents combined) and used them to rewrite the law on numerous occasions. As a candidate, Obama criticized Bush's prolific use of signing statements but did not entirely abandon the practice as president, issuing eight such statements in his first year in office.

# Work in the White House

Johanna Atienza was a twenty-year-old junior majoring in political science at a West Coast university when she learned from other students that her school had a Washington, D.C., internship program—and that it included the possibility of working in the White House. She was immediately interested: "What better way is there to learn about politics than from the inside?"

Johanna spent considerable time and effort on the application and then waited for the response. When she received the letter informing her of her acceptance, she was thrilled. In early January, she moved to Washington, D.C., and was assigned to work with the people who scheduled travel for the president and the first lady. Over the next three months, Johanna met and worked with some of the top officials in the White House. She also had the opportunity to meet the president and first lady.

What did Johanna learn from her three-month participation in the day-to-day life of White House politics that she was unlikely to learn in a classroom? First, she was struck by the incredible complexity of the presidency and Washington politics. Second, she gained tremendous respect for the people who work in the White House. They were dedicated people who worked long hours, often for little money.

- You can apply for the White House internship online at www.whitehouse.gov/government/whintern.html. Although the requirements vary with each presidential administration, students complete an application form that includes essay questions and provide two or three letters of recommendation. Once selected, interns must agree to a background check and a random drug test.

- Find out if your college offers course credit for internships in government. Although the internship is unpaid, students can usually arrange to earn course credits for their time, and, if they work with their home institution, they can use student loans to help cover the costs.

If a semester in Washington, D.C., does not fit into your schedule, there are many other ways to learn about the administration's policies and practices.

- Use the White House Web site to learn more about the president's policies. The WH Web page, www.whitehouse.gov, has links to at least a dozen top policy areas.

- Ask questions through the WH Web site. There are also links that will allow you to ask a question about the historical background of various presidential traditions.

- Listen to the president. The president records a weekly radio address that is broadcast on radio stations across the country. You can listen to the most recent recording, or search the archives to hear what the president has to say—in his own words and in his own voice.

# studyguide

## Practice Quiz

 Find a diagnostic Web Quiz with 31 additional questions on the StudySpace Web site: www.wwnorton.com/we-the-people

1. Which article of the Constitution established the presidency? *(p. 305)*
   a) Article I
   b) Article II
   c) Article III
   d) none of the above

2. What was the last American military involvement for which Congress declared war? *(p. 308)*
   a) World War II
   b) Korean War
   c) Vietnam War
   d) Iraq War

3. The War Powers Resolution of 1973 was an act passed by Congress that *(p. 308)*
   a) outlawed presidential use of executive agreements.
   b) created the National Security Council.
   c) granted the president the authority to declare war.
   d) stipulated that military forces must be withdrawn within sixty days in the absence of a specific congressional authorization for their continued deployment.

4. Which of the following does not require the advice and consent of the Senate? *(p. 310)*
   a) an executive agreement
   b) a treaty
   c) Supreme Court nominations
   d) All of the above require the advice and consent of the Senate.

5. What are the requirements for overriding a presidential veto? *(p. 311)*
   a) fifty percent plus one vote in both houses of Congress
   b) two-thirds vote in both houses of Congress
   c) three-fourths vote in both houses of Congress

   d) A presidential veto cannot be overridden by Congress.

6. When the president issues a rule or regulation that reorganizes or otherwise directs the affairs of the executive branch, such as the directives that established the Executive Office of the President and the Environmental Protection Agency, it is called *(p. 313)*
   a) an executive order.
   b) an executive mandate.
   c) administrative oversight.
   d) legislative initiative.

7. The Office of Management and Budget is part of *(p. 316)*
   a) the Executive Office of the President.
   b) the White House staff.
   c) the Kitchen Cabinet.
   d) both a and b.

8. How many people work for agencies within the Executive Office of the President? *(p. 316)*
   a) 25 to 50
   b) 700 to 1,000
   c) 1,500 to 2,000
   d) 4,500 to 5,000

9. Which of the following statements about vice presidents is *not* true? *(pp. 317–18)*
   a) The vice president succeeds the president in case of death, resignation, or incapacitation.
   b) The vice president casts the tie-breaking vote in the Senate when necessary.
   c) Presidential candidates typically select vice presidential candidates who are from their regions.
   d) Presidential candidates typically select vice presidential candidates who are likely to bring the support

of a state that would not otherwise support the ticket.

10. How has the role of the vice presidency changed since the 1970s? *(pp. 317–18)*
    a) the vice president's influence has decreased
    b) the vice president now appoints members of Supreme Court
    c) the vice president no longer helps the president win key states in an election
    d) the vice president's influence has increased

11. What are the three ways that presidents can expand their power? *(p. 319)*
    a) weakening national partisan institutions, avoiding popular appeals, and loosening their control of executive agencies
    b) strengthening national partisan institutions, using popular appeals, and bolstering their control of executive agencies
    c) weakening national partisan institutions, using popular appeals, and loosening their control of executive agencies
    d) strengthening national partisan institutions, avoiding popular appeals, and bolstering their control of executive agencies

12. When the president makes an announcement about his interpretation of a congressional enactment that he is signing into law, it is called *(p. 325)*
    a) a signing statement.
    b) an executive order.
    c) legislative initiative.
    d) executive privilege.

# Chapter Outline

 Find a detailed Chapter Outline on the StudySpace Web site: www.wwnorton.com/we-the-people

# Key Terms

 Find Flashcards to help you study these terms on the StudySpace Web site: www.wwnorton.com/we-the-people

**Cabinet** *(p. 314)* the secretaries, or chief administrators, of the major departments of the federal government. Cabinet secretaries are appointed by the president with the consent of the Senate

**commander in chief** *(p. 307)* the power of the president as commander of the national military and the state national guard units (when called into service)

**delegated powers** *(p. 306)* constitutional powers that are assigned to one governmental agency but that are exercised by another agency with the express permission of the first

**executive agreement** *(p. 310)* an agreement, made between the president and another country, that has the force of a treaty but does not require the Senate's "advice and consent"

**Executive Office of the President (EOP)** *(p. 316)* the permanent agencies that perform defined management tasks for the president. Created in 1939, the EOP includes the Office of Management and Budget, the Council of Economic Advisers, the National Security Council, and other agencies

**executive order** *(p. 313)* a rule or regulation issued by the president that has the effect and formal status of legislation

**expressed powers** *(p. 305)* specific powers granted to Congress in the Constitution

**inherent powers** *(p. 306)* powers claimed by a president that are not expressed in the Constitution but are inferred from it

**Kitchen Cabinet** *(p. 316)* an informal group of advisers to whom the president turns for counsel and guidance. Members of the official Cabinet may or may not also be members of the Kitchen Cabinet

**legislative initiative** *(p. 311)* the president's inherent power to bring a legislative agenda before Congress

**pocket veto** *(p. 311)* a veto that occurs when the president does not sign a passed bill within ten days of receiving it, and Congress has adjourned

**signing statement** *(p. 325)* an announcement made by the president when signing bills into

law, often presenting the president's interpretation of the law

**veto** *(p. 311)* the president's constitutional power to turn down a law. A presidential veto may be overridden by a two-thirds vote of each house of Congress

**War Powers Resolution** *(p. 308)* a resolution of Congress that the president can send troops into action abroad only by authorization of Congress, or if American troops are already under attack or serious threat

**White House staff** *(p. 316)* analysts and advisers to the president, often given the title "special assistant"

# For Further Reading

Aberbach, Joel, and Mark A. Peterson, eds. *The Executive Branch*. New York: Oxford University Press, 2005.

Crenson, Matthew, and Benjamin Ginsberg. *Presidential Power: Unchecked and Unbalanced*. New York: Norton, 2007.

Edwards, George. *Why the Electoral College Is Bad for America*. New Haven, CT: Yale University Press, 2004.

Fisher, Louis. *Presidential War Power*. Lawrence: University Press of Kansas, 2004.

Genovese, Michael. *Memo to a New President*. New York: Oxford University Press, 2008.

Genovese, Michael, and Robert J. Spitzer. *The Presidency and the Constitution*. New York: Palgrave/Macmillan, 2005.

Kernell, Samuel. *Going Public: New Strategies of Presidential Leadership*. Washington, DC: Congressional Quarterly Press, 2006.

Lowi, Theodore J. *The Personal President: Power Invested, Promise Unfulfilled*. Ithaca, NY: Cornell University Press, 1985.

Neustadt, Richard E. *Presidential Power: The Politics of Leadership from Roosevelt to Reagan*, rev. ed. New York: Free Press, 1990.

Pfiffner, James P. *The Modern Presidency*. New York: St. Martin's, 2008.

Rozell, Mark J., and Clyde Wilcox, eds. *The Clinton Scandal*. Washington, DC: Georgetown University Press, 2000.

Savage, Charles. *Takeover: The Return of the Imperial Presidency*. Boston: Little, Brown, 2007.

Skowronek, Stephen. *Presidential Leadership in Political Time*. Lawrence: University Press of Kansas, 2008.

Spitzer, Robert J. *President and Congress*. New York: McGraw-Hill, 1993.

Spitzer, Robert J. *The Presidential Veto: Touchstone of the American Presidency*. Albany: SUNY Press, 1988.

Warshaw, Shirley Anne. *The Co-Presidency of Bush and Cheney*. Stanford, CA: Stanford University Press, 2009.

# Recommended Web Sites

**Almanac of Policy Issues: War Powers Resolution**
www.policyalmanac.org/world/archive/war_powers_resolution.shtml
> The War Powers Resolution was passed in 1973 to define and limit the president's power during times of war. Read the full text of the resolution at this Web page.

**Dave Leip's Atlas of U.S. Presidential Elections**
www.uselectionatlas.org
> For information on upcoming and past presidential elections, refer to this Web page. Experiment with the electoral college calculator to see how your state could affect the electoral outcome.

**The National Archives: Executive Branch**
www.archives.gov/executive/
> Research official executive branch documents at the Executive Branch Web page, provided by the U.S. National Archives and Records Administration.

**Vicepresidents.com**
www.vicepresidents.com
> This Web site is dedicated to providing lots of interesting facts and archives about vice presidents, along with some lively humor.

**The White House**
www.whitehouse.gov
> This is the official Web site of the White House. Here you can read about current presidential news, the president's Cabinet, executive orders, and presidential appointments.

**White House Historical Association**
www.whitehousehistory.org
> The White House Historical Association is dedicated to the understanding, appreciation, and preservation of the White House. At its Web site you can find historical facts and take a detailed online tour of the numerous rooms and the property.

**The White House: Past First Ladies**
www.whitehouse.gov/history/firstladies/
> The first lady is an important resource for the president in his role as head of state. Read about the current and past first ladies on this Web site.

The Coast Guard—an agency within the federal bureaucracy—led the efforts to contain and clean up the Deepwater Horizon oil spill in 2010. These efforts included relocating endangered wildlife that was threatened by the spill. Here, pelicans rescued from the oil slick are loaded onto Coast Guard planes for release in a safer wildlife reserve.

# Bureaucracy

**11**

**WHAT GOVERNMENT DOES AND WHY IT MATTERS** Americans depend
on government bureaucracies to accomplish the most spectacular achievements as well as the most mundane. Yet they often do not realize that public
bureaucracies are essential for providing the services that they use every day
and that they rely on in emergencies. On a typical day, a college student might
check the weather forecast, drive on an interstate highway, mail the rent check,
drink from a public water fountain, check the calories on the side of a yogurt
container, attend a class, log on to the Internet, and meet a relative at the airport. Each of these activities is possible because of the work of a government
bureaucracy: the U.S. Weather Service, the U.S. Department of Transportation,
the U.S. Postal Service, the Environmental Protection Agency, the Food and
Drug Administration, the student loan programs of the U.S. Department of Education, the Advanced Research Projects Agency (which developed the Internet
in the 1960s), and the Federal Aviation Administration. Without the ongoing
work of these agencies, many of these common activities would be impossible,
unreliable, or more expensive. Even though bureaucracies provide essential
services that all Americans rely on, they are often disparaged by politicians and
the general public alike.

In emergencies, the national perspective on bureaucracy and, indeed, on "big government" shifts. After the September 11 terrorist attacks, all eyes turned to Washington. The federal government responded by strengthening and reorganizing the bureaucracy to undertake a whole new set of responsibilities designed to keep America safe. In the biggest government reorganization in over half a century, Congress created the Department of Homeland Security in 2002. The massive new department merged twenty-two existing agencies into a single department employing nearly 170,000 workers. Although the Bush administration presided over the creation of the Department of Homeland Security, Bush, like his Republican predecessors Ronald Reagan and George H. W. Bush, sought to roll back the regulatory role of the government.

Since coming to office, President Obama, like his Democratic predecessor Bill Clinton, has taken a different approach, one that reflects a greater belief in governmental action and the bureaucracy. Obama has appointed experienced state officials and scientific experts to important positions in major agencies and increased their funding. The White House has allowed agencies more latitude to make regulations than in the past. The Environmental Protection Agency (EPA), for example, determined that it would set standards for greenhouse gas emissions under the Clean Air Act. During Obama's first year, the Food and Drug Administration (FDA) took a more active role in regulating dietary supplements by placing warnings on such goods, while the Consumer Product Safety Commission has begun fining major toy companies for selling dangerous products, such as those containing lead.[1]

In the last two chapters, we examined the two branches of government— Congress and the presidency—that exercise ultimate responsibility over the bureaucracy. The numerous departments, agencies, offices, and bureaus that make up the bureaucracy exist because Congress created them by legal enactment. Congress oversees the activities of agencies, controls their funding, and can even rearrange or dismantle an agency. The president, as chief executive, can appoint top agency officials (with Senate approval), issue rules to govern agency behavior, control agency funding requests, and apply various other political pressures to compel agencies to respond to presidential priorities. Yet despite these many controls, members of Congress and presidents often express frustration at what they claim are the severe limits on the powers they can exercise to control the bureaucracy. These tensions suggest a separation of powers approach to studying the relationship between these three parts of the government.

## Bureaucracy Exists to Improve Efficiency

Bureaucracy is simply a form of organization. To appreciate the universality of bureaucracy, let us take the word and break it into its two main parts—*bureau* and *cracy*. *Bureau*, a French word, can mean either "office" or "desk." *Cracy* is the Greek word for "rule" or "form of rule." Putting *bureau* and *cracy* back together produces a very interesting definition: **bureaucracy** is the complex structure of offices, tasks, rules, and principles of organization that are employed by all large-scale institutions to coordinate effectively the work of their personnel. Each member of an organization has an office, meaning a place as well as a set of responsibilities. That is, each "office" is made up of a set of tasks that are specialized to the needs of the organization, and the person holding that office (or position) performs those specialized tasks. Specialization and repetition are essential to the efficiency of any organization. Therefore, when an organization is inefficient, it is almost certainly because it is not bureaucratized enough!

Bureaucracies not only perform specialized tasks that require routine action but also undertake politically controversial tasks that require them to exercise a great deal of discretion and professional judgment. In many areas of policy, Congress writes laws that are very broad and it is up to the bureaucracy to define what the laws will mean in practice. The decisions that bureaucrats make—often based on professional judgments—can themselves become politically contentious.

Both routine and exceptional tasks require the organization, specialization, and expertise found in bureaucracies. To provide these services, government bureaucracies employ specialists such as meteorologists, doctors, and scientists. To do their job effectively, these specialists require resources and tools (ranging from paper to blood samples); they have to coordinate their work with others (for example, the traffic engineers must communicate with construction engineers); and there must be effective outreach to the public (for example, private doctors must be made aware of health warnings). Bureaucracy provides a way to coordinate the many different parts that must work together in order to provide good services.

# The Size of the Federal Service Has Actually Declined

For decades, politicians from both parties have asserted that the federal government is too big. Ronald Reagan led the way with his 1981 statement that government was the problem, not the solution. Fifteen years later President Bill Clinton abandoned the traditional Democratic defense of government, declaring that "the era of big government is over." President George W. Bush voiced similar sentiments when he accepted his party's nomination for president in 2000, proclaiming "Big government is not the answer!" President Obama struck a different tone. Addressing Congress on the topic of health care reform, he noted that while Americans had a "healthy skepticism about government," they also believed that "hard work and responsibility should be rewarded by some measure of security and fair play" and recognized "that sometimes government has to step in to help deliver that promise."[2] Despite fears of bureaucratic growth getting out of hand, however, the federal service has hardly grown at all during the past thirty-five years; it reached its peak postwar level in 1968 with 3 million civilian employees plus an additional 3.6 million military personnel (a figure swollen by Vietnam). The number of civilian federal employees has since fallen to approximately 2.7 million in 2008; the number of military personnel totals only 1.4 million.[3]

The growth of the federal service is even less imposing when placed in the context of the total workforce and when compared to the size of state and local public employment. Figure 11.1 indicates that, since 1950, the ratio of federal employment to the total workforce has been steady, and in fact has *declined* slightly in the past thirty years. In 1950, there were 4.3 million state and local civil service employees (about 6.5 percent of the country's workforce). In 2007, there were just over 19 million (nearly 14 percent of the workforce). Federal employment, in contrast, exceeded 5 percent of the workforce only during World War II (not shown), and almost all of that temporary growth was military. After the demobilization, which continued until 1950 (as shown in Figure 11.1), the federal service has tended to grow at a rate that keeps pace with the economy and society. That is demonstrated by the lower line on Figure 11.1, which shows a constant relation between federal civilian employment and the size of the U.S. workforce. Variations in federal employment since 1946 have been in the military and are directly related to war and the Cold War (as shown by the top line on Figure 11.1).

Another useful comparison is to be found in Figure 11.2. Although the dollar increase in federal spending shown by the bars looks impressive, the trend line indicating the relation of federal spending to the Gross Domestic Product (GDP) remained close to what it had been in 1960. This changed in 2009, when the recession pushed spending way up, as the federal government sought to stimulate the economy and spending on other recession-related programs, such as unemployment insurance, rose. In 2009, the budget also reflected the costs of the wars in Iraq and Afghanistan for the first time.

In sum, the national government is indeed "very large," but it has not been growing any faster than the economy or the society. The same is roughly true of the growth pattern of state and local public personnel.

**FIGURE 11.1** Employees in the Federal Service and in the National Workforce, 1946–2008

Since 1950, the ratio of federal employment to the total workforce has gradually declined. The lower line in this figure shows that the federal service has tended to grow at a rate that keeps pace with the economy and society. The upper line shows that variations in federal employment since 1946 have been in the military and are directly related to war and the Cold War. When did military employment begin its sharp decline?

SOURCE: U.S. Census Bureau, "Federal Civilian Employment and Annual Payroll by Branch: 1970–2008," *Statistical Abstract of the United States 2010*, Table 484, www.census.gov; U.S. Census Bureau, "Department of Defense Personnel: 1960–2008," *Statistical Abstract of the United States 2010*, Table 498, www.census.gov (accessed 2/10/10).

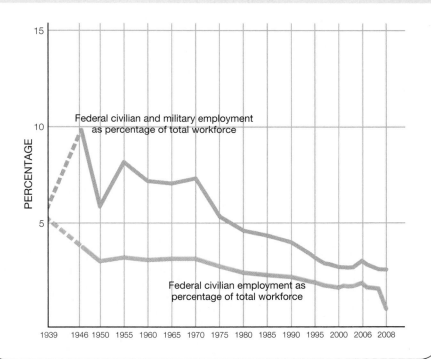

## Bureaucrats Fulfill Important Roles

Congress is responsible for making the laws, but, in most cases, legislation only sets the broad parameters for government action. Bureaucracies are reponsible for filling in the blanks by determining how the laws should be implemented. This requires bureaucracies to draw up much more detailed rules that guide the process of **implementation**. Bureaucracies also play a key role in enforcing the laws. Congress needs the bureaucracy to engage in rule making and implementation for several reasons. One is that bureaucracies employ people who have much more

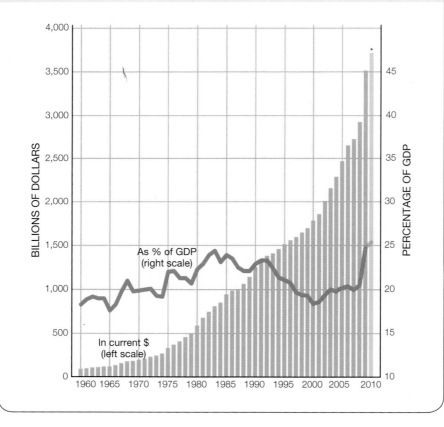

**FIGURE 11.2** Annual Federal Outlays, 1960–2010

As the bars on this figure indicate, when measured in dollars, federal government spending, which supports the federal bureaucracy, shows dramatic increases over time. But as the trend line shows, federal spending as a percentage of gross domestic product has experienced significant ups and downs over time. Federal spending jumped significantly in 2009, in large part due both to incorporation of funding for the Iraq and Afghanistan wars into the budget outlay calculation and to spending designed to stimulate the economy in the recession.

Data from 2010 is estimated.

SOURCE: Office of Management and Budget, "Table 1.3: Summary of Receipts, Outlays, and Surpluses or Deficits in Current Dollars, Constant (FY 2005) Dollars, and as Percentages of GDP: 1940–2015," www.whitehouse.gov (accessed 2/15/10).

specialized expertise in specific policy areas than do members of Congress. Decisions about how to achieve many policy goals—from managing the national parks to regulating air quality to ensuring a sound economy—rest on the judgment of specialized experts. A second reason that Congress needs bureaucracy is that because updating legislation can take many years, bureaucratic flexibility can ensure that laws are administered in ways that take new conditions into account. Finally, members of Congress often to prefer to delegate politically difficult decision making to bureaucrats.

One of the most important things that bureaucracies do is to issue rules. Rulemaking is exactly the same as legislation; in fact, it is often referred to as "quasi-legislation" that produces regulations by government agencies. The rules drawn up by government agencies provide more detailed and specific indications of what a policy actually will mean. For example, the Clean Air Act empowers the EPA to assess whether current or projected levels of air pollutants pose a threat to public health, to identify whether motor vehicle emissions are contributing to such pollution, and to create rules designed to regulate these emissions. Under the Bush administration, the EPA claimed it did not have the authority to regulate a specific group of pollutants commonly referred to as "greenhouse gases" (for example, carbon dioxide). In 2007, the Supreme Court ruled that the EPA did have that authority and had to provide a justification for not regulating such emissions.[4] In the first year of the Obama administration, the agency ruled that greenhouse gases did pose a threat to public health and that the emissions from motor vehicles contributed to greenhouse gas pollution.[5] The agency has now proposed new emission standards for automobiles, which would raise the average per vehicle emission rate for new vehicles to 35.5 miles per gallon starting in 2016.[6] Not only will this finding by the EPA have a significant effect on the automobile industry, in the future it could lead to far-reaching regulations governing all greenhouse gas–generating industries.

*The rules established by regulatory agencies have the force of law. In 2010, the car company Toyota was forced by federal regulators to recall six million vehicles in the U.S. owing to safety defects with some models.*

Once a new law is passed, the agency studies the legislation and proposes a set of rules to guide implementation. These proposed rules are then open to comment by anyone who wishes to weigh in. Representatives for the regulated industries and advocates of all sorts commonly submit comments. But anyone who wants to can go to www.regulations.gov to read proposed rules, enter their own comments, and view the comments of others. Once rules are approved, they are published in the Federal Register and have the force of law.

In addition to rule making, bureaucracies play an essential role in enforcing the laws. In enforcing the laws, bureaucracies exercise considerable power over private actors. For example, in 2009, the Consumer Product Safety Commission fined toy maker Mattel $2.3 million for selling toys that contained lead and another company, Mega Brands America, $1.1 million for failure to properly report a child fatality caused by one of its building sets.[7] In 2010, in order to comply with federal regulations, the auto manufacturer Toyota was forced to recall several car models after identifying problems with their gas pedals and accelerators. The National

Highway Traffic Safety Commission launched an investigation to discover when Toyota learned of the faults and could fine the auto company if it finds that Toyota did not promptly report the problems to regulators.[8]

**The Merit System: How to Become a Bureaucrat** Public bureaucrats are rewarded with greater job security than employees of most private organizations. More than a century ago, the federal government attempted to imitate business by passing the Civil Service Act of 1883, which was followed by almost universal adoption of equivalent laws in state and local governments. These laws required that appointees to public office be qualified, as measured by competitive examinations, for the job to which they are appointed. This policy came to be called the **merit system**; its purpose was to put an end to political appointments under the "spoils system," when government jobs were given out based on political connections rather than merit. Under the old spoils system, presidents filled up to two hundred thousand federal jobs with political friends and supporters. In 1881, President James A. Garfield wrote, "My day is frittered away with the personal seeking of people when it ought to be given to the great problems which concern the whole country."[9] Ironically, the final push to enact civil service reform occurred when a frustrated office seeker shot and killed President Garfield in 1881.

As a further safeguard against political interference (and to compensate for the lower-than-average pay given to public employees), merit system employees—genuine civil servants—were given a legal protection against being fired without a show of cause. Reasonable people may disagree about the value of such security and how far it should extend in the civil service, but the justifiable objective of this job protection—cleansing bureaucracy of political interference while upgrading performance—cannot be disputed.

## ● The Executive Branch Is Organized Hierarchically

Cabinet departments, agencies, and bureaus are the operating parts of the bureaucratic whole. Figure 11.3 is an organizational chart of one of the largest and most important of the fifteen **departments** (the largest subunit of the executive branch, each of which is headed by a department secretary), the Department of Agriculture. At the top is the head of the department, who in the United States is called the "secretary" of the department.[10] Below the secretary and the deputy secretary is a second tier of "undersecretaries" who have management responsibilities for one or more operating agencies, shown in the smaller print directly below each undersecretary. Those operating agencies are the third tier of the department, yet they are the highest level of responsibility for the actual programs around which the entire department is organized. This third tier is generally called the "bureau level." Each bureau-level agency usually operates under a statute, adopted by Congress, that set up the agency and gave it its authority and jurisdiction. The names of these bureau-level agencies are often quite well known to the public—the Forest Service and the Agricultural Research Service, for example. These are the so-called line agencies, or agencies that deal directly with the public. Sometimes these agen-

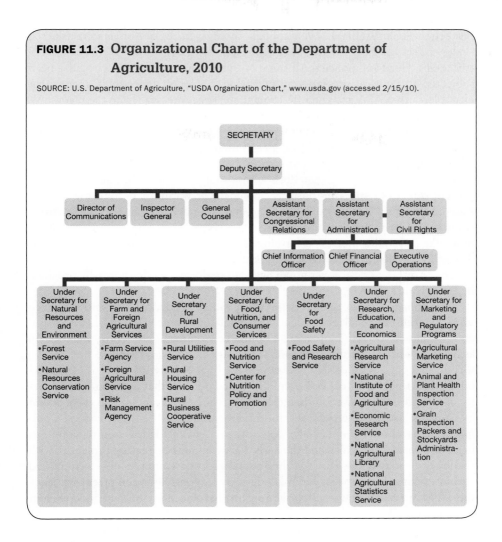

**FIGURE 11.3** Organizational Chart of the Department of Agriculture, 2010

SOURCE: U.S. Department of Agriculture, "USDA Organization Chart," www.usda.gov (accessed 2/15/10).

cies are officially called "bureaus," as in the Federal Bureau of Investigation (FBI), which is a part of the third tier of the Department of Justice. But "bureau" is also the conventional term for this level of administrative agency, even though many agencies or their supporters have preferred over the years to adopt a more palatable designation, such as "service" or "administration." Each bureau is, of course, subdivided into still other units, known as divisions, offices, or units—all are parts of the bureaucratic hierarchy.

Not all government agencies are part of Cabinet departments. Some **independent agencies** are set up by Congress outside the departmental structure altogether, even though the president appoints and directs the heads of these agencies. Independent agencies usually have broad powers to provide public services that are either too expensive or too important to be left to private initiatives. Some examples of independent agencies are the National Aeronautics and Space Administration (NASA), the Central Intelligence Agency (CIA), and the Environmental

Protection Agency (EPA). Even though these agencies are, in law, considered "independent" of direct presidential control, presidents use various means to control their actions and policies. All three of the just-mentioned agencies have been subjected to political pressures by presidents trying to direct their actions. For example, both NASA and the EPA came under great pressure from the George W. Bush administration to eliminate or downplay the threat posed by global warming by eliminating references to such terms as global warming, rising global temperatures, pollution, ice cap reduction, glacial melting, and ozone depletion in press releases and scientific reports. NASA's top climate scientist, James E. Hansen, went public with his complaint that Bush administration political appointees tried to prevent him from speaking publicly about global warming, despite the conclusions of NASA's scientific studies and those of other agencies and private scientific studies.[11] **Government corporations** are a third type of government agency but are more like private businesses performing and charging for a market service, such as delivering the mail (the United States Postal Service) or transporting railroad passengers (Amtrak). These government agencies perform a service normally provided by the private sector.

Yet a fourth type of agency is the independent regulatory commission, given broad discretion to make rules. The first regulatory agencies established by Congress, beginning with the Interstate Commerce Commission in 1887, were set up as independent regulatory commissions because Congress recognized that regulatory agencies are "minilegislatures," whose rules are exactly the same as legislation but require the kind of expertise and full-time attention that is beyond the capacity of Congress. Until the 1960s, most of the regulatory agencies that were set up by Congress, such as the Federal Trade Commission (1914) and the Federal Communications Commission (1934), were independent regulatory commissions. But beginning in the late 1960s and the early 1970s, all new regulatory programs, with two or three exceptions (such as the Federal Election Commission), were placed within existing departments and made directly responsible to the president. Since the 1970s, no major new regulatory programs have been established, independent or otherwise.

The different agencies of the executive branch can be classified into three main groups based on the services that they provide to the American public. The first category of agencies provides services and products that seek to promote the public welfare. The second group of agencies works to promote national security. The third group provides services that help to maintain a strong economy. Let us look more closely at what each set of agencies offers to the American public.

## Federal Bureaucracies Promote the Public Welfare

One of the most important activities of the federal bureaucracy is to promote the public welfare. Americans often think of government welfare as a single program that goes only to the very poor, but a number of federal agencies provide services, build infrastructure, and enact regulations designed to enhance the well-being of the vast majority of citizens. Take, for example, the National Institutes of Health (NIH), an agency of the Department of Health and Human Services (HHS).

Responsible for cutting-edge biomedical research, the NIH occupies a large cam- puslike complex with seventy-five buildings outside Washington, D.C. In its own labs and in the grants it provides to outside researchers, the NIH's central aim is to advance knowledge about health and diseases. Five of the scientists working in NIH labs have been awarded Nobel prizes for their research. The NIH is one of the leaders in experimenting with gene therapy, which is expected to open new pos- sibilities for curing diseases. HHS is also responsible for the two major health pro- grams provided by the federal government: Medicaid, which provides health care for low-income families and for many elderly and disabled people; and Medicare, which is the health insurance available to all elderly people in the United States.

A different notion of the public wel- fare but one highly valued by most Amer- icans is provided by the National Park Service, which is under the Department of the Interior. Created in 1916, the National Park Service is responsible for the care and upkeep of national parks. Since the nineteenth century, Americans have seen protection of the natural envi- ronment as an important public goal and have looked to federal agencies to imple- ment laws and administer programs that preserve natural areas and keep them open to the public.

The United States has no "Depart- ment of Regulation" but has many **regula- tory agencies**. Some of these are bureaus within departments, such as the Food and Drug Administration (FDA) within the Department of Health and Human Services, the Occupational Safety and Health Administration (OSHA) in the Department of Labor, and the Animal and Plant Health Inspection Service in the Department of Agriculture. As we saw earlier, other regulatory agencies are inde- pendent regulatory commissions, such as the Federal Communications Com- mission (FCC) and the Environmental Protection Agency (EPA). But whether departmental or independent, an agency or commission is regulatory if Congress delegates to it relatively broad powers over a sector of the economy or a type of commercial activity and authorizes it to make rules restricting the conduct of

*The federal bureaucracy plays an im- portant role in promoting public welfare. The EPA creates and enforces regulations related to the environment—for instance, preventing the pollution of groundwater. Here, an EPA manager examines a plastic liner that catches acid runoff from an aban- doned copper mine in Nevada (top). The Centers for Disease Control and Preven- tion, part of the Department of Health and Human Services, protects the health and safety of people through its work to reduce and eliminate infectious diseases, including avian flu and swine flu (bottom).*

people and businesses within that jurisdiction. Rules made by regulatory agencies have the force and effect of law.

The activities of these agencies seek to promote the welfare of all Americans, often working behind the scenes. The FDA, for example, works to protect public health by setting standards for food processing and inspecting plants to ensure that those standards are met. The EPA sets standards to limit polluting emissions from automobiles. The regulations required automobile manufacturers to change the way they design cars, and the result has been cleaner air in many metropolitan areas.

As we saw in Chapters 8 and 9, government agencies often develop close ties to the groups in society that they are supposed to regulate. This close political connection, summarized by the **iron triangle** relationship (see Figure 11.4), may push policies in a direction favorable to particular interests but inimical to the public interest.

## Federal Agencies Also Help Maintain a Strong Economy and Provide National Security

One of the remarkable features of American federalism is that the most vital agencies for the maintenance of the Union are located in state and local governments—namely, the police. But some agencies vital to maintaining national order and security do exist in the national government, and they can be grouped for convenience into three categories: (1) agencies for control of the sources of federal government revenue, (2) agencies for control of conduct defined as a threat to internal national security, and (3) agencies for defending American security from external threats. The departments of greatest influence in these three areas include Treasury, Justice, Homeland Security, Defense, and State.

In our capitalist economic system, the government does not directly run the economy. Yet many federal government activities are critical to maintaining a strong economy. Foremost among these are the agencies that are responsible for fiscal and monetary policy. Other agencies, such as the Internal Revenue Service (IRS), transform private resources into federal funds for public purposes. Tax policy may also strengthen the economy through decisions about whom to tax, how much, and when. Finally, the federal government, through such agencies as the Department of Transportation, the Commerce Department, and the Energy Department, may directly provide services or goods that bolster the economy.

**Fiscal and Monetary Agencies** The best term for government activity affecting or relating to money is **fiscal policy**, which is the use of taxing, monetary, and spending powers to manipulate the economy.[12]

The administration of fiscal policy occurs primarily in the Treasury Department. It is no contradiction to include the Treasury here as well as with the agencies for maintenance of the Union. This duplication indicates two things: first, that the Treasury is a complex department that performs more than one function of government; and second, that traditional controls have had to adapt to modern economic conditions and new technologies.

Today, in addition to collecting income, corporate, and other taxes, the Treasury is also responsible for managing the enormous national debt—over $9 trillion in

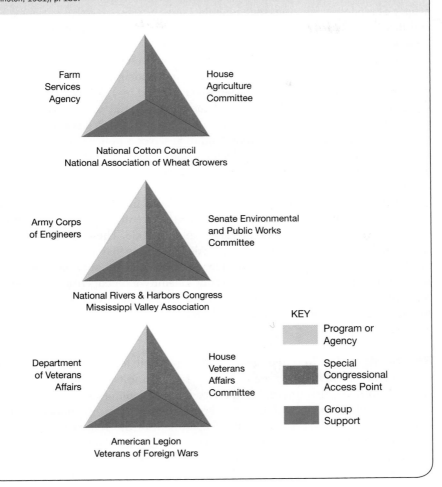

**FIGURE 11.4** Iron Triangles

SOURCE: Adapted from U.S. House of Representatives, *Report of the Subcommittee for Special Investigations of the Committee on Armed Services*, 86th Cong., 1st sess. (Washington, DC: Government Printing Office, 1960), p. 7. Reprinted from Theodore J. Lowi, *Incomplete Conquest: Governing America*, 2nd ed. (New York: Holt, Rinehart and Winston, 1981), p. 139.

Farm Services Agency

House Agriculture Committee

National Cotton Council
National Association of Wheat Growers

Army Corps of Engineers

Senate Environmental and Public Works Committee

National Rivers & Harbors Congress
Mississippi Valley Association

Department of Veterans Affairs

House Veterans Affairs Committee

American Legion
Veterans of Foreign Wars

KEY

Program or Agency

Special Congressional Access Point

Group Support

2010. (The national debt was less than one trillion dollars in 1980.)[13] Debt is not simply something the country owes; it is something a country has to manage and administer. The debt is also a fiscal instrument in the hands of the federal government that can be used—through manipulation of interest rates and through the buying and selling of government bonds—to slow down or to speed up the activity of the entire national economy, as well as to defend the value of the dollar in international trade. The Obama administration's first budget dramatically increased deficit spending in order to pump money into the economy to stimulate growth in the face of the most severe economic downturn since the Great Depression of the 1930s.

The Treasury Department is also responsible for printing the U.S. currency, but currency represents only a tiny proportion of the entire money economy. Most of the trillions of dollars used in the transactions of the private and public sectors of the U.S. economy exist in computerized accounts, not in currency.

Another important fiscal agency (although for technical reasons it is called an agency of monetary policy) is the **Federal Reserve System,** a system of twelve Federal Reserve Banks that facilitates exchanges of cash, checks, and credit; regulates member banks; and uses monetary policies to fight inflation and deflation, and is headed by the Federal Reserve Board. The Federal Reserve System (called simply the Fed) has authority over the interest rates and lending activities of the nation's most important banks. Congress established the Fed in 1913 as a clearinghouse responsible for adjusting the supply of money and credit to the needs of commerce and industry in different regions of the country. The Fed is also responsible for ensuring that banks do not overextend themselves, a policy that guards against a chain of bank failures during a sudden economic scare, such as occurred in 1929 and again in 2008. The Federal Reserve Board directs the operations of the twelve district Federal Reserve Banks, which are essentially "bankers' banks," serving the monetary needs of the hundreds of member banks in the national banking system.[14] The Treasury and the Federal Reserve took center stage when a string of bank failures threatened economic catastrophe in 2008. These agencies designed a $700 billion bailout package and persuaded Congress that a rapid response was needed to avert a worldwide depression. Although the Treasury and the Federal Reserve sprang into action when economic calamity loomed, critics charged that the crisis could have been prevented if these agencies had exercised more regulatory oversight over the financial sector during the previous decade.

**Revenue Agencies** **Revenue agencies** are responsible for collecting taxes. Examples include the Internal Revenue Service for income taxes and the Bureau of Alcohol, Tobacco, Firearms and Explosives for collection of taxes on the sales of those particular products. One of the first actions of Congress under President George Washington was to create the Department of the Treasury, and probably its oldest function is the collection of taxes on imports, called tariffs. Part of the newly created Department of Homeland Security since March 2003, federal customs agents are located at every U.S. seaport and international airport to oversee the collection of tariffs. But far and away the most important of the revenue agencies is the Internal Revenue Service (IRS), which will be our single case study in this section.

The IRS is responsive to political influences, especially given the fact that it must maintain cooperative relationships with the two oldest and most important congressional committees, the House Ways and Means Committee and the Senate Finance Committee. Nevertheless, the political patterns of the IRS are virtually the opposite of those of a clientele agency (an agency that serves or provides benefits to some specific group or "clientele" in society). As one expert put it, "probably no organization in the country, public or private, creates as much clientele *dis*favor as the Internal Revenue Service. The very nature of its work brings it into an adversary relationship with vast numbers of Americans every year."[15] Yet few scandals

*The Treasury Department helps maintain the economy in various ways. Here, Treasury Secretary Timothy Geithner meets with economic experts in 2009 to discuss oversight of the Troubled Assets Relief Program (TARP), which was designed to address the financial crisis that had deepened in 2008.*

have soiled its record. Complaints against the IRS have increased during the past few years. For example, one of 2008 presidential candidate Mike Huckabee's main campaign platform ideas was the abolition of the IRS. In its place, he proposed a nationwide federal sales tax that he called a "fair tax." But aside from the principle of the income tax, all the other complaints against the IRS are against its needless complexity, its lack of sensitivity and responsiveness to individual taxpayers, and its overall lack of efficiency. As one of its critics put it, "Imagine a company that's owed $216 billion plus interest, a company with a 22-percent error rate. A company that spent $4 billion to update a computer system—with little success. It all describes the Internal Revenue Service."[16] Again leaving aside the issue of the income tax itself, all the other complaints amount to just one big complaint: The IRS is not bureaucratic enough; it needs *more* bureaucratization. It needs to succeed with its new computer processing system; it needs vast improvement in its "customer services"; it needs long-term budgeting and other management control; and it needs to borrow more management and technology expertise from the private sector.

**Agencies for Internal Security** The task of maintaining domestic security changed dramatically after the terrorist attacks of September 11, 2001. The creation of the Department of Homeland Security in late 2002 signaled the high priority that domestic security would now have. The orientation of domestic agencies shifted as well, as agencies geared up to prevent terrorism, a task that differed greatly from their former charge of investigating crime. Along with this shift in responsibility, these agencies have acquired broad new powers—many of them controversial—including the power to detain terrorist suspects and to engage in extensive domestic intelligence-gathering about possible terrorists.

Prior to September 11, most of the effort put into maintaining national security took the form of legal work related to prosecuting federal crimes. The largest and most important unit of the Justice Department is the Criminal Division. Lawyers in the Criminal Division represent the United States government when it is the plaintiff enforcing the federal criminal laws, except for those cases (about 25 percent) specifically assigned to other divisions or agencies. Criminal litigation is handled by U.S. attorneys, who are appointed by the president. There is one U.S. attorney in each of the ninety-four federal judicial districts; he or she supervises the work of a number of assistant U.S. attorneys.

The Civil Division of the Justice Department deals with litigation in which the United States is the defendant being sued for injury and damages allegedly inflicted by a government official or agency. The missions of the other divisions of the Justice Department—Antitrust, Civil Rights, Environment and Natural Resources, and Tax—are described by their names.

When terrorism prevention took center stage, the Justice Department reoriented its activities accordingly. It was aided in its new mission by the USA PATRIOT Act, enacted soon after September 11. The act gave the Justice Department broad new powers, allowing the attorney general to detain any foreigner suspected of posing a threat to internal security. The Patriot Act also expanded the government's ability to use wiretaps and to issue search warrants without notifying suspects immediately. It required public libraries to keep lists of the public's book and Internet usage for federal inspection. Although initially popular with most Americans, these measures created concern about civil liberties. Despite these concerns, Congress renewed the act with only modest revisions in 2006.

Since 2001, the Justice Department has played a central role in setting the balance between national security and civil liberties. In 2007, high-profile congressional hearings revealed extensive conflicts between the Justice Department and the White House over the use of warrantless wiretapping in the United States. The hearings also exposed the fact that in 2005, Attorney General Alberto Gonzales secretly approved the use of severe methods of interrogation—many classified as torture under the Geneva Convention—even after Congress had passed a law forbidding torture.[17]

Since its creation in 2002, the Department of Homeland Security has also assumed a large role in domestic security (see Table 11.1), bringing under its umbrella such responsibilities as border safety and security (including immigration and customs); emergency preparedness; science-related concerns pertaining in particular to chemical, biological, and nuclear threats; and information and intelligence analysis and assessment. This new department has also faced competition from the FBI, and this competition initially resulted in some confusion and delay.

**Agencies for External National Security** Two departments occupy center stage in maintaining national security: the departments of State and Defense.

TABLE 11.1

## The Shape of a Domestic Security Department

| DEPARTMENT OF HOMELAND SECURITY | THE AGENCIES AND DEPARTMENTS THAT WERE MOVED TO THE MAIN DIVISIONS OF THE DEPARTMENT OF HOMELAND SECURITY: | DEPARTMENT OR AGENCY PREVIOUSLY UNDER: | FROM THE 2010 BUDGET REQUEST: | |
|---|---|---|---|---|
| | | | BUDGET REQUEST, IN MILLIONS: | ESTIMATED NUMBER OF EMPLOYEES: |
| Border and Transportation Security | U.S. Customs and Border Protection | Treasury Department | $11,437 | 58,105 |
| | Immigration and Customs Enforcement | Justice Department | $5,763 | 20,134 |
| | U.S. Citizenship and Immigration Services | Justice Department | $2,868 | 10,700 |
| | National Protection and Program Directorate (includes domestic preparedness) | General Services Administration | $1,959 | 2,584 |
| | Transportation Security Administration | Transportation Department | $7,794 | 51,949 |
| | Federal Law Enforcement Training Center | Treasury Department | $288 | 1,103 |
| Emergency Preparedness and Response | Federal Emergency Management Agency | Independent agency | $10,479 | 6,717 |
| Domestic Nuclear Detection Office | (new) | | $366 | 130 |
| Science and Technology | (multiple programs) | Department of Energy | $968 | 404 |
| Secret Service | Secret Service, including presidential protection units | Treasury Department | $1,710 | 7,055 |
| Coast Guard | Coast Guard | Transportation Department | $9,956 | 49,954 |
| Total DHS | | | $55,115 | 211,807 |

SOURCE: U.S. Department of Homeland Security, "Budget-in-Brief, Fiscal Year 2010," www.dhs.gov (accessed 2/16/10).

Although diplomacy is generally considered the primary task of the State Department, diplomatic missions are only one of its organizational dimensions. As of 2010, the State Department also included twenty-eight bureau-level units, each under the direction of an assistant secretary. Six of these are geographic or regional bureaus concerned with all problems within a defined region of the world; thirteen are "functional" bureaus, handling such things as economic and business affairs, intelligence and research, and international organizations. Four are bureaus of internal affairs, which handle such areas as security, finance and management, and legal issues.

These bureaus support the responsibilities of the elite of foreign affairs, the foreign service officers (FSOs), who staff U.S. embassies around the world and who hold almost all of the most powerful positions in the department below the rank of ambassador.[18] The ambassadorial positions, especially the plum positions in the major capitals of the world, are filled by presidential appointees, many of whom get their positions by having been important donors to the victorious political campaign.

Despite the importance of the State Department in foreign affairs, fewer than 20 percent of all U.S. government employees working abroad are directly under its authority. By far the largest number of career government professionals working abroad are under the authority of the Defense Department.

The creation of the Department of Defense by legislation between 1947 and 1949 was an effort to unify the two historic military departments, the War Department and the Navy Department, and to integrate them with a new department, the Air Force. Real unification, however, did not occur. The Defense Department simply added more pluralism to an already pluralistic national security establishment.

The American military, following worldwide military tradition, is organized according to a "chain of command"—a tight hierarchy of clear responsibility and rank, made clearer by uniforms, special insignia, and detailed organizational charts and rules of order and etiquette. The "line agencies" in the Department of Defense are the military commands, distributed geographically by divisions and fleets to deal with current or potential enemies. The "staff agencies," such as logistics, intelligence, personnel, research and development, quartermaster, and engineering, exist to serve the "line agencies." At the top of the military chain of command are chiefs of staff (called chief of naval operations in the Navy, and commandant in the Marines). These chiefs of staff also constitute the membership of the Joint Chiefs of Staff—the center of military policy and management.

America's primary political problem with its military has not been the historic one of how to keep the military out of politics (which is a perennial problem in many of the world's countries), but how to keep politics out of the military. In 2004, President George W. Bush and Congress came into sharp conflict over a $447 billion appropriations bill to cover military spending. Bush and the military supported the bill, but Congress inserted a provision to the bill that would have imposed a two-year delay in Bush's plans to close some military bases around the country. The Pentagon (the office building in Washington that serves as the headquarters for the American military, and which has become synonymous with the military services) also favored the closings. Bush threatened to veto the entire bill if the base-closing extension was kept in, and the Pentagon supported the closings by saying that they would help the military by saving tens of billions of dollars on unnecessary bases. Congress wanted the bases to stay open for a political reason—representatives feared that closing bases in an election year would result in job losses for which they would take the blame.[19]

The war on terrorism has given the Defense Department more control over policy decisions. For example, it took the lead in organizing the war against the Taliban in Afghanistan in 2001 and in the invasion of Iraq in 2003. In fact, some critics of the Iraq War argued that the postwar situation devolved into chaos at least partly because the State Department and the U.S. Agency for International Development (USAID, a civilian agency in charge of foreign aid and economic and social development in other nations) were kept out of American government decision making concerning the running of Iraq after the war. Even within American borders, the military now plays a greater role, as military planes now patrol airspace over major cities, and the National Guard has patrolled airports and subways—jobs traditionally reserved for civilian police forces.

**The 9/11 Commission and Reorganizing Security** In 2004, the National Commission on Terrorist Attacks upon the United States (the 9/11 Commission) issued a widely read report that called for a major reorganization of bureaucratic responsibilities for internal and external security. The report revealed that different departments of the American government had information that, if handled properly, might have prevented the attacks of September 11, 2001. The commission found that the federal government's attempts to improve security after September 11 still did not address the critical problems with duplication, prioritization, and coordination in the current system. To correct this, the commission made major recommendations designed to promote unity of effort across the bureaucracy.

Topping the list were proposals designed to bridge the divide between domestic and foreign security efforts. Prior to September 11, the FBI, which collects domestic information, did not talk to the CIA, and both the Defense Department and the National Security Agency (NSA) collected mountains of information that was not shared with either the FBI or the CIA. The 9/11 Commission's work prompted a major reorganization of the fragmented intelligence community. In 2005, a new office, the Director of National Intelligence (DNI), took over responsibility for coordinating the efforts of the sixteen different agencies that gather intelligence. The DNI reports directly to the president each morning.

There is considerable disagreement about whether the reorganization has built more effective intelligence capacities. In 2007, the Director of National Intelligence issued a surprising report declaring that Iran no longer had an active nuclear program. Called "one of the biggest reversals in the history of U.S. nuclear intelligence," the new report directly contradicted earlier accounts of the nuclear threat in Iran.[20] While some members of Congress viewed the revised report as a sign that the intelligence reorganization was working, others charged that the conclusions were politically motivated.[21]

Even with President Bush's backing, the road to such a major bureaucratic reorganization was politically difficult. Many interests, including the Department of

*After September 11, 2001, the federal government assumed a new role in airport security. With the passage of the Secure Aviation and Transportation Act, the federal government became involved with screening passengers and baggage.*

Defense and the CIA, lobbied fiercely to retain their autonomy and control over funds. However, the strong political momentum behind the report and its visibility in an election year where national security issues were front and center meant that the recommendations stood a good chance of becoming law.

## ● Several Forces Control Bureaucracy

Many people assume that bureaucracy and democracy are contradictory.[22] Americans cannot live with bureaucracy, they sometimes say, but, as this chapter shows, they also cannot live without it. The task is neither to retreat from bureaucracy nor to attack it, but to take advantage of its strengths while making it more accountable to the demands of democratic politics and representative government. This task will be the focus of the remainder of this chapter.

Two hundred years, millions of employees, and trillions of dollars after America's founding, we must return to James Madison's observation, "You must first enable the government to control the governed; and in the next place oblige it to control itself."[23] Today the problem is the same, only now the process has a name: administrative accountability. Accountability implies that some higher authority will guide and judge the actions of the bureaucracy. The highest authority in a democracy is *demos*—the people—and the guidance for bureaucratic action is the popular will. But the president and Congress must translate that ideal of accountability into practical terms.

# The President as Chief Executive Can Direct Agencies

In 1937, President Franklin Roosevelt's Committee on Administrative Management gave official sanction to an idea that had been growing increasingly urgent: "The president needs help." The national government had grown rapidly during the preceding twenty-five years, but the structures and procedures necessary to manage the burgeoning executive branch had not yet been established. The response to the call for "help" for the president initially took the form of three management policies: (1) All communications and decisions that related to executive policy decisions must pass through the White House; (2) In order to cope with such a flow, the White House must have adequate staffs of specialists in research, analysis, legislative and legal writing, and public affairs; and (3) The White House must have additional staff to follow through on presidential decisions—to ensure that those decisions are made, communicated to Congress, and carried out by the appropriate agency.

**Making the Managerial Presidency** Establishing a management capacity for the presidency began in earnest with FDR, but it did not stop there.[24] The story of the modern presidency can be told largely as a series of responses to the plea for managerial help. Indeed, each expansion of the national government into new policies and programs in the twentieth and twenty-first centuries has been accompanied by a parallel expansion of the president's management authority.

Presidents John Kennedy and Lyndon Johnson were committed to both government expansion and management expansion, in the spirit of their party's hero, FDR. President Nixon also strengthened and enlarged the managerial presidency, but for somewhat different reasons. He sought the strongest possible managerial hand because he had to assume that the overwhelming majority of federal employees had sympathies with the Democratic Party, which had controlled the White House and had sponsored governmental growth for twenty-eight of the previous thirty-six years.[25]

President Jimmy Carter was probably more preoccupied with administrative reform and reorganization than any other president in the twentieth century. His reorganization of the civil service will long be recognized as one of the most significant contributions of his presidency. The Civil Service Reform Act of 1978 was the first major revamping of the federal civil service since its creation in 1883. The 1978 act abolished the century-old Civil Service Commission (CSC) and replaced it with three agencies, each designed to handle one of the CSC's functions on the theory that the competing demands of these functions had given the CSC an "identity crisis." The Merit Systems Protection Board (MSPB) was created to defend competitive merit recruitment and promotion from political encroachment. A separate Federal Labor Relations Authority (FLRA) was set up to administer collective bargaining and individual personnel grievances. The third new agency, the Office of Personnel Management (OPM), was created to manage recruiting, testing, training, and the retirement system. The Senior Executive Service was also created at this time to recognize and foster "public management" as a profession and to facilitate the movement of top, "supergrade" career officials across agencies and departments.[26]

Carter also tried to impose a stringent budgetary process on all executive agencies. Called "zero-base budgeting," it was a method of budgeting from the bottom up, wherein each agency was required to rejustify its entire mission rather than merely its increase for the next year. Zero-base budgeting did not succeed, but the effort was not lost on President Reagan. Although Reagan gave the impression of being a laid-back president, he actually centralized management to an unprecedented degree. From Carter's "bottom-up" approach, Reagan went to a "top-down" approach, whereby the initial budgetary decisions would be made in the White House and the agencies would be required to fit within those decisions. This process converted the Office of Management and Budget (OMB) into an agency of policy determination and presidential management.[27] President George H. W. Bush took Reagan's centralization strategy even further in using the White House staff instead of Cabinet secretaries for managing the executive branch.[28]

President Clinton engaged in the most systematic effort to "change the way the government does business," a phrase he used often to describe the goal of his National Performance Review (NPR), one of the most important administrative reform efforts of the twentieth century. In September 1993, he launched the NPR, based on a set of 384 proposals drafted by a panel headed by Vice President Al Gore. The avowed goal of the NPR was to "reinvent government"—to make the federal bureaucracy more efficient, accountable, and effective. But this was little more than new language for the same management goal held by each of his predecessors. The NPR's original goal was to save more than $100 billion over five years, in large part by cutting the federal workforce by 12 percent (more than 270,000 jobs) by the end of 1999. By the end of 2000, $136 billion in savings was achieved, and the federal workforce had been cut by 426,200.[29]

Like his predecessors, George W. Bush pursued a strategy different from those of previous presidents. Bush dismantled Clinton's NPR and favored **privatization**— removing all or part of a program from the public sector to the private sector. Bush defended this approach by arguing that it saved the government money and placed work in the hands of more efficient private organizations. Yet privatization also came under criticism during the Iraq War, when the giant oil company Halliburton was given $9 billion in government contracts. Halliburton performed tasks ranging from supplying fuel for the military to providing cafeteria meals. Critics charged that Halliburton's costs were exorbitant: Pentagon auditors found that it overcharged the government by $61 million for the gas; Halliburton charged the government for forty-two thousand meals when it delivered only fourteen thousand. In 2004, the company was accused of more than $250 million in overcharges to the government. These findings undercut claims of efficiency. Adding to charges of favoritism was the fact that Bush's vice president, Dick Cheney, had served as Halliburton's CEO in the 1990s.[30] Privatization aside, the Bush administration's effort to limit the size of government ran headlong into the 2001 terrorist attacks on America, which impelled the administration to expand government, mostly in areas related to law enforcement, security, research, and intelligence. But critics contended that the Bush administration's distrust of the bureaucracy led it to exercise inappropriate political control. Political appointees occupied high agency positions that allowed them to suppress the work of agency experts when they threatened to undercut the administration's political goals.

Since Obama took office, his administration has sought to reinvigorate federal agencies, reflecting the Democrats' greater support for strong government institutions. Obama's approach to the managerial presidency features a deep belief in the importance of scientific expertise in government service. The president's appointments to head key regulatory agencies, including the EPA, OSHA, and the FDA, reflect this conviction. Some of the new agency leaders are well-known academic experts; others have won recognition for their achievements in state or local administrative settings.

## Congress Promotes Responsible Bureaucracy

Congress is constitutionally essential to responsible bureaucracy because ultimately the key to bureaucratic responsibility is legislation. When a law is passed and its intent is clear, the accountability for implementation of that law is also clear. Then the president knows what to "faithfully execute," and the responsible agency understands what is expected of it. But when Congress enacts vague legislation, agencies must resort to their own interpretations. The president and the federal courts often step in to tell agencies what the legislation intended. And so do the most intensely interested groups. Yet when everybody, from president to courts to interest groups, gets involved in the actual interpretation of legislative intent, to whom and to what is the agency accountable? Even when the agency wants to behave responsibly, how shall accountability be accomplished?

Congress's answer is **oversight**—the effort by Congress, through hearings, investigations, and other techniques, to exercise control over the activities of executive agencies by overseeing or supervising how legislation is carried out by the executive branch. The more power Congress has delegated to the executive, the more it has sought to reinvolve itself in directing the interpretation of laws through committee and subcommittee oversight of each agency. The standing committee system in Congress is well suited for oversight, inasmuch as most of the congressional committees and subcommittees have jurisdictions roughly parallel to one or more departments and agencies, and members of Congress who sit on these committees can develop expertise equal to that of the bureaucrats. Appropriations committees as well as authorization committees have oversight powers—as do their respective subcommittees. In addition to these, the Government Reform and Oversight Committee in the House and the Governmental Affairs Committee in the Senate have oversight powers not limited by departmental jurisdiction.

The best indication of Congress's oversight efforts is the use of public hearings, before which bureaucrats and other witnesses are summoned to discuss and defend agency budgets and past decisions. The data drawn from systematic studies of congressional committee and subcommittee hearings and meetings show quite dramatically that Congress has tried through oversight to keep pace with the expansion of the executive branch. Between 1950 and 1980, for example, the annual number of committee and subcommittee meetings in the House of Representatives rose steadily from 3,210 to 7,022; in the Senate, the number of such meetings rose from 2,607 to 4,265 (in 1975–76). Beginning in 1980 in the House and 1978 in the Senate, the number of committee and subcommittee hearings and meetings slowly began to decline, reaching 4,222 in the House and 2,597 in the Senate by the mid-1980s.

In the months after the terror attacks in 2001, Congress exercised little of its oversight powers around issues of national security. At the time it seemed more important to support the president. Since then, however, many congressional committees have convened hearings related to the war on terrorism. Congressional oversight increased dramatically after Democrats won control of Congress in the 2006 elections. They charged congressional Republicans with largely failing to oversee the executive because President George W. Bush, a Republican, opposed such oversight. Compared to the Republican-controlled Congress in 2005, the Democratic-controlled Congress held many more oversight hearings in 2007: in 2005 the House held a total of 579 oversight hearings; in only the first half of 2007 the number was 942. In 2005 the Republican Senate held 346 oversight hearings, while the Democrats in the first half of 2007 held 451.[31] Congress has held oversight hearings on a wide range of topics. Hearings have examined many different aspects of the Iraq and Afghanistan wars, including the use of government contractors. Congress has also been very active in overseeing programs related to the recession, including the Troubled Asset Relief Program (TARP), which was instituted to help bail out the banks in 2008. When trouble with Toyota vehicles surfaced in 2010, Congress exercised its oversight powers to determine whether the company knew of the problems and withheld information from the National Highway Traffic Safety Administration.

Although congressional oversight is potent because of Congress's power to make, and therefore to change, the law, often the most effective and influential lever over bureaucratic accountability is "the power of the purse"—the ability of the House and Senate committees and subcommittees on appropriations to increase or decrease funding of agencies, as well as to investigate agency activities, to control agency performance.

Oversight can also be carried out by individual members of Congress. Such inquiries addressed to bureaucrats are considered standard congressional "case work" and can turn up significant questions of public responsibility even when the motivation is only to meet the demand of an individual constituent. Oversight also takes place through communications between congressional staff and agency staff. The number of congressional staff has increased tremendously since the Legislative Reorganization Act of 1946, and the legislative staff, especially the staff of the committees, is just as professionalized and specialized as the staff of executive agencies. In addition, Congress has created for itself three large agencies whose obligations are to engage in constant research on problems taking place in or confronted by the executive branch. These are the General Accounting Office (GAO), the Congressional Research Service (CRS), and the Congressional Budget Office (CBO). Each of these agencies is designed to give Congress information independent of the information it can get directly from the executive branch through hearings and other communications.[32] Another source of information for oversight is direct from citizens through the Freedom of Information Act (FOIA), which gives ordinary citizens the right of access to agency files and agency data to determine whether derogatory information exists in the file about the citizens themselves and to learn about what the agency is doing in general.

# Navigate the Bureaucracy

To some, the idea of "getting involved" in something as complex as the federal, state, or even local bureaucracy can seem daunting. The bureaucracy has grown considerably in size in the last thirty-five or so years and now touches aspects of daily life ranging from protecting citizens from terrorist attacks, to protecting the environment, to making sure the food you eat is safe. These are all important issues that citizens should easily be able to get involved with, but given the size of bureaucracies, where do you jump in?

- Start with something simple. Ask yourself what political or social issue interests you and find out what bureaucratic agency is responsible for oversight and administering programs for that issue. For example, you may be concerned with the treatment of veterans returning from active service in places like Iraq and Afghanistan. The Department of Veterans Affairs (www.va.gov) would be a good place to start for information on what the government is doing to help those returning with physical and psychological injuries. You can try contacting someone at the VA via their Web site, but you may also consider checking out a veterans advocacy group.

- If you're interested in more active involvement in the bureaucracy, you should consider interning with a government agency in Washington, D.C. For example, you could earn academic credit while interning at bureaucratic agencies ranging from the Food and Drug Administration, to the Department of Housing and Urban Development, to the Department of Defense. One way to intern while earning academic credit is through attending the Washington Center (www.twc.edu). Many campuses across the country have a relationship with the Washington Center, and all you need to do is find your campus liaison. If your school does not already have a liaison, you'll need to find someone on campus who can serve as your adviser.

- Finally, you could think about being an "ombudsperson" to help people deal with the bureaucracy. Grandparents and other elderly relatives often need help navigating the Social Security system; new immigrants are often in the dark about what to do in order to become legal citizens; and many high school students need help filling out forms for financial aid. Try visiting VolunteerMatch (www.volunteermatch.org), a Web site that puts people together with individuals and groups who are in need of unpaid assistance.

## ● Democracy Can Control Bureaucracy

In the final analysis, the best approach for reconciling bureaucracy and democracy is to insist on clear rules and laws, maximum openness in agency decisions, clear rationales for those decisions, and accessible means for questioning and appealing those decisions. These methods apply equally to Congress and the bureaucracy. The very best approach for Congress to ensure accountability of the bureaucracy is for Congress to spend more time clarifying its legislative intent and less time on oversight. Bureaucrats are more responsive to clear legislative guidance than to anything else, and when Congress and the president are at odds about the interpretation of laws, bureaucrats can evade responsibility by playing off one branch against another. If Congress's intent in its laws is made clearer, it could then defer far more to presidential management and presidential maintenance of bureaucratic accountability. Moreover, clearer laws from Congress and clearer rules and decisions made by administrative agencies would reduce the need for courts to review those laws and decisions; judicial approaches to administrative accountability are the most expensive and time consuming, and therefore the least available to individual citizens.

Bureaucracy and democracy can be comfortable allies rather than warring adversaries. But make no mistake about it: Bureaucracy is here to stay. No reinvention of government, or radical decentralization of power, or substantial budget-cutting, or reductions in personnel can alter the necessity of bureaucracy or resolve the problem of reconciling bureaucracy with democracy.

# studyguide

## Practice Quiz ———————————————————————

 Find a diagnostic Web Quiz with 33 additional questions on the StudySpace Web site: www.wwnorton.com/we-the-people

1. Which of the following best describes the growth of the federal service in the past twenty-five years? *(p. 336)*
   a) rampant, exponential growth
   b) has grown at a rate roughly comparable to the growth of the economy
   c) decrease in the total number of federal employees
   d) vast, compared to the growth of the economy and the society

2. What task must bureaucrats perform if Congress charges them with enforcing a law through explicit directions? *(p. 337)*
   a) implementation
   b) interpretation
   c) lawmaking
   d) quasi-judicial decision making

3. Which of the following was *not* a component of the Civil Service Act of 1883? *(p. 340)*
   a) the merit system
   b) a job security system

c) a spoils system

d) All of the above were associated with the Civil Service Act of 1883.

4. Which of the following is *not* part of the executive branch? *(pp. 340–42)*
   a) Cabinet departments
   b) government corporations
   c) independent regulatory commissions
   d) All of the above are part of the executive branch.

5. Which of the following is an example of a government corporation? *(p. 342)*
   a) National Aeronautics and Space Administration (NASA)
   b) United States Postal Service
   c) National Science Foundation
   d) Federal Express

6. Which of the following is *not* an example of a clientele agency? *(p. 346)*
   a) Department of Justice
   b) Department of Commerce
   c) Department of Agriculture
   d) Department of Housing and Urban Development

7. Which of the following was *not* a part of the USA PATRIOT Act? *(p. 348)*
   a) a provision allowing the attorney general to detain any foreigner suspected of posing a threat to internal security
   b) a provision expanding the government's ability to use wiretaps
   c) a provision creating the Department of Homeland Security
   d) a provision requiring public libraries to keep lists of the public's book and Internet usage for federal inspection

8. Which of the following was a result of the recommendations of the 9/11 Commission? *(p. 351)*
   a) the invastion of Iraq in 2003
   b) the plan to build a memorial on the site of the World Trade Center

c) the merging of the FBI and the CIA
d) the sharing of information among the FBI, CIA, NSA, and other intelligence-gathering agencies

9. Which of the following has *not* been a method employed by presidents to reform bureaucracy? *(pp. 352–55)*
   a) administrative reorganization
   b) zero-base budgeting
   c) decreasing executive involvement in bureaucratic policy
   d) privatization

10. Which president instituted the bureaucratic reform of the National Performance Review? *(p. 354)*
    a) Richard Nixon
    b) Lyndon Johnson
    c) Jimmy Carter
    d) Bill Clinton

11. The concept of oversight refers to the effort made by *(p. 355)*
    a) Congress to make executive agencies accountable for their actions.
    b) the president to make Congress accountable for its actions.
    c) the courts to make executive agencies responsible for their actions.
    d) the states to make the executive branch accountable for its actions.

12. Which of the following is *not* an agency created by Congress to engage in constant research on problems taking place in or confronted by the executive branch? *(pp. 355–56)*
    a) Government Accountability Office
    b) Congressional Research Service
    c) Congressional Oversight Organization
    d) Congressional Budget Office

# Chapter Outline

 Find a detailed Chapter Outline on the StudySpace Web site: www.wwnorton.com/we-the-people

# Key Terms

Find Flashcards to help you study these terms on the StudySpace Web site: www.wwnorton.com/we-the-people

**bureaucracy** *(p. 335)* the complex structure of offices, tasks, rules, and principles of organization that are employed by all large-scale institutions to coordinate effectively the work of their personnel

**department** *(p. 340)* the largest subunit of the executive branch. The secretaries of the fifteen departments form the Cabinet

**Federal Reserve System** *(p. 346)* a system of twelve Federal Reserve Banks that facilitates exchanges of cash, checks, and credit; regulates member banks; and uses monetary policies to fight inflation and deflation

**fiscal policy** *(p. 344)* the use of taxing, monetary, and spending powers to manipulate the economy

**government corporation** *(p. 342)* a government agency that performs a service normally provided by the private sector

**implementation** *(p. 337)* the efforts of departments and agencies to translate laws into specific bureaucratic rules and actions

**independent agency** *(p. 341)* an agency that is not part of a Cabinet department

**iron triangle** *(p. 344)* the stable, cooperative relationship that often develops among a congressional committee, an administrative agency, and one or more supportive interest groups. Not all of these relationships are triangular, but the iron triangle is the most typical

**merit system** *(p. 340)* a product of civil service reform, in which appointees to positions in public bureaucracies must objectively be deemed qualified for those positions

**oversight** *(p. 355)* the effort by Congress, through hearings, investigations, and other techniques, to exercise control over the activities of executive agencies by overseeing or supervising how legislation is carried out by the executive branch

**privatization** *(p. 354)* removing all or part of a program from the public sector to the private sector

**regulatory agencies** *(p. 343)* agencies whose main job is to control some specific conduct in society through the issuance of rules and penalties if those rules are violated

**revenue agencies** *(p. 346)* agencies responsible for collecting taxes. Examples include the Internal Revenue Service for income taxes, the U.S. Customs Service for tariffs and other taxes on imported goods, and the Bureau of Alcohol, Tobacco, and Firearms for collection of taxes on the sales of those particular products

# For Further Reading

Arnold, Peri E. *Making the Managerial Presidency: Comprehensive Organization Planning.* Princeton, NJ: Princeton University Press, 1986.

Fesler, James W., and Donald F. Kettl. *The Politics of the Administrative Process.* Washington, DC: Congressional Quarterly Press, 2008.

Light, Paul C. *A Government Ill Executed: The Decline of the Federal Service and How to Reverse It.* Cambridge, MA: Harvard University Press, 2008.

Lowi, Theodore J. *The End of Liberalism.* New York: Norton, 1979.

Skowronek, Stephen. *Building a New American State: The Expansion of National Administrative Capacities, 1877–1920.* New York: Cambridge University Press, 1982.

Weiner, Tom. *Legacy of Ashes: The History of the CIA.* New York: Doubleday, 2007.

Wildavsky, Aaron, and Naomi Caiden. *The New Politics of the Budgetary Process*. New York: Longman, 2003.

Wilson, James Q. *Bureaucracy: What Government Agencies Do and Why They Do It*. New York: Basic Books, 1989.

Wood, B. Dan. *Bureaucratic Dynamics: The Role of Bureaucracy in a Democracy*. Boulder, CO: Westview, 1994.

# Recommended Web Sites

**Central Intelligence Agency**
www.cia.gov/about-cia/faqs/index.html
The Central Intelligence Agency (CIA) is one of several bureaucracies responsible for providing national security. A major problem facing this clandestine agency is how to provide security and meet the public's right to know what the government is doing. At the official Web site of the CIA, see what questions are often asked.

**Department of Homeland Security**
www.dhs.gov
The Department of Homeland Security was created after 9/11 to promote bureaucratic communication and domestic security. See what the department is doing to protect America from foreign threats.

**Federal Emergency Management Agency**
www.fema.gov
In the aftermath of Hurricane Katrina, the Federal Emergency Management Agency (FEMA) became infamous for its role in the disaster relief efforts. View the disaster history of your state and see what FEMA is currently doing to prevent disasters and assist Americans in need.

**Official U.S. Executive Branch Web Sites**
www.loc.gov/rr/news/fedgov.html
This resource page at the Library of Congress Web site provides links to every federal department, independent agency, and regulatory commission in the federal bureaucracy.

**Privatization.org**
www.privatization.org
Privatization is the removal of all or part of a program from the public sector to the private sector. This Web page, part of the Reason Foundation's Web site, promotes privatization and reform in all levels of the U.S. government.

**Project on Government Oversight**
www.pogo.org
The Project on Government Oversight is an independent, not-for-profit organization that seeks to make government more accountable by investigating corruption and misconduct. Originally set up to focus on the military, this organization now examines all types of government bureaucracies.

**U.S. Agency for International Development**
www.usaid.gov
In 1961 Congress created the U.S. Agency for International Development (USAID) to provide economic and social development assistance to foreign countries. Often criticized for promoting American values and foreign policy objectives, USAID is currently involved in numerous global issues.

In 2010, Barack Obama nominated former Solicitor General Elena Kagan to the Supreme Court, bringing the number of women justices to three. Kagan's nomination was approved by the Senate, and she was sworn in by Chief Justice John Roberts (right) in August 2010.

# 12

# The Federal Courts

**WHAT GOVERNMENT DOES AND WHY IT MATTERS** Many Americans think of the Supreme Court as a distant and mysterious institution whose decisions affect giant corporations, wealthy individuals, and powerful politicians. They see no direct relationship between the black-robed justices and the everyday lives of ordinary people. Occasionally, however, the Supreme Court is asked to hear questions that touch people's lives in a very direct way. One recent example is the 2007 case of *Morse v. Frederick*.[1] This case dealt with the policies of Juneau-Douglas High School in Juneau, Alaska. In 2002, the Olympic torch relay passed through Juneau on its way to Salt Lake City for the opening of the Winter Olympics. As the torch passed Juneau-Douglas High, a senior, Joseph Frederick, unfurled a banner that read, "BONG HITS 4 JESUS." The school's principal promptly suspended Frederick, who then brought suit for reinstatement, alleging that his free speech rights had been violated.[2]

Like most of America's public schools, Juneau-Douglas High prohibits assemblies or expressions at school events that advocate illegal drug use. Civil libertarians, see such policies as restricting students' right to free speech—a right that has been recognized by the Supreme Court since a 1969 case when it said an Iowa public school could not prohibit students from wearing antiwar armbands. Unfortunately for Frederick, today's Supreme Court is more conservative than its 1969 counterpart. Speaking for the Court's majority, Chief Justice John Roberts said that the First Amendment did not require schools to permit students to advocate illegal drug use. This decision affected not only Joseph Frederick but millions of other students whose views might be seen as inappropriate by school administrators.

Every year nearly 25 million cases are tried in American courts and one American in every nine is directly involved in litigation. Cases can arise from disputes between citizens, from efforts by government agencies to punish wrongdoing, or from citizens' efforts to prove that their rights have been infringed on as a result of government action—or inaction. Many critics of the U.S. legal system assert that Americans have become much too litigious (ready to use the courts for all purposes), and perhaps that is true. But the heavy use that Americans make of the courts is also an indication of the extent of conflict in American society. After all, it is far better that Americans seek to settle their differences through the courts rather than by fighting or feuding.

Unlike the two branches of government examined in the last two chapters, the courts are fundamentally undemocratic: their members are not elected (Supreme Court members serve for "lifetime during good behavior") and they are therefore insulated from public pressures. That does not mean that politics has no effect on court decisions—far from it. In addition, both Congress and the president have a hand in making law; judges can affect the meaning of law only through interpretation. That power, however, is an important one, as examples in this chapter will demonstrate. The courts not interpret the laws only passed by Congress and the decisions of presidents when challenges arise, they interpret and apply fundamental rights.

## key concepts

- Millions of cases come to trial in the United States every year.
- State and local courts handle the vast majority of court cases in America.
- The key power of the courts is judicial review.
- Only a tiny percentage of cases get to the Supreme Court, which tightly controls the flow of cases it hears.
- Court decisions are shaped by the justices' activism and ideology.

# ● The Legal System Settles Disputes

Originally, a "court" was the place where a sovereign ruled—where the king or queen governed. Settling disputes between citizens was part of governing. In modern democracies, courts and judges have taken over from kings the power to settle controversies by hearing the facts on both sides and deciding which side possesses greater merit. But since judges are not kings, they must have a basis for their authority. That basis in the United States is the Constitution and the law. Courts decide cases by hearing the facts on both sides of a dispute and applying the relevant law or principle to the facts.

## Court Cases Proceed under Criminal and Civil Law

Court cases in the United States proceed under two broad categories of law: criminal law and civil law.

Cases of **criminal law** involve the branch of law that deals with disputes or actions involving criminal penalties (as opposed to civil law). Criminal law regulates the conduct of individuals, defines crimes, and provides punishment for criminal acts. The government charges an individual with violating a statute (a law) that has been enacted to protect the public health, safety, morals, or welfare. In criminal cases, the government is always the **plaintiff** (the party that brings a complaint

*The courts have the authority to settle disputes not only between individuals and other private entities but also between individuals and the government. In "enemy combatant" cases, the Supreme Court ruled on the rights of prisoners being held in the U.S. base in Guantánamo, Cuba.*

or charges) and alleges that a criminal violation has been committed by a named **defendant** (the one against whom a complaint is brought in a criminal or civil case). Most criminal cases arise in state and municipal courts and involve matters from traffic offenses to robbery and murder. While the great bulk of criminal law is still a state matter, a large and growing body of federal criminal law deals with such matters as tax evasion, mail fraud, and the sale of narcotics. Defendants found guilty of criminal violations may be fined or sent to prison.

Cases of **civil law** involve disputes among individuals or between individuals and the government, including private law and governmental actions, to settle disputes that do not involve criminal penalties. Unlike criminal cases, the losers in civil cases cannot be fined or sent to prison, although they may be required to pay monetary damages for their actions. In a civil case, the one who brings a complaint is the plaintiff and the one against whom the complaint is brought is the defendant. The two most common types of civil cases involve contracts and torts. In a typical contract case, an individual or corporation charges that it has suffered because of another's violation of a specific agreement between the two. For example, the Smith Manufacturing Corporation may charge that Jones Distributors failed to honor an agreement to deliver raw materials at a specified time, causing Smith to lose business. Smith asks the court to order Jones to compensate it for the damage allegedly suffered. In a typical tort case, one individual charges that he or she has been injured by another's negligence or malfeasance. Medical malpractice suits are one example of tort cases. Another important area of civil law is administrative law, which involves disputes over the jurisdiction, procedures, or authority of administrative agencies. A plaintiff may assert, for example, that an agency did not follow proper procedures when issuing new rules and regulations. A court will then examine the agency's conduct in light of the Administrative Procedure Act, the legislation that governs agency rule making.

In deciding cases, courts apply statutes (laws) and legal **precedents** (prior decisions whose principles are used by judges as the basis for their decisions in present cases). State and federal statutes, for example, often govern the conditions under which contracts are and are not legally binding. Jones Distributors might argue that it was not obliged to fulfill its contract with the Smith Corporation because actions by Smith, such as the failure to make promised payments, constituted fraud under state law. Attorneys for a physician being sued for malpractice, on the other hand, may search for prior instances in which courts ruled that actions similar to those of their client did not constitute negligence. Such precedents are applied under the doctrine of *stare decisis*, a Latin phrase meaning "let the decision stand." It is the doctrine that a previous decision by a court applies as a precedent in similar cases until that decision is overruled.

## Types of Courts Include Trial, Appellate, and Supreme

In the United States, systems of courts have been established both by the federal government and by the governments of the individual states. Both systems have several levels, as shown in Figure 12.1. More than 99 percent of all court cases in the United States are heard in state courts. The overwhelming majority of criminal cases, for example, involve violations of state laws prohibiting such actions as murder, robbery, fraud, theft, and assault. If such a case is brought to trial, it

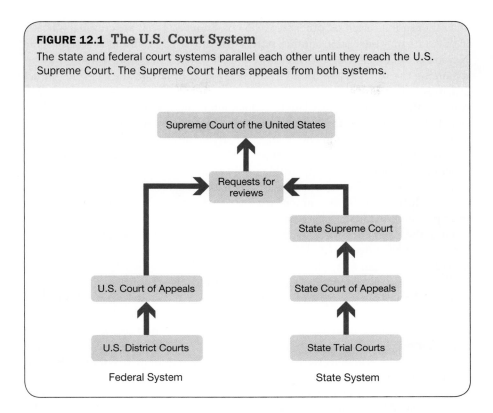

**FIGURE 12.1 The U.S. Court System**

The state and federal court systems parallel each other until they reach the U.S. Supreme Court. The Supreme Court hears appeals from both systems.

Supreme Court of the United States

Requests for reviews

State Supreme Court

U.S. Court of Appeals

State Court of Appeals

U.S. District Courts

State Trial Courts

Federal System

State System

will be heard in a state **trial court** (the first court to hear a criminal or civil case), in front of a judge and sometimes a jury, who will determine whether the defendant violated state law. If the defendant is convicted, he or she may appeal the conviction to a higher court, such as a state **court of appeals** (a court that hears the appeals of trial court decisions), and from there to a state's **supreme court** (the highest court in a particular state or in the United States; it serves an appellate function).

Similarly, in civil cases, most litigation is brought in the courts established by the state in which the activity in question took place. For example, a patient bringing suit against a physician for malpractice would file the suit in the appropriate court in the state where the alleged malpractice occurred. The judge hearing the case would apply state law and state precedent to the matter at hand. (It should be noted that most criminal and civil cases are settled before trial through negotiated agreements between the parties in which a defendant agrees to plead guilty in return for the state's agreement to reduce the severity of the criminal charge the defendant is facing. In criminal cases, these agreements are called **plea bargains**.)

Although each state has its own set of laws, these laws have much in common from state to state. Murder and robbery, obviously, are illegal in all states, although the range of possible punishments for those crimes varies from state to state. Some states, for example, provide for capital punishment (the death penalty) for murder and other serious offenses; other states do not. Some acts that are criminal offenses in one state may be legal in another state. Prostitution, for example, is legal in some Nevada counties, although it is outlawed in all other states. Considerable similarity among the states is also found in the realm of civil law. In the case of contract law, most states have adopted the Uniform Commercial Code (code used in many states in the area of contract law to reduce interstate differences in judicial decisions). In areas such as family law, however, which covers such matters as divorce and child custody arrangements, state laws vary greatly.

Cases are heard in the federal courts if they involve federal laws, treaties with other nations, or the U.S. Constitution; these areas are the official **jurisdiction** (the sphere of a court's power and authority) of the federal courts. In addition, any case in which the U.S. government is a party is heard in the federal courts. If, for example, an individual is charged with violating a federal criminal statute, such as evading the payment of income taxes, a federal prosecutor would bring charges before a federal judge. Civil cases involving the citizens of more than one state and in which more than $75,000 is at stake may be heard in either the federal or the state courts, usually depending on the preference of the plaintiff.

Federal courts serve another purpose in addition to trying cases within their jurisdiction: that of hearing appeals from state-level courts. Individuals found guilty of breaking a state criminal law, for example, can appeal their convictions to a federal court by raising a constitutional issue and asking a federal court to determine whether the state's actions were consistent with the requirements of the U.S. Constitution. An appellant might assert, for example, that the state court denied him or her the right to counsel, imposed excessive bail, or otherwise denied the appellant **due process of law**, defined as the right of every citizen against arbitrary action by national or state governments. Under such circumstances, an appellant can ask the federal court to overturn his or her conviction. Federal courts are not obligated to accept such appeals and will do so only if they feel that the issues raised have considerable merit and if the appellant has exhausted all possible remedies within the state courts. (This procedure is discussed in more detail later in this chapter.) The decisions of state supreme courts may also be appealed to the U.S. Supreme Court if the state court's decision has conflicted with prior U.S. Supreme Court rulings or has raised some important question of federal law. The U.S. Supreme Court accepts such appeals at its discretion.

In addition, in criminal cases, defendants who have been convicted in a state court may request a **writ of *habeas corpus*** from a federal district court. Sometimes known as the "Great Writ," because it is a fundamental safeguard of individual rights designed to prevent unlawful imprisonment, *habeas corpus* is a court order that the individual in custody be brought into court and shown the cause for detention. *Habeas corpus* is guaranteed by the Constitution and can be suspended only in cases of rebellion or invasion. Its historical purpose is to enable an accused person to challenge arbitrary detention and to force an open trial before a judge. But in 1867, Congress's distrust of southern courts led it to confer on federal courts the authority to issue writs of *habeas corpus* to prisoners already tried or being tried in state courts of proper jurisdiction where the constitutional rights of the prisoner were possibly being violated. This writ gives state prisoners a second channel toward Supreme Court review in case their direct appeal from the highest state court fails (see Figure 12.2). The writ of *habeas corpus* is discretionary; that is, the Court can decide which cases to review.

Although the federal courts hear only a small fraction of all the civil and criminal cases decided each year in the United States, their decisions are extremely important. It is in the federal courts that the Constitution and federal laws that govern all Americans are interpreted and their meaning and significance established. Moreover, it is in the federal courts that the powers and limitations of the increasingly powerful national government are tested. Finally, through their power to review the decisions of the state courts, it is ultimately the federal courts that dominate the American judicial system.

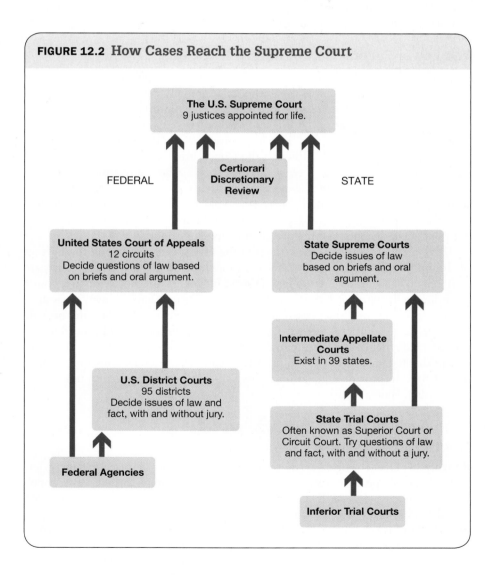

**FIGURE 12.2  How Cases Reach the Supreme Court**

The U.S. Supreme Court
9 justices appointed for life.

Certiorari Discretionary Review

FEDERAL                                    STATE

United States Court of Appeals
12 circuits
Decide questions of law based
on briefs and oral argument.

State Supreme Courts
Decide issues of law
based on briefs and oral
argument.

Intermediate Appellate Courts
Exist in 39 states.

U.S. District Courts
95 districts
Decide issues of law and
fact, with and without jury.

State Trial Courts
Often known as Superior Court or
Circuit Court. Try questions of law
and fact, with and without a jury.

Federal Agencies

Inferior Trial Courts

# The Federal Courts Hear a Small Percentage of All Cases

In 2008, federal district courts (the lowest federal level) received 349,969 cases. Though large, this number is approximately 1 percent of the number of cases heard by state courts. The federal courts of appeal listened to 61,104 cases in 2008 and about 15 percent of the verdicts were appealed to the U.S. Supreme Court. Most of the cases filed with the Supreme Court are dismissed without a ruling on their merits. The Court has broad latitude to decide what cases it will hear and generally listens to only those cases it deems to raise the most important issues. Out of over 10,000 appeals, only 83 cases were given full-dress Supreme Court review in its 2008–09 term (the nine justices actually sitting *en banc*—in full court—and hearing the lawyers argue the case).[3]

## The Lower Federal Courts Handle Most Cases

Most of the cases of original federal jurisdiction are handled by the federal district courts. **Original jurisdiction** is the authority to initially consider a case. It is distinguished from appellate jurisdiction, which is the authority to hear the appeals from a lower court's decision. Original jurisdiction courts are the courts that are responsible for discovering the facts in a controversy and creating the record on which a judgment is based. Although the Constitution gives the Supreme Court original jurisdiction in several types of cases, such as those affecting ambassadors and those in which a state is one of the parties, most original jurisdiction goes to the lowest courts—the trial courts. (In courts that have appellate jurisdiction, judges receive cases after the factual record is established by the trial court. Ordinarily, new facts cannot be presented before appellate courts.)

There are eighty-nine district courts in the fifty states, plus one in the District of Columbia and one in Puerto Rico, and three territorial courts. These courts are staffed by 679 federal district judges. District judges are assigned to district courts according to the workload; the busiest of these courts may have as many as twenty-eight judges. Only one judge is assigned to each case, except where statutes provide for three-judge courts to deal with special issues. The routines and procedures of the federal district courts are essentially the same as those of the lower state courts, except that federal procedural requirements tend to be stricter. States, for example, do not have to provide a grand jury, a twelve-member trial jury, or a unanimous jury verdict. Federal courts must provide all these things.

## The Appellate Courts Hear 20 Percent of Lower Court Cases

Roughly 20 percent of all lower court and federal agency cases are accepted for review by the federal appeals courts and by the Supreme Court in its capacity as an appellate court. There are thirteen U.S. Court of Appeals judicial districts, or circuits (with a total of 179 judges). Those districts consist of eleven that divide up the nation geographically, plus one for the District of Columbia, and one federal circuit (this court deals with patents, trademarks, international trade, and claims against the federal government—see Figure 12.3). So, for example, the Second Circuit includes New

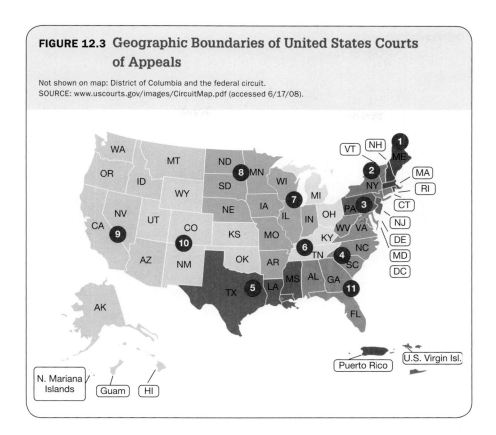

**FIGURE 12.3** Geographic Boundaries of United States Courts of Appeals

Not shown on map: District of Columbia and the federal circuit.
SOURCE: www.uscourts.gov/images/CircuitMap.pdf (accessed 6/17/08).

York, Connecticut, and Vermont; the Ninth Circuit includes California, Oregon, Washington State, Idaho, Montana, Nevada, and Arizona.

Except for cases selected for review by the Supreme Court, decisions made by the appeals courts are final. Because of this finality, certain safeguards have been built into the system. The most important is the provision of more than one judge for every appeals case. Each court of appeals has from six to twenty-eight permanent judgeships, depending on the workload of the circuit. Although normally three judges hear appealed cases, in some instances a larger number of judges sit together *en banc.*

Another safeguard is provided by the assignment of a Supreme Court justice as the circuit justice for each of the circuits. Since the creation of the appeals court in 1891, the circuit justice's primary duty has been to review appeals arising in the circuit in order to expedite Supreme Court action. The most frequent and best-known action of circuit justices is that of reviewing requests for stays of execution when the full Court is unable to do so—primarily during the summer, when the Court is in recess.

## The Supreme Court Is the Court of Final Appeal

The Supreme Court is America's highest court. Article III of the Constitution vests "the judicial power of the United States" in the Supreme Court, and this court is supreme in fact as well as form. The Supreme Court is the only federal court

## TABLE 12.1

### Supreme Court Justices, 2010 (in Order of Seniority)

| NAME | YEAR OF BIRTH | PRIOR EXPERIENCE | APPOINTED BY | YEAR OF APPOINTMENT |
|---|---|---|---|---|
| Antonin Scalia | 1936 | Law professor, federal judge | Reagan | 1986 |
| Anthony Kennedy | 1936 | Federal judge | Reagan | 1988 |
| Clarence Thomas | 1948 | Federal judge | George H. W. Bush | 1991 |
| Ruth Bader Ginsburg | 1933 | Federal judge | Clinton | 1993 |
| Stephen Breyer | 1938 | Federal judge | Clinton | 1993 |
| John G. Roberts, Jr. *Chief Justice* | 1955 | Federal judge | George W. Bush | 2005 |
| Samuel Alito | 1950 | Federal judge | George W. Bush | 2006 |
| Sonia Sotomayor | 1954 | Federal judge | Obama | 2009 |
| Elena Kagan | 1960 | Solicitor General, law school dean | Obama | 2010 |

established by the Constitution. The lower federal courts were created by Congress and can be restructured or, presumably, even abolished by the legislative branch. The Supreme Court is made up of a chief justice and eight associate justices (see Table 12.1). The **chief justice** presides over the Court's public sessions and conferences. In the Court's actual deliberations and decisions, however, the chief justice has no more authority than his colleagues. Each justice casts one vote. To some extent, the influence of the chief justice is a function of his or her own leadership ability. Some chief justices, such as the late Earl Warren, have been able to lead the court in a new direction. In other instances, forceful associate justices, such as the late Felix Frankfurter, are the dominant figures on the Court.

The Constitution does not specify the number of justices who should sit on the Supreme Court; Congress has the authority to change the Court's size. In the early nineteenth century, there were six Supreme Court justices; later there were seven. Congress set the number of justices at nine in 1869, and the Court has remained that size ever since. In 1937, President Franklin Roosevelt, infuriated by several Supreme Court decisions that struck down New Deal programs, asked Congress to enlarge the Court so that he could add a few sympathetic justices to the bench. Although Congress balked at Roosevelt's "court packing" plan, the Court gave in to FDR's pressure and began to take a more favorable view of his policy initiatives. The president, in turn, dropped his efforts to enlarge the Court. The Court's surrender to FDR came to be known as "the switch in time that saved nine."

## Judges Are Appointed by the President and Approved by the Senate

Federal judges are appointed by the president and are generally selected from among the more prominent or politically active members of the legal profession. Many federal judges previously served as state court judges or state or local prosecutors. Candidates for vacancies on the U.S. District Court are generally suggested to the president by a U.S. senator from the president's own party who represents the state in which the vacancy has occurred. Senators often see such a nomination as a way to reward important allies and contributors in their states. If the state has no senator from the president's party, the governor or members of the state's House delegation may make suggestions. In general, presidents endeavor to appoint judges who possess legal experience and good character and whose partisan and ideological views are similar to the president's own. Before the president makes a formal nomination, however, the senators from the candidate's own state must indicate that they support the nominee. This is an informal but seldom violated practice called **senatorial courtesy**. Because the Senate will rarely approve a nominee opposed by a senator from his or her own state, the president will usually not bother to present such a nomination to the Senate. Through this arrangement, senators are able to exercise veto power over appointments to the federal bench in their own states.

*In 2009, President Obama's first nominee to the Supreme Court, Sonia Sotomayor, was sworn in. Although a large Democratic majority in the Senate all but guaranteed Sotomayor would be confirmed, Republican senators grilled her for weeks on her approach to the law.*

President George W. Bush made the appointment of conservative judges a top priority. His appointments of John Roberts in 2005 and Samuel Alito in 2006 reflected this commitment, as both have voted in a consistently conservative direction since reaching the high court. As of 2010, five of the nine justices were appointed by Republicans. This majority, consisting of Chief Justice Roberts and Justices Alito, Kennedy, Scalia, and Thomas, has propelled the Court in a more conservative direction in a variety of areas. In 2009 and 2010, for example, in a series of 5–4 decisions, the Court overturned limits on corporate campaign spending, ruled that the Federal Communications Commission was justified in penalizing the use of expletives on the airwaves, and blocked a suit against former attorney general John Ashcroft by a terrorist suspect alleging that he had been mistreated in prison. Three members of the conservative bloc, Justices Alito, Thomas, and Roberts, are relatively young individuals who will likely serve on the Court for years, if not decades, to come. Through such judicial appointments presidents continue to exercise influence long after they have passed from the political scene.

Once the president has formally nominated an individual, the nominee must be considered by the Senate Judiciary Committee and confirmed by a majority vote in the full Senate. In recent years, the Senate Judiciary Committee has also sought to signal the president when it has had qualms about a judicial nomination. In recent years the judicial appointments process has been affected by increasing partisan conflict. Senate Democrats have sought to prevent Republican presidents from appointing conservative judges while Senate Republicans have worked to prevent Democratic presidents from appointing liberal judges. Historically, the Senate has confirmed nearly all of the presidents' lower federal court nominees, especially at the start of new presidential administrations. So, during the first eighteen months of Reagan's first term, the Senate confirmed 92 percent of his court nominees; in the first eighteen months of the first president Bush's term, it was 72 percent; for the start of Clinton's term, it was 67 percent; for the second President Bush, it was 59 percent; Obama's confirmation rate for his first eighteen months was the lowest ever: only 42 percent. This meant that 117 of 850 lower federal court positions (about 14 percent) were vacant. Law Professor Geoffrey Stone termed Obama's low confirmation rate "unprecedented."[4]

Two important reasons account for this declining rate of confirmation. The first is the just-mentioned rising partisan conflict in Congress, which has meant that the party opposed to the president has been more and more willing to take extreme measures to block presidential nominations and other initiatives. The second reason is that senators in the minority have been more and more willing to use the filibuster to block all Senate business. The power of the filibuster is reflected in the low confirmation rate for Obama court nominees, where he and fellow Democrats have been frustrated by Republicans even though the Democrats had a 59–41 vote Senate majority (60 votes are needed to end a filibuster).

Supreme Court nominations have also come to involve intense partisan struggle. Typically, after the president has named a nominee, interest groups opposed to the nomination have mobilized opposition in the media, the public, and the Senate. When President George H. W. Bush proposed conservative judge Clarence Thomas for the Court, for example, liberal groups launched a campaign to discredit Thomas. After extensive research into his background, opponents of the nomination were able to produce evidence suggesting that Thomas had sexually harassed a former subordinate, Anita Hill. Thomas denied the charge. After contentious Senate Judiciary Committee hearings, highlighted by testimony from both Thomas and Hill, Thomas narrowly won confirmation. During his presidency, George W. Bush's Supreme Court nominations of John Roberts and Samuel Alito won Senate approval with relatively little partisan acrimony. His lower federal court nominees, however, sparked considerable partisan feuding.

In 2009, when President Obama nominated federal judge Sonia Sotomayor to replace retiring justice David Souter, conservatives denounced Sotomayor as a "reverse racist" for her support of affirmative action. Many Republican senators, however, were reluctant to oppose a Hispanic nominee. For several years, the GOP has made efforts to attract America's rapidly growing Hispanic population. Republicans feared that opposing Sotomayor would undermine these efforts.[5] In the end, Sotomayor was easily confirmed, as was Obama's second nominee to the Court, Elena Kagan.

# The Power of the Supreme Court Is Judicial Review

One of the most important powers of the Supreme Court is the power of **judicial review**—the power of the courts to review and, if necessary, declare actions of the legislative and executive branches invalid or unconstitutional. The Supreme Court asserted this power in *Marbury v. Madison* (1803). The disputes can be over the constitutionality of federal or state laws, over the propriety or constitutionality of the court procedures followed, or over whether public officers are exceeding their authority. The Supreme Court's power of judicial review has come to mean review not only of lower court decisions but also of state legislation and acts of Congress. For this reason, the Supreme Court's decisions may alter the law of the land.

The Supreme Court's power of judicial review over lower court decisions has never been at issue. Nor has there been any serious quibble over the power of the federal courts to review administrative agencies in order to determine whether their actions and decisions are within the powers delegated to them by Congress. There has, however, been a great deal of controversy occasioned by the Supreme Court's efforts to review acts of Congress and the decisions of state courts and legislatures.

## Judicial Review Covers Acts of Congress

The Constitution does not expressly grant the Supreme Court the power of judicial review over congressional or other enactments, so some people have argued that the Court's later exercise of judicial review was improper. However, the Constitution's framers did discuss the matter, and according to historian Max Farrand, "it was generally assumed by the leading men in the convention that this power [judicial review] existed."[6] This question aside, the matter of judicial review was settled when the Supreme Court asserted the right in the 1803 case of

*Marbury v. Madison.* Even then, the court's assertion of the power was generally accepted, even by people who were not happy with the decision itself.[7] Since then, the president and Congress have often found reasons to criticize the court, but the idea of judicial review has never been seriously challenged. Still, the Supreme Court has been careful in using this power; since 1789, it has struck down fewer then 200 laws passed by Congress.

## Judicial Review Also Applies to State Actions

The logic of the **supremacy clause** of Article VI of the Constitution, which states that laws passed by the national government and all treaties "shall be the supreme Law of the Land" and superior to all laws adopted by any state or any subdivision, implies that the Court may review the constitutionality of state laws. Furthermore, in the Judiciary Act of 1789, Congress conferred on the Supreme Court the power to reverse state constitutions and laws whenever they are clearly in conflict with the U.S. Constitution, federal laws, or treaties.[8] This power gives the Supreme Court appellate jurisdiction over all of the millions of cases handled by American courts each year.

The supremacy clause of the Constitution not only established the federal Constitution, statutes, and treaties as the supreme law of the land but also provided that "the Judges in every State shall be bound thereby, any Thing in the Constitution or Laws of any State to the Contrary notwithstanding." Under this authority, the Supreme Court has frequently overturned state constitutional provisions or statutes and state court decisions it deems contrary to the federal Constitution or federal statutes.

The civil rights area abounds with examples of state laws that were overturned because the statutes violated guarantees of due process and equal protection contained in the Fourteenth Amendment to the Constitution. For example, in the 1954 case of *Brown v. Board of Education*, the Court overturned statutes from Kansas, South Carolina, Virginia, and Delaware that either required or permitted segregated public schools, on the basis that such statutes denied black schoolchildren equal protection of the law. In 1967, in *Loving v. Virginia*, the Court invalidated a Virginia statute prohibiting interracial marriages.[9]

State statutes in other subject matter areas are equally subject to challenge. In *Griswold v. Connecticut* (1965), the Court invalidated a Connecticut statute prohibiting the general distribution of contraceptives to married couples on the basis that the statute violated the couples' rights to marital privacy.[10]

Sometimes, court decisions are so broad and sweeping that they have the effect of changing the law, and legal practices, across the country. In the 1973 Supreme Court case of *Roe v. Wade*, for example, the Court ruled that a safe, legal abortion was a constitutionally protected right for women under most circumstances. This decision had the effect of striking down restrictive abortion laws in over forty states.

The 1963 case *Gideon v. Wainwright* extends the point. When the Supreme Court ordered a new trial for Clarence Earl Gideon because he had been denied the right to legal counsel,[11] it said to all trial judges and prosecutors that henceforth they would be wasting their time if they cut corners in trials of indigent defendants. It also invited thousands of prisoners to appeal their convictions. (See Chapter 4 for a further discussion of this case.)

In redressing wrongs, the courts sometimes call for a radical change in legal principle. Changes in race relations, for example, would probably have taken a great deal longer if the Supreme Court had not rendered the 1954 decision *Brown v. Board of Education* that redefined the rights of African Americans, striking down "separate but equal."

Similarly, the Supreme Court interpreted the doctrine of the separation of church and state so as to alter significantly the practice of religion in public institutions. For example, in a 1962 case, *Engel v. Vitale*, the Court declared that a once widely observed ritual—the recitation of a prayer by students in a public school—was unconstitutional under the establishment clause of the First Amendment.

Almost all the dramatic changes in the treatment of criminals and of persons accused of crimes have been made by the courts. The Supreme Court brought about a veritable revolution in the criminal process with three cases over less than five years: *Gideon v. Wainwright*, in 1963, was just discussed. *Escobedo v. Illinois*, in 1964, gave suspects the right to remain silent and the right to have counsel present during questioning. But the *Escobedo* decision left confusions that allowed differing decisions to be made by lower courts. In *Miranda v. Arizona*, in 1966, the Supreme Court cleared up these confusions by setting forth what is known as the *Miranda* rule: Arrested people must be informed prior to police interrogation that they have the right to remain silent, the right to be informed that anything they say can be held against them, and the right to counsel before and during police interrogation (see Chapter 4).[12]

One of the most significant changes brought about by the Supreme Court was the revolution in legislative representation unleashed by the 1962 case *Baker v. Carr*.[13] In this landmark case, the Supreme Court held that it could no longer avoid reviewing complaints about the apportionment of seats in state legislatures. Following that decision, the federal courts went on to force reapportionment of all state, county, and local legislatures in the country based on the principle of one person, one vote.

## Most Cases Reach the Supreme Court by Appeal

Given the millions of disputes that arise every year, the job of the Supreme Court would be impossible if it were not able to control the flow of cases and its own caseload. Cases that come first to the Supreme Court are very few in number. Original jurisdiction cases for the Supreme Court include (1) cases between the United States and one of the fifty states, (2) cases between two or more states, (3) cases involving foreign ambassadors or other ministers, and (4) cases brought by one state against citizens of another state or against a foreign country. The most important of these cases are disputes between states over land, water, or old debts. For example, New York and New Jersey have disagreed for years about who owns the small island on which the Statue of Liberty sits. This dispute was settled by the Supreme Court in 1999, when it ruled in favor of New Jersey's ownership. Generally, the Supreme Court deals with these cases by appointing a "special master," usually a retired judge, to actually hear the case and present a report. The Supreme Court then allows the states involved in the dispute to present arguments for or against the master's opinion.[14]

**Writs** Most cases reach the Supreme Court through the **writ of *certiorari***, which is granted whenever four of the nine justices agree to review a decision of a lower court (from the Latin "to make more certain"). The term *certiorari* is sometimes shortened to *cert*, and cases deemed to merit certiorari are referred to as "cert-worthy." An individual who loses in a lower federal court or state court and wants the Supreme Court to review the decision has ninety days to file a petition for a writ of *certiorari* with the clerk of the U.S. Supreme Court. There are two types of petitions, paid petitions and petitions *in forma pauperis* (in the form of a pauper). The former requires payment of filing fees, submission of a certain number of copies, and compliance with a variety of other rules. For *in forma pauperis* petitions, usually filed by prison inmates, the Court waives the fees and most other requirements. Petitions for thousands of cases are filed with the Court every year (see Figure 12.2).

Since 1972, most of the justices have participated in a "*certiorari* pool" in which their law clerks work together to evaluate the petitions. Each petition is reviewed by one clerk who writes a memo for all the justices participating in the pool summarizing the facts and issues and making a recommendation. Clerks for the other justices add their comments to the memo. After the justices have reviewed the memos, any one of them may place any case on the discuss list, which is circulated by the chief justice. If a case is not placed on the discuss list, it is automatically denied *certiorari*. Cases placed on the discuss list are considered and voted on during the justices' closed-door conference.

For *certiorari* to be granted, four justices must be convinced that the case satisfies Rule 10 of the Rules of the U.S. Supreme Court. Rule 10 states that *certiorari* is not a matter of right but is to be granted only when there are special and compelling reasons. These include conflicting decisions by two or more circuit courts, conflicts between circuit courts and state courts of last resort, conflicting decisions by two or more state courts of last resort, decisions by circuit courts on matters of federal law that should be settled by the Supreme Court, and a circuit court decision on an important question that conflicts with Supreme Court decisions. It should be clear from this list that the Court will usually take action under only the most compelling circumstances—when there are conflicts among the lower courts about what the law should be, when an important legal question has been raised in the lower courts but not definitively answered, or when a lower court deviates from the principles and precedents established by the high court.

As Figure 12.4 shows, the Court is inundated by appeals, and the number of appeals has skyrocketed over the years, even though the Court actually rules on less than 1 percent of these appeals. In addition to the judges themselves, others play important roles in shaping the flow of cases through the federal courts: the solicitor general, federal law clerks, and interest groups.

## The Solicitor General and Law Clerks Also Control the Flow of Cases

In addition to the judges themselves, two other entities play an important role in shaping the flow of cases through the federal courts: the solicitor general and federal law clerks.

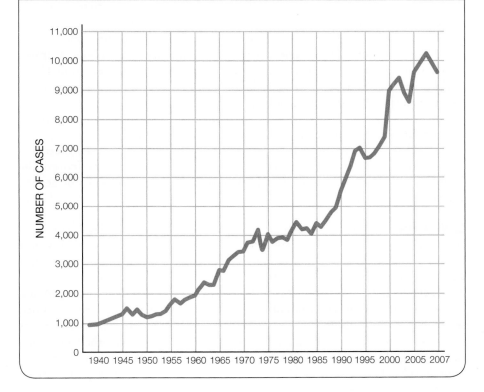

**FIGURE 12.4 Cases Filed in the U.S. Supreme Court, 1938–2007 Terms***

*Number of cases filed in term starting in year indicated.

SOURCES: Years 1938–69, 1970–83, 1984–99: reprinted with permission from *The United States Law Week* (Washington, DC: Bureau of National Affairs), vol. 56, 3102; vol. 59, 3064; vol. 61, 3098; vol. 63, 3134; vol. 65, 3100; vol. 67, 3167; vol. 69, 3134 (copyright © Bureau of National Affairs Inc.); and 2000–05 U.S. Bureau of the Census. *Statistical Abstract of the United States*; 2006–07: Office of the Clerk, Supreme Court of the United States.

**The Solicitor General** If any single person has greater influence than individual judges over the federal courts, it is the **solicitor general** of the United States. The solicitor general is the third-ranking official in the Justice Department (below the attorney general and the deputy attorney general) but is the top government lawyer in virtually all cases before the Supreme Court in which the government is a party. The solicitor general controls the flow of cases by screening them before any agency of the federal government can appeal them to the Supreme Court; indeed, the justices rely on the solicitor general to "screen out undeserving litigation and furnish them with an agenda to government cases that deserve serious consideration."[15] More than half the Supreme Court's total workload consists of cases under the direct charge of the solicitor general. Typically, more requests for appeals are rejected than are accepted by the solicitor general. Agency heads may lobby the president or otherwise try to circumvent the solicitor general, and a few of the independent agencies have a legal right to make direct appeals, but these are almost inevitably doomed to **per curiam** rejection—rejection through a brief, unsigned opinion by an appellate court, usually rejecting a petition to review the decision of a lower court, and that amounts to reaffirmation of the lower court's opinion—if the solicitor general refuses to participate. Congress has given only a few agencies, including the Federal Communications Commission, the Federal Maritime Commission, and in some cases the Department of Agriculture (even though it is not an independent agency), the right to appeal directly to the Supreme Court without going through the solicitor general.

The solicitor general can enter a case even when the federal government is not a direct litigant by writing an **amicus curiae** ("friend of the court") brief. A "friend of the court" is not a direct party to a case but seeks to assist the Supreme Court in reaching a decision by presenting additional briefs. Thus, when the government has such an interest, the solicitor general can file as *amicus curiae*, or a federal court can invite such a brief because it wants an opinion in writing. The solicitor general also has the power to invite others to enter cases as *amici curiae*.

In addition to exercising substantial control over the flow of cases, the solicitor general can shape the arguments used before the federal courts. Indeed, the Supreme Court tends to give special attention to the way the solicitor general characterizes the issues.

**Law Clerks** Every federal judge employs law clerks to research legal issues and assist with the preparation of opinions. Each Supreme Court justice is assigned four clerks. The clerks are almost always honors graduates of the nation's most prestigious law schools. A clerkship with a Supreme Court justice is a great honor and generally indicates that the fortunate individual is likely to reach the very top of the legal profession. The work of the Supreme Court clerks is a closely guarded secret, but some justices rely heavily on their clerks for advice in writing opinions and in deciding whether an individual case ought to be heard by the Court. In a recent book, a former law clerk to the late justice Harry Blackmun charged that Supreme Court justices yielded "excessive power to immature, ideologically driven clerks, who in turn use that power to manipulate their bosses."[16]

**Lobbying for Access: Interests and the Court** At the same time that the Court exercises discretion over which cases it will review, groups and forces in society often seek to persuade the justices to listen to their problems. Interest groups use several different strategies to get the Court's attention. Lawyers representing these groups try to choose the proper client and the proper case, so that the issues in question are most dramatically and appropriately portrayed. They also have to pick the right district or jurisdiction in which to bring the case. Sometimes they even have to wait for an appropriate political climate.

Congress will sometimes provide interest groups with legislation designed to facilitate their use of litigation. One important recent example is the 1990 Americans with Disabilities Act (ADA), enacted after intense lobbying by public interest and advocacy groups. The ADA, in conjunction with the 1991 Civil Rights Act,

*In 2005, the Supreme Court decided two cases involving displays of the Ten Commandments on government property. Christian activists paid close attention to the wording of the decisions, which allowed such displays in some circumstances.*

opened the way for disabled individuals to make effective use of the courts to press their interests.

The two most notable users of the pattern of cases strategy in recent years have been the National Association for the Advancement of Colored People (NAACP) and the American Civil Liberties Union (ACLU). For many years, the NAACP (and its Defense Fund—now a separate group) has worked through local chapters and with many individuals to encourage litigation on issues of racial discrimination and segregation. Sometimes it distributes petitions to be signed by parents and filed with local school boards and courts, deliberately sowing the seeds of future litigation. The NAACP and the ACLU often encourage private parties to bring suit and then join the suit as *amici curiae*.

## The Supreme Court's Procedures Mean Cases May Take Months or Years

**The Preparation** The Supreme Court's decision to accept a case is the beginning of what can be a lengthy and complex process (see Figure 12.5). First, the attorneys on both sides must prepare **briefs**—written documents that may be several hundred pages long in which the attorneys explain why the Court should rule in favor of their client. Briefs are filled with referrals to precedents specifically chosen to show that other courts have frequently ruled in the same way that the Supreme Court is being asked to rule. The attorneys for both sides muster the most compelling precedents they can in support of their arguments.

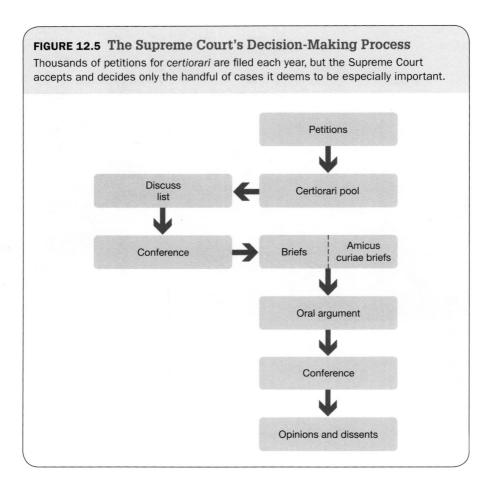

**FIGURE 12.5 The Supreme Court's Decision-Making Process**

Thousands of petitions for *certiorari* are filed each year, but the Supreme Court accepts and decides only the handful of cases it deems to be especially important.

As the attorneys prepare their briefs, they often ask sympathetic interest groups for their help. Groups are asked to file *amicus curiae* briefs that support the claims of one or the other litigant. In a case involving separation of church and state, for example, liberal groups such as the ACLU and Citizens for the American Way are likely to be asked to file *amicus* briefs in support of strict separation, whereas conservative religious groups are likely to file *amicus* briefs advocating increased public support for religious ideas. Often, dozens of briefs will be filed on each side of a major case. *Amicus* filings are a primary method used by interest groups to lobby the Court. By filing these briefs, groups indicate to the Court where their group stands and signal to the justices that they believe the case to be an important one.

**Oral Argument** The next stage of a case is **oral argument**, in which attorneys for both sides appear before the Court to present their positions and answer the justices' questions. Each attorney has only a half hour to present his or her case, and this time includes interruptions for questions. Certain members of the Court, such as Justice Antonin Scalia, are known to interrupt attorneys dozens of times. Others, such as Justice Clarence Thomas, seldom ask questions. For an attorney, the opportunity to argue a case before the Supreme Court is a singular honor and a mark of professional distinction. It can also be a harrowing experience, as justices interrupt a carefully prepared presentation to ask pointed questions. Oral argument can be very important to the outcome of a case. It allows justices to better understand the heart of the case and to raise questions that might not have been addressed in the opposing side's briefs. It is not uncommon for justices to go beyond the strictly legal issues and ask opposing counsel to discuss the implications of the case for the Court and the nation at large.

**The Conference** Following oral argument, the Court discusses the case in its Wednesday or Friday conference. The chief justice presides over the conference and speaks first; the other justices follow in order of seniority. The Court's conference is secret, and no outsiders are permitted to attend. The justices discuss the case and eventually reach a decision on the basis of a majority vote. If the Court is divided, a number of votes may be taken before a final decision is reached. As the case is discussed, justices may try to influence or change one another's opinions. At times, this may result in compromise decisions.

**Opinion Writing** After a decision has been reached, one of the members of the majority is assigned to write the majority opinion (an **opinion** is the written explanation of the Supreme Court's decision in a particular case). This assignment is made by the chief justice, or by the most senior justice in the majority if the chief justice is on the losing side. The assignment of the opinion can make a significant difference to the interpretation of a decision, because the majority opinion states the court's legal conclusion or result, and whoever writes this opinion is shaping the law. Lawyers and judges in the lower courts will examine the opinion carefully to ascertain the Supreme Court's meaning. Differences in wording and emphasis can have important implications for future litigation. Once the majority opinion is drafted, it is circulated to the other justices. Some members of the majority may decide that they cannot accept all the language of the opinion and therefore write "concurring" opinions that support the decision but offer a somewhat different rationale or emphasis. In assigning an opinion, serious thought must be given to the impression the case will make on lawyers and on the public, as well as to the probability that one justice's opinion will be more widely accepted than another's.

One of the more dramatic instances of this tactical consideration occurred in 1944, when Chief Justice Harlan F. Stone chose Justice Felix Frankfurter to write the opinion in the "white primary" case *Smith v. Allwright*. The chief justice believed that this sensitive case, which overturned the southern practice of prohibiting black participation in nominating primaries, required the efforts of the most brilliant and scholarly jurist on the Court. But the day after Stone made the assignment, Justice Robert H. Jackson wrote a letter to Stone urging a change of assignment. In his letter, Jackson argued that Frankfurter, a foreign-born Jew from New England, would not win the South with his opinion, regardless of its brilliance. Stone accepted the advice and substituted Justice Stanley Reed, an American-born Protestant from Kentucky and a southern Democrat in good standing.[17]

*On several occasions, Justice Ruth Bader Ginsburg has read her dissenting opinions aloud from the bench, to emphasize her strong disagreement with the majority.*

**Dissent** Justices who disagree with the majority decision of the Court may choose to publicize their disagreement in the form of a **dissenting opinion** (written by a justice in the minority in a particular case in which the justice wishes to express his or her reasoning in the case). Dissents can be used to express opposition to an outcome or to signal to defeated political forces in the nation that their position is supported by at least some members of the Court. Because there is no need to please a majority, dissenting opinions can be more eloquent and less guarded than majority opinions. Some of the greatest writing in the history of the Court is found in dissents, and some of the most famous justices, such as Oliver Wendell Holmes, Louis D. Brandeis, and William O. Douglas, were notable dissenters. In the single 1952–53 Court term, Douglas wrote thirty-five dissenting opinions. In the 1958–59 term, he wrote eleven dissents. During the latter term, justices Frankfurter and Harlan wrote thirteen and nine dissents, respectively.

Dissent plays a special role in the work and impact of the Court because it amounts to an appeal to lawyers all over the country to keep bringing cases of the sort at issue. Therefore, an effective dissent influences the flow of cases through the Court as well as the arguments that will be used by lawyers in later cases. Even more important, dissent emphasizes the fact that, although the Court speaks with a single opinion, it is the opinion only of the majority—and one day the majority might go the other way.

## Supreme Court Decisions Are Influenced by Activism and Ideology

The Supreme Court explains its decisions in terms of law and precedent. But although law and precedent do have an effect on the Court's deliberations and eventual decisions, it is the Supreme Court that decides what laws actually mean and what importance precedent will actually have. Throughout its history, the Court has shaped and reshaped the law. In the late nineteenth and early twentieth centuries, for example, the Supreme Court held that the Constitution, law, and precedent permitted racial segregation in the United States. Beginning in the late 1950s, however, the Court found that the Constitution prohibited segregation on the basis of race and indicated that the use of racial categories in legislation was always suspect. By the 1970s and 1980s, the Court once again held that the Constitution permitted the use of racial categories—when such categories were needed to help members of minority groups achieve full participation in American society. In the 1990s, the Court began to retreat from this position, too, indicating that governmental efforts to provide extra help to racial minorities could represent an unconstitutional infringement on the rights of the majority.

Although it is not the only relevant factor, the prime explanation for these movements is shifts in judicial philosophy. These shifts, in turn, result from changes in the Court's composition as justices retire and are replaced by new justices who, as we saw earlier, tend to share the philosophical outlook of the president who appointed them.

**Activism and Restraint** One element of judicial philosophy is the issue of activism versus restraint. Over the years, some justices have believed that courts should narrowly interpret the Constitution according to the stated intentions of its framers and defer to the views of Congress when interpreting federal statutes. Justice Frankfurter, for example, advocated judicial deference to legislative bodies and avoidance of the "political thicket" in which the Court would entangle itself by deciding questions that were essentially political rather than legal in character. Advocates of **judicial restraint** (refusing to go beyond the clear words of the Constitution in interpreting its meaning) are sometimes called "strict constructionists," because they look strictly to the words of the Constitution in interpreting its meaning.

The alternative to restraint is **judicial activism**. Activist judges such as the former chief justice Earl Warren believed that the Court should go beyond the words of the Constitution or a statute to consider the broader societal implications of its decisions. Activist judges sometimes strike out in new directions, promulgating new interpretations or inventing new legal and constitutional concepts when they believe these to be socially desirable. For example, Justice Harry Blackmun's decision in *Roe v. Wade* was based on a constitutional right to privacy that is not found in the words of the Constitution. Blackmun and the other members of the majority in the *Roe* case argued that the right to privacy was implied by other constitutional provisions. The idea of privacy is in fact an old one, extending back to the nineteenth century (see Chapter 4). However, its extension to abortion carved a new legal path, making it an example of judicial activism.

Activism and restraint are sometimes confused with liberalism and conservatism. For example, conservative politicians often castigate "liberal activist" judges and call for the appointment of conservative jurists who will refrain from reinterpreting the law. To be sure, some liberal jurists are activists and some conservatives have been advocates of restraint, but the relationship is by no means one to one. Indeed, the Rehnquist Court, dominated by conservatives, was among the most activist courts in American history, striking out in new directions in such areas as federalism and election law. During its 2006–07 term, the conservative Roberts Court overturned a number of its own precedents. Liberal commentators accused the Court's conservative majority of having no more respect for precedent than a "wrecking ball."

**Political Ideology** The second component of judicial philosophy is political ideology. The liberal or conservative outlooks of justices play an important role in their decisions. Indeed, the philosophy of activism versus restraint is, to a large extent, a smokescreen for political ideology. For the most part, liberal judges have been activists, willing to use the law to achieve social and political change, whereas conservatives have been associated with judicial restraint. Interestingly, however,

# Become an Advocate for Justice

Do you think you can't affect the outcome of justice? Think again. Thousands of socially conscious youth convened in Jena, Louisiana, in 2007 to protest the sentences of the so-called Jena 6. After black students at a local high school sat beneath a campus tree that was historically claimed by white students, nooses were found dangling from the same tree. Racial tensions were exacerbated when the justice system appeared to treat white students lightly while coming down hard on black students who behaved similarly. Whites who assaulted black students were tried as juveniles and given light sentences. Five of the six black students who retaliated by assaulting

a white classmate were charged with attempted murder. In order to protest the perceived injustice of the criminal justice system to black defendants, more than 10,000 demonstrators, including a large number of young people, descended on the city of Jena for marches and vigils. Their presence helped to overturn the original sentences of the Jena 6.

If protesting what you believe to be an injustice in the court system isn't for you, there are plenty of other things that you can do.

- Help wrongfully convicted inmates. The Innocence Project assists prison inmates who may be vindicated through the use of DNA testing and has helped to exonerate more than 200 inmates serving lengthy sentences or even facing the death penalty. By visiting the project's Web site (www.innocenceproject.org), you can find out about things that you can do to help.

- Draw attention to the courts' role in key issues. Recent decisions declaring un-

constitutional legislation that defines marriage as a union between a man and woman have drawn considerable criticism from those opposed to what some call "legislating from the bench." Talk to friends and family about what role the courts should play in settling policy disputes. Consider writing a letter to a newspaper about whether the courts should take a more or less active role.

- Along similar lines, you can explore perspectives on the court's role in society. There are a variety of membership groups who are organized around a very clear idea of how the courts should interface with civil society. Check out the Web sites of the Federalist Society for Law and Public Policy Studies (www.fed-soc.org) and the People for the American Way (www.pfaw.org).

- Listen to Supreme Court media files. The Web site for Oyez (www.oyez.org) has links to Supreme Court oral arguments and opinion announcements.

in recent years some conservative justices who have long called for restraint have actually become activists in seeking to undo some of the work of liberal jurists over the past three decades.

From the 1950s to the 1980s, the Supreme Court took an activist role in such areas as civil rights, civil liberties, abortion, voting rights, and police procedures. For example, the Supreme Court was more responsible than any other governmental institution for breaking down America's system of racial segregation. The Supreme Court virtually prohibited states from interfering with the right of a woman to seek an abortion and sharply curtailed state restrictions on voting rights. And it was the Supreme Court that placed restrictions on the behavior of local police and prosecutors in criminal cases. In a series of decisions between 1989 and 2008, however, the conservative justices appointed by Reagan, George H. W. Bush, and George W. Bush were able to swing the Court to a more conservative position on civil rights, affirmative action, abortion rights, property rights, criminal procedure, voting rights, desegregation, and the power of the national government.

**Unpredictability** Despite predictions about how active a new member of the Court is likely to be, or his or her ideological point of view, justices often behave differently on the Court than the presidents who nominate them expect. By one estimate, about a quarter of all justices appointed to the Court have behaved differently from what the presidents who appointed them predicted. Two of Republican president Dwight Eisenhower's appointees to the Court, William Brennan and Earl Warren, turned out to be far more liberal and activist than Eisenhower anticipated. (Eisenhower was once quoted as saying that these two appointments were the biggest mistakes of his presidency.) One of Democratic president John F. Kennedy's Court nominees, Byron White, proved to be a leading conservative on the court. Former Republican president George H. W. Bush's nominee David Souter often sided with the liberal members of the Court.

All in all, presidents Reagan and Bush senior and junior were relatively successful in pushing the federal courts, including the Supreme Court, in a more conservative direction, by virtue of appointing more conservative justices. Taking the twelve years of the Reagan and first Bush presidencies together, the two appointed about two-thirds of all federal judges. The impact of these more conservative judges will be felt for years to come, especially when combined with President George W. Bush's conservative appointees. However, an element of unpredictability remains in the appointment process, because it is difficult to know how a court nominee will actually vote in the wide range of cases that the courts consider, and because, protected by lifetime tenure, each justice is free to follow his or her conscience and interpret the law accordingly.

## The Judiciary Was Designed to Protect Liberty

In the original conception of the framers, the judiciary was to be the institution that would protect individual liberty from the government. As we saw in Chapter 2, the framers believed that in a democracy the great danger was what they termed "tyranny of the majority"—the possibility that a popular majority, "united or actuated by some common impulse or passion," would "trample on the rules of justice."[18] The framers hoped that the courts would protect liberty from the potential excesses of democracy. And for most of American history, this was precisely the role played by the federal courts. The courts' most important decisions were those that protected the freedoms—to speak, worship, publish, vote, and attend school—of groups and individuals whose political views, religious beliefs, or racial or ethnic backgrounds made them unpopular.

Today, Americans of all political persuasions seem to view the courts as useful instruments through which to pursue their goals rather than as protectors of individual rights. Liberals and conservatives alike hope to use the courts as instruments of social policy. One side wants to ban abortion and the other to promote school integration. One side hopes to help business maintain its profitability, whereas the other wants to enhance the power of workers in the workplace. These may all be noble goals, but they present a basic dilemma for students of American government. If the courts are simply one more set of policy-making institutions, then who is left to protect the liberty of individuals?

# studyguide

## Practice Quiz

 Find a diagnostic Web Quiz with 33 additional questions on the StudySpace Web site: www.wwnorton.com/we-the-people

1. What is the name for the body of law that involves disputes between private parties? *(p. 366)*
   a) civil law
   b) privacy law
   c) household law
   d) common law

2. By what term is the practice of the courts to uphold precedent known? *(p. 366)*
   a) *certiorari*
   b) *stare decisis*
   c) rule of four
   d) senatorial courtesy

3. Where do most trials in America take place? *(p. 366)*
   a) state and local courts
   b) appellate courts

   c) federal courts
   d) the Supreme Court

4. The term "writ of *habeas corpus*" refers to *(p. 368)*
   a) a court order that an individual in custody be brought into court and shown the cause for his or her detention.
   b) a criterion used by courts to screen cases that no longer require resolution.
   c) a decision of at least four of the nine Supreme Court justices to review a decision of a lower court.
   d) a brief, unsigned decision by an appellate court, usually rejecting a petition to review the decision of a lower court.

5. Under what authority is the number of Supreme Court justices decided? *(p. 372)*
   a) the president
   b) the chief justice
   c) Congress
   d) the Constitution

6. The Supreme Court's decision in *Marbury v. Madison* was important because *(p. 375)*
   a) it invalidated state laws prohibiting interracial marriage.
   b) it ruled the recitation of prayers in public schools are unconstitutional under the establishment clause of the First Amendment.
   c) it established that arrested people have the right to remain silent, the right to be informed that anything they say can be held against them and the right to counsel before and during police interrogation.
   d) it established the power of judicial review.

7. Which of the following cases involved the "right to privacy"? *(p. 376)*
   a) *Griswold v. Connecticut*
   b) *Brown v. Board of Education*
   c) *Schneckloth v. Bustamante*
   d) *Marbury v. Madison*

8. Which of the following Supreme Court cases did not involve the rights of criminal suspects? *(p. 377)*
   a) *Miranda v. Arizona*
   b) *Escobedo v. Illinois*
   c) *Baker v. Carr*
   d) *Gideon v. Wainwright*

9. Which of the following is *not* included in the original jurisdiction of the Supreme Court? *(p. 377)*
   a) cases between the United States and one of the fifty states
   b) cases involving challenges to the constitutionality of state laws
   c) cases between two or more states
   d) cases involving foreign ambassadors or other ministers

10. Which of the following does not influence the flow of cases heard by the Supreme Court? *(p. 378)*
    a) the Supreme Court itself
    b) the solicitor general
    c) the attorney general
    d) law clerks

11. Which government official is responsible for arguing the federal government's position in cases before the Supreme Court? *(p. 379)*
    a) the vice president
    b) the attorney general
    c) the U.S. district attorney
    d) the solicitor general

12. A justice who favored going beyond the words of the Constitution to consider the broader societal implications of the Supreme Court's decisions would be considered an advocate of which judicial philosophy? *(p. 385)*
    a) judicial restraint
    b) judicial activism
    c) judicial constitutionalism
    d) *stare decisis*

## Chapter Outline

Find a detailed Chapter Outline on the StudySpace Web site:
www.wwnorton.com/we-the-people

# Key Terms

 Find flashcards to help you study these terms on the StudySpace Web site: www.wwnorton.com/we-the-people

**amicus curiae** *(p. 379)* literally, "friend of the court"; individuals or groups who are not parties to a lawsuit but who seek to assist the Supreme Court in reaching a particular decision by presenting additional briefs

**briefs** *(p. 381)* written documents in which attorneys explain, using case precedents, why the court should find in favor of their client

**chief justice** *(p. 372)* justice on the Supreme Court who presides over the Court's public sessions

**civil law** *(p. 366)* the branch of law that deals with disputes that do not involve criminal penalties

**court of appeals** *(p. 367)* a court that hears the appeals of trial court decisions

**criminal law** *(p. 365)* the branch of law that regulates the conduct of individuals, defines crimes, and provides punishment for criminal acts

**defendant** *(p. 366)* the one against whom a complaint is brought in a criminal or civil case

**dissenting opinion** *(p. 384)* a decision written by a justice in the minority in a particular case in which the justice wishes to express his or her reasoning in the case

**due process of law** *(p. 368)* the right of every citizen against arbitrary action by national or state governments

**judicial activism** *(p. 385)* judicial philosophy that posits that the Court should go beyond the words of the Constitution or a statute to consider the broader societal implications of its decisions

**judicial restraint** *(p. 385)* judicial philosophy whose adherents refuse to go beyond the clear words of the Constitution in interpreting its meaning

**judicial review** *(p. 375)* the power of the courts to review and if necessary declare actions of the legislative and executive branches invalid or unconstitutional. The Supreme Court asserted this power in *Marbury v. Madison* (1803)

**jurisdiction** *(p. 368)* the sphere of a court's power and authority

**opinion** *(p. 383)* the written explanation of the Supreme Court's decision in a particular case

**oral argument** *(p. 382)* stage in Supreme Court procedure in which attorneys for both sides appear before the Court to present their positions and answer questions posed by justices

**original jurisdiction** *(p. 370)* the authority to initially consider a case. Distinguished from appellate jurisdiction, which is the authority to hear the appeals from a lower court's decision

**per curiam** *(p. 380)* a brief, unsigned decision by an appellate court, usually rejecting a petition to review the decision of a lower court

**plaintiff** *(p. 365)* the individual or organization that brings a complaint or charges in court

**plea bargains** *(p. 367)* negotiated agreements in criminal cases in which a defendant agrees to plead guilty in return for the state's agreement to reduce the severity of the criminal charge the defendant is facing

**precedent** *(p. 366)* prior case whose principles are used by judges as the basis for their decisions in present cases

**senatorial courtesy** *(p. 373)* the practice whereby the president, before formally nominating a person for a federal judgeship, seeks the indication that senators from the candidate's own state support the nomination

**solicitor general** *(p. 379)* the top government lawyer in all cases before the Supreme Court in which the government is a party

**stare decisis** *(p. 366)* literally, "let the decision stand." The doctrine that a previous decision by a court applies as a precedent in similar cases until that decision is overruled

**supremacy clause** *(p. 376)* clause in Article VI of the Constitution that states that laws passed by the national government and all treaties "shall be the supreme law of the land" and superior to all laws adopted by any state or any subdivision

**supreme court** *(p. 367)* the highest court in a particular state or in the United States.

This court primarily serves an appellate function

**trial court** *(p. 367)* the first court to hear a criminal or civil case

**writ of certiorari** *(p. 378)* a decision of at least four of the nine Supreme Court justices to review a decision of a lower court; from the Latin "to make more certain"

**writ of habeas corpus** *(p. 368)* a court order that the individual in custody be brought into court and shown the cause for detention. *Habeas corpus* is guaranteed by the Constitution and can be suspended only in cases of rebellion or invasion

# For Further Reading

Abraham, Henry. *The Judicial Process*, 7th ed. New York: Oxford University Press, 1998.

Baum, Lawrence. *The Supreme Court*, 10th ed. Washington, DC: Congressional Quarterly Press, 2009.

Cross, Frank. *Decision Making in the U.S. Courts of Appeals*. Stanford, CA: Stanford University Press, 2007

Epstein, Lee. *Constitutional Law for a Changing America*. Washington, DC: Congressional Quarterly Press, 2007.

Fisher, Louis. *Constitutional Dialogues*. Princeton, NJ: Princeton University Press, 1988.

Greenberg, Jan Crawford. *Supreme Conflict: The Inside Story of the United States Supreme Court*. New York: Penguin, 2008.

Hall, Kermit L., Kermit Hall, James Ely, and Joel Grossman. *The Oxford Companion to the Supreme Court*. New York: Oxford University Press, 2005.

Irons, Peter. *A People's History of the Supreme Court*. New York: Penguin, 2006.

Johnson, Timothy R. *Oral Arguments and Decision Making on the U.S. Supreme Court*. Albany, NY: SUNY Press, 2004.

O'Brien, David M. *Storm Center: The Supreme Court in American Politics*, 8th ed. New York: Norton, 2008.

Rosen, Jeffrey. *The Supreme Court: The Personalities and Rivalries that Defined America*. New York: Holt, 2007.

Spitzer, Robert J., ed. *Politics and Constitutionalism*. Albany, NY: SUNY Press, 2000.

Spitzer, Robert J. *Saving the Constitution from Lawyers*. New York: Cambridge University Press, 2008.

Sunstein, Cass. *Are Judges Political?* Washington, DC: Brookings, 2006.

Toobin, Jeffrey. *The Nine: Inside the Secret World of the Supreme Court*. New York: Anchor, 2008.

Ward, Artemus. *Deciding to Leave: The Politics of Retirement from the U.S. Supreme Court*. Albany, NY: SUNY Press, 2003.

## Recommended Web Sites

**Balkinization**
http://balkin.blogspot.com
Balkinization is a widely read blog on constitutional, legal, and judicial issues, organized by Jack Balkin of Yale University Law School.

**Concourts**
www.concourts.net
The U.S. Supreme Court has the responsibility of examining and interpreting the Constitution. The Concourts Web site assumes a comparative perspective and looks at systems of constitutional review in over 150 countries.

**The Constitution Project**
www.constitutionproject.org
The Constitution Project is a bipartisan think-tank that examines constitutional issues.

**FindLaw**
http://findlaw.com
FindLaw's Web site provides answers to most legal questions and helps individuals find legal counsel.

**Justice Talking**
justicetalking.org
*Justice Talking* is a public radio program that examines current legal issues and important court cases.

**Law and Courts Section of the American Political Science Association (APSA)**
www.law.nyu.edu/lawcourts
This organized section of the APSA contains a variety of resources from academic experts on legal and judicial matters.

**Legal Information Institute**
www.law.cornell.edu
The Legal Information Institute at Cornell University is a wonderful Web site for conducting legal research.

**Office of the Solicitor General**
www.usdoj.gov/osg
The solicitor general conducts litigation on behalf of the U.S. Supreme Court and has a tremendous amount of control over the cases that it hears. See what cases are currently being considered by this powerful official of the Justice Department.

**U.S. Courts**
www.uscourts.gov
The U.S. court system consists of trial, appellate, and supreme courts. The U.S. Courts Web site provides a look at the different types of courts in the federal judiciary.

**U.S. Supreme Court**

**www.scotusblog.com**

This U.S. Supreme Court blog is updated frequently each day with reporting on Supreme Court news and issues.

**www.supremecourtus.gov**

The Web site for the U.S. Supreme Court provides information on recent decisions. Take a moment to read some oral arguments, briefs, or court opinions.

**U.S. Supreme Court Media**

**www.oyez.org**

The Web site for U.S. Supreme Court Media has a great search engine for finding information on such landmark cases as *Marbury v. Madison, Miranda v. Arizona,* and *Roe v. Wade.*

Health care is an area of domestic policy that has been controversial. Although most Americans support universal access to health care, they disagree about the best way to ensure high-quality health care. As Congress considered various proposals in 2009 and 2010, the debate heated up.

# Domestic Policy

**WHAT GOVERNMENT DOES AND WHY IT MATTERS** Public policy refers to the decisions, rules, and regulations produced by the government. This chapter gives much of its attention to one broad subcategory of public policy: social policy. Social policies are important because they promote a range of public goals found in most public policies. The first is to protect against the risks and insecurities that most people face over the course of their lives. These include illness, disability, temporary unemployment, and the reduced earning capability that comes with old age. Most spending on social welfare in the United States goes to programs, such as Social Security and medical insurance for the elderly, that serve these purposes. These are widely regarded as successful and popular (though expensive) programs.

Comprehensive health care reform is more controversial. Most Americans support universal access to health care, but, when it comes to specific proposals, they often express doubts. Democrats experienced the public's ambivalence about health reform when they sought to make major changes to the system in 2010. Although the Democratic Congress succeeded in enacting landmark health reform legislation, the reform remained an issue in the 2010 elections as Republicans appealed to voters' worries about the impact and cost of the new law.

Another goal of social policy—to alleviate poverty—has long generated contro-versy in the United States. Americans take pride in their strong work ethic and prize the value of self-sufficiency. As a result, the majority of Americans express suspicions that the able-bodied poor will not try hard enough to support them-selves. Yet Americans also recognize that poverty may be the product of past inequality of opportunity. Since the 1960s, a variety of educational programs and income-assistance policies have sought to end poverty and promote equal oppor-tunity. Much progress has been made toward these goals. However, the dispro-portionate rates of poverty among minorities suggest that our policies have not solved the problem of unequal opportunity.

In the last several chapters, we examined the parts of the government that make policy: Congress, the presidency, the bureaucracy, and the courts. This and the next chapter examine that which is produced by the government—namely, public policy. Many, many books have been written about public policy, and it is not possible to cover the whole range of policies in a single chapter. So this and the next chapter will divide the subject in half and focus on a few selected examples. This chapter will focus on domestic policy, meaning policies that shape what happens within our nation's borders. The next chapter will examine foreign policy, meaning policies that shape America's relations with the other nations of the world.

In this chapter, we will examine the different approaches to achieving policy goals. We will then examine one broad area of domestic public policy, called social policy. We focus on social policy because much of the government's annual bud-get goes to social programs, because such spending is often controversial, and because it illustrates how the government tries to accomplish its goals.

## **key**concepts

- Public policy is made through the use of various techniques of control exercised by the government, including promotional techniques, regulation, and redistribution.

- The modern welfare state, dating from the 1930s, supports the idea of equality.

- Government spending on social programs for the nonworking poor has declined in recent years.

- Most social policy spending goes to the middle class.

- Government policies, including education, employment, housing, and health, can break the cycle of poverty.

# Public Policy Is Government Coercion

Most of this book has focused on how government gets things done. This chapter, and the next, will focus on what the government produces, called **public policy**. Public policy can be defined simply as a purpose or goal expressed by the government that is backed by a sanction (a reward or punishment). Public policy can be a law, a rule, a regulation, or an order. It can include a law passed by Congress, a presidential directive, a Supreme Court ruling, or a rule issued by a bureaucratic agency.

In trying to achieve some purpose, public policy is inherently coercive, even when motivated by the best and most benign intentions. Note that the word "policy" shares a common origin with the word "police." Both terms come from the Greek words *polis* and *politeia*, which refer to the political community and the sources of public authority. Thus the coercion that is the basis of public policy is necessary in order for the policy to be carried out, regardless of whether one agrees or disagrees with the particular policy in question. So it is important to remember that although the idea of coercion seems inherently negative, it is in fact a vital and necessary part of governing. (If overused or misused, coercion can obviously be harmful.)

# The Tools for Making Policy Are Techniques of Control

Techniques of control are to policy makers what tools are to a carpenter. There is a limited number of techniques that the government can use, each with its own logic and limitations. An accumulation of experience helps us to understand when a certain technique is likely to work. Still, just as carpenters will have different ideas about the best tool for a job, so policy makers will disagree about which techniques work best and when. What we offer here is a workable elementary handbook of techniques that will be useful for analyzing policy.

Table 13.1 lists some important techniques of control available to policy makers. These techniques can be grouped into three categories: promotional, regulatory, and redistributive policies.

## Promotional Policies Get People to Do Things by Giving Them Rewards

Promotional policies are the carrots of public policy. Their purpose is to encourage people to do something they might not otherwise do or to get people to do more of what they are already doing. Sometimes the purpose is merely to compensate people for something done in the past. Promotional techniques can be classified into at least two separate types: subsidies and contracting.

**Subsidies** Subsidies are simply government grants of cash or other valuable commodities, such as land, to individuals or organizations that are used to promote activities desired by the government, to reward political support, or to buy off political opposition. Subsidies were the dominant form of public policy of the national government and the state and local governments throughout the nineteenth

**TABLE 13.1**

## Techniques Of Public Control

| TYPE OF POLICY | TECHNIQUES | DEFINITIONS AND EXAMPLES |
|---|---|---|
| Promotional | Subsidies and grants of cash, land, etc. | "Patronage" is the promotion of private activity through what recipients consider "benefits" (example: in the nineteenth century the government encouraged westward settlement by granting land to those who went west) |
| | Contracts | Agreements with individuals or firms in the "private sector" to purchase goods or services |
| | Licenses | Unconditional permission to do something that is otherwise illegal (franchise, permit) |
| Regulatory | Criminal penalties | Heavy fines or imprisonment, loss of citizenship |
| | Civil penalties | Less onerous fines, probation, public exposure, restitution |
| | Administrative regulations | Setting interest rates, maintaining standards of health and safety, investigating and publicizing wrongdoing |
| | Subsidies and contracts | Can be considered regulatory when certain conditions are attached (example: the government refuses to award a contract to firms that show no evidence of affirmative action in hiring) |
| | Regulatory taxes | Taxes that keep consumption or production down (liquor, gas, cigarette taxes) |
| | Expropriation | "Eminent domain"— the power to take private property for public use |
| Redistributive | Taxes | Altering the redistribution of money by changing taxes or tax rules |
| | Budgeting and spending through subsidies and contracts | Deficit spending to pump money into the economy when it needs a boost; creating a budget surplus by cutting spending or increasing taxes to discourage consumption in inflationary times |
| | Fiscal use of credit and interest (monetary techniques) | Changing interest rates to affect both demand or money and consumption (example: the Federal Reserve Board raises interest rates to slow economic growth and ward off inflation) |

century. They continue to be an important category of public policy at all levels of government.

During the nineteenth century, subsidies in the form of land grants were given to farmers and to railroad companies to encourage western settlement. Substantial cash subsidies have traditionally been given to shipbuilders to help build the com-mercial fleet and to guarantee the use of their ships as military personnel carriers in time of war. Policies using the subsidy technique have continued to be plentiful in the twentieth century, even after the 1990s, when there was widespread public and official hostility toward subsidies. For example, in 2007, the annual value of corporate subsidies not including agriculture was estimated at $92 billion.[1] Crop subsidies alone, implemented by the Department of Agriculture, amounted to about $18 billion in 2007.

Subsidies have always been a technique favored by politicians because subsidies can be treated as "benefits" that can be spread widely in response to many demands that might otherwise produce profound political conflict. Subsidies can, in other words, be used to buy off the opposition. And once subsidies exist, the threat of their removal becomes a very significant technique of control.

**Contracting** Like any corporation, a government agency must purchase goods and services by contract. The law requires open bidding for a substantial propor-tion of these contracts because government contracts are extremely valuable to businesses in the private sector and because the opportunities and incentives for abuse are very great. But contracting is more than a method of buying goods and services. Contracting is also an important technique of policy because government agencies are often authorized to use their **contracting power** (the power of govern-ment to set conditions on companies seeking to sell goods or services to govern-ment agencies) as a means of encouraging corporations to improve themselves, as a means of helping to build up whole sectors of the economy, and as a means of encouraging certain desirable goals or behavior, such as equal employment oppor-tunity. For example, the infant airline industry of the 1930s was nurtured by the national government's lucrative contracts to carry airmail.

Military contracting has long been a major element in government spending. So tight was the connection between defense contractors and the federal govern-ment during the Cold War that as he was leaving office, President Eisenhower warned the nation to beware of the powerful "military-industrial complex." After the Cold War, as military spending and production declined, major defense con-tractors began to look for alternative business activities to supplement the reduced demand for weapons. For example, Lockheed Martin, the nation's largest defense contractor, began to bid on contracts related to welfare reform. Since the terrorist attacks of 2001, however, the military budget has been awash in new funds and military contractors are flooded with business. President Bush increased the Pen-tagon budget by more than 7 percent a year, requesting so many weapons systems that one observer called the budget a "weapons smorgasbord."[2] Military contractors geared up to produce not only weapons for foreign warfare but also surveillance systems to enhance domestic security.

## Regulatory Policies Are Rules Backed by Penalties

If promotional policies are the carrots of public policy, regulatory policies can be considered the sticks. Regulation is a technique of control in which the govern-ment adopts rules imposing restrictions on the conduct of private citizens. It comes in several forms, but every regulatory technique shares a common trait: direct government control of conduct. The conduct may be regulated because people feel it is harmful to others, or threatens to be, such as drunk driving or false advertising. Or the conduct may be regulated because people think it's immoral, whether it is harming anybody or not, such as prostitution, gambling, or drinking. Because there are many forms of regulation, we have subdivided them here: (1) police regulation, through civil and criminal penalties, (2) administrative regulation, (3) regulatory taxation, and (4) expropriation.

**Police Regulation** "Police regulation" comes closest to the traditional exercise of police power—a power traditionally reserved to the states to regulate the health, safety, and morals of its citizens. After a person's arrest and conviction, these techniques are administered by courts and, where necessary, penal institutions. They are regulatory techniques.

Civil penalties usually refer to fines or some other form of material restitution (such as public service) as a sanction for violating civil laws or common law principles, or committing negligence. Civil penalties can range from a five-dollar fine for a parking violation to a more onerous penalty for late payment of income taxes to the much more onerous penalties for violating antitrust laws against unfair competition or environmental protection laws against pollution. Criminal penalties usually refer to imprisonment but can also involve heavy fines and the loss of certain civil rights and liberties, such as the right to vote.

**Administrative Regulation** Police regulation addresses conduct considered immoral. In order to eliminate such conduct, strict laws have been passed and severe sanctions enacted. But what about conduct that is not considered morally wrong but that may have harmful consequences? For example, there is nothing morally wrong with radio or television broadcasting. But government regulates broadcasting on a particular frequency or channel because there would be virtual chaos if everybody could broadcast on any frequency at any time.

This kind of conduct is thought of less as *policed* conduct and more as *regulated* conduct. When conduct is said to be regulated, the purpose is rarely to eliminate the conduct but rather to influence it toward more appropriate channels, toward more appropriate locations, or toward certain qualified types of persons, all for the purpose of minimizing injuries or inconveniences. This type of regulation is sometimes called administrative regulation because the controls are given over to civilian agencies rather than to the police, and the rules are made by regulatory agencies and commissions. Each regulatory agency has extensive powers to keep a sector of the economy under surveillance and also has powers to make rules dealing with the behavior of individual companies and people. But these administrative agencies have fewer powers of punishment than the police and the courts have, and the administrative agencies generally rely on the courts to issue orders enforcing the rules and decisions made by the agencies.

Table 13.1 listed subsidies and contracts as examples of both promotional and regulatory policies; although these techniques might normally be thought of as strictly promotional policies, they can also be used as techniques of administrative regulation. It all depends on whether the law sets serious conditions on eligibility for the subsidy or contract. To put it another way, the government can use the threat of losing a valuable subsidy or contract to improve compliance with the goals of regulation. For example, the threat of removal of the subsidies called "federal aid to education" has had a very significant influence on the willingness of schools to cooperate in the desegregation of their student bodies and faculties. For another example, social welfare subsidies (benefits) can be lowered to encourage or force people to take low-paying jobs, or they can be increased to calm political unrest when they are engaging in political protest.[3]

**Regulatory Taxation** In many instances, the primary purpose of a tax is not to raise revenue but to influence conduct, often to discourage or eliminate an activity altogether by making it too expensive for most people. Such taxes are called regulatory taxes. For example, since the end of Prohibition, although there has been no penalty for the production or sale of alcoholic beverages, the alcohol industry has not been free from regulation. First, all alcoholic beverages have to be licensed, allowing only those companies that are "bonded" to put their product on the market. Beyond that, federal and state taxes on alcohol are made disproportionately high, on the theory that, in addition to the revenue gained, less alcohol will be consumed. The same is true of cigarette taxes.

**Expropriation** Confiscation of property with or without compensation for a public use, or expropriation, is a widely used technique of control in the United States, especially in land-use regulation. Almost all public works, from highways to parks to government office buildings, involve the forceful taking of some private property in order to assemble sufficient land and the correct distribution of land for the necessary construction.

We generally call the power to expropriate eminent domain (the right of government to take private property for public use), a power that is recognized as inherent in any government. The Fifth Amendment of the U.S. Constitution surrounds this expropriation power with important safeguards against abuse, so that government agencies in the United States are not permitted to use that power except through a strict due process, and they must offer "fair market value" for the land sought.[4]

Forcing individuals to work for a public purpose is another form of expropriation. The draft of young men for the armed forces, court orders to strikers to return to work, and sentences for convicted felons to do community service are examples of the regular use of expropriation in the United States.

## Redistributive Policies Affect Broad Classes of People

Redistributive policies (also called macroeconomic policies) are usually of two types—fiscal and monetary—but they have a common purpose: to control people by manipulating the entire economy rather than by regulating people directly. (*Macroeconomic* refers to the economy as a whole.) Whereas regulatory policies focus on individual conduct, redistributive policies seek to control conduct more indirectly by altering the conditions of conduct or manipulating the environment of conduct.

*In the early days of the Depression, much of the assistance for the destitute was provided by private groups, through projects such as New York City soup kitchens. Just a few years later, the government became responsible for providing food to needy families.*

**Fiscal Policies** Fiscal policies are the government's use of taxing, monetary, and spending powers to manipulate the economy. Personal and corporate income taxes, which raise most of the U.S. government's revenues, are the most prominent examples. While the direct purpose of an income tax is to raise revenue, each tax has a different impact on the economy, and government can plan for that impact. After passing major tax cuts in 2001, President Bush proposed and Congress passed a sweeping new round of cuts in 2003. Bush's plan was intended to promote investment by reducing taxes on most stock dividends, to spur business activity by offering tax breaks to small businesses, and to stimulate the economy by reducing the tax rates for all taxpayers. In 2006, Congress extended the rate reductions on dividends and capital gains, a move that estimates show will cost the treasury $70 billion over five years. To help pay for the $940 billion cost (over ten years) of President Obama's health care reform, enacted in 2010, the law calls for increasing the Medicare payroll tax for individuals making over $200,000 and for married couples making over $250,000.

Taxes became a major issue in the closing weeks of the presidential race in 2008. Republican candidate John McCain pledged not to raise taxes and labeled Barack Obama a "redistributionist." Obama, for his part, defended his plan to roll back the Bush cuts and stuck with his pledge to raise taxes on the 3 percent of households who make more than $250,000 a year. The debate recapped a classic partisan division, with Republicans arguing that any tax increase harms the economy and Democrats contending that taxes are needed to support public programs and that it is only fair for high earners to pay a larger share of taxes than those with lower incomes.

**Monetary Policies** Monetary policies allow government to regulate the economy through the manipulation of the supply of money are credit. America's most powerful institution in this area of monetary policy is the Federal Reserve Board (the Fed), the governing board of the Federal Reserve System, consisting of a chair and six other members, all appointed by the president with the consent of the Senate. The Fed can affect the total amount of credit available through the interest (called the discount rate) it charges on the loans it extends to member banks. If the Fed significantly decreases the discount rate, it can give a boost to a sagging economy. During 2001, the Fed cut interest rates eleven times to combat the combined effects of recession and the terrorist attacks. In the steep recession that began in 2008, the Fed acted aggressively. By December 2008, it had cut rates nine times, from a high in September 2007 of 4.75 percent to a historically low zero percentage rate. Moreover, the Federal Reserve kept interest rates at that level well into 2010 in an attempt to encourage new lending and thus economic growth.[5] If the Fed raises the discount rate, it can put a brake on the economy because the higher discount rate also increases the general interest rates charged by leading private banks to their customers. Although the Federal Reserve is responsible for ensuring high employment as well as price stability, it has been particularly important in fighting inflation. During the late 1970s and early 1980s, with inflation at record high levels, Federal Reserve Chairman Paul Volcker aggressively raised interest rates in order to dampen inflation. Although his actions provoked a sharp recession, they raised the stature of the Fed, demonstrating its ability to manage the economy.

**Spending Power as Fiscal Policy** Perhaps the most important redistributive technique of all is the most familiar one: the "spending power," which is a combination of subsidies and contracts. Government can use these techniques to achieve policy goals far beyond buying goods and services and regulating individual conduct. This is why subsidies and contracts show up yet again in Table 13.1 as redistributive techniques.

Agricultural subsidies are one example of the national government's use of its purchasing power as a fiscal or redistributive technique. And since the 1930s, the federal government has attempted to raise and to stabilize the prices of several important agricultural products, such as corn and wheat, by authorizing the Department of Agriculture to buy enormous amounts of these commodities if prices on the market fall below a fixed level.

# ● Social Policy and the Welfare System Buttress Equality

For much of American history, local governments and private charities were in charge of caring for the poor. During the 1930s, when this largely private system of charity collapsed in the face of widespread economic destitution, the federal government created the beginnings of an American welfare state. The idea of the welfare system was new; it meant that the national government would oversee programs designed to promote economic security for all Americans—not just for the poor. The American system of social welfare includes many different policies enacted over the years since the Great Depression. Because each program is governed by distinct rules, the kind and level of assistance available varies widely.

## The History of the Government Welfare System Dates Only to the 1930s

There has always been a welfare system in America. But until 1935, it was almost entirely private, composed of an extensive system of voluntary philanthropy through churches and other religious groups, ethnic and fraternal societies, communities and neighborhoods, and philanthropically inclined rich individuals. Most often it was called "charity," and although it was private and voluntary, it was thought of as a public obligation.

The traditional approach of charity crumbled in 1929 before the stark reality of the Great Depression. During the Depression, misfortune became so widespread and private wealth shrank so drastically that private charity was out of the question and the distinction between deserving and undeserving became impossible to draw. Around 20 percent of the workforce immediately became unemployed; this figure grew as the Depression stretched into years. Moreover, few of the unemployed had any monetary resources or any family farm on which to fall back. Banks failed, wiping out the savings of millions who had been prudent enough or fortunate enough to have any savings at all. Thousands of businesses failed as well, throwing middle-class Americans onto the bread lines along with unemployed laborers, dispossessed farmers, and those who had never worked in any capacity whatsoever. The Great Depression proved to Americans that poverty could be a result of imperfections in the economic system as well as of individual irresponsibility. It also forced Americans to alter drastically their standards regarding who was deserving and who was not.

Once poverty and dependency were accepted as problems inherent in the economic system, a large-scale public policy approach was not far away. By the time President Franklin D. Roosevelt took office in 1933, the question was not whether there was to be a public welfare system but how generous or restrictive that system would be.

## The Social Security Act of 1935 Was the Foundation of the Welfare System

If the welfare state were truly a state, its founding would be the Social Security Act of 1935. This act created two separate categories of welfare: contributory and noncontributory. Table 13.2 lists the key programs in each of these categories, with the year of their enactment and recent figures on the number of Americans they benefit and their cost to the federal government.

**Contributory Programs** The category of welfare programs that are financed by taxation or other mandatory contributions by their present or future recipients can justifiably be called "forced savings"; these programs force working Americans

## Public Welfare Programs

The biggest public welfare programs are the insurance or contributory programs, including old age insurance (what we commonly call Social Security), Medicare (health care for seniors), and unemployment insurance. The noncontributory programs of the public assistance system are generally smaller and less expensive. Which group does the government spend more money on—the elderly or poor families with children?

| TYPE OF PROGRAM | YEAR ENACTED | NUMBER OF RECIPIENTS IN 2007 (IN MILLIONS) | FEDERAL AND STATE OUTLAYS IN 2007 (IN BILLIONS) |
| --- | --- | --- | --- |
| **Contributory (Insurance) System** | | | |
| Old-Age, Survivors, and Disability Insurance | 1935 | 50.9** | $615.2** |
| Medicare | 1965 | 45.2* | $455.1* |
| Unemployment Compensation | 1935 | 7.6 | $30.1 |
| **Noncontributory (Public Assistance) System** | | | |
| Medicaid | 1965 | 57.8** | $269.9** |
| Food Stamps | 1964 | 28.4** | $34.6** |
| Supplemental Security Income (cash assistance for aged, blind, disabled) | 1974 | 7.4 | $42.1 |
| School Lunch Program | 1946 | 31.0** | $8.3** |
| Temporary Assistance to Needy Families | 1996 | 3.9 | $26.9 |
| State Children's Health Insurance Policy* | 1997 | 7.4* | $6.9* |

*2008 data.
**Number of units, Section 8 Housing and low-cost public housing; 2006 data.
SOURCES: U.S. Census Bureau, *2010 Statistical Abstract*, www.census.gov (accessed 3/20/10).

to set aside a portion of their current earnings to provide income and benefits during their retirement years. These **contributory programs** are what most people have in mind when they refer to **Social Security** or social insurance, a contributory welfare program into which working Americans contribute a percentage of their wages, and from which they receive cash benefit after retirement. Under the original contributory program, old-age insurance, the employer and the employee were each required to pay equal amounts, which in 1937 were set at 1 percent of the first $3,000 of wages, to be deducted from the paycheck of each employee and matched by the same amount from the employer. This percentage has increased over the years; the contribution in 2010 was 7.65 percent subdivided as follows: 6.2 percent on the first $106,800 of income for Social Security benefits, plus 1.45 percent on all earnings for Medicare.[6] Social Security mildly redistributes wealth from higher- to lower-income people, and it quite significantly redistributes wealth from younger workers to older retirees.

Congress increased Social Security benefits every two or three years during the 1950s and 1960s. The biggest single expansion in contributory programs since 1935 was the establishment in 1965 of **Medicare**, a form of national health insurance for the elderly and the disabled, which provides substantial medical services to elderly persons who are already eligible to receive old-age, survivors', and disability insurance under the original Social Security system. In 2003, Congress added a prescription drug benefit to the package of health benefits for the elderly. Social Security benefits and costs are adjusted through **indexing** (periodic adjusting of social benefits or wages to account for increases in the cost of living), whereby benefits paid out under contributory programs are modified annually by **cost-of-living adjustments (COLAs)**—changes made to the level of benefits of a government program based on the rate of inflation—designed to increase benefits to keep up with the rate of inflation. But, of course, Social Security taxes (contributions) also increased after almost every benefit increase.

**Noncontributory Programs** Social programs that provide assistance to people based on demonstrated need rather than any contribution they have made—**noncontributory programs**—are also known as "public assistance programs," or, derisively, as "welfare." Until 1996, the most important noncontributory program was Aid to Families with Dependent Children (AFDC, originally called Aid to Dependent Children, or ADC), which provided federal funds, administered by the states, for children living with parents or relatives who fell below state standards of need. It was founded in 1935 by the original Social Security Act. In 1996, Congress abolished AFDC and replaced it with the Temporary Assistance to Needy Families (TANF) block grant. Eligibility for public assistance is determined by **means testing**, a procedure that requires applicants to show a financial need for assistance. Between 1935 and 1965, the government created programs to provide housing assistance, school lunches, and food stamps to other needy Americans.

As with contributory programs, the noncontributory public assistance programs also made their most significant advances in the 1960s and 1970s. The largest single category of expansion was the establishment in 1965 of **Medicaid**, a program that provides extended medical services to all low-income persons who have already established eligibility through means testing under AFDC or TANF. Noncontributory programs underwent another major transformation in the 1970s in the level of benefits they provide. Besides being means tested, noncontributory programs are provided by the national government to the states as incentives to establish the programs (see Chapter 3). Thus from the beginning there were considerable disparities in benefits from state to state. The national government sought to rectify the disparities in levels of old-age benefits in 1974 by creating the "means

*After 1935, the federal government created new programs to help poor families. For example, the federally funded school lunch program provides nutritious meals for needy children.*

test"–based Supplemental Security Income (SSI) program to augment benefits for the aged, the blind, and the disabled. SSI provides uniform minimum benefits across the entire nation and includes mandatory COLAs. States are allowed to be more generous if they wish, but no state is permitted to provide benefits below the minimum level set by the national government. As a result, twenty-five states increased their own SSI benefits to the mandated level. The program is financed from general revenues rather than from Social Security contributions.

The TANF program is also administered by the states and, as with the old-age benefits just discussed, benefit levels vary widely from state to state (see Figure 13.1). In 2008, the states' monthly TANF benefits varied from $170 in Mississippi to $923 in Alaska. In 2010, the nationally defined poverty level for a family of three was $18,310 a year, or $1,526 a month.[7]

The number of people receiving AFDC benefits expanded in the 1970s, in part because new welfare programs had been established in the mid-1960s: Medicaid (discussed earlier) and **food stamps**, which are coupons that can be exchanged for food at most grocery stores. These programs provide what are called **in-kind benefits**—noncash goods and services provided by the government that the beneficiary would otherwise have to pay for in cash. In addition to simply adding on the cost of medical services and food to the level of benefits given to AFDC recipients, the possibility of receiving Medicaid benefits provided an incentive for poor Americans to establish their eligibility for AFDC, which would also establish their eligibility to receive Medicaid. At the same time, the government significantly expanded its publicity efforts to encourage the dependent unemployed to establish their eligibility for these various programs.

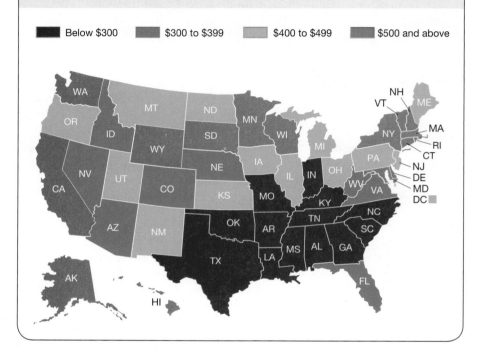

**FIGURE 13.1  Monthly Spending on TANF Benefits**

Spending on TANF benefits varies widely across the country. In thirteen states, monthly benefits for a family of three are below $300; in fourteen states, they are above $500 a month. In which regions does spending on TANF benefits tend to be higher? In which regions is it generally lower?

SOURCES: Figures for January 1996, 2000, 2002, and 2005: Congressional Research Services Report, "The Temporary Assistance for Needy Families (TANF) Block Grant: Responses to Frequently Asked Questions" (Table 6), www.nationalaglawcenter.org/assets/crs/RL32760.pdf.

## Welfare Reform Has Dominated the Welfare Agenda in Recent Years

The Republicans controlling the White House and the Senate in the 1980s initially had welfare reform very high on their agenda. They proceeded immediately, with the cooperation of many Democrats, to cut the rate of increase of all the major social welfare programs, including the contributory social insurance programs and the noncontributory, "need-based" programs. However, very little was actually cut in either type of program, and the welfare system quickly began to expand again. After 1984, expenditures for public assistance programs began to increase at a rate about equal to the rate of general economic growth (called the Gross Domestic Product, or GDP). Moreover, no public assistance programs were terminated, despite Republican criticisms of them.

The Republicans took control of both houses of Congress in 1995, based on their "Contract with America," which included a promise to introduce a bill to "reduce illegitimacy, control welfare spending, and reduce welfare dependence."

The Republican welfare bill removed the federal guarantee of assistance, forced 1.5 million welfare recipients to work by 2000, denied public aid to legal immigrants who are not citizens, and granted states wide discretion in administering welfare programs.

During the 104th Congress (1995–96), President Clinton twice vetoed proposals for welfare reform, arguing that they would harm children. However, in August 1996, the president signed a third bill similar to the previous proposals. This major reform of welfare abolished AFDC and replaced the federal guarantee of assistance to the poor with block grants to the states through the new TANF program. This program allows states to deny assistance to legal immigrants and requires the head of each family receiving welfare to work within two years or lose assistance. The legislation also establishes a lifetime limit of five years on the receipt of assistance.

After this law was enacted, the number of families receiving assistance dropped by 60 percent nationwide (see Figure 13.2).[8] The sharp decline in the number of recipients was widely hailed as a sign that welfare reform was working. Indeed, former welfare recipients have been more successful at finding and keeping jobs than many critics of the law predicted. One important indicator of how welfare has changed is the proportion of funds it provides in cash assistance. Before the 1996 reform, assistance was provided largely in the form of a cash grant. By 2008, 70 percent of welfare funds were allocated for noncash assistance and 30 percent for cash assistance. This means that an increasing proportion of welfare funds is spent on such costs as assistance with transportation to work, temporary shelter, or

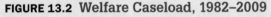

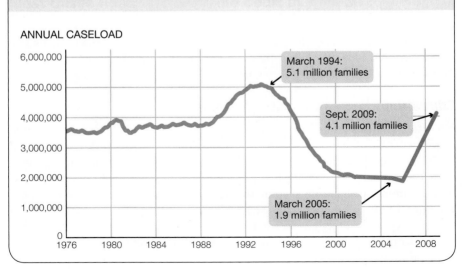

**FIGURE 13.2 Welfare Caseload, 1982–2009**

Welfare caseloads began to decline even before the 1996 reform. They continued to plummet in the years after welfare reform. Welfare caseloads remained low even during the recession of the early 2000s. Why do you think they rose again by 2009?

SOURCE: U.S. Department of Health and Human Services, www.acf.hhs.gov (accessed 5/7/10).

ANNUAL CASELOAD

March 1994: 5.1 million families

Sept. 2009: 4.1 million families

March 2005: 1.9 million families

one-time payments for emergencies so that people do not go on the welfare rolls. The orientation of assistance has shifted away from subsidizing people who are not in the labor force toward addressing temporary problems that low-income people face and providing assistance that facilitates work.[9] The law has been less successful in other respects: researchers have found no clear evidence that it has helped reduce out-of-wedlock births. And critics point out that most former welfare recipients are not paid enough to pull their families out of poverty. Moreover, many families eligible for food stamps and Medicaid stopped receiving these benefits when they left the welfare rolls. The law has helped reduce welfare caseloads, but it has done little to reduce poverty.[10]

Since 1996, two different perspectives on TANF reform have emerged. Democrats have proposed changes that would make the welfare law "an antipoverty weapon."[11] They hope to increase spending on child care, allow more education and training, and relax time limits for those working and receiving welfare benefits. Republicans, by contrast, have proposed stricter work requirements and advocated programs designed to promote marriage among welfare recipients.[12] In 2005 Congress renewed the TANF program and added new funding to promote marriage and two-parent families. As the economy soured in 2008 and 2009, welfare rolls began to move upward but at a very slow rate. The American Recovery and Reinvestment Act of 2009 included a TANF Emergency Fund that provided money for states to create subsidized jobs for low-income parents and young adults. Despite these measures, many advocates for the poor worried that the state TANF programs were not assisting enough poor families.[13]

## ● The Cycle of Poverty Can Be Broken by Education, Employment, Health, and Housing Policies

The welfare state not only supplies a measure of economic security but also provides opportunity. The American belief in equality of opportunity makes such programs particularly important. Programs that provide opportunity keep people from falling into poverty, and they offer a hand up to those who are poor. At their best, opportunity policies allow all individuals to rise as high as their talents will take them. Four types of policies are most significant in opening opportunity: education policies, employment policies, health policies, and housing policies.

### Education Policies Provide Life Tools

Education is highly valued in America, a belief reflected in the fact that the vast majority of the education provided to Americans comes from public educational institutions financed through state, local, and (to a lesser extent) national government education policy. Less well appreciated is the fact that education is an extremely important factor in shaping the distribution and redistribution of wealth and opportunity in America. This assertion is supported by the fact that a person's lifelong income is directly correlated with his or her level of education. In other words, people with more education earn more in their lifetimes than people with less education.

Compared to state and local efforts, the role of national government education policy is limited. Moreover, the most important national education policies have come only since World War II: the GI Bill of Rights of 1944, the National Defense Education Act (NDEA) of 1958, the Elementary and Secondary Education Act of 1965 (ESEA), and various youth and adult vocational training acts since 1958. Note, however, that since the GI Bill was aimed almost entirely at postsecondary schooling, the national government did not really enter the field of elementary education until after 1957.[14]

What finally brought the national government into elementary education was embarrassment over the fact that the Soviet Union had beaten the United States into space with the launching of the satellite Sputnik. The national policy under NDEA was aimed specifically at improving education in science and mathematics. General federal aid for education did not come until ESEA in 1965, which allocated funds to school districts with substantial numbers of children from families who were unemployed or earning very little.

President Clinton's education program included more federal aid for preschool programs for needy children, national education standards coupled with teachers' incentives, and, at the postsecondary level, scholarships for minorities and an ambitious national service program available to all students to earn credit toward college tuition. Clinton's most concrete achievement in education policy was the Improving America's Schools Act of 1994, also known as Goals 2000, which aimed to reverse federal policies dating back to the 1960s that set lower academic standards for schools in poorer school districts than for those in wealthier ones. Goals 2000 set uniform national standards for educational achievement from the wealthiest to the poorest school districts, and committed $400 million in federal funds to help establish these standards. The logic of the old system was that it was unfair to expect disadvantaged children to perform at the same level as children from wealthier backgrounds. But the result, not surprisingly, was to discourage children in poor school districts from achieving academic excellence.

President George W. Bush's most prominent policy achievement in education was the No Child Left Behind Act of 2001, which enacted stronger federal requirements for student testing and school accountability. It required every child in grades three through eight to be tested yearly for proficiency in math and reading, with the scores to serve as a basis for judging schools. Parents with children in schools whose scores are poor have the right to transfer their

*Education policy is the most important means of providing equal opportunity for all Americans. President George W. Bush's 2001 No Child Left Behind Act, an education reform bill passed by overwhelmingly bipartisan majorities in Congress, imposes stronger national requirements for school accountability and testing.*

children to a better school or to get funds for tutoring and summer programs. Since enactment, some states have rebelled against what they considered an "unfunded mandate," meaning that the government failed to provide the funds necessary to comply with the law. Teachers objected that "teaching to the test" undermined critical thinking skills. In some states, up to half the schools failed to meet the new standards, resulting in a costly remedial challenge. Under the federal law, they were required to improve student performance by providing such new services as supplemental tutoring, longer school days, and additional summer school. By 2004, the federal government decided to relax some of the law's requirements. When No Child Left Behind came up for reauthorization in 2007, Congress was unable to reach an agreement on a new bill. The current provisions of the act remained in effect, and it was left to a future Congress to work out the difficult compromises needed to reauthorize the legislation.

Faced with these conflicts, the Obama administration sought a major overhaul of No Child Left Behind. Obama's proposal kept some features of the original law, including its emphasis on testing and standards. Yet the president's approach broadened the criteria for evaluating schools to include attendance and graduation rates. It also made academic progress, rather than test results, the main criteria for judging a school's academic success. Parts of the president's blueprint for reform immediately attracted controversy. One contentious issue was a proposal to change the criteria for allocating $14 billion in federal assistance to schools (called Title I funds) from a per pupil formula to a system of competitive grants. The idea aroused intense opposition because it would greatly increase federal power over schools and alter longstanding patterns of funding. The provisions for holding teachers accountable for student achievement provoked antagonism. Teachers' unions charged that the president's plan made the teachers responsible for achievement but gave them no authority over education.[15] Although teachers' unions are a major Democratic backer, Democratic members of Congress appeared supportive of the president's proposals. Even so, controversies over the president's plan promised a vigorous legislative debate over the reform of No Child Left Behind.

## Employment and Training Programs Mean Steady Incomes

Considering the importance that Americans attach to work and the high value they place on education, it is somewhat surprising that the United States does not have a strong system for employment and job training. Such programs have two goals. One is to prepare entry-level workers for new jobs or to retrain workers whose jobs have disappeared. A second goal is to provide public jobs during economic downturns when sufficient private employment is not available. Since the 1930s, the American employment and training systems have fared poorly in terms of expenditures, stability, and results.[16]

The first public employment programs were launched during Roosevelt's New Deal. These programs were created to use the power of the federal government to get people back to work again. But by the end of the 1930s, questions about corruption and inefficiency in employment programs reduced support for them.

Not until the 1960s did the federal government try again. This time, as part of the War on Poverty, government programs were designed to train and retrain workers, primarily the poor, rather than to provide them with public employment. For the most part, the results of these programs were disappointing. It proved very difficult to design effective training policies in the federal system; lack of coordination and poor administration plagued the Great Society training programs.

In 1982, Congress created a new program that supported local efforts at job training. The Job Training Partnership Act (JTPA) became the primary federal program supporting job training. In addition to retraining adult workers, JTPA provides funding for summer jobs for youth. President Clinton placed an especially high value on creating a strong system of job training. Clinton's program made use of tax credits and direct subsidies to employers to set up apprentice-training jobs for young people and was to be part of a more ambitious national system that was called "lifelong learning." It was inspired by training programs that exist in some European countries, and it coupled national initiatives with community organizations and administration. Yet Clinton's initiatives in job training remained small, as budgetary pressures and congressional skepticism limited his legislative achievements.

As part of its efforts to stimulate the economy and to assist the unemployed, the Obama administration enacted a variety of grant programs aimed at offering training for dislocated workers and young people as well as tax credits for employers who retain workers or hire new workers. Obama also promoted the idea of "green jobs" and sought to kick-start growth in jobs connected to reducing America's carbon footprint. The legislation provided funding for a number of training programs that prepared workers for jobs in the energy sector. In his first budget, the president proposed to provide seed funding for clean energy technology. Although there is considerable enthusiasm for the idea of green jobs, sparking such fundamental change in the American economy is a difficult task that will take many years to accomplish.

## Health Policies Mean Fewer Sick Days

Until recent decades, no government in the United States—national, state, or local—concerned itself directly with individual health. But public responsibility was always accepted for *public* health. After New York City's newly created Board of Health was credited with holding down a cholera epidemic in 1867, most states followed with the creation of statewide public health agencies. Within a decade, the results were obvious. Between 1884 and 1894, for example, Massachusetts's rate of infant mortality dropped from 161.3 per 1,000 to 141.4 per 1,000.[17] Reductions in mortality rates during the late nineteenth century may be the most significant contribution ever made by government to human welfare.

The U.S. Public Health Service (USPHS) has been in existence since 1798 but was a small part of public health policy until after World War II. Established in 1937, but little noticed for twenty years, was the National Institutes of Health (NIH), an agency within the USPHS created to do biomedical research. Between 1950 and 2008, NIH expenditures by the national government increased from $160 million to $28 billion. NIH research on the link between smoking and disease led to one of the most visible public-health campaigns in American history. Today, NIH's focus has turned to cancer and acquired immunodeficiency syndrome (AIDS). As with smoking, this work on AIDS has resulted in massive public-health education as well as new products and regulations. In 2011, federal spending on AIDS-related programs was $27 billion.

Other, recent commitments to the improvement of public health are the numerous laws aimed at cleaning up and defending the environment (including the creation in 1970 of the Environmental Protection Agency) and laws attempting to improve the health and safety of consumer products (regulated by the Consumer Product Safety Commission, created in 1972). Health policies aimed directly at the poor include Medicaid and nutritional programs, particularly food stamps and the school lunch program. As Figure 13.3 shows, the government has committed

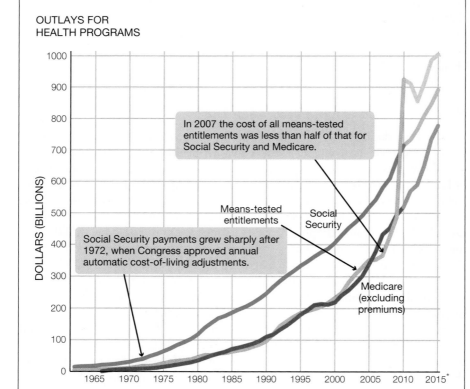

### FIGURE 13.3 Federal Social Spending, 1962–2015*

Social Security and Medicare, the main entitlement programs that provide pensions and health insurance for people over sixty-five, have grown dramatically since 1962. The federal government spends far more on these two programs, which benefit all elderly people regardless of income, than it does on means-tested programs, which benefit the poor.

SOURCE: Office of Management and Budget, The President's Budget, Historical Tables, Table 8.1, Outlays by Budget Enforcement Act Category, 1962–2015; Table 16.1, Outlays for Health Programs, 1962–2015, www.whitehouse.gov (accessed 3/12/10).

OUTLAYS FOR HEALTH PROGRAMS

In 2007 the cost of all means-tested entitlements was less than half of that for Social Security and Medicare.

Means-tested entitlements

Social Security

Social Security payments grew sharply after 1972, when Congress approved annual automatic cost-of-living adjustments.

Medicare (excluding premiums)

*2010–2015 are estimates.

large resources to health care programs. While these programs yield great benefits by providing health care to millions, the cost of these programs has risen dramatically in recent years—far more than the rate of inflation—prompting growing calls for major changes in spending and funding.

The Obama administration and the Democratic Congress pressed forward with comprehensive health care reform. Seeking to avoid the conflicts that broke out in Congress over the Clintons' failed health care reform proposal, Obama offered Congress broad principles for reform, not a detailed proposal. The administration aimed to cover most Americans who lacked health insurance with a reform strategy that built on the existing system. The congressional plans for reform had three key features: the first was the creation of state-based insurance exchanges where individuals could buy health insurance, along with insurance regulation that would prohibit insurers from denying benefits for a variety of reasons such as preexisting conditions; the second was a provision requiring uninsured individuals to purchase health insurance; and the third was a set of subsidies to help the uninsured and small businesses purchase insurance as well as an expansion of Medicaid and the State Children's Health Insurance Program (SCHIP). One controversial provision was a "public option" that would allow individuals to purchase government-provided insurance from the insurance exchange. Aware that this idea had become a flashpoint for opponents, Democratic congressional leaders ultimately dropped it from consideration in their final negotiations.

Even so, opponents branded the reform proposals as "big government" and sometimes as "socialism," a charge that has been levied against health reform initiatives since the 1940s. Republicans closed ranks against the proposal, meaning that all the credit—or blame—for the act would fall on the Democrats. This put the Democrats in a precarious position: if they failed to enact the legislation, they could be charged with having wasted a year when Congress should have been addressing the country's economic problems. But if they succeeded, they had to defend legislation that had become less popular over the course of 2009.

Democrats won enactment of comprehensive health care reform through a set of complex parliamentary maneuvers early in 2010, but the politics of health care reform continued to loom large in the 2010 congressional elections. Republicans appealed to ongoing public uncertainty about the new legislation and promised to repeal it if they won control of Congress.

## Housing Policies Provide Residential Stability

The United States has one of the highest rates of homeownership in the world, and the central thrust of federal housing policy has been to promote homeownership. The federal government has traditionally done much less to provide housing for low-income Americans who cannot afford to buy homes. Federal housing programs were first created in the 1930s depression period when many Americans found themselves unable to afford housing. Through public housing for low-income families, which originated in 1937 with the Wagner-Steagall National Housing Act, and subsidized private housing after 1950, the percentage of American families living in overcrowded conditions was reduced from 20 percent in 1940 to 9 percent in 1970. Federal policies made an even greater contribution to reducing

# Take an Active Stance on Social Problems

As this chapter illustrates, social policy affects all aspects of our lives, including whether we have national educational standards, the qualifications for unemployment benefits, the provision of health care and Social Security, and much more. The decisions we make as a society concerning issues such as these reflect our national values. So, when we increase spending on federal grants for higher education we make a commitment to expanding access to college for low- and middle-income students. When we require welfare recipients to move to work or risk losing their benefits, we emphasize our commitment to self-reliance.

Social policy also reflects what we believe about responsibility. It illustrates what we think about our responsibility to each other and what we are willing to do for each other as members of a shared polity. With so many issues, it may be hard to decide what to support or what you want the government to do. Certainly, many people feel so overwhelmed or intimidated that they opt out of the debate altogether. But with a little effort, you can educate yourself about the issues and take an active role in the national conversation.

- You can start by thinking through debates over major social policies and finding out where you fit. Two issues that have been debated recently are health care reform and immigration. A good place to start developing a deeper understanding of these issues is the Public Agenda Foundation (www.publicagenda.org/issues /issuehome.cfm), which lays out what advocates on all sides say.

- Many people across the political spectrum see an important role for non profit organizations, including faith-based groups, to work with (or instead of) government in providing key services to those in need. The Roundtable on Religion and Social Policy www.religionand socialpolicy.org, provides independent analysis of this phenomenon.

- Immigration reform is a perennial issue in American politics. As much as we like to think of ourselves as the proverbial "melting pot," the influx of immigrants, many of whom are here illegally, challenges our embrace of diversity. Working through a campus organization, you might stage a debate with experts on both sides of the issue. Groups to contact include the American Civil Liberties Union (www.aclu.org), American Conservative Union (www.conservative.org), National Council of La Raza (www.nclr.org), and the Asian American Legal Defense and Education Fund (www.aaldef.org).

"substandard" housing, defined by the U.S. Census Bureau as dilapidated houses without hot running water and without some other plumbing. In 1940, almost 50 percent of American households lived in substandard housing. By 1950, this had been reduced to 35 percent; by 1975, the figure was reduced further to 8 percent.[18] Despite these improvements in housing standards, federal housing policy until the 1970s was largely seen as a failure. Restricted to the poorest of the poor, marked by racial segregation and inadequate spending, public housing contributed to the problems of the poor by isolating them from shopping, jobs, and urban amenities. Dilapidated high-rise housing projects stood as a symbol of the failed American policy of "warehousing the poor." By the 1980s, the orientation of housing policy had changed: Most federal housing policy for low-income Americans came in the form of housing vouchers (called Section 8 vouchers) that provided recipients with support to rent in the private market. While this program did not promote the same isolation of the poor, it was often useless in expensive housing markets where the vouchers provided too little money to cover rental costs.

In 2007 and 2008, a home loan crisis presented the government with a different kind of housing problem. During the housing boom of the early 2000s, many homeowners received loans that they later could not afford to repay. As a result, millions of homeowners were in danger of losing their homes as they defaulted on their mortgage payments. Moreover, the magnitude of bad debt harmed banks and threatened to destabilize the entire economy. The federal government responded with a plan that would delay interest rate increases that were the cause of the problem for some homeowners. Even so, many people lost their homes and the broader economy felt the strain as the effects of the defaulted loans filtered through the economic system.

## ● Social Policy Spending Benefits the Middle Class More Than the Poor

The two categories of social policy—contributory and noncontributory—generally serve different groups of people. We can understand much about the development of social policy by examining which constituencies benefit from different policies.

The strongest and most generous programs are those in which the beneficiaries are widely perceived as deserving of assistance and also are politically powerful. Because Americans prize work, constituencies who have "earned" their benefits in some way or those who cannot work because of a disability are usually seen as most deserving of government assistance. Politically powerful constituencies are those who vote as a group, lobby effectively, and mobilize to protect the programs from which they benefit.

When we study social policies from a group perspective, we can see that senior citizens and the middle class receive the most benefits from the government's social policies and that children and the working poor receive the fewest. In addition, America's social policies do little to change the fact that minorities and women are more likely to be poor than white Americans and men.

## Senior Citizens Now Receive over a Third of All Federal Dollars

The elderly are the beneficiaries of the two strongest and most generous social policies: old-age pensions (what we call Social Security) and Medicare (medical care for the elderly). As these programs have grown, they have provided most elderly Americans with economic security and have dramatically reduced the poverty rate among the elderly. In 1959, before very many people over the age of sixty-five received social insurance, the poverty rate for the elderly was 35 percent; by 2009, it had dropped to 9.7 percent.[19] Because of this progress, many people call Social Security the most effective antipoverty program in the United States. This does not mean that the elderly are rich, however; in 2008, the median income of elderly households was $29,744, well below the national median income. The aim of these programs is to provide security and prevent poverty rather than to assist people once they have become poor. And they have succeeded in preventing poverty among most of the aged.[20]

One reason that Social Security and Medicare are politically strong is that the elderly are widely seen as a deserving population. They are not expected to work, because of their age. Moreover, both programs are contributory, and a work history is a requirement for receiving a Social Security pension. But these programs are also strong because they serve a constituency that has become quite powerful. The elderly are a very large group: in 2008, there were 38.9 million Americans over the age of sixty-five. Because Social Security and Medicare are not means tested, they are available to all former workers and their spouses over the age of sixty-five, whether they are poor or not. The size of this group is of such political importance because the elderly turn out to vote in higher numbers than the rest of the population.

In addition, the elderly have developed strong and sophisticated lobbying organizations that can influence policy making and mobilize elderly Americans to defend these programs against proposals to cut them. One important and influential organization that defends the interests of older people in Washington is AARP (formerly the American Association of Retired Persons). AARP had 40 million members in 2010, amounting to one-fifth of all voters. It also has a sophisticated

*Recent reports have estimated that the Social Security system will be unable to pay full benefits by 2041. Former president Bush advocated creating private retirement accounts as a way of reforming Social Security.*

lobbying organization in Washington that employs 28 lobbyists and a staff of 165 policy analysts.[21] Although AARP is the largest and the strongest organization of the elderly, other groups, such as the Alliance for Retired Americans, to which many retired union members belong, also lobby Congress on behalf of the elderly.

These lobbying groups are among the most powerful in America. They mobilize their supporters and work with legislators to block changes they believe will hurt the elderly. Because of the tremendous political strength of the elderly, Social Security has been nicknamed the "third rail of American politics: touch it and you die."[22] In the case of Medicare reform, for example, AARP had long opposed any reform that allowed private health care firms to provide Medicaid benefits. But in 2003, AARP switched its position and endorsed the Bush administration's bill to provide prescription drug benefits through the involvement of private firms. AARP's endorsement of the plan was decisive to its passage. In 2005, AARP's opposition to President Bush's plan to partially privatize Social Security was decisive in killing the plan. In 2009 and 2010, AARP came out in support of health care reform, although it avoided endorsing any specific bill. Thousands of members left the organization in protest, but AARP is so large that their actions had little impact.

## The Middle Class Benefits from Social Policies

Americans don't usually think of the middle class as benefiting from social policies, but government action promotes the social welfare of the middle class in a variety of ways. First, medical care and pensions for the elderly help the middle class by relieving them of the burden of caring for elderly relatives. Before these programs existed, old people were more likely to live with and depend financially on their adult children. Many middle-class families whose parents and grandparents are in nursing homes rely on Medicaid to pay nursing-home bills.

In addition, the middle class benefits from what some analysts call the "shadow welfare state."[23] These are the social benefits that private employers offer to their workers—medical insurance and pensions, for example. The federal government subsidizes such benefits by not taxing the payments that employers and employees make for health insurance and pensions. These **tax expenditures**, as they are called, are an important way in which the federal government helps ensure the social welfare of the middle class. (Such programs are called "tax expenditures" because the federal government helps finance them through the tax system by providing tax deductions for private employers for amounts spent on health insurance and other benefits rather than by direct spending.) Another key tax expenditure that helps the middle class is the tax exemption on mortgage interest payments: Taxpayers can deduct the amount they have paid in interest on a mortgage from the income they report on their tax return. By not taxing these payments, the government makes homeownership less expensive.

People often don't think of these tax expenditures as part of social policy because they are not as visible as the programs that provide direct payments or services to beneficiaries. But tax expenditures represent a significant federal investment: They cost the national treasury some $945 billion a year and make it easier

*In 2008, as a growing number of Americans found they could not afford the mortgages on their homes, the government authorized measures to help people keep their homes. Critics of the government's response said that the measures did not do enough to help homeowners and were intended mainly to help big financial companies.*

and less expensive for working Americans to obtain health care, save for retirement, and buy homes. These programs are very popular with the middle class, so Congress rarely considers reducing them. On the few occasions when public officials have tried to limit these programs—with proposals to limit the amount of mortgage interest that can be deducted, for example—they have quickly retreated. These programs are simply too popular among Americans whose power comes from their numbers at the polling booth.

## The Working Poor Receive Fewer Benefits

People who are working but are poor or are just above the poverty line receive only limited assistance from government social programs. This is somewhat surprising, given that Americans value work so highly. But the working poor are typically employed in jobs that do not provide pensions or health care; often they are renters because they cannot afford to buy homes. This means they cannot benefit from the shadow welfare state that subsidizes the social benefits enjoyed by most middle-class Americans. At the same time, however, they cannot get assistance through programs such as Medicaid and TANF, which are largely restricted to the nonworking poor.

Two government programs do assist the working poor: the Earned Income Tax Credit (EITC) and food stamps. The EITC was implemented in 1976 to provide poor workers some relief from increases in the taxes that pay for Social Security.

As it has expanded, the EITC has provided a modest wage supplement for the working poor, allowing them to catch up on utility bills or pay for children's clothing. Poor workers can also receive food stamps. These two programs help supplement the income of poor workers, but they offer only modest support. Because the wages of less-educated workers have declined significantly over the past fifteen years and minimum wages have not kept pace with inflation, the problems of the working poor remain acute.

Even though the working poor may be seen as deserving, they are not politically powerful because they are not organized. There is no equivalent to AARP for the poor. Nonetheless, because work is highly valued in American society, politicians find it difficult to cut the few social programs that help the working poor. In 1995, efforts to cut the EITC were defeated by coalitions of Democrats and moderate Republicans, although Congress did place new restrictions on food stamps and reduced the level of spending on this type of aid.

## Spending for the Nonworking Poor Is Declining

The only nonworking, able-bodied poor people who receive federal cash assistance are parents who are caring for children. The primary source of cash assistance for these families was AFDC and now is the state-run TANF program, but they also rely on food stamps and Medicaid. Able-bodied adults who are not caring for children are not eligible for federal assistance other than food stamps. Many states provide small amounts of cash assistance to such individuals through programs called "general assistance," but in the past decade, many states have abolished or greatly reduced their general assistance programs in an effort to encourage these adults to work. Thus, the primary reason the federal government provides any assistance to able-bodied adults is because they are caring for children. Although Americans don't like to subsidize adults who are not working, they do not want to harm children.

AFDC was the most unpopular social spending program, and as a result, spending on it declined after 1980. Under TANF, states receive a fixed amount of federal funds, whether the welfare rolls rise or fall. Because the number of people on welfare has declined so dramatically since 1994—by nearly 50 percent—states have had generous levels of federal resources for the remaining welfare recipients. Many states, however, have used the windfall of federal dollars to cut taxes and indirectly support programs that benefit the middle class, not the poor.[24] Welfare recipients have little political power to resist cuts in their benefits.

## Minorities, Women, and Children Are Most Likely to Face Poverty

Minorities, women, and children are disproportionately poor. Much of this poverty is the result of disadvantages rooted in the position of these groups in the labor market. African Americans and Latinos tend to be economically less well off than the rest of the American population. Much of this economic inequality stems from the fact that minority workers tend to have low-wage jobs. Minorities are also more likely to become unemployed and to remain unemployed for longer periods of time than are white Americans. African Americans, for example, typically have experienced twice as much unemployment as other Americans have. The combination of low-wage jobs and unemployment often means that minorities are less likely to have jobs that give them access to the shadow welfare state. They are more likely to fall into the precarious categories of the working poor or the nonworking poor.

In the past several decades, policy analysts have begun to talk about the "feminization of poverty," or the fact that women are more likely to be poor than men are. This problem is particularly acute for single mothers, who are more than twice as likely to fall below the poverty line than the average American (see Figure 13.4). When the Social Security Act was passed in 1935, the main programs for poor

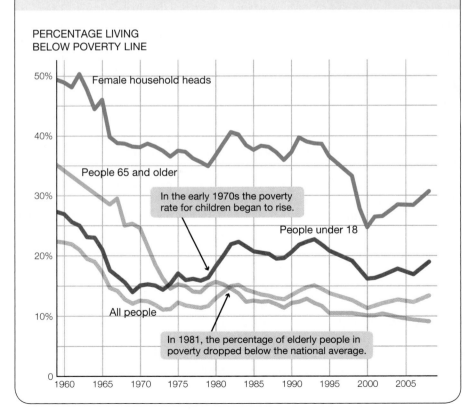

**FIGURE 13.4 Poverty Level in the United States, 1960–2008**

Poverty among all Americans has declined markedly since 1960. However, the rate of progress has varied significantly across groups. Female-headed households have made the slowest progress, although poverty rates for this group have dropped sharply since 1994. Which group has seen the greatest reduction in its poverty level since 1960?

SOURCES: U.S. Census Bureau Current Population Survey, www.census.gov (accessed 3/14/10); Carmen DeNavas-Walt, Bernadette D. Proctor, Jessica C. Smith, *Income, Poverty, and Health Insurance Coverage in the United States: 2008*, Table 1, U.S. Government Printing Office, Washington, D.C., 2009, p.6, www.census.gov (accessed 3/14/10).

PERCENTAGE LIVING
BELOW POVERTY LINE

Female household heads

People 65 and older

In the early 1970s the poverty rate for children began to rise.

People under 18

All people

In 1981, the percentage of elderly people in poverty dropped below the national average.

women were Aid to Dependent Children (ADC) and survivors' insurance for widows. The framers of the act believed that ADC would gradually disappear as more women became eligible for survivors' insurance. The social model behind the Social Security Act was that of a male breadwinner with a wife and children. Women were not expected to work, and if a woman's husband died, ADC or survivors' insurance would help her stay at home and raise her children. The framers of Social Security did not envision today's large number of single women heading families. At the same time, they did not envision that so many women with children would also be working. This combination of changes helped make AFDC (the successor program to ADC) more controversial. Many people ask, why shouldn't welfare recipients work, if the majority of women who are not on welfare work?

One of the most troubling issues related to American social policy is the number of American children who live in poverty. The rate of child poverty in 2008 was 19.0 percent—5.8 percent higher than that of the population as a whole. These high rates of poverty stem in part from the design of American social policies. Because these policies do not generously assist able-bodied adults who aren't working, and because these policies offer little help to the working poor, the children of these adults are likely to be poor as well.

As child poverty has grown, several lobbying groups have emerged to represent children's interests; the best known of these is the Children's Defense Fund. But even with a sophisticated lobbying operation and although their numbers are large, poor children do not vote and therefore wield little political power.

# studyguide

## Practice Quiz

 Find a diagnostic Web Quiz with 33 additional questions on the StudySpace Web site: www.wwnorton.com/we-the-people

1. Which is *not* an example of a regulatory technique of public control? *(pp. 400–01)*
   a) licenses
   b) civil penalties
   c) expropriation
   d) criminal penalties

2. The power of government to set conditions on companies seeking to sell goods or services to government agencies is called *(p. 399)*
   a) administrative regulation.
   b) police power.
   c) eminent domain.
   d) contracting power.

3. The Fed's raising or lowering of the discount rate is an example of *(p. 403)*
   a) subsidizing.
   b) regulatory taxation.
   c) monetary policy.
   d) fiscal policy.

4. America's welfare state was constructed initially in response to *(pp. 403–04)*
   a) World War II.
   b) political reforms of the Progressive era.
   c) the Great Depression.
   d) the growth of the military-industrial complex.

5. Which of the following is *not* an example of a contributory program? *(pp. 405–06)*
   a) Social Security
   b) Medicare
   c) food stamps
   d) All of the above are examples of contributory programs.

6. In 1996, as part of welfare reform, Aid to Families with Dependent Children was abolished and replaced by *(p. 406)*
   a) the Earned Income Tax Credit.
   b) Aid to Dependent Children.
   c) Supplemental Security Income.
   d) Temporary Assistance to Needy Families.

7. Means testing requires that applicants for welfare benefits show *(p. 406)*
   a) that they are capable of getting to and from their workplace.
   b) that they have the ability to store and prepare food.
   c) some definite need for assistance plus an inability to provide for it.
   d) that they have the time and resources to take full advantage of federal educational opportunities.

8. Which of the following are examples of in-kind benefits? *(p. 407)*
   a) Medicaid and food stamps
   b) Social Security payments and cost-of-living adjustments
   c) Medicare and unemployment compensation
   d) None of the above are examples of in-kind benefits.

9. Which of the following is *not* aimed at breaking the cycle of poverty? *(p. 410)*
   a) drug policies
   b) education policies
   c) employment training programs
   d) health policies

10. What event prompted the federal government to enter the field of elementary education? *(p. 411)*
    a) the Great Depression
    b) World War II
    c) the Soviet Union's launching of *Sputnik*
    d) the civil rights movement

11. Who are the chief beneficiaries of the "shadow welfare state"? *(p. 419)*
    a) the rich
    b) the nonworking poor
    c) the working poor
    d) the middle class

12. Which of the following statements best describes the poverty level in the United States since 1960? *(p. 422)*
    a) It has declined equally among all groups.
    b) It has declined overall but has fallen at different rates for different groups.
    c) It has increased equally among all groups.
    d) It has increased overall but has risen at different rates for different groups.

## Chapter Outline

Find a detailed Chapter Outline on the StudySpace Web site: www.wwnorton.com/we-the-people

## Key Terms

Find Flashcards to help you study these terms on the StudySpace Web site: www.wwnorton.com/we-the-people

**contracting power** *(p. 399)* the power of government to set conditions on companies seeking to sell goods or services to government agencies

**contributory programs** *(p. 405)* social programs financed in whole or in part by taxation or other mandatory contributions by their present or future recipients. The most important example is Social Security, which is financed by a payroll tax

**cost-of-living adjustments (COLAs)** *(p. 406)* changes made to the level of benefits of a government program based on the rate of inflation

**Fiscal Policy** *(p. 402)* the government's use of taxing monetary, and spending powers to manipulate the economy

**food stamps** *(p. 407)* coupons that can be exchanged for food at most grocery stores; the largest in-kind benefits program

**indexing** *(p. 406)* periodic adjusting of social benefits or wages to account for increases in the cost of living

**in-kind benefits** *(p. 407)* noncash goods and services provided to needy individuals and families by the federal government that the beneficiary would otherwise have to pay for in cash

**means testing** *(p. 406)* a procedure by which potential beneficiaries of a public assistance program establish their eligibility by demonstrating a genuine need for the assistance

**Medicaid** *(p. 406)* a federally financed, state-operated program providing medical services to low-income people

**Medicare** *(p. 406)* a form of national health insurance for the elderly and the disabled

**Monetary Policy** *(p. 403)* an effort to regulate the economy through the manipulation of the supply of money and credit. America's most powerful institution in this area of monetary policy is the Federal Reserve Board

**noncontributory programs** *(p. 406)* social programs that provide assistance to people based on demonstrated need rather than any contribution they have made

**public policy** *(p. 397)* a purpose or goal expressed by the government that is backed by a sanction (a reward or punishment)

**Social Security** *(p. 405)* a contributory welfare program into which working Americans contribute a percentage of their wages and from which they receive cash benefits after retirement

**subsidies** *(p. 397)* government grants of cash or other valuable commodities such as land to individuals or organizations; used to promote activities desired by the government, to reward political support, or to buy off political opposition

**tax expenditures** *(p. 419)* government subsidies provided to employers and employees through tax deductions for amounts spent on health insurance and other benefits; these are one way the government helps to ensure the social welfare of the middle class

# For Further Reading

Campbell, Andrea Louise. *How Policies Make Citizens: Senior Political Activism and the American Welfare State*. Princeton, NJ: Princeton University Press, 2005.

Gutman, Amy. *Democratic Education*. Princeton, NJ: Princeton University Press, 1987.

Hacker, Jacob S. *The Great Risk Shift: Why American Jobs, Families, Health Care, and Retirement Aren't Secure—and How We Can Fight Back*. New York: Oxford University Press, 2006.

Howard, Christopher. *The Welfare State Nobody Knows: Debunking Myths about U.S. Social Policy*. Princeton, NJ: Princeton University Press, 2007.

Katz, Michael. *In the Shadow of the Poorhouse: A Social History of Welfare in America*. New York: Basic Books, 1986.

Katznelson, Ira, and Margaret Weir. *Schooling for All: Race, Class, and the Democratic Ideal*. New York: Basic Books, 1985.

Krugman, Paul. *Peddling Prosperity: Economic Sense and Nonsense in the Age of Diminished Expectations*. New York: Norton, 1994.

Light, Paul. *Artful Work: The Politics of Social Security Reform*. New York: Random House, 1985.

Marmor, Theodore R., Jerry L. Mashaw, and Phillip L. Harvey. *America's Misunderstood Welfare State*. New York: Basic Books, 1990.

Mettler, Suzanne. *Soldiers to Citizens: The GI Bill and the Making of the Greatest Generation*. New York: Oxford University Press, 2005.

Patterson, James T. *America's Struggle against Poverty, 1900–1994*. Cambridge, MA: Harvard University Press, 1994.

Schwarz, John E. *America's Hidden Success: A Reassessment of Twenty Years of Public Policy*. New York: Norton, 1988.

Spitzer, Robert J. *The Politics of Gun Control*. Washington, DC: Congressional Quarterly Press, 2008.

Weir, Margaret, Ann Orloff, and Theda Skocpol, eds. *The Politics of Social Policy in the United States*. Princeton, NJ: Princeton University Press, 1988.

# Recommended Web Sites

**Center for Retirement Research**
http://crr.bc.edu
Americans pay for their retirement with a mix of Social Security, employer-sponsored savings plans, and private savings. This Web site provides analyses of the challenges that face all aspects of the current arrangements and includes a downloadable "Social Security Fix-It Book."

**Center on Budget and Policy Priorities**
www.cbpp.org
The Center on Budget and Policy Priorities is a nonpartisan, liberal-leaning, nonprofit organization that provides timely data and analysis of social programs that serve low-income Americans. It also studies economic and social changes that affect the well-being of low-income people. Areas of research include the Earned Income Tax Credit, food assistance, Social Security, and climate change. It focuses on national programs as well as state and local policies.

**Libertarian Party**
www.lp.org
Contrary to many other Americans, libertarians believe that social programs pose a threat to personal freedom and should be eliminated. Go to the Libertarian Party's Web site to read the organization's opinions and positions on most current social policies.

**Medicare**
www.medicare.gov
Health care is one of the largest and most controversial social programs in the United States. At the Medicare Web site, find out what services the Department of Health and Human Services provides.

**Modern American Poetry: The Great Depression**
www.english.uiuc.edu/maps/depression/depression.htm
The Great Depression changed American opinion about the causes of and responsibility for poverty. This Web site, by Cary Nelson at the University of Illinois at Urbana-Champaign, provides information, statistics, and photos of this historical period as well as analysis of poems by Depression-era writers.

**Poverty.com**
**www.poverty.com**
Poverty is a problem that exists in the United States and around the world. Read about how poverty, hunger, and related problems affect people in other areas countries.

**Public Agenda**
**www.publicagenda.com**
Public Agenda is a nonpartisan organization that tries to bridge the gap between American leaders and public opinion on current social, domestic, and foreign-policy issues.

**U.S. Department of Education**
**www.ed.gov**
The U.S. Department of Education is dedicated to providing equal access to education and improving academic programs throughout America. At the department's Web site, you can learn about the No Child Left Behind Act and other policies.

Foreign policy often involves finding a balance between cooperation and promoting U.S. interests. Here, President Obama meets with President Hamid Karzai of Afghanistan to discuss the ongoing war there.

# 14

# Foreign Policy

**WHAT GOVERNMENT DOES AND WHY IT MATTERS** Ever since George Washington, in his Farewell Address, warned the American people "to have . . . as little political connection as possible" with foreign nations and to "steer clear of permanent alliances," Americans have been distrustful of foreign policy. But, despite their distrust, the United States has been forced to pursue its national interests in the world through a variety means, including diplomacy, economic policy, and precisely the sorts of entangling alliances with other nations and involvements with international organizations that would have troubled Washington.

America has also fought a large number of wars. Though Americans like to regard themselves as a peaceful people, since our own Civil War, American forces have been deployed abroad on hundreds of occasions for major conflicts as well as minor skirmishes. Writing in 1989, historian Geoffrey Perret commented that no other nation, "has had as much experience of war as the United States."[1] America has not become less warlike in the years since Paret published his observation. Between 1989 and the present, American forces have fought two wars in the Persian Gulf and a war in Afghanistan, while engaging in lesser military actions in Panama, Kosovo, Somalia and elsewhere. Every year, of course, America's military arsenal and defense budget dwarfs those of other nations. America currently spends more than $600 billion per year on its military and weapons programs—a figure that represents more than one-third of the world's total military expenditure and nearly ten times the amount spent by the Chinese People's Republic, the nation that currently ranks second to the U.S. in overall military outlays.

An old American adage asserts that "politics stops at the water's edge." The point of this saying is that if we fail to work together to protect our nation's political, economic, and security interests in the wider world, we will all suffer. In today's world, however, the water's edge does not neatly demarcate the difference of interests between "us" and "them." As the global economic crisis that deepened in 2008 revealed, "our" economic interests and "their" economic interests are intertwined. Environmental concerns are global, not national. And even in the realm of security interests, some risks and threats are shared and require international rather than national responses. Or national government, created to further our national interests, must find ways of acting internationally and striking the right balance between competition and cooperation in the international arena.

Generally speaking, the term *foreign policy* refers to the programs and policies that determine America's relations with other nations and foreign entities. Foreign policy includes diplomacy, military and security policy, international human rights policies, and various forms of economic policy such as trade policy and international energy policy. Of course, foreign policy and domestic policy are not completely separate categories but are, instead, closely intertwined. Take security policy, for example. Defending the nation requires the design and manufacture of tens of billions of dollars in military hardware. The construction and procurement of this military equipment involves a host of economic policies, and paying for it shapes America's fiscal policies.

In this chapter, we will first examine the main goals and purposes of American foreign policy. We will then discuss the actors and institutions that shape foreign policy. Next, we will analyze the instruments that policy makers have at their disposal to implement foreign policy.

## key concepts

- The main goals of American foreign policy are security, prosperity, and improving the world
- American foreign policy is shaped by the president, Congress, and private interests
- The American government uses diplomacy, military force, and money to achieve its goals

# Foreign Policy Goals Are Related

Although U.S. foreign policy has a number of purposes, three main goals stand out. These are security, prosperity, and the creation of a better world. These goals are closely intertwined.

## Security Is Based on Military Strength

To many Americans, the chief purpose of the nation's foreign policy is protection of America's security in an often hostile world. Traditionally, the United States has been concerned about threats that might emanate from other nations, such as Nazi Germany during the 1940s and then Soviet Russia until the Soviet Union's collapse in the late 1980s. Today, American security policy is concerned not only with the actions of other nations but also with the activities of terrorist groups and other hostile **non-state actors**.[2] To protect the nation's security from foreign threats, the United States has built an enormous military apparatus and a complex array of intelligence-gathering institutions, such as the Central Intelligence Agency (CIA), charged with evaluating and anticipating challenges from abroad.[3]

During the eighteenth and nineteenth centuries, the United States believed that its security was based on its geographic isolation. We were separated by two oceans from European and Asian powers, and many Americans thought that our security would be best preserved by remaining aloof from international power struggles. This policy was known as **isolationism**. In his 1796 farewell address, President George Washington warned Americans to avoid permanent alliances with foreign powers, and in 1823, President James Monroe warned foreign powers not to meddle in the Western Hemisphere. Washington's warning and what came to be called the Monroe Doctrine were the cornerstones of the U.S. foreign policy of isolationism until the end of the nineteenth century. The United States saw itself as the dominant power in the Western Hemisphere and, indeed, believed that its "manifest destiny" was to expand from sea to sea. The rest of the world, however, should remain at arm's length.

In the twentieth century, technology made oceans less of a barrier to foreign threats, and the world's growing economic interdependence meant that the United States could no longer ignore events abroad. At the beginning of the twentieth century, despite its isolationist sentiments, the United States entered World War I on the side of Great Britain and France when the Wilson administration concluded that America's economic and security interests would be adversely affected by a German victory. In 1941, America was drawn into World War II when Japan attacked the U.S. Pacific fleet anchored at Pearl Harbor, Hawaii. Even before the Japanese attack forced America to fight, the Roosevelt administration had already concluded that the United States had to act to prevent a victory by the German-Japanese-Italian Axis alliance.

Abandoning isolationism after World War II, the United States developed a new security policy known as **deterrence**, the development and maintenance of military strength to discourage attack, designed to "contain" the growing power of the Soviet Union. By the end of the 1940s, the Soviets had built a huge empire and enormous military forces. Most threatening of all, the Soviet Union had built nuclear weapons and intercontinental bombers capable of attacking the United States. Some

Americans argued that we should attack the Soviets before it was too late. This policy is known as **preventive war**. Others said that we should show our peaceful intentions and attempt to placate the Soviets. This policy is called **appeasement**.

The policies that the United States actually adopted, deterrence and containment, could be seen as midway between preventive war and appeasement. A nation pursuing a policy of deterrence, on the one hand, signals its peaceful intentions, but on the other hand indicates its willingness and ability to fight if attacked. Thus, during the era of confrontation with the Soviet Union between the late 1940s and 1990, known as the **Cold War**, the United States frequently asserted that it had no intention of attacking the Soviet Union. At the same time, however, the United States built a huge military force, including an arsenal of nuclear weapons and intercontinental missiles, and frequently asserted that in the event of a Soviet attack, it had the ability and will to respond with overwhelming force. The Soviet Union announced that its nuclear weapons were also intended for deterrent purposes. Eventually the two sides possessed such enormous arsenals of nuclear missiles that each potentially had the ability to destroy the other in the event of war. This heavily armed standoff came to be called a posture of mutually assured destruction. During the 1962 Cuban Missile Crisis, the United States and the U.S.S.R. came to the brink of war when President Kennedy declared that the Soviet Union must remove its nuclear missiles from Cuba and threatened to use force if the Soviets refused. After an extremely intense several weeks, the crisis was defused by a negotiated compromise in which the Soviets agreed to remove their missiles in exchange for a U.S. guarantee that it would not invade Cuba. The two superpowers had come so close to nuclear war that the leaders of both nations sought ways of reducing tensions. This effort led to a period of détente in which a number of arms control agreements were signed and the threat of war was reduced.

In 1991, the Soviet Union collapsed, partly because its huge military expenditures undermined its creaky and inefficient centrally planned economy. The new Russia, though still a formidable and sometimes unfriendly power, posed less of a threat to the United States. Americans celebrated the end of the Cold War and believed that the enormous expense of America's own military forces might be reduced. Within several years of the Soviet collapse, however, a new set of security threats emerged, requiring new policy responses. The September 11 terrorist attacks demonstrated a threat against which some security scholars had long warned. The threat was that non-state actors and so-called rogue states might acquire significant military capabilities, including nuclear weapons, and would not be affected by America's deterrent capabilities.

Unlike **nation-states**, countries with governments and fixed borders, terrorist groups are non-state actors having no fixed geographic location that can be attacked. Terrorists may believe that they can attack and melt away, leaving the United States with no one against whom to retaliate. Hence, the threat of massive retaliation does not deter them. Rogue states are nations with unstable and erratic leaders who seem to pursue policies driven by ideological or religious fervor rather than careful consideration of economic or human costs. The United States considers North Korea and Iran rogue states.

To counter these new security threats, the George W. Bush administration shifted from a policy of deterrence to one of **preemption**. Preemption is often used as

*Military force is the most visible instrument of foreign policy and may become necessary when other options fail. The use of force, however, almost always engenders unanticipated consequences and problems, as America's experience in Iraq has shown.*

another name for preventive war or willingness to strike first in order to prevent an enemy attack. The United States declared that it would not wait to be attacked but would, if necessary, take action to disable terrorist groups and rogue states before they can do us harm. The Bush administration's "global war on terror" is an expression of this notion of preemption, as was the U.S. invasion of Iraq. The United States has also refused to rule out the possibility that it would attack North Korea or Iran if it deemed those nations' nuclear programs to be an imminent threat to American security interests. The Obama administration declared that it would endeavor to establish constructive dialogues with North Korea, Iran, and other hostile states. However, Obama did not necessarily renounce the Bush Doctrine for those states that declined to become constructively engaged.

## Economic Prosperity Helps All Nations

A second major goal of U.S. foreign policy is promoting American prosperity. America's international economic policies are intended to expand employment opportunities in the United States, to maintain access to foreign energy supplies at a reasonable cost, to promote foreign investment in the United States, and to lower the prices Americans pay for goods and services.

The most important international organization for promoting trade is the **World Trade Organization (WTO)**, which officially came into being in 1995. The WTO grew out of the **General Agreement on Tariffs and Trade (GATT)**, established in 1947. Since World War II, GATT had brought together a wide range of nations for regular negotiations designed to reduce barriers to trade. Such barriers, many

believed, had contributed to the breakdown of the world economy in the 1930s and had helped to cause World War II. The WTO has 151 members worldwide, including the United States. Similar policy goals are pursued in regional arrangements, such as the **North American Free Trade Agreement (NAFTA),** a trade treaty among the United States, Canada, and Mexico to lower and eliminate tariffs among the three countries.

Working toward freer trade has been an important goal of each presidential administration since World War II. Yet as globalization has advanced, concerns about free trade and about the operation of the WTO, in particular, have grown. Critics believe that the WTO does not pay sufficient attention to the concerns of developing nations and to such issues as environmental degradation, human rights, and labor practices, including the use of child labor in many countries. The major problem in WTO negotiations has been conflicts between poor, developing nations and rich, developed countries.

*Managing relations with China has been an important part of the Obama administration's foreign policy. In 2010, President Obama met with Chinese president Hu Jintao in Washington as part of the nuclear security summit.*

## America Seeks a Better World

A third goal of American policy is to make the world a better place for all its inhabitants. The main forms of policy that address this goal are international environmental policy, international human rights policy, and international peacekeeping. The United States also contributes to international organizations such as the World Health Organization that work for global health and against hunger. These policies are often seen as secondary to the other goals of American foreign policy, forced to give way if they interfere with security or foreign economic policy. Moreover, although the United States spends billions annually on security policy and hundreds of millions on trade policy, we spend relatively little on environmental, human rights, and peacekeeping efforts. Some critics charge that America has the wrong priorities, spending far more to make war than to protect human rights and the global environment. Nevertheless, a number of important American foreign policy efforts are, at least in part, designed to make the world a better place.

In the realm of international environmental policy, the United States supports a number of international efforts to protect the environment. These include the United Nations Framework Convention on Climate Change, an international

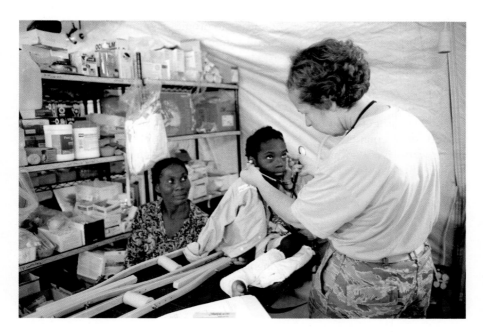

*U.S. foreign policy also promotes humanitarian goals around the world, such as helping Haitians following a devastating earthquake in 2010.*

agreement to study and ameliorate harmful changes in the global environment, and the Montreal Protocol, an agreement signed by more than 150 countries to limit the production of substances potentially harmful to the world's ozone layer. Other nations have severely criticized the United States for withdrawing from the 1997 Kyoto Protocol, an agreement setting limits on emissions of greenhouse gases from industrial countries. The United States has asserted that the Kyoto Protocol would be harmful to American economic interests. Although the United States is concerned with the global environment, national economic interests took precedence in this case. In preparation for the 2012 expiration of the Kyoto agreement, world leaders gathered in Copenhagen, Denmark, in 2009 to begin the process of negotiating a new climate treaty. The Copenhagen Climate Summit, however, failed to produce a binding international agreement and ended with the United States, Europe, and China blaming one another for the lack of concrete results.

The same national priorities seem apparent in the area of human rights policy. The United States has a long-standing commitment to human rights and is a party to most major international agreements concerning human rights. These include the International Covenant on Civil and Political Rights, the International Convention against Torture, the Convention on the Elimination of All Forms of Racial Discrimination, and various agreements to protect children. The State Department's Bureau of Democracy, Human Rights and Labor works cooperatively with international organizations to investigate and focus attention on human rights abuses. In 1998, the United States enacted the International Religious Freedom Act, which calls on all governments to respect religious freedom.

Although the United States is committed to promoting human rights, this commitment has a lower priority in American foreign policy than the nation's security concerns and economic interests. Thus, the United States is likely to overlook human rights violations by its major trading partners, such as China, and remain silent in the face of human rights violations by such allies as Saudi Arabia. Nevertheless, human rights concerns do play a role in American foreign policy.

Another form of U.S. policy designed to improve the condition of the world is support for international peacekeeping efforts. At any point in time, a number of border wars, civil wars, and guerrilla conflicts are flaring somewhere in the world, usually in its poorer regions. These wars often generate humanitarian crises in the form of casualties, disease, and refugees. In cooperation with international agencies and other nations, the United States funds a number of efforts to keep the peace in volatile regions and to deal with the health care and refugee problems associated with conflict. In 2007, the United States provided more than $1 billion in funding for United Nations peacekeeping operations in Bosnia, Kosovo, Sierra Leone, Lebanon, the Democratic Republic of Congo, and East Timor. As the world's wealthiest nation, the United States also recognizes an obligation to render assistance to nations facing crises and emergencies.

## ● American Foreign Policy Is Shaped By Government and Non-Government Actors

As we have seen, domestic policies are made by governmental institutions and influenced by a variety of interest groups, political movements, and even the mass media. The same is true in the realm of foreign policy. The president and his chief advisers are the principal architects of U.S. foreign policy. However, the Congress, the bureaucracy, the courts, political parties, interest groups, and trade associations also play important roles in this realm. Often, the president and Congress are at odds over foreign policy. When the Democrats took control of Congress in 2006, they vowed to force the president to end the war in Iraq. The president vowed to resist the Democrats' efforts and generally prevailed. Ethnic lobbies such as the pro-Israel lobby and the Armenian lobby also seek to affect foreign policy. In 2007, the Armenian lobby persuaded Congress to condemn Turkey's actions in 1915, which led to the deaths of more than one million Armenians. The president feared that Turkey, an important U.S. ally, would be offended and blocked the effort. Let us examine the major institutions and forces shaping American foreign policy.

### The President Leads Foreign Policy

Most American presidents have been domestic politicians who set out to make their place in history through achievements in domestic policy. A standard joke during Bill Clinton's 1992 campaign, extending well into his first year, was that he had learned his foreign policy at the International House of Pancakes. Thus, it was not unusual that President George W. Bush had virtually no foreign-policy

*Obama's appointment of Hillary Clinton—one of the most prominent politicians in the country—as secretary of state reflected his commitment to diplomacy. Here, Clinton meets with Palestinian Prime Minister Salam Fayyad.*

preparation prior to taking office. He had traveled very little outside the United States, and he had had virtually no foreign experience as governor of Texas.

Nonetheless, Bush was decisive in the initiatives he took to define America's national interest for his administration. Examples include revival of the controversial nuclear missile shield ("Star Wars"); abandonment of the Anti-Ballistic Missile (ABM) treaty, which alienated Russia; changes in policy priorities away from humanitarian and environmental goals toward a far stronger emphasis on national security; and turning America's concerns (by degree or emphasis) away from Europe toward an "Asia-first" policy.

September 11 and its aftermath immensely accentuated the president's role and his place in foreign policy.[4] By 2002, foreign policy was the centerpiece of the Bush administration's agenda. In a June 1 speech at West Point, the "**Bush Doctrine**" of preemptive war was announced. Bush argued that "our security will require all Americans . . . to be ready for preemptive action when necessary to defend our liberty and to defend our lives." Bush's statement was clearly intended to justify his administration's plans to invade Iraq, but it had much wider implications for international relations, including the central role of the American president in guiding foreign policy.

By 2010, Obama had put his own stamp on American foreign policy, altering the conduct of America's war in Afghanistan and seeking to compel the Israelis and Palestinians to accept a Middle East peace deal. Obama also sought to more fully engage America's allies, who had been miffed by the previous administration's tendency to engage in unilateral action.

## The Bureaucracy Implements and Informs Policy Decisions

The major foreign policy actors in the bureaucracy are the secretaries of the departments of State, Defense, and the Treasury; the Joint Chiefs of Staff (JCOS), especially the chair of the JCOS; and the director of the Central Intelligence Agency (CIA). Since 1947, a separate unit in the White House has overseen the vast foreign policy establishment for the purpose of synthesizing all the messages arising out of the bureaucracy and helping the president make his own foreign policy. This is the National Security Council (NSC). It is a "subcabinet" made up of the major players just listed, plus others each president was given the authority to add. Since the profound shake-up of September 11, two additional key players have been added. The first was the secretary of the new Department of Homeland Security (DHS). The second was imposed at the top as the war in Iraq was becoming a quagmire: a director of national intelligence, to collate and coordinate intelligence coming in from multiple sources and to report a synthesis of all this to the president, on a daily basis.

Since the creation of the CIA and the Department of Defense in 1947, the secretary of defense and the director of the CIA have often been rivals engaged in power struggles for control of the intelligence community.[5] For the most part, secretaries of defense have prevailed in these battles, and the Defense Department today controls more than 80 percent of the nation's intelligence capabilities and funds. The creation of the position of director of national intelligence in 2005 to coordinate all intelligence activities set off new Washington power struggles as the "intelligence czar" faced opposition from both the CIA and the Department of Defense.

In the wake of 9/11, military and law enforcement agencies have increased their role in America's foreign policy making.[6] For example, in recent years, American ambassadors have complained that they have been relegated to secondary status as the White House has looked to military commanders for information, advice, and policy implementation. For every region of the world, the U.S. military has assigned a "combatant commander," usually a senior general or admiral, to take charge of operations in that area. In many instances, these combatant commanders, who control troops, equipment, and intelligence capabilities, have become the real eyes, ears, and spokespersons for American foreign policy in their designated regions.

## Congress's Legal Authority Can Be Decisive

Although the Constitution gives Congress the power to declare war (see Table 14.1), Congress has exercised this power on only five occasions: the War of 1812, the Mexican War (1846), the Spanish-American War (1898), World War I (1917), and World War II (1941). For the first 150 years of American history, Congress's role was limited because the United States' role in world affairs was limited. The Senate's treaty power was and is an important entrée of the Senate into foreign policy making. Since World War II and the continual involvement of the United States in international security and foreign aid, Congress as a whole has become a

## Principal Foreign-Policy Provisions of the Constitution

| | POWERS GRANTED | |
| --- | --- | --- |
| | PRESIDENT | CONGRESS |
| War power | Commander in chief of armed forces | Provide for the common defense; declare war |
| Treaties | Negotiate treaties | Ratification of treaties by two-thirds majority (Senate) |
| Appointments | Nominate high-level government officials | Confirm president's appointments (Senate) |
| Foreign commerce | No explicit powers, but treaty negotiation and appointment powers pertain | Explicit power "to regulate foreign commerce" |
| General powers | Executive power; veto | Legislative power; power of the purse; oversight and investigation |

major foreign policy maker because most modern foreign policies require financing, which requires action by both the House of Representatives and the Senate. For example, Congress's first act after September 11 was to authorize the president to use "all necessary and appropriate force," coupled with a $40 billion emergency appropriations bill for homeland defense. And although President Bush believed he possessed the constitutional authority to invade Iraq, he still sought congressional approval, which he received in October 2002.

Not only does the president need Congress to provide funding for foreign and military policy initiatives, but, under the Constitution, many presidential agreements with foreign nations also have to be approved by Congress. Article II, Section 2, of the Constitution declares that proposed treaties with other nations must be submitted by the president to the Senate and approved by a two-thirds vote. Because this "supermajority" is usually difficult to achieve, presidents generally prefer a different type of agreement with other nations called an **executive agreement**. An executive agreement is similar to a treaty and has the force of law but usually requires only a simple majority vote (that is, 50 percent plus one) in both houses of Congress for approval, rather than the Senate's "advice and consent."

Another aspect of Congress's role in foreign policy is the Senate's power to confirm the president's nominations of Cabinet members, ambassadors, and other high-ranking officials (such as the director of the CIA, but not the director of the NSC). A final constitutional power of Congress is the regulation of "commerce with foreign nations."

Other congressional players are the foreign policy, military policy, and intelligence committees: in the Senate, these are the Foreign Relations Committee, the Armed Services Committee, the Intelligence Committee and the Homeland

Security and Governmental Affairs Committee; in the House, these are the Foreign Affairs Committee, the Intelligence Committee, the Homeland Security Committee, and the Armed Services Committee. Usually, a few members of these committees who have spent years specializing in foreign affairs become trusted members of the foreign policy establishment and are influential makers of foreign policy. In fact, several members of Congress have left the legislature to become key foreign affairs cabinet members.

## Interest Groups Pressure Foreign Policy Decisionmakers

Although the president, the executive-branch "bureaucracy," and Congress are the true makers of foreign policy, the "foreign policy establishment" is a much larger arena, including what can properly be called the shapers of foreign policy—a host of unofficial, informal players, people who possess varying degrees of influence, depending on their prestige, their reputation, their socioeconomic standing, and—most important—the party and ideology that are dominant at a given moment.

By far the most important category of nonofficial player is the interest group—that is, the interest group to which one or more foreign policy issues are of longstanding and vital relevance. Most of these groups are "single-issue" groups and are therefore most active when their particular issue is on the agenda.

Another type of interest group with a well-founded reputation for influence in foreign policy is made up of people with strong attachments to and identification with their country of national origin. The interest group with the reputation for the greatest influence is Jewish Americans, whose family and emotional ties to Israel make them one of the most alert and active interest groups in the whole field of foreign policy. In 2010, a dispute between Israel and the Obama administration over Israel's construction of new Jewish housing in Jerusalem led to an intense effort by American Jews to generate congressional support for Israel's position. Similarly, Americans of Irish heritage, despite having lived in the United States for two, three, or four generations, still maintain vigilance about American policies toward Ireland and Northern Ireland; some even contribute to the Irish Republican Army. Many other ethnic and national interest groups wield similar influence over American foreign policy.

A third type of interest group is devoted to human rights. Such groups are made up of people who,

*Interest groups like Amnesty International may influence foreign policy by lobbying the government directly and by raising public awareness of certain issues.*

instead of having self-serving economic or ethnic interests in foreign policy, are genuinely concerned about the welfare and treatment of people throughout the world—particularly those who suffer under harsh political regimes. A relatively small but often quite influential example is Amnesty International, whose exposés of human-rights abuses have altered the practices of many regimes around the world. In recent years, the Christian right has been a vocal advocate for the human rights of Christians who are persecuted in other parts of the world, most notably in China, for their religious beliefs. For example, the Christian Coalition joined groups such as Amnesty International in lobbying Congress to restrict trade with countries that permit attacks against religious believers.

A related type of group is the ecological or environmental group, sometimes collectively called "greens." Groups of this nature often depend more on demonstrations than on the usual forms and strategies of influence in Washington—lobbying and using electoral politics, for example. Demonstrations in strategically located areas can have significant influence on American foreign policy.

## The Media Are Sometimes Muzzled

The balancing of security against freedom of the press has become increasingly difficult with the increased power of the media that has resulted from significant developments in communications and information technology. Iraq is a compelling case in point. During the first few weeks of the invasion in 2003, nearly 600 embedded journalists (plus a number of "free-floating" U.S. and non-U.S. journalists) provided the most intensive coverage in the history of war, and without any question for the first time the coverage was instantaneous, visual, annotated, and in color—not only on television but on the front pages of the major newspapers and online as well.

Take special note of the word *embedded*. No matter how delicately put, embedding involved the management of the journalists in a deal to provide access and protection in return for "responsible" reporting, a deal that led to the widespread suspicion and fear that not only the journalists but also the news itself was being managed. The suspicion grew as the war changed after the regime of Saddam Hussein was deposed, the Iraqi armed forces dispersed, and the entire civil government that had been dominated by the Hussein Baathist Party was decommissioned. Quite simply, the situation changed from a conventional, organized war to an ambiguous, insurgent war. This was the end of any practice of embedding and the beginning of fewer but freer-floating journalists, a change that also meant the expansion of dissent and open criticism accompanying the reports. "News management" to any degree was no longer possible.

## Putting It Together

Let's make a few tentative generalizations to frame the remainder of this chapter. First, when an important foreign policy decision has to be made under conditions of crisis—where time is of the essence—the influence of the presidency is at its strongest. Second, within those time constraints, access to the decision is limited almost exclusively to the narrowest definition of the foreign-policy establishment. The arena for participation is tiny; any discussion at all is limited to the officially and constitutionally designated players.[7] As time becomes less restricted, even when the decision to be made is of great importance, the arena of participation expands to include more government players and more nonofficial, informal players—the most concerned interest groups and the most important journalists. In other words, the arena becomes more pluralistic and, therefore, less distinguishable from the politics of domestic policy making. Third, because there are so many other countries with power and interests on any given issue, there are severe limits on the choices the United States can make. That is, U.S. policy makers engage in strategic interaction with policy makers in other nations; their choices are made both in reaction to and in anticipation of these strategic interactions. As one author concludes, in foreign affairs, "policy takes precedence over politics."[8] Thus even though foreign policy making in noncrisis situations may closely resemble the pluralistic politics of domestic policy making, foreign policy making is still a narrower arena with fewer participants.

## ● Tools of American Foreign Policy Include Diplomacy, Force, and Money

We will deal here with those instruments of American foreign policy most important in the modern epoch: diplomacy, the United Nations, the international monetary structure, economic aid, collective security, and military deterrence. Each of these instruments will be evaluated in this section for its utility in the conduct of American foreign policy, and each will be assessed in light of the history and development of American values.

### Diplomacy Is the Master Policy Tool

We begin this treatment of instruments with diplomacy because it is the instrument to which all other instruments should be subordinated, although they seldom are. **Diplomacy** is the representation of a government to other foreign governments. Its purpose is to promote national values or interests by peaceful means. According to Hans Morgenthau, "a diplomacy that ends in war has failed in its primary objective."[9]

Diplomacy, by its very nature, is overshadowed by spectacular international events, dramatic initiatives, and meetings among heads of state or their direct personal representatives. The traditional American distrust of diplomacy continues today, albeit in weaker form. Impatience with or downright distrust of diplomacy has been built not only into all the other instruments of foreign policy but also into the modern presidential system itself.[10] So much personal responsibility has been heaped on the presidency that it is difficult for presidents to entrust any of their authority or responsibility in foreign policy to professional diplomats in the State Department and other bureaucracies.

Distrust of diplomacy has also produced a tendency among all recent presidents to turn frequently to military and civilian personnel outside the State Department to take on a special diplomatic role as direct personal representatives of the president. As discouraging as it is to those who have dedicated their careers

*The United Nations is sometimes an important instrument of American foreign policy. In trying to build international support for the U.S. case against Iraq, President Bush went before the General Assembly and urged the United Nations to compel Iraq to disarm. Two months later, the UN Security Council gave its qualified support to Bush's position.*

to foreign service to have personal appointees chosen over their heads, it is probably even more discouraging when they are displaced from a foreign-policy issue as soon as relations with the country they are posted in begin to heat up. When a special personal representative is sent abroad to represent the president, that envoy holds a status higher than that of the local ambassador, and the embassy becomes the envoy's temporary residence and base of operation. Despite the impressive professionalization of the American foreign service—with advanced training, competitive exams, language requirements, and career commitment—this practice of displacing career ambassadors with political appointees and with special personal presidential representatives occurs often.

The significance of diplomacy and its vulnerability to politics may be better appreciated as we proceed to the other instruments. Diplomacy was an instrument more or less imposed on Americans as the prevailing method of dealing among nation-states in the nineteenth century. The other instruments to be identified and assessed below are instruments that Americans self-consciously crafted for themselves to take care of their own chosen place in the world affairs of the second half of the twentieth century and beyond. They therefore better reflect American culture and values than diplomacy does.

## The United Nations Is the World's Congress

The utility of the **United Nations (UN)** to the United States as an instrument of foreign policy can be too easily underestimated, because the United Nations is a very large and unwieldy institution with few powers and no armed forces to implement its rules and resolutions. An organization of nations founded in 1945 to be a channel for negotiation and a means of settling international disputes peaceably, the UN has had frequent successes in providing a forum for negotiation and on some occasions a means of preventing international conflicts from spreading. On a number of occasions, the UN has been a convenient cover for U.S. foreign-policy goals. Its supreme body is the UN General Assembly, comprising one representative of each of the 192 member states; each member representative has one vote, regardless of the size of the country. Important issues require a two-thirds majority vote, and the annual session of the General Assembly runs only from September to December (although it can call extra sessions). It has little organization that can make it an effective decision-making body, with only six standing committees, few tight rules of procedure, and no political parties to provide priorities and discipline. Its defenders are quick to add that although it lacks armed forces, it relies on the power of world opinion; and this is not to be taken lightly. The powers of the United Nations devolve mainly to its "executive committee," the UN Security Council, which alone has the real power to make decisions and rulings that member states are obligated by the UN Charter to implement. The Security Council may be called into session at any time, and each member (or a designated alternate) must be present at UN Headquarters in New York at all times. It is composed of fifteen members: five are permanent (the victors of World War II), and ten are elected by the General Assembly for two-year, nonrepeatable terms. The five permanent members are China, France, Russia, the United Kingdom, and the United States. Each of the fifteen members has only one vote, and a nine-vote majority of the fifteen is required on all substantive matters. But each of the five permanent members also has a negative vote, a "veto," and one veto is sufficient to reject any substantive proposal.

The UN can serve as a useful forum for international discussions and an instrument for multilateral action. Most peacekeeping efforts to which the United States contributes, for example, are undertaken under UN auspices.

## The International Monetary Structure Helps Provide Economic Stability

Fear of a repeat of the economic devastation that followed World War I brought the United States together with its allies (except the U.S.S.R) to Bretton Woods, New Hampshire, in 1944 to create a new international economic structure for the postwar world. The result was two institutions: the International Bank for Reconstruction and Development (commonly called the World Bank) and the International Monetary Fund.

The World Bank was set up to finance long-term capital. Leading nations took on the obligation of contributing funds to enable the World Bank to make loans to capital-hungry countries. (The U.S. quota has been about one-third of the total.)

The **International Monetary Fund (IMF)** was set up to provide for the short-term flow of money. After the war, the dollar, instead of gold, was the chief means by which the currencies of one country would be "changed into" currencies of another country for purposes of making international transactions. To permit debtor countries with no international balances to make purchases and investments, the IMF was set up to lend dollars or other appropriate currencies to needy member countries to help them overcome temporary trade deficits. For many years after World War II, the IMF, along with U.S. foreign aid, in effect constituted the only international medium of exchange.

During the 1990s, the IMF returned to a position of enhanced importance through its efforts to reform some of the largest debtor nations and formerly communist countries to bring them more fully into the global capitalist economy. The future of the IMF, the World Bank, and all other private sources of international investment will depend in part on extension of more credit to the Third World and other developing countries, because credit means investment and productivity. But the future may depend even more on reducing the debt that is already there from previous extensions of credit.

## Economic Aid Has Two Sides

Every year, the United States provides nearly $30 billion in economic assistance to other nations. Some aid has a humanitarian purpose, such as helping to provide health care, shelter for refugees, or famine relief. A good deal of American aid, however, is designed to promote American security interests or economic concerns. For example, the United States provides military assistance to a number of its allies in the form of advanced weapons or loans to help them purchase advanced weapons. Such loans generally stipulate that the recipient must purchase the designated weapons from American firms. In this way, the United States hopes to bolster its security and economic interests with one grant. The two largest recipients of American military assistance are Israel and Egypt, American allies that fought two wars against one another. The United States believes that its military assistance allows both to feel sufficiently secure to remain at peace with one another.

Aid is an economic carrot. Sanctions are an economic stick. Economic sanctions that the United States employs against other nations include trade embargoes, bans on investment, and efforts to prevent the World Bank or other international institutions from extending credit to a nation against which the United States has a grievance. Sanctions are most often employed when the United States seeks to weaken what it considers a hostile regime or when it is attempting to compel some particular action by another regime. In recent years, the United States has maintained economic sanctions against Iran and North Korea in an effort to prevent those nations from pursuing nuclear weapons programs.

## Collective Security Is Designed to Deter War

In 1947, most Americans hoped that the United States could meet its world obligations through the United Nations and economic structures alone. But most foreign-policy makers anticipated the need for military entanglements at the time of drafting the original UN Charter by insisting on language that recognized the right of all nations to provide for their mutual defense independent of the United Nations. And almost immediately after enactment of the Marshall Plan, designed to promote European economic recovery, the White House and a parade of State and Defense Department officials followed up with an urgent request to the Senate to ratify, and to both houses of Congress to finance, mutual defense alliances.

At first quite reluctant to approve treaties providing for national security alliances, the Senate ultimately agreed with the executive branch. The first collective security agreement was the Rio Treaty (ratified by the Senate in September 1947), which created the Organization of American States (OAS). This was the model treaty, anticipating all succeeding collective security treaties by providing that an armed attack against any of its members "shall be considered as an attack against all the American States," including the United States. A more significant break with U.S. tradition against peacetime entanglements came with the North Atlantic Treaty (signed in April 1949), which created the **North Atlantic Treaty Organization (NATO)**. Comprising of the United States, Canada, and most of Western Europe, NATO was formed in 1948 to counter the perceived threat from the Soviet Union. ANZUS, a treaty tying Australia and New Zealand to the United States, was signed in September 1951. Three years later, the Southeast Asia Treaty created the Southeast Asia Treaty Organization (SEATO).

In addition to these multilateral treaties, the United States entered into a number of **bilateral treaties**—treaties between two countries. As one author has observed, the United States has been a *producer* of security, whereas most of its allies have been *consumers* of security.[11]

This pattern has continued in the post–Cold War era, and its best illustration is in the Persian Gulf War, where the United States provided the initiative, the leadership, and most of the armed forces, even though its allies were obliged to reimburse over 90 percent of the cost.

It is difficult to evaluate collective security and its treaties because the purpose of collective security as an instrument of foreign policy is prevention, and success of this kind has to be measured in terms of what did *not* happen. Critics have argued that U.S. collective security treaties posed a threat of encirclement to the Soviet Union, forcing it to produce its own collective security, particularly the Warsaw Pact.[12] Nevertheless, no one can deny the counterargument that more than sixty years have passed without a world war.

## Military Force Is "Politics by Other Means"

The most visible instrument of foreign policy is, of course, military force. The United States has built the world's most imposing military, with army, navy, marine, and air force units stationed in virtually every corner of the globe. The United States spends nearly as much on military might as the rest of the world combined (Figure 14.1). The famous Prussian military strategist Carl von Clausewitz called war "politics by other means." By this he meant that nations used force not simply to demonstrate their capacity for violence. Rather, force or the threat of force is a tool nations must sometimes use to achieve their foreign policy goals. Military force may be needed to protect a nation's security interests and economic concerns. Ironically, force may also be needed to achieve humanitarian goals. For example, without international military protection, the people who have taken refuge in camps in the Darfur region of Sudan would be at the mercy of the violent Sudanese regime.

# Make Your Voice Heard in Foreign Policy

On April 4, 2008, a group of students at the University of Utah staged a "die in" to raise awareness about the genocide in Darfur, Sudan. Following in the footsteps of thousands of students nationwide, these young men and women spent five minutes lying in silence to symbolize the victims who had died or been displaced since the conflict began. These students helped draw attention to an international issue that they cared about.

You may feel you do not know enough about U.S. foreign policy to get involved in current issues and debates. Fortunately, there are many easily accessible resources available to help you learn, and, once you've educated yourself, many outlets for action.

- *Take the test.* You can test your own geographic knowledge by taking a quiz from National Geographic at nationalgeographic.com/roper2006/. You can see how well you do—and how you compare to other young adults worldwide.

- *Educate yourself.* The Council on Foreign Relations (cfr.org) is a nonpartisan, nonprofit organization that has numerous resources for educating yourself about the key issues in U.S. foreign policy. You can link to background materials to learn about the key issues facing the nation and the world.

- *Join an advocacy group.* As you learn more about key issues, you may find yourself developing support for a particular perspective or side in the debate. There are groups working to influence public policy from every perspective. Visiting their Web sites and taking advantage of their educational materials, as well as the opportunities they offer to get more involved, will provide you a means of adding your voice to those of others who share your values. For example, if you are concerned about the war in Iraq, you could check out the National Youth & Student Peace Coalition (nyspc.org). Or, if you think U.S. foreign policy should be more oriented toward reflecting key American values of equality and justice, then you can read the materials and sign the petitions at justforeignpolicy.org. Finally, if you want to work to ensure that the American troops in Afghanistan and Iraq receive the support they need, look into moveamericaforward.org.

- *Educate your fellow students.* You may find that you are so moved by some of the foreign policy issues that you want to share your knowledge with other students. Many of the national organizations have resources to help students start campus chapters. STAND, for example, will provide you with training in establishing a group on campus, instructions on how to advocate effectively, and even help you to find speakers to bring to campus.

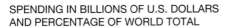

### FIGURE 14.1 Military Spending, 2008

NOTE: 2008 total military spending: $1. 473 trillion

SOURCE: Center for Arms Control and Non-Proliferation, www.armscontrolcenter.org/policy/securityspending
/articles/fy09_dod_request_global/(accessed 4/22/09).

SPENDING IN BILLIONS OF U.S. DOLLARS
AND PERCENTAGE OF WORLD TOTAL

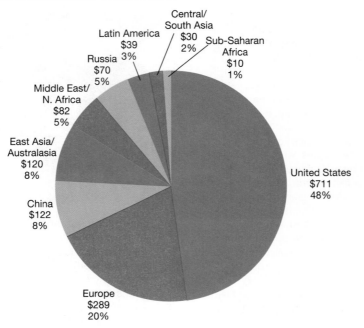

Central/
South Asia
$30
2%

Latin America
$39
3%

Sub-Saharan
Africa
$10
1%

Russia
$70
5%

Middle East/
N. Africa
$82
5%

East Asia/
Australasia
$120
8%

China
$122
8%

United States
$711
48%

Europe
$289
20%

Though force is sometimes necessary, military force is generally seen as a last re-sort and avoided if possible because of a number of problems commonly associated with its use. First, the use of military force is extremely costly in both human and financial terms. In the past fifty years, tens of thousands of Americans have been killed and hundreds of billions of dollars spent in America's military operations.

Second, the use of military force is inherently fraught with risk. However care-fully policy makers and generals plan for military operations, results can seldom be fully anticipated. Variables ranging from the weather to unexpected weapons and tactics deployed by opponents may upset the most careful calculations and turn military operations into costly disasters or convert maneuvers that were expected to be quick and decisive into long, drawn-out, expensive struggles. For example, American policy makers expected to defeat the Iraqi army quickly and easily in 2003—and they did. Policy makers did not anticipate, however, that American forces would still be struggling years later to defeat the insurgency that arose in the war's aftermath.

Finally, in a democracy, any government that chooses to address policy problems through military means is almost certain to encounter political difficulties Generally speaking, the American public will support relatively short and decisive military engagements. If, however, a conflict drags on, producing casualties and expenses with no clear outcome, the public loses patience and opposition politicians point to the government's lies and ineptitude. Korea, Vietnam, and Iraq are all examples of protracted conflicts whose domestic political repercussions brought down the governments that decided military force was needed.

Thus, military force remains a major foreign policy tool, but the use of military force is fraught with risk and is not to be undertaken lightly.

## Arbitration Resolves Disputes

The final foreign policy tool we shall consider is dispute arbitration. Arbitration is the resolution of a disagreement by a neutral third party. International arbitration is sometimes seen as a form of "soft power" as distinguished from military force, economic sanctions, and other coercive foreign policy instruments. The United States will occasionally turn to international tribunals to resolve disputes with other countries. For example, in February 2008, the U.S. government asked the International Court of Justice to resolve a long-standing dispute with Italy over American property confiscated by the Italian government more than forty years ago.

# studyguide

## Practice Quiz

 Find a diagnostic Web Quiz with 31 additional questions on the StudySpace Web site: www.wwnorton.com/we-the-people

1. Which of the following terms best describes the American posture toward the world prior to the middle of the twentieth century? *(p. 431)*
   a) interventionist
   b) isolationist
   c) unilateralist
   d) none of the above

2. Which of the following terms describes the idea that the development and maintenance of military strength discourages attack? *(p. 431)*
   a) deterrence
   b) containment

   c) "minuteman" theory of defense
   d) detente

3. The Cold War refers to the *(p. 432)*
   a) competition between the United States and Canada over Alaska.
   b) the years between World War I and World War II when the United States and Germany were hostile to one another.
   c) the period of struggle between the United States and the Soviet Union between the late 1940s and the late 1980s.
   d) the economic competition between the United States and Japan today.

4. Which of the following statements about the General Agreement on Tariffs and Trade is *not* true? *(p. 433)*
   a) It set many of the rules governing international trade.
   b) It was the precursor to the World Trade Organization.
   c) It was designed to reduce barriers to trade.
   d) It was in existence from 1791 to 1947.

5. The shaping of American foreign policy is *(p. 436)*
   a) dominated entirely by the president.
   b) dominated entirely by Congress.
   c) dominated entirely by interest groups.
   d) highly pluralistic, involving a large mix of both official and unofficial players.

6. The Bush Doctrine refers to *(p. 437)*
   a) the idea that the United States should not allow foreign powers to meddle in the Western Hemisphere.
   b) the idea that the United States should avoid future wars by giving in to the demands of hostile foreign powers.
   c) the idea that the United States should take preemptive action against threats to its national security.
   d) the idea that the United States should never take preemptive action against threats to its national security.

7. An agreement made between the president and another country that has the force of a treaty but requires only a majority vote in both houses of Congress for approval is called *(p. 439)*
   a) an executive order.
   b) an executive agreement.
   c) a diplomatic decree.
   d) arbitration.

8. Which of the following statements about the United Nations is *not* true? *(pp. 443–44)*
   a) It gives every country one vote in the General Assembly.
   b) It has a powerful armed forces to implement its decisions.
   c) It was founded in 1945.
   d) It was designed to be a channel for negotiation and a means of settling international disputes peaceably.

9. Which of the following was *not* an important international economic institution created in the 1940s? *(p. 444)*
   a) the Federal Reserve
   b) the World Bank
   c) the International Monetary Fund
   d) All three are important international economic institutions created in the 1940s.

10. Which of the following was dedicated to the relief, reconstruction, and economic recovery of Western Europe? *(p. 445)*
    a) the Marshall Plan
    b) the Lend-Lease Act
    c) the General Agreement on Tariffs and Trade
    d) the North American Free Trade Agreement

11. The North Atlantic Treaty Organization was formed in 1948 by the United States, *(p. 446)*
    a) Canada, and most of Eastern Europe.
    b) Canada, and Mexico.
    c) Canada, and most of Western Europe.
    d) Canada, and the United Kingdom.

12. Which statement best describes the United States' military spending compared to other countries? *(p. 446)*
    a) The United States spends significantly more than any other country in the world.
    b) The United States spends significantly more than any other country in the world except for China.
    c) The United States spends significantly less than any other country in the world.
    d) The United States spends about the same as most other countries in the world.

# Chapter Outline

Find a detailed Chapter Outline on the StudySpace Web site:
www.wwnorton.com/we-the-people

# Key Terms

Find Flashcards to help you study these terms on the
StudySpace Web site: www.wwnorton.com/we-the-people

**appeasement** *(p. 432)* effort to forestall war by giving in to the demands of a hostile power

**bilateral treaties** *(p. 446)* treaties made between two nations

**Bush Doctrine** *(p. 437)* foreign policy based on the idea that the United States should take preemptive action against threats to its national security

**Cold War** *(p. 432)* the period of hostilities, but no direct war, between the United States and the former Soviet Union between the late 1940s and about 1990

**deterrence** *(p. 431)* the development and maintenance of military strength as a means of discouraging attack

**diplomacy** *(p. 442)* the representation of a government to other foreign governments

**executive agreement** *(p. 439)* an agreement, made between the president and another country, that has the force of a treaty but does not require the Senate's "advice and consent"

**General Agreement on Tariffs and Trade (GATT)** *(p. 433)* international trade organization, in existence from 1947 to 1995, that set many of the rules governing international trade

**International Monetary Fund (IMF)** *(p. 444)* an institution established in 1944 that provides loans and facilitates international monetary exchange

**isolationism** *(p. 431)* desire to avoid involvement in the affairs of other nations

**nation-state** *(p. 432)* a political entity consisting of people with some common cultural experience (nation) who also share a common political authority (state), recognized by the sovereignties (nation-states)

**non-state actors** *(p. 431)* groups other than nation-states that attempt to play a role in the international system. Terrorist groups are one type of non-state actor

**North American Free Trade Agreement (NAFTA)** *(p. 434)* trade treaty between the United States, Canada, and Mexico to lower and eliminate tariffs between the three countries

**North Atlantic Treaty Organization (NATO)** *(p. 446)* a treaty organization, comprising the United States, Canada, and most of Western Europe, formed in 1948 to counter the perceived threat from the Soviet Union

**preemption** *(p. 432)* the principle that allows the national government to override state or local actions in certain policy areas. In foreign policy, the willingness to strike first in order to prevent an enemy attack

**preventive war** *(p. 432)* policy of striking first when a nation fears that a foreign foe is comtemplating hostile action

**United Nations (UN)** *(p. 443)* an organization of nations founded in 1945 to serve as a channel for negotiation and a means of settling international disputes peaceably. The UN has had frequent successes in providing a forum for negotiation and on some occasions a means of preventing international conflicts from spreading. On a number of occasions, the UN has supported U.S. foreign policy goals

**Word Trade Organization (WTO)** *(p. 433)* international organization promoting free trade that grew out of the General Agreement on Tariffs and Trade

# For Further Reading

Art, Robert. *The Use of Force: Military Power and International Politics*. New York: Rowman and Littlefield, 2009.

Bacevich, Andrew. *The New American Militarism: How Americans Are Seduced by War*. New York: Oxford University Press, 2006.

Daalder, Ivo H., and James M. Lindsay. *American Unbound—The Bush Revolution in Foreign Policy*. Washington, DC: Brookings Institution Press, 2003.

Fisk, Robert. *The Great War for Civilization: The Conquest of the Middle East*. New York: Knopf, 2005.

Gaddis, John L. *The Cold War: A New History*. New York: Penguin, 2005.

Jentleson, Bruce. *American Foreign Policy—The Dynamics of Choice in the 21st Century*. 4th ed. New York: Norton, 2010.

Johnson, Chalmers. *The Sorrows of Empire*. New York: Henry Holt, 2004.

Kagan, Robert. *Dangerous Nation*. New York: Knopf, 2006.

Kaufman, Joyce. *A Concise History of U.S. Foreign Policy*. New York: Rowman and Littlefield, 2010.

Kennan, George F. *Around the Cragged Hill: A Personal and Political Philosophy*. New York: Norton, 1993.

Mandelbaum, Michael. *The Case for Goliath: How America Acts as the World's Government in the 21st Century*. Washington, DC: Public Affairs Press, 2005.

Mearsheimer, John J., and Stephen M. Walt. *The Israel Lobby and U.S. Foreign Policy*. New York: Farrar Straus and Giroux, 2008.

Pious, Richard M. *The War on Terrorism and the Rule of Law*. Los Angeles: Roxbury, 2006.

Renshon, Stanley. *National Security in the Obama Administration*. New York: Routledge, 2009.

# Recommended Web Sites

**American Israel Public Affairs Committee**
www.aipac.org
   Interest groups are some of the main shapers of foreign policy. One of the top lobbies in the nation, the American Israel Public Affairs Committee (AIPAC) works to strengthen the U.S.-Israel relationship.

**Foreign Policy Association**
www.fpa.org
   This nonprofit organization tries to generate interest in and draw attention to global issues and policies.

**International Monetary Fund**
www.imf.org
**World Trade Organization**
www.wto.org
   The International Monetary Fund (IMF) and the World Trade Organization (WTO) have been considered instruments of modern American foreign policy. Read about how these organizations are trying to promote capitalism, free trade, and economic development.

**National Security Council**
www.whitehouse.gov/nsc/

The National Security Council was formed in 1947 and consists of senior advisers and Cabinet officials who keep the president informed on all matters of national security and foreign policy.

**Peterson Institute for International Economics**
www.iie.com

The Peterson Institute for International Economics is dedicated to analyzing international economic policy. Take a minute to review some of the studies that have influenced the policies of such international organizations as NAFTA, the WTO, and the IMF.

**United Nations**
www.un.org

Founded in 1945, the United Nations (UN) promotes international peace and security. Visit the UN Web site for information on the General Assembly, the Security Council, economic and social development, and humanitarian issues.

**U.S. Department of State**
www.state.gov

The U.S. Department of State is the primary bureaucratic department for American diplomacy and national security.

**U.S. Senate: Treaties**
http://senate.gov

The most important foreign policy task of the Senate is reviewing and approving treaties. Learn more about the Senate's treaty-making powers and find information about treaty action at this U.S. Senate Web site.

# The Declaration of Independence

In Congress, July 4, 1776

The unanimous Declaration of the thirteen united States of America,

When in the Course of human events, it becomes necessary for one people to dissolve the political bands which have connected them with another, and to assume among the powers of the earth, the separate and equal station to which the Laws of Nature and of Nature's God entitle them, a decent respect to the opinions of mankind requires that they should declare the causes which impel them to the separation.

We hold these truths to be self-evident, that all men are created equal, that they are endowed by their Creator with certain unalienable Rights, that among these are Life, Liberty and the pursuit of Happiness.—That to secure these rights, Governments are instituted among Men, deriving their just powers from the consent of the governed.—That whenever any Form of Government becomes destructive of these ends, it is the Right of the People to alter or to abolish it, and to institute new Government, laying its foundation on such principles and organizing its powers in such form, as to them shall seem most likely to effect their Safety and Happiness. Prudence, indeed, will dictate that Governments long established should not be changed for light and transient causes; and accordingly all experience hath shewn, that mankind are more disposed to suffer, while evils are sufferable, than to right themselves by abolishing the forms to which they are accustomed. But when a long train of abuses and usurpations, pursuing invariably the same Object evinces a design to reduce them under absolute Despotism, it is their right, it is their duty, to throw off such Government, and to provide new Guards for their future security.—Such has been the patient sufferance of these Colonies; and such is now the necessity which constrains them to alter their former Systems of Government. The history of the present King of Great Britain is a history of repeated injuries and usurpations, all having in direct object the establishment of an absolute Tyranny over these States. To prove this, let Facts be submitted to a candid world.

He has refused his Assent to Laws, the most wholesome and necessary for the public good.

He has forbidden his Governors to pass Laws of immediate and pressing importance, unless suspended in their operation till his Assent should be obtained; and when so suspended, he has utterly neglected to attend to them.

He has refused to pass other Laws for the accommodation of large districts of people, unless those people would relinquish the right of Representation in the Legislature, a right inestimable to them and formidable to tyrants only.

He has called together legislative bodies at places unusual, uncomfortable, and distant from the depository of their public Records, for the sole purpose of fatiguing them into compliance with his measures.

He has dissolved Representative Houses repeatedly, for opposing with manly firmness his invasions on the rights of the people.

He has refused for a long time, after such dissolutions, to cause others to be elected; whereby the Legislative powers, incapable of Annihilation, have returned to the People at large for their exercise; the State remaining in the mean time exposed to all the dangers of invasion from without, and convulsions within.

He has endeavoured to prevent the population of these States; for that purpose obstructing the Laws for Naturalization of Foreigners; refusing to pass others to encourage their migrations hither, and raising the conditions of new Appropriations of Lands.

He has obstructed the Administration of Justice, by refusing his Assent to Laws for establishing Judiciary powers.

He has made Judges dependent on his Will alone, for the tenure of their offices, and the amount and payment of their salaries.

He has erected a multitude of New Offices, and sent hither swarms of Officers to harrass our people, and eat out their substance.

He has kept among us, in times of peace, Standing Armies without the Consent of our legislatures.

He has affected to render the Military independent of and superior to the Civil power.

He has combined with others to subject us to a jurisdiction foreign to our constitution, and unacknowledged by our laws; giving his Assent to their Acts of pretended Legislation:

For Quartering large bodies of armed troops among us:

For protecting them, by a mock Trial, from punishment for any Murders which they should commit on the Inhabitants of these States:

For cutting off our Trade with all parts of the world:

For imposing Taxes on us without our Consent:

For depriving us in many cases, of the benefits of Trial by Jury:

For transporting us beyond Seas to be tried for pretended offences:

For abolishing the free System of English Laws in a neighboring Province, establishing therein an Arbitrary government, and enlarging its Boundaries so as to render it at once an example and fit instrument for introducing the same absolute rule into these Colonies:

For taking away our Charters, abolishing our most valuable Laws, and altering fundamentally the Forms of our Governments:

For suspending our own Legislatures, and declaring themselves invested with power to legislate for us in all cases whatsoever.

He has abdicated Government here, by declaring us out of his Protection and waging War against us.

He has plundered our seas, ravaged our Coasts, burnt our towns, and destroyed the lives of our people.

He is at this time transporting large Armies of foreign Mercenaries to compleat the works of death, desolation and tyranny, already begun with circumstances of Cruelty & perfidy scarcely paralleled in the most barbarous ages, and totally unworthy the Head of a civilized nation.

He has constrained our fellow Citizens taken Captive on the high Seas to bear Arms against their Country, to become the executioners of their friends and Brethren, or to fall themselves by their Hands.

He has excited domestic insurrections amongst us, and has endeavoured to bring on the inhabitants of our frontiers, the merciless Indian Savages, whose known rule of warfare, is an undistinguished destruction of all ages, sexes and conditions.

In every stage of these Oppressions We have Petitioned for Redress in the most humble terms: Our repeated Petitions have been answered only by repeated injury. A Prince whose character is thus marked by every act which may define a Tyrant, is unfit to be the ruler of a free people.

Nor have We been wanting in attentions to our British brethren. We have warned them from time to time of attempts by their legislature to extend an unwarrantable jurisdiction over us. We have reminded them of the circumstances of our emigration and settlement here. We have appealed to their native justice and magnanimity, and we have conjured them by the ties of our common kindred to disavow these usurpations, which, would inevitably interrupt our connections and correspondence. They too have been deaf to the voice of justice and of consanguinity. We must, therefore, acquiesce in the necessity, which denounces our Separation, and hold them, as we hold the rest of mankind, Enemies in War, in Peace Friends.

We, Therefore, the Representatives of the United States of America, in General Congress, Assembled, appealing to the Supreme Judge of the world for the rectitude of our intentions, do, in the Name, and by Authority of the good People of these Colonies, solemnly publish and declare, That these United Colonies are, and of Right ought to be Free and Independent States; that they are Absolved from all Allegiance to the British Crown, and that all political connection between them and the State of Great Britain, is and ought to be totally dissolved; and that as Free and Independent States, they have full Power to levy War, conclude Peace, contract Alliances, establish Commerce, and to do all other Acts and Things which Independent States may of right do. And for the support of this Declaration, with a firm reliance on the protection of divine Providence, we mutually pledge to each other our Lives, our Fortunes and our sacred Honor.

The foregoing Declaration was, by order of Congress, engrossed, and signed by the following members:

*John Hancock*

**NEW HAMPSHIRE**
*Josiah Bartlett*
*William Whipple*
*Matthew Thornton*

**MASSACHUSETTS BAY**
*Samuel Adams*
*John Adams*
*Robert Treat Paine*
*Elbridge Gerry*

**RHODE ISLAND**
*Stephen Hopkins*
*William Ellery*

**CONNECTICUT**
*Roger Sherman*
*Samuel Huntington*
*William Williams*
*Oliver Wolcott*

**NEW YORK**
*William Floyd*
*Philip Livingston*
*Francis Lewis*
*Lewis Morris*

**NEW JERSEY**
*Richard Stockton*
*John Witherspoon*
*Francis Hopkinson*
*John Hart*
*Abraham Clark*

**PENNSYLVANIA**
*Robert Morris*
*Benjamin Rush*
*Benjamin Franklin*
*John Morton*
*George Clymer*
*James Smith*
*George Taylor*
*James Wilson*
*George Ross*

**DELAWARE**
*Caesar Rodney*
*George Read*
*Thomas M'Kean*

**MARYLAND**
*Samuel Chase*
*William Paca*
*Thomas Stone*
*Charles Carroll, of Carrollton*

**VIRGINIA**
*George Wythe*
*Richard Henry Lee*
*Thomas Jefferson*
*Benjamin Harrison*
*Thomas Nelson, Jr.*
*Francis Lightfoot Lee*
*Carter Braxton*

**NORTH CAROLINA**
*William Hooper*
*Joseph Hewes*
*John Penn*

**SOUTH CAROLINA**
*Edward Rutledge*
*Thomas Heyward, Jr.*
*Thomas Lynch, Jr.*
*Arthur Middleton*

**GEORGIA**
*Button Gwinnett*
*Lyman Hall*
*George Walton*

*Resolved,* That copies of the Declaration be sent to the several assemblies, conventions, and committees, or councils of safety, and to the several commanding officers of the continental troops; that it be proclaimed in each of the United States, at the head of the army.

# The Articles of Confederation

Agreed to by Congress November 15, 1777;
ratified and in force March 1, 1781

To all whom these Presents shall come, we the undersigned Delegates of the States affixed to our Names, send greeting. Whereas the Delegates of the United States of America, in Congress assembled, did, on the fifteenth day of November, in the Year of Our Lord One thousand Seven Hundred and Seventy seven, and in the Second Year of the Independence of America, agree to certain articles of Confederation and perpetual Union between the States of Newhampshire, Massachusetts-bay, Rhodeisland and Providence Plantations, Connecticut, New-York, New-Jersey, Pennsylvania, Delaware, Maryland, Virginia, North-Carolina, South-Carolina and Georgia in the words following, viz. Articles of Confederation and perpetual Union between the states of Newhampshire, Massachusetts-bay, Rhodeisland and Providence Plantations, Connecticut, New-York, New-Jersey, Pennsylvania, Delaware, Maryland, Virginia, North-Carolina, South-Carolina and Georgia.

Art. I. The Stile of this confederacy shall be "The United States of America."

Art. II. Each state retains its sovereignty, freedom and independence, and every Power, Jurisdiction and right, which is not by this confederation expressly delegated to the United States, in Congress assembled.

Art. III. The said states hereby severally enter into a firm league of friendship with each other, for their common defence, the security of their Liberties, and their mutual and general welfare, binding themselves to assist each other, against all force offered to, or attacks made upon them, or any of them, on account of religion, sovereignty, trade, or any other pretence whatever.

Art. IV. The better to secure and perpetuate mutual friendship and intercourse among the people of the different states in this union, the free inhabitants of each of these states, paupers, vagabonds and fugitives from Justice excepted, shall be entitled to all privileges and immunities of free citizens in the several states; and the people of each state shall have free ingress and regress to and from any other state, and shall enjoy therein all the privileges of trade and commerce, subject to the same duties, impositions and restrictions as the inhabitants thereof respectively, provided that such restriction shall not extend so far as to prevent the removal of property imported into any state, to any other state, of which the Owner is an inhabitant; provided also that no imposition, duties or restriction shall be laid by any state, on the property of the united states, or either of them.

If any Person guilty of, or charged with treason, felony, or other high misdemeanor in any state, shall flee from Justice, and be found in any of the united states, he shall, upon demand of the Governor or executive power, of the state from which he fled, be delivered up and removed to the state having jurisdiction of his offence.

Full faith and credit shall be given in each of these states to the records, acts and judicial proceedings of the courts and magistrates of every other state.

Art. V. For the more convenient management of the general interests of the united states, delegates shall be annually appointed in such manner as the legislature of each state shall direct, to meet in Congress on the first Monday in November, in every year, with a power reserved to each state, to recall its delegates, or any of them, at any time within the year, and to send others in their stead, for the remainder of the Year.

No state shall be represented in Congress by less than two, nor by more than seven Members; and no person shall be capable of being a delegate for more than three years in any term of six years; nor shall any person, being a delegate, be capable of holding any office under the united states, for which he, or another for his benefit receives any salary, fees or emolument of any kind.

Each state shall maintain its own delegates in a meeting of the states, and while they act as members of the committee of the states.

In determining questions in the united states, in Congress assembled, each state shall have one vote.

Freedom of speech and debate in Congress shall not be impeached or questioned in any Court, or place out of Congress, and the members of congress shall be protected in their persons from arrests and imprisonments, during the time of their going to and from, and attendance on congress, except for treason, felony, or breach of the peace.

Art. VI. No state without the Consent of the united states in congress assembled, shall send any embassy to, or receive any embassy from, or enter into any conference, agreement, or alliance or treaty with any King, prince or state; nor shall any person holding any office or profit or trust under the united states, or any of them, accept of any present, emolument, office or title of any kind whatever from any king, prince or foreign state; nor shall the united states in congress assembled, or any of them, grant any title of nobility.

No two or more states shall enter into any treaty, confederation or alliance whatever between them, without the consent of the united states in congress assembled, specifying accurately the purposes for which the same is to be entered into, and how long it shall continue.

No state shall lay any imposts or duties, which may interfere with any stipulations in treaties, entered into by the united states in congress assembled, with any king, prince or state, in pursuance of any treaties already proposed by congress, to the courts of France and Spain.

No vessels of war shall be kept up in time of peace by any state, except such number only, as shall be deemed necessary by the united states in congress assembled, for the defence of such state, or its trade; nor shall any body of forces be kept up by any state, in time of peace, except such number only, as in the judgment of the united states, in congress assembled, shall be deemed requisite to garrison the forts necessary for the defence of such state; but every state shall always keep up a well regulated and disciplined militia, sufficiently armed and accoutred, and shall provide and constantly have ready for use, in public stores, a due number of field pieces and tents, and a proper quantity of arms, ammunition and camp equipage.

No state shall engage in any war without the consent of the united states in congress assembled, unless such state be actually invaded by enemies, or shall have received certain advice of a resolution being formed by some nation of Indians to invade such state, and the danger is so imminent as not to admit of a delay, till the united states in congress asssembled can be consulted; nor shall any state grant commissions to any ships or vessels of war, nor letters of marque or reprisal, except it be after a declaration of war by the united states in congress assembled, and then only against the kingdom or state and the subjects thereof, against which war has been so declared, and under such regulations as shall be established by the united states in congress assembled, unless such state be infested by pirates; in which case vessels of war may be fitted out for that occasion, and kept so long as the danger shall continue, or until the united states in congress assembled shall determine otherwise.

Art. VII. When land-forces are raised by any state for the common defence, all officers of or under the rank of colonel, shall be appointed by the legislature of each state respectively, by whom such forces shall be raised, or in such manner as such state shall direct, and all vacancies shall be filled up by the state which first made the appointment.

Art. VIII. All charges of war, and all other expences that shall be incurred for the common defence or general welfare, and allowed by the united states in congress assembled, shall be defrayed out of a common treasury, which shall be supplied by the several states in proportion to the value of all land within each state, granted to or surveyed for any Person, as such land and the buildings and improvements thereon shall be estimated according to such mode as the united states in congress assembled, shall from time to time direct and appoint.

The taxes for paying that proportion shall be laid and levied by the authority and direction of the legislatures of the several states within the time agreed upon by the united states in congress assembled.

Art. IX. The united states in congress assembled, shall have the sole and exclusive right and power of determining on peace and war, except in the cases mentioned in the sixth article—of sending and receiving ambassadors—entering into treaties and alliances, provided that no treaty of commerce shall be made whereby the legislative power of the respective states shall be restrained from imposing such imposts and duties on foreigners, as their own people are subjected to, or from prohibiting the exportation of any species of goods or commodities whatsoever—of establishing rules for deciding in all cases, what captures on land or water shall be legal, and in what manner prizes taken by land or naval forces in the service of the united states shall be divided or appropriated—of granting letters of marque and reprisal in times of peace—appointing courts for the trial of piracies and felonies committed on the high seas and establishing courts for receiving and determining finally appeals in all cases of captures, provided that no member of congress shall be appointed a judge of any of the said courts.

The united states in congress assembled shall also be the last resort on appeal in all disputes and differences now subsisting or that hereafter may arise between two or more states concerning boundary, jurisdiction or any other cause whatever; which authority shall always be exercised in the manner following. Whenever the legislative or executive authority or lawful agent of any state in controversy with another shall present a petition to congress stating the matter in question and praying for a hearing, notice thereof shall be given by order of congress to the legislative or executive authority of the other state in controversy, and a day assigned for the appearance of the parties by their lawful agents, who shall then be directed to appoint by joint consent, commissioners or judges to constitute a court for hearing and determining the matter in question: but if they cannot agree, congress shall name three persons out of each of the united states, and from the list of such persons each party shall alternately strike out one, the petitioners beginning, until the number shall be reduced to thirteen; and from that number not less than seven, nor more than nine names as congress shall direct, shall in the presence of congress be drawn out by lot, and the persons whose names shall be so drawn or any five of them, shall be commissioners or judges, to hear and finally determine the controversy, so always as a major part of the judges who shall hear the cause shall agree in the determination: and if either party shall neglect to attend at the day appointed, without shewing reasons, which congress shall judge sufficient, or being present shall refuse to strike, the congress shall proceed to nominate three persons out of each state, and the secretary of congress shall strike in behalf of such party absent or refusing; and the judgment and sentence of the court to be appointed, in the manner before prescribed, shall be final and conclusive; and if any of the parties shall refuse to submit to the authority of such court, or to appear to defend their claim or cause, the court shall nevertheless proceed to pronounce sentence, or judgment, which shall in like manner be final and decisive, the judgment or sentence and other proceedings being in either case transmitted to congress, and lodged among the acts of congress for the security of the parties concerned: provided that every commissioner, before he sits in judgment, shall take an oath to be administered by one of the judges of the supreme or superior court of the state, where the cause shall be tried, "well and truly to hear and determine the matter in question, according to the best of his judgment, without favour, affection or hope of reward:" provided also, that no state shall be deprived of territory for the benefit of the united states.

All controversies concerning the private right of soil claimed under different grants of two or more states, whose jurisdictions as they may respect such lands, and the states which passed such grants are adjusted, the said grants or either of them being at the same time claimed to have originated antecedent to such settlement of jurisdiction, shall on the petition of either party to the congress of the united states, be finally determined as near as may be in the same manner as is before prescribed for deciding disputes respecting territorial jurisdiction between different states.

The united states in congress assembled shall also have the sole and exclusive right and power of regulating the alloy and value of coin struck by their own authority, or by that of the respective states—fixing the standard of weights and measures throughout the united states—regulating the trade and managing all affairs with the Indians, not members of any of the states, provided that the legislative right of any state within its own limits be not infringed or violated—establishing and regulating post-offices from one state to another, throughout all the united states, and exacting such postage on the papers passing thro' the same as may be requisite to defray the expences of the said office—appointing all officers of the land forces, in the service of the united states, excepting regimental officers—appointing all the officers of the naval forces, and commissioning all officers whatever in the service of the united states—making rules for the government and regulation of the said land and naval forces, and directing their operations.

The united states in congress assembled shall have authority to appoint a committee, to sit in the recess of congress, to be denominated "A Committee of the States," and to consist of one delegate from each state; and to appoint such other committees and civil officers as may be necessary for managing the general affairs of the united states under their direction—to appoint one of their number to preside, provided that no person be allowed to serve in the office of president more than one year in any term of three years; to ascertain the necessary sums of Money to be raised for the service of the united states, and to appropriate and apply the same for defraying the public expenses—to borrow money, or emit bills on the credit of the united states, transmitting every half year to the respective states an account of the sums of money so borrowed or emitted,—to build and equip a navy—to agree upon the number of land forces, and to make requisitions from each state for its quota, in proportion to the number of white inhabitants in such state; which requisition shall be binding, and thereupon the legislature of each state shall appoint the regimental officers, raise the men and cloath, arm and equip then in a soldier like manner, at the expense of the united states; and the officers and men so cloathed, armed and equipped shall march to the place appointed, and within the time agreed on by the united states in congress assembled: But if the united states in congress assembled shall, on consideration of circumstances judge proper that any state should not raise men, or should raise a smaller number than its quota, and that any other state should raise a greater number of men than the quota thereof, such extra number shall be raised, officered, cloathed, armed and equipped in the same manner as the quota of such state, unless the legislature of such state shall judge that such extra number cannot be safely spared out of the same, in which case they shall raise officer, cloath, arm and equip as many of such extra number as they judge can be safely spared. And the officers and men so cloathed, armed and equipped, shall march to the place appointed, and within the time agreed on by the united states in congress assembled.

The united states in congress assembled shall never engage in a war, nor grant letters of marque and reprisal in time of peace, nor enter into any treaties or alliances, nor coin money, nor regulate the value thereof, nor ascertain the sums and expenses necessary for the defence and welfare of the united states, or any of them, nor emit bills, nor borrow money on the credit of the united states, nor appropriate money, nor agree upon the number of vessels of war, to be built or purchased, or the number of land or sea forces to be raised, nor appoint a commander in chief of the army or navy, unless nine states assent to the same: nor shall a question on any other point, except for adjourning from day to day be determined, unless by the votes of a majority of the united states in congress assembled.

The congress of the united states shall have power to adjourn to any time within the year, and to any place within the united states, so that no period of adjournment be for a longer duration than the space of six Months, and shall publish the Journal of their proceedings monthly, except such parts thereof relating to treaties, alliances or military operations, as in their judgment require secrecy; and the yeas and nays of the delegates of each state on any question shall be entered on the Journal, when it is desired by any delegate; and the delegates of a state, or any of them, at his or their request shall be furnished with a transcript of the said Journal, except such parts as are above excepted, to lay before the legislatures of the several states.

Art. X. The committee of the states, or any nine of them, shall be authorised to execute, in the recess of congress, such of the powers of congress as the united states in congress assembled, by the consent of nine states, shall from time to time think expedient to vest them with; provided that no power be delegated to the said committee, for the exercise of which, by the articles of confederation, the voice of nine states in the congress of the united states assembled is requisite.

Art. XI. Canada acceding to this confederation, and joining in the measures of the united states, shall be admitted into, and entitled to all the advantages of this union: but no other colony shall be admitted into the same, unless such admission be agreed to by nine states.

Art. XII. All bills of credit emitted, monies borrowed and debts contracted by, or under the authority of congress, before the assembling of the united states, in pursuance of the present confederation, shall be deemed and considered as a charge against the united states, for payment and satisfaction whereof the said united states and the public faith are hereby solemnly pledged.

Art. XIII. Every state shall abide by the determinations of the united states in congress assembled, on all questions which by this confederation are submitted to them. And the Articles of this confederation shall be inviolably observed by every state, and the union shall be perpetual; nor shall any alteration at any time hereafter be made in any of them; unless such alteration be agreed to in a congress of the united states, and be afterwards confirmed by the legislatures of every state.

And Whereas it hath pleased the Great Governor of the World to incline the hearts of the legislatures we respectively represent in congress, to approve of, and to authorize us to ratify the said articles of confederation and perpetual union. Know Ye that we the undersigned delegates, by virtue of the power and authority to us given for that purpose, do by these presents, in the name and in behalf of our respective constituents, fully and entirely ratify and confirm each and every of the said articles of confederation and perpetual union, and all and singular the matters and things therein contained: And we do further solemnly plight and engage the faith of our respective constituents, that they shall abide by the determinations of the united states in congress assembled, on all questions, which by the said confederation are submitted to them. And that the articles thereof shall be inviolably observed by the states we respectively represent, and that the union shall be perpetual. In Witness whereof we have hereunto set our hands in Congress. Done at Philadelphia in the state of Pennsylvania the ninth day of July, in the Year of our Lord one Thousand seven Hundred and Seventy-eight, and in the third year of the independence of America.

# The Constitution of the United States of America

[PREAMBLE]
We the People of the United States, in Order to form a more perfect Union, establish Justice, insure domestic Tranquility, provide for the common defence, promote the general Welfare, and secure the Blessings of Liberty to ourselves and our Posterity, do ordain and establish this Constitution for the United States of America.

## Article I

### SECTION 1
[LEGISLATIVE POWERS]
All legislative Powers herein granted shall be vested in a Congress of the United States, which shall consist of a Senate and House of Representatives.

### SECTION 2
[HOUSE OF REPRESENTATIVES, HOW CONSTITUTED, POWER OF IMPEACHMENT]
The House of Representatives shall be composed of Members chosen every second Year by the People of the several States, and the Electors in each State shall have the Qualifications requisite for Electors of the most numerous Branch of the State Legislature.

No Person shall be a Representative who shall not have attained to the Age of twenty five Years, and been seven Years a Citizen of the United States, and who shall not, when elected, be an Inhabitant of that State in which he shall be chosen.

Representatives and *direct Taxes*[1] shall be apportioned among the several States which may be included within this Union, according to their respective Numbers, *which shall be determined by adding to the whole Number of free Persons, including those bound to Service for a Term of Years, and excluding Indians not taxed, three fifths of all other Persons.*[2] The actual Enumeration shall be made within three Years after the first Meeting of the Congress of the United States, and within every subsequent Term of ten Years, in such Manner as they shall by Law direct. The Number of Representatives shall not exceed one for every thirty Thousand, but each State shall have at Least one Representative; *and until such enumeration shall be made, the State of New Hampshire shall be entitled to chuse three, Massachusetts eight, Rhode-Island and Providence Plantations one, Connecticut five, New-York six, New Jersey four, Pennsylvania eight, Delaware one, Maryland six, Virginia ten, North Carolina five, South Carolina five, and Georgia three.*[3]

When vacancies happen in the Representation from any State, the Executive Authority thereof shall issue Writs of Election to fill such Vacancies.

The House of Representatives shall chuse their Speaker and other Officers; and shall have the sole Power of Impeachment.

---

[1]Modified by Sixteenth Amendment.

[2]Modified by Fourteenth Amendment.

[3]Temporary provision.

## SECTION 3

[THE SENATE, HOW CONSTITUTED, IMPEACHMENT TRIALS]

The Senate of the United States shall be composed of two Senators from each State, *chosen by the Legislature thereof,*[4] for six Years; and each Senator shall have one Vote.

Immediately after they shall be assembled in Consequence of the first Election, they shall be divided as equally as may be into three Classes. The Seats of the Senators of the first Class shall be vacated at the Expiration of the second Year, of the second Class at the Expiration of the fourth Year, and of the third Class at the Expiration of the sixth Year, so that one third may be chosen every second Year; *and if Vacancies happen by Resignation, or otherwise, during the Recess of the Legislature of any State, the Executive thereof may make temporary Appointments until the next Meeting of the Legislature, which shall then fill such Vacancies.*[5]

No Person shall be a Senator who shall not have attained to the Age of thirty Years, and been nine Years a Citizen of the United States, and who shall not, when elected, be an Inhabitant of that State for which he shall be chosen.

The Vice President of the United States shall be President of the Senate, but shall have no Vote, unless they be equally divided.

The Senate shall chuse their other Officers, and also a President pro tempore, in the Absence of the Vice President, or when he shall exercise the Office of President of the United States.

The Senate shall have the sole Power to try all Impeachments. When sitting for that Purpose, they shall be on Oath or Affirmation. When the President of the United States is tried, the Chief Justice shall preside: And no Person shall be convicted without the Concurrence of two thirds of the Members present.

Judgment in Cases of Impeachment shall not extend further than to removal from Office, and disqualification to hold and enjoy any Office of honor, Trust or Profit under the United States: but the Party convicted shall nevertheless be liable and subject to Indictment, Trial, Judgment and Punishment, according to Law.

## SECTION 4

[ELECTION OF SENATORS AND REPRESENTATIVES]

The Times, Places and Manner of holding Elections for Senators and Representatives, shall be prescribed in each State by the Legislature thereof; but the Congress may at any time by Law make or alter such Regulations, except as to the Places of chusing Senators.

*The Congress shall assemble at least once in every Year, and such Meeting shall be on the first Monday in December, unless they shall by Law appoint a different Day.*[6]

## SECTION 5

[QUORUM, JOURNALS, MEETINGS, ADJOURNMENTS]

Each House shall be the Judge of the Elections, Returns and Qualifications of its own Members, and a Majority of each shall constitute a Quorum to do Business;

---

[4]Modified by Seventeenth Amendment.

[5]Modified by Seventeenth Amendment.

[6]Modified by Twentieth Amendment.

but a smaller Number may adjourn from day to day, and may be authorized to compel the Attendance of absent Members, in such Manner, and under such Penalties as each House may provide.

Each House may determine the Rules of its Proceedings, punish its Members for disorderly Behaviour, and, with the Concurrence of two thirds, expel a Member.

Each House shall keep a Journal of its Proceedings, and from time to time publish the same, excepting such Parts as may in their Judgment require Secrecy; and the Yeas and Nays of the Members of either House on any questions shall, at the Desire of one fifth of those Present, be entered on the Journal.

Neither House, during the Session of Congress, shall, without the Consent of the other, adjourn for more than three days, nor to any other Place than that in which the two Houses shall be sitting.

## SECTION 6
[COMPENSATION, PRIVILEGES, DISABILITIES]
The Senators and Representatives shall receive a Compensation for their Services, to be ascertained by Law, and paid out of the Treasury of the United States. They shall in all Cases, except Treason, Felony and Breach of the Peace, be privileged from Arrest during their Attendance at the Session of their respective Houses, and in going to and returning from the same; and for any Speech or Debate in either House, they shall not be questioned in any other Place.

No Senator or Representative shall, during the Time for which he was elected, be appointed to any civil Office under the Authority of the United States, which shall have been created, or the Emoluments whereof shall have been encreased during such time; and no Person holding any Office under the United States, shall be a Member of either House during his Continuance in Office.

## SECTION 7
[PROCEDURE IN PASSING BILLS AND RESOLUTIONS]
All Bills for raising Revenue shall originate in the House of Representatives; but the Senate may propose or concur with Amendments as on other Bills.

Every Bill which shall have passed the House of Representatives and the Senate, shall, before it become a Law, be presented to the President of the United States: If he approve he shall sign it, but if not he shall return it, with his Objections to that House in which it shall have originated, who shall enter the Objections at large on their Journal, and proceed to reconsider it. If after such Reconsideration two thirds of that House shall agree to pass the Bill, it shall be sent, together with the Objections, to the other House, by which it shall likewise be reconsidered, and if approved by two thirds of that House, it shall become a Law. But in all such Cases the Votes of both Houses shall be determined by yeas and Nays, and the Names of the Persons voting for and against the Bill shall be entered on the Journal of each House respectively. If any Bill shall not be returned by the President within ten Days (Sundays excepted) after it shall have been presented to him, the Same shall be a Law, in like Manner as if he had signed it, unless the Congress by their Adjournment prevent its Return, in which Case it shall not be a Law.

Every Order, Resolution, or Vote to which the Concurrence of the Senate and House of Representatives may be necessary (except on a question of Adjournment) shall be presented to the President of the United States; and before the

Same shall take Effect, shall be approved by him, or being disapproved by him, shall be repassed by two thirds of the Senate and House of Representatives, according to the Rules and Limitations prescribed in the Case of a Bill.

## SECTION 8
[POWERS OF CONGRESS]
The Congress shall have Power

To lay and collect Taxes, Duties, Imposts and Excises, to pay the Debts and provide for the common Defence and general Welfare of the United States; but all Duties, Imposts and Excises shall be uniform throughout the United States;

To borrow Money on the credit of the United States;

To regulate Commerce with foreign Nations, and among the several States, and with the Indian Tribes;

To establish an uniform Rule of Naturalization, and uniform Laws on the subject of Bankruptcies throughout the United States;

To coin Money, regulate the Value thereof, and of foreign Coin, and fix the Standard of Weights and Measures;

To provide for the Punishment of counterfeiting the Securities and current Coin of the United States;

To establish Post Offices and post Roads;

To promote the Progress of Science and useful Arts, by securing for limited Times to Authors and Inventors the exclusive Right to their respective Writings and Discoveries;

To constitute Tribunals inferior to the supreme Court;

To define and punish Piracies and Felonies committed on the high Seas, and Offences against the Law of Nations;

To declare War, grant Letters of Marque and Reprisal, and make Rules concerning Captures on Land and Water;

To raise and support Armies, but no Appropriation of Money to that Use shall be for a longer Term than two Years;

To provide and maintain a Navy;

To make Rules for the Government and Regulation of the land and naval Forces;

To provide for calling forth the Militia to execute the Laws of the Union, suppress Insurrections and repel Invasions;

To provide for organizing, arming, and disciplining, the Militia, and for governing such Part of them as may be employed in the Service of the United States, reserving to the States respectively, the Appointment of the Officers, and the Authority of training the Militia according to the discipline prescribed by Congress;

To exercise exclusive Legislation in all Cases whatsoever, over such District (not exceeding ten Miles square) as may, by Cession of particular States, and the Acceptance of Congress, become the Seat of the Government of the United States, and to exercise like Authority over all Places purchased by the Consent of the Legislature of the State in which the Same shall be, for the Erection of Forts, Magazines, Arsenals, dock-Yards, and other needful Buildings;—And

To make all Laws which shall be necessary and proper for carrying into Execution the foregoing Powers, and all other Powers vested by this Constitution in the Government of the United States, or in any Department or Officer thereof.

## SECTION 9
[SOME RESTRICTIONS ON FEDERAL POWER]

*The Migration or Importation of such Persons as any of the States now existing shall think proper to admit, shall not be prohibited by the Congress prior to the Year one thousand eight hundred and eight, but a Tax or duty may be imposed on such Importation, not exceeding ten dollars for each Person.*[7]

The Privilege of the Writ of Habeas Corpus shall not be suspended, unless when in Cases of Rebellion or Invasion the public Safety may require it.

No Bill of Attainder or ex post facto Law shall be passed.

*No Capitation, or other direct, Tax shall be laid, unless in Proportion to the Census or Enumeration herein before directed to be taken.*[8]

No Tax or Duty shall be laid on Articles exported from any State.

No Preference shall be given by any Regulation of Commerce or Revenue to the Ports of one State over those of another; nor shall Vessels bound to, or from, one State, be obliged to enter, clear, or pay Duties in another.

No Money shall be drawn from the Treasury, but in Consequence of Appropriations made by Law; and a regular Statement and Account of the Receipts and Expenditures of all public Money shall be published from time to time.

No Title of Nobility shall be granted by the United States: And no Person holding any Office of Profit or Trust under them, shall, without the Consent of the Congress, accept of any present, Emolument, Office, or Title, of any kind whatever, from any King, Prince, or foreign State.

## SECTION 10
[RESTRICTIONS UPON POWERS OF STATES]

No State shall enter into any Treaty, Alliance, or Confederation; grant Letters of Marque and Reprisal; coin Money; emit Bills of Credit; make any Thing but gold and silver Coin a Tender in Payment of Debts; pass any Bill of Attainder, ex post facto Law, or Law impairing the Obligation of Contracts, or grant any Title of Nobility.

No State shall, without the Consent of the Congress, lay any Imposts or Duties on Imports or Exports, except what may be absolutely necessary for executing it's inspection Laws: and the net Produce of all Duties and Imposts, laid by any State on Imports or Exports, shall be for the Use of the Treasury of the United States; and all such Laws shall be subject to the Revision and Control of the Congress.

No State shall, without the Consent of Congress, lay any Duty of Tonnage, keep Troops, or Ships of War in time of Peace, enter into any Agreement or Compact

---

[7]Temporary provision.

[8]Modified by Sixteenth Amendment.

with another State, or with a foreign Power, or engage in War, unless actually invaded, or in such imminent Danger as will not admit of delay.

## Article II

### SECTION 1

[EXECUTIVE POWER, ELECTION, QUALIFICATIONS OF THE PRESIDENT]

The executive Power shall be vested in a President of the United States of America. *He shall hold his Office during the Term of four Years, and, together with the Vice President, chosen for the same Term, be elected, as follows*[9]

Each State shall appoint, in such Manner as the Legislature thereof may direct, a Number of Electors, equal to the whole Number of Senators and Representatives to which the State may be entitled in the Congress: but no Senator or Representative, or Person holding an Office of Trust or Profit under the United States, shall be appointed an Elector.

*The electors shall meet in their respective States, and vote by ballot for two Persons, of whom one at least shall not be an Inhabitant of the same State with themselves. And they shall make a List of all the Persons voted for, and of the Number of Votes for each; which List they shall sign and certify, and transmit sealed to the Seat of the Government of the United States, directed to the President of the Senate. The President of the Senate shall, in the Presence of the Senate and House of Representatives, open all the Certificates, and the Votes shall then be counted. The Person having the greatest Number of Votes shall be the President, if such Number be a Majority of the whole Number of Electors appointed; and if there be more than one who have such Majority, and have an equal Number of Votes, then the House of Representatives shall immediately chuse by Ballot one of them for President; and if no Person have a Majority, then from the five highest on the List the said House shall in like Manner chuse the President. But in chusing the President, the Votes shall be taken by States, the Representation from each State having one Vote; A quorum for this Purpose shall consist of a Member or Members from two thirds of the States, and a Majority of all the States shall be necessary to a Choice. In every Case, after the Choice of the President, the person having the greatest Number of Votes of the Electors shall be the Vice President. But if there should remain two or more who have equal Votes, the Senate shall chuse from them by Ballot the Vice President.*[10]

The Congress may determine the Time of chusing the Electors, and the Day on which they shall give their Votes; which Day shall be the same throughout the United States.

No Person except a natural born Citizen, or a Citizen of the United States, at the time of the Adoption of this Constitution, shall be eligible to the Office of President; neither shall any Person be eligible to that Office who shall not have attained to the Age of thirty five Years, and been fourteen Years a Resident within the United States.

---

[9]Number of terms limited to two by Twenty-second Amendment.

[10]Modified by Twelfth and Twentieth Amendments.

In Case of the Removal of the President from Office, or his Death, Resignation, or Inability to discharge the Powers and Duties of the said Office, the Same shall devolve on the Vice President, and the Congress may by Law provide for the Case of Removal, Death, Resignation or Inability, both of the President and Vice President, declaring what Officer shall then act as President, and such Officer shall act accordingly, until the Disability be removed, or a President shall be elected.

The President shall, at stated Times, receive for his Services, a Compensation, which shall neither be increased nor diminished during the Period for which he shall have been elected, and he shall not receive within that Period any other Emolument from the United States, or any of them.

Before he enter on the Execution of his Office, he shall take the following Oath or Affirmation:—"I do solemnly swear (or affirm) that I will faithfully execute the Office of President of the United States, and will to the best of my Ability, preserve, protect and defend the Constitution of the United States."

## SECTION 2

[POWERS OF THE PRESIDENT]

The President shall be Commander in Chief of the Army and Navy of the United States, and of the Militia of the several States, when called into the actual Service of the United States; he may require the Opinion, in writing, of the principal Officer in each of the executive Departments, upon any Subject relating to the Duties of their respective Offices, and he shall have Power to grant Reprieves and Pardons for Offences against the United States, except in Cases of Impeachment.

He shall have Power, by and with the Advice and Consent of the Senate, to make Treaties, provided two thirds of the Senators present concur; and he shall nominate, and by and with the Advice and Consent of the Senate, shall appoint Ambassadors, other public Ministers and Consuls, Judges of the supreme Court, and all other Officers of the United States, whose Appointments are not herein otherwise provided for, and which shall be established by Law: but the Congress may by Law vest the Appointment of such inferior Officers, as they think proper, in the President alone, in the Courts of Law, or in the Heads of Departments.

The President shall have Power to fill up all Vacancies that may happen during the Recess of the Senate, by granting Commissions which shall expire at the End of their next Session.

## SECTION 3

[POWERS AND DUTIES OF THE PRESIDENT]

He shall from time to time give to the Congress Information of the State of the Union, and recommend to their Consideration such Measures as he shall judge necessary and expedient; he may, on extraordinary Occasions, convene both Houses, or either of them, and in Case of Disagreement between them, with Respect to the Time of Adjournment, he may adjourn them to such Time as he shall think proper; he shall receive Ambassadors and other public Ministers; he shall take Care that the Laws be faithfully executed, and shall Commission all the Officers of the United States.

## SECTION 4

[IMPEACHMENT]

The President, Vice President and all civil Officers of the United States, shall be removed from Office on Impeachment for, and Conviction of, Treason, Bribery, or other high Crimes and Misdemeanors.

## Article III

### SECTION 1

[JUDICIAL POWER, TENURE OF OFFICE]

The judicial Power of the United States, shall be vested in one supreme Court, and in such inferior Courts as the Congress may from time to time ordain and establish. The Judges, both of the supreme and inferior Courts, shall hold their Offices during good Behaviour, and shall, at stated Times, receive for their Services, a Compensation, which shall not be diminished during their Continuance in Office.

### SECTION 2

[JURISDICTION]

The judicial Power shall extend to all Cases, in Law and Equity, arising under this Constitution, the Laws of the United States, and Treaties made, or which shall be made, under their Authority;—to all Cases affecting Ambassadors, other public Ministers and Consuls;—to all Cases of admiralty and maritime Jurisdiction;—to Controversies to which the United States shall be a Party;—to Controversies between two or more States;—*between a State and Citizens of another State;*—between Citizens of different States,—between Citizens of the same State claiming Lands under Grants of different States, *and between a State*, or the Citizens thereof, *and foreign States, Citizens or Subjects.*[11]

In all Cases affecting Ambassadors, other public Ministers and Consuls, and those in which a State shall be Party, the supreme Court shall have original Jurisdiction. In all the other Cases before mentioned, the supreme Court shall have appellate Jurisdiction, both as to Law and Fact, with such Exceptions, and under such Regulations as the Congress shall make.

The Trial of all Crimes, except in Cases of Impeachment, shall be by Jury; and such Trial shall be held in the State where the said Crimes shall have been committed; but when not committed within any State, the Trial shall be at such Place or Places as the Congress may by Law have directed.

### SECTION 3

[TREASON, PROOF, AND PUNISHMENT]

Treason against the United States, shall consist only in levying War against them, or in adhering to their Enemies, giving them Aid and Comfort. No Person shall be convicted of Treason unless on the Testimony of two Witnesses to the same overt Act, or on Confession in open Court.

---

[11]Modified by Eleventh Amendment.

The Congress shall have Power to declare the Punishment of Treason, but no Attainder of Treason shall work Corruption of Blood, or Forfeiture except during the Life of the Person attainted.

## Article IV

### SECTION 1

[FAITH AND CREDIT AMONG STATES]

Full Faith and Credit shall be given in each State to the public Acts, Records, and judicial Proceedings of every other State. And the Congress may by general Laws prescribe the Manner in which such Acts, Records and Proceedings shall be proved, and the Effect thereof.

### SECTION 2

[PRIVILEGES AND IMMUNITIES, FUGITIVES]

The Citizens of each State shall be entitled to all Privileges and Immunities of Citizens in the several States.

A Person charged in any State with Treason, Felony or other Crime, who shall flee from Justice, and be found in another State, shall on Demand of the executive Authority of the State from which he fled, be delivered up, to be removed to the State having Jurisdiction of the Crime.

*No person held to Service or Labour in one State, under the Laws thereof, escaping into another, shall, in Consequence of any Law or Regulation therein, be discharged from such Service or Labour, but shall be delivered up on Claim of the Party to whom such Service or Labour may be due.*[12]

### SECTION 3

[ADMISSION OF NEW STATES]

New States may be admitted by the Congress into this Union; but no new State shall be formed or erected within the Jurisdiction of any other State; nor any State be formed by the Junction of two or more States, or Parts of States, without the Consent of the Legislatures of the States concerned as well as of the Congress.

The Congress shall have Power to dispose of and make all needful Rules and Regulations respecting the Territory or other Property belonging to the United States; and nothing in this Constitution shall be so construed as to Prejudice any Claims of the United States, or of any particular State.

### SECTION 4

[GUARANTEE OF REPUBLICAN GOVERNMENT]

The United States shall guarantee to every State in this Union a Republican Form of Government, and shall protect each of them against Invasion; and on Application of the Legislature, or of the Executive (when the Legislature cannot be convened), against domestic Violence.

---

[12]Repealed by Thirteenth Amendment.

## Article V

[AMENDMENT OF THE CONSTITUTION]

The Congress, whenever two thirds of both Houses shall deem it necessary, shall propose Amendments to this Constitution, or, on the Application of the Legislatures of two thirds of the several States, shall call a Convention for proposing Amendments, which, in either Case, shall be valid to all Intents and Purposes, as Part of this Constitution, when ratified by the Legislatures of three fourths of the several States, or by Conventions in three fourths thereof, as the one or the other Mode of Ratification may be proposed by the Congress; *Provided that no Amendment which may be made prior to the Year One thousand eight hundred and eight shall in any Manner affect the first and fourth Clauses in the Ninth Section of the first Article;*[13] and that no State, without its Consent, shall be deprived of its equal Suffrage in the Senate.

## Article VI

[DEBTS, SUPREMACY, OATH]

All Debts contracted and Engagements entered into, before the Adoption of this Constitution, shall be as valid against the United States under this Constitution, as under the Confederation.

This Constitution, and the Laws of the United States which shall be made in Pursuance thereof; and all Treaties made, or which shall be made, under the Authority of the United States, shall be the supreme Law of the Land; and the Judges in every State shall be bound thereby, any Thing in the Constitution or Laws of any State to the Contrary notwithstanding.

The Senators and Representatives before mentioned, and the Members of the several State Legislatures, and all executive and judicial Officers, both of the United States and of the several States, shall be bound by Oath or Affirmation, to support this Constitution; but no religious Test shall be required as a Qualification to any Office or public Trust under the United States.

## Article VII

[RATIFICATION AND ESTABLISHMENT]

The Ratification of the Conventions of nine States, shall be sufficient for the Establishment of this Constitution between the States so ratifying the Same.[14]

Done in Convention by the Unanimous Consent of the States present the Seventeenth Day of September in the Year of our Lord one thousand seven hundred

---

[13]Temporary provision.

[14]The Constitution was submitted on September 17, 1787, by the Constitutional Convention, was ratified by the conventions of several states at various dates up to May 29, 1790, and became effective on March 4, 1789.

and Eighty seven and of the Independence of the United States of America the Twelfth. *In Witness* whereof We have hereunto subscribed our Names,

*G:⁰ WASHINGTON—*
*Presidt. and deputy from Virginia*

**NEW HAMPSHIRE**
*John Langdon*
*Nicholas Gilman*

**MASSACHUSETTS**
*Nathaniel Gorham*
*Rufus King*

**CONNECTICUT**
*Wm. Saml. Johnson*
*Roger Sherman*

**NEW YORK**
*Alexander Hamilton*

**NEW JERSEY**
*Wil: Livingston*
*David Brearley*
*Wm. Paterson*
*Jona: Dayton*

**PENNSYLVANIA**
*B Franklin*
*Thomas Mifflin*
*Robt. Morris*
*Geo. Clymer*
*Thos. FitzSimons*
*Jared Ingersoll*
*James Wilson*
*Gouv Morris*

**DELAWARE**
*Geo: Read*
*Gunning Bedford jun*
*John Dickinson*
*Richard Bassett*
*Jaco: Broom*

**MARYLAND**
*James McHenry*
*Dan of St Thos. Jenifer*
*Danl. Carroll*

**VIRGINIA**
*John Blair—*
*James Madison Jr.*

**NORTH CAROLINA**
*Wm. Blount*
*Richd. Dobbs Spaight*
*Hu Williamson*

**SOUTH CAROLINA**
*J. Rutledge*
*Charles Cotesworth*
   *Pinckney*
*Charles Pinckney*
*Pierce Butler*

**GEORGIA**
*William Few*
*Abr Baldwin*

# Amendments to the Constitution

*Proposed by Congress and Ratified by the Legislatures of the Several States, Pursuant to Article V of the Original Constitution.*

*Amendments I–X, known as the Bill of Rights, were proposed by Congress on September 25, 1789, and ratified on December 15, 1791.*

## Amendment I
[FREEDOM OF RELIGION, OF SPEECH, AND OF THE PRESS]

Congress shall make no law respecting an establishment of religion, or prohibiting the free exercise thereof; or abridging the freedom of speech, or of the press; or the right of the people peaceably to assemble, and to petition the Government for a redress of grievances.

## Amendment II
[RIGHT TO KEEP AND BEAR ARMS]

A well regulated Militia, being necessary to the security of a free State, the right of the people to keep and bear Arms, shall not be infringed.

## Amendment III
[QUARTERING OF SOLDIERS]

No Soldier shall, in time of peace be quartered in any house, without the consent of the Owner, nor in time of war, but in a manner to be prescribed by law.

## Amendment IV
[SECURITY FROM UNWARRANTABLE SEARCH AND SEIZURE]

The right of the people to be secure in their persons, houses, papers, and effects, against unreasonable searches and seizures, shall not be violated, and no Warrants shall issue, but upon probable cause, supported by Oath or affirmation, and particularly describing the place to be searched, and the persons or things to be seized.

## Amendment V
[RIGHTS OF ACCUSED PERSONS IN CRIMINAL PROCEEDINGS]

No person shall be held to answer for a capital, or otherwise infamous crime, unless on a presentment or indictment of a Grand Jury, except in cases arising in the land or naval forces, or in the Militia, when in actual service in time of War or in public danger; nor shall any person be subject for the same offence to be twice put in jeopardy of life or limb; nor shall be compelled in any criminal case to be a witness against himself, nor be deprived of life, liberty, or property, without due process of law; nor shall private property be taken for public use, without just compensation.

## Amendment VI
[RIGHT TO SPEEDY TRIAL, WITNESSES, ETC.]

In all criminal prosecutions, the accused shall enjoy the right to a speedy and public trial, by an impartial jury of the State and district wherein the crime shall have been committed, which district shall have been previously ascertained by law, and to be informed of the nature and cause of the accusation; to be confronted with the witnesses against him; to have compulsory process for obtaining witnesses in his favor, and to have the Assistance of Counsel for his defence.

## Amendment VII
[TRIAL BY JURY IN CIVIL CASES]
In suits at common law, where the value in controversy shall exceed twenty dollars, the right of trial by jury shall be preserved, and no fact tried by a jury, shall be otherwise reexamined in any Court of the United States, than according to the rules of the common law.

## Amendment VIII
[BAILS, FINES, PUNISHMENTS]
Excessive bail shall not be required, nor excessive fines imposed, nor cruel and unusual punishments inflicted.

## Amendment IX
[RESERVATION OF RIGHTS OF PEOPLE]
The enumeration in the Constitution, of certain rights, shall not be construed to deny or disparage others retained by the people.

## Amendment X
[POWERS RESERVED TO STATES OR PEOPLE]
The powers not delegated to the United States by the Constitution, nor prohibited by it to the States, are reserved to the States respectively, or to the people.

## Amendment XI
[PROPOSED BY CONGRESS ON MARCH 4, 1794; DECLARED RATIFIED ON JANUARY 8, 1798.]
[RESTRICTION OF JUDICIAL POWER]
The Judicial power of the United States shall not be construed to extend to any suit in law or equity, commenced or prosecuted against one of the United States by Citizens of another State, or by Citizens or Subjects of any Foreign State.

## Amendment XII
[PROPOSED BY CONGRESS ON DECEMBER 9, 1803; DECLARED RATIFIED ON SEPTEMBER 25, 1804.]
[ELECTION OF PRESIDENT AND VICE PRESIDENT]
The Electors shall meet in their respective states and vote by ballot for President and Vice-President, one of whom, at least, shall not be an inhabitant of the same state with themselves; they shall name in their ballots the person voted for as President, and in distinct ballots the person voted for as Vice-President, and they shall make distinct lists of all persons voted for as President, and of all persons voted for as Vice-President, and of the number of votes for each, which lists they shall sign and certify, and transmit sealed to the seat of the government of the United States, directed to the President of the Senate;—the President of the Senate shall, in presence of the Senate and House of Representatives, open all the certificates and the votes shall then be counted;—The person having the greatest number of votes for President,

shall be the President, if such number be a majority of the whole number of Electors appointed; and if no person have such majority, then from the persons having the highest numbers not exceeding three on the list of those voted for as President, the House of Representatives shall choose immediately, by ballot, the President. But in choosing the President, the votes shall be taken by states, the representation from each state having one vote; a quorum for this purpose shall consist of a member or members from two-thirds of the states, and a majority of all the states shall be necessary to a choice. And if the House of Representatives shall not choose a President whenever the right of choice shall devolve upon them, before the fourth day of March next following, then the Vice-President shall act as President, as in the case of the death or other constitutional disability of the President.—The person having the greatest number of votes as Vice-President, shall be the Vice-President, if such number be a majority of the whole number of Electors appointed, and if no person have a majority, then from the two highest numbers on the list, the Senate shall choose the Vice-President; a quorum for the purpose shall consist of two-thirds of the whole number of Senators, and a majority of the whole number shall be necessary to a choice. But no person constitutionally ineligible to the office of President shall be eligible to that of Vice-President of the United States.

### Amendment XIII
[PROPOSED BY CONGRESS ON JANUARY 31, 1865; DECLARED RATIFIED ON DECEMBER 18, 1865.]

### SECTION 1
[ABOLITION OF SLAVERY]
Neither slavery nor involuntary servitude, except as a punishment for crime whereof the party shall have been duly convicted, shall exist within the United States, or any place subject to their jurisdiction.

### SECTION 2
[POWER TO ENFORCE THIS ARTICLE]
Congress shall have power to enforce this article by appropriate legislation.

### Amendment XIV
[PROPOSED BY CONGRESS ON JUNE 13, 1866, DECLARED RATIFIED ON JULY 28, 1868.]

### SECTION 1
[CITIZENSHIP RIGHTS NOT TO BE ABRIDGED BY STATES]
All persons born or naturalized in the United States, and subject to the jurisdiction thereof, are citizens of the United States and of the State wherein they reside. No State shall make or enforce any law which shall abridge the privileges or immunities of citizens of the United States; nor shall any State deprive any person of life, liberty, or property, without due process of law; nor deny to any person within its jurisdiction the equal protection of the laws.

### SECTION 2
[APPORTIONMENT OF REPRESENTATIVES IN CONGRESS]
Representatives shall be apportioned among the several States according to their respective numbers, counting the whole number of persons in each State, excluding

Indians not taxed. But when the right to vote at any election for the choice of electors for President and Vice-President of the United States, Representatives in Congress, the Executive and Judicial officers of a State, or the members of the Legislature thereof, is denied to any of the male inhabitants of such State, being twenty-one years of age, and citizens of the United States, or in any way abridged, except for participation in rebellion, or other crime, the basis of representation therein shall be reduced in the proportion which the number of such male citizens shall bear to the whole number of male citizens twenty-one years of age in such State.

## SECTION 3
[PERSONS DISQUALIFIED FROM HOLDING OFFICE]
No person shall be a Senator or Representative in Congress, or elector of President and Vice-President, or hold any office, civil or military, under the United States, or under any State, who, having previously taken an oath, as a member of Congress, or as an officer of the United States, or as a member of any State legislature, or as an executive or judicial officer of any State, to support the Constitution of the United States, shall have engaged in insurrection or rebellion against the same, or given aid or comfort to the enemies thereof. But Congress may by a vote of two-thirds of each House, remove such disability.

## SECTION 4
[WHAT PUBLIC DEBTS ARE VALID]
The validity of the public debt of the United States, authorized by law, including debts incurred for payment of pensions and bounties for services in suppressing insurrection or rebellion, shall not be questioned. But neither the United States nor any State shall assume or pay any debt or obligation incurred in aid of insurrection or rebellion against the United States, or any claim for the loss or emancipation of any slave; but all such debts, obligations and claims shall be held illegal and void.

## SECTION 5
[POWER TO ENFORCE THIS ARTICLE]
The Congress shall have power to enforce, by appropriate legislation, the provisions of this article.

## Amendment XV
[PROPOSED BY CONGRESS ON FEBRUARY 26, 1869;
DECLARED RATIFIED ON MARCH 30, 1870.]

## SECTION 1
[NEGRO SUFFRAGE]
The right of citizens of the United States to vote shall not be denied or abridged by the United States or by any State on account of race, color, or previous condition of servitude.

## SECTION 2
[POWER TO ENFORCE THIS ARTICLE]
The Congress shall have power to enforce this article by appropriate legislation.

## Amendment XVI

[PROPOSED BY CONGRESS ON JULY 2, 1909; DECLARED RATIFIED ON FEBRUARY 25, 1913.]
[AUTHORIZING INCOME TAXES]

The Congress shall have power to lay and collect taxes on incomes, from whatever source derived, without apportionment among the several States, and without regard to any census or enumeration.

## Amendment XVII

[PROPOSED BY CONGRESS ON MAY 13, 1912; DECLARED RATIFIED ON MAY 31, 1913.]
[POPULAR ELECTION OF SENATORS]

The Senate of the United States shall be composed of two Senators from each State, elected by the people thereof, for six years; and each Senator shall have one vote. The electors in each State shall have the qualifications requisite for electors of the most numerous branch of the State legislatures.

When vacancies happen in the representation of any State in the Senate, the executive authority of such State shall issue writs of election to fill such vacancies: *Provided,* That the legislature of any State may empower the executive thereof to make temporary appointments until the people fill the vacancies by election as the legislature may direct.

This amendment shall not be so construed as to affect the election or term of any Senator chosen before it becomes valid as part of the Constitution.

## Amendment XVIII

[PROPOSED BY CONGRESS DECEMBER 18, 1917; DECLARED RATIFIED ON JANUARY 29, 1919.]

### SECTION 1

[NATIONAL LIQUOR PROHIBITION]

*After one year from the ratification of this article the manufacture, sale, or transportation of intoxicating liquors within, the importation thereof into, or the exportation thereof from the United States and all territory subject to the jurisdiction thereof for beverage purposes is hereby prohibited.*

### SECTION 2

[POWER TO ENFORCE THIS ARTICLE]

*The Congress and the several States shall have concurrent power to enforce this article by appropriate legislation.*

### SECTION 3

[RATIFICATION WITHIN SEVEN YEARS]

*This article shall be inoperative unless it shall have been ratified as an amendment to the Constitution by the legislatures of the several States, as provided in the Constitution, within seven years from the date of the submission hereof to the States by the Congress.*[1]

---

[1]Repealed by Twenty-first Amendment.

## Amendment XIX

[PROPOSED BY CONGRESS ON JUNE 4, 1919; DECLARED RATIFIED ON AUGUST 26, 1920.]
[WOMAN SUFFRAGE]

The right of citizens of the United States to vote shall not be denied or abridged by the United States or by any State on account of sex.

Congress shall have power to enforce this article by appropriate legislation.

## Amendment XX

[PROPOSED BY CONGRESS ON MARCH 2, 1932; DECLARED RATIFIED ON FEBRUARY 6, 1933.]

### SECTION 1
[TERMS OF OFFICE]

The terms of the President and Vice President shall end at noon on the 20th day of January, and the terms of Senators and Representatives at noon on the 3d day of January, of the years in which such terms would have ended if this article had not been ratified; and the terms of their successors shall then begin.

### SECTION 2
[TIME OF CONVENING CONGRESS]

The Congress shall assemble at least once in every year, and such meeting shall begin at noon on the 3d day of January, unless they shall by law appoint a different day.

### SECTION 3
[DEATH OF PRESIDENT-ELECT]

If, at the time fixed for the beginning of the term of the President, the President elect shall have died, the Vice President elect shall become President. If a President shall not have been chosen before the time fixed for the beginning of his term, or if the President elect shall have failed to qualify, then the Vice President elect shall act as President until a President shall have qualified; and the Congress may by law provide for the case wherein neither a President elect nor a Vice President elect shall have qualified, declaring who shall then act as President, or the manner in which one who is to act shall be selected, and such person shall act accordingly until a President or Vice President shall have qualified.

### SECTION 4
[ELECTION OF THE PRESIDENT]

The Congress may by law provide for the case of the death of any of the persons from whom the House of Representatives may choose a President whenever the right of choice shall have devolved upon them, and for the case of the death of any of the persons from whom the Senate may choose a Vice President whenever the right of choice shall have devolved upon them.

### SECTION 5
[AMENDMENT TAKES EFFECT]

Sections 1 and 2 shall take effect on the 15th day of October following the ratification of this article.

## SECTION 6

This article shall be inoperative unless it shall have been ratified as an amendment to the Constitution by the legislatures of three-fourths of the several States within seven years from the date of its submission.

### Amendment XXI

[PROPOSED BY CONGRESS ON FEBRUARY 20, 1933; DECLARED RATIFIED ON DECEMBER 5, 1933.]

## SECTION 1

[NATIONAL LIQUOR PROHIBITION REPEALED]

The eighteenth article of amendment to the Constitution of the United States is hereby repealed.

## SECTION 2

[TRANSPORTATION OF LIQUOR INTO "DRY" STATES]

The transportation or importation into any State, Territory, or Possession of the United States for delivery or use therein of intoxicating liquors, in violation of the laws thereof, is hereby prohibited.

## SECTION 3

[RATIFICATION WITHIN SEVEN YEARS]

This article shall be inoperative unless it shall have been ratified as an amendment to the Constitution by conventions in the several States, as provided in the Constitution, within seven years from the date of the submission hereof to the States by the Congress.

### Amendment XXII

[PROPOSED BY CONGRESS ON MARCH 21, 1947; DECLARED RATIFIED ON FEBRUARY 27, 1951.]

## SECTION 1

[TENURE OF PRESIDENT LIMITED]

No person shall be elected to the office of President more than twice, and no person who has held the office of President or acted as President, for more than two years of a term to which some other person was elected President shall be elected to the office of the President more than once. But this Article shall not apply to any person holding the office of President when this Article was proposed by the Congress, and shall not prevent any person who may be holding the office of President, or acting as President, during the term within which this Article becomes operative from holding the office of President or acting as President during the remainder of such term.

## SECTION 2

[RATIFICATION WITHIN SEVEN YEARS]

This article shall be inoperative unless it shall have been ratified as an amendment to the Constitution by the legislatures of three-fourths of the several States within seven years from the date of its submission to the States by the Congress.

## Amendment XXIII

[PROPOSED BY CONGRESS ON JUNE 16, 1960; DECLARED RATIFIED ON MARCH 29, 1961.]

### SECTION 1

[ELECTORAL COLLEGE VOTES FOR THE DISTRICT OF COLUMBIA]

The District constituting the seat of Government of the United States shall appoint in such manner as the Congress may direct:

A number of electors of President and Vice President equal to the whole number of Senators and Representatives in Congress to which the District would be entitled if it were a State, but in no event more than the least populous State; they shall be in addition to those appointed by the States, but they shall be considered, for the purposes of the election of President and Vice President, to be electors appointed by a State; and they shall meet in the District and perform such duties as provided by the twelfth article of amendment.

### SECTION 2

[POWER TO ENFORCE THIS ARTICLE]

The Congress shall have power to enforce this article by appropriate legislation.

## Amendment XXIV

[PROPOSED BY CONGRESS ON AUGUST 27, 1962; DECLARED RATIFIED ON JANUARY 23, 1964.]

### SECTION 1

[ANTI-POLL TAX]

The right of citizens of the United States to vote in any primary or other election for President or Vice President, for electors for President or Vice President, or for Senator or Representative of Congress, shall not be denied or abridged by the United States or any State by reason of failure to pay any poll tax or other tax.

### SECTION 2

[POWER TO ENFORCE THIS ARTICLE]

The Congress shall have power to enforce this article by appropriate legislation.

## Amendment XXV

[PROPOSED BY CONGRESS ON JULY 6, 1965; DECLARED RATIFIED ON FEBRUARY 10, 1967.]

### SECTION 1

[VICE PRESIDENT TO BECOME PRESIDENT]

In case of the removal of the President from office or his death or resignation, the Vice President shall become President.

### SECTION 2

[CHOICE OF A NEW VICE PRESIDENT]

Whenever there is a vacancy in the office of the Vice President, the President shall nominate a Vice President who shall take the office upon confirmation by a majority vote of both houses of Congress.

## SECTION 3

[PRESIDENT MAY DECLARE OWN DISABILITY]

Whenever the President transmits to the President pro tempore of the Senate and the Speaker of the House of Representatives his written declaration that he is unable to discharge the powers and duties of his office, and until he transmits to them a written declaration to the contrary, such powers and duties shall be discharged by the Vice President as Acting President.

## SECTION 4

[ALTERNATE PROCEDURES TO DECLARE AND TO END PRESIDENTIAL DISABILITY]

Whenever the Vice President and a majority of either the principal officers of the executive departments, or of such other body as Congress may by law provide, transmit to the President pro tempore of the Senate and the Speaker of the House of Representatives their written declaration that the President is unable to discharge the powers and duties of his office, the Vice President shall immediately assume the powers and duties of the office as Acting President.

Thereafter, when the President transmits to the President pro tempore of the Senate and the Speaker of the House of Representatives his written declaration that no inability exists, he shall resume the powers and duties of his office unless the Vice President and a majority of either the principal officers of the executive department, or of such other body as Congress may by law provide, transmit within four days to the President pro tempore of the Senate and the Speaker of the House of Representatives their written declaration that the President is unable to discharge the powers and duties of his office. Thereupon Congress shall decide the issue, assembling within forty eight hours for that purpose if not in session. If the Congress, within twenty one days after receipt of the latter written declaration, or, if Congress is not in session, within twenty one days after Congress is required to assemble, determines by two-thirds vote of both Houses that the President is unable to discharge the powers and duties of his office, the Vice President shall continue to discharge the same as Acting President; otherwise, the President shall resume the powers and duties of his office.

## Amendment XXVI

[PROPOSED BY CONGRESS ON MARCH 23, 1971; DECLARED RATIFIED ON JULY 1, 1971.]

## SECTION 1

[EIGHTEEN-YEAR-OLD VOTE]

The right of citizens of the United States, who are eighteen years of age or older, to vote shall not be denied or abridged by the United States or by any State on account of age.

## SECTION 2

[POWER TO ENFORCE THIS ARTICLE]

The Congress shall have power to enforce this article by appropriate legislation.

## Amendment XXVII

[PROPOSED BY CONGRESS ON SEPTEMBER 25, 1789; DECLARED RATIFIED ON MAY 8, 1992.]
[CONGRESS CANNOT RAISE ITS OWN PAY]

No law varying the compensation for the services of the Senators and Representatives, shall take effect, until an election of representatives shall have intervened.

# The Federalist Papers

## No. 10: Madison

Among the numerous advantages promised by a well constructed Union, none deserves to be more accurately developed than its tendency to break and control the violence of faction. The friend of popular governments never finds himself so much alarmed for their character and fate, as when he contemplates their propensity to this dangerous vice. He will not fail therefore to set a due value on any plan which, without violating the principles to which he is attached, provides a proper cure for it. The instability, injustice, and confusion introduced into the public councils have, in truth, been the mortal diseases under which popular governments have everywhere perished, as they continue to be the favorite and fruitful topics from which the adversaries to liberty derive their most specious declamations. The valuable improvements made by the American constitutions on the popular models, both ancient and modern, cannot certainly be too much admired; but it would be an unwarrantable partiality to contend that they have as effectually obviated the danger on this side, as was wished and expected. Complaints are everywhere heard from our most considerate and virtuous citizens, equally the friends of public and private faith and of public and personal liberty, that our governments are too unstable, that the public good is disregarded in the conflicts of rival parties, and that measures are too often decided, not according to the rules of justice and the rights of the minor party, but by the superior force of an interested and overbearing majority. However anxiously we may wish that these complaints had no foundation, the evidence of known facts will not permit us to deny that they are in some degree true. It will be found, indeed, on a candid review of our situation, that some of the distresses under which we labor have been erroneously charged on the operation of our governments; but it will be found, at the same time, that other causes will not alone account for many of our heaviest misfortunes; and, particularly, for that prevailing and increasing distrust of public engagements and alarm for private rights which are echoed from one end of the continent to the other. These must be chiefly, if not wholly, effects of the unsteadiness and injustice with which a factious spirit has tainted our public administration.

By a faction I understand a number of citizens, whether amounting to a majority or minority of the whole, who are united and actuated by some common impulse of passion, or of interest, adverse to the rights of other citizens, or to the permanent and aggregate interests of the community.

There are two methods of curing the mischiefs of faction: the one, by removing its causes; the other, by controlling its effects.

There are again two methods of removing the causes of faction: the one, by destroying the liberty which is essential to its existence; the other, by giving to every citizen the same opinions, the same passions, and the same interests.

It could never be more truly said than of the first remedy, that it is worse than the disease. Liberty is to faction what air is to fire, an aliment without which it instantly expires. But it could not be a less folly to abolish liberty, which is essential to political life, because it nourishes faction, than it would be to wish the annihilation of air, which is essential to animal life, because it imparts to fire its destructive agency.

The second expedient is as impracticable, as the first would be unwise. As long as the reason of man continues fallible, and he is at liberty to exercise it, different opinions will be formed. As long as the connection subsists between his reason and his self-love, his opinions and his passions will have a reciprocal influence on each other; and the former will be objects to which the latter will attach themselves. The diversity in the faculties of men, from which the rights of property originate, is not less an insuperable obstacle to a uniformity of interests. The protection of these faculties is the first object of Government. From the protection of different and unequal faculties of acquiring property, the possession of different degrees and kinds of property immediately results; and from the influence of these on the sentiments and views of the respective proprietors, ensues a division of the society into different interests and parties.

The latent causes of faction are thus sown in the nature of man; and we see them everywhere brought into different degrees of activity, according to the different circumstances of civil society. A zeal for different opinions concerning religion, concerning Government, and many other points, as well of speculation as of practice; an attachment to different leaders ambitiously contending for pre-eminence and power; or to persons of other descriptions whose fortunes have been interesting to the human passions, have in turn divided mankind into parties, inflamed them with mutual animosity, and rendered them much more disposed to vex and oppress each other, than to co-operate for their common good. So strong is this propensity of mankind to fall into mutual animosities, that where no substantial occasion presents itself, the most frivolous and fanciful distinctions have been sufficient to kindle their unfriendly passions, and excite their most violent conflicts. But the most common and durable source of factions has been the various and unequal distribution of property. Those who hold and those who are without property have ever formed distinct interests in society. Those who are creditors, and those who are debtors, fall under a like discrimination. A landed interest, a manufacturing interest, a mercantile interest, a moneyed interest, with many lesser interests, grow up of necessity in civilized nations, and divide them into different classes, actuated by different sentiments and views. The regulation of these various and interfering interests forms the principal task of modern Legislation, and involves the spirit of party and faction in the necessary and ordinary operations of Government.

No man is allowed to be judge in his own cause, because his interest would certainly bias his judgment and, not improbably, corrupt his integrity. With equal, nay with greater reason, a body of men are unfit to be both judges and parties at the same time; yet what are many of the most important acts of legislation but so many judicial determinations, not indeed concerning the rights of single persons, but concerning the rights of large bodies of citizens; and what are the different classes of legislators but advocates and parties to the causes which they determine? Is a law proposed concerning private debts? It is a question to which the creditors are parties on one side and the debtors on the other. Justice ought to hold the balance between them. Yet the parties are, and must be, themselves the judges; and the most numerous party, or in other words, the most powerful faction must be expected to prevail. Shall domestic manufacturers be encouraged, and in what degree, by restrictions on foreign manufacturers? are questions which would be differently decided by the landed and the manufacturing classes, and probably by neither with a sole regard to justice and the public good. The apportionment of taxes on the various descriptions of property is an act which seems to require the most exact impartiality; yet there is, perhaps, no legislative act in which greater opportunity and temptation are given to a predominant party to trample on the rules of justice. Every shilling with which they overburden the inferior number is a shilling saved to their own pockets.

It is in vain to say that enlightened statesmen will be able to adjust these clashing interests and render them all subservient to the public good. Enlightened statesmen will not always be at the helm. Nor, in many cases, can such an adjustment be made at all without taking into view indirect and remote considerations, which will rarely prevail over the immediate interest which one party may find in disregarding the rights of another or the good of the whole.

The inference to which we are brought is that the *causes* of faction cannot be removed and that relief is only to be sought in the means of controlling its *effects.*

If a faction consists of less than a majority, relief is supplied by the republican principle, which enables the majority to defeat its sinister views by regular vote. It may clog the administration, it may convulse the society; but it will be unable to execute and mask its violence under the forms of the Constitution. When a majority is included in a faction, the form of popular government, on the other hand, enables it to sacrifice to its ruling passion or interest both the public good and the rights of other citizens. To secure the public good and private rights against the danger of such a faction, and at the same time to preserve the spirit and the form of popular government, is then the great object to which our enquiries are directed. Let me add that it is the great desideratum by which alone this form of government can be rescued from the opprobrium under which it has so long labored and be recommended to the esteem and adoption of mankind.

By what means is this object attainable? Evidently by one of two only. Either the existence of the same passion or interest in a majority at the same time must be prevented, or the majority, having such co-existent passion or interest, must be rendered, by their number and local situation, unable to concert and carry into effect schemes of oppression. If the impulse and the opportunity be suffered to coincide, we well know that neither moral nor religious motives can be relied on as an adequate control. They are not found to be such on the injustice and violence of individuals, and lose their efficacy in proportion to the number combined together, that is, in proportion as their efficacy becomes needful.

From this view of the subject it may be concluded that a pure Democracy, by which I mean a Society consisting of a small number of citizens, who assemble and administer the Government in person, can admit of no cure for the mischiefs of faction. A common passion or interest will, in almost every case, be felt by a majority of the whole; a communication and concert results from the form of Government itself; and there is nothing to check the inducements to sacrifice the weaker party or an obnoxious individual. Hence it is that such Democracies have ever been spectacles of turbulence and contention; have ever been found incompatible with personal security or the rights of property; and have in general been as short in their lives as they have been violent in their deaths. Theoretic politicians, who have patronized this species of Government, have erroneously supposed that by reducing mankind to a perfect equality in their political rights, they would at the same time be perfectly equalized and assimilated in their possessions, their opinions, and their passions.

A Republic, by which I mean a Government in which the scheme of representation takes place, opens a different prospect and promises the cure for which we are seeking. Let us examine the points in which it varies from pure Democracy, and we shall comprehend both the nature of the cure and the efficacy which it must derive from the Union.

The two great points of difference between a Democracy and a Republic are: first, the delegation of the Government, in the latter, to a small number of citizens elected by the rest; secondly, the greater number of citizens and greater sphere of country over which the latter may be extended.

The effect of the first difference is, on the one hand, to refine and enlarge the public views by passing them through the medium of a chosen body of citizens, whose wisdom may best discern the true interest of their country and whose patriotism and love of justice will be least likely to sacrifice it to temporary or partial considerations. Under such a regulation it may well happen that the public voice, pronounced by the representatives of the people, will be more consonant to the public good than if pronounced by the people themselves, convened for the purpose. On the other hand, the effect may be inverted. Men of factious tempers, of local prejudices, or of sinister designs, may, by intrigue, by corruption, or by other means, first obtain the suffrages, and then betray the interests of the people. The question resulting is, whether small or extensive Republics are most favorable to the election of proper guardians of the public weal; and it is clearly decided in favor of the latter by two obvious considerations.

In the first place it is to be remarked that however small the Republic may be, the Representatives must be raised to a certain number in order to guard against the cabals of a few; and that however large it may be they must be limited to a certain number in order to guard against the confusion of a multitude. Hence, the number of Representatives in the two cases not being in proportion to that of the Constituents, and being proportionally greatest in the small Republic, it follows that if the proportion of fit characters be not less in the large than in the small Republic, the former will present a greater option, and consequently a greater probability of a fit choice.

In the next place, as each Representative will be chosen by a greater number of citizens in the large than in the small Republic, it will be more difficult for unworthy candidates to practise with success the vicious arts by which elections are too often carried; and the suffrages of the people being more free, will be more likely to centre on men who possess the most attractive merit and the most diffusive and established characters.

It must be confessed that in this, as in most other cases, there is a mean, on both sides of which inconveniencies will be found to lie. By enlarging too much the number of electors, you render the representative too little acquainted with all their local circumstances and lesser interests; as by reducing it too much, you render him unduly attached to these, and too little fit to comprehend and pursue great and national objects. The Federal Constitution forms a happy combination in this respect; the great and aggregate interests being referred to the national, the local and particular to the State legislatures.

The other point of difference is the greater number of citizens and extent of territory which may be brought within the compass of Republican than of Democratic Government; and it is this circumstance principally which renders factious combinations less to be dreaded in the former than in the latter. The smaller the society, the fewer probably will be the distinct parties and interests composing it; the fewer the distinct parties and interests, the more frequently will a majority be found of the same party; and the smaller the number of individuals composing a majority, and the smaller the compass within which they are placed, the more easily will they concert and execute their plans of oppression. Extend the sphere and you take in a greater variety of parties and interests; you make it less probable that a majority of the whole will have a common motive to invade the rights of other citizens; or if such a common motive exists, it will be more difficult for all who feel it to discover their own strength and to act in unison with each other. Besides other impediments, it may be remarked, that where there is a consciousness of unjust or dishonorable purposes, communication is always checked by distrust in proportion to the number whose concurrence is necessary.

Hence, it clearly appears that the same advantage which a Republic has over a Democracy in controlling the effects of faction is enjoyed by a large over a small republic—is enjoyed by the Union over the States composing it. Does this advantage consist in the substitution of representatives whose enlightened views and virtuous sentiments render them superior to local prejudices and to schemes of injustice? It will not be denied that the representation of the Union will be most likely to possess these requisite endowments. Does it consist in the greater security afforded by a greater variety of parties, against the event of any one party being able to outnumber and oppress the rest? In an equal degree does the increased variety of parties comprised within the Union increase this security? Does it, in fine, consist in the greater obstacles opposed to the concert and accomplishment of the secret wishes of an unjust and interested majority? Here again the extent of the Union gives it the most palpable advantage.

The influence of factious leaders may kindle a flame within their particular States but will be unable to spread a general conflagration through the other States: a religious sect may degenerate into a political faction in a part of the Confederacy; but the variety of sects dispersed over the entire face of it must secure the national Councils against any danger from that source: a rage for paper money, for an abolition of debts, for an equal division of property, or for any other improper or wicked project, will be less apt to pervade the whole body of the Union than a particular member of it; in the same proportion as such a malady is more likely to taint a particular county or district than an entire State.

In the extent and proper structure of the Union, therefore, we behold a republican remedy for the diseases most incident to Republican Government. And according to the degree of pleasure and pride we feel in being republicans ought to be our zeal in cherishing the spirit and supporting the character of federalist.

PUBLIUS

## No. 51: Madison

To what expedient, then, shall we finally resort, for maintaining in practice the necessary partition of power among the several departments as laid down in the constitution? The only answer that can be given is that as all these exterior provisions are found to be inadequate the defect must be supplied, by so contriving the interior structure of the government as that its several constituent parts may, by their mutual relations, be the means of keeping each other in their proper places. Without presuming to undertake a full development of this important idea I will hazard a few general observations which may perhaps place it in a clearer light, and enable us to form a more correct judgment of the principles and structure of the government planned by the convention.

In order to lay a due foundation for that separate and distinct exercise of the different powers of government, which to a certain extent is admitted on all hands to be essential to the preservation of liberty, it is evident that each department should have a will of its own; and consequently should be so constituted that the members of each should have as little agency as possible in the appointment of the members of the others. Were this principle rigorously adhered to, it would require that all the appointments for the supreme executive, legislative, and judiciary magistracies should be drawn from the same fountain of authority, the people, through channels having no communication whatever with one another. Perhaps such a plan of constructing the several departments would be less difficult in practice than it may in contemplation appear. Some difficulties, however, and some additional expense would attend the execution of it. Some deviations, therefore, from the principle must be admitted. In the constitution of the judiciary department in particular, it might be inexpedient to insist rigorously on the principle: first, because peculiar qualifications being essential in the members, the primary consideration ought to be to select that mode of choice which best secures these qualifications; second, because the permanent tenure by which the appointments are held in that department must soon destroy all sense of dependence on the authority conferring them.

It is equally evident that the members of each department should be as little dependent as possible on those of the others for the emoluments annexed to their offices. Were the executive magistrate, or the judges, not independent of the legislature in this particular, their independence in every other would be merely nominal.

But the great security against a gradual concentration of the several powers in the same department consists in giving to those who administer each department the necessary constitutional means and personal motives to resist encroachments of the others. The provision for defence must in this, as in all other cases, be made commensurate to the danger of attack. Ambition must be made to counteract ambition. The interest of the man must be connected with the constitutional rights of the place. It may be a reflection on human nature that such devices should be necessary to control the abuses of government. But what is government itself but the greatest of all reflections on human nature? If men were angels, no government would be necessary. If angels were to govern men, neither external nor internal controls on government would be necessary. In framing a government which is to be administered by men over men, the great difficulty lies in this: You must first enable the government to control the governed; and in the next place oblige it to control itself. A dependence on the people is, no doubt, the primary control on the government; but experience has taught mankind the necessity of auxiliary precautions.

This policy of supplying, by opposite and rival interests, the defect of better motives, might be traced through the whole system of human affairs, private as well as public. We see it particularly displayed in all the subordinate distributions of power, where the constant aim is to divide and arrange the several offices in such a manner as that each may be a check on the other; that the private interest of every individual may be a sentinel over the public rights. These inventions of prudence cannot be less requisite in the distribution of the supreme powers of the State.

But it is not possible to give to each department an equal power of self-defense. In republican government, the legislative authority necessarily predominates. The remedy for this inconveniency is to divide the legislature into different branches; and to render them, by different modes of election and different principles of action, as little connected with each other as the nature of their common functions and their common dependence on the society will admit. It may even be necessary to guard against dangerous encroachments by still further precautions. As the weight of the legislative authority requires that it should be thus divided, the weakness of the executive may require, on the other hand, that it should be fortified. An absolute negative on the legislature appears, at first view, to be the natural defense with which the executive magistrate should be armed. But perhaps it would be neither altogether safe nor alone sufficient. On ordinary occasions it might not be exerted with the requisite firmness, and on extraordinary occasions it might be perfidiously abused. May not this defect of an absolute negative be supplied by some qualified connection between this weaker branch of the stronger department, by which the latter may be led to support the constitutional rights of the former, without being too much detached from the rights of its own department?

If the principles on which these observations are founded be just, as I persuade myself they are, and they be applied as a criterion to the several State constitutions, and to the federal Constitution, it will be found that if the latter does not perfectly correspond with them, the former are infinitely less able to bear such a test.

There are, moreover, two considerations particularly applicable to the federal system of America, which place that system in a very interesting point of view.

*First.* In a single republic, all the power surrendered by the people is submitted to the administration of a single government; and usurpations are guarded against by a division of the government into distinct and separate departments. In the compound republic of America, the power surrendered by the people is first divided between two distinct governments, and then the portion allotted to each subdivided among distinct and separate departments. Hence a double security arises to the rights of the people. The different governments will control each other, at the same time that each will be controlled by itself.

*Second.* It is of great importance in a republic not only to guard the society against the oppression of its rulers, but to guard one part of the society against the injustice of the other part. Different interests necessarily exist in different classes of citizens. If a majority be united by a common interest, the rights of the minority will be insecure. There are but two methods of providing against this evil: The one by creating a will in the community independent of the majority—that is, of the society itself; the other, by comprehending in the society so many separate descriptions of citizens as will render an unjust combination of a majority of the whole very improbable, if not impracticable. The first method prevails in all governments possessing an hereditary or self-appointed authority. This, at best, is but a precarious security; because a power independent of the society may as well espouse the unjust views of the major as the rightful interests of the minor party, and may possibly be turned against both parties. The second method will be exemplified in the federal republic of the United States. Whilst all authority in it will be derived from and dependent on the society, the society itself will be broken into so many parts, interests and classes of citizens, that the rights of individuals, or of the minority, will be in little danger from interested combinations of the majority. In a free government the security for civil rights must be the same as that for religious rights. It consists in the one case in the multiplicity of interests, and in the other in the multiplicity of sects. The degree of security in both cases will depend on the number of interests and sects; and this may be presumed to depend on the extent of country and number of people comprehended under the same government. This view of the subject must particularly recommend a proper federal system to all the sincere and considerate friends of republican government: Since it shows that in exact proportion as the territory of the Union may be formed into more circumscribed Confederacies, or States, oppressive combinations of a majority will be facilitated; the best security, under the republican form, for the rights of every class of citizens, will be diminished; and consequently the stability and independence of some member of the government, the only other security, must be proportionally increased. Justice is the end of government. It is the end of civil society. It ever has been and ever will be pursued until it be obtained, or until liberty be lost in the pursuit. In a society under the forms of which the stronger faction can readily unite and oppress the weaker, anarchy may as truly be said to reign as in a state of nature, where the weaker individual is not secured against the violence of the stronger: And as, in the latter state, even the stronger individuals are prompted, by the uncertainty of their condition, to submit to a government which may protect the weak as well as themselves: So, in the former state, will the more powerful factions or parties be gradually induced, by a like motive, to wish for a government which will protect all parties, the weaker as well as the more powerful. It can be little doubted that if the State of Rhode Island was separated from the Confederacy and left to itself, the insecurity of rights under the popular form of government within such narrow limits would be displayed by such reiterated oppressions of factious majorities that some power altogether independent of the people would soon be called for by the voice of the very factions whose misrule had proved the necessity of it. In the extended republic of the United States, and among the great variety of interests, parties, and sects which it embraces, a coalition of a majority of the whole society could seldom take place on any other principles than those of justice and the general good; and there being thus less danger to a minor from the will of the major party, there must be less pretext, also, to provide for the security of the former, by introducing into the government a will not dependent on the latter, or, in other words, a will independent of the society itself. It is no less certain than it is important, notwithstanding the contrary opinions which have been entertained, that the larger the society, provided it lie within a practicable sphere, the more duly capable it will be of self-government. And happily for the *republican cause*, the practicable sphere may be carried to a very great extent by a judicious modification and mixture of the *federal principle*.

PUBLIUS

# Presidents and Vice Presidents

| | PRESIDENT | VICE PRESIDENT |
|---|---|---|
| 1 | George Washington *(Federalist 1789)* | John Adams *(Federalist 1789)* |
| 2 | John Adams *(Federalist 1797)* | Thomas Jefferson *(Dem.-Rep. 1797)* |
| 3 | Thomas Jefferson *(Dem.-Rep. 1801)* | Aaron Burr *(Dem.-Rep. 1801)*<br><br>George Clinton *(Dem.-Rep. 1805)* |
| 4 | James Madison *(Dem.-Rep. 1809)* | George Clinton *(Dem.-Rep. 1809)*<br><br>Elbridge Gerry *(Dem.-Rep. 1813)* |
| 5 | James Monroe *(Dem.-Rep. 1817)* | Daniel D. Tompkins *(Dem.-Rep. 1817)* |
| 6 | John Quincy Adams *(Dem.-Rep. 1825)* | John C. Calhoun *(Dem.-Rep. 1825)* |
| 7 | Andrew Jackson *(Democratic 1829)* | John C. Calhoun *(Democratic 1829)*<br><br>Martin Van Buren *(Democratic 1833)* |
| 8 | Martin Van Buren *(Democratic 1837)* | Richard M. Johnson *(Democratic 1837)* |
| 9 | William H. Harrison *(Whig 1841)* | John Tyler *(Whig 1841)* |
| 10 | John Tyler *(Whig and Democratic 1841)* | |
| 11 | James K. Polk *(Democratic 1845)* | George M. Dallas *(Democratic 1845)* |
| 12 | Zachary Taylor *(Whig 1849)* | Millard Fillmore *(Whig 1849)* |

| PRESIDENT | VICE PRESIDENT |
|---|---|
| 13  Millard Fillmore *(Whig 1850)* | |
| 14  Franklin Pierce *(Democratic 1853)* | William R. D. King *(Democratic 1853)* |
| 15  James Buchanan *(Democrat 1857)* | John C. Breckinridge *(Democrat 1857)* |
| 16  Abraham Lincoln *(Republican 1861)* | Hannibal Hamlin *(Republican 1861)* <br><br> Andrew Johnson *(Unionist 1865)* |
| 17  Andrew Johnson (Unionist 1865) | |
| 18  Ulysses S. Grant *(Republican 1869)* | Schuyler Colfax *(Republican 1869)* <br><br> Henry Wilson *(Republican 1873)* |
| 19  Rutherford B. Hayes *(Republican 1877)* | William A. Wheeler *(Republican 1877)* |
| 20  James A. Garfield *(Republican 1881)* | Chester A. Arthur *(Republican 1881)* |
| 21  Chester A. Arthur *(Republican 1881)* | |
| 22  Grover Cleveland *(Democratic 1885)* | Thomas A. Hendricks *(Democratic 1885)* |
| 23  Benjamin Harrison *(Republican 1889)* | Levi P. Morton *(Republican 1889)* |
| 24  Grover Cleveland *(Democratic 1893)* | Adlai E. Stevenson *(Democratic 1893)* |
| 25  William McKinley *(Republican 1897)* | Garret A. Hobart *(Republican 1897)* <br><br> Theodore Roosevelt *(Republican 1901)* |

| PRESIDENT | VICE PRESIDENT |
|---|---|
| 26 Theodore Roosevelt<br>*(Republican 1901)* | Charles W. Fairbanks<br>*(Republican 1905)* |
| 27 William H. Taft<br>*(Republican 1909)* | James S. Sherman<br>*(Republican 1909)* |
| 28 Woodrow Wilson<br>*(Democratic 1913)* | Thomas R. Marshall<br>*(Democratic 1913)* |
| 29 Warren G. Harding<br>*(Republican 1921)* | Calvin Coolidge<br>*(Republican 1921)* |
| 30 Calvin Coolidge<br>*(Republican 1923)* | Charles G. Dawes<br>*(Republican 1925)* |
| 31 Herbert Hoover<br>*(Republican 1929)* | Charles Curtis<br>*(Republican 1929)* |
| 32 Franklin D. Roosevelt<br>*(Democratic 1933)* | John Nance Garner<br>*(Democratic 1933)*<br><br>Henry A. Wallace<br>*(Democratic 1941)*<br><br>Harry S. Truman<br>*(Democratic 1945)* |
| 33 Harry S. Truman<br>*(Democratic 1945)* | Alben W. Barkley<br>*(Democratic 1949)* |
| 34 Dwight D. Eisenhower<br>*(Republican 1953)* | Richard M. Nixon<br>*(Republican 1953)* |
| 35 John F. Kennedy<br>*(Democratic 1961)* | Lyndon B. Johnson<br>*(Democratic 1961)* |
| 36 Lyndon B. Johnson<br>*(Democratic 1963)* | Hubert H. Humphrey<br>*(Democratic 1965)* |
| 37 Richard M. Nixon<br>*(Republican 1969)* | Spiro T. Agnew<br>*(Republican 1969)*<br><br>Gerald R. Ford<br>*(Republican 1973)* |

| PRESIDENT | VICE PRESIDENT |
|-----------|----------------|
| 38  Gerald R. Ford *(Republican 1974)* | Nelson Rockefeller *(Republican 1974)* |
| 39  James E. Carter *(Democratic 1977)* | Walter Mondale *(Democratic 1977)* |
| 40  Ronald Reagan *(Republican 1981)* | George H. W. Bush *(Republican 1981)* |
| 41  George H. W. Bush *(Republican 1989)* | J. Danforth Quayle *(Republican 1989)* |
| 42  William J. Clinton *(Democratic 1993)* | Albert Gore, Jr. *(Democratic 1993)* |
| 43  George W. Bush *(Republican 2001)* | Richard B. Cheney *(Republican 2001)* |
| 44  Barack H. Obama *(Democratic 2009)* | Joseph R. Biden, Jr. *(Democratic 2009)* |

# glossary

**affirmative action**   government policies or programs that seek to address past injustices against specified groups by making special efforts to provide members of these groups with access to educational and employment opportunities

**agency representation**   the type of representation by which representatives are held accountable to their constituency if they fail to represent that constituency properly. This is the incentive for good representation when the personal backgrounds, views, and interests of the representative differ from those of his or her constituency

**agenda setting**   the power of the media to bring public attention to particular issues and problems

**amendment**   a change added to a bill, law, or constitution

*amicus curiae*   literally, "friend of the court"; individuals or groups who are not parties to a lawsuit but who seek to assist the Supreme Court in reaching a decision by presenting additional briefs

**Antifederalists**   those who favored strong state governments and a weak national government, and were opponents of the constitution proposed at the American Constitutional Convention of 1787

**appeasement**   effort to forestall war by giving in to the demands of a hostile power

**appropriations**   the amounts of money approved by Congress in statutes (bills) that each unit or agency of government can spend

**Articles of Confederation**   America's first written constitution; served as the basis for America's national government until 1789

**authoritarian government**   a system of rule in which those in power hold absolute authority over the people, although other institutions may operate independently of the government

**bicameral**   a two-chambered legislature; opposite of unicameral

**bilateral treaties**   treaties made between two nations

**bill**   a proposed law that has been sponsored by a member of Congress and submitted to the clerk of the House or Senate

**Bill of Rights**   the first ten amendments to the Constitution, which guarantee certain rights and liberties to the people

**bills of attainder**   laws that decree a person guilty of a crime without a trial

**block grants**   federal grants that allow states considerable leeway or discretion in how the funds should be spent

**briefs**   written documents in which attorneys explain, using case precedents, why the court should find in favor of their client

*Brown v. Board of Education*   the 1954 Supreme Court decision that struck down the "separate but equal" doctrine as fundamentally unequal. This case eliminated state power to use race as a criterion of discrimination in law and provided the national government with the power to intervene by exercising strict regulatory policies against discriminatory actions

**bureaucracy**   the complex structure of offices, tasks, rules, and principles of organization that are employed by all large-scale institutions to coordinate effectively the work of their personnel

**Bush Doctrine** foreign policy based on the idea that the United States should take preemptive action against threats to its national security

**Cabinet** the secretaries, or chief administrators, of the major departments of the federal government. Cabinet secretaries are appointed by the president with the consent of the Senate

**categorical grants** congressional grants given to states and localities on the condition that expenditures be limited to a problem or group specified by law

**checks and balances** mechanisms through which each branch of government is able to participate in and influence the activities of the other branches. Major examples include the presidential veto power over congressional legislation, the power of the Senate to approve presidential appointments, and judicial review of congressional enactments

**chief justice** justice on the Supreme Court who presides over the Court's public sessions

**citizenship** informed and active membership in a political community

**civil law** a system of jurisprudence, including private law and governmental actions, to settle disputes that do not involve criminal penalties

**civil liberties** areas of personal freedom with which governments are prevented from interfering

**civil rights** legal or moral claims that citizens are entitled to make on government

**"clear and present danger" test** test to determine whether speech is protected or unprotected, based on its capacity to present a "clear and present danger" to society

**closed primary** a primary election where only registered members of a political party may vote

**cloture** a rule allowing three-fifths of the members in the U.S. Senate to set a time limit on debate over a given bill

**Cold War** the period of hostilities, but no direct war, between the United States and the former Soviet Union between the late 1940s and about 1990

**collective goods** benefits, sought by groups, that are broadly available and cannot be denied to nonmembers

**commander in chief** the power of the president as commander of the national military and the state national guard units (when called into service)

**commerce clause** Article 1, Section 8, of the Constitution, which delegates to Congress the power "to regulate Commerce with foreign Nations, and among the several States and with the Indian Tribes." The Supreme Court interpreted this clause in favor of national power over the economy

**concurrent powers** powers exercised by both the federal and the state governments

**confederation** a system of government with a weak national government but strong states or provinces

**conference committee** a joint committee created to work out a compromise on House and Senate versions of a piece of legislation

**conservative** today this term refers to those who generally support the social and economic status quo and are suspicious of efforts to introduce new political formulae and economic arrangements. Conservatives believe that a large and powerful government poses a threat to citizens' freedom

**constituency** the district and its people comprising the area from which an official is elected

**constitutional government** a system of rule in which governmental power is both described in, and limited by, a governing constitution

**containment** the policy used by the United States during the Cold War to restrict the expansion of communism and limit the influence of the Soviet Union

**contracting power** the power of government to set conditions on companies seeking to sell goods or services to government agencies

**contributory programs** social programs financed in whole or in part by taxation or other mandatory contributions by their present or future recipients. The most important example is Social Security, which is financed by a payroll tax

**cooperative federalism** federalism existing since the New Deal era in which grants-in-aid have been used strategically to encourage states and localities to pursue nationally defined goals, with national and state governments sharing powers and resources via intergovernmental cooperation

**cost-of-living adjustments (COLAs)** changes made to the level of benefits of a government program based on the rate of inflation

**court of appeals** a court that hears the appeals of trial court decisions

**criminal law** the branch of law that deals with disputes or actions involving criminal penalties (as opposed to civil law); it regulates the conduct of individuals, defines crimes, and provides punishment for criminal acts

**de facto** literally, "by fact"; practices that occur even when there is no legal enforcement, such as school segregation in much of the United States today

**de jure** literally, "by law"; legally enforced practices, such as school segregation in the South before the 1960s

**defendant** the one against whom a complaint is brought in a criminal or civil case

**delegated powers** constitutional powers that are assigned to one governmental agency but that are exercised by another agency with the express permission of the first

**democracy** a system of rule where popular wishes and preferences regularly and systematically shape who controls the government and what the government does

**department** the largest subunit of the executive branch. The secretaries of the fifteen departments form the Cabinet

**deterrence** the development and maintenance of military strength as a means of discouraging attack

**devolution** a policy to remove a program from one level of government by delegating it or passing it down to a lower level of government, such as from the national government to the state and local governments

**diplomacy** the representation of a government to other foreign governments

**direct democracy** a system of rule that permits citizens to vote directly on laws and policies

**dissenting opinion** a decision written by a justice in the minority in a particular case in which the justice wishes to express his or her reasoning in the case

**divided government** the condition in American government wherein the presidency is controlled by one party while the opposing party controls one or both houses of Congress

**double jeopardy** the Fifth Amendment right providing that a person cannot be tried twice for the same crime

**dual citizenship** the status of being governed by both the U.S. federal government and the individual's state government

**dual federalism** the system of government that prevailed in the United States from 1789 to the 1930s, in which the powers of the national government and the states were considered entirely separate and distinct from each other; during this time, the states possessed a vast amount of governing power

**due process of law** the right of every citizen to be protected against arbitrary action by national or state governments

**elastic clause** a phrase in Article 1, Section 8, of the Constitution (also known as the necessary and proper clause), which provides Congress with the authority to make all laws "necessary and proper" to carry out the other powers given to Congress

**electoral college** the presidential electors from each state who meet after the popular election to cast ballots for president and vice president

**electoral realignment** the point in history when a new party supplants the ruling party, becoming in turn the dominant political force. In the United States, this has tended to occur roughly every thirty years

**eminent domain**  the right of government to take private property for public use

**equal protection clause**  provision of the Fourteenth Amendment guaranteeing citizens "the equal protection of the laws." This clause has served as the basis for the civil rights of African Americans, women, and other groups

**equal time rule**  the requirement that broadcasters provide candidates for the same political office equal opportunities to communicate their messages to the public

**equality of opportunity**  a widely shared American ideal that all people should have the freedom to use whatever talents and wealth they have to reach their fullest potential

**establishment clause**  the First Amendment clause that says that "Congress shall make no law respecting an establishment of religion." This means that a "wall of separation" exists between church and state

***ex post facto* laws**  laws that declare an action to be illegal after it has been committed

**exclusionary rule**  the ability of courts to exclude evidence obtained in violation of the Fourth Amendment

**executive agreement**  an agreement, made between the president and another country, that has the force of a treaty but does not require the Senate's "advice and consent"

**Executive Office of the President (EOP)**  the permanent agencies that perform defined management tasks for the president. Created in 1939, the EOP includes the Office of Management and Budget, the Council of Economic Advisers, the National Security Council, and other agencies

**executive order**  a rule or regulation issued by the president that has the effect and formal status of legislation

**expressed powers**  specific powers granted to Congress in the Constitution

**fairness doctrine**  A Federal Communications Commission requirement for broadcasters who air programs on controversial issues to provide time for opposing views. The FCC ceased enforcing this doctrine in 1985

**Federal Reserve System**  a system of twelve Federal Reserve Banks that facilitates exchanges of cash, checks, and credit; regulates member banks; and uses monetary policies to fight inflation and deflation

**federalism**  a system of government in which power is divided, by a constitution, between the central (national) government and regional (state) governments

**Federalist Papers**  a series of essays written by James Madison, Alexander Hamilton, and John Jay supporting the ratification of the Constitution

**Federalists**  those who favored a strong national government and supported the constitution proposed at the American Constitutional Convention of 1787

**Fifteenth Amendment**  one of three Civil War amendments; guaranteed voting rights for African American men

**fighting words**  speech that directly incites damaging conduct

**filibuster**  a tactic used by members of the Senate to prevent action on legislation they oppose by continuously holding the floor and speaking until the majority backs down. Once given the floor, senators have unlimited time to speak, and it requires a vote of three-fifths of the Senate to end a filibuster

**fiscal policy**  the use of taxing, monetary, and spending powers to manipulate the economy

**527 committee**  nonprofit independent groups that receive and disburse funds to influence the nomination, election, or defeat of candidates. Named after Section 527 of the Internal Revenue Code, which defines and provides tax-exempt status for nonprofit advocacy groups

**food stamps**  coupons that can be exchanged for food at most grocery stores; the largest in-kind benefits program

**Fourteenth Amendment** one of three Civil War amendments; guaranteed equal protection and due process

**framing** the power of the media to influence how events and issues are interpreted

**free exercise clause** the First Amendment clause that protects a citizen's right to believe and practice whatever religion one chooses

**free riders** those who enjoy the benefits of collective goods but did not participate in acquiring them

**full faith and credit clause** provision from Article IV, Section 1 of the Constitution, requiring that the states normally honor the public acts and judicial decisions that take place in another state

**General Agreement Tariffs and Trade (GATT)** international trade organization, in existence from 1947 to 1995, that set many of the rules governing international trade

**general revenue sharing** the process by which one unit of government fields a portion of its tax income to another unit of government, according to an established formula. Revenue sharing typically involves the national government providing money to state governments

**gerrymandering** the process of redrawing legislative district boundary lines to provide political advantage or disadvantage

**government** institutions and procedures through which a territory and its people are ruled

**government corporation** a government agency that performs a service normally provided by the private sector

**grand jury** jury that determines whether sufficient evidence is available to justify a trial; grand juries do not rule on the accused's guilt or innocence

**grants-in-aid** programs through which Congress provides money to state and local governments on the condition that the funds be employed for purposes defined by the federal government

**grassroots mobilization** a lobbying campaign in which a group mobilizes its membership to contact government officials in support of the group's position

**Great Compromise** the agreement reached at the Constitutional Convention of 1787 where representation in the House of Representatives would be apportioned according to the number of inhabitants in each state, but in the Senate each state would have an equal vote regardless of its population

**habeas corpus** a court order demanding that an individual in custody be brought into court and shown the cause for detention

**home rule** power delegated by the state to a local unit of government to manage its own affairs

**impeachment** the formal charge by the House of Representatives that a government official has committed "Treason, Bribery, or other high Crimes and Misdemeanors"

**implementation** the efforts of departments and agencies to carry out the objectives of the organization as laid down by its board of directors (if a private company) or by law (if a public agency)

**implied powers** powers derived from the necessary and proper clause of Article I, Section 8, of the Constitution. Such powers are not specifically expressed, but are implied through the expansive interpretation of delegated powers

**incorporation** the process by which court decisions have required the states to follow parts of the Bill of Rights based on the use or application of the Fourteenth Amendment

**incumbency** the ability to retain office election after election

**incumbent** a candidate running for a position that he or she already holds

**independent agency** an agency that is not part of a Cabinet department

**indexing** periodic process of adjusting social benefits or wages to account for increases in the cost of living

**informational benefits** special newsletters, periodicals, training programs, conferences, and other information provided to members of groups to entice others to join

**inherent powers** powers claimed by a president that are not expressed in the Constitution, but are inferred from it

**in-kind benefits** noncash goods and services provided to needy individuals and families by the federal government that the beneficiary would otherwise have to pay for in cash

**institutional advertising** advertising designed to create a positive image of an organization

**interest group** a voluntary membership association organized to pursue a common interest or interests, through political participation, toward the ultimate goal of getting favorable public policy decisions from government

**International Monetary Fund (IMF)** an institution that provides loans and facilitates international monetary exchange

**iron triangle** the stable, cooperative relationships that often develop between a congressional committee, an administrative agency, and one or more supportive interest groups. Similar relationships with more than three parties exist, but the iron triangle is the most typical

**isolationism** desire to avoid involvement in the affairs of other nations

**joint committee** a legislative committee formed of members of both the House and the Senate

**judicial activism** judicial philosophy that posits that the court should go beyond the words of the Constitution or a statute to consider the broader societal implications of its decisions

**judicial restraint** judicial philosophy whose adherents refuse to go beyond the clear words of the Constitution in interpreting its meaning

**judicial review** the power of the courts to rule on the constitutionality of actions of the legislative and executive branches, or the states. The Supreme Court asserted this power in *Marbury v. Madison* (1803)

**jurisdiction** the sphere of a court's power and authority

**Kitchen Cabinet** an informal group of advisers to whom the president turns for counsel and guidance. Members of the official Cabinet may or may not also be members of the Kitchen Cabinet

**laissez-faire capitalism** an economic system in which the means of production and distribution are privately owned and operated for profit with minimal or no government interference

**legislative initiative** the president's implied power to bring a legislative agenda before Congress

**libel** a written statement, made in "reckless disregard of the truth," which is considered damaging to a victim because it is "malicious, scandalous, and defamatory"

**liberal** today, one who generally supports political and social reform; extensive governmental intervention in the economy; the expansion of federal social services; more vigorous efforts on behalf of the poor, minorities, and women; and greater concern for consumers and the environment

**liberty** freedom from government control

**limited government** a government whose powers are defined and limited by a constitution

**lobbying** a strategy by which organized interests seek to influence the passage of legislation or other public policy by exerting direct pressure on members of the legislature or others in government

**logrolling** a legislative practice wherein agreements are made between legislators in voting for or against a bill. Unlike bargaining, parties to logrolling have nothing in common but their desire to exchange support

**majority leader** the elected leader of the majority party in the House of Representatives or in the Senate. In the House, the majority leader is subordinate in the party hierarchy to the Speaker of the House

**majority party** the party that holds the majority of legislative seats in either the House or the Senate

**majority rule/minority rights** the democratic principle that a government follows the preferences of the majority of voters but protects the interests of the minority

**material benefits** special goods, services, or money provided to members of groups to entice others to join

**means testing** a procedure by which potential beneficiaries of a public assistance program establish their eligibility by demonstrating a genuine need for the assistance

**measurement error** failure to identify the true distribution of opinion within a population because of errors such as ambiguous or poorly worded questions

**Medicaid** a federally financed, state-operated program providing medical services to low-income people

**Medicare** a form of national health insurance for the elderly and the disabled

**membership association** an organized group in which members play a substantial role, sitting on committees and engaging in group projects

**merit system** a product of civil service reform, in which appointees to positions in public bureaucracies must objectively be deemed qualified for the position

**minority leader** the elected leader of the minority party in the House or Senate

**minority party** the party that holds a minority of legislative seats in either the House or the Senate

**Miranda rule** the requirement, articulated by the Supreme Court in *Miranda v. Arizona* (1966), that persons under arrest must be informed prior to police interrogation of their rights to remain silent and to have the benefit of legal counsel

**monetary policy** an effort to regulate the economy through the manipulation of the supply of money and credit. America's most powerful institution in this area of monetary policy is the Federal Reserve Board

**multiple-member district** an electorate that selects all candidates at large from the whole district; each voter is given the number of votes equivalent to the number of seats to be filled

**nation-state** a political entity consisting of people with some common cultural experience (nation) who also share a common political authority (state), recognized by the sovereignties (nation-states)

**necessary and proper clause** from Article I, Section 8 of the Constitution, it provides Congress with the authority to make all laws necessary and proper to carry out its expressed powers

**New Federalism** policy of Presidents Nixon and Reagan to return power to the states through block grants

**New Jersey Plan** a framework for the Constitution, introduced by William Paterson, which called for equal state representation in the national legislature regardless of population

**New Politics movement** a political movement that began in the 1960s and 1970s, made up of professionals and intellectuals for whom the civil rights and antiwar movements were formative experiences. The New Politics movement strengthened public-interest groups

**news enclave** a group seeking specialized information not provided by the mainstream media

**nomination** the process through which political parties select their candidates for election to public office

**noncontributory programs** social programs that provide assistance to people based on demonstrated need rather than any contribution they have made

**non-state actors** groups other than nation-states that attempt to play a role in the international system. Terrorist groups are one type of non-state actor

**North American Free Trade Agreement (NAFTA)** trade treaty between the

United States, Canada, and Mexico to lower and eliminate tariffs between the three countries

**North Atlantic Treaty Organization (NATO)** a treaty organization, comprising the United States, Canada, and most of Western Europe, formed in 1948 to counter the perceived threat from the Soviet Union

**open primary** a primary election in which registered voters decide on the day of the primary in which party's primary they will participate

**opinion** the written explanation of the Supreme Court's decision in a particular case

**oral argument** stage in Supreme Court procedure in which attorneys for both sides appear before the Court to present their positions and answer questions posed by justices

**original jurisdiction** the authority to initially consider a case. Distinguished from appellate jurisdiction, which is the authority to hear the appeals from a lower court's decision

**oversight** the effort by Congress, through hearings, investigations, and other techniques, to exercise control over the activities of executive agencies by overseeing or supervising how legislation is carried out by the executive branch

**party identification** an individual voter's psychological ties to one party or another

**party unity vote** a roll-call vote in the House or Senate in which at least 50 percent of the members of one party take a particular position and are opposed by at least 50 percent of the members of the other party. Party votes are rare today, although they were fairly common in the nineteenth century

**patronage** the resources available to higher officials, including making partisan appointments to offices, and conferring grants, licenses, or special favors to supporters

***per curiam*** decision by an appellate court, without a written opinion, that refuses to review the decision of a lower court; amounts to reaffirmation of the lower court's opinion

**plaintiff** the individual or organization that brings a complaint or charges in court

**plea bargains** negotiated agreements in criminal cases in which a defendant agrees to plead guilty in return for the state's agreement to reduce the severity of the criminal charge the defendent is facing

**pluralism** the theory that all interests are and should be free to compete for influence in the government. The outcome of this competition is compromise and moderation

**plurality system** a type of electoral system in which, to win a seat in the parliament or other representative body, a candidate need only receive the most votes in the election, not necessarily a majority of the votes cast

**pocket veto** a presidential veto that occurs if the president does not sign a given piece of legislation passed during the final ten days of a legislative session if Congress, by its adjournment, prevents the bill from being returned to it

**police power** power reserved to the government to regulate the health, safety, and morals of its citizens

**political action committee (PAC)** a private group that raises and distributes funds for use in election campaigns

**political efficacy** the ability to influence government and politics

**political equality** the right to participate in politics equally, based on the principle of "one person, one vote"

**political parties** organized groups that attempt to influence the government by electing their members to important government offices

**political socialization** the process by which people learn political attitudes and beliefs

**politics** conflict over the leadership, structure, and policies of governments

**popular sovereignty** a principle of democracy in which political authority rests ultimately in the hands of the people

**pork barrel (or pork)** appropriations made by legislative bodies for local projects that are often not needed but that are created to help local representatives win re-election in their home districts

**power** influence over a government's leadership, organization, or policies

**precedent** prior case whose principles are used by judges as the basis for their decisions in present cases

**preemption** the principle that allows the national government to override state or local actions in certain policy areas

**preventive war** policy of striking first when a nation fears that a foreign foe is contemplating hostile action

**preferred freedoms** certain protections in the Bill of Rights, such as free speech and free press, that are considered even more important than other freedoms

**primary elections** elections used to select a party's candidate for the general election

**priming** preparing the public to take a particular view of an event or political actor

**prior restraint** an effort by a government agency to block the publication of material it deems libelous or harmful in some other way; censorship. In the United States, the courts forbid prior restraint except under the most extraordinary circumstances

**private bill** a bill in Congress to provide a specific person with some kind of relief, such as a special exemption from immigration quotas

**privatization** removing all or part of a program from the public sector to the private sector

**privileges and immunities clause** provision from Article IV, Section 2 of the Constitution, that citizens of one state should be entitled to similar treatment in other states

**probability sampling** a method used by pollsters to select a sample in which every individual in the population has an equal probability of being selected as a respondent so that the correct weight can be given to all segments of the population

**proportional representation** a multiple-member district system that allows each political party representation in proportion to its percentage of the total vote

**public opinion** citizens' attitudes about political issues, leaders, institutions, and events

**public opinion polls** scientific instruments for measuring public opinion

**public policy** a purpose or goal expressed by the government that is backed by a sanction (a reward or punishment)

**purposive benefits** selective benefits of group membership that emphasize the purpose and accomplishments of the group

**push polling** a polling technique in which the questions are designed to shape the respondent's opinion

**random digit dialing** polls in which respondents are selected at random from a list of ten-digit telephone numbers, with every effort made to avoid bias in the construction of the sample

**random sampling** a method of measuring popular opinion whereby a small group of people, randomly selected from the population as a whole, may be considered representative, as long as every person had an equal chance of being picked

**recall** removal of a public official by popular vote

**redistricting** the process of redrawing election districts and redistributing legislative representatives. This happens every ten years to reflect shifts in population or in response to legal challenges to existing districts

**referendum** the practice of referring a measure proposed or passed by a legislature to the vote of the electorate for approval or rejection

**regulatory agencies** agencies whose main job is to control some specific conduct in society through the issuance of rules and penalties if those rules are violated

**representative democracy/republic** a system of government that gives citizens a regular opportunity to elect government officials

**reserved powers** the Tenth Amendment to the Constitution that aims to reserve powers to the states

**revenue agencies** agencies responsible for collecting taxes. Examples include the Internal Revenue Service for income taxes, the U.S. Customs Service for tariffs and other taxes on imported goods, and the Bureau of Alcohol, Tobacco, and Firearms for collection of taxes on the sales of those particular products

**right of rebuttal** a Federal Communications Commission regulation giving individuals the right to have the opportunity to respond to personal attacks made on a radio or television broadcast

**right to privacy** the right to be let alone, which has been interpreted by the Supreme Court to entail free access to birth control and abortions

**roll-call vote** a vote in which each legislator's yes or no vote is recorded as the clerk calls the names of the members alphabetically

**sample** a small group selected by researchers to represent the most important characteristics of an entire population

**select committee** a (usually) temporary legislative committee set up to highlight or investigate a particular issue or address an issue not within the jurisdiction of existing committees

**selection bias** polling error that arises when the sample is not representative of the population being studied, which create errors in overrepresenting or underrepresenting some opinions

**senatorial courtesy** the practice whereby the president, before formally nominating a person for a federal judgeship, seeks the indication that senators from the candidate's own state support the nomination

**seniority** priority or status ranking given to an individual on the basis of length of continuous service on a committee in Congress

**"separate but equal" rule** doctrine that public accommodations could be segregated by race but still be equal

**separation of powers** the division of governmental power among several institutions that must cooperate in decision making

**signing statement** an announcement made by the president when signing bills into law, often presenting the president's interpretation of the law

**single-member district** an electorate that is allowed to select only one representative from each district; the normal method of representation in the United States

**slander** an oral statement, made in "reckless disregard of the truth," which is considered damaging to the victim because it is "malicious, scandalous, and defamatory"

**Social Security** a contributory welfare program into which working Americans contribute a percentage of their wages, and from which they receive cash benefits after retirement

**sociological representation** a type of representation in which representatives have the same racial, ethnic, religious, or educational backgrounds as their constituents. It is based on the principle that if two individuals are similar in background, character, interests, and perspectives, then one could better represent the other's views

**solicitor general** the top government lawyer in all cases before the Supreme Court where the government is a party

**solidary benefits** selective benefits of a group membership of an emotional nature that include friendship, networking, and consciousness-raising

**Speaker of the House** the chief presiding officer of the House of Representatives. The Speaker is elected at the beginning of every Congress on a straight party vote. The Speaker is the most important party and House leader, and can influence the legislative agenda, the fate of individual pieces of legislation, and members' positions within the House

**speech plus** speech accompanied by conduct or physical activity such as sit-ins, picketing, and demonstrations; protection of this form of speech under the First

Amendment is conditional, and restrictions imposed by state or local authorities are acceptable if properly balanced by considerations of public order

**staff organization** type of membership group in which a professional staff conducts most of the group's activities

**standing committee** a permanent committee with the power to propose and write legislation that covers a particular subject, such as finance or appropriations

***stare decisis*** literally, "let the decision stand." The doctrine that a previous decision by a court applies as a precedent in similar cases until that decision is overruled

**states' rights** the principle that the states should oppose the increasing authority of the national government. This principle was most popular in the period before the Civil War

**strict scrutiny** test, used by the Supreme Court in racial discrimination cases and other cases involving civil liberties and civil rights, which places the burden of proof on the government rather than on the challengers to show that the law in question is constitutional

**subsidies** government grants of cash or other valuable commodities such as land to individuals or organizations; used to promote activities desired by the government, to reward political support, or to buy off political opposition

**suffrage** the right to vote; also called franchise

**supremacy clause** Article VI of the Constitution, which states that laws passed by the national government and all treaties "shall be the supreme law of the land" and superior to all laws adopted by any state or any subdivision

**supreme court** the highest court in a particular state or in the United States. This court primarily serves an appellate function

**tax expenditures** government subsidies provided to employers and employees through tax deductions for amounts spent on health insurance and other benefits; these represent one way the government helps to ensure the social welfare of the middle class

**term limits** legally set limits on the number of terms an elected official can serve

**third parties** parties that organize to compete against the two major American political parties

**Thirteenth Amendment** one of three Civil War amendments; abolished slavery

**Three-fifths Compromise** the agreement reached at the Constitutional Convention of 1787 that stipulated that for purposes of the apportionment of congressional seats, five slaves would count as three free persons

**totalitarian government** a system of rule in which the government not only exercises great power, but seeks to impose its will by suppressing any and all other groups and individuals in society that might pose a challenge to its power

**trial court** the first court to hear a criminal or civil case

**turnout** the percentage of eligible individuals who actually vote

**two-party system** a political system in which only two parties have a realistic opportunity to compete effectively for control of the government

**tyranny** oppressive and unjust government that employs cruel and unjust use of power and authority

**unfunded mandates** regulations or conditions for receiving grants that impose costs on state and local governments for which they are not reimbursed by the federal government

**unitary system** a governing system that gives most power to the federal or national government

**United Nations (UN)** an organization of nations founded in 1945 to serve as a channel for negotiation and a means of settling international disputes peaceably.

The UN has had frequent successes in providing a forum for negotiation and on some occasions a means of preventing international conflicts from spreading. On a number of occasions, the UN has supported U.S. foreign policy goals

**veto** the president's constitutional power to prevent a bill from becoming a law. A presidential veto may be overridden by a two-thirds vote of each house of Congress

**Virginia Plan** a framework for the Constitution, introduced by Edmund Randolph, which provided for a system of representation in the national legislature based upon the population of each state

**War Powers Resolution** a resolution of Congress that the president can send troops into action abroad only by authorization of Congress, or if American troops are already under attack or serious threat

**whips** party members in the House or Senate who are responsible for coordinating the party's legislative strategy, building support for key issues, and counting votes

**White House staff** analysts and advisers to the president, often given the title "special assistant"

**World Trade Organization (WTO)** international organization promoting free trade that grew out of the General Agreement on Tariffs and Trade

**writ of *certiorari*** a decision of at least four of the nine Supreme Court justices to review a decision of a lower court; from the Latin "to make more certain"

**writ of *habeas corpus*** a court order that the individual in custody be brought into court and shown the cause for detention. *Habeas corpus* is guaranteed by the Constitution and can be suspended only in cases of rebellion or invasion

# endnotes

## Chapter 1

1. Pew Research Center, "Senate Legislative Process a Mystery to Many," January 28, 2010, http://people-press.org/report/586/; "Public Knows Basic Facts about Financial Crisis" April 9, 2009, http://pewresearch.org/pubs/1179/economic-news-iq-quiz.
2. See Eugen Weber, *Peasants into Frenchmen: The Modernization of Rural France, 1870–1914* (Stanford, CA: Stanford University Press, 1976), chap. 5.
3. See V. O. Key, *Politics, Parties, and Pressure Groups* (New York: Crowell, 1964), p. 201.
4. Harold Lasswell, *Politics: Who Gets What, When, How* (New York: Meridian Books, 1958).
5. Susan B. Carter, Scott Sigmund Gartner, Michael R. Haines, Alan L. Olmsted, Richard Sutch, and Gavin Wright, eds., *Historical Statistics of the United States: Millennial Edition Online*, Table Aa145–184, Population, By Sex and Race: 1790–1990 (New York: Cambridge University Press, 2006). Current data available at U.S. Census Bureau, www.census.gov (accessed 4/15/10).
6. Carter et al., *Historical Statistics of the United States*, Table Aa145–184, Population, By Sex and Race: 1790–1990.
7. Carter et al., *Historical Statistics of the United States*, Table Aa145–184, Population, By Sex and Race: 1790–1990; Table Aa2189–2215, Hispanic Population Estimates.
8. U.S. Census Bureau, "Statistical Abstract of the United States," www.census.gov (accessed 11/13/07); Claude S. Fischer and Michael Hout, *A Century of Difference: How America Changed in the Last One Hundred Years* (New York: Russell Sage Foundation, 2006), p. 36.
9. Carter et al., *Historical Statistics of the United States*, Table Aa22–35, Selected Population Characteristics.
10. Michael B. Katz and Mark J. Stern, *One Nation Divisible: What America Was and What It Is Becoming* (New York: Russell Sage Foundation, 2006), p. 16.
11. Carter et al., *Historical Statistics of the United States*, Table Aa145–184, Population, By Sex and Race: 1790–1990.
12. U.S. Census Bureau, "Annual Estimates of the Population by Sex, Race, and Hispanic or Latino Origin for the United States: April 1, 2000, to July 1, 2006 (NC-EST2006-03)," www.census.gov/popest/national/asrh/NC-EST2006-srh .html (accessed 10/17/07).
13. U.S. Census Bureau, "Population Profile of the United States: Dynamic Version," www.census.gov/population/pop-profile/dynamic/ForeignBorn.pdf (accessed 12/2/07).

14. Jeffrey S. Passel, "Size and Characteristics of the Unauthorized Migrant Population in the U.S.," Pew Hispanic Center, March 7, 2006, www.pewhispanic.org/files/reports/61.pdf (accessed 10/17/07).

15. Anthony Faiola, "States' Immigrant Policies Diverge," *Washington Post,* October 15, 2007, p. A1.

16. Fischer and Hout, *A Century of Difference,* p. 187; The Pew Forum on Religion and Public Life, http://pewforum.org/world-affairs/countries/?CountryID=222 (accessed 10/17/07).

17. Fischer and Hout, *A Century of Difference,* p. 187; The Pew Forum on Religion and Public Life, http://pewforum.org/world-affairs/countries/?CountryID=222 (accessed 10/17/07).

18. Carter et al., *Historical Statistics of the United States,* Table Aa125-144, Population, By Age: 1900–2000; U.S. Census Bureau, "National Population Estimates," www.census.gov/popest/national/asrh/ (accessed 10/17/07).

19. Michael R. Haines, "Population Characteristics," *Historical Statistics of the United States,* pp. 1–21.

20. Constitution of the United States of America, Article I, Section 2; U.S. Census Bureau, "Congressional Apportionment: Census 2000 Brief," www.census.gov/prod/2001pubs/c2kbr01-7.pdf (accessed 10/20/07).

21. Herbert McClosky and John Zaller, *The American Ethos: Public Attitudes toward Capitalism and Democracy* (Cambridge, MA: Harvard University Press, 1984), p. 19.

22. J. R. Pole, *The Pursuit of Equality in American History* (Berkeley: University of California Press, 1978), p. 19.

## Chapter 2

1. Michael Kammen, *A Machine That Would Go of Itself* (New York: Vintage, 1986), p. 22.

2. The social makeup of colonial America and some of the social conflicts that divided colonial society are discussed in Jackson Turner Main, *The Social Structure of Revolutionary America* (Princeton, NJ: Princeton University Press, 1965).

3. George B. Tindall and David E. Shi, *America: A Narrative History,* 8th ed. (New York: Norton, 2009), p. 194.

4. For a discussion of events leading up to the Revolution, see Charles M. Andrews, *The Colonial Background of the American Revolution* (New Haven, CT: Yale University Press, 1924).

5. See Carl Becker, *The Declaration of Independence* (New York: Knopf, 1942).

6. See Merrill Jensen, *The Articles of Confederation* (Madison: University of Wisconsin Press, 1970).

7. Reported in Samuel E. Morrison, Henry Steele Commager, and William Leuchtenberg, *The Growth of the American Republic* (New York: Oxford University Press, 1969), vol. 1, p. 244.

8. Quoted in Morrison et al., *The Growth of the American Republic,* vol. 1, p. 242.

9. Charles A. Beard, *An Economic Interpretation of the Constitution of the United States* (New York: Macmillan, 1913).

10. Madison's notes, along with the somewhat less complete records kept by several other participants in the convention, are available in a four-volume set. See

Max Farrand, ed., *The Records of the Federal Convention of 1787*, 4 vols., rev. ed. (New Haven, CT: Yale University Press, 1966).

11. Farrand, ed., *The Records of the Federal Convention of 1787*, vol. 2, p. 10.
12. E. M. Earle, ed., *The Federalist* (New York: Modern Library, 1937), No. 71.
13. Earle, ed., *The Federalist*, No. 62.
14. Max Farrand, *The Framing of the Constitution of the United States* (New Haven, CT: Yale University Press, 1962), 49.
15. Richard E. Neustadt, *Presidential Power* (New York: Wiley, 1960), p. 33.
16. Melancton Smith, quoted in Herbert J. Storing, *What the Anti-Federalists Were For* (Chicago: University of Chicago, 1981), p. 17.
17. Earle, ed., *The Federalist*, No. 57.
18. "Essays of Brutus," No. 15, in Storing, ed., *The Complete Anti-Federalist*.
19. Earle, ed., *The Federalist*, No. 10.
20. Earle, ed., *The Federalist*, No. 51.
21. Garry Wills, *A Necessary Evil* (New York: Simon & Schuster, 1999), p. 297.

## Chapter 3

1. Kim Geiger, "Senate Bill Pushes Phone Driving Ban." *Los Angeles Times*, October 14, 2009, p. A16.
2. Dan Ring, "8,100 Gay, Lesbian Couples Marry after 2004 Decision," *Springfield Republican*, May 17, 2006, p. 1.
3. www.ncsl.org/IssuesResearch/HumanServices/SameSexMarriage/tabid/16430/Default.aspx (accessed February 2, 2010).
4. *Hicklin v. Orbeck*, 437 U.S. 518 (1978).
5. *Sweeny v. Woodall*, 344 U.S. 86 (1953).
6. Marlise Simons, "France Won't Extradite American Convicted of Murder," *New York Times*, December 5, 1997, p. A9.
7. A good discussion of the constitutional position of local governments is in York Willbern, *The Withering Away of the City* (Bloomington: Indiana University Press, 1971). For more on the structure and theory of federalism, see Thomas R. Dye, *American Federalism: Competition among Governments* (Lexington, MA: Lexington Books, 1990), chap. 1; and Martha Derthick, "Up-to-Date in Kansas City: Reflections on American Federalism" (the 1992 John Gaus Lecture), *PS: Political Science & Politics* 25 (December 1992): 671–75.
8. For a good treatment of the contrast between national political stability and social instability, see Samuel P. Huntington, *Political Order in Changing Societies* (New Haven, CT: Yale University Press, 1968), chap. 2.
9. *McCulloch v. Maryland*, 4 Wheaton 316 (1819).
10. *Gibbons v. Ogden*, 9 Wheaton 1 (1824).
11. The Sherman Antitrust Act, adopted in 1890, for example, was enacted not to restrict commerce, but rather to protect it from monopolies, or trusts, so as to prevent unfair trade practices and to enable the market again to become self-regulating. Moreover, the Supreme Court sought to uphold liberty of contract to protect businesses. For example, in *Lochner v. New York*, 198 U.S. 45 (1905), the Court invalidated a New York law regulating the sanitary conditions and hours of labor of bakers on the grounds that the law interfered with liberty of contract.
12. Kenneth T. Palmer, "The Evolution of Grant Policies," in *The Changing Politics of Federal Grants*, by Lawrence D. Brown, James W. Fossett, and Kenneth T. Palmer (Washington, DC: Brookings, 1984), p. 15.

13. Palmer, "The Evolution of Grant Policies," p. 6.
14. The key case in this process of expanding the power of the national government is generally considered to be *NLRB v. Jones & Laughlin Steel Corporation*, 301 U.S. 1 (1937), in which the Supreme Court approved federal regulation of the workplace and thereby virtually eliminated interstate commerce as a limit on the national government's power.
15. *U.S. v. Darby Lumber Co.*, 312 U.S. 100 (1941).
16. W. John Moore, "Pleading the 10th," *National Journal*, July 29, 1995, p. 1940.
17. *Printz v. United States*, 521 U.S. 898 (1997).
18. *Seminole Indian Tribe v. Florida*, 517 U.S. 44 (1996).
19. *Federal Maritime Commission v. Carolina State Ports Authority*, 535 U.S. 743 (2002).
20. *Nevada Department of Human Resources v. Hibbs*, 538 U.S. 721 (2003).
21. Morton Grozdins, *The American System*, ed. Daniel J. Elazar (Chicago: Rand McNally, 1966).
22. See Terry Sanford, *Storm Over the States* (New York: McGraw-Hill, 1967).
23. James L. Sundquist with David W. Davis, *Making Federalism Work* (Washington, DC: Brookings, 1969), p. 271. Wallace was mistrusted by the architects of the War on Poverty because he was a strong proponent of racial segregation. He believed in "states' rights," which meant that states, not the federal government, should decide what liberty and equality meant.
24. See Don Kettl, *The Regulation of American Federalism* (Baton Rouge: Louisiana State University Press, 1983).
25. Eliza Newlin Carney, "Power Grab," *National Journal*, April 11, 1998, p. 798.
26. See Advisory Commission on Intergovernmental Relations, *Federal Regulation of State and Local Governments: The Mixed Record of the 1980s* (Washington, DC: Advisory Commission on Intergovernmental Relations, July 1993).
27. Advisory Commission on Intergovernmental Relations, *Federal Regulation of State and Local Governments*, p. iii.
28. Advisory Commission on Intergovernmental Relations, *Federal Regulation of State and Local Governments*, p. 51.
29. Robert Frank, "Proposed Block Grants Seen Unlikely to Cure Management Problems," *Wall Street Journal*, May 1, 1995, p. 1.
30. Judith Havemann, "Scholars Question Whether Welfare Shift Is Reform," *Washington Post*, April 20, 1995, p. A8.
31. "Political License in New York," *New York Times*, September 29, 2007, p. A14.
32. Sarah Kershaw, "Eight States to Press Bush on Insurance Coverage of Children," *New York Times*, October 2, 2007, p. B1.
33. *Massachusetts v. Environmental Protection Agency*, 127 S. Ct. 1438 (2007).
34. Kate Phillips, "South Carolina Governor Rejects Stimulus Money," *New York Times*, March 20, 2009, http://thecaucus.blogs.nytimes.com/2009/03/20/round-2-omb-rejects-sc-governors-stimulus-plan/ (accessed 10/06/2009).
35. Robert Pear and J. David Goodman, "Governors' Fight Over Stimulus May Define G.O.P.," *New York Times*, February 22, 2009, www.nytimes.com/2009/02/23/us/politics/23governors.html (accessed 10/07/2009).
36. The White House, Office of the Press Secretary, Memorandum for the Heads of Executive Departments and Agencies, Subject: Preemption, May 20, 2009, http://theusconstitution.org/blog.histroy/wp-content/uploads/2009/05/obama-preemption-memo-5202009.pdf (accessed 10/17/09).

37. Carrie Johnson, "U.S. Eases Stance on Medical Marijuana," *Washington Post*, October 20, 2009, p. 1.

## Chapter 4

1. Clinton Rossiter, ed., *The Federalist Papers* (New York: New American Library, 1961), No. 84, p. 513.
2. Rossiter, ed., *The Federalist Papers*, No. 84, p. 513.
3. Let there be no confusion about the words "liberty" and "freedom." They are synonymous and interchangeable. "Freedom" comes from the German *Freiheit*. "Liberty" is from the French *liberté*. Although people sometimes try to make them appear to be different, both of them have equal concern with the absence of restraints on individual choices of action.
4. *Barron v. Baltimore*, 7 Peters 243, 246 (1833).
5. The Fourteenth Amendment also seems designed to introduce civil rights. The final clause of the all-important Section 1 provides that no state can "deny to any person within its jurisdiction the equal protection of the laws." It is reasonable to conclude that the purpose of this provision was to obligate the state governments as well as the national government to take *positive* actions to protect citizens from arbitrary and discriminatory actions, at least those based on race.
6. For example, *The Slaughterhouse Cases*, 16 Wallace 36 (1883).
7. *Chicago, Burlington and Quincy Railroad Company v. Chicago*, 166 U.S. 226 (1897).
8. *Gitlow v. New York*, 268 U.S. 652 (1925).
9. *Near v. Minnesota*, 283 U.S. 697 (1931); *Hague v. C.I.O.*, 307 U.S. 496 (1939).
10. Quoted in Henry J. Abraham, *Freedom and the Court: Civil Rights and Liberties in the United States*, 6th ed. (New York: Oxford University Press, 1994), p. 14.
11. *Abington School District v. Schempp*, 374 U.S. 203 (1963).
12. *Engel v. Vitale*, 370 U.S. 421 (1962).
13. *Doe v. Santa Fe Independent School District*, 530 U.S. 290 (2000).
14. *Wallace v. Jaffree*, 472 U.S. 38 (1985).
15. *Lynch v. Donnelly*, 465 U.S. 668 (1984).
16. *Zelman v. Simmons-Harris*, 536 U.S. 639 (2002).
17. *Zelman v. Simmons-Harris*, 536 U.S. 639 (2002).
18. *Van Orden v. Perry*, 545 U.S. 677 (2005).
19. *McCreary v. ACLU*, 545 U.S. 844 (2005).
20. *West Virginia State Board of Education v. Barnette*, 319 U.S. 624 (1943). The case it reversed was *Minersville School District v. Gobitus*, 310 U.S. 586 (1940).
21. *Employment Division, Department of Human Resources of Oregon v. Smith*, 494 U.S. 872 (1990).
22. *Wisconsin v. Yoder*, 406 U.S. 205 (1972).
23. Adam Liptak, "Justices, 5-4, Reject Corporate Campaign Spending Limit," *New York Times*, January 22, 2010, A1.
24. David D. Kirkpatrick, "Lobbies' New Power: Cross Us, And Our Cash Will Bury You," *New York Times*, January 22, 2010, A1.
25. *Abrams v. U.S.*, 250 U.S. 616 (1919).
26. *U.S. v. Carolene Products Company*, 304 U.S. 144 (1938), note 4. This footnote is one of the Court's most important doctrines. See Alfred H. Kelly, Winfred A. Harbison, and Herman Belz, *The American Constitution: Its Origins and Development*, 7th ed. (New York: Norton, 1991), vol. 2, pp. 519–23.

27. *Schenk v. U.S.*, 249 U.S. 47 (1919).
28. *Stromberg v. California*, 283 U.S. 359 (1931).
29. *Texas v. Johnson*, 488 U.S. 884 (1989).
30. *United States v. Eichman*, 496 U.S. 310 (1990).
31. *Virginia v. Black*, 528 U.S. 343 (2003).
32. For a good general discussion of "speech plus," see Louis Fisher, *American Constitutional Law* (New York: McGraw-Hill, 1990), pp. 544–46. The case upholding the buffer zone against the abortion protesters is *Madsen v. Women's Health Center*, 114 S.Ct. 2516 (1994).
33. *Near v. Minnesota*, 283 U.S. 697 (1931).
34. *New York Times v. U.S.*, 403 U.S. 731 (1971).
35. *Branzburg v. Hayes*, 408 U.S. 656 (1972).
36. *New York Times v. Sullivan*, 376 U.S. 254 (1964).
37. *Roth v. U.S.*, 354 U.S. 476 (1957).
38. Concurring opinion in *Jacobellis v. Ohio*, 378 U.S. 184 (1964).
39. *Miller v. California*, 413 U.S. 15 (1973).
40. *Reno v. American Civil Liberties Union*, 521 U.S. 844 (1997).
41. *U.S. v. American Library Association*, 539 U.S. 194 (2003).
42. *Chaplinsky v. State of New Hampshire*, 315 U.S. 568 (1942). This case was reaffirmed in a much more famous and important case decided at the height of the cold war, when the Supreme Court held that "there is no substantial public interest in permitting certain kinds of utterances: the lewd and obscene, the profane, the libelous, and the insulting or 'fighting' words—those which by their very utterance inflict injury or tend to incite an immediate breach of the peace."
43. *Broadcasting Company v. Acting Attorney General*, 405 U.S. 1000 (1972).
44. *Board of Trustees of the State University of New York v. Fox*, 492 U.S. 469 (1989). This case arose from an attempt to sell Tupperware in a dormitory on the State University of New York (SUNY) Cortland campus.
45. *City Council v. Taxpayers for Vincent*, 466 U.S. 789 (1984).
46. *Posadas de Puerto Rico Associates v. Tourism Company of Puerto Rico*, 479 U.S. 328 (1986).
47. *Bethel School District v. Fraser*, 478 U.S. 675 (1986).
48. *Hazelwood v. Kuhlmeier*, 484 U.S. 260 (1988).
49. *Morse v. Frederick*, 06-278 (2007).
50. *U.S. v. Miller*, 307 U.S. 174 (1939). This view has been accepted in over forty lower federal court decisions from the 1940s to the present.
51. *Presser v. Illinois*, 116 U.S. 252 (1886).
52. *D.C. v. Heller*, 07-290 U.S. 5268 (2008).
53. 08–1521 (2010).
54. *Horton v. California*, 496 U.S. 128 (1990).
55. *Mapp v. Ohio*, 367 U.S. 643 (1961). Although Mapp went free in this case, she was later convicted in New York on narcotics trafficking charges and served nine years of a twenty-year sentence.
56. For a good discussion of the issue, see Fisher, *American Constitutional Law*, pp. 884–89.
57. *Brendlin v. California*, 06-820 (2007).
58. *Safford Unified School District No. 1 v. Redding*, 08–479 (2009).
59. *Gideon v. Wainwright*, 372 U.S. 335 (1963). For a full account of the story of the trial and release of Clarence Earl Gideon, see Anthony Lewis, *Gideon's Trumpet*

(New York: Random House, 1964). See also David O'Brien, *Storm Center,* 2nd ed. (New York: Norton, 1990).

60. *Furman v. Georgia,* 408 U.S. 238 (1972).

61. *Gregg v. Georgia,* 428 U.S. 153 (1976).

62. *Baze v. Rees,* 553 U.S. 35 (2008).

63. *Griswold v. Connecticut,* 381 U.S. 479 (1965).

64. *Griswold v. Connecticut,* concurring opinion. In 1972, the Court extended the privacy right to unmarried women: *Eisenstadt v. Baird,* 405 U.S. 438 (1972).

65. *Roe v. Wade,* 410 U.S. 113 (1973).

66. *Lawrence v. Texas,* 539 U.S. 558 (2003).

67. *Missouri ex rel. Gaines v. Canada,* 305 U.S. 337 (1938).

68. *Brown v. Board of Education of Topeka, Kansas,* 347 U.S. 483 (1954).

69. For good treatments of this long stretch of the struggle of the federal courts to integrate the schools, see Paul Brest and Sanford Levinson, *Processes of Constitutional Decision-Making: Cases and Materials,* 2nd ed. (Boston: Little, Brown, 1983), pp. 471–80; and Alfred Kelly et al., *The American Constitution: Its Origins and Development,* 6th ed. (New York: Norton, 1983), pp. 610–16.

70. Pierre Thomas, "Denny's to Settle Bias Cases," *Washington Post,* May 24, 1994, p. A1.

71. John A. Powell, "Segregated Schools Ruling Not All Bad: In Rejecting Seattle's Integration Bid Top Court Majority Also Held that Avoiding Racial Isolation is a Legitimate Public Goal," *Newsday,* July 16, 2007, p. A33.

72. See especially *Katzenbach v. McClung,* 379 U.S. 294 (1964). Almost immediately after passage of the Civil Rights Act of 1964, a case was brought challenging the validity of Title II, which covered discrimination in public accommodations. Ollie's Barbecue was a neighborhood restaurant in Birmingham, Alabama. It was located eleven blocks away from an interstate highway and even farther from railroad and bus stations. Its table service was for whites only; there was only a take-out service for blacks. The Supreme Court agreed that Ollie's was strictly an intrastate restaurant, but since a substantial proportion of its food and other supplies were bought from companies outside the state of Alabama, there was a sufficient connection to interstate commerce; therefore, racial discrimination at such restaurants would "impose commercial burdens of national magnitude upon interstate commerce." Although this case involved Title II, it had direct bearing on the constitutionality of Title VII.

73. In 1970, this act was amended to outlaw for five years literacy tests as a condition for voting in all states.

74. See Douglas S. Massey and Nancy A. Denton, *American Apartheid: Segregation and the Making of the Underclass* (Cambridge, MA: Harvard University Press, 1993), chap. 7.

75. www.naacp.org (accessed May 4, 2010).

76. See Jane J. Mansbridge, *Why We Lost the ERA* (Chicago: University of Chicago Press, 1986); and Gilbert Steiner, *Constitutional Inequality* (Washington, DC: Brookings, 1985).

77. See *Frontiero v. Richardson,* 411 U.S. 677 (1973).

78. *Meritor Savings Bank v. Vinson,* 477 U.S. 57 (1986).

79. *Franklin v. Gwinnett County Public Schools,* 503 U.S. 60 (1992).

80. *U.S. v. Virginia,* 518 U.S. 515 (1996).

81. *Ledbetter v. Goodyear Tire and Rubber Co.* 127 S. Ct. 2162 (2007).

82. *Lau v. Nichols*, 414 U.S. 563 (1974).

83. Dick Kirschten, "Not Black and White," *National Journal*, March 2, 1991, p. 497.

84. See the discussion in Robert A. Katzmann, *Institutional Disability: The Saga of Transportation Policy for the Disabled* (Washington, DC: Brookings, 1986).

85. For example, after pressure from the Justice Department, one of the nation's largest rental-car companies agreed to make special hand-controls available to any customer requesting them. See "Avis Agrees to Equip Cars for Disabled," *Los Angeles Times*, September 2, 1994, p. D1.

86. Supreme Court of the United States, *Gross. FBL Financial Service, Inc., No. 08–411*, www.supremecourtus.gov (accessed 10/22/2009).

87. *Bowers v. Hardwick*, 478 U.S. 186 (1986).

88. Quoted in Joan Biskupic, "Gay Rights Activists Seek a Supreme Court Test Case," *Washington Post*, December 19, 1993, p. A1.

89. *Romer v. Evans*, 517 U.S. 620 (1996).

90. *Lawrence v. Texas*, 539 U.S. 558 (2003).

91. For excellent coverage of the political and constitutional issues surrounding the actions of states on same-sex marriage, see Kenneth Kersch, "Full Faith and Credit for Same-Sex Marriages?" *Political Science Quarterly*, 112, 117–36 (Spring 1997).

92. From Lyndon B. Johnson, *The Vantage Point* (New York: Holt, Rinehart and Winston, 1971), p. 166.

93. The Department of Health, Education, and Welfare (HEW) was the cabinet department charged with administering most federal social programs. In 1980, when education programs were transferred to the newly created Department of Education, HEW was renamed the Department of Health and Human Services.

94. *Regents of the University of California v. Bakke*, 438 U.S. 265 (1978).

95. See, for example, *United Steelworkers v. Weber*, 443 U.S. 193 (1979); and *Fullilove v. Klutznick*, 448 U.S. 448 (1980).

96. *Ward's Cove v. Atonio*, 490 U.S. 642 (1989).

97. *Grutter v. Bollinger*, 539 U.S. 306 (2003).

98. *Gratz v. Bollinger*, 539 U.S. 244 (2003).

## Chapter 5

1. Carol Glynn, et al., *Public Opinion*, 2nd ed. (Boulder, CO: Westview, 2004), p. 293.

2. Benjamin Ginsberg, *The American Lie: Government by the People and Other Political Fables* (Boulder, CO: Paradigm, 2007), p. 79.

3. Erika Falk, et al., "Legislative Issue Advertising in the 108th Congress," Annenberg Public Policy Center, March 2005.

4. For a discussion of the political beliefs of Americans, see Harry Holloway and John George, *Public Opinion* (New York: St. Martin's, 1986). See also Paul R. Abramson, *Political Attitudes in America* (San Francisco: Freeman, 1983).

5. See Angus Campbell et al., *The American Voter* (New York: Wiley, 1960), p. 147.

6. CNN Poll, 2009.

7. CNN Poll, 2009.

8. CBS News/*New York Times* Poll, 2008.

9. Elisabeth Noelle-Neumann, *The Spiral of Silence* (Chicago: University of Chicago Press, 1984).

10. O. R. Holsti, "A Widening Gap between the Military and Society? Some Evidence, 1976–1996," *International Security* 23 (Winter 1998–1999), 5–42.
11. Gerald F. Seib and Michael K. Frisby, "Selling Sacrifice," *Wall Street Journal*, February 5, 1993, p. 1.
12. Michael K. Frisby, "Clinton Seeks Strategic Edge with Opinion Polls," *Wall Street Journal*, June 24, 1996, p. A16.
13. James Carney, "Playing by the Numbers," *Time*, April 11, 1994, p. 40.
14. See Gillian Peele, *Revival and Reaction* (Oxford, UK: Clarendon, 1985). See also Connie Paige, *The Right-to-Lifers* (New York: Summit, 1983).
15. Jason DeParle, "The Clinton Welfare Bill Begins Trek in Congress," *New York Times*, July 15, 1994, p. 1.
16. Joe Queenan, "Birth of a Notion," *Washington Post*, September 20, 1992, p. C1.
17. Herbert Asher, *Polling and the Public* (Washington, DC: Congressional Quarterly Press, 2001), p. 64.
18. John Goyder, Keith Warriner, and Susan Miller, "Evaluating Socioeconomic Status Bias in Survey Nonresponse," *Journal of Officiating Statistics* 18, no. 1 (2002).
19. Anthony Man, "Cell Phone Use Soars, Forcing Pollsters to Change Methods," Fort Lauderdale Sun-Sentinel, March 31, 2010, http://articles.sun-sentinel.com (accessed May 5, 2010). Thanks to Wittenberg University student Jordan Leishman for his assistance.
20. Michael Kagay and Janet Elder, "Numbers Are No Problem for Pollsters, Words Are," *New York Times*, August 9, 1992, p. E6.
21. William Saletan, "Push Me, Poll You," *Slate*, February 15, 2000.
22. Mike McIntire, "Mayoral Race Has Whodunit: The Anti-Ferrer Pollster Calls," *New York Times*, August 30, 2005, p. B1.
23. "Dial S for Smear," *Memphis Commercial Appeal*, September 22, 1996, p. 6B.
24. Benjamin I. Page and Robert Y. Shapiro, "Effects of Public Opinion on Policy," *American Political Science Review* 77 (March 1983): 175–90.
25. Robert A. Erikson, Gerald Wright, and John McIver, *Statehouse Democracy: Public Opinion and Democracy in the American States* (New York: Cambridge University Press, 1994).
26. The results of separate studies by the political scientists Lawrence Jacobs, Robert Shapiro, and Alan Monroe were reported by Richard Morin in "Which Comes First, the Politician or the Poll?" *Washington Post National Weekly Edition*, February 10, 1997, p. 35.

## Chapter 6

1. Benjamin Ginsberg and Martin Shefter, *Politics by Other Means* (New York: Basic Books, 1990), p. 24.
2. CNN.com/Inside Politics, February 18, 2003.
3. Samantha M. Shapiro, "The Dean Connection," *New York Times Magazine*, December 7, 2003, p. 58.
4. David Perlmutter, "Photojournalism in Crisis," *Editor and Publisher*, August 2006. www.editorandpublisher.com/eandp/columns/shoptalk_display.jsp?vnu_content_id=1003019475, (accessed 1/13/10).
5. U.S. Bureau of the Census, *Statistical Abstract of the United States: 1994* (Washington, DC: Department of Commerce, 1994), pp. 567, 576.
6. *Red Lion Broadcasting Company v. FCC*, 395 U.S. 367 (1969).

7. For a criticism of the increasing consolidation of the media, see the essays in Patricia Aufderheide et al., *Conglomerates and the Media* (New York: New York University Press, 1997).

8. See Leo Bogart, "Newspapers in Transition," *Wilson Quarterly*, special issue, 1982; and Richard Harwood, "The Golden Age of Press Diversity," *Washington Post*, July 22, 1994, p. A23.

9. See Benjamin Ginsberg, *The Captive Public* (New York: Basic Books, 1986).

10. Michael Dawson, "Structure and Ideology: The Shaping of Black Public Opinion," paper presented to the 1995 meeting of the Midwest Political Science Association, Chicago, Illinois, April 7, 1995.

11. See the discussions in Gary Paul Gates, *Air Time* (New York: Harper & Row, 1978); Edward Jay Epstein, *News from Nowhere* (New York: Random House, 1973); Michael Parenti, *Inventing Reality* (New York: St. Martin's, 1986); Herbert Gans, *Deciding What's News* (New York: Vintage, 1980); and W. Lance Bennett, *News: The Politics of Illusion* (New York: Longman, 1986).

12. See Tom Burnes, "The Organization of Public Opinion," in *Mass Communication and Society*, ed. James Curran (Beverly Hills, CA: Sage, 1979), pp. 44–230. See also David Altheide, *Creating Reality* (Beverly Hills, CA: Sage, 1976).

13. David Garrow, *Protest at Selma* (New Haven, CT: Yale University Press, 1978).

14. Quoted in Stephen Ansolabehere, Roy Behr, and Shanto Iyengar, *The Media Game* (New York: MacMillan, 1993), p. 142.

15. Katherine Q. Seelye, "Obama Plays Convincing Obama in Skit Mocking Clinton," *New York Times*, November 5, 2007, p. A17.

16. Jonah Goldberg, "Reporters Hate Guns," *Brill's Content*, February 2000, p. 53.

17. Jeff Cohen, "NRA Defines Debate," *Brill's Content*, February 2000, p. 52.

18. Doris Graber, *Mass Media and American Politics* (Washington, DC: Congressional Quarterly Press, 1993), p. 384.

19. Philip M. Taylor, *War and the Media* (Manchester, UK: Manchester University Press, 1992), pp. 67–75.

20. Herbert I. Schiller, *The Mind Manager* (Boston: Beacon Press, 1973): Edward S. Herman and Noam Chomsky, *Manufacturing Consent* (New York: Pantheon, 1988).

21. Graber, *Mass Media and American Politics*, p. 53.

22. See Martin Linsky, *Impact: How the Press Affects Federal Policymaking* (New York: Norton, 1986).

23. For a good discussion of how to evaluate media biases see Don Hazen and Julie Winokur, eds., *We the Media* (New York: New Press, 1997).

## Chapter 7

1. Alan Greenblatt, "With Major Issues Fading, Capitol Life Lures Fewer," *Congressional Quarterly Weekly Report*, October 25, 1997, p. 2625.

2. See Walter Dean Burnham, *Critical Elections and the Mainsprings of American Electoral Politics* (New York: Norton, 1970). See also James L. Sundquist, *Dynamics of the Party System* (Washington, DC: Brookings, 1983).

3. Benjamin Ginsberg, *The Consequences of Consent* (New York: Random House, 1982), chap. 4.

4. For a discussion of third parties in the United States, see Daniel Mazmanian, *Third Parties in Presidential Election* (Washington, DC: Brookings, 1974).

5. See Maurice Duverger, *Political Parties* (New York: Wiley, 1954).

6. Walter Dean Burnham, "The End of American Party Politics, *Transaction* 7 (1969): 12–22.

7. Raymond J. La Raja, "Political Parties in the Era of Soft Money," Sandy L. Maisel, S. L. (ed.), *The Parties Respond: Changes in American Parties and Campaigns*, Fourth Edition, (Boulder, CO: Westview Press, 2002), pp.163–88.

8. On the limited polarization among ordinary voters, see Morris P. Fiorina, with Samuel J. Abrams and Jeremy C. Pope, *Culture War? The Myth of a Polarized America* (New York: Pearson-Longman, 2004); on growing partisan attachment among a subset of voters, see Alan Abramowitz and Kyle Saunders, "Why Can't We All Just Get Along? The Reality of a Polarized America," *The Forum* 3.2 (2005).

9. Robert Jackman, "Political Institutions and Voter Turnout in the Democracies," *American Political Science Review* 81 (June 1987): p. 420.

10. Helen Dewar, "'Motor Voter' Agreement Is Reached," *Washington Post*, April 28, 1993, p. A6.

11. Erik Austin and Jerome Chubb, *Political Facts of the United States since 1789* (New York: Columbia University Press, 1986), pp. 378–79.

12. *League of United Latin American Citizens v. Wilson*, CV-94-7569 (C.D. Calif.) (1995).

13. No. 08-205 (2010)

14. Dan Eggen and T. W. Farnam, "Super PACs Alter Campaign," *The Washington Post*, Sept. 28, 2010, 1.

15. Brody Mullins and Danny Yadron, "GOP Groups Launch Massive Ad Blitz: Alliance Spends $50 Million on Competitive House Races Where Democrats Have Moore Money Now," *The Wall Street Journal*. Oct. 13, 2010. A4; Michael Luo and Griff Palmer, "Outside Groups on the right Flexed Muscles in House Races," *The New York Times*, Nov. 4, 2010, P6.

16. Tom Curry, msnbc.com, www.msnbc.com.

17. Michael Luo and Jeff Zeleny, "Straining to Reach Money Goal, Obama Presses Donors," *New York Times*, September 9, 2008, p.1.

18. *Buckley v. Valeo*, 424 U.S. 1 (1976).

## Chapter 8

1. Dan Eggen and Kimberly Kindy, "Familiar Players in Health Bill Lobbying," *Washington Post*, July 6, 2009, p. 1.

2. Clinton Rossiter, ed., *The Federalist Papers* (New York: New American Library, 1961), No. 10, p. 83.

3. Rossiter, ed., *Federalist Papers*, No. 10.

4. The best statement of the pluralist view is in David Truman, *The Governmental Process* (New York: Knopf, 1951), chap. 2.

5. E. E. Schattschneider, *The Semisovereign People* (New York: Holt, Rinehart and Winston, 1960), p. 35.

6. Betsy Wagner and David Bowermaster, "B.S. Economics," *Washington Monthly*, November 1992, pp. 19–21.

7. Mancur Olson, *The Logic of Collective Action* (Cambridge, MA: Harvard University Press, 1965).

8. Timothy Penny and Steven Schier, *Payment Due: A Nation in Debt, a Generation in Trouble* (Boulder, CO: Westview, 1996), pp. 64–65.

9. Kay Lehman Schlozman and John T. Tierney, *Organized Interests and American Democracy* (New York: Harper & Row, 1986), p. 60.

10. John Herbers, "Special Interests Gaining Power as Voter Disillusionment Grows," *New York Times*, November 14, 1978.

11. For discussions of lobbying, see Allan J. Cigler and Burdett A. Loomis, eds., *Interest Group Politics* (Washington, DC: Congressional Quarterly Press, 1983). See also Jeffrey M. Berry, *Lobbying for the People* (Princeton, NJ: Princeton University Press, 1977).

12. "The Swarming Lobbyists," *Time*, August 7, 1978, p. 15.

13. Leslie Wayne and Michael Moss, "Bailout for Airlines Showed the Weight of a Mighty Lobby," *New York Times*, October 10, 2001, p. A1.

14. John P. Heinz, Edward O. Laumann, Robert L. Nelson, and Robert H. Salisbury, *The Hollow Core: Private Interests in National Policy Making* (Cambridge, MA: Harvard University Press, 1993), p. 96. See also Schlozman and Tierney, *Organized Interests and American Democracy*, chap. 13.

15. David Kirkpatrick, "Congress Finds Ways of Avoiding Lobbyist Limits," *Washington Post*, February 11, 2007, p. 1.

16. A number of important policy domains, such as the environmental and welfare arenas, are controlled not by a highly structured and unified iron triangle but by a concern with the issues in question. Activists and interest groups recognized as being involved in the area are sometimes called "stakeholders" and are customarily invited to testify before congressional committees or give their views to government agencies considering action in their domain.

17. *Roe v. Wade*, 410 U.S. 113 (1973).

18. *Webster v. Reproductive Health Services*, 492 U.S. 490 (1989).

19. *Brown v. Board of Education of Topeka, Kansas*, 347 U.S. 483 (1954).

20. See, for example, *Duke Power Co. v. Carolina Environmental Study Group*, 438 U.S. 59 (1978).

21. E. Pendleton Herring, *Group Representation before Congress* (New York: McGraw-Hill, 1936).

22. Michael Weisskopf, "Energized by Pulpit or Passion, the Public is Calling," *Washington Post*, February 1, 1993, p. 1

23. Julia Preston, "Grass Roots Roared and Immigration Bill Collapsed," *New York Times*, June 10, 2007, p. 1.

24. Richard L. Burke, "Religious-Right Candidates Gain as GOP Turnout Rises," *New York Times*, November 12, 1994, p. 10.

25. Elisabeth R. Gerber, *The Populist Paradox* (Princeton NJ: Princeton University Press, 1999), p. 6.

26. Olson, *The Logic of Collective Action*.

## Chapter 9

1. The historian Garry Wills refers to the idea that the three branches were designed to be coequal as an "extraordinary misperception". *A Necessary Evil* (New York: Simon & Schuster, 1999), p. 84.

2. For data on occupational backgrounds of the members of the 105th Congress, see *Congressional Quarterly Weekly Report*, January 4, 1997.

3. Marian D. Irish and James Prothro, *The Politics of American Democracy*, 5th ed. (Englewood Cliffs, NJ: Prentice Hall, 1971), p. 352.

4. For some interesting empirical evidence see Angus Campbell, Philip Converse, Warren Miller, and Donald Stokes, *Elections and the Political Order* (New York: Wiley, 1966), chap. 11.

5. Dennis Conrad, "AP Impact: House Members Spent $20.3M on Mailing to Constituents," *Cortland Standard*, December 28, 2007, p. 24.

6. John S. Saloma, *Congress and the New Politics* (Boston: Little, Brown, 1969), pp. 184–85. A 1977 official report using less detailed categories came up with almost the same impression of Congress's workload. Commission on Administrative Review, *Administrative Reorganization and Legislative Management*, House Doc. #95-232 (September 28, 1977), vol. 2, especially pp. 17–19.

7. See Barbara C. Burrell, *A Woman's Place Is in the House: Campaigning for Congress in the Feminist Era* (Ann Arbor: University of Michigan Press, 1994); and David Broder, "Key to Women's Political Parity: Running," *Washington Post*, September 8, 1994, p. A17.

8. "Did Redistricting Sink the Democrats?" *National Journal*, December 17, 1994, p. 2984.

9. *Miller v. Johnson*, 515 U.S. 900 (1995).

10. Timothy Eagan, "Built with Steel, Perhaps, but Greased with Pork," *New York Times*, April 10, 2004, p. A1.

11. Tom Hamburger and Richard Simon, "Everybody Will Know If It's Pork," *Los Angeles Times*, January 6, 2007, p. A1.

12. David Clarke, "Earmarks: Here to Stay or Facing Extinction," *Congressional Quarterly (CQ) Weekly*, March 16, 2009, p. 613. Jared Allen, "Lawmakers Purshing for Earmark Reform Think Obama Boosted Their Chances," *The Hill*, January 30, 2010, www.thehill.com (accessed 1/31/10).

13. www.house.gov/stark/services.html.

14. Congressional Quartely, *Guide to the Congress of the United States*, 2nd ed. (Washington, DC: Congressional Quarterly Press, 1976), pp. 229–310.

15. Kelly McCormack, "Private Bills" *The Hill*, May 9, 2007, http://thehill.com/cover-stories/private-bills-2007-05-08.html (accessed 3/20/08).

16. Richard Fenno, Jr., *Home Style: House Members in Their Districts* (Boston: Little, Brown, 1978).

17. Edward Epstein, "Pelosi Proud of Dems' Work in First 100 Days," *San Francisco Chronicle*, March 29, 2007, p. A1.

18. http://home.ourfuture.org/cloture_vote_chart.html (accessed 1/13/10); Steven R. Hurst, "Analysis: Republicans Setting Filibuster Record," March 1, 2010, Associated Press, www.msnbc.msn.com/id/35643530/ns/politics-capitol_hill (accessed 3/17/10).

19. See John W. Kingdon, *Congressmen's Voting Decisions* (New York: Harper & Row, 1973), chap. 3; and R. Douglas Arnold, *The Logic of Congressional Action* (New Haven, CT: Yale University Press, 1990).

20. Daniel Franklin, "Tommy Boggs and the Death of Health Care Reform," *Washington Monthly*, April 1995, p. 36.

21. Holly Idelson, "Signs Point to Greater Loyalty on Both Sides of the Aisle," *Congressional Quarterly Weekly Report*, December 19, 1992, p. 3849.

22. "GOP Leadership PACs' Fundraising Far Outstrips 1997–98," *Congressional Quarterly Weekly Report*, August 15, 1999, p. 1991.
23. Carl Hulse, "Even Some in G.O.P. Call for More Oversight of Bush," *New York Times*, May 31, 2004, p. A13.
24. Elizabeth Williamson, "Revival of Oversight Role Sought; Congress Hires More Investigators, Plans Subpeonas," *Washington Post*, April 25, 2007, p. A1.
25. Thomas E. Mann, Molly Reynolds, and Peter Hoey, "A New, Improved Congress?" *New York Times*, August 26, 2007, p. 11.
26. Peter Grier, "Financial Crisis Inquiry Commission: Top bankers contrite, sort of," *Christian Science Monitor*, Jan. 13, 2010, www.csmonitor.com (accessed 2/5/10).
27. Robert J. Spitzer, "The Presidency: The Clinton Crisis and Its Consequences," in *The Clinton Scandal and the Future of American Government*, eds. Mark J. Rozell and Clyde Wilcox (Washington, DC: Georgetown University Press, 2000), pp. 7–10.
28. Carroll J. Doherty, "Impeachment: How It would Work," *Congressional Quarterly Weekly Report*, January 31, 1998, p. 222.

## Chapter 10

1. "The Cover-Up Continues," *New York Times*, Oct. 26, 2009, p. A20.
2. *In re Neagle*, 135 U.S. 1 (1890).
3. James G. Randall, *Constitutional Problems under Lincoln* (New York: Appleton, 1926), ch. 1.
4. Edward S. Corwin, *The President: Office and Powers*, 4th rev. ed. (New York: New York University Press, 1957), p. 229.
5. These statutes are contained mainly in Title 10 of the United States Code, Sections 331, 332, and 333.
6. The best study covering all aspects of the domestic use of the military is that by Adam Yarmolinsky, *The Military Establishment* (New York: Harper & Row, 1971). Probably the most famous instance of a president's unilateral use of the power to protect a state "against domestic violence" was in dealing with the Pullman Strike of 1894. The famous Supreme Court case that ensued was *In re Debs*, 158 U.S. 564 (1895).
7. Dan Slater, "Bush Pardon Party Goes Out with a Whimper," *Wall Street Journal*, January 20, 2009, http://blogs.wsj.com (accessed 3/20/10).
8. In *United States v. Pink*, 315 U.S. 203 (1942), the Supreme Court confirmed that an executive agreement is the legal equivalent of a treaty, despite the absence of Senate approval. This case approved the executive agreement that was used to establish diplomatic relations with the Soviet Union in 1933. An executive agreement, not a treaty, was used in 1940 to exchange "fifty over age destroyers" for ninety-nine-year leases on some important military bases.
9. There is a third source of presidential power implied from the provision for "faithful execution of the laws." This is the president's power to impound funds—that is, to refuse to spend money Congress has appropriated for certain purposes. One author referred to this as a "retroactive veto power" (Robert E. Goosetree, "The Power of the President to Impound Appropriated Funds," *American University Law Review*, January 1962). Many modern presidents used this impoundment power freely and to considerable effect, and Congress occasionally delegated such power to the president by statute. But in reaction to the Watergate scandal, Congress adopted the

Budget and Impoundment Control Act of 1974, which was designed to circumscribe the president's ability to impound funds by requiring that the president spend all appropriated funds unless both houses of Congress consent to an impoundment within forty-five days of a presidential request. Therefore, since 1974, the use of impoundment has declined significantly. Presidents have either had to bite their tongues and accept unwanted appropriations or had to revert to the older and more dependable but politically limited method of vetoing the entire bill.

10. For a different perspective, see William F. Grover, *The President as Prisoner: A Structural Critique of the Carter and Reagan Years* (Albany: State University of New York Press, 1988).

11. For more on the veto, see Robert J. Spitzer, *The Presidential Veto: Touchstone of the American Presidency* (Albany: State University of New York Press, 1988).

12. A substantial portion of this section is taken from Theodore J. Lowi, *The Personal President* (Ithaca, NY: Cornell University Press, 1985), pp. 141–50.

13. All the figures since 1967, and probably 1957, are understated, because additional White House staff members were on "detail" service from the military and other departments (some secretly assigned) and are not counted here because they were not on the White House payroll.

14. Article I, Section 3, provides that "The Vice-President . . . shall be President of the Senate, but shall have no Vote, unless they be equally divided." This is the only vote the vice president is allowed.

15. Shirley Anne Warshaw, *The Keys to Power* (New York: Longman, 2000) pp. 100–108.

16. Barton Gellman and Jo Becker, "Angler: The Cheney Vice Presidency," *Washington Post*, June 24, 2007, p. A1.

17. David Ignatius, "A Skeptical Biden's Role," *RealClearPolitics.com*, November 26, 2009. www.realclearpolitics.com (accessed 4/14/10).

18. Samuel Kernell, *Going Public: New Strategies of Presidential Leadership* 3rd ed. (Washington, DC: Congressional Quarterly Press, 1997); also, Jeffrey K. Tulis, *The Rhetorical Presidency* (Princeton, NJ: Princeton University Press, 1987).

19. Tulis, *The Rhetorical Presidency*, 91.

20. Sidney M. Milkis, *The President and the Parties* (New York: Oxford, 1993), 97

21. James MacGregor Burns, *Roosevelt: The Lion and the Fox* (New York: Harcourt, Brace, 1956), 317.

22. Kernell, *Going Public*, 79.

23. Lowi, *The Personal President*.

24. Lowi, *The Personal President*, 11.

25. Harold W. Stanley and Richard G. Niemi, *Vital Statistics on American Politics, 2001–2002* (Washington, DC: Congressional Quarterly Press, 2001), 250–51.

26. Milkis, *The President and the Parties*, 128.

27. Milkis, *The President and the Parties*, 160.

28. The classic critique of this process is Theodore J. Lowi, *The End of Liberalism* (New York: Norton, 1969).

29. Kenneth Culp Davis, *Administrative Law Treatise* (St. Paul: West Publishing, 1958), 9.

30. Presidential Memorandum on Regulatory Review, January 30, 2009 www .gpoaccess.gov (accessed 3/3/10).

31. A complete inventory is provided in Harold C. Relyea, "Presidential Directives: Background and Review," Congressional Research Service Report 98–611 (Washington, DC: Library of Congress, November 9, 2001).

32. Terry M. Moe and William G. Howell, "The Presidential Power of Unilateral Action," *Journal of Law, Economics and Organization* 15. 1 (January 1999): 133–34.

33. *Youngstown Sheet & Tube Co. V. Sawyer*, 346 U.S. 579 (1952).

34. Todd Gaziano, "The New 'Massive Resistance,'" *Policy Review* (May-June 1998): 283.

35. Mark Killenback, "A Matter of Mere Approval: The Role of the President in the Creation of Legislative History," 48 *University of Arkansas Law Review* 239 (1995).

36. Philip Cooper, *By Order of the President* (Lawrence: University Press of Kansas, 2002), p. 201.

37. Edward S. Corwin, *The President: Office and Powers*, 4th rev. ed. (New York: New York University Press, 1957), p. 283.

38. Cooper, p. 201.

39. Cooper p. 216.

## Chapter 11

1. John B. Judis, "The Quiet Revolution," *New Republic*, February 1, 2010, www.tnr.com (accessed 2/2/10).

2. "Obama's Health Care Speech to Congress," *New York Times*, September 9, 2009, www.nytimes.com (accessed 2/10/10).

3. U.S. Census Bureau, "Federal Civilian Employment and Annual Payroll by Branch: 1970–2008," *Statistical Abstract of the United States 2010*, Table 484, www.census.gov; U.S. Census Bureau, "Department of Defense Personnel: 1960–2008," *Statistical Abstract of the United States 2010*, Table 498, www.census.gov (accessed 2/10/10).

4. Linda Greenhouse, "Justices Say E.P.A. Has Power to Act on Harmful Gases," *New York Times*, April 3, 2007, www.nytimes.com (accessed 2/15/10).

5. Environmental Protection Agency, "Endangerment and Cause or Contribute Findings for Greenhouse Gases under the Clean Air Act," http://epa.gov (accessed 2/16/10).

6. John M. Broder, "U.S. Issues Limits on Greenhouse Gas Emissions From Cars," *New York Times*, April 2, 2010, p. 81.

7. John B. Judis, "The Quiet Revolution," *New Republic*, February 1, 2010, www.tnr.com (accessed 2/2/10).

8. Greg Gardner, "U.S. Probes Toyota Recall," *Detroit Free Press*, www.freep.com (accessed 2/16/10).

9. Quoted in Leonard D. White, *The Republican Era* (New York: Free Press, 1958), p. 6.

10. As of 2010, salaries for GS-15 federal employees in Washington, D.C., could range from $99,628 to $129,517; salaries for the Senior Executive Service could range between $119,554 and $179,700 annually. Office of Personnel Management, "Salaries and Wages," www.opm.gov/oca/payrates/index.htm (accessed 6/3/10).

11. Andrew C. Revkin, "Call for Openness at NASA Adds to Reports of Pressure," *New York Times*, February 16, 2006, p. 20; Richard Simon and Janet Wilson, "EPS Staff Sought Influence of Former Chief on California Warming Law," *Los Angeles Times*, February 27, 2008, p. 1.

12. See Paul Peterson, *The Price of Federalism* (Washington, DC: Brookings Institution, 1995), for a recent argument that "redistribution" is the distinctive function of the national government in the American federal system.

13. *Budget of the United States Government, FY 1998: Analytical Perspectives* (Washington, DC: U.S. Government Printing Office, 1997), Table 12-2, p. 219.

14. For an excellent political analysis of the Fed, see Donald Kettl, *Leadership at the Fed* (New Haven, CT: Yale University Press, 1986).

15. George E. Berkley, *The Craft of Public Administration* (Boston: Allyn & Bacon, 1975), p. 417. Emphasis added.

16. Correspondent Kelli Arena, "Overhauling the IRS," CNN Financial Network, March 7, 1997.

17. David Johnston, "Bush Intervened in Dispute over N.S.A. Eavesdropping," *New York Times*, May 16, 2007, p. A1; Scott Shane, David Johnston, and James Risen, "Secret U.S. Endorsement of Severe Interrogations," *New York Times*, October 4, 2007, p. A1.

18. For more detail, consult John E. Harr, *The Professional Diplomat* (Princeton, NJ: Princeton University Press, 1972), p. 11; and Nicholas Horrock, "The CIA Has Neighbors in the 'Intelligence Community,'" *New York Times*, June 29, 1975, sec. 4, p. 2. See also Roger Hilsman, *The Politics of Policy Making in Defense and Foreign Affairs*, 3rd ed. (Englewood Cliffs, NJ: Prentice Hall, 1993).

19. Carl Hulse, "House Approves $447 Billion in Spending for Military," *New York Times*, May 21, 2004, p. A16.

20. David E. Sanger and Steven Lee Myers, "Notes from Secret Iran Talks Led to U.S. Reversal," *New York Times*, December 7, 2007, p. 4.

21. Mark Mazzetti, "New Data, New Methods, New Conclusion," *New York Times*, December 5, 2007, p. 12; Peter Baker and Dafna Linzer, "Diving Deep, Unearthing a Surprise," *Washington Post*, December 8, 2007, p. A9; Jon Ward, "NIE Authors Accused of Partisan Politics," *Washington Times*, December 7, 2007, p. A1.

22. The title was inspired by a book by Charles Hyneman, *Bureaucracy in a Democracy* (New York: Harper, 1950). For a more recent effort to describe the federal bureaucracy and to provide some guidelines for improvement, see Patricia W. Ingraham and Donald F. Kettl, eds., *Agenda for Excellence: Public Service in America* (Chatham, NJ: Chatham House, 1992).

23. Clinton Rossiter, ed., *The Federalist Papers* (New York: New American Library, 1961), No. 51, p. 322.

24. The title of this section was inspired by Peri Arnold, *Making the Managerial Presidency* (Princeton, NJ: Princeton University Press, 1986).

25. See Richard Nathan, *The Plot That Failed: Nixon and the Administrative Presidency* (New York: Wiley, 1975), pp. 68–76.

26. For more details and evaluations, see David Rosenbloom, *Public Administration* (New York: Random House, 1986), pp. 186–221; Charles H. Levine and Rosslyn Kleeman, "The Quiet Crisis in the American Public Service," in *Agenda for Excellence: Public Service in America*, ed. Patricia Ingraham and Donald Kettl (Chatham, NJ: Chatham House, 1992); and Patricia Ingraham and David Rosenbloom, "The State of Merit in the Federal Government," in *Agenda for Excellence*.

27. Lester Salamon and Alan Abramson, "Governance: The Politics of Retrenchment," in *The Reagan Record*, ed. John Palmer and Isabel Sawhill (Cambridge, MA: Ballinger, 1984), p. 40.

28. Colin Campbell, "The White House and the Presidency under the 'Let's Deal' President," in *The Bush Presidency: First Appraisals*, ed. Colin Campbell and Bert A. Rockman (Chatham, NJ: Chatham House, 1991), pp. 185–222.
29. See National Partnership for Reinventing Government, http://govinfo.library .unt.edu/npr/index.htm (accessed 9/10/08).
30. Joshua Chaffin, "Democrats Probe High Cost of Halliburton," *Financial Times*, February 17, 2004, p. 10; Laura Rich, "On the Job in Iraq," *New York Times*, May 23, 2004, pp. 3–6.
31. Thomas E. Mann, Sarah Binder, and Molly Reynolds, "Is the Broken Branch on the Mend?" Brookings Institution, 2007, pp. 11–12, www.brookings.edu/~/ media/Files/rc/papers/2007/0904governance_mann/0904governance_mann .pdf (accessed 1/2/08).
32. The Office of Technology Assessment (OTA) was a fourth research agency serving Congress until 1995. It was one of the first agencies scheduled for elimination by the 104th Congress. Until 1983, Congress had still another tool of legislative oversight: the legislative veto. Each agency operating under such provisions was obliged to submit to Congress every proposed decision or rule, which would then lie before both chambers for thirty to sixty days. If Congress took no action by one-house or two-house resolution explicitly to veto the proposed measure during the prescribed period, it became law. In 1983, the Supreme Court declared the legislative veto unconstitutional on the grounds that it violated the separation of powers—the resolutions Congress passed to exercise its veto were not subject to presidential veto, as required by the Constitution. See *Immigration and Naturalization Service v. Chadha*, 462 U.S. 919 (1983).

## Chapter 12

1. No. 551 U.S. 393 (2007).
2. Charles Lane, "Court Backs School on Speech Curbs," *Washington Post*, June 26, 2007, p. A6.
3. U.S. Bureau of the Census, *Statistical Abstract of the United States* (Washington, DC: Government Printing Office, 2009).
4. Geoffrey R. Stone, "Republican Obstruction on Judges," *Huffington Post*, August 17, 2010, www.huffingtonpost.com (accessed 8/20/10).
5. Peter Wallsten and Richard Simon, "Sotomayor Nomination Splits GOP," *Los Angeles Times*, May 27, 2009, http://articles.latimes.com (accessed 11/12/09).
6. Max Farrand, *The Framing of the Constitution of the United States* (New Haven, CT: Yale University Press, 1913), p. 157.
7. C. Herman Pritchett, *The American Constitution* (New York: McGraw-Hill, 1959), p. 138.
8. The Supreme Court affirmed this review power in *Martin v. Hunter's Lessee*, 1 Wheat. 304 (1816).
9. *Brown v. Board of Education*, 347 U.S. 483 (1954); *Loving v. Virginia*, 388 U.S. 1 (1967).
10. *Griswold v. Connecticut*, 381 U.S. 479 (1965).
11. *Gideon v. Wainwright*, 372 U.S. 335 (1963).
12. *Engel v. Vitale*, 370 U.S. 421 (1962); *Gideon v. Wainwright*, 372 U.S. 335 (1963); *-Escobedo v. Illinois*, 378 U.S. 478 (1964); and *Miranda v. Arizona*, 384 U.S. 436 (1966).

13. *Baker v. Carr*, 369 U.S. 186 (1962).
14. Walter F. Murphy, "The Supreme Court of the United States," in *Encyclopedia of the American Judicial System*, ed. Robert J. Janosik (New York: Scribner's, 1987).
15. Robert Scigliano, *The Supreme Court and the Presidency* (New York: Free Press, 1971), p. 161. For an interesting critique of the solicitor general's role during the Reagan administration, see Lincoln Caplan, "Annals of the Law," *The New Yorker*, August 17, 1987, pp. 30–62.
16. Edward Lazarus, *Closed Chambers* (New York: Times Books, 1998), p. 6.
17. *Smith v. Allwright*, 321 U.S. 649 (1994).
18. Clinton Rossiter, ed., *The Federalist Papers* (New York: New American Library, 1961), No. 10, p. 78.

## Chapter 13

1. *Cato Handbook for Policymakers*, 7th ed. (Washington, DC: Cato Institute, 2009), p. 281, www.cato.org (accessed 3/19/10).
2. James Dao, "The Nation; Big Bucks Trip Up the Lean New Army," *New York Times*, February 10, 2002, sec. 4, p. 5.
3. For an evaluation of the policy of withholding subsidies to carry out desegregation laws, see Gary Orfield, *Must We Bus?* (Washington, DC: Brookings Institution, 1978). For an evaluation of the use of subsidies to encourage work or to calm political unrest, see Frances Fox Piven and Richard Cloward, *Regulating the Poor: The Functions of Public Welfare* (New York: Random House, 1971).
4. For an evaluation of the politics of eminent domain, see Theodore J. Lowi and Benjamin Ginsberg, *Poliscide* (New York: Macmillan, 1976), p. 235 and *passim*, and especially chaps. 11 and 12, written by Julia and Thomas Vitullo-Martin.
5. The Federal Reserve Board, *Intended Federal Funds Rate, 1990 to present*, www .federalreserve.gov/fomc/fundsrate.htm (accessed 3/8/10).
6. Social Security Online, "Contribution and Benefit Base," www.ssa.gov/OACT/COLA/cbb.html (accessed 6/11/10).
7. Liz Schott and Zachary Levinson, "TANF Benefits are Low and Have Not Kept Pace with Inflation," Washington DC: Center on Budget and Policy Priorities, November 24, 2008, www.cbpp.org (accessed 3/11/10).
8. U.S. Department of Health and Social Services, Administration for Children and Families, "TANF Total Number of Recipients, Fiscal Year 2009," www.acf.hhs.gov (accessed 3/12/10).
9. Center for Law and Social Policy, "Analysis of Fiscal Year 2006 TANF and MOE Spending by States," http://clasp.org (accessed 4/9/08).
10. See the discussion of the law and the data presented in House Ways and Means Committee Print, WMCP: 106-14, 2000 Green Book, Section 7, Temporary Assistance for Needy Families (TANF), http://frwebgate.access.gpo.gov (accessed 3/26/08); Rebecca M. Blank, "Evaluating Welfare Reform in the United States," *Journal of Economic Literature* 40 (December 2002): 1105–66.
11. Robert Pear, "House Democrats Propose Making the '96 Welfare Law an Antipoverty Weapon," *New York Times*, January 24, 2002, p. A22.
12. Robin Toner, "Welfare Chief Is Hoping to Promote Marriage," *New York Times*, February 19, 2002, p. A1.
13. LaDonna Pavetti and Dottie Rosenbaum, "Creating a Safety Net That Works When the Economy Doesn't: The Role of the Food Stamps and TANF Programs,"

Washington, DC: Center on Budget and Policy Priorities, February 25, 2010, www .cbpp.org (accessed 3/12/10).

14. There were a couple of minor precedents. One was the Smith-Hughes Act of 1917, which made federal funds available to the states for vocational education at the elementary and secondary levels. Second, the Lanham Act of 1940 made federal funds available to schools in "federally impacted areas," that is, areas with an unusually large number of government employees and/or where the local tax base was reduced by large amounts of government-owned property.

15. Sam Dillon, "Obama Proposes Sweeping Change in Education Law," *New York Times*, March 14, 2010, p. A1.

16. For an analysis of employment and training initiatives since the 1930s, see Margaret Weir, *Politics and Jobs* (Princeton, NJ: Princeton University Press, 1992).

17. Morton Keller, *Affairs of State: Public Life in Nineteenth Century America* (Cambridge, MA: Belknap Press of Harvard University Press, 1977), p. 500.

18. John E. Schwarz, *America's Hidden Success*, 2nd ed. (New York: Norton, 1988), pp. 41–42.

19. U.S. Bureau of the Census, (in place of 1997 *Statistical Abstract*) http://blogs .findlaw.com (accessed 6/11/10).

20. See, for example. Theodore R. Marmor, Jerry L. Mashaw, and Philip L. Harvey, *America's Misunderstood Welfare State* (New York: Basic Books, 1990), p. 156; Carmen DeNavas-Walt, Bernadette D. Proctor, Jessica C. Smith, *Income, Poverty, and Health Insurance Coverage in the United States: 2008*, Table 1, Income and Earnings Summary Measures by Selected Characteristics: 2007 and 2008, U.S. Government Printing Office, Washington, DC, 2009, p.6, www.census.gov (accessed 3/14/10).

21. Burdett A. Loomis and Allen J. Cigler, "Introduction: The Changing Nature of Interest Group Politics," in *Interest Group Politics*, 4th ed., ed. Burdett A. Loomis and Allan J. Cigler (Washington, DC: Congressional Quarterly Press, 1995), p. 12.

22. See Senator Bob Kerrey's remarks quoted in David S. Broder, "Deficit Doomsday," *Washington Post*, August 7, 1994, p. C9.

23. See Beth Stevens, "Blurring the Boundaries: How the Federal Government Has Influenced Welfare Benefits in the Private Sector," in *The Politics of Social Policy in the United States*, ed. Margaret Weir, Ann Orloff, and Theda Skocpol (Princeton, NJ: Princeton University Press, 1988), pp. 122–48.

24. Frances Fox Piven and Richard Cloward, *Poor People's Movements* (New York: Pantheon, 1977), chap. 5.

## Chapter 14

1. Geoffrey Perret, *A Country Made by War* (New York: Random House, 1989), 558.

2. Rupert Smith, *The Utility of Force: The Art of War in the Modern World* (New York: Vintage, 2008).

3. D. Robert Worley, *Shaping U.S. Military Forces: Revolution or Relevance in a Post–Cold War World* (Westport, CT.: Praeger Security International, 2006).

4. Matthew Crenson and Benjamin Ginsberg, *Presidential Power: Unchecked and Unbalanced* (New York: Norton, 2007).

5. Benjamin Ginsberg, *The American Lie: Government by the People and Other Political Fables* (Boulder, CO.: Paradigm, 2007).

6. Paul R. Pillar, *Terrorism and American Foreign Policy* (Washington, D.C.: Brookings Institution Press, 2003).

7. One confirmation of this is found in Theodore Lowi, *The End of Liberalism: The Second Republic of the United States*, 2nd ed. (New York: Norton, 1979), 127–30; another is found in Stephen Krasner, "Are Bureaucracies Important?" *Foreign Policy* 7 (Summer 1972): 159–79. However, it should be noted that Krasner was writing his article in disagreement with Graham T. Allison, "Conceptual Models and the Cuban Missile Crisis," *American Political Science Review* 63, no. 3 (September 1969): 689–718.

8. Peterson, "The President's Dominance in Foreign Policy Making," p. 232.

9. Hans Morgenthau, *Politics among Nations*, 2nd ed. (New York: Knopf, 1956), p. 505.

10. See Theodore Lowi, *The Personal President: Power Invested, Promise Unfulfilled* (Ithaca, NY: Cornell University Press, 1985), pp. 167–69.

11. George Quester, *The Continuing Problem of International Politics* (Hinsdale, IL: Dryden Press, 1974), 229.

12. The Warsaw Pact was signed in 1955 by the Soviet Union, the German Democratic Republic (East Germany), Poland, Hungary, Czechoslovakia, Romania, Bulgaria, and Albania. Albania later dropped out. The Warsaw Pact was terminated in 1991.

# answer key

**Chapter 13**

1. a
2. d
3. c
4. c
5. c
6. d
7. c
8. a
9. a
10. c
11. d
12. b

**Chapter 14**

1. b
2. a
3. c
4. d
5. c
6. c
7. d
8. b
9. a
10. a
11. c
12. a

# photo credits

# index

Page numbers in *italics* refer to tables, figures, and illustrations.

Clinton, George, 49
Clinton, Hillary, 8, 184
closed primary, 220
cloture, 285–86
CNN, 169, 177, 318
coalition, use of term, 211
coercion, 66, 397
Cohen, Jeff, 187
cold war:
    collective security treaties in,
      445–46
    end of, 431–32, 446
    peace dividend from, 431–32
collective goods, 242
collective security, 445–46
college students, loans for, 197–98
Columbine High School, Colorado,
    187
comedy shows, public opinion influ-
    enced by, 184, 186
comity, 45, 68
commander-in-chief, president as, 307
commerce, *see* trade and commerce
commerce clause, 72–73, 76, 86
commercial speech, 106
committees, congressional, 279,
    280–82
    assignments to, 289–90
    bills reported out of, 283
    conference, 282, 286
    deliberation on legislative proposals
      by, 283–86
    foreign policy roles of, 440
    joint, 281
    oversight by, 292–93, 355–56
    permanent, 280
    powers of, 293
    select, 280–81
    seniority in, 282
    staffers of, 282
    standing, 280
    and two-party system, 202–3
Common Cause, 238, 241, 247
Communications Decency Act
    (1996), 105, 175
community:

participation of citizens in, 8
    personal liberty vs., 17, *17*
competition, free, 19
concurrent powers, 67
confederation, 34, 65
conference, committees, 282, 286
conference, use of term, 277
Congo, 436
Congress, U.S., *240*, *245*, 265–301
    access to, 250, 251, 253
    access to floor in, 290
    in Articles of Confederation, 34, 38
    balances in, 51
    as bicameral legislature, 267–68
    block grants of, 80
    and bureaucracy, 354
    and campaign funding, 254–55
    and civil rights, 117–18, 120–22,
      125, 131
    committee system of, 202, 279,
      280–82, 283–86, 289–90,
      292–93, 355–56, 439
    conservative coalition in, 203
    constituency services by, 267,
      270–71, 275–77, 287
    constitutional amendments
      proposed by, 45–46, 52–53
    Constitution as basis of, 41–44,
      304
    debate in, 283–86
    direct patronage in, 275–77
    in divided government, 206
    foreign policy made by, 265–66,
      271, 438–39
    grants-in-aid from, 78
    in Great Compromise, 39
    impeachment powers of, 295
    implied power of, 65
    incumbency and, 271–74
    influences on decisions of, 287–90
    in iron triangle, 250, 251
    and judiciary, 44–45, 376
    legislative agenda in, 279
    legislative intent of, 356
    legislative powers of, 266, 277
    legislative process in, 283–86

direct, 12, 258–60
education in, 145–46
"excessive," 41, 43
interest group influence on, 259
Jacksonian, 11
majority rule with minority rights in, 21
media in, 169
popular sovereignty in, 20
public opinion in, 160–61, 190–91
representative, 12, 20, 50
in U.S., 12
use of term, 23
voting as important in, 21
Democratic Party, 203, 206–8, 273, 275
and Great Depression, 208
historical origins of, *200*, 206–7
Jeffersonian Republicans, 203, 206
and New Deal, 208
Progressive program adopted by, 210–11
racial policies of, 146–47
Denny's restaurants, 118–19
departments, 340
deterrence, 442
Developing (Third) World, 445, 446
devolution, 77, 86
Dewey, Thomas, *158*
diplomacy:
distrust of, 442–43
in foreign policy, 442–43
presidential powers of, 307, 310
use of term, 443
direct democracy, 12, 258–60
direct mail, campaign funding via, 227–29
Director of National Intelligence, 438
Disability Rights and Education Fund, 125
disabled Americans, civil rights of, 126, 380–81
discount rate, 403
dissenting opinions, 384
district courts, 370
divided government, 206

doctrine of incorporation, 96–97
Dole, Robert J., 77
domestic policy, 395–427
*see also* public policy
double jeopardy, 110
Douglas, William O., 113, 384
Drudge Report, 173
dual citizenship, 92
dual federalism, 69, 77, 78
due process of law, 92, 94, 95
amendments incorporating issue of, 108–9
in civil rights issues, 376–77
in court system, 368
rights of criminally accused under, 108–9

earmarked funds, 275
Earned Income Tax Credit (EITC), 420
East India Company, 31–32, *32*
East Timor, 436
economic agencies:
federal, 342, 344–46
and security policy, 423
economic inequality, 20
economic interest groups, 440
Economic Opportunity Act (1964), 78
education:
in all-male schools, 125
bilingual, 125
in democracy, 145–46
finance of, 411
gender discrimination in, 123
interest groups in, 240
life tools via, 410–12
and political opinions, 145–46
and school prayers, 377
segregation in, 115–20, *118*, 252, 376
sexual harassment in, 125
and training programs, 412–13
vouchers and, 97
Education Act (1972), Title IX of, 123

Hitler, Adolf, 9, 10
Hobbes, Thomas, 29
Hobbs Anti-Racketeering Act (1946), 326
Holmes, Oliver Wendell, 100, 384
Homeland Security Department, U.S., 309, 313, 348
  congressional oversight of, 358
  creation of, 4, 334
  divisions of, 349, 438
home rule, 68
Hoover, Herbert, 74, 208
hostile environment harassment, 123
House of Representatives, U.S., 21
  Armed Services Committee of, 440
  committees of, 280–82, 346, 355
  contrasted with Senate, 267–68
  debate in, 283–86
  direct popular election of, 42, 43
  Foreign Affairs Committee of, 440
  Homeland Security Committee of, 440
  impeachment powers of, 295
  and institutional racism, 41
  Intelligence Committee of, 440
  local interests served by, 267
  Oversight and Government Reform Committee of, 293, 355
  party leadership in, 277–80
  powers of, 43, 292–93
  re-election to, 272–73
  requirements for candidates to, 201
  Select Committee on Energy Dependence and Global Warming of, 280
  Speaker of, 269, 277, 277
  state representation in, 39–40
  term of office in, 42, 43, 267
  Three-fifths Compromise and, 39–40
  Ways and Means Committee of, 280
  women in, 269
  see also Congress, U.S.
housing:
  policies, 413–15

  segregation in, 115, 116–17, 120–22
  subsidized, 413–15
Housing and Urban Development Department, U.S. (HUD), 120–22, 343
Huckabee, Mike, 347
human rights interest groups, 440–41
Hurricane Katrina, 269, 355
Hussein, Saddam, 308, 310

IBM, 240
ideology:
  and interest groups, 243–44
  political, 148–49, 384–85, 387
"I Have a Dream" (King), 117
immigrants, immigration, 13–16
  Asian, 15
  and ethnic diversity, 12–16
  European, 12–14
  Latin American, 13, 15
  religious affiliations of, 14–16
Immigration Reform and Control Act (1986), 124
immigration reform bill, 253–54
impeachment:
  and Clinton trial, 181, 181, 295
  grounds for, 295
  use of term, 295
implementation, by bureaucracy, 337
implied powers, 65
Improving America's Schools Act (1994), 411
income tax, 346–47
incorporation, 96–97
incumbency, 200, 271–74
independent agencies, 341
independent regulatory commissions, 342
independent spending, of campaign funds, 228
indexing, 406
inflation, 402
influence, see power
informational benefits, 243

redistricting, 273–74
*Red Lion Broadcasting v. FCC*, 176
redress of grievances, 95
Reed, Stanley, 384
referenda, 202, 220
Reform Party, 210
*Regents of the University of California v. Bakke*, 129–31
registration, to vote, 201, 217–20
regulation, forms of, 399–401
regulatory agencies, 342, 343
regulatory review, 323–24
regulatory taxes, 401
regulatory techniques, 398, 399–401
  administrative regulation, 400–401
  expropriation, 401
  police regulation, 400
  regulation forms, 400–401
  taxation, 401
Rehabilitation Act (1973), 125
Rehnquist, William H., 111, 385
Reid, Harry, 8
religion:
  establishment clause, 97
  freedom of, 17, 96, 97–100
  free exercise of, 99–100
  interest groups in, 243–44
  and public opinion, 153
  separation of church and state, 98–99, 377
religious affiliation, of immigrants, 14–16
religious Right, 243–44, 253, 256
*Reno v. ACLU*, 105
representation, 267–71
  agency, 269, 270–71
  in bicameral legislature, 267–68
  proportional, 211
  simple theory of, 287
  sociological, 269, 273
representative democracy, 12, 20, 50
republic, 12
Republican Party, 203, 273, 275
  antiabortion factions in, 153
  beginnings of, 203, 210

Contract with America of, 279, 289, 408
  as GOP, 143
  historical origins of, 207–8, *207*
  social programs scaled back by, 147, 408–9
  and voting rights for freed slaves, 11–12
Republicans, Jeffersonian, *200*
reserved powers, 66
revenue agencies, 346–47
revenue sharing, 80
Rice, Condoleezza, 318
right of rebuttal, 176
"right to die" movement, 114
"right to life" movement, 153
Rio Treaty (1947), 446
Roberts, John G., Jr., 372, *373*, 374, 375, 385
Robinson, Michael, 188
*Roe v. Wade*, 113, 153, 250–52, 376, 385
roll-call votes, 215, 288
Rome, imperial treasury of, 344
*Romer v. Evans*, 128
Roosevelt, Eleanor, *318*
Roosevelt, Franklin D., 157, 180, 205, 307, 311, 321, *321*, 404
  and bureaucracy, 353
  "fireside chats" of, 321
  and New Deal, 74, 76, 208, 211, 412
  and Supreme Court, 372
  and World War II, 151–52, 304
Roosevelt, Theodore, 320
Rotary International, 243
royalists, 30
rule-making, bureaucratic, 339
Rumsfeld, Donald, 168, 293

Safe Drinking Water Act Amendments (1986), 326
Salazar, Antonio, 10
sample, in polls, 155
sampling frame, 155

and "Use of Force" resolution, 308
September 11 Commission (National Commission on Terrorist Attacks upon the United States), 351
Service Employees International Union, 229
Seventeenth Amendment, 43
sexual harassment, 123
shadow welfare state, 420
Shays, Christopher, 293
Shays, Daniel, 36, *36*
Shays's Rebellion, 36, *36*
Sheehan, Margaret, 188
*Shelley v. Kraemer,* 115
Shell Oil, 240
Sherman, Roger, 33
"shield laws," 104
shopkeepers, artisans, and laborers, 30, 31, 36
Sierra Club, 241, 247
Sierra Leone, 436
signing statements, 325–26
*Silent Scream, The,* 153
Simpson, O. J., 178
single-member-district plurality system, 211
Sixth Amendment, 112
*60 minutes II,* 168
slander, 104
slaves, slavery, 13, 14, 325
    abolition of, 11–12, 114
    as citizens vs. property, 39–40
    freeing of, 11–12, 114
    populations of, 39–40
*Smith v. Allwright,* 383
social class:
    elitist bias and, 239, 245
    middle class, 11, 421
    political opinion and, 143–45
social groups:
    balance of power among, 231
    party identification by, *213*
    as source of values, 143–45
social inequality, 20
social institutions, totalitarian, 10
Socialists, 148

socialization, political, 142–47
social policy:
    Republican Party and, 147, 408
    and welfare state, 404–10
    *see also* welfare system
Social Security, 208, 404–7, 418, *418*, 425
sociological representation, 269, 273
soft money, 255
soldiers, quartering of, 96
solicitor general, 379–80
solidary benefits, 243
"sophomore surge," 272
Sotomayor, Sonia, *373*, 375
Souter, David H., 387
Southeast Asia Treaty Organization (SEATO), 446
Southern Christian Leadership Conference (SCLC), 117, 253
Southern Manifesto (1956), 76
southern planters, 30, 34, 35, 38, 40, 41
southern states, and segregation, 77–78
sovereignty, popular, 20
Soviet Union:
    in cold war, 431–32, 446
    collapse of, 10
    totalitarian government in, 9, 10
    and Warsaw Pact, 446
Speaker of the House, 269, 277, *277*
speech:
    commercial, 106
    expressive, 106
    fighting words, 106
    First Amendment and, 100–106
    freedom of, 11, 17, 95, 96, 100–106, *102*, 253, 363–64
    libel and slander, 104
    limits on protection of, 104–6
    obscenity and pornography, 104–5
    political, 100–102
    in public schools, 106
    symbolic, 102–3, *102*
    truth and, 100

on abortion issue, 113, 153,
250–52, 376, 387
activism vs. restraint in, 385
on apportionment, 377
and birth control issue, 113
briefs of, 381
on campaign finance, 101–2
on campaign funding, 228
cases heard in, 368, 378
chief justice of, 372
and civil liberties, 96–97, 101,
113–14, 385, 387
and civil rights, 76, 114–20, *114*,
123, 127, 129–31, 252, 376,
384, 385, 387
and congressional powers, 76, 376
Constitution interpreted by, 72–73,
366, 368, 384
Constitution provision for, 42, 45
and death penalty, 112–13
dissenting opinions in, 384
and enemy combatant cases, *365*
and establishment clause, 98–99
and exclusionary rule, 109
FCC appeals to, 380
Federal Maritime Commission
appeals to, 380
and federal power, 76–77
and freedom of assembly and
petition, 103
and free exercise clause, 99–100
and free press, 103–4
and free speech, 100–106, *102*
influences on, 384
and interstate commerce, 72–73,
76, 119
and judicial review, 44–45,
375–76, 380
justices appointed to, 371, 374
justices (current) of, 371
lobbying for access to, 380–81
majority opinion in, 384
and "Miranda rights," 111, 377
on one person, one vote, 377
opinion writing in, 383
oral arguments to, 382–83

on police procedures, 387
political ideology in, 374, 384–85,
387
powers of, 42, 45, 46
and privacy issues, 113–14, 128
and racial redistricting, 274
on right to bear arms, 106–8
on search and seizure, 108–9
and separation of church
and state, *99*
and sexual harassment, 123
size of, 374
and states' rights, 73–74
and supremacy clause, 376
unpredictability of, 387
on voting rights, 387
and women's rights, 250–52
writs to, 378
supreme courts, of states, 367
symbolic speech, 102–3, *102*

Taliban, 351
talk radio, 171
tariffs, 346
taxes, taxation:
colonial conflict over, 30–31
debate on cuts in, 402–3
income tax, 346–47
and Internet, 79
and political socialization, 141
regulatory, 401
Republicans on, 402
tax expenditures, 419
Tea Act (1773), 31–32
Tea Party movement, 182, 226
Teamsters Union, 240
Telecommunications Act (1996), 79,
105, 175, 177
Temporary Assistance to Needy
Families (TANF), 406, 407, 409,
420, 421
Tenth Amendment:
and federal powers, 76
as reserved power amendment, 66
and state powers, 66, 76–77
and states' rights, 74, 76

on Constitution's probable future, 28

and foreign policy caution, 429

and Treasury Department foundation, 346

*Washington Post*, 190, 191

*Washington Times*, 191

Watergate:

and media, 188

reform in aftermath of, 254

scandals in aftermath of, 254

weapons of mass destruction (WMDs), 308

Weather Service, U.S., 333

*Webster v. Reproductive Health Services*, 251–52

*Weekly Standard*, 191

welfare system:

AFDC, 406, 407, 409, 420–21

and charity, 404

COLAs in, 406

contributory programs in, 404–6, 418

Economic Opportunity Act and, 78

EITC, 420

expenditures for, 408

food stamps, 407, 420

Great Depression and, 404

history of, 404

in-kind programs in, 407

Medicaid, 78, 79, 407

Medicare, 406, 418

need-based programs in, 407

New Deal and, 74

noncontributory programs in, 406–7

for nonworking poor, 420

and poverty, 395–96, 421–23

public assistance programs in, 406–7

reform of, 408–10

and senior citizens, 418–19

shadow welfare state in, 420

social policy and, 395–96, 404–10

Social Security, 404–7, 418

SSI, 407

state powers in, 78

TANF, 406, 407, 409, 421

tax expenditures in, 420

unfunded mandates in, 79–80

voluntary philanthropy and, 404

and working poor, 420

*West Virginia State Board of Education v. Barnette*, 99

Whig Party, 203–5, 206–7, 210

whip system, 278, 290–91

White, Byron R., 387

White House staff, 316, 353

Wills, Garry, 52

Wilson, James, 38, 40

Wilson, Joseph, 104, 310

Wilson, Woodrow, 320, 321, 431

women:

civil rights for, 247, 250–52, 253, 376

congressional representation of, 269, 273

and gender discrimination, 122–24

and poverty, 421–23

and sexual harassment, 123

voting rights for, 12

Women's Equity Action League (WEAL), 122

Woodward, Bob, 188

work, freedom to, 20

working poor, 420

World Bank, 444

World Trade Organization (WTO), 433–34

World War I, 309, 431

World War II, 151–52, *153*, 309, 336, 431

Wright, Jeremiah, 216

writ of *certiorari*, 378

writ of *habeas corpus*, 378

Yates, Robert, 39, 50

Young, Don, 275

YouTube, *172*, 174

*Zelman v. Simmons-Harris*, 98

zero-based budgeting, 353

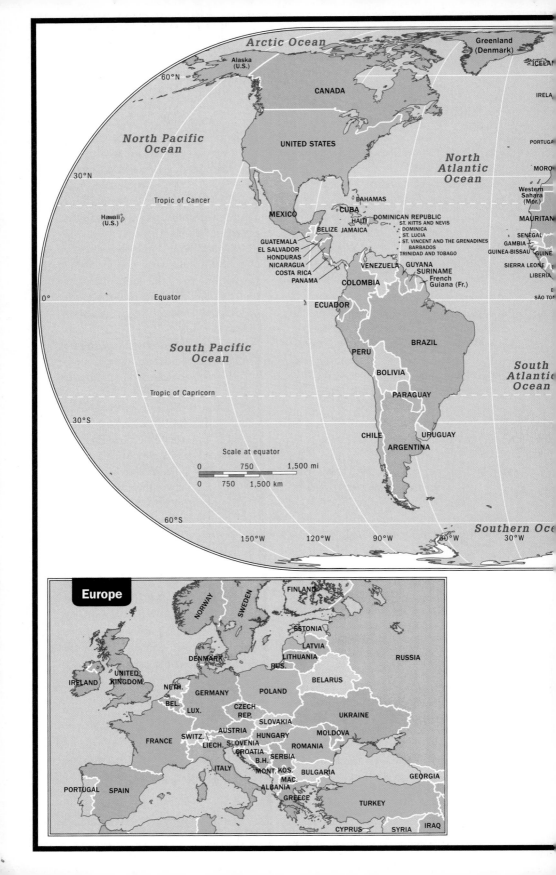

Arctic Ocean

Greenland (Denmark)

ICELA

Alaska (U.S.)

60°N

CANADA

IRELA

North Pacific Ocean

UNITED STATES

North Atlantic Ocean

PORTUGA

MORO

30°N

Tropic of Cancer

Western Sahara (Mor.)

BAHAMAS

MAURITAN

Hawaii (U.S.)

MEXICO

CUBA

DOMINICAN REPUBLIC

HAITI

ST. KITTS AND NEVIS

DOMINICA

SENEGAL

BELIZE JAMAICA

ST. LUCIA

ST. VINCENT AND THE GRENADINES

GAMBIA

GUATEMALA

BARBADOS

GUINEA-BISSAU GUINE

EL SALVADOR

TRINIDAD AND TOBAGO

SIERRA LEONE

HONDURAS

VENEZUELA GUYANA

LIBERIA

NICARAGUA

SURINAME

E

COSTA RICA

French

SÃO TOM

PANAMA

COLOMBIA

Guiana (Fr.)

0°

Equator

ECUADOR

South Pacific Ocean

BRAZIL

South Atlanti Ocean

PERU

Tropic of Capricorn

BOLIVIA

PARAGUAY

30°S

Scale at equator

0    750    1,500 mi

0    750    1,500 km

CHILE

URUGUAY

ARGENTINA

60°S

Southern Oce

150°W    120°W    90°W    30°W

30°W

Europe

NORWAY SWEDEN FINLAND

ESTONIA

LATVIA

DENMARK

LITHUANIA

RUSSIA

RUS.

IRELAND UNITED KINGDOM

BELARUS

NETH.

GERMANY

POLAND

BEL.

LUX.

CZECH REP.

UKRAINE

SLOVAKIA

AUSTRIA

MOLDOVA

FRANCE SWITZ.

HUNGARY

LIECH. SLOVENIA

ROMANIA

CROATIA

B.H.

SERBIA

ITALY

MONT. KOS.

BULGARIA

GEORGIA

MAC.

ALBANIA

PORTUGAL SPAIN

GREECE

TURKEY

CYPRUS

SYRIA IRAQ

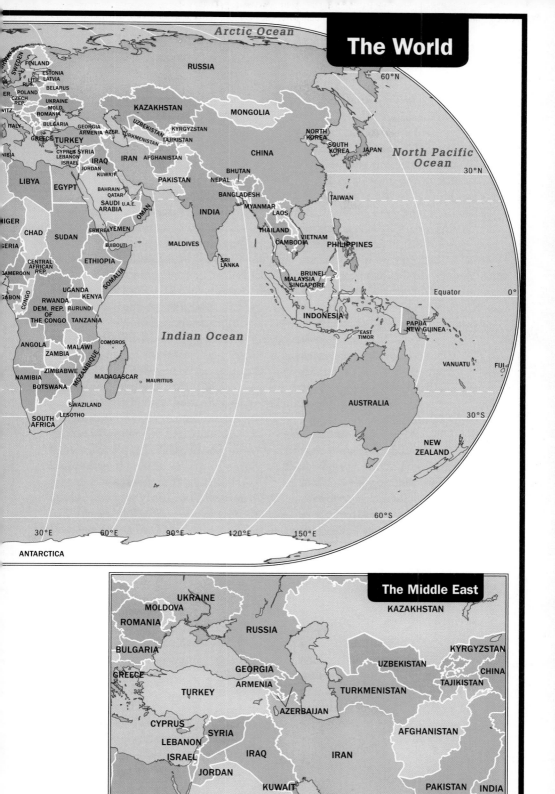

# The World

Arctic Ocean

SWEDEN
FINLAND
NORWAY
ESTONIA
LITH. LATVIA
RUS.
BELARUS
POLAND
GER.
CZECH REP.
ITALY
ROMANIA
BULGARIA
GREECE
TURKEY
CYPRUS SYRIA
LEBANON
ISRAEL
JORDAN
KUWAIT
BAHRAIN
QATAR
SAUDI ARABIA
U.A.E.

RUSSIA

KAZAKHSTAN

UZBEKISTAN
KYRGYZSTAN
TURKMENISTAN
TAJIKISTAN

MONGOLIA

60°N

GEORGIA
ARMENIA AZER.

IRAQ
IRAN
AFGHANISTAN

CHINA

NORTH KOREA
SOUTH KOREA
JAPAN

North Pacific Ocean

30°N

LIBYA
EGYPT

PAKISTAN
NEPAL
BHUTAN

TAIWAN

NIGER
CHAD
SUDAN
ERITREA YEMEN
DJIBOUTI

BANGLADESH
INDIA
MYANMAR
LAOS
THAILAND
VIETNAM
CAMBODIA

PHILIPPINES

NISIA

GERIA
CAMEROON

OMAN

MALDIVES

SRI LANKA

CENTRAL AFRICAN REP.
ETHIOPIA
SOMALIA

BRUNEI
MALAYSIA
SINGAPORE

GABON
CONGO
UGANDA
KENYA
RWANDA
BURUNDI
DEM. REP. OF THE CONGO
TANZANIA

INDONESIA

Equator
0°

EAST TIMOR

PAPUA NEW GUINEA

Indian Ocean

ANGOLA
ZAMBIA
MALAWI
COMOROS

VANUATU
FIJI

NAMIBIA
BOTSWANA
ZIMBABWE
MOZAMBIQUE
MADAGASCAR
MAURITIUS

SWAZILAND
SOUTH AFRICA
LESOTHO

AUSTRALIA

30°S

NEW ZEALAND

60°S

30°E
60°E
90°E
120°E
150°E

ANTARCTICA

# The Middle East

UKRAINE
MOLDOVA
ROMANIA
BULGARIA
GREECE
RUSSIA
GEORGIA
TURKEY
ARMENIA
AZERBAIJAN
CYPRUS
SYRIA
LEBANON
ISRAEL
IRAQ
JORDAN
KUWAIT
EGYPT
SAUDI ARABIA
BAHRAIN
QATAR

KAZAKHSTAN
KYRGYZSTAN
UZBEKISTAN
CHINA
TURKMENISTAN
TAJIKISTAN
AFGHANISTAN
IRAN
PAKISTAN
INDIA